55 *Victorian Prose Writers Before 1867*, edited by William B. Thesing (1987)

56 *German Fiction Writers, 1914-1945*, edited by James Hardin (1987)

57 *Victorian Prose Writers After 1867*, edited by William B. Thesing (1987)

58 *Jacobean and Caroline Dramatists*, edited by Fredson Bowers (1987)

59 *American Literary Critics and Scholars, 1800-1850*, edited by John W. Rathbun and Monica M. Grecu (1987)

60 *Canadian Writers Since 1960*, Second Series, edited by W. H. New (1987)

61 *American Writers for Children Since 1960: Poets, Illustrators, and Nonfiction Authors*, edited by Glenn E. Estes (1987)

62 *Elizabethan Dramatists*, edited by Fredson Bowers (1987)

63 *Modern American Critics, 1920-1955*, edited by Gregory S. Jay (1988)

64 *American Literary Critics and Scholars, 1850-1880*, edited by John W. Rathbun and Monica M. Grecu (1988)

65 *French Novelists, 1900-1930*, edited by Catharine Savage Brosman (1988)

66 *German Fiction Writers, 1885-1913*, 2 parts, edited by James Hardin (1988)

67 *Modern American Critics Since 1955*, edited by Gregory S. Jay (1988)

68 *Canadian Writers, 1920-1959*, First Series, edited by W. H. New (1988)

69 *Contemporary German Fiction Writers*, First Series, edited by Wolfgang D. Elfe and James Hardin (1988)

70 *British Mystery Writers, 1860-1919*, edited by Bernard Benstock and Thomas F. Staley (1988)

71 *American Literary Critics and Scholars, 1880-1900*, edited by John W. Rathbun and Monica M. Grecu (1988)

72 *French Novelists, 1930-1960*, edited by Catharine Savage Brosman (1988)

73 *American Magazine Journalists, 1741-1850*, edited by Sam G. Riley (1988)

74 *American Short-Story Writers Before 1880*, edited by Bobby Ellen Kimbel, with the assistance of William E. Grant (1988)

75 *Contemporary German Fiction Writers*, Second Series, edited by Wolfgang D. Elfe and James Hardin (1988)

76 *Afro-American Writers, 1940-1955*, edited by Trudier Harris (1988)

77 *British Mystery Writers, 1920-1939*, edited by Bernard Benstock and Thomas F. Staley (1988)

78 *American Short-Story Writers, 1880-1910*, edited by Bobby Ellen Kimbel, with the assistance of William E. Grant (1988)

79 *American Magazine Journalists, 1850-1900*, edited by Sam G. Riley (1988)

80 *Restoration and Eighteenth-Century Dramatists*, First Series, edited by Paula R. Backscheider (1989)

81 *Austrian Fiction Writers, 1875-1913*, edited by James Hardin and Donald G. Daviau (1989)

82 *Chicano Writers*, First Series, edited by Francisco A. Lomelí and Carl R. Shirley (1989)

83 *French Novelists Since 1960*, edited by Catharine Savage Brosman (1989)

84 *Restoration and Eighteenth-Century Dramatists*, Second Series, edited by Paula R. Backscheider (1989)

85 *Austrian Fiction Writers After 1914*, edited by James Hardin and Donald G. Daviau (1989)

86 *American Short-Story Writers, 1910-1945*, First Series, edited by Bobby Ellen Kimbel (1989)

87 *British Mystery and Thriller Writers Since 1940*, First Series, edited by Bernard Benstock and Thomas F. Staley (1989)

88 *Canadian Writers, 1920-1959*, Second Series, edited by W. H. New (1989)

89 *Restoration and Eighteenth-Century Dramatists*, Third Series, edited by Paula R. Backscheider (1989)

90 *German Writers in the Age of Goethe, 1789-1832*, edited by James Hardin and Christoph E. Schweitzer (1989)

91 *American Magazine Journalists, 1900-1960*, First Series, edited by Sam G. Riley (1990)

92 *Canadian Writers, 1890-1920*, edited by W. H. New (1990)

93 *British Romantic Poets, 1789-1832*, First Series, edited by John R. Greenfield (1990)

94 *German Writers in the Age of Goethe: Sturm und Drang to Classicism*, edited by James Hardin and Christoph E. Schweitzer (1990)

95 *Eighteenth-Century British Poets*, First Series, edited by John Sitter (1990)

96 *British Romantic Poets, 1789-1832*, Second Series, edited by John R. Greenfield (1990)

97 *German Writers from the Enlightenment to Sturm und Drang, 1720-1764*, edited by James Hardin and Christoph E. Schweitzer (1990)

98 *Modern British Essayists*, First Series, edited by Robert Beum (1990)

99 *Canadian Writers Before 1890*, edited by W. H. New (1990)

100 *Modern British Essayists*, Second Series, edited by Robert Beum (1990)

101 *British Prose Writers, 1660-1800*, First Series, edited by Donald T. Siebert (1991)

102 *American Short-Story Writers, 1910-1945*, Second Series, edited by Bobby Ellen Kimbel (1991)

103 *American Literary Biographers*, First Series, edited by Steven Serafin (1991)

104 *British Prose Writers, 1660-1800*, Second Series, edited by Donald T. Siebert (1991)

105 *American Poets Since World War II*, Second Series, edited by R. S. Gwynn (1991)

106 *British Literary Publishing Houses, 1820-1880*, edited by Patricia J. Anderson and Jonathan Rose (1991)

107 *British Romantic Prose Writers, 1789-1832*, First Series, edited by John R. Greenfield (1991)

108 *Twentieth-Century Spanish Poets*, First Series, edited by Michael L. Perna (1991)

109 *Eighteenth-Century British Poets*, Second Series, edited by John Sitter (1991)

110 *British Romantic Prose Writers, 1789-1832*, Second Series, edited by John R. Greenfield (1991)

111 *American Literary Biographers*, Second Series, edited by Steven Serafin (1991)

112 *British Literary Publishing Houses, 1881-1965*, edited by Jonathan Rose and Patricia J. Anderson (1991)

113 *Modern Latin-American Fiction Writers*, First Series, edited by William Luis (1992)

114 *Twentieth-Century Italian Poets*, First Series, edited by Giovanna Wedel De Stasio, Glauco Cambon, and Antonio Illiano (1992)

115 *Medieval Philosophers*, edited by Jeremiah Hackett (1992)

(Continued on back endsheets)

Dictionary of Literary Biography® • Volume One Hundred Forty-Three

American Novelists Since World War II
Third Series

American Novelists Since World War II
Third Series

Edited by
James R. Giles
Northern Illinois University
and
Wanda H. Giles
Northern Illinois University

A Bruccoli Clark Layman Book
Gale Research Inc.
Detroit, Washington, D.C., London

To the people who taught us to read, the greatest gift we have had, for their grace and their passion, and in respect

Matthew J. Bruccoli
Edwin Harrison Cady
Jim Corder
James Melville Cox
Orville Clements
Earley Davis
J. Hubert Dunn
Georges Edelen
Richard Ellmann
Warren G. French
Roger and Eva Walker Giles
Rudolph P. Gottfried
Georgia M. and Knofel P. Hancock
Joseph W. Jones
Lyle Kendall
Gordon Mills
Alene Payton
Wallace Stegner
Clara Stephens
Edna Copeland Teaford
Maxine Turnage
Ruth Farlow Uyesugi
Yvor Winters
Samuel Yellen

And, always in hope, for Morgan

Contents

Plan of the Series

... Almost the most prodigious asset of a country, and perhaps its most precious possession, is its native literary product — when that product is fine and noble and enduring.

Mark Twain*

The advisory board, the editors, and the publisher of the *Dictionary of Literary Biography* are joined in endorsing Mark Twain's declaration. The literature of a nation provides an inexhaustible resource of permanent worth. We intend to make literature and its creators better understood and more accessible to students and the reading public, while satisfying the standards of teachers and scholars.

To meet these requirements, *literary biography* has been construed in terms of the author's achievement. The most important thing about a writer is his writing. Accordingly, the entries in *DLB* are career biographies, tracing the development of the author's canon and the evolution of his reputation.

The purpose of *DLB* is not only to provide reliable information in a convenient format but also to place the figures in the larger perspective of literary history and to offer appraisals of their accomplishments by qualified scholars.

The publication plan for *DLB* resulted from two years of preparation. The project was proposed to Bruccoli Clark by Frederick C. Ruffner, president of the Gale Research Company, in November 1975. After specimen entries were prepared and typeset, an advisory board was formed to refine the entry format and develop the series rationale. In meetings held during 1976, the publisher, series editors, and advisory board approved the scheme for a comprehensive biographical dictionary of persons who contributed to North American literature. Editorial work on the first volume began in January 1977, and it was published in 1978. In order to make *DLB* more than a reference tool and to compile volumes that individually have claim to status as literary history, it was decided to organize volumes by topic, period, or genre. Each of these freestanding volumes provides a biographical-bibliographical guide and overview for a particular area of literature. We are convinced that this organization — as opposed to a single alphabet method — constitutes a valuable innovation in the presentation of reference material. The volume plan necessarily requires many decisions for the placement and treatment of authors who might properly be included in two or three volumes. In some instances a major figure will be included in separate volumes, but with different entries emphasizing the aspect of his career appropriate to each volume. Ernest Hemingway, for example, is represented in *American Writers in Paris, 1920–1939* by an entry focusing on his expatriate apprenticeship; he is also in *American Novelists, 1910–1945* with an entry surveying his entire career. Each volume includes a cumulative index of the subject authors and articles. Comprehensive indexes to the entire series are planned.

With volume ten in 1982 it was decided to enlarge the scope of *DLB*. By the end of 1986 twenty-one volumes treating British literature had been published, and volumes for Commonwealth and Modern European literature were in progress. The series has been further augmented by the *DLB Yearbooks* (since 1981) which update published entries and add new entries to keep the *DLB* current with contemporary activity. There have also been *DLB Documentary Series* volumes which provide biographical and critical source materials for figures whose work is judged to have particular interest for students. One of these companion volumes is entirely devoted to Tennessee Williams.

We define literature as the *intellectual commerce of a nation:* not merely as belles lettres but as that ample and complex process by which ideas are generated, shaped, and transmitted. *DLB* entries are not limited to "creative writers" but extend to other figures who in their time and in their way influenced the mind of a people. Thus the series encompasses historians, journalists, publishers, and screenwriters. By this means readers of *DLB* may be aided to perceive literature not as cult scripture in the keeping of intellectual high priests but firmly positioned at the center of a nation's life.

*From an unpublished section of Mark Twain's autobiography, copyright by the Mark Twain Company

DLB includes the major writers appropriate to each volume and those standing in the ranks immediately behind them. Scholarly and critical counsel has been sought in deciding which minor figures to include and how full their entries should be. Wherever possible, useful references are made to figures who do not warrant separate entries.

Each *DLB* volume has a volume editor responsible for planning the volume, selecting the figures for inclusion, and assigning the entries. Volume editors are also responsible for preparing, where appropriate, appendices surveying the major periodicals and literary and intellectual movements for their volumes, as well as lists of further readings. Work on the series as a whole is coordinated at the Bruccoli Clark Layman editorial center in Columbia, South Carolina, where the editorial staff is responsible for accuracy of the published volumes.

One feature that distinguishes *DLB* is the illustration policy – its concern with the iconography of literature. Just as an author is influenced by his surroundings, so is the reader's understanding of the author enhanced by a knowledge of his environment. Therefore *DLB* volumes include not only drawings, paintings, and photographs of authors, often depicting them at various stages in their careers, but also illustrations of their families and places where they lived. Title pages are regularly reproduced in facsimile along with dust jackets for modern authors. The dust jackets are a special feature of *DLB* because they often document better than anything else the way in which an author's work was perceived in its own time. Specimens of the writers' manuscripts are included when feasible.

Samuel Johnson rightly decreed that "The chief glory of every people arises from its authors." The purpose of the *Dictionary of Literary Biography* is to compile literary history in the surest way available to us – by accurate and comprehensive treatment of the lives and work of those who contributed to it.

The *DLB* Advisory Board

Introduction

The United States just after World War II assumed virtually a new identity, and the writing from the late 1940s sometimes seems to have come out of just about as many viewpoints, theories, memories, and readings as there were people living at the time. They write and talk — oral history took on a significance during the postwar years that would grow throughout the rest of the century, informing some branches of American literature — about the monumentality of experience: the end of the last "good war," the rise of the United States in international politics and commerce, the opening of the universities to nontraditional classes and ethnic groups, the expansion of the literary canon, the new freedoms and strengths of women and ethnic groups, the horror and power of weaponry, decolonization and the explosion of new nations with special relationships to one of the two great powers, and the cold war that was a state of hostilities without declaration which nonetheless controlled world events and alliances.

The ordinary American who had hit the road in the Dust Bowl years moved even beyond that drift, and artists and writers found seven U.S. servicemen raising a united flag on a Pacific atoll; income growing so that the chicken in every pot hoped for by President Herbert Hoover was not a worry so long as there was a hundred-dollar-down house in which to cook it; and large families becoming fashionable, affordable, and socially favored as home and civic life became a myth that would call to, but baffle and elude, writers for the rest of the century, never providing its own, earlier unquestioned, definition. Crime and violence grew in stunning proportion to prewar experience, the juvenile delinquents of the 1950s leading eventually to the drive-by shooters and jack burglars of the 1990s, a far move from the shoot-outs and urban violence of Mark Twain's West or Theodore Dreiser's and Frank Norris's cities and their psychological and economic cruelties.

And maybe at the beginning of all of this Technicolor, as Tom Wolfe would call it in the 1960s, when it began to dazzle and burn too brightly, stood one image that opened the time — the nurse and the sailor in Times Square celebrating the end of World War II with a kiss vibrant with youth, hope, optimism, strength, confidence, love, and the black and white of anonymity. What this couple conveyed in the 1945 *Life* photograph was not new to human experience, but the expressions of it, the vitality and confidence, came out of victory in this war, with the expansion and importance it handed to the United States. Moreover, photographs themselves became an American icon in a nation of cameras and their images, with family albums continuing their domestic popularity, but with new technological potential: television, forensic imaging, computer enhancement. World wars do not create literature; simply, they destroy nearly everything in their paths. But at the end there is that couple, kissing, laughing, dancing with the hope of a new age, the fearlessness of conquerers in a world where only two decades earlier they or their families were probably, like most Americans, isolated, rural, onlooking.

The undeniable logic behind the tradition of designating 1945 as the beginning of a new era of the American novel is that it was also the year when the United States discovered itself one of only two world superpowers. For the generation who had fought the Great War (1914–1918), home had always been reality. It *was* a long way to Tipperary, but there was no question that everyone planned to come right back. The trip that began with the siege of Pearl Harbor has never ended. Home *is* now the undefinable myth and the political battleground. James Jones tried to identify and mourn it in *Some Came Running* (1958), and he made a finer attempt from Paris — his short stories, *The Ice-Cream Headache and Other Stories* (1968). Other expatriates in Europe included Chester Himes, who had learned before leaving the United States that his home country could not foster his genius; neither was it a home for James Baldwin.

Writers who stayed in this country would try to find homes — Stephen King, in *The Eyes of the Dragon* (1984), tried to wrest a home from terror, and his *Cujo* (1981), with its Saint Bernard, and *Christine* (1983), a celebration of the family car, follow the home-seeking trail. The most poignant search may have been that of Native Americans — N. Scott Momaday's youthful essay on how he feels on being Indian reveals the most painful truth of Indian literature: that he was not sure of who he was, much less where he lived as a "Native" American raised on reservations afforded by the U.S. government. And one among many women who have struggled over the concept of home, which has suffocated and defined them, is Sue Miller, who also writes of photography, in the postwar years more a domestic and a communications boon than ever before. The settings of Miller's novels are houses (for example, those in *Family Pictures* 1990; *For Love*, 1993), commanding even if nearly empty. Ross Lockridge's *Raintree County* (1948), one of the big books of the century, is the search by a man throughout time and place for the place in which he and his family have lived for generations. And two of the major authors – John Updike and Toni Morrison – write often on the nature of identity as it is frustrated and occasionally exalted in home and family. The Times Square kiss is an emblem: the couple in the kiss may well be strangers.

Almost as soon as the kiss was over, Americans became richer and busier than ever before. For some it was small changes – the replacement of chicken by steaks, the consumerism that assaulted the soul (Jones, *Some Came Running;* Updike, *Couples*, 1968). And the country no longer luxuriated in ignorance of international affairs. It could not continue looking on; now it made and implemented decisions. Under President Harry S Truman, Americans undertook the rebuilding of Europe, formerly the center of the worlds of intellect and style. The plan was to use Yankee technology and American generosity. But even as the most clearly powerful and intact of countries, the United States could not escape being touched by the profound insecurity and moral uncertainty that were a part of the war's legacy. The full disclosure of the horrors of the Holocaust forced the West to question as never before the inherent decency of human beings. The American technology that destroyed Hiroshima, John Hersey's ravaged city (1946), forced the nation to confront a newly discovered human potential: the extinction of all life, made possible by brilliant minds and malleable matter. Americans could hardly ignore the fact that the powerful instruments for human annihilation were the clear result of technology, in which they had for so long posited an almost religious faith.

After helping rebuild some of Europe with the Marshall Plan, the nation assumed a responsibility to stop the spread of communism and thus involved itself in the only-somewhat-undeclared conflict with the Soviet Union, rung in by Winston Churchill in his "iron curtain" speeches of the 1940s and perhaps ended in the collapse of the Soviet bloc in 1989. For the United States the first crisis of the cold war began just five years after World War II, earlier believed to be a defining, limiting event in international warfare. In 1950, when Communist North Korea invaded South Korea, U.S. troops went to aid the besieged Asian nation as part of a United Nations police action to force out the invading North Koreans. The Korean conflict lasted until its ambiguous ending in 1953, but forty years later, when the unconquered North Korea adapted the nuclear weaponry of World War II, the ambiguity was once more a live issue. Korea would be the first, but not the last, tragically indecisive, brutalizing post–World War II experience for the United States in Asia. By the end of the police action, more than 150,000 American casualties (killed and wounded) fell in Korea. The urge to fight, so long resisted before World War II, was not slow to return to the American household.

What happened in Korea from 1950 to 1953 was never officially called a war; it was the Korean conflict, a palatable political noun spoon-fed to a weary generation of only somewhat young men. Whatever it was called, it forced Americans to realize that there were real limitations to the power of even the strongest of nations, an idea that contributed significantly to a pervasive sense of instability and uncertainty in the United States, back wherever home was. In 1952 Americans elected as their president Dwight D. Eisenhower, the former commander in chief of the Allied forces in Europe; some of his political strength was his common touch, the famous smile that met a national need for reassurance and stability. But he was a general, not a father to the country; and the 1950s were haunted by another new kind of nightmare, and the dominant images were far from kisses – congressional committee rooms and microfilm in pumpkins; the tough, smug Roy Cohn and the finally exasperated counsel Joseph Welch, with his gentle outrage: "Have you no decency, sir?" Decency had once been a given in U.S. manners and morals; its loss, or at least diminution, was one of the grave blows of the postwar years. Joseph McCarthy, a senator from Wisconsin, had largely inspired the witch-hunt for Communists in places of influence in the United States, but he was joined readily enough by a still-unsettled and war-prone American nation. Writers and other creative people soon found themselves favorite targets of McCarthyism, with the blacklists that isolated friend from friend and destroyed the careers of suspected Communists, certainly including writers, in the motion-picture, radio, and television industries, and in academia. Ironically, Irwin Shaw, whose *The Young Lions* (1948) was the most optimistic of the major post–World War II novels because of Shaw's declared "faith in the decency of the American people," would be among those blacklisted.

The national insecurity and loss of faith in moral certainty inevitably touched the young American writers who began publishing in the late 1940s and early 1950s. Not surprising, several of them – Norman Mailer (*The Naked and the Dead,* 1948), Jones (*From Here to Eternity,* 1951), and Gore Vidal (*Williwaw,* 1951) – first published war novels; and a recurrent theme in this early World War II fiction is a warning against the imminent danger of an American fascism. Mailer and Jones, in their first published novels, create American generals who openly and unapologetically preach the necessity that strong leaders control the weak and directionless masses. And this thematic concern was not limited to the war novelists; Saul Bellow's *Dangling Man* (1944), William Styron's *Lie Down in Darkness* (1951), and Himes's *If He Hollers Let Him Go* (1945) express anxiety about the existence of grave internal threats to the preservation of American democracy. J. D. Salinger's *The Catcher in the Rye* (1951), not an overtly political novel, presented Holden Caulfield – youth in rebellion against a corrupt society and the "phonies" who profited from it – an emblematic figure for his entire decade. And even Shaw, with his abiding faith in the common American, wrote, in short stories and *The Troubled Air* (1951), specific protests against McCarthyism and the repression of the freedom of people whose lifework was words.

In contrast Herman Wouk violated the fictional logic of his otherwise powerful and honest novel *The Caine Mutiny* (1951) by imposing on it an arbitrary ending that seems to advocate adherence to authority, however incompetent or even corrupt. It is impossible to estimate the cost during the 1950s of self-censorship to American literature and to American culture in general. What is clear, though, is that the spirit of the times – a decade now remembered for full-blown emphasis on idealized family life, consumption of goods, and unquestioning adherence to newly created traditional values – caused serious American writers simply to retreat from any sense of involvement in, or commitment to, the dominant culture of the nation. The clearest example of a literary repudiation of mainstream American society came from the talented group of writers known as the Beat Generation. Jack Kerouac, Allen Ginsberg, and Lawrence Ferlinghetti were among the best known of the Beats, writers who sought in Zen Buddhism, jazz, and drugs antidotes to what they perceived as the sterile confor-

mity of American life. In a bit of historical foreshadowing, California – specifically San Francisco, and even more specifically San Francisco's City Lights bookstore – was the center of the Beat movement; later the city would be home to the passive rebels of the 1960s counterculture.

Zen would not prove to be the only foreign philosophy of significant influence on American literature and American culture in the years following World War II. French existentialism, with its emphasis on the absence of any ethical system in the external universe and the resulting need for each individual to discover or create individual moral truths, had a strong appeal for postwar writers. A kind of fiction that can be called existential realism began to appear on the American literary scene during the 1950s. The work of most of the important writers to emerge in the United States since 1945 contains at least existential overtones. For one remarkable example, perhaps the main consistency in the constantly evolving literary career of Mailer has been his self-definition as an American existentialist.

Despite the considerable importance of the 1950s to American literature, 1961 and 1962 more clearly represented the end of one era of the American novel and the beginning of another. In these two years, at the beginning of what would prove to be one of the most turbulent decades in American history, Ernest Hemingway committed suicide and William Faulkner died. The work of these men constituted the triumph of modernism in American fiction; and they had dominated the national literary scene for more than three decades. Indeed, only the American Renaissance writers (Nathaniel Hawthorne, Herman Melville, Ralph Waldo Emerson, Henry David Thoreau, and Edgar Allan Poe) had been so central and vital to American literature for so long as the Lost Generation, that group of young men born in the late 1890s who wrote, beginning in the 1920s, from Europe on themes of alienation and rejection of parochial American cultural norms. (Other than Hemingway's *The Sun Also Rises* [1926], in which the term *lost generation* was first used, other classics include F. Scott Fitzgerald's *The Great Gatsby* [1925] and *Tender Is the Night* [1934].) Hemingway and Faulkner, leading literary figures in their generation, produced a body of writing distinguished by its revolutionary sophistication in narrative technique and approach to characterization. Strongly influenced by the innovations in narration associated with Henry James and James Joyce, their work moved American fiction beyond William Dean Howells's "reality of the commonplace."

By the 1960s, however, the Hemingway-Faulkner legacy had begun to have an inhibiting effect on the American novel. It was increasingly difficult to surpass the innovations in modernist technique found in such Lost Generation masterpieces as Faulkner's *The Sound and the Fury* (1929) and *Absalom, Absalom!* (1936) and *The Sun Also Rises*. A result of the brilliance of these works was that, to later American writers, modernism was the only valid mode for the twentieth-century novel, but a few had already rebelled against the limitations of modernist technique. Bellow, who had published two novels during the 1940s that conformed to the narrative and structural conventions of modernism, rediscovered in *The Adventures of Augie March* (1953) the formal freedom inherent in Twain's nineteenth-century legacy of the frontier picaresque novel. American novelists searched for narrative structures that would liberate them from the restraints of modernism throughout the 1960s.

The social and political turbulence of that decade contributed to the intensely felt need of many writers to escape virtually any kind of limitations on their art. Few, if any, periods in American history have begun so hopefully or ended so chaotically as the 1960s. In 1960 John F. Kennedy, the country's youngest president, was elected. Kennedy's youth, his search for a New Frontier, and his often-quoted inaugural appeal seemed to promise a revival of American idealism. The young, academically brilliant administration perceived no limits: the nation was promised a man on the moon within the decade. And existing technology was there for the using: television had in the 1950s become the primary source of entertainment and information for most Americans; and, despite critical lamentations over its genuine potential for superficiality, Kennedy instinctively grasped its potential for forming public opinion through the visual sharing of public experience. He had achieved the presidency in part because his appearance against Vice-president Richard Nixon in a series of debates had won him the confidence of the American television audience, and he performed masterfully on television throughout his brief term in office.

This administration was confronted with the civil rights movement, symbolized in Dr. Martin Luther King, Jr., but led by many — the most nearly realized twentieth-century example of Thomas Jefferson's expected internal revolution. Not wanting to offend the Southern wing of the Democratic party, the president first offered only verbal support to the cause of civil rights.

But — when pictures of Freedom Riders and other civil rights protesters in the South under attack by water hoses, clubs, police dogs, and bombs began to dominate the national news on television screens throughout the nation — the civil rights movement quickly became the central beneficiary of the youthful idealism to which Kennedy had appealed. The president and his brother, Attorney General Robert Kennedy, saw the inevitability of a direct role in the struggle for American civil rights, which in some ways climaxed on 17 June 1963, when King delivered his "I Have a Dream" speech to a crowd of more than two hundred thousand in Washington, D.C., and such heroes of the movement as Bernice Regan of Sweet Honey in the Rock demanded freedom.

Their torment expressed the smothering brutalities of real experience that had found passionate voice in such novels as Richard Wright's *Native Son* (1940), William Attaway's *Blood on the Forge* (1941), and Ann Petry's *The Street* (1946) and that would later find literary voice in Morrison, who in 1993 received the first Nobel Prize for Literature awarded to a black American. Words came to be the most effective weapons for the people struggling in the civil rights movement. With the witness of these men and women, Washington came to see the necessity of passing a federal civil rights bill aimed at ending the barriers — and the bloodshed — legitimized by racial segregation in this country. The civil rights struggle inspired a new activism among Americans — writers, artists, entertainers, students, housewives, clergy, teachers — and Pete Seeger's "Wasn't That a Time?" expresses the peculiar combination of innocence, wonder, and corruption that the creative community experienced and translated. Novels of the 1960s by black authors, preceded in the recent past by the occasional Willard Motley (such as *Knock on Any Door*, 1947) or the many popular novels of Frank Yerby, came out of the earlier struggle of such writers as novelist and essayist Baldwin (*Go Tell It on the Mountain*, 1954; *Notes of a Native Son*, 1955) and Ralph Ellison, whose great work, *Invisible Man* (1952), emerged with a clarity and brilliance of voice rarely seen — or possible — in his own country of birth.

The nation was in a state of turmoil when on 22 November 1963 President Kennedy was assassinated. Frame 313 became the new American icon, and few events have been so devastating to the American sense of spirit as this murder and those that followed it in Dallas in the next three days. In a few seconds the illusory confidence of inexperience — still intact domestically — ended. By the end of the weekend a young policeman would also die by gunfire, and so would the alleged assassin – another young, undefined man, someone who may once have heard Kennedy's call to do what he could for his country. In the young president's death there was no second chance, no relief, no easy comprehension. The nation gathered in living rooms, churches, schools, and even department-store furniture showrooms, watching the ceremony of grief. In an extended television event, the last for this television president, the country found some shared solace in watching the lying in state, the funeral, and the processions to the Capitol, the cathedral, and Arlington National Cemetery.

The murders that followed, however, introduced other kinds of shock. Officer J. D. Tippitt was an American Everyman: young, married, with children; he could have been anyone. And when, on live television, Kennedy's accused assassin, Lee Harvey Oswald, was shot to death by a Dallas nightclub owner, the killing was an early example of the power of television to stun its audience through the immediacy of image and the quickness with which anarchy emerged from the high energy and political commitment of the dead president. Some people were already wondering whether such a passive medium as the novel could remain viable to an audience trained to respond so quickly. And Oswald's death, moreover, intensified an already-present element of doubt and uncertainty first expressed by the artistic community. Further, it seemed impossible that so slight and insignificant a figure as Oswald could have a significant or decisive effect on American history, and suspicion of conspiracy in the president's death will possibly always haunt the American mind. In years that followed, several books with assassination-plot motifs appeared, among them Bryan Wooley's *November 22* (1981) and Vance Bourjaily's *Man Who Knew Kennedy* (1967).

The nation seemed briefly to rediscover some stability and moral certainty when Kennedy's successor, Lyndon B. Johnson, a Texan who was expected to sympathize with the segregationist South, brilliantly secured the passage of the 1964 Civil Rights Act in a Congress he knew profoundly. Thus the old-style Southern politician provided the legislative centerpiece so long sought. That a new stability had arrived seemed especially certain when Johnson was reelected in 1964 in a landslide victory over conservative Barry Goldwater, a Westerner who had voted against the civil rights bill. But it was a short triumph, a small domestic peace. Events overseas would quickly shatter the national recovery and war on poverty.

Not long after Americans first read Hersey's *Hiroshima*, events had begun in Southeast Asia that would bring a new war, one that devastated the spirit in a way not earlier experienced by Americans. Few people knew or noticed that in the 1950s the United States, in an attempt to halt the spread of communism in Asia, had committed itself to defending a corrupt and authoritarian regime in a small Southeast Asian half-nation. As the political situation deteriorated, President Kennedy sent American military advisers to South Vietnam, and after the Johnson election in 1964 the United States became heavily involved in a miserable, confusing war in a country that few Americans had previously known. Throughout the next four years increasing numbers of American resources and troops were poured into a struggle doomed from the first – and with the historic example of the French fall in Vietnam shouting the futility to those who could listen.

The horror and hopelessness of the American effort was, again via television, brought home to the nation in 1968. Amid repeated assurances by the U.S. government and military that the war was going well, the North Vietnamese forces launched a devastatingly effective offensive against American and South Vietnamese forces during a term of negotiated cease-fire. As it did throughout the war, television brought shattering images of horror and destruction into the homes of Americans – the naked, crying Vietnamese girl whose clothing had been burned away by napalm, running toward the cameras of a nation who had supplied it; a South Vietnamese general (thus on the side of the United States) executing a bound prisoner with a pistol shot to the head, the death shown (though nearly suppressed by nationalistic sentiment) in the film *Hearts and Minds* (1974). For the first time in the century – in a national mood far from the loyalty, cooperation, and sacrifice of World War II – a reaction, and even revulsion, against the nation's involvement in a military action took to the streets, the newspapers and journals, even the classrooms of the mid 1960s.

More and more young Americans of draft age refused to accept induction into the armed services, and antiwar demonstrations became almost a ritual of daily life on college campuses across the nation. Hardly noticed in its beginnings, a counterculture of young men and women devoted to opposition to the war, experimentation with sex and drugs, and rebellion against everything associated with middle-class tradition (the establishment) was highly visible throughout urban America. The residential section of San Francisco surrounding Haight and Ashbury streets was soon identified as the center of the youth-dominated counterculture. It was the "Age of Aquarius" in San Francisco (and on the stages of *Hair* [1967] productions in New York and London), the time of a "dirty little war" in Southeast Asia. Across the United States an overidentified generation gap erupted – an expression of the personal isolation that replaced international political isolation. The dirtiness of the war, besides the massive casualties suffered, had to do with a new kind of racial conflict that ripped apart the fabric of national unity in the last half of the 1960s: African-Americans, especially in the urban centers in the North and on the West Coast, were outraged by the disproportionate number of young black men being drafted to serve in Vietnam ground forces and in addition came to believe that resources of potential use in America's inner cities were being wasted in Southeast Asia. The Watts section of Los Angeles in 1965 and the black neighborhoods of Detroit in 1967 suffered massive outbreaks of rioting and looting, and the television images of the late 1960s were body bags and coffins coming off planes at the edges of burning cities.

All the tensions that had been building throughout the 1960s seemed to explode in the years between 1968 and 1970. On 4 April 1968 Martin Luther King was assassinated in Memphis; and on 5 June of that same year Robert Kennedy, in a campaign for the presidency, was shot and killed – on television – in Los Angeles just after winning the California Democratic primary. In the summer, national television audiences saw the spectacle of antiwar demonstrators at the Democratic National Convention in Chicago under assault by armed officers in what the federally ordered Walker Report later called a "police riot." In 1970 National Guard troops fired on and killed student protesters at two universities, Kent State in Ohio and Jackson State in the Mississippi capital.

In 1969 an American did indeed land on the moon; still, Neil Armstrong's walk there, hard to celebrate as first anticipated in the early 1960s, represented one of the few seemingly unequivocal triumphs for American technology in the decade. Yet for the novelist, and especially for the writer of science fiction, even this revolutionary scientific breakthrough had ominous overtones. Now what had recently belonged to the world of fantasy had become one more aspect of reality; like so many other major historical events during the 1960s, Armstrong's adventure on the moon was visible on television as it occurred. From then on – indeed, from Alan Shepard's 1961 *Gemini* rocket ride – *astronaut* be-

came a part of the vocabulary of ordinary Americans rather than a concept reserved for science fiction. Space science was always national news, but, until the walk on the moon, television images were limited primarily to takeoffs and landings, with the occasional verbal thrust ("Godspeed, John Glenn") also made for a watching audience.

Inevitably a decade marked by such relentless turmoil dramatically affected the American novel. It in fact called into even more serious question than in the previous decade the traditional mimetic role of the novel; American writers and critics began to wonder whether fiction could hope to capture such an elusive reality. Even at the beginning of the decade, Philip Roth expressed genuine doubt on this question:

> The American writer in the middle of the 20th century has his hands full in trying to understand, and then describe, and then make *credible* much of the American reality. It stupefies, it sickens, it infuriates, and finally it is even a kind of embarrassment to one's own meager imagination. The actuality is continually outdoing our talents, and the culture tosses up figures almost daily that are the envy of any novelist.

Throughout the rest of the 1960s echoes of Roth's pessimistic analysis, usually with some variations in emphasis, became commonplace in literary magazines. Mailer, among others, wondered whether the mass media's daily barrage of information and news effectively buried any objective and potentially verifiable reality that might exist. In the 1960s it became somewhat fashionable to issue pronouncements on the death of the novel. It was, after all, a time of so much death.

But a genre that had been so central to Western culture for so long would not pass quickly into oblivion. Already seeking alternatives to modernism and traditional realism, American novelists began to invent ways to revitalize the novel. The most venturesome found routes to use the chaos and contradictions of the time creatively. First in short stories and then in a novel, *Snow White* (1967), Donald Barthelme perfected his technique of narrative collage, a device that deliberately *appeared* to echo the fragmentation and randomness of American culture and society. In his first novel, *V.* (1963), Thomas Pynchon transformed the national obsession with plots and conspiracies into an elaborate historical tour de force; in *Gravity's Rainbow* (1973) he would explore an even darker and more complex landscape. Two World War II novels, one published at the beginning and the other at the end of the 1960s and based on different modes of narrative experimentation, depicted what almost seemed another war than the one described in the late 1940s and early 1950s by Jones, Mailer, and Shaw. With the title of his first novel, *Catch-22* (1961), Joseph Heller coined a phrase that has since become part of the English and American vocabulary for the description of bureaucratic and technological irrationality and insanity. Kurt Vonnegut, Jr., a prisoner of war in Dresden, Germany – a city of irreplaceable cultural importance and no great military significance when the U.S. Air Force destroyed it in a World War II technique known as fire bombing – combined in *Slaughterhouse-Five* (1969) literary realism with science fiction to capture and convey the technological horror that he had witnessed. This was beyond the power of television, a smashing together of internal and external realities and voices incomprehensible through chronological reportage and images.

John Barth, in a 1967 essay provocatively titled "The Literature of Exhaustion," concisely expressed the rationale for the continuous search in the 1960s for innovation in fictional technique. Careless readers saw the essay as simply another pronouncement on the death of the novel; and Barth sometimes seems to encourage precisely this kind of misinterpretation. At one point, for instance, he says that he is "inclined to agree" with those who believe that "the novel, if not narrative literature generally, if not the printed word altogether, has by this hour of the world just about shot its bolt." But the essay turns out to be a plea for the revitalization of the novel. Barth asserts that contemporary writers of fiction who ignore the work of such literary innovators as the Argentine writer Jorge Luis Borges, the Irish playwright Samuel Beckett, and the Russian-born novelist Vladimir Nabokov are doomed to create outdated and irrelevant fiction. Self-consciousness in narration is the key to creating the kind of art that Barth believes has validity; people need, he says, "novels which imitate the form of the Novel, by an author who imitates the role of Author."

The self-conscious, experimental fiction that Barth advocated and that he, Barthelme, Vonnegut, Pynchon, Heller, and others wrote was given different labels, the most common one probably being *metafiction*. Assuredly their work marked a movement of the American novel away from modernism and toward postmodernism; where Hemingway and Faulkner had perfected techniques ranging from narrative minimalism to complex variations on the stream of consciousness to prevent any overt intrusion of an authorial presence that would de-

stroy the reader's suspension of disbelief, the 1960s practitioners of metafiction devised elaborate methods to expedite precisely such intrusions. In his 1971 critical study *City of Words,* Tony Tanner provides an analysis of the fascination that such elaborate and often self-reflective alternative "realities" as labyrinths, mirrors, and libraries held for these writers. In many ways Barth's novel *Giles Goat-Boy* (1966) epitomizes 1960s metafiction in using a mode of ironic mysticism and a mock-academic settings.

Other writers, responding to the sense that contemporary reality had become too complex and chaotic to be captured by traditional realistic fiction, would attempt to erase the commonly accepted boundaries between fact and fiction. Describing contemporary events, Truman Capote in *In Cold Blood* (1965) and Mailer in *The Armies of the Night* (1968; he would use the technique in such later works as *The Executioner's Song,* 1979) combined objective reporting with fictional subjectivity to produce a genre variously called nonfiction fiction, faction, or the New Journalism, the latter the province of Wolfe, whose one novel, *Bonfire of the Vanities* (1987), would come out of years of observation of the complex realities of New York City life. Other writers – for instance, Styron in *The Confessions of Nat Turner* (1967) – chose instead to fictionalize the historic past. Styron's book is not at all the same thing as the popular historical novel; nor is it a glorious revelation of the mythic past, as is Lockridge's *Raintree County.* It is instead a meditation on the connections between past and present American racial hatred and guilt. Finally, for all the speculation during the 1960s that traditional literary realism could no longer capture external reality, it was that decade which saw the publication of at least two novels, Hubert Selby's *Last Exit to Brooklyn* (1964) and Joyce Carol Oates's *them* (1969), that would alone have revitalized the tradition of American literary naturalism.

One must use care to avoid overgeneralizing the influence of the 1960s on the American novel. It is easy to find self-destructive artifacts: Jones, far from his literary home, the U.S. Army, wrote in Paris *Go to the Widow-Maker* (1967) and *The Merry Month of May* (1971) – two novels that lessened his reputation and commented pessimistically on the fallen times. Still, the decade was a climactic and defining one for the novel and for American literature in general, and it at least resulted in a recognition of the need to reexamine long-standing assumptions about the viability of literary realism and modernism closely, even if such examination resulted in the reaffirmation of either or both of these modes of writing.

For the United States the 1970s, while eventually a calmer decade than the preceding one, still had traumatic moments. In 1970 President Nixon at last started the process of extricating the United States from its military involvement in Vietnam by bombing and then invading the neighboring nation of Cambodia, which housed Vietcong bases. By the middle of the next year most American ground troops had been withdrawn from Vietnam, though a peace settlement was not signed until January 1973, after Nixon, in an echo of Truman in 1945, had ordered heavy bombing of the North. The war left a legacy of division and recrimination that has yet to end. The men and women who served in Vietnam did not receive the kind of homecoming that had traditionally been the reward for returning American veterans of overseas combat.

Nor, after the traditional parades, was life ever wholly fine for returning veterans or those who stayed at home. Women, for example, were required to come to expanded productive life outside the home during the absence of men in war, but there was no room for them when the veterans reclaimed their jobs. And not all veterans returned to jobs or were able to work. Every war has produced disabilities among veterans; additionally, the wars after World War II have produced large numbers of addicted men and women, as the opiates of survival in other countries became the opiates of culture shock on return to a consumerist, unthreatened civilian nation. Drug addiction among veterans is a new phenomenon in the middle class; before the 1960s the few references to it came in occasional pieces – references, for example, to "the drunken Ira Hayes," a Pima Indian who raised the flag on Iwo Jima but could not live in reservation America. By 1985 the Kentucky teenagers in Bobbie Ann Mason's *In Country* would know more about "dope" in Vietnam than did the mothers of the men and women who went to war there. Stephen King also writes on the addiction of his generation as a result of Vietnam.

The conquering heroes of World War II changed in only eight years to the largely neglected forces returning home from Korea. The Vietnam veterans came home to a place where to be ignored was good fortune. The other option was to be openly denounced for having fought in an immoral war. No clear and easily comprehensible justification of the U.S. involvement in Vietnam was ever articulated. When the war ended inconclusively after the deaths of more than fifty-six thousand American soldiers, overwhelmingly of the lower class and often people of color ("Three-Five-Zero-Zero" in *Hair* is virtually whispered; the song about the dirty little war reflected a war that had become a dirty little secret), the nation wanted above all to try to forget the entire experience. It has never been forgotten, though in time acceptance of the experience and its responsibilities has begun to seem possible, and the building of the Vietnam War Memorial was one of the rare healing acts in the public art of this country. Talking and writing about Vietnam have come slowly, and only recently have such writers as Tim O'Brien, Larry Heinemann, and Mason been free to explore the experience of the U.S. fighting contingent in Vietnam and in the United States after the war.

It was U.S. mass media that began a realistic evaluation of the war and its legacy. Between 1978 and 1990 award-winning American films explored the horrific nature of military combat in Vietnam and/or the postwar suffering of those who survived it; among the best are *The Deer Hunter* (1978), *Coming Home* (1978), *Platoon* (1986), and *Born on the Fourth of July* (1989). By the late 1980s even television, especially in the series *China Beach,* was beginning to examine the suffering, and the political and moral ambiguity, of the war. The novelists on the war are a small group, most of them Vietnam veterans; they have so far produced a small, distinguished body of war fiction. They have used a variety of literary approaches that echo both the early realistic-naturalistic World War II novels of Mailer, Jones, and Shaw and the later postmodernist works of Heller and Vonnegut. Heinemann's *Close Quarters* (1977) and *Paco's Story* (1987) are written in a predominantly realistic mode, while O'Brien's *Going After Cacciato* (1978) experiments with postmodernist narration. Mason's *In Country* was the first novel to observe the domestic war: the returns to individual and civil ignorance of the horror of modern warfare; the mysterious sicknesses that followed the fighting; and the curious, insensitive, invasive, compassionate, and chaotic response of the people who stayed at home. The near helplessness of women after war has seldom been so uncompromisingly stated as in Mason's descriptions of the pot of geraniums held on Mamaw's lap in the long journey from western Kentucky to the Wall, where she at first experiences the agony of not being able to "see" her son and then, with the help of unknown friends, gives him her flowers.

Initially, the landslide reelection of President Nixon in 1972 and the 1973 Paris treaty that, for the United States at least, ended the war promised the fulfillment of a national longing for unity and stability. That illusion was shattered when a pre-election burglary of Democratic national headquarters in the Watergate apartment/office/shopping/dining complex in Washington, D.C., barely noticed when it occurred, mushroomed into a complex scandal that reached finally into the White House itself and, in August 1974, forced Nixon to become the first American president to resign from office. A crucial factor in his downfall was television, which broadcast the U.S. Senate's investigation into the Watergate burglary and its subsequent coverup by the president and his key advisers. Key participants in the Senate hearings were quickly transformed into heroes, villains, and icons. The hearings themselves seemed at times to be a hybrid of the morality play and soap opera as they introduced American television viewers to a bizarre underground of laundered money, Cuban-American superpatriots, and renegade CIA agents. Himes was not the only novelist to write out of this environment, but he deals with it brilliantly in his detective novels, which newly expanded that form. The hearings dramatized a sequence of actual events that were clearly improbable, if not "unreal."

Just as Roth had lamented more than a decade earlier, the literary imagination was severely challenged to match, and then replicate, such a surrealistic reality. Certainly the elaborate, if ultimately ineffectual, attempt by the president's men (and one woman, at least – Rose Mary Wood) to destroy any traces of administration involvement in what was simultaneously a ridiculous and potentially sinister episode appeared to validate the obsession of Pynchon and other postmodern writers with vast and ultimately impenetrable plots and conspiracies. Other writers handled the Watergate affair in reportage, most prominently Robert Woodward and Carl Bernstein in *All the President's Men* (1974).

The sense of national instability, severely affected by the presidential resignation, was not erased in the 1970s. The Nixon presidency was followed by the administrations of Gerald Ford and Jimmy Carter, which remained free of scandal but were nevertheless perceived as unfocused and ineffectual; and in 1992 Updike's title *Memories of the Ford Administration* would give readers pause: there was little to remember. But in the early 1980s a politician at least as adroit as John F. Kennedy in the use of television to create dramatic and instantaneous images assumed the presidency: Ronald Reagan, a former motion-picture actor called "the great communicator" because of his intuitive mastery of mass media, became the first American president since Eisenhower to complete two terms in office. The Reagan presidency represented a return to

political conservatism and a repudiation of much of the liberal Democratic agenda that had dominated national politics since Franklin D. Roosevelt's New Deal and was the direct result of a national movement away from political activism. Thus, while it represented something of a new national consensus, it alienated many traditional liberals and much of the old intellectual community.

During this period of national malaise and nondirection, serious American writers became more alienated from the national mainstream than at any time since the 1920s at least. This alienation was partly, but certainly not entirely, the result of national politics. To a significant degree it was related to an evolving ideology in academic circles that denied the traditional role of the novel as the literary genre of the middle class. In fact, the influence of the French thinkers Michel Foucault and Jacques Derrida led to new theories – first structuralism and then deconstruction – that questioned traditional assumptions about the nature and purpose of literature and of writing itself. Most structuralists argued that literary texts were interrelated and were not primarily the creation of individual writers but the product of the structure of society's dominant ideas and values. Deconstructionists held that, because of the uncertainty of language itself, all writing most inevitably negates its own apparent meanings. Since these two theories assert that the traditional belief in an individual author of a novel is merely a convention and that the elusiveness of language constantly negates the possibility of any consistent theme or intent in any piece of writing, they challenged and repudiated the traditional view of the novel as a controlled individual work designed to speak to a mass audience.

This new emphasis on the fundamentally arbitrary nature of literature and thus of critical judgments about it led to an extensive reexamination of the accepted canon of American literature. Beginning in the 1970s feminist critics, merging some aspects of structuralist theory with the ideas of the French psychoanalyst Jacques Lacan, argued that the canon had traditionally been established by white males and thus reflected an arbitrary and limited approach to American writing. The feminist critical agenda resulted in more than one kind of benefit for American literary studies. It led to the rediscovery of a few previously undervalued American women writers of the past, among them Kate Chopin, Tillie Olsen, Zora Neale Hurston, Anzia Yezierska, and Meridel Le Sueur. It also inspired new thinking about the proper subject matter for the novel by asserting that books written by men have tended to undervalue, if not to ignore or misperceive completely, the value of women, even in their customary nurturing roles. Finally, it brought a new awareness of the stereotypes that male writers have often imposed on female characters and an awareness of contemporary women writing to counter such stereotypes.

The same impulses that have affected feminist literary thinking have inspired, especially in academia, a view of literature and the novel in particular as being most important as a form of cultural study. This approach to literature has resulted in a new interest in writers from traditionally marginalized social groups. Beginning in the 1970s such black women writers as Morrison, Alice Walker, Gayl Jones, and Toni Cade Bambara began to exercise an influence on the American novel comparable to that already enjoyed by Bellow, Roth, and other Jewish-American writers. Maxine Hong Kingston, Amy Tan, and many other young Asian-American novelists have made their initial contributions to the national literature, as have Chicano writers Sandra Cisneros, Raymond Barrio, Rudolfo Anaya, and Rolando Hinojosa-Smith, among the first Hispanics to celebrate their ethnicity since John Rechy (*City of Night*, 1963). Finally the fiction and poetry, perhaps engendered by the 1930s writings of D'Arcy McNickle, of Momaday, whose *House Made of Dawn* (1968) was the first contemporary Indian novel, and of such later writers as Louise Erdrich, Leslie Marmon Silko, and James Welch have inspired a Native American literary renaissance.

The contemporary American novel reflects so rich a cultural diversity that it is difficult to think that until the postwar period scholars innocently defined the novel as a hidebound masculine volume. The considerable benefit of newer, broader, and more precise thinking has inevitably resulted in the questioning of old assumptions about the role of the American novelist as the voice of national consensus. Few today speak of the national mission of the American writer with the confident assurance of Emerson or Howells. Fewer successfully play the part of a national man of letters as Edmund Wilson did so recently, and as Frederick Exley admired in *Pages from a Cold Island* (1975). For different reasons and in different ways, postmodernist novelists such as Pynchon and even writers speaking for socially marginalized groups must assume that they are addressing much more restricted and limited audiences than the traditional middle-class readership of fiction. There are, in addition, more prosaic reasons for the contemporary alienation of the serious American novelist from the middle class.

Television has been the communications medium of choice for middle-class America for nearly five decades; and for almost that long writers and others have regretted its shallowness and superficiality. Inevitably the ubiquitous presence of television in America has trained its audience to respond more readily to instantaneous visual images than to the printed page. Beginning in the 1950s paperback reprints evolved as a means of making the novel accessible to the middle class, but the paperback-publishing industry has itself been adversely affected by inflationary pressures. A dramatic example of the cost of fiction came in 1992 when Mailer's long novel, *Harlot's Ghost*, broke the thirty-dollar-a-copy barrier in hardback. In direct response to the exorbitant cost of hardback fiction, Bellow has published two novellas — *A Theft* and *The Bellarosa Connection* (both 1989) — as paperback originals.

Still, in spite of all these pressures, some quite serious and important postwar novelists have tried to speak to, and sometimes on behalf of, middle-class America. Updike's centrality to the postwar American novel owes in no small part to his evocation, in four volumes, of the financial and spiritual troubles of his fictional Toyota dealer, Rabbit Angstrom. In *Rabbit, Run* (1960), *Rabbit Redux* (1971), *Rabbit Is Rich* (1980), and *Rabbit at Rest* (1990), Updike depicts the morally ambiguous social rise of an ordinary American and thus echoes the fiction of Howells and Sinclair Lewis. It is a tribute to the versatile nature of Updike's considerable talent that he can, in other work, echo, usually for satiric purposes, the methodology of literary deconstruction.

Other postwar American novelists of impressive talent have revitalized old fictional genres traditionally associated with popular culture. In *Horseman, Pass By* (1961) and *Moving On* (1970) Larry McMurtry wrote a kind of novel that can best be described as the contemporary Western, in which he investigates an ongoing conflict between the debased values of twentieth-century Texas with the state's legacy of frontier freedom. In 1986 McMurtry won the Pulitzer Prize for fiction — not for one of his contemporary Westerns but for *Lonesome Dove,* a novel structured around a trail drive, a familiar plot device to any student of the popular culture of the American West. Somewhat similarly Stephen King has attained enormous popularity by revitalizing and making contemporary political observations through the genres of Gothic and horror fiction; Elmore Leonard, among others, has brought new perspectives to the detective novel.

The late 1950s and 1960s pronouncements on the novel's demise to the contrary, American fiction since World War II has been, and continues to be, vital indeed. A 1968 anthology of post–1945 American fiction, *How We Live: Contemporary Life in Contemporary Fiction*, edited by Penny Chapin Hills and L. Rust Hills, illustrates this point by closing with a list of three hundred living American fiction writers of at least some significance. Twenty-five years later an even-longer list is easily developed. Even if no contemporary American writers can be said to hold the kind of Olympian prominence enjoyed by the two modernist giants Hemingway and Faulkner – and no intelligent bets are being placed (it is, for example, risky to ignore the witty and profoundly wise Eudora Welty) – post–World War II American fiction is distinguished by a richer diversity of achievement than at any other time in the nation's history.

– Wanda H. Giles and James R. Giles

Acknowledgments

This book was produced by Bruccoli Clark Layman, Inc. Karen L. Rood is senior editor for the *Dictionary of Literary Biography* series. David Marshall James was the in-house editor.

Production coordinator is George F. Dodge. Photography editors are Dennis Lynch and Joseph Matthew Bruccoli. Layout and graphics supervisor is Penney L. Haughton. Copyediting supervisor is Bill Adams. Typesetting supervisor is Kathleen M. Flanagan. Julie E. Frick is editorial associate. The production staff includes Phyllis A. Avant, Joseph Matthew Bruccoli, Ann M. Cheschi, Melody W. Clegg, Patricia Coate, Wilma Weant Dague, Brigitte B. de Guzman, Denise W. Edwards, Sarah A. Estes, Joyce Fowler, Laurel M. Gladden, Stephanie C. Hatchell, Rebecca Mayo, Kathy Lawler Merlette, Pamela D. Norton, Delores I. Plastow, Patricia F. Salisbury, and William L. Thomas, Jr.

Walter W. Ross and Deborah M. Chasteen did library research. They were assisted by the following librarians at the Thomas Cooper Library of the University of South Carolina: Linda Holderfield and the interlibrary-loan staff; reference librarians Gwen Baxter, Daniel Boice, Faye Chadwell, Cathy Eckman, Gary Geer, Qun "Gerry" Jiao, Jean Rhyne, Carol Tobin, Carolyn Tyler, Virginia Weathers, Elizabeth Whiznant, and Connie Widney; circulation-department head Thomas Marcil; and acquisitions-searching supervisor David Haggard. Special thanks are due to Roger Mortimer and the Staff of Special Collections at the Thomas Cooper Library. The following librarians generously provided material: William Cagle and Joel Silver of the Lilly Library, Indiana University, and Ann Freudenberg, Kendon Stubbs, and Edmund Berkeley, Jr., of the University of Virginia Library.

American Novelists Since World War II
Third Series

Dictionary of Literary Biography

Vance Bourjaily

(17 September 1922 –   )

William A. Francis
University of Akron

See also the Bourjaily entry in *DLB 2: American Novelists Since World War II, First Series.*

BOOKS: *The End of My Life* (New York: Scribners, 1947; London: W. H. Allen, 1963);

The Hound of Earth (New York: Scribners, 1955); republished as *The Hounds of Earth* (London: Secker & Warburg, 1956);

The Violated (New York: Dial, 1958; London: W. H. Allen, 1962);

Confessions of a Spent Youth (New York: Dial, 1960; London: W. H. Allen, 1961);

The Unnatural Enemy (New York: Dial, 1963; London: W. H. Allen, 1965);

The Man Who Knew Kennedy (New York: Dial, 1967; London: W. H. Allen, 1967);

Brill Among the Ruins (New York: Dial, 1970; London: W. H. Allen, 1971);

Country Matters: Collected Reports from the Fields and Streams of Iowa and Other Places (New York: Dial, 1973);

Now Playing at Canterbury (New York: Dial, 1976);

A Game Men Play (New York: Dial, 1980);

The Great Fake Book (New York: Weidenfeld & Nicolson, 1986);

Old Soldier (New York: Donald I. Fine, 1990);

Fishing by Mail: The Outdoor Life of a Father and Son, by Bourjaily and Philip Bourjaily (New York: Atlantic Monthly, 1993).

PLAY PRODUCTIONS: *The Quick Years,* New York, Actors' and Writers' Theatre, 25 November 1953;

$4000, libretto by Bourjaily, music by Tom Turner, Iowa City, University of Iowa, July 1969.

OTHER: *discovery,* six issues, edited by Bourjaily (New York: Pocket Books, 1952–1955);

"The Lost Art of Writing for Television," in *Writing in America,* edited by John Fischer and Robert B. Silvers (New Brunswick, N. J.: Rutgers University Press, 1960), pp. 108–124;

"A Certain Kind of Work," in *Afterwords: Novelists on Their Novels,* edited by Thomas McCormack (New York: Harper & Row, 1969), pp. 177–191.

SELECTED PERIODICAL PUBLICATIONS – UNCOLLECTED:
FICTION
"The Amish Farmer," *Esquire,* 94 (October 1980): 92–99;

"The Duchess," *Southern Review,* 25 (January 1989): 199–220.

NONFICTION
"The Girl in the Abstract Bed," drawings by Tobias Schneebaum, *Mademoiselle,* 40 (November 1954): 112–113;

"An Epitaph for Biafra," *New York Times Magazine,* 25 January 1970, pp. 32–33, 85–87;

"My Father's Life," *Esquire,* 101 (March 1984): 98–100;

"The Final Act," *American Heritage,* 35 (June–July 1984): 31–35;

"Red Lewis' Town Is Kinder to Him Than He Was to It," *Smithsonian,* 16 (December 1985): 46–57.

In Vance Bourjaily's ten novels, spanning nearly fifty years, he has observed with a critical but compassionate eye the devastating impact of World War II on the American psyche, along with the subsequent corrosive force of the cold-war era

Vance Bourjaily (photograph by Jeff Smoot)

and its markings of suspicion and paranoia. In the society that Bourjaily describes the once-nurturing institutions of church and school are emptied of promise, as is the fabled American dream. Alone, misguided, and often exhausted, Bourjaily's protagonists struggle to preserve their humanity in a nation that "seems . . . to have used up its citizens' energy – the only national resource worth calculating – in too short and bright a flash." This passage from *The Hound of Earth* (1955) echoes in all his novels, describing the elemental conflict his characters must resolve if they are to survive amid the chaos of the age. His protagonists draw on what inner resources they possess and confront the paradoxes and dilemmas that circumscribe their humanity and limit their self-discovery. Some are not so successful, but at least they begin to see the truth about themselves; others, seeing the truth, make the compromises their consciences will allow. Sympathetically portrayed, Bourjaily's characters are sustained by the restorative powers of nature, the transcendental powers of music and song, and the indistinguishable powers of life and love, all of which constitute the thematic center of his novels.

Bourjaily was born on 17 September 1922 in Cleveland, Ohio. (The surname is derived from the Arabic *Abu-jaily* [father of men] and is attributed to an ancestor whose children were all male.) He was

the second of three sons born to Lebanon native Monte Ferris Bourjaily, a journalist, and Ohio native Barbara Webb Bourjaily, a journalist and author of popular romance fiction. Monte Ferris Bourjaily became the general manager of United Feature Syndicate and was the founder of Globe Syndicate. He edited and published works by writers such as Heywood Broun, Westbrook Pegler, and Eleanor Roosevelt. The Bourjailys left Cleveland when Vance was an infant, and he grew up in Connecticut and New York. Following his parents' separation when he was about eleven, he lived near Winchester, Virginia, with his mother and stepfather.

Bourjaily's love of stories was fostered by his mother at an early age. She read to him from the works of Joseph Conrad, Charles Dickens, and Emily Dickinson, as well as from children's classics. Later he read boys' books, stories by Sir Arthur Conan Doyle, and novels by Sinclair Lewis, especially *Arrowsmith* (1925). Logan Pearsall Smith's essays in *Trivia* impressed on him the pleasures of a lovely writing style. He discovered the fiction of F. Scott Fitzgerald and Nathanael West at Solebury prep school in Pennsylvania, but he was expelled as a sophomore for smoking. The influence these writers had on Bourjaily is evident in his references to them in his stories and allusions to them in the titles of his novels.

After graduation from Handley High School in Winchester in 1939, Bourjaily planned to attend Harvard University, but family finances prevented his doing so. Instead, he spent the fall of 1939 in Winchester writing a series of philosophical essays, "Not to Confound My Elders," which portray a young man planning to write about his life experiences. The essays are darkened by the shadow of the inevitable war; he thought of himself as a member of another lost generation. He believed that not writing from experience would essentially be dishonest and propagandistic. With his mother's help he tried to have the essays published. Her agent discussed the manuscript with Maxwell Perkins, who said that the essays might be published as a stunt but that it would be damaging to a young man who was someday going to be a writer. These months spent in Winchester are captured in "The Poozle Dreamers" (*Confessions of a Spent Youth,* 1960). Bourjaily never did go to Harvard, but after his year of writing he entered Bowdoin College in Brunswick, Maine. He interrupted his studies from 1942 to 1944 to serve as a volunteer ambulance driver for the American Field Service, and from 1944 to 1946 he served in the army.

After his discharge Bourjaily went back to Virginia, where he spent six months completing the first draft of *The End of My Life* (1947). He showed the manuscript to Perkins, who recommended changes. In December 1946 Bourjaily married Bettina Yensen. He returned to Bowdoin, from which he graduated in 1947, shortly after *The End of My Life* was published. He turned immediately to his next novel, "The Sun Follower," which was never published. From 1949 to 1950 he was a staff writer for the *San Francisco Chronicle.*

During the early 1950s the Bourjailys lived for more than two years in Mexico City, where he wrote *The Quick Years,* a play that was produced in New York in November 1953. In New York he cofounded *discovery,* which presented poems and stories by new writers, and he wrote television scripts for live broadcasts. In 1957 Bourjaily accepted a teaching position at the University of Iowa's Writers Workshop, where he remained until 1980, when he left to teach creative writing at the University of Arizona. Since 1985 he has been a member of the Louisiana State University M.F.A. program in creative writing, which he directed for seven years.

The End of My Life is the story of Skinner Galt's ill-prepared passage from idyllic, irresponsible college life to the barbaric realities of war. In New York — where he waits for passage to Cairo to serve as a volunteer in the ambulance corps — Skinner and his girlfriend, Cindy (short for Cinderella), an actress, create a never-never land in which they play at life while grim news of war is reported from the front. Skinner, as his name indicates, cannot get beneath the surface, or skin, of life. He reads but does not comprehend T. S. Eliot's profoundly disturbing *Waste Land* (1922). Skinner reduces complex worldviews and ideologies to a game of football in which the YES team (Abraham Lincoln, Mark Twain, and Karl Marx) plays the NO team (Voltaire, Jonathan Swift, and Eliot), and Skinner is the ball.

Skinner is a friendly, witty, and engaging man, yet — for reasons never made clear — he is self-destructive. In Syria and Italy, where he experiences the bloodshed of war, he also discovers his hatred of the military authority that abuses the values he had been taught at home. He withdraws, becomes a loner, and turns his destructive isolation on Cindy by ending their correspondence. His close friend Rod, a homosexual and a gifted musician, goes AWOL into an Arab city and takes on a new identity. Skinner realizes that he and his friends have not been prepared emotionally for the inevitable war. The props of adolescence fall away; the "pre-war neurotics" try to cope with their enlarged death wishes and bouts of self-pity, from which little illumination comes. The "nice, small war . . . with clear-cut issues" that they hoped to find engulfs them in its senseless bestiality. Their immunity as ambulance drivers cannot shield them from their destructive negativism, their existential irresponsibility. In the climax of the novel Skinner is involved in the death of a pretty young nurse whom he drives to the front near Capua, Italy, to observe the fighting. She is killed when a German pilot strafes the road. He begins to feel guilt for his complicity in her death, but in his cell he finds sanctuary from his guilt in a deathlike listlessness. He is on the threshold of his rite of passage to a responsible adult life, but the novel ends before he makes the passage. Skinner can only imagine a future when war ends and peace and hope return.

The End of My Life was well received by reviewers, many of whom said that Bourjaily showed promise. They praised its excellent dialogue, sense of scene, uncompromising honesty, and clearly delineated characters. Bourjaily's debt to Fitzgerald and Ernest Hemingway was noted. Some critics were disappointed, however, that Bourjaily did not explain the source of Skinner's nihilism.

Eight years intervened between the publication of Bourjaily's first novel and his second, *The Hound of Earth,* which dramatizes the disturbing realization that peace comes with treaties but wars con-

Dust jacket for Bourjaily's 1976 novel, in which the narrative structure is modeled after Geoffrey Chaucer's Canterbury Tales

tinue unarrested in the hearts and souls of the combatants, who must negotiate their own terms of peace. Allerd Pennington, the guilt-driven protagonist, had unknowingly contributed to the development of the atomic bomb that destroyed Hiroshima. He goes AWOL, abandons his family and friends, changes his name to Clark, and spends seven years as an exile in the United States. His progress through the country metaphorically parallels the journeys of Meriwether Lewis and William Clark in their nineteenth-century exploration of the Louisiana Territory. Bourjaily maps the cold-war period in a nation whose shallow materialism is grotesquely dramatized in a San Francisco department store during the Christmas season of Pennington's last days of exile prior to his arrest.

The novel castigates a self-indulgent, materialistic society that has lost touch with the nation's history and the true meaning of the American dream, which has been perverted to signify extraordinary wealth, possessions, and power. The fragile values

of love, spirituality, and comradeship have been supplanted by bizarre sexuality, obsession with religious trappings and combative holiday shopping for tawdry toys, and backstabbing friends who betray Pennington to FBI agent Casper Usez, whose first name honors one of the Magi and whose gift to Pennington is compassion and understanding. Usez tries to reason with Pennington, but Pennington will not be convinced that his work on the atomic bomb was not an unforgivable sin against mankind. And yet he cannot forsake all others: he is drawn to a young man who needs his help and to a girl he begins to love. In allowing himself to be arrested by Usez, he sets aside pious guilt and affirms what he had all along denied – his humanity, the Hound of Earth that no one escapes. In *The Hound of Earth,* which mitigates the pessimism of *The End of My Life,* Bourjaily found the major theme that resonates in all his later works: compassion, which teaches that everyone suffers together.

Reviewers of *The Hound of Earth* acknowledged Bourjaily's rich portrayal of character and the evocative pre-Christmas setting along with the fast pace of the chase story. But many of them were not satisfied with the development of the fine idea promised in the story. They noted the lack of insight into Pennington's struggle of conscience over the seven years of his self-imposed exile.

In 1955, soon after completing *The Hound of Earth* but before moving to his teaching position at the University of Iowa, Bourjaily turned to *The Violated* (1958), the most ambitious of his first three novels. The germ of the idea for this novel came to him in Mexico, where he heard an account of children putting on a performance of *Hamlet*. Intrigued and wondering how they might do this, he began writing a novel with the opening lines, "Look. In a condemned house in Brooklyn, some children are performing *Hamlet*." The novel was completed in Iowa, where Bourjaily's teaching position allowed him free time to revise and polish the manuscript for publication in August 1958.

The action of the story turns around the children's extraordinary performance of *Hamlet,* which Bourjaily makes into a metaphor of the inarticulate, depersonalized urban society of the late 1950s. The play within the novel is unduly long, yet it is an effective device. It is "The Mousetrap" in which Sheila Walle, who directs the production and plays Hamlet, catches "Mousie," her Gertrude-like mother, who offends her child as well as her husband. Sheila's poignant attack on her mother engages the adult characters in debilitating guilt. Intuitively the players chafe their parents' feelings and, in the single aborted performance, catch the reflections of men and women unable to relate to their children and to one another.

The spirit of compassion that overtakes Pennington in *The Hound of Earth* is muted in *The Violated,* in which many characters give and receive pain, commit adultery, and abuse and even destroy one another, but they almost never rise above their limitations in order to embrace life and love. They are violated by one another and by a force about which Bourjaily speaks in a note for the book's dust jacket: "their inability to communicate, to love, to comprehend, to create . . . neurotic commitments to preposterous goals or, more tragically, to no goals at all."

The action of the novel begins in 1957 with the performance of *Hamlet,* but the time quickly shifts back to the early 1930s and the adolescent years of the major characters, Tom and Ellen Beniger and their friends Guy and Eddie, whose lives are shaped by their parents' failure to love. This is the violation they in turn will pass on to the child actors. The congenital violation has physical and psychological manifestations: Tom has asthma and an unspecified chest pain; Ellen is an alcoholic; Eddie develops a grotesque, dwarfish body; and Guy, sexually violated as a boy, seduces women and keeps score in his diary. Largely as a result of their failure to communicate, the characters become isolated, and their inner cores are numbed. Sheila's play temporarily shocks them into life and self-examination, which are frustrating and confusing for them. Numbness, forgetfulness, and a death-in-life existence overtake them.

In the final chapter of this long novel Bourjaily moves beyond 1957 to the next decade and the next generation's failures: deaths, divorces, and suicide. In a sad, cynical conclusion Bourjaily shows the four-year-old son of one of the *Hamlet* cast members (the suicide) being molded into an actor through speech and dance lessons. The cycle of violation continues like that of a Greek tragedy in this dark, nihilistic novel devoid of the spiritual regeneration that flows from compassionate understanding and love.

Confessions of a Spent Youth is an autobiographical novel written over a period of eight years. The narrator's literary name, Ulysses Snow Davids Quincy, derives from Thomas De Quincey's *Confessions of an English Opium Eater* (1822). *Quince,* as he is called by friends, also suggests a near rhyme with *Vance.* Although Bourjaily covers some of the same episodes included in *The End of My Life,* his intention was not to repudiate his first novel but, as he says in "A Certain Kind of Work" (1969), "to see

the same kind of experience, which it dealt with romantically, with tough, early-middle-aged clarity." *Confessions of a Spent Youth* is a much fuller and richer work, and its positive view of life differentiates it from Skinner's story.

Quince recounts his war experiences fifteen years after his discharge. From this detached viewpoint he realizes that "the things we learn by experience, while interesting enough, are never really clear until they no longer apply to the lives we are living." This distancing allows Quince – and Bourjaily – to distinguish between the accumulation of raw, naturalistic experiences to which he had dedicated himself at seventeen and the careful analysis of the meaning of those experiences, which include certain elements found in American literature: sexual initiation, drinking, college life, first love, religious doubt, and violation of established codes. The earnest, confessional mode Bourjaily adopts seeks to correct the stereotypes found in the realistic novels that shaped young Quince's attitudes toward life.

Quince is a picaresque hero who crosses many thresholds on his travels. He also takes on different identities, which are subtly applied to him along mythic lines. Bourjaily playfully associates Quince with Hermes, messenger of the gods and guide to the underworld as well as patron of travelers, thieves, and healers. Quince-Hermes reveals the hell of a venereal-disease ward and transports bodies of dead soldiers back from the line. The Fisher King story of Eliot's *Waste Land,* which Skinner read without understanding, is also threaded throughout the novel. At the end of his travels – his quest for who he is – Quince visits a town named Dayport (the promise of the light and time that await him) to begin to make a life for himself. The older Quince voices the major theme of the novel: "I was always a tourist in the worlds of your world, and never found the one in which I could belong until I learned to make my own." Some reviewers dismissed *Confessions of a Spent Youth* as a pretentious, ineffective imitation of De Quincey's *Confessions* and faulted the novel's gratuitous sexuality. Others praised Bourjaily's vitality of style, intellectual honesty, and successful creation of a modern representative hero searching for the meaning of his experiences.

The idea for *The Man Who Knew Kennedy* (1967; the title is taken from Sinclair Lewis's *The Man Who Knew Coolidge,* 1928) began with an invitation Bourjaily received to write a story honoring President John F. Kennedy for inclusion in a commemorative anthology. The project failed, but Bourjaily decided to turn his story into a novel, so he put aside "Expedition," his novel in progress. Kennedy's 1963 assassination and the darkening of Camelot, his

Washington, D.C., are paralleled in *The Man Who Knew Kennedy* by the self-destruction of Dave Doremus, the man who met Kennedy when they were recuperating in a military hospital. Dave has many of Kennedy's qualities and ambitions and is a true member of the president's generation. The unraveling of Dave's business ventures and his failures in marriage are a paradigm for his generation's destiny of premature decline and death after a short burst of hope and promise, as seen in *The Violated*.

The erratic course of the nation without Kennedy is dramatized when Dave, his friend Barney, and their wives go on a Caribbean cruise. For the two men this voyage re-creates images of their halcyon days of sailing off the Maine coast shortly after the war. The cruise takes them near San Salvador, which Dave insists on "discovering" as Columbus had done centuries earlier. It is an innocent attempt to find origins, to return to the beginnings before the nation became old and greedy and bound up in frequent wars (Vietnam looms on the horizon). But the two couples cannot escape the present. Dave leaves abruptly to answer the desperate call of Sunny Brown, a singer to whom he had once been married. When Barney reaches New Haven, he learns of Dave's and Sunny's suicides.

An honorable businessman, Barney tries to find a solid foundation in a shifting world. This is not easy for a man who espouses the creed, "The first lesson of our times: take all the false security you can get in this world. It's the only kind there is." He returns to his hardwood company and finds assurance in the beauty of wood in an age of plastic and veneer. Family sustains him, and in the closing pages of the novel he takes his children to Arlington National Cemetery to stand before the eternal flame at Kennedy's grave. It is an act of faith meant to be imprinted in the minds of his children. At this tender moment Kennedy's quotation reassures him: "We are not here to curse the darkness, but to light a candle." Life goes on with renewed meaning for Barney, who has lost a president and a friend, but there is an ominous sense that other Lee Harvey Oswalds lurk everywhere to bring down the good men, whose successors do not walk in the light of Camelot.

The Man Who Knew Kennedy sold well and was a Literary Guild selection. It was reviewed widely, but the notices were mixed. Unfavorable reviews cited weaknesses in plot and characterization. Bourjaily was faulted for not being more explicit about why the twentieth century is out of joint or why Dave is driven to suicide. Reviews in a more positive tone praised the elegiac novel's powerful nostalgia and sentimental reminiscences as well as the development of vivid secondary characters.

Brill Among the Ruins (1970), the later-chosen title for "Expeditions," is Bourjaily's most successful novel both in the development of its plot and the incisive portrait of its hero, Bob Brill. In the novel, which was nominated for the 1970 National Book Award, Bourjaily reveals the inner life of a complex hero whose extraordinarily high standards are offset by his human failings. Like *The Man Who Knew Kennedy*, *Brill Among the Ruins* is an elegiac novel. The object of mourning in the latter is the violation of the flagging American spirit by the Vietnam War, conducted by two vulgarians: "Johnson's vulgarity was deadlier; Nixon's more depressing." The war is mirrored in the embattled Midwest, which is threatened from within by loggers, arrogant hunters, land developers, and farmers seeding their land with poisonous chemicals that are carried into the nearby Mississippi River.

In despair Brill sets off for a pre-Columbian archaeology site in Mexico where he sees in the distant past the origins of America's decline: European violation of the aboriginal people and the imposition of European values; the introduction of deadly diseases; and Christian license to rape and pillage the land. In this setting Brill, the man from Rosetta, Illinois, learns to decipher the coded past and realizes that he has one last chance to take a stand against the arrogance of politicians and the cozy ignorance of a smug, complacent American society destined for ruin. In addition he must repair the unity of his fractious family.

Brill Among the Ruins is a poignant, entirely credible story about the wonder of life wrested from the ruins (and runes) of postwar society by a man who is not paralyzed by the events of the century but who heroically confronts the clownish vulgarians who steer America toward oblivion. Despite its excellence *Brill Among the Ruins* received mixed reviews. It was faulted for its abbreviated sentences and stylistic coyness, its quick turns in plot and subplot, and its fantastic element. More sensitive reviewers responded to the novel's penetrating portrait of Brill, the excellent passages on archaeology, and the depiction of the abrasive times and indifferent middle-class values and of the positing of individual responsibilities when attractive escape routes abound.

Bourjaily's seventh novel, *Now Playing at Canterbury* (1976), consists of stories in which each first-person narrator, according to Bourjaily, is distinctly not the author. Each narrator is characterized through the story told and the narrative method used, as in Geoffrey Chaucer's *Canterbury Tales* (circa 1387). Bourjaily presents a comedy of manners (chapter 1); a story called "See Sato in the Funny Papers" (chapter 5), in which comic-strip balloons contain lines of dialogue; a gothic tale called "The Maneaters of Dueyville" (chapter 13); a Chaucerian rhymed-couplet story called "A Bad Spring for Everybody's Wife" (chapter 15); and a Joycean tale (chapter 17). The connecting point of the somewhat uneven stories is a tragic opera, *$4000,* for which Bourjaily wrote the libretto. (*$4000* was performed at the University of Iowa in July 1969.)

The narrators are gathered in celebration of art at the dedication of a new performing-arts building on the campus of State University. The novel features good cheer, both ribald and sublime humor, grotesque people and events, accounts of the visceral sexuality of the castrati, and ever-present music. The journey with which the novel begins – "Here we go. The quest is on again" – is for stories, which the novel celebrates. Through the gaiety and tears of the storytellers, life is celebrated: "Every man is his own Homer, blind, caught in the endless wonder of the words, of the cries, of the shouts, of the laughter, of the tears of the things of the stories of our lives." An intricate, complex book, *Now Playing at Canterbury* is greater than the sum of its parts: it is Bourjaily's tour de force. Reviewers responded positively to the festive spirit of the book but occasionally complained about the meandering structure and the tedious details of some stories.

According to Bourjaily in a 1988 interview with William A. Francis, *A Game Men Play* (1980) was written in response to the "turgid, baroque, overwritten, [and] far too melodramatic" fiction he read in 1977 as a National Book Award judge. He concluded that those novels were "full of Byzantine plotting . . . unnecessary densities of prose and . . . prose ornaments." He decided then, in reaction to those novels, that *A Game Men Play* was to have a straightforward story line, and the prose was to be free of metaphors and other figures of speech. The novel's hero, C. K. "Chink" Peters, like the prose, is lean, sinewy, and unpretentious. The story is part pastoral meditation, part thriller. During World War II Chink was an intelligence officer required to perform bloody deeds, which he did with little feeling. After the war ended, he was a CIA agent playing the game men play, but he dreamed of a life of his own.

Early in the novel, aboard a freighter carrying thoroughbred horses to New Zealand, Chink thinks about two lovely girls whose recent violent deaths in Manhattan were reported in a San Francisco paper. He had taught them equestrian skills when they were younger and living near him in Virginia.

Dust jacket for Bourjaily's 1980 novel, a thriller featuring a former CIA agent

Chink's ocean passage takes him back in time to thoughts of his parents and youth. He reflects on his solitary life as a horseman in northern California and is eager to return to the quiet life he has made for himself. But, once the journey ends, he is called back into his old ways to play the game men play, one of intrigue and suspense.

Summoned to New York by the girls' father, Chink becomes immersed in a thrilling, tangled plot of lies and deceptions. He solves the murders, but in doing so he discovers far more disturbing truths about the pitiful human condition of the late twentieth century. Unlike Skinner and Pennington, however – as well as the characters in *The Violated,* who have few inner resources to pull them through times of despair – Chink makes a Spartan affirmation of love, duty, comradeship, and especially life itself. Yet he distances himself from society and finds peace in the solitude of the land and the horses he trains. The prose style and dramatic action of *A Game Men Play* are a union of sound and sense. Reviewers praised the novel's sheer storytelling plea-

Dust jacket for Bourjaily's 1990 novel, which focuses on two brothers, one of whom has AIDS

sure, rich assortment of characters, fast pace, quick wit, and effective plotting.

Bourjaily's love of traditional jazz is central to *The Great Fake Book* (1986). The technical challenge he posed for himself was to write a novel in which the author is simply not present, a challenge he first met in *Now Playing at Canterbury*. He removed himself as commentator in *The Great Fake Book* by writing a form of epistolary novel made up not only of letters but also of telephone conversations, recorded messages, the narrator's notes to himself, and the notes of Mike Mizzourin interspersed between the pages of a fake book, which is in the possession of a retired newspaper editor who releases the pages a few at a time to Charlie, Mike's son. In exchange for the letters Charlie promises to find out information about the editor's former mistress.

Musicians used the illegal fake book, a compendium of more than a thousand songs, to play a wide variety of music. Mike notes in his copy that "*the Great Fake Book* [is the] *book of the great fake life*

without which real life would be unbearable." Events in the life of Mike, who died thirty years earlier, are slowly revealed to Charlie through the pages he receives from the retired editor. The reader follows both stories, one embedded in the other, past and present intertwined. Mike's voice from the past tells of his struggle to become a musician; the small-town intrigues and treacheries that follow him to his death in New York; the gothic characters with whom he is caught up, including young Evaun, whom he loves; and the courtship of Livia, Charlie's mother.

Charlie discovers that the national and international intrigues of 1980 in which he is entangled are variations of his father's complex life following World War II. Livia, a lovely fashion model when she met Mike, refuses to tell Charlie the events leading to his father's death. Silence and anger freeze her in the buried past. Only when Charlie forces her to reveal truths about his father does she become alive by writing a long, fascinating letter to him. The mystery of the past and the power of music that vitalized it make storytellers of Mike, Charlie, and Livia. And stories, like the Great Fake Book, make life bearable. Reviewers generally praised *The Great Fake Book* for its vitality, fast pace, and carefully delineated characters.

Old Soldier (1990) is Bourjaily's shortest novel. Its plot is crisp and strong, its characters and setting vivid. The thematic heart of the novel is the love between two brothers, Joe and Tommy McKay. Through the eyes of Joe, an old soldier, the reader sees Tommy, a homosexual musician who has just learned that he has AIDS. The brothers are bonded in their love of bagpipes, the outdoors (fishing for landlocked salmon in Maine), and Tommy's son, Little Joe, from a long-ago marriage. In its rush from the promises of life and love to Tommy's heroic self-sacrifice at the climax of the novel, the story unfolds with an almost breathless pace, short chapters, and brisk dialogue.

Old Soldier is a plaintive novel of lost expectations, as symbolized by Tommy's playing of Patrick Mor's "Cumha na Cloinne" (Lament for the Children). The fishing scenes in northern Maine convey some of the mystery of life that Henry David Thoreau and Hemingway captured in their reflections on nature. But the idyllic moments are shattered when nearby campers, believing that Tommy's disease is contagious, attack the brothers and try to drive them away. In the struggle Tommy is wounded. Knowing that his blood is infectious, he sacrifices himself in the river. Joe mourns his brother's passing by playing the slow music of "The

Braes of Locheil" and then releases the bagpipe into the swift, deep water. Landlocked like the salmon that "couldn't use the air that kept us alive, anymore than we could use theirs," Joe returns to his namesake nephew to be the father Tommy never could.

With the exception of *The Violated* and *The Man Who Knew Kennedy*, which both enjoyed good sales and publication in paperback, Bourjaily's novels have not sold widely. Perhaps the untimely death of Perkins in 1947 adversely affected Bourjaily's prospects for commercial success. Furthermore, in a 1988 interview with William Parrill, Bourjaily observed that, at the Dial Press, "I never had the same two people as editor and publisher twice. It got pretty confusing after a while." Editor-author relationships aside, Bourjaily, a private man, has not sought publicity to promote his books. He takes a philosophical view about his reputation as a novelist. In a 1977 interview with Matthew J. Bruccoli, Bourjaily observed: "Each time there has been a book I've been, if not optimistic, at least hopeful that I would make some money and get more general recognition. . . . But meanwhile, I suppose, one constructs a life of what satisfactions are available."

Bourjaily's reputation rests on his ability to tell wonderful stories with vivid, surprising details. He creates multidimensional characters who are motivated by high, often unattainable, aspirations; are entirely human; and come to terms with the world they did not make. Bourjaily's novels depict the common man struggling – often heroically, often paradoxically – to live with the contradictions that define society. Rich language, brisk dialogue, subtle wit, and broad humor converge in Bourjaily's novels, in which closeness to the land and celebration of story and song are his hallmarks.

Interviews:

Harry T. Moore, Interview, in *Talks with Authors*, edited by Charles F. Madden (Carbondale: Southern Illinois University Press, 1968), pp. 201–214;

Matthew J. Bruccoli, "Vance Bourjaily," in *Conversations with Writers I* (Detroit: Bruccoli Clark/Gale, 1977), pp. 2–23;

Steve Wilbers, "Inside the Iowa Writers' Workshop: Interviews with Donald Justice, Marvin Bell, and Vance Bourjaily," *North American Review*, 262 (Summer 1977): 7–15;

Michael J. Bandler, "Portrait of an Author Reading," *Chicago Tribune Book World*, 20 January 1980, pp. 1–2;

William A. Francis, "A Converstion about Names with Novelist Vance Bourjaily," *Names*, 34 (December 1986): 355–363;

Francis, "From Jazz to Joyce: A Conversation with Vance Bourjaily," *Literary Review*, 31 (Summer 1988): 403–414;

William Parrill, "The Art of the Novel: An Interview with Vance Bourjaily," *Louisiana Literature*, 5 (Fall 1988): 3–20;

Dinty W. Moore, "An Interview with Vance Bourjaily," *AWP Chronicle*, 22 (February 1990): 1–4.

References:

John W. Aldridge, *After the Lost Generation: A Critical Study of the Writers of Two Wars* (New York: McGraw-Hill, 1951), pp. 121–132;

Aldridge, Introduction to Bourjaily's *The End of My Life* (New York: Arbor House, 1984), pp. xi-xvii;

Robert W. DeLancey, "Man and Mankind in the Novels of Vance Bourjaily," *English Record*, 10 (Winter 1959): 2–6;

Harris Dienstfrey, "The Novels of Vance Bourjaily," *Commentary*, 31 (April 1961): 360–363;

William A. Francis, "The Motif of Names in Bourjaily's *The Hound of Earth*," *Critique*, 17, no. 3 (1976): 64–72;

Francis, "The Novels of Vance Bourjaily: A Critical Analysis," Ph.D. dissertation, Case Western Reserve University, 1975;

Francis, "Vance Bourjaily's *The Man Who Knew Kennedy*: A Novel of Camelot Lost," *Literary Onomastics Studies*, 14 (1987): 199–211;

William McMillen, "The Public Man and the Private Novel: Bourjaily's *The Man Who Knew Kennedy*," *Critique*, 17, no. 3 (1976): 86–95;

John M. Muste, "The Fractional Man as Hero: Bourjaily's *Confessions of a Spent Youth*," *Critique*, 17, no. 3 (1976): 73–85;

Muste, "The Second Major Subwar: Four Novels by Vance Bourjaily," in *The Shaken Realist*, edited by Melvin J. Friedman and John B. Vickery (Baton Rouge: Louisiana State University Press, 1970), pp. 311–326;

"The Role of the Writer in America," *Voices*, 2 (Spring 1962): 3–27;

Evelyn Shakir, "Pretending to Be Arab: Role-playing in Vance Bourjaily's 'The Fractional Man,'" *MELUS*, 9 (Spring 1982): 7–21.

Papers:

The major manuscript collection of Bourjaily's published and unpublished works is located in the library of Bowdoin College, Brunswick, Maine. The University of Iowa library has a small collection of his manuscripts.

Harry Crews

(7 June 1935 –   )

Michael P. Spikes
Arkansas State University

See also the Crews entry in *DLB 6: American Novelists Since World War II, Second Series.*

BOOKS: *The Gospel Singer* (New York: Morrow, 1968);

Naked in Garden Hills (New York: Morrow, 1969);

This Thing Don't Lead to Heaven (New York: Morrow, 1970);

Karate Is a Thing of the Spirit (New York: Morrow, 1971; London: Secker & Warburg, 1972);

Car (New York: Morrow, 1972; London: Secker & Warburg, 1973);

The Hawk Is Dying (New York: Knopf, 1973; London: Secker & Warburg, 1974);

The Gypsy's Curse (New York: Knopf, 1974; London: Secker & Warburg, 1975);

A Feast of Snakes (New York: Atheneum, 1976; London: Secker & Warburg, 1977);

A Childhood: The Biography of a Place (New York & London: Harper & Row, 1978; London: Secker & Warburg, 1979);

Blood and Grits (New York & London: Harper & Row, 1979);

Florida Frenzy (Gainesville: University Press of Florida, 1982);

Two (Northridge, Cal.: Lord John, 1984);

All We Need of Hell (New York & London: Harper & Row, 1987);

The Knockout Artist (New York & London: Harper & Row, 1988);

Body (New York & London: Poseidon, 1990);

Madonna at Ringside (Northridge, Cal.: Lord John, 1991);

Scar Lover (New York & London: Poseidon, 1992).

SELECTED PERIODICAL PUBLICATIONS – UNCOLLECTED: "Getting It Together," *Writer,* 84 (June 1971): 9–11;

"Why I Live Where I Live," *Esquire,* 94 (September 1980): 46–47.

Harry Crews, circa 1992 (photograph by Maggie Powell)

Harry Crews has primarily written novels – his thirteenth was published in 1992 – though he has also authored a highly acclaimed autobiography and many essays. One of the most original and provocative writers of the contemporary South, he creates fictional worlds and describes real ones that have variously fascinated and repulsed his critics but have almost never left them indifferent. Crews's universe is grim and often surreal, filled with physical freaks and emotional misfits, bizarre perversions and obsessions, and extravagant acts of violence. As Allen Shepherd observes, "Reading Crews is not something one wants to do too much of at a single sitting; the intensity of his vision is unsettling."

Crews relates in *A Childhood: The Biography of a Place* (1978) that he was born and raised in dire poverty in rural south Georgia. His stepfather – like Harry's father, who died when his son was a small child – was a tenant farmer who worked long, back-breaking hours, barely making enough to support his family. The environment in which the young Crews lived was stark and bleak, full of all manner of suffering and hardships, though it also afforded moments of love, close family ties, and simple pleasures.

In 1953, at age seventeen, Crews enlisted in the Marine Corps, in which he served for three years. After his discharge in 1956 he enrolled at the University of Florida on the GI Bill. As he observed in a 1983 interview with Kay Bonetti, "I didn't go to the university because I thought somebody'd teach me how to write. . . . I went there because it was a place to be for four years, and I would get money from the government." Midway through his college career he took a year and a half off to see the country on his Triumph motorcycle.

In an autobiographical sketch included with his first novel, *The Gospel Singer* (1968), he notes:

> I headed west one bright spring morning with seven dollars and fifty-five cents in my pocket, and during the following year I was in jail in Glenrock, Wyoming, beaten in a fair fight by a one-legged Blackfoot Indian on a reservation in Montana, washed dishes in Reno, Nevada, picked tomatoes outside San Francisco, had the hell scared out of me in a YMCA in Colorado Springs, Colorado, by a man who thought he was Christ, and made friends in Chihuahua, Mexico, with a Mexican airline pilot who made a fetish of motorcycle saddlebags.

Following this beatnik *wanderjahr,* Crews returned to the University of Florida, where he studied with Andrew Lytle, whose instruction and friendship were vital to Crews's early development as a writer. After receiving his B.A. in 1960 and his M.S.Ed. in 1962, Crews taught English for five years at Broward Community College in Fort Lauderdale, Florida, supporting his wife, Sally, and their son Byron (their youngest son, Patrick, died in 1961). In 1968 he became a creative-writing instructor at his alma mater, where he still teaches today.

Not a typical academic, Crews has long been known for his barroom brawling, heavy drinking, and general hard living, though, as he claimed in a 1992 interview with Ruth Ellen Rasche, he is presently sober, having dried out after being "drunk for about nine years." In this interview he related the story of one of his colleagues telling a PBS reporter

that "people like Harry Crews should not be allowed on university campuses for young people to watch self-destruct." Crews still spends time in bars and pool halls, yet now doing research for his books rather than imbibing. "When I'm doing that [listening and observing in a pool hall]," he said, "that's just as important as an 18th century scholar poring over dusty, huge books in the stacks of the library in search of something he needs to know."

Recognition was slow in coming for Crews. He wrote seriously for more than ten years, churning out scores of short stories and four novels without publishing anything. His persistence, however, finally paid off with *The Gospel Singer*. This novel centers around the misadventures and destruction of the title character. The Gospel Singer is from a small, depressing Georgia town, Enigma, which he left as a young man in order to market his good looks and exceptional voice in the city but to which he has returned as the book opens, principally to see his longtime lover, MaryBell. His relationship with her contains and reflects the central conflicts in his life: the need to maintain a public persona versus knowledge of his true self; the desire for fame and fortune versus feelings of guilt for exploiting others; and the longing for innocence versus a compulsion toward evil.

MaryBell was a childhood playmate and sweetheart of the Gospel Singer, but she became much more than that early in his ministry after a service in which he accidentally converted her. Enflamed with adoration and girlish love, she gave herself to this man who, without really thinking, succumbed to his lustful desires. This incident initiated a squalid, clandestine affair. He lies to her about his other sexual involvements, subtly deceives her into believing he intends marriage, and finally turns her into a bitter nymphomaniac whom he fears.

The Gospel Singer no more wanted to convert MaryBell than he wants to convert the legions of others he has led to Christ. He knows he is a hypocrite – maintaining a public facade of innocence and singing God's praise as if he means it, though performing sheerly for financial reward – and he feels guilty about it. Nonetheless, in order to sustain the popularity and wealth he so craves, he continues the charade. Crews accents the Gospel Singer's depravity and misery by associating him with the attractions in a freak show that follows him around the country, drawing on his audiences; he is as inwardly grotesque as they are outwardly deformed.

The Gospel Singer never gets to see MaryBell, at least not alive, when he returns to Enigma. Upon

*Dust jacket for Crews's third novel, which focuses on the residents
and staff of a rural Georgia nursing home*

arrival he discovers that she has been murdered by Willalee Bookatee Hull, a close black friend of his from childhood. Willalee, who has also been converted by the Gospel Singer and has founded a church in his honor, killed MaryBell out of resentment and anger over her revelation to him of the Gospel Singer's secret sins. By the end of the book, the Gospel Singer is so racked with pain over the role he has played in the downfall of MaryBell and Willalee and so repulsed by his audiences' search for salvation through him that, at the urging of his manager Didymus, he confesses his sins before a large crowd gathered at a revival service at which he is scheduled to sing. Deeply disappointed in their savior's frailty, the mob falls upon him, lynching their idol along with Willalee, whom they have dragged out of jail.

Through his depiction of the Gospel Singer, Crews comments on the hidden deformity that often underlies seeming perfection, the devastating consequences of living a lie, and the compulsion to wallow in acknowledged evil. Through his depiction of MaryBell and the other admirers, Crews highlights the gullibility of the common man and woman, their desperate need for messiahs to compensate for their inner lackings, and the irrational violence and hatred that can erupt when this need is not met.

Walter Sullivan wrote in the *Sewanee Review* (1969) that *The Gospel Singer* "has all the hallmarks of a first novel: it is energetic but uneven, competent but clumsy, not finally satisfactory but memorable." Crews's book may be uneven and clumsy in places, but its high energy, finely drawn characters, and compelling message more than make up for its relatively minor flaws and render it not merely memorable but highly satisfactory. Crews's second novel, *Naked in Garden Hills* (1969), is in many respects even more accomplished than his first. Jean Stafford in the *New York Times Book Review* (13 April 1969) called it "southern Gothic at its best" and asserted that it "lives up to and beyond the shining promise of Mr. Crews's first novel." *Naked in Garden Hills* is set in a central Florida town, Garden Hills, that once boasted a prosperous phosphate mine but now, as the story begins, is destitute and virtually deserted because of the mine's closing. Crews relates in the essay "Getting It Together" (1971) that this setting, like the one for *The Gospel Singer,* grew out of a real-life experience. He and his wife once drove through a Georgia town named Enigma, prompting him to set his first book there, and on a trip between Fort Lauderdale and Tampa he happened upon a foul-smelling phosphate plant that he determined to make the locale of his second novel. Crews's fictional phosphate-plant town was developed by the character Jack O'Boylan, who acquired the property from a land speculator who committed suicide. Eventually, when the mine ceases to be profitable, O'Boylan unloads the property on one of the novel's central characters, Fat Man. Throughout the novel the few residents remaining in Garden Hills long for the Godot-like O'Boylan to return to restore prosperity to their wasteland. But O'Boylan, like Godot, never arrives.

The strength of the book lies in its vividly drawn characters. Their lives are as barren and pathetic as their environment, yet they evoke sympathy and, in at least one case, admiration of sorts. Fat Man is five feet tall, weighs six hundred pounds, drinks Metrecal by the case, and has to have an attendant, a washed-up jockey named Jester, help him perform the most basic daily routines. His sad, impotent quest for love and meaning has rendered his life and body grotesque. Motherless and the son of an insane father, he sought understanding at college in the arms of a male track star who finally rejected him. As the owner of Garden Hills, he presides over nothing, his existence as wasted and bloated with emptiness as his town.

In the end Fat Man winds up as a freakish exhibit in a bizarre discotheque. The creator of this establishment, Dolly Ferguson, returned to Garden Hills after being exploited and generally made a fool in New York City. Her hunger for power and acceptance leads her to attempt a sexual relationship with Fat Man. She craves the love she has never found as well as the prestige and control she believes will come through aligning herself with the town's owner. When her seduction fails, her rejection drives her to humiliate Fat Man — whose attendant has deserted him for Dolly — by luring him, helpless and starving, into a cage at her discotheque.

Certainly, Dolly's callous ambition and sense of vengeance are not praiseworthy, but her effort to rejuvenate her dead life and the community through her business venture, as tasteless as it may be, is admirable. The hurt feelings that lead her to mistreat Fat Man are at least understandable. Fat Man, Dolly, Jester, and the rest of the characters are terribly flawed and, to varying degrees, failed individuals, but they are all finally redeemed by their longings and vulnerabilities.

This Thing Don't Lead to Heaven (1970) is not, despite its many merits, as impressive a work as either of Crews's first two novels. Several of the characters here are weakly sketched, and some of the themes are insufficiently developed. *This Thing Don't Lead to Heaven* was generally not as well received by critics as were *The Gospel Singer* and *Naked in Garden Hills.* Shepherd observes that "adjectives such as 'uninteresting,' 'disgusting,' 'repetitious,' and 'preposterous' set the tone of reviews." The book concerns death and deformities, literal and figurative, and how people attempt to deal with them.

The residents of the nursing home in Cumesh, Georgia, where the story takes place, attempt to delay and deny death through, among other things, attempted sexual adventures and vicarious participation in the Doris Day movie that blares away at a drive-in theater near the home. Axel, who owns and runs the home, tries to conquer the deadness and sterility in her malformed personal life by entering into a romantic relationship with Junior Bledsoe, who capitalizes on death by selling funeral plots. Jefferson Davis Munroe, a midget masseur, rails against his spiritual barrenness, which originates in a loveless home life, and his physical deformity by administering life-restoring massages and aligning himself with Carlita, a Cuban woman who practices voodoo and may possibly, Munroe believes, correct his bodily defects with her magic.

All the old people at the home will, of course, eventually die. Munroe never grows. No one can undo the lack of love in Axel's life before she meets Junior. Through the Carlita-Munroe and Axel-Junior relationships Crews suggests, however, the possibility of at least temporarily and partially staving off spiritual death through love and mutual need. This redemptive theme — which is not as forcefully expressed as it might have been because of the lack of development of such characters as Junior and Carlita — contrasts markedly with the more dismal picture Crews paints in his first two books. In *This Thing Don't Lead to Heaven,* as in the other texts, he focuses on the downtrodden and the emotionally and physically crippled, but, unlike the first two books, this one offers a measure of hope for these people.

In *Karate Is a Thing of the Spirit* (1971) Crews is even more insistent on the importance of love. All the major characters seek to fill inner vacancies or to overcome outward defeats. Karate, which Crews once studied, is initially the primary medium through which they try to achieve these goals. In his search for direction and companionship John Kaimen, a young drifter, is drawn to the practice of this rigorous discipline in community with a group of others who live a monastic existence in an old motel on a south Florida beach. Their leader, Belt, has become a karate master, a "tranquility freak," in an effort to compensate for his dishonorable discharge – he ran in the face of enemy fire in Korea – from the army. Gaye Nell O'Dell, a karate adept and beauty queen, wants the success, power, and independence that eluded her mother because of an unwanted pregnancy.

These and other characters in the novel all find, at least in the beginning and to a degree, the purposes they seek through the love of karate and the sense of belonging that their group affords. Ironically, however, the outward toughness and inner mastery that these karate devotees achieve ultimately papers over failures, inner weaknesses, and insecurities. Crews seems to suggest that those who appear strongest are often deeply flawed, that those most devoted to displays of strength are frequently those who are, at some profound level, weakest or afraid of being weak.

Fanatical allegiance to karate proves to be not enough for either John or Gaye Nell, who becomes pregnant through a relationship with him. At first she is adamantly against having the child, fearing the same sort of fate her mother suffered, and persuades John to help her abort the fetus through vicious sex. But in the midst of their lovemaking he has a revelatory experience, realizing that all that really matters to him is Gaye Nell and their unborn infant. His love prevails; she forgets about being a beauty queen and karate master, choosing instead to be a mother and John's companion. In the final scene the two speed away from Belt and company in Belt's microbus. Though it may be true, as John Deck observed in the *New York Times Book Review* (25 April 1971), that this resolution "approach[es] the sentimental," Crews still manages to make his point: devotion to self-mastering disciplines such as karate or beauty-pageant competition can bring meaning and purpose up to a point, but ultimately the deepest satisfaction comes from the natural, simple experience of love and intimacy between two people.

In the essay "Why I Live Where I Live" (1980) Crews calls the automobile "that abomina-

tion before the Lord." His fifth novel, *Car* (1972), may be read as an extended exposition on this theme. The book, applauded by *Newsweek* (6 March 1972) shortly after it first appeared as "his best yet," is about Herman Mack, who sets out to eat a Ford Maverick piece by piece. The car is carved up into half-ounce cubes that Mack ingests each day and then passes the next morning. Both the eating and the defecation are conducted as public ceremonies. In fact, much of Herman's motive for engaging in this stunt is the fame and money that it brings. Huge crowds gather each day for the performances, the events are televised, and the defecated cubes are sold for exorbitant prices to adoring fans. The pieces of the Maverick function as a sort of automotive Eucharist that is consumed by a devoted worshiper while a congregation of sympathetic onlookers watches.

Other examples of this perverse alliance with automobiles can be seen in Herman's sister, Junell, who can enjoy sex only when in a car, and in a prostitute named Margo whose life is forever altered after a sexual experience on the hood of a Corvette. Through his surreal, Kafkaesque tale Crews is obviously criticizing America's love affair with the car. The crass, glitzy, shallow, consumer culture that generates this love produces the sort of superficial, hollow individuals who can associate the most intimate of human activities with a technological product and who can revel in the trivial sensationalism of ingesting and excreting a piece of machinery.

Herman never finishes eating the car. After consuming a large portion of the Maverick's front end, he is physically and psychologically sickened and refuses to go any farther. His twin brother, Mister, takes over for him, fearing financial ruin for the entire family if the project is not completed. In the last scene in which he appears, Mister is on the verge of killing himself in a desperate effort to fulfill their obligation to finish the car. Herman's withdrawal from the project reflects a spiritual growth – a rebellion against consumer values – which Mister, the promoters of the act, and the fanatical masses never achieve. The novel ends with Herman and a reformed Margo lovingly holding hands in an old Rolls Royce parked in a junkyard that Herman's father owns. Neither has escaped cars completely, but both have come to value intimacy and understanding over the heartless, showy, materialistic ethic of the automobile and the consumer society that revolves around it.

Crews's sixth novel, *The Hawk Is Dying* (1973), was hailed by Shepherd as "arguably his best novel." It is certainly one of his most thought pro-

Dust jacket for Crews's 1988 novel, which concerns the rise and fall of a professional boxer

voking. George Gattling, the protagonist, is a middle-aged man who, as the novel opens, is desperately unhappy with his plight. He has a boring job – selling automobile upholstery – and a vacant personal life – living with a sister for whom he cares little and having an unfaithful young girlfriend. One of his few pleasures is watching over his sister's mentally retarded son, Fred.

George attempts to escape the emptiness and tedium of his existence by training hawks. The first few he captures die, but he eventually manages to keep one alive. This hawk becomes George's constant companion and principal reason for living. He is attracted to its fierce wildness and independence, its death-dealing majesty. George – subconsciously wishing he were so wild, free, and majestic himself – attempts to live vicariously through the hawk by training it to hunt for him. This process involves a degree of taming and control that makes the bird precisely the opposite of what he admires. On the

one hand, then, George is admirable for forsaking his mundane existence and seeking out primal freedom and regal self-esteem through the hawk, but, on the other hand, his secondhand acquisition of these qualities comes at the price of abuse, of sorts, of this magnificent creature.

A similar ambiguity arises in relation to Fred's death by drowning in his water bed. It is never clear exactly how the death occurs – it may be just an accident, or George may play a role in it – but it is clear that George wishes the death, apparently out of love. He sees Fred as being trapped, much like himself, in a meaningless existence and wants to free him from it. But this freedom is purchased through abuse. Whether the abuse is real or merely desired makes little difference; George imposes emancipation by inflicting his engulfing will on another. The situation parallels that of George and the hawk: his intentions of freeing Fred are admirable, but George's imposition of a death sentence – if only in his mind – is reprehensible. Is George then a hero or a heel, someone who triumphs or who fails? It is difficult, perhaps impossible, finally to say.

Crews's books often feature freaks: Foot, the leader of the freak show, in *The Gospel Singer;* Jester, the midget jockey, in *Naked in Garden Hills;* and Jefferson Davis Munroe in *This Thing Don't Lead to Heaven.* Perhaps the most compelling of all Crews's physical grotesques, however, is Marvin Molar, the narrator and central figure in his seventh novel, *The Gypsy's Curse* (1974). Marvin is a deaf-mute with no legs who lives in a gym. He earns a living by performing acrobatic freak acts for gawking audiences. As in most of his other novels involving freaks, Crews uses a physically deformed character to highlight the spiritual deformities of both that character and the other, so-called normal, characters. Marvin's spiritual deformity is his obsession with a gorgeous woman, Hester, who has a special hold on him because she represents all that he is not but would love to be: outwardly whole, an object of attention because of attractiveness rather than abnormality.

The novel is a classic study of a man who sells his soul for the love of a destructive, sirenlike beauty. Hester's spell leads Marvin to abet in, through his failure to control her, the death of his close friend and father figure, Al, who owns the gym where Marvin lives. Eventually Marvin brutally murders Hester in a jealous rage when he catches her in the arms of another man – an act that leaves him in the Florida state penitentiary at the end of the book. His feelings of inferiority and physical abnormality drive him to annihilate that which he can never possess.

As pronounced as they are, Marvin's inner flaws – symbolized in and largely precipitated by his outer ones – are finally no match for the spiritual malformations of other characters who have no visible defects. The audiences of "normals" who gape at his acts show considerable small-mindedness and cruelty through their condescending, sometimes outrightly derisive treatment of the legless deaf-mute. Physically perfect Hester is a spiritual monster who uses and abuses almost everyone with whom she comes into contact. As in many of Crews's books, in *The Gypsy's Curse* it is much easier to sympathize and identify with the physically deformed individual, whose inner problems are at least understandable, than it is with many of the outwardly unmarred characters, whose interior flaws are freakish in sinister ways.

Jonathan Yardly (*New York Times Book Review,* 3 June 1974) called *The Gypsy's Curse* a work in

which its author "seems at last to be rounding his formidable talents into shape." But Crews's eighth novel, *A Feast of Snakes* (1976), is even better. M. M. Leber (*Library Journal,* 15 January 1976) observed, "This is Crews at his best." This grim, oppressive tale of a washed-up former high-school football star raises such issues as the effects of despair and hopelessness on the individual, the degree to which one is responsible for one's fate, and the emptiness and impotence of machismo. As the novel opens, Joe Lon Mackey, two years out of Mystic High, is trapped in an abysmal marriage, stuck in a job – manager of his father's small-town liquor store – he detests, tormented by thoughts of lost gridiron glory, and generally miserable in the present and hopeless about the future.

Joe Lon's situation only gets worse as the story – which concerns the activities surrounding an annual rattlesnake roundup in Mystic, Georgia – progresses. He becomes increasingly bitter, depressed, and helpless. He feels humiliated by the accomplishments of his high-school sweetheart, Berenice, who returns home from the University of Georgia for a visit. He treats his wife, Elfie, with escalating hatred and violence and feels more and more guilty about his behavior. He becomes convinced that there is no way he can overcome his illiteracy and lack of work skills and thus escape his menial job. His misery and despair finally lead him to mass murder, as he guns down a group of people gathered at the roundup festivities. The result, in turn, is his own death: the survivors in the crowd hurl him into a pit filled with rattlesnakes.

The reader may view Joe Lon as a victim of circumstances who deserves sympathy, perhaps even admiration, for lashing out at the end in the manner he does. One might argue that he is truly trapped in a dead-end existence; thus his murderous outburst represents an understandable and heroic, if ultimately futile, attempt to vent his pent-up rage and obliterate a world aligned against him. One might also argue, however, that Joe Lon makes little or no effort to alter his condition, that he wallows in self-pity, that his shooting spree is inexcusable and wholly reprehensible. Given this second reading the book is a morality play about failure of nerve rather than a lesson in fate.

Read either way *A Feast of Snakes* condemns the macho, tough-guy ethic by which Joe Lon and others in the novel, such as Sheriff Buddy Matlow and Joe Lon's father, live. These men exhibit violent, hypermasculine behavior: the sheriff rapes his attractive female prisoners, Joe Lon's father trains fighting dogs and drives his wife to suicide through his cruelty, and Joe Lon abuses his spouse and finally commits murder. Their actions conclude in their downfalls: the sheriff is castrated and dies; Joe Lon's father is left empty and alone; and Joe Lon is hurled into the rattlesnake pit.

As well as being an accomplished novelist, Crews is also a master of nonfiction. Nowhere does he better demonstrate his talent for documentary prose than in his 1978 autobiography, *A Childhood: The Biography of a Place,* though he admits that the line between reality and fiction blurs. Here he recollects, through fascinating vignettes, the events of his early years growing up in Bacon County, Georgia. William White (*Library Journal,* 15 September 1978) noted that "[Crews] tells it well and feelingly, without a false note." Robert Sherrill (*New York Times Book Review,* 24 December 1978) remarked, "Crews's reminiscences are different, fresh, and very touching." Many of the stories in Crews's autobiography focus on the hardships and violence of his youth. In one tale a man cuts off the hand of another man who trespasses on his property. There is an account of pulling worms from the throats of malnourished children to keep them from choking. Crews tells of his bout with a mysterious childhood illness that left him crippled for months. He talks about his father, who died of a heart attack from overwork.

As vicious and bad as things were, however, there were also happy times and love. Crews fondly remembers the pleasure he and a young black friend took from making up stories about the people in the pictures in the Sears-Roebuck catalogue. He recounts many acts of concern and sacrifice shown by friends and family. Perhaps the ultimate lesson of the book is captured in its epigraph: "Survival is triumph enough." The brutal circumstances in which Crews was raised required him to summon enormous courage simply to get by. *A Childhood* is also useful for understanding Crews's novels. The sort of rough, crude, poor, and uneducated characters that he depicts in his autobiography often appear in his fiction.

Though ostensibly about subjects ranging from L. L. Bean to Charles Bronson — and revealing, as Frank W. Shelton notes, "a unique perspective on the modern South" — the journalistic essays comprising Crews's next two books, *Blood and Grits* (1979) and *Florida Frenzy* (1982), are, in the final analysis, simply more autobiography. As Allen Lacy (*Chronicle Review,* 16 April 1979) observes about *Blood and Grits,* the book "is ultimately about Harry Crews." Almost all the wide-ranging pieces in these collections originally appeared elsewhere:

in the column Crews wrote for *Esquire* in the mid 1970s and in such magazines as *Playboy* and *Playgirl.* There is a significant overlap between the two volumes; five of the pieces in *Florida Frenzy* were earlier published in *Blood and Grits.*

Crews uses these essays as a forum for expressing an array of personal attitudes and beliefs. For example, in several pieces he vents his disgust for urban, middle-class America. In an essay on L. L. Bean (*Blood and Grits*) Crews chuckles over the fact that American men spend thousands of dollars on Bean's rugged outdoor clothing, even though the vast majority of them have never been anywhere near the wilds where such clothes would be necessary or truly useful. These men play at being rough and tough, wearing their stylish gear to the supermarket. In another entry in *Blood and Grits* Crews muses on the savage, murderous nature that he believes lies buried somewhere deep inside everyone. After a reading he gave at the University of Texas, he happened on the tower in the middle of the campus from which Charles Whitman shot and killed twelve people. Crews is fascinated, feeling a certain frightening, horrible kinship with the crazed killer. In *Florida Frenzy* there are essays on dogfighting and cockfighting that celebrate Crews's love for blood sports. In other pieces he discusses such diverse subjects as why he enjoys teaching at the university and why he likes living in Gainesville. *Blood and Grits* and *Florida Frenzy* not only give one glimpses into the multifaceted mind of Crews the man, but they, like *A Childhood,* can also help one better understand his fiction, for his essays raise issues and broach themes that repeatedly appear, in less direct and immediate guises, in his novels.

Crews's next novel, *All We Need of Hell* (1987), received mixed reviews. Russell Banks (*New York Times Book Review,* 1 February 1987) dubbed it an "excellent, edgy novel," while, at the other extreme, Shepherd (*Georgia Review,* Fall 1987) declared that "Crews's good work is very good, but this novel isn't it and it is well to say so." The story — the opening pages of which are lifted directly from a short-fiction piece in *Florida Frenzy* — centers around Duffy Deeter, a forty-year-old Gainesville, Florida, lawyer who originally appeared in *A Feast of Snakes.*

As the novel begins, Duffy is a driven, essentially unhappy man. In addition to being intent on winning in the courtroom, he feels that he must also excel on the track, on the handball court, in the weight room, and in the bedroom. Duffy is almost a parody of the middle-aged macho stud who is obsessed with competition and winning, desperately attempting to maintain his youthful vigor and viril-

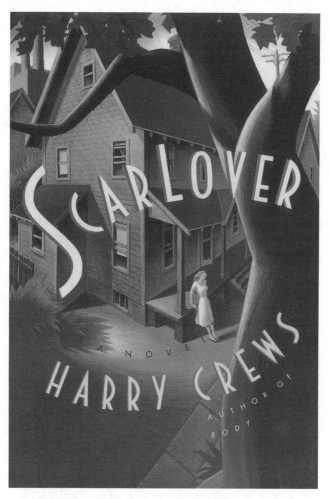

Dust jacket for Crews's 1992 novel, about a former marine who overcomes his emotional scars to find love and happiness in Florida during the 1950s

ity through manly physical activities, and intent on showing off his superiority. His attitude and approach to life are perhaps best summed up in the opening episode in the novel where, in order to prolong his sexual performance, he fantasizes about concentration-camp scenes while making love to his beautiful young mistress. To Duffy, sex is not for love, or even for pleasure, but is rather a competition sport in which he joylessly attempts to prove to himself and his lover what a superb sexual athlete he is.

Ironically, Duffy's efforts to be a winner have contributed to grave defeats in his personal life. His neglect of his wife, Tish, has helped destroy his marriage, though she certainly adds to the problem through her selfishness, affairs, and lavish spending. Furthermore, Duffy has no control over or real connection with his nine-year-old son, Felix. The fat, hopelessly out-of-shape child exasperates his

health-conscious father by refusing to exercise and bingeing on candy bars. As in *A Feast of Snakes,* Crews criticizes the macho ethic. Duffy's hypermasculine posturing is comic in its exaggeration, destructive to his relationships, and finally unsatisfying.

Unlike Joe Lon Mackey, however, Duffy has a savior, a black man named Tump Walker, a cocaine-using running back for the Miami Dolphins who decks Duffy in a handball game early in the book. But, unlike Duffy, Tump possesses certain traditionally feminine qualities, such as the ability to nurture and sensitivity toward the needs of others. Through these attributes Tump shapes up Felix, helps Duffy establish a more meaningful relationship with his son, and is the catalyst in reuniting Duffy with Tish.

There is some truth in Christopher Lehmann-Haupt's charge in the *New York Times* (12 January

1987) that "there is something decidedly forced and even sentimental about this turn of events [that Tump Walker precipitates]." Felix's transformation is a bit sudden and hard to believe, and the Duffy-Tish reunion smacks too much of a contrived, clichéd happily-ever-after ending. Nonetheless, Crews makes a valiant and, at least to a degree, successful attempt to show that forgiveness, friendship, and love are finally superior to, more life enhancing than puffed-up, egocentric, undiluted machismo.

In a 1990 interview with William Walsh, Crews observed that "I never would have written *The Knockout Artist* [1988] if I hadn't spent a good bit of my young manhood around a fight gymnasium with boxers, managers, or if my brother hadn't been a fighter." Crews's tenth novel – praised by Charles Nicol (*New York Times Book Review*, 1 May 1988) as "carefully plotted" and "skilled storytelling . . . [with] plenty of bizarre local color" – is about a young man, Eugene Talmadge Biggs, whose background is similar to Crews's. Like Crews, Eugene comes from Bacon County, Georgia, where he was raised in poverty.

When Eugene arrives in Jacksonville, Florida, looking for work, he meets Budd Jenkins, the foreman of a sheet-metal shop where Eugene finally gains employment. Budd introduces him to boxing, trains him, gets him a few fights with nobodys whom he easily defeats, and eventually procures him a spot on the undercard of a bout at Madison Square Garden. Eugene, out of his league in New York, is quickly dispatched by a superior fighter, and this defeat marks the beginning of the end of his boxing career. After being knocked out several more times by no-name fighters, his competitive days in the ring conclude when he is decked in a match in New Orleans.

Following this fight Budd deserts him, and Eugene – alone and angry in his dressing room – hits his own jaw, rendering himself unconscious. Abandoned in New Orleans, Eugene parlays the ability to knock himself out into a freak act that he peddles before perverted audiences in kinky underworld settings. Humiliated by his failed career and abandonment by Budd, Eugene continues to denigrate himself for money in these degrading spectacles.

Eugene is eventually taken in by Charity, a beautiful, rich, young graduate student in psychology at Tulane University. She uses him as a subject for her dissertation and generally treats him like an overgrown pet. The bulk of the novel is the story of Eugene's struggle to free himself from his double prostitution: to Charity, who provides lavishly for him in exchange for his sexual services and cooperation in her experiment, and to his freak act, in which he exchanges his dignity for dollars. But this man – who is bought, owned, and sold by others – succeeds in transforming himself into a free, dignified individual. With the financial backing of Oyster boy – a kinky, big-time New Orleans businessman whose shady sponsorship Eugene finally drops – and the aid of Pete – a friend who eventually becomes a burden to be discarded – Eugene becomes the manager of a young fighter, Jacques Deverouge, whom he treats with all the love and respect he never received from Budd.

This fulfilling work gives Eugene self-respect and financial stability, motivating and allowing him to quit performing his knockout exhibitions. It also gives him the courage to break with Charity. At the end of the book he puts a pistol in her mouth, forcing her to burn the tapes she has made of his intimate confessions during their lovemaking and severing all emotional and financial dependence on her. The fact that he does not kill Charity is a sign of just how much control he has attained over his life. Unlike Marvin Molar, who is so consumed by Hester that he must annihilate what he cannot have, Eugene is not an emotional hostage to Charity and is thus able simply to release this woman who has become meaningless to him. In the book's final scene Eugene rides out of New Orleans with Jacques, leaving behind all his shame and servitude. Of all Crews's characters, Eugene is perhaps the most admirable and heroic, the one who most thoroughly changes his life for the better and triumphs over his circumstances.

Robert H. Donahugh's assessment of Crews's next novel, *Body* (1990), in *Library Journal* (August 1990) is apt: "Not as powerful or controlled as the author's *A Feast of Snakes* or as surrealistic and fascinating as *The Knockout Artist,* this is still a taut, readable book that the author's fans will savor." *Body* is perhaps most distinguished by its humor. Many of Crews's books contain large doses of comedy, usually of the black or mocking variety, but none provides as much as *Body*. The central subject, however, is decidedly serious. Shereel Dupont, a female bodybuilder, is competing for the Ms. Cosmos title in Miami, Florida. Under the demanding tutelage of her trainer, Russell "Muscle" Morgan, who first appeared as a minor character in *The Gypsy's Curse,* Shereel has endured the excruciating pain and monumental sacrifices necessary to mold her body into competitive shape. Her chief challenger, a black woman named Marvella Washington, is trained by Wallace the Wall, a former champion.

Much of the humor involves Shereel's redneck relatives and fiancé, all from Waycross, Georgia. They do not understand why Dorothy Turnipseed – Shereel's real name – does what she does; why the grotesquely muscled male competitors, who lounge about the pool, look the way they look; why the prissy hotel clerk, Julian Lipschitz, and the pompous hotel manager, Dexter Friedkin, act the way they act. Crews gives hilarious descriptions of the country-hick habits of Nail, Shereel's fiancé; Alphonse, her father; Earnestine, her mother; Motor and Turner, her brothers; and Earline, her sister. He constructs brilliantly comic interchanges between them and Julian, Dexter, and those associated with the contest. The humor cuts two ways, highlighting the naiveté and down-home simplicity of the Georgia clan as well as accenting the absurdity of the more sophisticated folk they encounter.

Crews, however, is not merely making fun of his creations. As comical as they are, Shereel's family and fiancé are also loving and protective of their kin and demonstrate a great deal of common sense. Nail, a Vietnam War hero, is not one to be trifled with when it comes to Shereel; on the last page of the novel he kills himself and a judge responsible for her defeat in the Ms. Cosmos contest. The bodybuilders, in many ways ridiculous in their excesses, are also sadly obsessed with their sport. Billy Bat, a contestant in the men's competition, falls in love with Earline, Shereel's fat sister, primarily because she is – at some primally sensual level – what he wishes he were: free to digest all the rich, calorie-laden foods he desires. His lust for Earline is both amusing and a sad reflection on the prison he has constructed for himself out of his austere goals.

Shereel is the only character in the book who is hardly funny at all. Her desperate desire, fueled by Russell, to be number one eventually leads to her suicide; she slashes her wrists in a bathtub after coming in second to Marvella. All traces of comedy in *Body* are, then, finally snuffed out in a *Feast of Snakes*-like ending in which Shereel is unable to live with what she has become. Her demise is perhaps easier to sympathize with than Joe Lon Mackey's because she makes a more obvious effort to become what she envisions. But, like Joe Lon, she may be criticized for bowing to – rather than attempting to overcome – defeat.

Scar Lover (1992) takes place in Jacksonville, Florida, during the mid 1950s. Pete Butcher, the central character, is a Marine Corps veteran who lives in a boardinghouse and earns his living stacking blocks of cellophane in a hot boxcar. As the book begins, he is a loner, professing to have no desire to get involved in other people's problems and wanting even less to divulge his own. Like his Rastafarian coworker, George, Pete has ugly scars, ones not visible on his back as George's are, but ones in his heart and psyche. Pete feels a repulsive attraction for the U-shaped brands that George's wife, Linga, has burned into her husband's back to signify their years of marriage. This contradictory attitude – one of repulsion and attraction – toward George's outer scars symbolizes Pete's true feelings about his own, and others', inner scars.

Despite his surface disgust for people's foibles, Pete is also fascinated by them. The novel traces his progress in facing and coping with wounds and blemishes – his transformation from one who lacks the nerve to confront his and others' personal difficulties into one who has the courage to probe and manage them. *Scar Lover* is one of Crews's happy-ending novels, like *Karate Is a Thing of the Spirit* and *The Knockout Artist,* in which the protagonist faces down his demons and conquers them.

Pete's primary scar is the guilt he harbors over his younger brother's severe mental deficiency. Years prior to the novel's opening, he had accidentally hit his four-year-old sibling in the head with a hammer, leaving him mentally disabled. By the end of the book Pete is literally and figuratively able to embrace his past mistake. After years of separation he is reunited with his brother, welcoming him with open arms – he actually kisses the hammer scars on his brother's forehead – and going so far as to take on his permanent care. But Pete will not have to mind the boy by himself. He becomes, along with his brother, part of a family, willingly entangling himself in all its difficulties.

This involvement has its roots in Pete's first encounter with Sarah, a young woman with whom he forms a sexual relationship early in the novel but from whom he nonetheless wishes to maintain his emotional distance. Gradually, however, he comes to acknowledge her on the most intimate level. He learns to accept her cantankerous, cancer-ridden mother, and he ceases to run from Sarah's own health problems. When her father has a fatal heart attack, he helps the two women cope with the death and its aftermath. In sum, Pete falls in love with Sarah, complete with connections and scars. In the end he, Sarah, her mother, and his brother are united, ready to face the future with all its hazards. Pete has become a true scar lover, realizing that genuine happiness and fulfillment lie not in dodging the trials and tribulations of life but rather in facing up to and attacking them.

As Rasche notes, Crews's next novel will deal with a south Florida man who raises giant pigs and alligators. There is no reason to believe that this book will be any less impressive than his other books generally have been. Few writers can equal the strength and weird energy of Crews's vision in his best works. *Scar Lover,* though not without its detractors, is at least as forceful and innovative as his early novels. Even in his generally negative review of the book, George Stade (*New York Times Book Review,* 15 March 1992) admits that "the first third of the novel . . . is pure gold, pure Harry Crews, with plenty of the grim humor and enraged charity that have become his trademark." Readers can no doubt expect many more fine novels and essays from this prolific and accomplished writer.

Interviews:

Anne Foata, Interview, *Recherche Anglaises et Américaines,* 5 (May 1972): 207–225;

V. Sterling Watson, "Arguments over an Open Wound: An Interview with Harry Crews," *Prairie Schooner,* 48 (Spring 1974): 60–74;

David K. Jeffrey and Donald R. Noble, "Harry Crews: An Interview," *Southern Quarterly,* 19 (Winter 1981): 65–79;

Kay Bonetti, Interview, *Missouri Review,* 6 (Winter 1983): 145–164;

Hank Nuwer, "The Writer Who Plays with Pain: Harry Crews," *Rendezvous,* 21 (Fall 1985): 55–67;

William Walsh, Interview, *Pembroke Magazine,* 22 (1990): 121–129;

Ruth Ellen Rasche, "Blue Eyed Boy," *University of Florida Today,* 17 (November 1992): 11–13.

References:

Larry W. DeBord and Gary L. Long, "Harry Crews on the American Dream," *Southern Quarterly,* 20 (Spring 1982): 35–53;

David K. Jeffrey, ed., *A Grit's Triumph: Essays on the Works of Harry Crews* (Port Washington, N.Y.: Associated Faculty Press, 1983);

William J. Schafer, "Partial People: The Novels of Harry Crews," *Mississippi Quarterly,* 41 (Winter 1987–1988): 69–88;

John Seelye, "Georgia Boys: The Redclay Satyrs of Erskine Caldwell and Harry Crews," *Virginia Quarterly Review,* 56 (Autumn 1980): 612–626;

Frank W. Shelton, "The Nonfiction of Harry Crews: A Review," *Southern Literary Journal,* 16 (Spring 1984): 135;

Allen Shepherd, "Matters of Life and Death: The Novels of Harry Crews," *Critique,* 20 (April 1979): 53–62.

Frederick Exley

(28 March 1929 – 17 June 1992)

Thomas Deegan
Saint Xavier University

See also the Exley entry in *DLB Yearbook: 1981.*

BOOKS: *A Fan's Notes: A Fictional Memoir* (New York: Random House, 1968; New York & London: Harper & Row, 1968; London: Weidenfeld & Nicolson, 1970);
Pages from a Cold Island (New York: Random House, 1975);
Last Notes from Home (New York: Random House, 1988; London: Viking, 1990).

SELECTED PERIODICAL PUBLICATIONS –
UNCOLLECTED: "Poem from a Man at Middle Age," *Esquire,* 79 (May 1973): 234;
"Holding Penalties Build Men," *Inside Sports,* 3 (November 1981): 105–109;
"The Laureate of Alexandria Bay," *Esquire,* 105 (March 1986): 214–218;
"A Fan's Note," *American Film,* 11 (September 1986): 33–36;
"A Fan's Further Notes," *Esquire,* 107 (June 1987): 150–152;
"If Nixon Could Possess the Soul of This Woman, Why Can't I?," *Esquire,* 112 (December 1989): 208–213;
"The Last Great Saloon," *Gentlemen's Quarterly,* 60 (December 1990): 290–295, 340–342.

Frederick Exley's literary output over some twenty years amounts to only three novels: *A Fan's Notes* (1968), *Pages from a Cold Island* (1975), and *Last Notes from Home* (1988), plus enough magazine articles to fill a small volume. None of his novels has been a strong seller, and only *A Fan's Notes* was a critical success. This fine novel has attracted a devoted following, a readership of college students and hopeful writers, rather like that of J. D. Salinger in the 1950s. Perhaps his appeal, especially to younger readers, lies in his romantic rebellion against hypocrisy and repressiveness, what he calls the madness of America. Following in the literary tradition of mixing fiction and

autobiography, Exley writes in a confessional mode, his persona on an edge, but facing an even madder American culture. As he remarks in *Last Notes from Home,* Exley is outraged at the "obscene spectacle America has become" but realizes that he must confront the truth of this America, whatever risks to him and his protagonists. For some readers his success is his criticism of contemporary America. But his true strength is his merciless self-scrutiny, done in a style that is both funny and heartbreaking, with close observations of people and incidents that constitute a unique, formidable voice in contemporary American literature.

The son of Earl Exley, a telephone lineman, and Charlotte Merkley Exley, Frederick was born in Watertown, New York, on 28 March 1929. His older brother, William, became the central character in *Last Notes from Home;* Frederick also had a twin, Frances, and a younger sister, Constance. He attended Watertown public schools through graduation from high school, then studied for a year at John Jay High School in Katonah, New York, to raise his grades enough to get into college. He played football and basketball and at John Jay was named to an interscholastic all-star basketball team. Exley once called this period at John Jay "the most productive year of my life," a time when he felt he was living up to his potential. He recounts his sports experience and the influence of his football coach in "Holding Penalties Build Men" (1981) and *Last Notes from Home.* When that time ended, he humored his father by attending Hobart College in Geneva, New York, as a predental student and then transferred as an English major to the University of Southern California, graduating in 1953.

Over the next fifteen years Exley drifted unsuccessfully through several jobs. He also developed a serious affinity for alcohol, which he discusses throughout his writing. In a belated imitation of the men who in the 1930s "laid around and played around this old world too long," he wan-

Frederick Exley

dered from New York to Chicago, working public relations for some railroads then breathing their last gasps of commercial life. Then came other short-term jobs in several cities, perhaps most painful the two years in the 1960s when he taught high-school English in rural New York. He despised his students' lack of interest and achievement and the school's policy of passing them on to get them out. He recalls this misery in *A Fan's Notes:* "I would go through the motions of teaching and try to prevent my students' believing my contempt was leveled at them. Not succeeding, I found that by the Thanksgiving holiday the majority of my students despised me, I loathed them, and we moved warily about each other snarling like antic cats."

His personal life failed along with his on-the-job performances. He married twice and had two children. His first marriage, to Francena Fritz, lasted from 1967 to 1970 and produced a daughter, Pamela Rae. His second marriage (1970–1974), to Nancy Glenn, lasted only a year longer and also produced a daughter, Alexandra.

In 1958 Exley had entered a mental hospital for the first of three extended stays. His drifting

years of personal erosion were unsurprising, but other by-products were not. During his second hospitalization he began writing what would become *A Fan's Notes.*

Exley's writing is dominated by a preoccupation with writing itself, especially the role of the writer. He believes in the redemptive power of literature: its power to bring order out of chaos, to make sense of life. For him a writer's is the highest calling; and the finest form of worship is reading and cherishing another's work. His works are sprinkled with references to other writers, living and dead; and he searches intently for his place among them.

Another near-obsession of Exley's writing is his concern with the notion of home – the importance of roots in a nation of strangers. Like James Joyce of Dublin and, later, William Kennedy of Albany, Exley always writes about Watertown, his hometown. He explained this interest to Mary Cantwell in 1976: "I dislike intensely the new mobility and lack of heritage and lack of roots. I'm always trying to suggest to the reader what a flimsy thing home is." He extends the "flimsiness" – that is, elusiveness – of home further, to the fragility of life itself. In large measure his books are laden with what he calls "the burdens of grief," stories of life's ordinary unfairness and catastrophes. Exley once remarked that his work is about the longing to connect with something or someone outside oneself. In his novels his narrators become increasingly aware of the bonds of love.

Exley, indeed a loner, writes novels full of outcasts. Against the conformity demanded by society, he is interested in originals, people who fail to do the quintessentially American thing of fitting in, of celebrating America's dream of its own success. His cast of characters is a counterculture: eccentrics, mavericks, misfits, liars, obsessives, madmen, criminals – each of them perhaps Exley's own alter ego. But they both publicly and privately exhibit courage, strength, and discipline – a kind of competent professionalism in the face of adversity.

In *A Fan's Notes* Exley remembers a time when his father took him to meet Steve Owen, the coach of the New York Giants:

> Owen asked, "Are you tough?"
> "Pardon, sir?"
> "*Are you tough?*"
> "I don't know, sir."
> Owen looked at my father. "Is he tough, Mr. Exley?"
> Though more than anything I wanted my father to say that I was, I was not surprised at his answer. "It's too soon to tell."

Toughness is a theme that runs through Exley's work, and his books are to some extent homages to people who exhibit a professional grit – Frank Gifford, the New York Giants football player and sports commentator (*A Fan's Notes*); the American writer Edmund Wilson (*Pages from a Cold Island*); and Exley's brother, William (*Last Notes from Home*). Exley maintains a love/envy relationship with these heroes and examines them as participants in American history.

The obvious differences among these three men suggest polarities and contradictions of Exley's work as he tries to express the complexity of modern experience. Thomas R. Edwards notes that Exley uses such polarities to portray himself as "an intractably inconsolable romantic" confronting the madness of America and says correctly that for Exley "health and disease, strength and weakness, are parts of the same idea." Edwards states that Exley also depicts "athleticism and its decline into drunkenness and paranoia, romance and sexual adventurism, performance and impotence, pride in

family and place and the need to escape them, personal honor and a fascination with criminality."

Random House published *A Fan's Notes* in 1968 after it was rejected by fourteen other publishers. Exley subtitles the novel "a fictional memoir" and in a prefatory note disclaims the factual basis of the events in his book: "I have drawn freely from the imagination and adhered only loosely to the pattern of my past life. To this extent, and for this reason, I ask to be judged as a writer of fantasy." In a later interview, however, Exley admitted that he "had to build a kind of disguise around" some of the characters in the book, especially his former wife Francena, to avoid litigation, "but the major part was done straight." The question of truth is perennial in the criticism of autobiographical fiction. The scenes rendered in this novel are colored by memory and embellished by the resources of the imagination. They are further shaped by the author's need to bring pattern and coherence to the raw material of his life. Exley's confessional mode nevertheless suggests that he is using this novel to restructure his past and to give meaning to the present.

In *A Fan's Notes* Exley depicts "that long malaise, my life," the agonizing story of a romantic idealist who fails at everything, including every job he tries over a period of fifteen years, marriage, and parenthood. A former athlete reduced to being a spectator on the sidelines, he is an alcoholic sponging off his friends and ending his nights in drunken brawls or in strangers' beds. Finally, he is a mental patient. At a climactic point in the novel he is jailed by a Miami judge who calls him "a fatuous lunatic." Yet in this strangely powerful book Exley tells a tale of grief with such honesty and such lack of self-pity that the reader is compelled to follow him. Further appealing is Exley's personal style, the blend of rage with critical insight, outrageous humor with sensitive intelligence, and raunchy sex with spiritual longing.

A Fan's Notes opens some time around 1962 with a drunken Exley sitting in a bar in Watertown, awaiting the telecast of a New York Giants–Dallas Cowboys game. He suffers a "seizure" and fears a heart attack. Instead his illness is the result of his prolonged excessive drinking. This memento mori causes him to examine the life that has fallen this far. Quoting from Nathaniel Hawthorne's *Fanshawe* (1828) in the epigraph to the book, he provides a self-diagnosis: "If his inmost heart could have been laid open, there would have been discovered that dream of undying fame; which, dream as it is, is more powerful than a thousand realities." Exley the incurable romantic needs success and fame, but,

*Dust jacket for Exley's first book, about a former athlete who sinks into
alcoholism and mental illness*

having failed in so many ways, he is reduced to a
life of fandom – hence the title of the novel.

Exley as narrator says he drinks "to check the
mental exhilaration produced by extended sobriety."
He inherited this burden of the need for fame from his
father, Earl, a local sports hero and figure of toughness:

> Other men might inherit from their fathers a head for
> figures, a gold pocket watch all encrusted with the oxi-
> dized green of age, or an eternally astonished expres-
> sion; from mine I acquired this need to have my name
> whispered in reverential tones. . . . I wanted the wealth
> and the power that fame would bring; and finally I
> wanted love – or said that I did, though I know now
> that what I wanted was the adulation of the crowd. "Oh,
> Jesus, Pop! *Why? Why? Why?*" I have always been sorry
> I didn't shout that humiliation. Had my father found the
> words to tell me why he so needed the Crowd, I might
> have saved my soul and now be a farm-implement sales-

man living sublimely content in Shaker Heights with my
wife Marylou and six spewling brats.

After Exley's graduation from college and his
father's death, he transferred his hero worship from
lineman Earl Exley to New York Giants star and former BMOC Frank Gifford, whom Exley knew as a
student at the University of Southern California. As
he explains in "A Fan's Further Notes" (1987), "I'd
written a book in which Frank Gifford had been my
narrator's alter ego, the narrator and Gifford being, as
it were, the light and dark sides of the American psyche." Exley said he felt a kinship with Gifford because
they both had been born during the Depression and
had working-class fathers and poor homes. Exley felt
he knew a terrifying ache that drove Gifford.

Another attraction for Exley was football, for
him a pristine arena against a world of phoniness, as
he writes in *A Fan's Notes:*

Why did football bring me to life? I can't say precisely. Part of it was my feeling that football was an island of directness in a world of circumspection.... It smacked of something old, something traditional, something unclouded by legerdemain and subterfuge. It had that kind of power over me, drawing me back with the force of something known, scarcely remembered, elusive as integrity – perhaps it was no more than the force of a forgotten childhood. Whatever it was, I gave myself up to the Giants utterly. The recompense I gained was the feeling of being alive.

But fandom was more dangerous than that for the alcoholic Exley; it provided him with an identity and a sense of meaning that were increasingly missing in his own life. As Edwards notes, "Fans are, however briefly and benignly, crazy. They are not just fanciers or fantasists but fanatics, caught up in a desire that's literally self-destructive, a desire not to be what they are."

A Fan's Notes presents Exley's confrontation with the American dream, a conflict that begins in earnest with his postgraduate attempt "to take on New York City." But he experiences, and runs from, a problem common in the first grasp for fame: he wants its wealth and its power, but he is unwilling or unable to trade his sense of integrity for it. He experiences New York as a process of submitting to conformity and self-compromise; he would like to believe, this young man, that New York fails him, and not the reverse.

He renders his confrontation with the American dream in a sequence involving his love, at age twenty-six, for Bunny Sue Allorgee, the Daisy to his Gatsby. Bunny Sue represents the essential attraction/repulsion dilemma of romantic dreams. She "was so very American," a heartbreakingly beautiful Big Ten coed. "She was the Sweetheart of Sigma Chi – well, no, not precisely; precisely she was the only sophomore in the history of Michigan or Illinois or Indiana to be chosen, above all those other honey-dipped girls, Homecoming Queen. And finally, she was Chicago's impossible, nearly obscene gift to me."

But Exley comes to recognize the horror of his dream of life with Bunny Sue when he visits her parents in the fictional midwestern suburb of Heritage Heights – the meeting that ends everything. Her family represents to him the horrible shallowness of middle-class American life. In a flash he sees his future:

I suddenly saw myself consigned to the breakfast nook with Poppy [Bunny Sue's father], our Giant tuques pulled down about our ears, our tongues lapping at the Pabst cans, our ears glued to the radio, now and again raising our eyes to look self-consciously at one another and to make not very funny jokes about the women-folk in the other room, jokes that, sadly, admitted our helplessness before the jewel they carried between their legs.

In the face of this honest vision Exley is literally struck impotent. He later realizes that "my inability to couple has not been with [Bunny Sue] but with some aspect of America with which I could not have lived successfully." But he should have made this realization sooner, on a shopping trip with Bunny Sue:

She purchased seven pair of blue panties, a pair for every day of the week, with Monday, Tuesday, etc., embroidered at a place very close to the crotch. "Pretty corny, huh?" she said to nobody in particular; then to the salesgirl, "Is it all right if I wear Tuesday's on Saturday?" Here she turned to me and winked.... That morning was the first day in my life I recognized there were times when I needed a drink; I needed one then as badly, I expect, as I ever had or ever would again.

After Bunny Sue, Exley tells of his retreat from the city and further from reality, his descent through drink and meaningless sex, and his eventual madness. He ends up in Watertown sunken in the apathy of depression, lying on his mother's davenport, eating Oreo cookies, watching soap operas, and talking to his mother's dog. He is then admitted to the state mental hospital.

Reviews of *A Fan's Notes* failed to appear for three months after publication, but, when they came, they were generous. Giving the novel high critical praise, they quickly established Exley as an important new literary find. Sales, however, were small: fewer than nine thousand copies of the hardcover edition. Gradually, though, *A Fan's Notes* became a cult classic, emerging in eight paperback editions, the most recent of which was the prestigious Vintage Contemporaries series. Christopher Lehmann-Haupt, writing in the *New York Times* (23 December 1968), called *A Fan's Notes* "such a singularly moving, entertaining, *funny* book. ... Mostly it's because Exley's character and experience are familiar enough to identify with (and therefore to fear) and at the same time mad and extreme and bizarre enough to separate him from us (and therefore to pity). One gets involved without getting hurt." Several critics compared Exley with F. Scott Fitzgerald; Mike McGrady, in *Newsday* (19 July 1969), asserted *A Fan's Notes* to be "the best novel written in the English language since *The Great Gatsby*." A minority, including Stanley Reynolds of the *New Statesman* (30 January 1970), found the "novel ram-

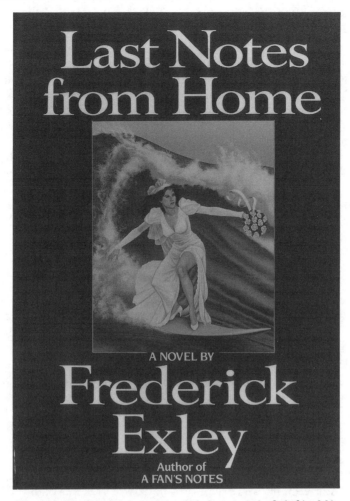

Dust jacket for Exley's last novel, in which the protagonist finds friendship and love on his way to attend his brother's funeral in Hawaii

bling, unclear, repetitious, and written in that curious overblown American style. . . . The effect here is rather like getting buttonholed by a drunk in a bar."

A Fan's Notes was nominated for the National Book Award, won the William Faulkner Award for the best novel of 1968, and received the National Institute of Arts and Letters Rosenthal Award. As a result of its publication Exley received a Rockefeller Foundation grant. A 1972 film version, starring Jerry Orbach, was made by Warner Bros. Exley, who was paid thirty-five thousand dollars for the film rights, thought the finished product "bore no relation to anything I'd written."

After *A Fan's Notes* was published, Exley lived almost a year in New York, awaiting his fame. He spent much of his time in the Lion's Head, a literary bar in Greenwich Village, the setting of his article "The Last Great Saloon" (1990). In fall 1968, fortified with a fifty-thousand-dollar advance from Ran-

dom House and ten thousand dollars from the Rockefeller grant, Exley began work on *Pages from a Cold Island,* the second volume of what he now projected as a trilogy. Despite the generous reviews of *A Fan's Notes,* Exley was depressed by its poor sales. It was less a matter of money than of personal need. In 1976 he told Cantwell, "I'm the best known writer to other writers in America, but I want to be loved by the public too." Exley notes in *Pages from a Cold Island* that, because of the confessional nature of *A Fan's Notes,* "I was summarily and disparagingly dismissed as having 'shot my wad.' . . . I had not published until I was in my late thirties; I was cognizant that after years of excessive drinking, three times resulting in my incarceration in insane asylums, I hadn't the zest or the wit . . . to produce what the boys at The Lion's Head called 'a shelf.' " He later admitted that his subsequent writing was an attempt to create another novel whose quality would match that of his first. At least with the burden of fame unceremoniously lifted, Exley could turn to *Pages from a Cold Island.*

In fall 1969 Exley moved to Singer Island, Riviera Beach, Florida, taking up residence at the Seaview Hotel, where he continued to work on *Pages from a Cold Island.* The "cold" of the title refers not to the island but to his despondent state of mind as he looked back on "America's journey through the Sixties," which had begun with the promise of President John F. Kennedy's inaugural address and had ended in fall 1969 at Chappaquiddick, another cold island. In *Pages from a Cold Island* he realizes his life is going nowhere. His wife has left (just before publication of *A Fan's Notes*), and he has escaped to Florida, where his only acquaintances are fringe people: barflies, beach bums, and prostitutes. At one point, feeling the book was not working, he put its 480 pages of typescript in the trunk of his Chevrolet Nova for three years. In a state of depression he came close to suicide for the second time in his life.

Two events saved the book and its author. Two days after his suicide attempt he read a magazine article about Gloria Steinem and decided that by interviewing her he might get the book back on track and "lift the pages from the gloom in which they wallowed." And in 1972 Exley moved back to the Watertown area, settling in Alexandria Bay, New York, on the Saint Lawrence River, twenty-three miles north of his birthplace. This relocation was for him an important homecoming and reconciliation. There he was among old school friends whom he valued, and his mother and two sisters lived nearby. For the rest of his life Exley divided his time between this place and Singer Island. He read the death notice of Edmund Wilson, his most revered writer, in the *Watertown Tribune* the day after Wilson's death on 12 June 1972. Three weeks later Exley went to Wilson's hometown to meet his secretary, Mary Pcolar; his wife and daughter; and some of Wilson's friends. Exley's purpose was to include Wilson in his book.

Exley's homage to Wilson is the center of *Pages from a Cold Island.* As with Gifford in *A Fan's Notes,* Exley's fanhood derives first from his respect for Wilson as a significant public figure of his time, "a man [who] could live with the truth so long and survive," and perhaps Exley's recognition that Wilson led a coherent literary life in contrast to his own undisciplined one. Exley's admiration also derives from his sense of kinship with an autobiographical writer who exposed the hypocrisy and shallowness of American life, loved upstate New York, and was practically his neighbor. Wilson's ancestral home in Talcottville, New York, attracted Exley with his newfound connection to home and continuity.

Pages from a Cold Island is divided into Exley's encounters with a few public figures who dominated the American landscape of the 1960s: Wilson, Steinem, and, to a lesser extent, Norman Mailer. It also recounts Exley's residence in the Iowa Writers Workshop during the 1972 fall term. The predominant subject of the book is the literary life, exemplified mainly by Wilson. When Exley discusses Wilson in an Iowa Writers Workshop class, he sums up Wilson's significance: " 'Your real literary life,' I offered as my one piece of tendentiousness, 'will begin the day you accept the conditions, apartness, confusion, loneliness, work, and *work, and work* — the conditions so many of your peers have already accepted and that Edmund Wilson and his stone house so vividly and hauntingly evoke.' "

Exley also seeks a kinship with Steinem through life parallels — both were Depression-era babies who got an education and were shaped by the same events of the 1960s — all the while cognizant of her splendid success and his failure. But here Exley is not Steinem's abject fan. He has no real sympathy with the women's liberation movement, and he suspects in her a smug insincerity, wanting to talk with her to see "that she cared." His interview with this reluctant subject goes poorly because she quickly senses his arrogant antagonism as he playacts the interviewer. But this section of the book works better than the Wilson section. Exley's comic insincerity as the bad boy — alternately worshipful and lustful, believing "the missionary rigidity with which she approached matters left her hopelessly vulnerable" to contradictions, poking fun at the cool and haughty woman who takes herself seriously — is actually strangely endearing. In the last section of the book Exley recounts a failed meeting with Mailer — an incident he perhaps intended for a third major section of the book.

The book ends with Exley's experience at the Iowa Writers Workshop. Again he has difficulty in the role of teacher. His students this time are too intense for him, and by the end of the term he "had to belt back a half-dozen double vodkas before even going down the hill to confront this group." He devotes much space to his sexual liaison with April, a student who is a "Miss Middle America to a heartbreaking fault" in the mold of Bunny Sue.

Reviews of *Pages from a Cold Island* were mixed, and the praise it received was decidedly milder than that accorded *A Fan's Notes,* to which it was inevitably compared. Many critics sensed that its faults arose out of Exley's desperate need to write another book. The negative reviews expressed several concerns, including Exley's failure to bring his subjects to life and to make the reader care about them. Other criticisms were that he did not bring the book's disparate parts together into a coherent whole and that its title betrays the fact that it is just pages of writing, a series of magazine pieces held together under the heading of American life in the 1960s. According to Alfred Kazin in the *New York Times Book Review* (20 April 1975), "much as I enjoy reading Exley, I am depressed by how instantly perishable it all seems. It's too much of an act – the act it had to be to get itself written. So it's not a novel either, but a magazine-smart piece of writing by a very good writer who is afraid of letting us see the dilemma that made this book necessary."

A Fan's Notes works well because in it Exley is a true fan – unaffected, passionate, and pathetic. In *Pages from a Cold Island* he is too competitively engaged with Steinem and Mailer to treat them as he does Gifford, too jealous of their success to allow them their fame. He intrudes so much in his interview with Steinem that it emerges as a story about an interview rather than a profile of her. In addition, the scattered anecdotes and occasional insights into Wilson's complex character do not emerge as a compelling portrait of Wilson, but rather an account of Exley's quest for that portrait. *A Fan's Notes* is an intense, deeply felt book. By comparison *Pages from a Cold Island* is slack, digressive, gossipy, and sometimes even petty. Like *A Fan's Notes, Pages from a Cold Island* did not sell well and was quickly remaindered.

Last Notes from Home completes Exley's autobiographical trilogy. The dust jacket blurb calls it "a novel," and Exley describes it as a work of fiction, claiming he has "never written about Frederick Exley except as he exists as a created character." Nevertheless the book centers on the death of Exley's older brother, Col. William Exley, a retired army officer to whom Exley refers as "the Brigadier." The book begins with Exley's 1973 trip to Hawaii with his mother to visit his brother, who is dying of cancer. The colonel's ensuing death and burial provide the overall narrative-structuring element in the novel. But, as in *Pages from a Cold Island,* Exley digresses from this subject, interweaving many stories.

Another plot element is Exley's involvement with two individuals he meets on the flight to Hawaii. Both are larger-than-life free spirits who fabricate their personal histories: a drunken Irishman, James O'Twoomey – perhaps an oddball public-relations man, perhaps an IRA terrorist, perhaps a

con man and criminal – who perhaps for a time takes Exley captive; and Robin Glenn, a beautiful and accommodating airline stewardess who eventually marries Exley. The narrative meanders from the stories of these characters in 1973, moving forward into later years and backward into Exley's reminiscences of his adolescent years in Watertown, including his high-school athletic experiences, family conflicts, and teenage lust. There are also stories of various friends and acquaintances, past and present. The book ends with Exley's marriage to Glenn and a scene of her on a surfboard, riding the waves at Waikiki Beach, dressed in her grandmother's wedding gown.

As in Exley's previous novels, *Last Notes from Home* abounds in wild humor, drinking, sex, and self-destructive behavior, all presented with precisely remembered detail. Here again Exley uses the confessional mode, first addressing James Arness, who played Sheriff Matt Dillon on the television series *Gunsmoke,* and then Alissa Tunstall-Phinn, the narrator's former psychiatrist and lover. The disparate material gains coherence and structure through Exley's themes. A central idea is the complex nature of his love for his brother, a much-decorated military hero who survived combat in World War II, Korea, and Vietnam, only to die of cancer at forty-six.

William is the Gifford of this novel – a man who exhibited toughness, a combination of machismo, strength, and courage, while participating on the public stage of American life. He is the heroic achiever against whom Exley gauges his own human failings and the failures of American society. His love for William is complicated, though, by guilt born of their sibling rivalry. Exley fundamentally disagreed with America's military involvement in Vietnam; he hoped one day to sit around a pool with his brother and come to understand "the mid-20th-century nightmare."

There are other deaths besides William's in *Last Notes from Home.* Exley's lament for the dead and for others' misfortunes brings moments of poignancy that are among his best. One of these sections recounts his love over a period of four years for his high-school sweetheart, Cassandra McIntyre, who eventually dies as a result of anorexia nervosa. She represents a youthful life force stifled by society's repressive demand for conformity: "I loved her more than any woman I ever knew. . . . It took me a quarter of a century and a lot of living even to say good-bye to Cass."

Despite the novel's definite strengths, reviews again had a tone of disappointment. Exley fans, who had waited thirteen years for its publication, were not impressed. Some reviewers who had praised *A Fan's Notes* sadly noted a falloff from its standards in terms of style, narrative technique, characterization, and tone. While praising aspects of *Last Notes from Home,* some reviewers criticized its haphazard construction – especially if it is to be called a novel – its choppy narrative style, and lack of compelling material. After *Last Notes from Home* Exley continued to live in Alexandria Bay, devoting his writing mainly to magazine pieces, including "A Fan's Further Notes," an account of his attendance – at Gifford's invitation – at Super Bowl XXI in January 1987 (New York Giants versus Denver Broncos). Gifford had read *A Fan's Notes* and was genuinely flattered by Exley's portrayal, and they became friends.

Exley died at Alexandria Bay on 17 June 1992 after suffering a stroke. His work has yet to receive the scholarly critical attention it deserves. There is no book-length critical or biographical study, and few scholarly essays have appeared. Some critics consider *A Fan's Notes* Exley's only clear success. Others find in all his work a sustained assessment of American culture, a stylistic originality, and a courage and passion that mark him as a great writer. Larry McMurtry called Exley "in a rough way, a kind of American Dante." In "The Last Great Saloon" Exley observes:

> And it wasn't until last year, when I reached 60 and realized I had behind me only three novels and enough articles to fill a volume, that it occurred to me that though I never drink a jot while writing, I do little else when not working and that . . . the periods of work were retreating relentlessly against the onslaught of the drunken times. For all that, I am yet unable to apologize for the quality of my limited output or rue what might have been.

Bob Loomis, Exley's editor at Random House, commented, "*Last Notes* is really a book about love – or rather the compulsive search for it – told by a narrator whose macho demeanor can't even begin to cover up the overwhelming rage and compassion that rule his heart."

References:

Mary Cantwell, "The Hungriest Writer: One Fan's Notes on Frederick Exley," *New York Times,* 13 September 1992, pp. 30–31;

Cantwell, "The Sad, Funny, Paranoid, Loving Life of a Male American Writer – Frederick Exley," *Mademoiselle,* 82 (June 1976): 63–68, 126;

C. Barry Chabot, "The Alternative Vision of Frederick Exley's *A Fan's Notes*," *Critique,* 19, no. 1 (1977): 87–100;

Thomas R. Edwards, "A Case of the American Jitters," *New York Review of Books,* 19 January 1989, pp. 36–37;

Jane Howard, "Frederick Exley," *People,* 30 (14 November 1988): 163–167;

Donald R. Johnson, "The Hero in Sports Literature and Exley's *A Fan's Notes*," *Southern Humanities Review,* 13 (Summer 1979): 233–244;

Steven Shoemaker, "Barth, Schleiermacher, and a New York Giants Fan," *Religion in Life,* 44 (Spring 1972): 18–28;

Philip Sterling, "Frederick Exley's *A Fan's Notes:* Football as Metaphor," *Critique,* 22, no. 1 (1980): 39–46.

Papers:

Exley's papers and manuscripts are at the University of Rochester, New York.

Chester Himes

(29 July 1909 – 12 November 1984)

Robert J. Butler
Canisius College

See also the Himes entries in *DLB 2: American Novelists Since World War II, First Series* and *DLB 76: Afro-American Writers, 1940–1955.*

BOOKS: *If He Hollers Let Him Go* (Garden City, N.Y.: Doubleday, Doran, 1945; London: Falcon Press, 1947);

Lonely Crusade (New York: Knopf, 1947; London: Falcon Press, 1950);

Cast the First Stone (New York: Coward-McCann, 1952);

The Third Generation (Cleveland: World, 1954);

The Primitive (New York: New American Library, 1955);

For Love of Imabelle (Greenwich, Conn.: Fawcett, 1957); expanded as *La Reine des pommes,* translated by Minnie Danzas (Paris: Gallimard, 1958); revised as *A Rage in Harlem* (New York: Avon, 1965; London: Panther, 1969);

Il pleut des coups durs, translated by C. Wourgaft (Paris: Gallimard, 1958); republished as *The Real Cool Killers* (New York: Avon, 1959; London: Panther, 1969);

Couché dans le pain, translated by J. Hérisson and H. Robillot (Paris: Gallimard, 1959); republished as *The Crazy Kill* (New York: Avon, 1959; London: Panther, 1968);

Dare-dare, translated by Pierre Verrier (Paris: Gallimard, 1959); republished as *Run Man, Run* (New York: Putnam, 1966; London: Muller, 1967);

Tout pour plaire, translated by Yves Malartic (Paris: Gallimard, 1959); republished as *The Big Gold Dream* (New York: Avon, 1960; London: Panther, 1968);

Imbroglio negro, translated by J. Fillion (Paris: Gallimard, 1960); republished as *All Shot Up* (New York: Avon, 1960; London: Panther, 1969);

Ne nous énervons pas!, translated by Fillion (Paris: Gallimard, 1961); republished as *The Heat's On* (New York: Putnam, 1966; London: Muller,

Chester Himes (Gale International Portrait Gallery)

1966); republished as *Come Back Charleston Blue* (Harmondsworth, U.K.: Penguin, 1974);

Pinktoes (Paris: Olympia, 1961; expurgated edition, New York: Putnam/Stein & Day, 1965; London: Barker, 1965);

Une affaire de viol, translated by André Mathieu (Paris: Editions Les Yeux Ouverts, 1963); republished as *A Case of Rape* (Washington, D.C.: Howard University Press, 1984);

Retour en Afrique, translated by Pierre Sergent (Paris: Plon, 1964); republished as *Cotton Comes to Harlem* (New York: Putnam, 1965; London: Muller, 1966);

Blind Man with a Pistol (New York: Morrow, 1969; London: Hodder & Stoughton, 1969); republished as *Hot Day, Hot Night* (New York: Dell, 1970);

The Quality of Hurt: The Autobiography of Chester Himes (Garden City, N.Y.: Doubleday, 1972; London: M. Joseph, 1973);

Black on Black: Baby Sister and Selected Writings (Garden City, N.Y.: Doubleday, 1973; London: M. Joseph, 1975);

My Life of Absurdity: The Autobiography of Chester Himes (Garden City, N.Y.: Doubleday, 1976);

Plan B, translated by Hélène Devaux-Minie (Paris: Lieu Commun, 1983).

OTHER: "Democracy Is for the Unafraid," in *Primer for White Folks,* edited by Bucklin Moon (New York: Doubleday, Doran, 1945), pp. 479–483;

"Dilemma of the Negro Novelist in the United States," in *Beyond the Angry Black,* edited by John A. Williams (New York: Cooper Square, 1966), pp. 52–58.

SELECTED PERIODICAL PUBLICATIONS – UNCOLLECTED: "*Native Son:* Pros and Cons," *New Masses,* 35 (21 May 1940): 23–24;

"Now Is the Time! Here Is the Place!," *Opportunity,* 20 (September 1942): 271–273, 284;

"A Letter of Protest to His Publishers from Chester Himes in Spain," *Negro Digest,* 18 (May 1969): 98.

Chester Bomar Himes's career extended from the mid 1930s to the mid 1980s, a time of enormous social change and racial turmoil in the United States. His work is remarkable for the honesty, intensity, and artistic skill with which it represents such a pivotal and turbulent period. Central to his writing is an unusually bold treatment of interracial sex as well as a frank and graphic portrayal of the persistent violence that characterizes race relationships in America. Himes mastered a wide variety of fictional forms, including the short story, the protest novel, the detective novel, and the satiric novel. In addition, he was an accomplished polemical writer and journalist. A controversial figure throughout his career, he was, for the most part, underappreciated in America and, according to H. Bruce Franklin, was "not only one of the most neglected major American authors, but also one of the most misunderstood." Himes was better received in Europe, where he lived for the last thirty-one years of his life. French critics in particular placed a high value on his work, regarding him as an important

Afro-American writer especially gifted in the realms of the detective novel and protest fiction.

In most of his writing Himes draws heavily from his experiences; therefore, his readers should have a detailed and accurate understanding of his extraordinary life. As Gilbert H. Muller observes, Himes was driven throughout his career by a "need to validate [his] life in art," using his writing to probe in a relentlessly honest way important aspects of his experiences. Consequently, Muller stresses that "Himes's fiction can be treated in part as a single autobiographical text." Like many modern American writers, such as Theodore Dreiser, James T. Farrell, and Richard Wright, who operated largely within the naturalistic tradition, Himes grounded his literature in the reality he knew from firsthand experience, subtly transforming that material to produce an art notable for its power and authenticity.

Chester Bomar Himes was born on 29 July 1909 in Jefferson City, Missouri, to parents just two generations removed from slavery. His father, Joseph Sandy Himes, taught blacksmithing and wheelwrighting as the head of the Mechanical Department at Lincoln Institute, a local black college. (The senior Himes later taught these subjects as well as Negro history at Alcorn A&M University in Mississippi and Branch Normal College in Arkansas.) Chester's mother, Estelle Bomar Himes, was a schoolteacher who instructed him and his brother Joseph at home until they were in eighth grade. Chester's family on his father's side was descended from field slaves and on his mother's side came from house slaves and white owners his mother believed were related to English nobility.

Unlike Wright – an Afro-American novelist with whom Himes is often compared and who came from an environment of grinding poverty – Himes originated from a middle-class background. His brother Joseph, whom Himes characterizes in the first volume of his autobiography, *The Quality of Hurt* (1972), as an "internationally known sociologist," graduated with honors from Oberlin College and then went to Ohio State University, where he earned a doctorate. He had a long, distinguished career as a teacher and scholar at North Carolina College in Durham. Chester's eldest brother, Edward, attended Atlanta University and later became an important union leader in Harlem. Himes's cousin Henry Lee Moon graduated from Howard University and worked as an editor for two important black publications, the *Crisis* and the *Amsterdam News.* He also served the NAACP as its publicity director and a member of its executive board.

Scanning the surface of Himes's family background and considering the fact that he became a well-known novelist, one is tempted to read his life as a classic American success story, a narrative of his own and his family's "rise" to great social and personal success, overcoming the effects of slavery in just three generations. But, as Himes's fiction and two autobiographies emphatically reveal, nothing could be further from the truth. For underneath the outward stability and relatively high social status of Himes's early life were what he regarded as tremendous "hurts," physical and psychological traumas that ultimately led him to view his life in disturbingly existential terms as a series of "absurdities."

Two events in Himes's early teen years are particularly vivid examples of these traumas. When Chester was thirteen and working toward a high-school diploma at Branch Normal College, he and his brother Joseph were to give a demonstration in the use of explosives as a part of the school's awards ceremony. Their mother forbade Chester to participate in the event because he had misbehaved earlier in the day. When Joseph attempted to perform the demonstration alone, the chemicals blew up in his face, blinding him for life. In efforts to locate proper medical attention for Joseph, Himes's family was forced to move first to Saint Louis and then to Cleveland, places where his father was never able to find adequate work and where the Himeses accordingly experienced severe economic difficulties for many years. Because the chemistry demonstration was Chester's idea and because he was not able to help his brother in carrying it out, he suffered enormous guilt about the incident for the rest of his life. As he reveals in *The Quality of Hurt,* "That one moment in my life hurt me as much as all the others put together. It still does, half a century later."

Another event that left lasting scars on Himes took place in 1926 when he was working as a busboy in a Cleveland hotel in an attempt to earn money for college. After being on the job for only a few days, Himes fell forty feet down an elevator shaft that was inadvertently left open by hotel personnel. He suffered severe injuries, including three broken vertebrae, several broken teeth, deep facial lacerations, and a fractured arm. This accident left Himes with serious back problems for the rest of his life.

But perhaps the most damaging "hurts" Himes underwent as a child were social and psychological. As physically painful as were the accidents he and his brother experienced, even more damaging to Himes was the fact that both of them were denied treatment at white hospitals and had to settle for inadequate medical attention at poorly equipped black hospitals. The social divisions within his family and the racial splits in American society deeply wounded Himes as a child and continued to trouble him for the rest of his life. Separated from other blacks because of his family's social status, he was also profoundly excluded from white society because of his race. In the second volume of his autobiography, *My Life of Absurdity* (1976), he argues that his persistent alienation, which stemmed from the huge gap between the democratic ideals of American society and the racist practices that subverted these ideals, resulted in his living an "absurd" life: "If one lives in a country where racism is held valid and practiced in all ways of life, eventually . . . one comes to feel the absurdity of life." While writers such as Wright and Alice Walker have made their contributions to Afro-American literature in compelling explorations of the bleak poverty of the black experience, Himes probes — in equally powerful ways — the physical, psychological, and spiritual wounding of middle-class black Americans.

These deep wounds were dramatically evident in Himes's family life. The racial polarities of American society were clear to him when he observed his parents, for his father was black-skinned and heavily Negroid in his features while his mother, an octoroon, could pass for white. Estelle, who identified strongly with the white side of her lineage and romanticized its supposed origins in English nobility, was openly critical of her husband's lower social background as a descendant of field slaves. Always insisting that her children "live up to our heritage" — that is, the genteel side of her family — she unwittingly induced in Himes a negative view of his father in particular and ordinary black people in general. While Himes felt a "strange, fierce love that survived everything" for his mother, he became ashamed of his father, seeing him as an Uncle Tom who came from a "tradition derived from an inherited slave mentality which accepts the premise that whites knew best, and that blacks should accept what whites offer and be thankful." For example, Himes became lastingly bitter when his father insisted that he settle quickly with the Cleveland hotel whose neglect had resulted in the elevator accident. His mother, however, wanted to sue the hotel for a much larger financial award. Himes never forgave his father for not pressing his case more aggressively against the white people who owned the hotel.

Seeing his parents as "the complete opposite" of each other, Himes suffered from a painful psychological division that, once implanted in him as a child, dominated his imagination for the rest of his life. He thus came to view himself – and each of his protagonists, who are often shadows of himself – as a fundamentally split person. One side of him aspired to the outward success his mother's ancestry claimed as his natural birthright, and the other part of him was profoundly suspicious of that success because he feared it would turn him into his father, a frustrated man Himes felt had traded his personal integrity for a slightly higher rung on the social ladder. Himes and his protagonists, therefore, are especially dramatic illustrations of what W. E. B. Du Bois, in *The Souls of the Black Folk* (1903), characterizes as one of the enduring problems of most American blacks – their being split in two by a social system that imposes a "double consciousness" on them: "One ever feels this twoness – an American, a Negro: two souls, two thoughts, two unreconciled strivings; two warring ideals in one dark body whose dogged strength alone keeps it from being torn asunder."

These divisions are evident in all phases of Himes's life and are central preoccupations in most of his writing. Much of his loneliness as a child can be attributed to his not being able to identify fully with either blacks or whites. (One of the modern American novels Himes particularly admired was William Faulkner's *Light in August* [1932], wherein the central character, Joe Christmas, is afflicted with precisely the same problem.) As the fortunes of his family declined, particularly after Joseph's medical problems depleted their financial resources, Himes experienced more and more psychological turmoil and came to see himself as two opposite people in one dark body. Part of him was driven toward success; he became an excellent student who was placed several grade levels ahead to high school. He played school sports with such "suicidal intensity" that he incurred injuries that troubled him for many years. He scored fourth highest on the IQ test given to all entering freshmen at Ohio State University, where he enrolled in 1926 in order to realize his boyhood dream of becoming a physician. While at Ohio State, Himes eagerly engaged in a quest to fit into conventional college life and the white society beyond it by becoming a typical "Joe College" student of the 1920s. He pledged a fraternity in his first semester, undertook an extremely ambitious social schedule, and desperately acquired all the trappings of a conventionally successful college student: "I bought a coonskin coat for three hundred dollars, a long-stemmed pipe, a Model T Ford roadster, and I became a collegian."

But, while Himes was going to such extremes to cultivate this outward aspect of his personality, another part of his nature was also developing: a rebellious inner self completely at odds with his outer self. While living in Saint Louis, for example, he had developed the habit of skipping school and roaming the streets of this "strange, big city" for secret adventures. While at Ohio State he began to frequent the bars and whorehouses of Columbus's black slums. Unsure of himself with the coeds at Ohio State and overcome with an "inferiority complex" that made him feel ill at ease on campus, he descended into the underworld of the ghetto, where his ego was bolstered by "older, amoral women." As he came to resent the "in-group distinctions" of middle-class black students and the standoffish quality of the overall "white environment" at school, he consciously rebelled against them with his unconventional nightlife. He was asked to withdraw from college after bringing some fellow students to a downtown whorehouse. Exhausted by the conflicting demands of his opposed identities, Himes became physically ill at the end of the 1927 fall semester and never returned to school.

Sharply divided by these "schizophrenic impulses," Himes soon rejected his public role of successful student and prospective doctor, consciously developing the persona of street-smart hustler. Returning to Cleveland after leaving college, he immediately began work at a ghetto nightclub. He exalted in this "new life" and cultivated the alter ego of "Little Katzi," a small-time crook engaged in gambling, bootlegging, and robbery. In summer 1928 he was arrested for stealing guns in Detroit and was given a suspended sentence of two years. A few days before he planned to return to Ohio State, he stole a car, wrote several bad checks, and was again arrested and given another suspended sentence. By this time he was smoking opium and had developed a reputation for extreme violence; indeed, his fellow hustlers warned people that "Little Katzi will kill you" if crossed. In late November 1928 he was arrested for armed robbery after breaking into the house of a wealthy white family, holding them at gunpoint, and stealing more than fifty-three thousand dollars in valuables. On 27 December 1928 he was sentenced to twenty-five years of hard labor in prison. He withdrew into the grim underworld of Ohio State Penitentiary, later recalling, "I would do my time and the outside world could fuck itself."

His prison experience, paradoxically, proved to be salvific, for it created a new identity that, if it could not heal the sharp divisions of his prior life, could at least make these divisions bearable by coherently representing them in art. While in prison Himes became a writer. Finding the penitentiary a microcosm of the society that had driven him into self-destructive behavior, he initially responded to it with characteristic "violent seizures of rage." Eventually, however, he learned to redirect and master that rage by writing stories about prison life that not only provided him with money, which he needed to avoid the more brutal forms of prison work, but also gave him a new self-image that he respected and valued. Indeed, Himes came to see writing as his "salvation."

His first story, "To What Red Hell," describes the 1930 fire at the penitentiary that killed three hundred inmates, a fate Himes narrowly escaped by being transferred earlier in the day to a part of the prison unaffected by the fire. This story was published in *Esquire* in October 1934, and a second one, "The Night's for Crying," also appeared in that magazine in January 1937. It centers on a vicious killer, Black Boy, on death row for a senseless murder. While incarcerated, Himes also placed several stories in black newspapers such as the *Atlantic World,* the *Pittsburgh Courier,* and the *Baltimore Afro-American.*

It is difficult to overstate the importance of prison on Himes's personal and literary development. As Franklin notes, "Himes's achievement as a writer of fiction, indeed, his very existence as an author, comes directly from his experience in prison, which shaped his imagination and determined his outlook on American society." Some of Himes's best stories concern prison life, and his third novel, *Cast the First Stone* (1952), is set in prison. Like Malcolm X – who underwent a profound change of consciousness in a penitentiary that trapped his body but drove him inward to a new sense of self – Himes came to see his years in prison as a kind of conversion experience, insisting that he "grew to manhood in the Ohio State Penitentiary" because there he was able to become "dependent on no one but myself" and develop the "basic patterns of survival" he needed to protect himself from "self-destruction."

When Himes was released from prison in 1936 after serving seven and a half years of his sentence, he immediately began to rebuild his life. He married Jean Johnson, a black woman he knew from his days as a hustler in Cleveland. This marriage, although far from perfect, lasted fourteen years and gave him the emotional and psychological stability that was missing from his earlier life and was necessary for his writing at the time. Between

Lesley Packard Himes, 1959

1936 and 1945, when he published his first novel, *If He Hollers Let Him Go,* Himes supported himself and his wife with a variety of jobs. He worked in Cleveland as a bellhop and a waiter and then enlisted in the Works Progress Administration as a laborer and later as a research assistant in the Cleveland Public Library. In 1939 he was employed in the Ohio Writers' Project, writing unsigned editorials for the *Cleveland Daily News.* When World War II began, his WPA employment abruptly ended, and he lived for several months at Malabar Farms, Louis Bromfield's artist colony, in Pleasant Valley, Ohio. While there he was encouraged by Bromfield to complete "Black Sheep," a long novel based on his prison experience. In hopes of getting this work turned into a film, Himes and his wife took a Greyhound bus to Los Angeles in 1940.

Himes's four years in wartime Los Angeles were of critical importance to him because there he saw with full clarity the racism and violence of

American life that became the center of his next two published novels and remained serious concerns for him throughout his career. As thousands of black and white workers, many of them from the South, converged on Los Angeles in the early 1940s to work in war industries, the old patterns of segregation were used by employers despite President Franklin D. Roosevelt's executive order mandating integration in all war-related labor. Himes worked in twenty-three different menial jobs during the first three years of the war, even though he was well qualified for a much higher level of employment. He was skilled in carpentry, plumbing, electrical wiring, roofing, and reading blueprints – talents he had picked up from his father, who had taught them in various black schools. Moreover, Himes's prison experience had involved the operation of many machine tools, and his years as a writer had made him an excellent typist. Nevertheless, he was employed as a laborer while more prestigious and highly paid jobs went almost exclusively to whites.

The literary result of Himes's war-related labor experience was *If He Hollers Let Him Go,* which came directly from "the accumulation of . . . racial hurts" that he received in Los Angeles. Bob Jones, the protagonist, heads west seeking the American dream of expanded possibilities but finds a racist environment that imposes severely limited roles on him. When he steps out of these roles, he is threatened with serious punishments, including prison and even death. Although Los Angeles is in a "war boom," the best that black men can do for work is the sort of token position Jones receives as "leaderman," a supervisor of black mechanics. To make matters worse, the Japanese bombing of Pearl Harbor has created a racial paranoia in California resulting in the imprisonment of thousands of Japanese-Americans in internment camps as well as the increased scrutiny of blacks.

Jones is, for the most part, Himes's self-portrait. Both have gone west from Cleveland and have attended Ohio State University. Each has aspired to be a doctor but has given up this hope, realizing that such ambitions do not square with the hard facts of racial life in America. Moreover, Jones has "puttered around" in an artist commune named Karamu and has also worked with a theater group in Cleveland, clear parallels to Himes's experience at Bromfield's writers' colony and his work with the Ohio Writers' Project.

Even more significant is that Jones, like his creator, is a profoundly divided man. One part of him hungers for success in mainstream America, as evidenced by his studying medicine at Ohio State and working hard to make the football team. This outward self falls in love with Alice Harrison, a light-skinned Negro whose father is Wellington L. P. Harrison, "one of the richest Negroes in the city if not the whole West Coast." Attracted to Alice because he believes that "she'd still make the grade in the white man's world," Jones senses that marrying her will guarantee his success in that world. But another part of him recoils from this success because he feels he will pay a steep price for it: his identity as an individual black man. This inner self rebels vigorously against both the white system symbolized by his bosses at Atlas Shipbuilding and the black middle class represented by Alice and her family. This rebellious self, similar to the personality of "Little Katzi" that Himes developed after withdrawing from college, expresses itself in two ways: physical violence toward white men and verbal abuse toward white women.

After being called a "nigger" by Johnny Stoddart, a white coworker who objects to his winning a crap game at Atlas, Jones resolves "to murder him cold-bloodedly." Like Wright's Bigger Thomas, who feels empowered by killing a white person, Jones relishes the thought of shooting Stoddart. As he stalks the white man, he thinks, "I wanted him to feel as scared and powerless and unprotected as I felt every goddamned morning I woke up." Although he never acts on these murderous impulses toward white men, he does act on his aggression toward Madge Perkins, a white woman who refuses to work with him by exclaiming, "I ain't gonna work with no nigger." Regarding her as a grotesque symbol of a white social order that tantalizes, frustrates, and wants to "screw" him, he answers her insult by shouting, "Screw you, then, you cracker bitch," thus losing his position as leaderman and putting himself at risk of being fired.

Most of the narrative is furiously driven by the duality of conflicting selves in Jones. Because he alternates wildly between desires to marry the "aristocratic" Alice and to demean the sluttish Madge, many of the novel's key scenes take the form of his attempts to court Alice or to attack white people such as Madge. By the end of the book Jones resolves to repress his inner self, which wants to take on the white world, and to act instead in terms of his public self, which wants to marry Alice and thus become part of the system. He attempts to achieve a "new life" with Alice, assuring her that he has already made up his mind to conform to the expectations of mainstream America. Indeed, he feels that becoming an integral part of Alice's middle-class world will finally release him from slavery itself, allowing him to cross "the river Jordan to the promised land."

But, just as Himes begins to construct this extremely conventional and sentimental ending, he brilliantly dismantles it, replacing it with a boldly naturalistic conclusion much truer to the facts of American life. When Jones returns to Atlas to apologize and thus recover his position as leaderman, he accidentally bumps into Madge, who is avoiding work by sleeping in an empty room. In a scene closely resembling the episode in *Native Son* (1940) in which Bigger Thomas finds himself alone with Mary Dalton in her bedroom, Jones is struck with "overwhelming fear" and a "raw wild panic." Both he and Madge are "trapped" in the roles a racist society insists that they perform. Although Jones wants to leave the room, he cannot. One part of himself is attracted to Madge as America's forbidden fruit, and she wants to use him sexually, threatening to accuse him of rape if he leaves. When some white employees demand entrance to the room, Jones locks the door and engages in a brutal fight with Madge. The scene ends when the "mob" outside uses an acetylene torch to cut the lock off the door and almost lynches Jones after Madge accuses him of trying to rape her.

At the end of the novel Jones survives his ordeal but loses nearly everything he values – his freedom, his individuality, and all prospects of a "successful" life with Alice. His situation at the end of the novel closely resembles Himes's own in 1927 when he withdrew from college and began the criminal activity that soon resulted in his imprisonment. For Jones gets his own kind of prison: the U.S. Army. The judge who tries him for the alleged rape of Madge decides to give him a break by forcing him to sign up for military service instead of sending him to jail. But for Jones there is little distinction between the highly regimented world of prison and the equally regimented world of the army, since both are punishments imposed on him by a racist social system that defines his place as a black man.

If Himes's first published novel describes his loss of faith in modern America by finally locating its central character in a situation comparable to his own when he was sentenced to prison in 1928, his second novel, *Lonely Crusade* (1947), can be seen, initially at least, in a more hopeful light. Its protagonist is in the more positive situation that Himes confronted when he was released from prison in 1936. Like Himes – who discovered a potential "salvation" for himself as a writer and soon married a woman whom he loved deeply – Lee Gordon at the beginning of the novel is empowered by two things

that allow him to transcend suicidal despair: his work as union organizer at Comstock Aircraft Organization and his marriage to Ruth Gordon. The book therefore starts off in an optimistic way, with its central character feeling "a new lease on life" when he is hired by the union council to serve as an organizer. The job provides him with increased pay and self-respect, thus allowing him "again [to] be a husband to his wife."

Although the first pages of *Lonely Crusade* promise to go beyond the dark nihilism of *If He Hollers Let Him Go,* the reader soon finds that Gordon's happiness and faith in the future are based on a flimsy foundation. Even though he has a bachelor's degree from California State University at Los Angeles, he lives in a racist society that will not let him reap the fruits of his education or compete with whites on an equal footing. Like Jones, who suffers from low self-esteem and repeatedly imagines himself as a collared dog, Lee sees himself as "lower than a dog," plagued by a sense of "inner disparagement." Frustrated by his lack of confidence and the limited roles that further erode his self-image, he often envisions himself in antiheroic terms, thinking, "He was no medicine man, no Marcus Garvey, no black Messiah." (In a similar way Jones observes that he will "never be a hero" and finally has to accept the bleak options open to him.)

As *Lonely Crusade* progresses, Lee's antiheroic status is emphasized when his sources of affirmation at the beginning of the novel are undercut and ultimately reduced to absurdity. His marriage to Ruth in particular is undermined by his persistent insecurity and the racist environment that strips him of manhood. Consumed by self-doubt, Lee seeks compensatory ego gratification by beating up his wife and blaming her for most of his problems, imagining her as the "vessel of his impotency." Lee's sharply divided nature brings the most harm to his marriage. Part of him hates Ruth, but another part loves her deeply and feels that "in his distress, she was his haven." The part of him that hates his black wife is inevitably drawn to Jackie Forks, a white Communist organizer with whom Lee has an affair that severely damages and perhaps destroys his marriage.

After his marriage with Ruth is compromised when she finds out about his affair with Jackie, Lee's political involvements also dissolve into meaninglessness. The Communist party is portrayed throughout the novel as intent on crudely manipulating people with its self-serving power games rather than helping laborers fight against capitalism and work toward a more just society. Luther

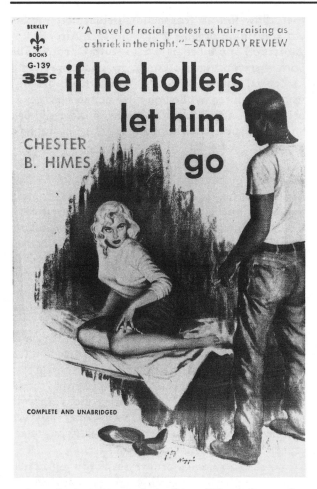

Cover for the 1958 paperback edition of Himes's first novel

ture – he can commit himself to the union and its fight against the police and Comstock. Lee clearly chooses this second course when he participates in the union's demonstration against the company; on the last page of the novel he carries the union banner in an attempt to lead the workers.

But Himes surrounds Lee's support of the union with powerful ironies, strongly undercutting any heroic meaning that might otherwise emerge from his actions. Lee has already lost most of his faith in the union because of its racism and dishonesty, and he clearly realizes that "nothing could save him – not even the union." Furthermore, Lee's quixotic gesture of marching despite the warnings of police is clearly suicidal, since an officer is training his revolver on Lee as he protests and will almost certainly shoot him. All that the reader can conclude about Lee at the end is that "he was alone now" – dispossessed, like Jones, of his previous beliefs and trying to salvage his manhood in a world that fights his every effort to become a man.

Because Himes's first two books are acted out in wartime California and center on similar antiheroic protagonists, they almost read like one continuous novel. In many ways they rank among Himes's most impressive literary achievements, but, because of their extraordinarily frank treatment of race, sex, and violence, they received disappointing reviews. Critics were particularly harsh in their judgments of *Lonely Crusade*. As Himes points out in *The Quality of Hurt*:

> Everyone hated the book. The communist review *The New Masses* hit the stands with a vitriolic three-page attack.... *The Daily Worker* and the *People's Voice* launched attacks. *Ebony* magazine ran an editorial ... in which it said: "The character of Lee Gordon is psychotic, as is the author, Chester Himes." *The Atlantic Monthly* said "Hate runs through this book like a streak of yellow bile."

Feeling that readers disliked his first two novels because they "came too close to the truth," Himes became embittered about the critical response to his work and had difficulty writing for the next five years. Late in his life he ranked the negative reception of *Lonely Crusade* with the most damaging psychological wounds he had ever received: "Of all the hurts I had suffered before – my brother's accident, my own accident, being kicked out of college, my parents' divorce, my term in prison, and my racial hell on the West Coast ... the rejection of *Lonely Crusade* hurt me the most." At this point Himes "decided to leave the United States forever if I got a chance."

McGregor – a black Communist organizer who betrays both his fellow union members and party coworkers when he accepts bribes from Lewis Foster, the vice-president of Comstock – finally admits to Lee, "What the hell does I know about Marx? Or give a damn 'bout him? But I knows how to be a nigger and make it pay." From top to bottom Communist officials are portrayed as no better than Luther because they are blatant opportunists who will lie, cheat, and kill to achieve their self-interested political goals.

Like Jones, then, Lee ends up trapped and alone, facing two equally self-destructive alternatives as he confronts an essentially absurd situation. Feeling strongly "impelled to run," he can skip bail, escape to another part of the country, change his name, and try again to establish a new life. But this course will activate his old doubt about there being "something missing" in the "essence of [his] manhood." Like Jones, who finally enters the army, Lee has a second alternative, which is collective in na-

From 1947 to 1953, however, Himes lacked the financial resources to move to Europe, so he lived in the New York City area, working at low-paying jobs as dishwasher, porter, bellhop, and caretaker of several estates. In 1948 he attended Yaddo, the writers' colony in Saratoga Springs, New York, but throughout this period he found it extremely difficult to write, working sporadically on *The Third Generation* (1954), a novel about his family's history, and "The Black Sheep," a fictionalized account of his prison years. The latter novel was published as *Cast the First Stone,* the last book he completed in the United States. The novel is set in an unspecified prison during the 1940s and, like Willard Motley's *Knock on Any Door* (1947) and other "raceless" novels popular during the late 1940s and early 1950s, focuses almost exclusively on white characters. However, Jim Monroe, a white man from Mississippi, resembles Himes in several ways. He has suffered a serious back injury as a child, has attended college, and has been given a twenty-five-year sentence for armed robbery. Moreover, he has narrowly escaped a fire in the prison that killed several hundred inmates.

Cast the First Stone is notable for its direct treatment of homosexual love. Although Himes briefly treats Alice Harrison's lesbian flirtations in *If He Hollers Let Him Go,* he makes a male-male relationship a central concern in *Cast the First Stone.* Much of Monroe's personal growth stems from his involvement with Duke Dido, a younger man who provides him with love and understanding he has never known. In the early drafts of the novel these characters consummate their relationship, but in the published version Himes was forced by nervous editors to tone down this part of the novel, making their relationship curiously platonic. In any event Dido's influence on Monroe is pivotal, moving him to a new awareness of himself as a human being and rejecting the prison's definition of him as a numbered object.

Several other factors also contribute to Monroe's achieving the same kind of growth that Himes experienced in prison. Monroe gains a certain amount of economic independence from the prison system by developing an extremely lucrative gambling operation, becoming a kind of celebrity to his fellow convicts. More important, he develops a strong intellectual friendship with a prisoner named Metz, with whom he discusses literature, law, and religion. Their exchanges stimulate him to read widely and to make the first moves toward becoming a writer. His metamorphosis is completed during the fire in the prison on Easter Monday. This experience becomes a powerful epiphany to him of how American society brutalizes minorities by trapping them in unsafe conditions and then showing a macabre kind of relief when they are destroyed. Thus shocked into a lucid awareness of the social environment that helped to make him a criminal, Monroe is psychologically liberated at the end of the novel by an existential consciousness that shows him "the way to freedom."

Himes revealed in a letter to Carl Van Vechten (18 February 1947) that he wrote *Cast the First Stone* to "escape my past" by gaining a truer understanding of the social forces that had molded him into a criminal, and he underwent a process of purgation and liberation in completing this novel after struggling with it for more than twelve years. The twelve-hundred-dollar advance provided by his publisher enabled him to begin a new life in France. The move transformed his life and reactivated him as a writer. But, unlike Wright, whose exile in France led him to write about world events and gradually to distance himself from a close analysis of black life in America, Himes continued to make the American racial dilemma the chief focus of his writing throughout his thirty-one-year exile in Europe, which gave him a new perspective on his native country.

Himes left for France on 3 April 1953 and, except for several brief returns, remained abroad for the rest of his life. Depressed by his failing marriage and the hostile reaction of American critics to his work, he was encouraged by French reviewers' favorable responses to *Lonely Crusade,* ranking it with works by Faulkner, F. Scott Fitzgerald, and Ernest Hemingway as one of the best American books published in France in 1952. Moreover, Himes initially saw France as a place where he would not be victimized as a black person. As he observes in *The Quality of Hurt:* "I got along all right with people of other nationalities, the French and the Spanish. I forgot I was black with them. But the Americans and the English always made a point of reminding me I was black, as though it were a stigma, and this brought out the worst in me." Although Himes's actual experience in France and Spain later caused him to revise this high estimate of French and Spanish racial tolerance, he nevertheless benefited greatly from his expatriation.

Himes's living in Paris put him in frequent contact with such black American exiles as Wright, James Baldwin, and William Gardner Smith. Although Himes, by temperament and conviction a loner, was careful not to become too closely associated with other writers and avoided becoming part of a literary school or aesthetic movement, he did get to know a group of black artists and intellectuals who gathered at the Café Tournon. He profited immensely from his association with other writers and formed a particularly important relationship with Wright. Although these two fiercely individualistic men certainly had their quarrels and fell out with each other over personal and literary matters, Himes stressed that he "respected Wright more than anyone else I knew," looking up to him as a black writer who achieved success in the larger literary world without compromising his integrity as a black man. For the first time in his life Himes was independent but not alone. He was closely associated with an important black writer who in many ways shared his vision and could encourage him in his work. This literary friendship enabled him to grow steadily as a novelist.

Europe stimulated Himes in another important way, freeing him from the repressive puritanism of American culture that had always divided his personality and stifled his art. Paris offered him the intellectual freedom that he had desired since his prison years but could never find in America. He eagerly devoured the works of such French existentialists as Albert Camus, Jean Cocteau, and Jean-Paul Sartre, finding their absurdist visions of life a liberation from the grim determinism he had endorsed in America. An important part of the existential freedom in which Himes exulted while living in Paris was sexual in nature. Himes observed that "sex and writing were my two obsessions," but he had found himself both sexually impotent and imaginatively deadlocked while living in America. But he felt strongly that the radically free sexuality in which he indulged while living in Paris rekindled his literary fires.

While en route to Europe aboard the *Ile de France,* Himes began an affair with Willa Thompson, a white Philadelphia heiress whom he described as "completely uninhibited." When this relationship ended, he began an extravagant affair with a twenty-two-year-old German woman, Marlene Behrens, that ended with her being committed to a sanitarium after a suicide attempt. Himes then started a long relationship with another white woman, Lesley Packard, whom he later married and with whom he lived for the rest of his life. Thus released from the social, racial, and artistic restraints of American life that had led to a five-year period of greatly reduced literary activity, Himes underwent a remarkable progress of artistic revitalization in Europe. After three years in France he had published two autobiographical novels, *The Third Generation* and *The Primitive* (1955), and was

beginning the work in detective fiction that made him a world-famous writer.

Himes got the idea for *The Third Generation* in summer 1950 when he discovered parts of the manuscript for a novel about his family's history that his mother had been writing late in her life. Although he did not use any of this material – most of it was set during slavery and dealt with issues that he felt would not interest a contemporary American audience – his mother's work reawakened his interest in his family's past and stimulated his desire to come to terms with it. The novel that emerged five years later examines a black family that is an exact replica of Himes's own, and this book is probably more revealing of his painful feelings toward his parents than his two volumes of autobiography.

Originally titled "The Cord," *The Third Generation* is Himes's attempt to cut himself away from the traumatic experiences of childhood and to give birth to a new self divorced from his family. The father in the novel, William Taylor, is a black professor only two generations removed from the humiliations of field slavery. He marries Lillian Manning, a light-skinned mulatto who sees herself as a woman "only one-thirty-second part Negro" in whose "veins flowed some of the most aristocratic blood in all the South." The family begins to disintegrate when the parents are unable to decide how their children should be raised. William argues that they should be brought up "to prepare them for the reality of being black," while his wife, who sees blackness as "the embodiment of evil," wants to deny their Negro roots altogether and rear them as white people. As was the case in Himes's home, "the battle of color raged continuously," resulting in an acrimonious divorce and a precipitous descent into poverty.

The Third Generation may be viewed as Himes's most naturalistic work, for it not only studies in minute detail the actual circumstances of his experience but also informs that experience with a determinism that comes close to being absolute. The Taylors are initially restricted (tailored) by the biological fact of their racial origins and then are doubly punished by social conditioning, since their mixed racial origins exclude them from both white and black communities. After eleven-year-old Tom Taylor is blinded, the family's economic situation quickly deteriorates, and they are forced to endure bleak poverty in the urban environments of Saint Louis and Cleveland. It seems as if the Taylors are not only threatened by social, biological, and racial forces beyond their understanding and control but are also under some sort of divine injunction as well. The novel's title ominously echoes an Old Testament curse: "I, the Lord thy God am a jealous God, visiting the iniquity of the fathers upon the children unto the third and fourth generation of them that hate me" (Exodus 20:5).

Feeling hemmed in by his environment and vaguely cursed by the gods of his world, Charles Taylor, the book's young protagonist, uses the same strategy employed by the Jews in Exodus – he escapes from an existence that seems designed to destroy him. But the place he will go where things will be much different is never made clear, since no promised land appears on any of his horizons. He is left with the experience of complete disorientation resulting from radical alienation. Cutting the cord from the old life, he senses his new life as a sustained birth trauma. Or, to use his own metaphor, his life has become a book that is falling apart: "It was as if a madman had snatched pages from a treasured book, the story stopping eerily in the middle of a sentence, a gaping hole left in the lives of all the characters, the senses groping futilely to fill the missing parts gone, now the meaning all distorted as if coming suddenly and unexpectedly into a street of funny mirrors." For people such as Charles, who are part of the third generation after the abolition of slavery, twentieth-century American life may offer only new forms of emotional and psychological bondage that are just as crippling.

The Primitive also centers on a protagonist who must contend with modern kinds of enslavement as he is caught painfully between white and black worlds. Jesse Robinson, a struggling black novelist in Harlem who is forced to work as a porter in order to survive, tries to break out of this economic trap when he aggressively challenges white America's ultimate taboo by having an affair with a wealthy white woman, Kriss Cummings. But the orgies that Jesse experiences with Kriss over a six-day period in her posh Gramercy Park apartment fail to liberate either of them because each is unable either to understand or transcend the rigid stereotypes that govern race and sex in America. Kriss – who perceives black men as erotic "primitives" who are valuable only when they can block out the pain of her life by satisfying her extraordinary libidinal appetites – makes it clear that she will give Jesse the financial security he needs to pursue his writing only if he can live out on a daily basis the role of the black stud. (At one point she thinks, "If she could sleep with him and immediately afterward have him beheaded, she would enjoy his company.") And Jesse can only invert rather than dissolve the labels Kriss neurotically imposes on him. Enraged by her

view of him as a superlover, he becomes a superhater – a stereotyped black beast who murders her in a fit of drunken rage. Like most of the interracial affairs in Himes's fiction, the relationship between Jesse and Kriss is pathological because it is driven by environmental determinants that convert love into hate and sex into violence.

Himes regarded *The Primitive* as his favorite book and often remarked about the pleasures he experienced while writing it. As he observed in a 1963 letter to novelist John A. Williams:

> I wrote *The Primitive* sitting in the sun in a house in ... Mallorca filled with tranquilizer pills and everything was crystal clear to me and no more horrible than the life of Jesse from a distance of five thousand miles and five years ... and it amused me in the same grotesque morbid ... fashion which I would be amused seeing a white man who was chasing a Negro boy suddenly fall and break his neck.

In sharp contrast to the characters in *The Primitive* who are destroyed because they fail to see either themselves or their culture in any clear way, Himes – aided by a temporal distance of five years and a spatial distance of five thousand miles – was beginning to assume a fruitful new life in Europe because he could now see in a lucid, detached way the American problems that had formerly reduced him to an impotent rage.

Although they were published in the early years of Himes's exile in Europe, both *The Third Generation* and *The Primitive* look backward to his faltering career in America rather than point forward to the distinctively new career he was establishing abroad. Both are naturalistic protest novels that envision black people as victims of a racist system that denies them humanity and severely penalizes them for stepping out of the limited roles extended to blacks in America. If Himes had continued writing in this vein, his European exile would have been meaningless in artistic terms. It would have given him merely a freer opportunity to play out literary impulses that he was beginning to regard as superficial.

By 1955 Himes had a strong desire to break away from "the tradition of Richard Wright," which he felt used naturalistic techniques crudely to explore a deterministic view of life. He wanted to develop a different style that would allow him to capture his unique experience and probe in a fuller way the deeper, hidden dimensions of black life. As he explains in *My Life of Absurdity:*

Cover for the 1969 paperback edition of Himes's 1966 novel,
featuring detectives Grave Digger Jones and Coffin
Ed Johnson

I had the creative urge, but the old used forms for the black American writer did not fit my creations. I wanted to break through that barrier that labeled me as a protest writer. I knew the life of an American black needed another image than just the victim of racism. We were more than just victims. . . . We were unique individuals, funny but not clowns, solemn but not serious, hurt but not suffering, sexualists but not whores in the usual sense of the word; we had a tremendous love of life, a love of sex, a love of ourselves. We were absurd.

A rather strange coincidence helped Himes to find a way of breaking through the limits of protest writing. While investigating the possibility of publishing *The Primitive* at Gallimard, Himes bumped into Marcel Duhamel, who had translated *If He Hollers Let*

Him Go into French. Duhamel was greatly impressed by the terse realism of that novel and suggested that Himes consider writing detective fiction in the manner of such hard-boiled American realists as Raymond Chandler and Dashiell Hammett. Duhamel, who was editing a line of crime thrillers for Gallimard called *La Série Noire* (The Black Series), offered Himes an advance of one thousand dollars to write a book for the series.

Because Himes was nearly destitute at the time, he was in no position to turn down such an offer, even though he initially believed that he might be prostituting his talents to write popular thrillers. However, he soon found that the modern detective novel was precisely the literary form he needed to express his vision of black American life in wildly absurdist terms. While working on his first crime thriller, *For Love of Imabelle* (1957), he found himself fascinated by the "strange, violent, unreal stories" he was telling, some of which he had picked up in prison and as a hustler in Cleveland. By the time he had finished the book, he was convinced that he had uncovered a new literary space for Afro-American writers, one that could enable them to explore and express in fresh ways "the American black's secret mind."

Himes published nine detective novels – seven of which were originally published in French translations – between 1957 and 1969, including *For Love of Imabelle, The Real Cool Killers* (1959), *The Crazy Kill* (1959), *The Big Gold Dream* (1960), *All Shot Up* (1960), *Cotton Comes to Harlem* (1965), *The Heat's On* (1966), *Run Man, Run* (1966), and *Blind Man with a Pistol* (1969). All but *Run Man, Run* have as their central characters two black detectives, Grave Digger Jones and Coffin Ed Johnson, who attempt in various ways to maintain at least a marginal kind of order in a disintegrating urban world threatened by crime, violence, and racism. As Stephen F. Millikin notes, most of these books follow a common plot formula, beginning with a bizarre "opening scene of violence" that involves "Harlem characters in a crime that is apparently inexplicable." Himes's detectives then employ a variety of police methods ranging from subtle deduction to not-so-subtle physical intimidation to solve the crime, thus bringing a fragile peace to the Harlem community. Himes's early detective novels stick rather closely to this formula, often at the expense of character development and narrative diversity, but his later crime thrillers undertake bold departures from this pattern.

For Love of Imabelle, for example, follows most of the conventions of popular American detective novels. Like the fiction of Chandler, Hammett, and Mickey Spillane, it takes place in a sinister urban setting, a dark underworld of vice and crime. Its two black detectives – like their counterparts in such books as Hammett's *The Maltese Falcon* (1930) and Chandler's *The Big Sleep* (1939) – are hardboiled loners who are deeply cynical about society in general and the police bureaucracy in particular. Their chief task is to transcend the corruption of society and the red tape of their jobs, solving crime and imposing "order" on an essentially violent world.

Unlike Himes's later crime thrillers – in which the detectives confront mysteries that are in some ways unsolvable and encounter extreme forms of evil and violence that tax even their case-hardened

sensibilities – *For Love of Imabelle* provides the detectives with a problem that is clear-cut and easy to solve in a definite way. All they have to do is apprehend the con artists who have executed a well-known Harlem fraud known as "The Blow." An innocent man named Jackson has been bilked out of fifteen hundred dollars on the promise that such an amount can be increased to fifteen thousand dollars by using a special chemical process that alters the print on ten-dollar bills. Jackson, who needs the extra money so that he can marry Imabelle, the girl of his dreams, has lost both his cash and his prospects for marriage. After more than a hundred pages of chase scenes in which Coffin Ed and Grave Digger relentlessly stalk the criminals through an exotic landscape redolent of funky blues music and hustlers who dress in "cashmere, melton, mink and muskrat," the villains are killed and Jackson is free to marry Imabelle.

As Himes continued to work over a twelve-year period with detective fiction – a genre he described as providing him with "more pleasure" than any other type of literature he had written – he found many new possibilities in its apparently simple form. To use a term given prominence in recent years by such critics as Henry Louis Gates and Houston Baker, Himes "signified" on the form of the detective novel, repeating its conventions yet also carefully revising them to express new meanings particularly relevant to the Afro-American experience. *The Heat's On,* first published in France as *Ne nous énervons pas!* (1961), is a vivid example of how Himes transformed the popular detective novel. The exotic Harlem setting of *For Love of Imabelle* here becomes a darkly surrealistic world that reflects both the highly pressurized minds of the characters and the hellish quality of the society in which they are forced to live.

Early in *The Heat's On* a Harlem street scene is described as a kind of nightmare: "Vaguely human shapes hung from the dark open windows of the front apartments, like an amphitheater of ghosts; and the windows of the block apartments were ablaze with lights as though the next war had begun." Populating this "steaming bedlam" are such grotesque figures as an albino giant named Pinkie, a humpbacked dwarf named Jake, and an evangelist called Sister Heavenly, whose face has "the shrunken, dried-up, leathery look of a monkey's." To reinforce this vision of modern hell, Himes uses an extensive pattern of heat imagery. The entire novel is fired to the boiling point with many kinds of heat, including the physical sort, which nearly causes a riot midway through the novel, and the psychological type, which puts most of the novel's characters on the edge of violence.

Caught in such an oppressive, nearly demonic world, Coffin Ed and Grave Digger must rely on increasingly violent and illegal means to carry out their mission of making Harlem a "decent, peaceful city for people to live in." In the novel's opening scene, for example, Grave Digger kills a suspected heroin pusher when he punches him in the stomach to force him to vomit the drugs he has swallowed in an attempt to hide the evidence of his crime. From this point on, Himes's detectives use ever-more-violent tactics to solve mysteries and bring criminals to justice.

After Grave Digger is seriously wounded in a shoot-out with drug dealers, Coffin Ed becomes "a civilian on a manhunt" as he stalks the men who have nearly killed his partner. Armed with a nickel-plated .38 revolver, a hunting knife, and a huge blackjack – and honed to a fine pitch of alertness on Benzedrine and coffee – he begins to resemble and even act like a "homicidal maniac." The novel's climactic scenes are similar to a Western showdown, as Ed overpowers criminals with extreme violence. At the end of the novel he faces his enemies in classic Western fashion, "shooting from the hip" to kill three hit men from the syndicate.

As in *For Love of Imabelle,* the novel ends with mysteries solved, criminals defeated, and order restored. But *The Heat's On* is ultimately a much more disturbing book because the order achieved is so fragile and temporary. The forces of chaos are stronger and reveal themselves in more intense and widespread violence. Twelve people are brutally murdered, a dog is eviscerated, and a house is blown to smithereens with nitroglycerin. In order to contain such "mother-rapin' senseless violence," the detectives are forced to go "beyond the line ... of human restraint," descending to the level of criminals themselves. In the book's crowning irony, the real villains are never caught or punished. Even though Coffin Ed and Grave Digger are able to round up petty dope pushers such as Jake and mid-level distributors such as Sister Heavenly, they are never able to get at the real source of the cancer eating away at Harlem – the syndicate.

Cotton Comes to Harlem, first published as *Retour en Afrique* (1964), is an even darker work because it compounds the pessimistic social vision of *The Heat's On* with a bitterly ironic humor comparable to the black humor of such novels as Joseph Heller's *Catch-22* (1961) and Kurt Vonnegut's *Slaughterhouse-Five* (1969). Although Himes's earlier detective novels contain snatches of dark comedy, in *Cotton Comes*

to Harlem he employs it as a central device that suffuses all parts of the novel and greatly intensifies the bleakness of its vision. Grave Digger's diagnosis of the crime problem in Harlem is a vivid example of this bitterly reductive humor. Angered by the police commissioner's directive that crime must be controlled by something other than "brute force," he quips: "We got the highest crime rate on earth among the colored people of Harlem. And there ain't but three things to do about it: Make the criminals pay for it – you don't want to do that; pay the people to live decently – you ain't going to do that; so all that's left is let 'em eat one another up."

Postmodern dark comedy abounds in such a Hobbesian world, and most of the novel's major scenes produce a laughter that intensifies pain by robbing the reader of belief rather than providing the psychic relief of traditional comedy. When Coffin Ed reads the news accounts of violence in Harlem, he is both appalled by its enormity and oddly amused by the trivial reasons that trigger it: "Man kills wife with an ax for burning the breakfast pork chops . . . man kills another for spilling beer on his new suit . . . woman stabs man fourteen times, no reason given."

The two major swindles that Grave Digger and Coffin Ed must prevent from being foisted on the people of Harlem also produce a weird combination of horror and mirth that finally intensifies the pain rather than relieving it. Colonel Robert J. Calhoun's Back to Southland Movement – with its flamboyant posters of "conk-haired black cotton pickers clad in overalls that resembled Italian-tailored suits" and its extravagant offers to Harlemites of a Shangri-la in the Mississippi of the early 1960s – might at first seem wildly funny, but this fraud becomes depressing when one realizes how it will simply reenslave black people in an even more hopeless situation than that which they must currently endure. In a similar way the Rev. Deke O'Malley's Back to Africa Movement, with its bizarre pageantry and outrageous promises, might be funny were it not for the fact that such a con game will result in hundreds of honest people being robbed of their hard-earned cash and dreams.

The book's central metaphor, a bale of cotton filled with eighty-seven thousand dollars in stolen money, is artfully used by Himes to create sinister black-humor effects. It initially generates laughter because it is apparently so incongruous with a modern urban setting. (Grave Digger at one point muses, "With income taxes and hydrogen bombs and black revolutions, who thinks of a bale of cotton?") As various people struggle to gain possession of the bale of cotton through a wild assortment of she-nanigans, it continues to produce laughter. But, when the metaphor is thoughtfully considered, it evokes a much more disturbed reaction because it clearly suggests that Harlem is a modern plantation controlled by new forces of slavery. Not only are people physically enslaved by the money in the bale of cotton – to the point where they will easily kill for it – but they are also psychologically trapped by the dreams of a romanticized past in the South, or in Africa, as symbolized by the cotton. By giving ownership of the cotton to a junkyard worker, Himes suggests that everything it represents should be junked and replaced by newer, more humanizing values. But the novel never makes clear what these values might be.

By the time Himes had completed his final crime thriller, *Blind Man with a Pistol,* he had completely inverted the form of the detective novel. He thus gave shape to an ultimately absurdist vision of life wherein all forms of rational order – personal, social, political, and literary – either collapse or are reduced to meaninglessness. As Robert Skinner remarks, *Blind Man with a Pistol* "shows Himes at his most bitter and most distrustful" – indeed, it represents the end point in a long process of growing disillusionment and despair.

One of the first signs of how much more pessimistic *Blind Man with a Pistol* is than Himes's earlier detective fiction is the greatly reduced effectiveness of Grave Digger and Coffin Ed. While in previous books their heroic individualism and ability to act effectively against the forces of chaos are Harlem's only bulwark against rampant crime leading to social anarchy, here they are presented as aging warriors unable to carry out their mission. No longer "the big, loose-jointed colored men" of *The Heat's On* or the "big, dangerous men" of *Cotton Comes to Harlem,* they are described as gray-haired and "thicker around their middles." Harlem punks joke about Grave Digger's acid-scarred face and call him a "black Frankenstein," something that now inspires his anxiety rather than the rage he would have felt as a younger man. Moreover, police regulations forbid both Coffin Ed and Grave Digger from using the aggressive tactics that work so effectively to fight crime in the earlier novels. As a result they become much less forceful as central characters, not appearing in the novel until the fourth chapter and remaining on the margins of the novel's action in many key scenes. In a sense they have become "invisible men" who observe rather than control social reality. As they drive their patrol cars at night, "they could see in the dark streets but couldn't be seen."

Blind Man with a Pistol presents an absurdist vision in which violence is completely out of control on all levels and American society is on the verge of a total breakdown. In the preface to the novel Himes reveals that he was inspired to write the book after a friend told him the story of a blind man with a pistol who shot at a white man who had slapped him on the subway. But the blind man mistakenly killed an innocent black man. For Himes this became a metaphor of the anarchy spreading through America in the late 1960s:

> I thought, damn right, sounds just like today's news, riots in the ghettos, war in Vietnam, masochistic doings in the Middle East. And then I thought of some of our loudmouthed leaders urging our vulnerable soul brothers on to getting themselves killed, and thought further that all unorganized violence is like a blind man with a pistol.

This absurdist parable distills the essence of the novel's meaning. Set on Nat Turner's Day, when Harlem celebrates an unsuccessful rebellion that ended in a bloodbath, the novel describes an anarchic world "where anything can happen" because nobody is in control of the raw violence that seems to explode in every major scene.

Marcus Mackenzie, a sincere but naive person who wants to solve the "Negro Problem" with a commitment to peace and Christian love, organizes a "March of Brotherhood" across the heart of Harlem, but it degenerates into pointless fighting when it collides with two other protest marches, one organized by Black Power activists and the other by a group calling themselves the Black Jesus movement. This strange riot, described as a "free-for-all scramble" ending in random looting, calls into question three political strategies used in the 1960s to solve America's racial problems, defining each as irrational. Those who march for the supposedly nonviolent Brotherhood are high on sex and create an "orgy" that scandalizes even the most sophisticated Harlemites. The Black Power marchers are high on marijuana and resemble "Nazi SS troopers in black face." The Black Jesus marchers, who claim they will save the world with their fundamentalist religious beliefs, are in fact drunk and also out of control. When these three political forces collide, spontaneous fighting erupts, which for Himes is a perfect revelation of the world of black humor: "It was all just a big joke. Three different kinds of protest parades."

Blind Man with a Pistol presents a fundamentally evil world that has gone mad. The novel's early scenes are strikingly different from those

Dust jacket for Himes's 1969 book, his final crime novel

opening such books as *The Heat's On* and *Cotton Comes to Harlem* because they focus on more disturbing kinds of evil and grubby tasks that are far from heroic. Whereas Himes's earlier crime thrillers begin with basically greedy people trying to victimize innocent Harlemites, *Blind Man with a Pistol* opens with a grotesque episode in which a black Mormon named Reverend Sam advertises for "fertile womens" after three of his wives have mysteriously died and have been secretly buried in the basement of his temple, a converted funeral parlor. The purpose of this scene is not to provide Himes's detectives with a praiseworthy task but to define a world that is irremediably corrupt. (Significantly, Coffin Ed and Grave Digger never get involved in this part of the novel's action.)

The novel's second scene pictures a white man, John Henderson, who leers at young black men while lost in fantasies of stripping off his clothes and letting himself be "ravished." Whereas in earlier novels Grave Digger and Coffin Ed are

given the heroic challenge of saving Harlem's hardworking and honest people from swindlers and murderers, here they are given the job of finding out who killed Henderson after one of his sexual encounters has gone bad. Although they eventually find his killers, this crime's solution has little positive effect – it neither restores social order nor helps any people for whom Coffin Ed and Grave Digger care.

During his European exile Himes wrote one other novel about Harlem, *Pinktoes* (1961), which was published to great popular acclaim in Paris. Begun five years earlier as "Mamie Mason," the novel is strikingly different in tone and outlook from his cycle of detective novels. In a letter to Van Vechten dated 25 April 1956, Himes described *Pinktoes* as "an experiment in good will," a whimsical satire on the moral foibles, social pretensions, and sexual excesses of white liberals and the black middle class. Entering the world of *Pinktoes* after experiencing Himes's detective fiction, the reader finds a radically different fictive universe. Black humor is replaced by a surprisingly gentle, even tolerant, kind of satire. Himes's rage subsides in favor of a bemused detachment as he contemplates the sexual misadventures of a wide range of distinguished people who claim to be working toward a solution of the "Negro Problem," but in fact they are more interested in orgies and interracial sex.

Joe Mason, a consultant on interracial harmony for a major political party, spends most of his working hours making love to his white secretary in his office behind closed doors. His wife, Mamie, widely known throughout Harlem as "the Hostess with the Mostess," devotes herself to creating elaborate parties in their fashionable apartment for people interested in integration. Although these parties usually begin with serious discussions of how American race relations can be improved through better education, economic change, and a more democratic political system, they almost always end up with people ambling off to various bedrooms after consuming enormous quantities of food and drink.

Unlike *If He Hollers Let Him Go,* where sex between the races invariably explodes into violence, and unlike *The Primitive,* where an affair between a white woman and a black man exposes the terrible racial problems at the root of American society, the interracial sex in *Pinktoes* is described in an offhand, comic manner. At best it produces some uncommonly intense pleasures that brighten the routine lives of the major characters. At worst it produces some amusing squabbles and embarrassments that are happily resolved at the end of the book when Mamie presides over her annual Masked Ball at the Savoy Ballroom. Pledged to support "racial unification" on both cultural and personal levels, Mamie's legions of black and white friends act out in an altogether pleasurable way their sexual fantasies. When Mamie in her welcoming remarks pleads for everyone to indulge in "more . . . interracial . . . intercourse" (perhaps unaware of the double entendre she offers to her delighted audience), the novel ends in a burst of Rabelaisian frenzy to which Himes gives his complete approval.

While *Pinktoes* is a curiously, uncharacteristically happy book in Himes's canon, his last novel, *Plan B* (1983), is an unrelievedly bitter book that is much more consistent with the rest of his fiction. Begun in the early 1970s but never completed, it is the logical extension of *Blind Man with a Pistol,* rejecting the unorganized violence pictured so terrifyingly in that novel and arguing instead for blacks to use systematically organized violence as a means of transforming American society. In a 1972 interview

with Hoyt W. Fuller, Himes revealed that he was at work on the "definitive book on Black Revolution," a novel that would describe "massive, extreme violence" against an incurably racist and capitalistic "white establishment." He initially built the novel around two stories that he had written in the late 1960s – "Tang," which describes a Harlem junkie's brutal murder of his wife, and "Prediction," about a race war raging throughout the United States. Coffin Ed and Grave Digger appear briefly in *Plan B* but are dropped from the action when Himes shifts the focus of the novel to an unnamed black revolutionary figure who massacres hundreds of white policemen as they parade down Main Street in a major American city.

His health failing and his imagination drawn in several directions by narrative fragments that he could not assimilate into a coherent story, Himes abandoned the manuscript in the mid 1970s to devote his remaining energy to writing his autobiography. *Plan B* was published in its incomplete form by a minor Paris press a year before Himes died of Parkinson's disease in Moraira, Spain, on 12 November 1984. It is perhaps fitting that his last novel appeared in such a fragmentary form, since Himes finally saw his life as equally "absurd," a discontinuous mix of events that could not be coherently fashioned into an orderly narrative with a clearly formulated meaning. The final sentence of *My Life of Absurdity* vividly conveys this sense of his experience as an essentially random flow of events: "For all its inconsistencies, its contradictions, its humiliations, its hurts, its ecstasies and its absurdities; that's my life – the third generation out of slavery."

Himes's work, however, definitely helped to shape Afro-American fiction in many clear and significant ways. His unflinchingly honest portrayal of American racial problems from the 1930s to the 1970s prepared the ground for such militant writers as Amiri Baraka, Don L. Lee, and John A. Williams. His brilliant experiments with surrealism and black humor inspired such metafictionists as Ishmael Reed and Clarence Major, who used Himes's detective novels as models to help them deconstruct standard fictional discourse in order to present Afro-American life as fundamentally absurd. Himes's bold treatment of interracial sex and homosexuality created literary space later explored by such writers as James Baldwin, Gayl Jones, and Alice Walker.

For all these reasons, Himes's work should be rescued from the critical misinterpretations that plagued his literary efforts. Falsely labeled early in his career as a protest writer who oversimplified American reality in order to expound on a narrow political thesis, Himes was always deeply suspicious of any kind of political ideology. For this reason such books as *If He Hollers Let Him Go* and *Lonely Crusade* are much more complex than generally supposed and deserve much more careful analysis. Later accused of selling out to popular tastes by writing a series of crime potboilers, Himes in fact experimented shrewdly with the form of the detective novel and, as Skinner rightly observes, gave "new life to one of the few truly American genres."

Himes's remarkable two-volume autobiography offers not only an important history of American society from the early part of the twentieth century to the black urban rebellions of the late 1960s but also possesses the literary excellence that merits the kind of critical study given to more widely accepted autobiographies, such as *The Autobiography of Malcolm X* (1965) and Wright's *Black Boy* (1945). For a great variety of reasons Himes has been what Muller calls "a forgotten figure in contemporary American literature," and it is time to give his work the attention it deserves and to acknowledge his important place in Afro-American letters.

Interviews:

John A. Williams, "My Man Himes: An Interview with Chester Himes," in *Armistad 1,* edited by Williams and Charles F. Harris (New York: Random House, 1970), pp. 25–94;

Hoyt W. Fuller, "Traveller on the Long, Rough, Lonely Old Road: An Interview with Chester Himes," *Black World,* 21 (March 1972): 4–22, 87–98.

Bibliography:

Michael Fabre, "A Tentative Check List: A Selected Bibliography of Chester Himes," *Black World,* 21 (March 1972): 76–78.

References:

H. Bruce Franklin, *Prison Literature in America* (New York: Oxford University Press, 1978), pp. 181–237;

Addison Gayle, *The Way of the New World* (Garden City, N.Y.: Doubleday, 1975), pp. 181–191;

A. Robert Lee, "Hurts, Absurdities, and Violence: The Contrary Dimensions of Chester Himes,"

Journal of American Studies, 12 (April 1978): 99–114;

James Lundquist, *Chester Himes* (New York: Ungar, 1976);

Edward Margolies, *Native Sons: A Critical Study of Twentieth-Century Negro Authors* (New York: Lippincott, 1968), pp. 87–101;

Margolies, "The Thrillers of Chester Himes," *Studies in Black Literature* (June 1970): 1–11;

Stephen F. Millikin, *Chester Himes: A Critical Appraisal* (Columbia: University of Missouri Press, 1976);

Gilbert H. Muller, *Chester Himes* (Boston: Twayne, 1989);

Raymond Nelson, "Domestic Harlem: The Detective Fiction of Chester Himes," *Virginia Quarterly Review* (Spring 1972): 260–276;

Ralph Reckley, Sr., "The Oedipal Complex and Intraracial Conflict in Chester Himes' *The Third Generation,*" *CLA Journal,* 21 (December 1977): 275–281;

Reckley, "The Use of the Doppelganger or Double in Chester Himes' *Lonely Crusade,*" *CLA Journal,* 20 (June 1977): 448–458;

Ishmael Reed, "The Author and His Works, Chester Himes: Writer," *Black World,* 21 (March 1972): 24–38;

John Reilly, "Chester Himes's Harlem Tough Guys," *Journal of Popular Culture,* 9 (Spring 1976): 935–947;

Robert Skinner, *Two Guns from Harlem: The Detective Fiction of Chester Himes* (Bowling Green, Ohio: Bowling Green State University Popular Press, 1989);

Robert P. Smith, Jr., "Chester Himes in France and the Legacy of the Roman Policier," *CLA Journal,* 25 (September 1981): 18–27;

Richard Yarborough, "The Quest for the American Dream in Three Afro-American Novels," *MELUS,* 8 (Winter 1981): 33–59.

Papers:

Many of Himes's papers are held at the Beinecke Rare Book and Manuscript Library, Yale University. Some materials are held in the archives of the Julius Rosenwald Fund, Fisk University, Nashville, Tennessee.

James Jones

(6 November 1921 – 9 May 1977)

Allen Shepherd
University of Vermont

See also the Jones entry in *DLB 2: American Novelists Since World War II, First Series.*

BOOKS: *From Here to Eternity* (New York: Scribners, 1951; London: Collins, 1952);

Some Came Running (New York: Scribners, 1957; London: Collins, 1959);

The Pistol (New York: Scribners, 1959; London: Collins, 1959);

The Thin Red Line (New York: Scribners, 1962; London: Collins, 1963);

Go to the Widow-Maker (New York: Delacorte, 1967; London: Collins, 1967);

The Ice-Cream Headache and Other Stories (New York: Delacorte, 1968; London: Collins, 1968);

The Merry Month of May (New York: Delacorte, 1971; London: Collins, 1971);

A Touch of Danger (New York: Doubleday, 1973; London: Collins, 1973);

Viet Journal (New York: Delacorte, 1974);

WW II: A Chronicle of Soldiering (New York: Grosset & Dunlap, 1975);

Whistle (New York: Delacorte, 1978; London: Collins, 1978).

Collection: *The James Jones Reader,* edited by James R. Giles and J. Michael Lennon (Seacaucus, N.J.: Carol, 1991).

James Jones's principal claim to attention is his World War II trilogy. *From Here to Eternity* (1951) is a narrative of the peacetime army, concluding with the Japanese attack on Pearl Harbor. *The Thin Red Line* (1962) recounts the taking of Guadalcanal in 1943, and *Whistle,* posthumously published in 1978, is the story of wounded veterans returned for hospital treatment in the United States. Closely related to the trilogy is a novella, *The Pistol* (1959), set in Hawaii at the same time as *From Here to Eternity.* These four books offer a bleak, supremely professional, highly antiromantic account of the anonymous, uncelebrated enlisted man's World War II that is unmatched in American literature.

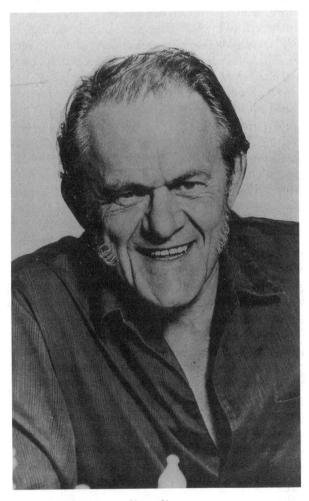

James Jones

James Jones was born on 6 November 1921 in the small town of Robinson, Illinois, to Ramon and Ada Blessing Jones. The family had been socially prominent and prosperous but suffered hard times during the author's childhood. "I . . . grew up," Jones remembered, "in an atmosphere of hot emotions and boiling recriminations covered with a thin but resilient skin of gentility." Upon graduation from high school he took his father's advice and enlisted in the U.S. Army Air Corps in 1939. He was sent to Hawaii, where he transferred to the infantry, housed at Schofield Barracks.

Jones experienced the Japanese attack on nearby Pearl Harbor; was wounded at Guadalcanal; was shipped stateside to Army General Hospital in Memphis, Tennessee, where he was awarded a Purple Heart and the Bronze Star; and was discharged from the service in 1944. At this time he met Lowney Handy, the wife of oil executive Harry Handy, and under her tutelage began his literary apprenticeship. Jones completed a novel about embittered veterans, "They Shall Inherit the Laughter," which Maxwell Perkins at Scribners rejected. He did, however, express interest in a sketch about two characters in the peacetime army – a piece that, after five years of unremitting labor, Jones developed into *From Here to Eternity*.

If it is not his best book (some would argue that *The Thin Red Line* is that), *From Here to Eternity* displays most of Jones's strengths and many of his limitations. With good reason David Dempsey – who in the *New York Times Book Review* (25 February 1952) wrote the most important review of the novel – termed it "the work of a major new American novelist," the product of "an original and utterly honest talent." The novel won the National Book Award in 1952 against such contenders as J. D. Salinger's *The Catcher in the Rye* and was made into a highly successful 1953 film that garnered eight Academy Awards.

From Here to Eternity is an inside narrative of the peacetime army. The principal figures are Pvt. Robert E. Lee Prewitt and 1st Sgt. Milton Anthony Warden. Prewitt, a good welterweight boxer and a fine bugler, has transferred from a soft berth in the rear echelon to an infantry company because of his stubborn belief that a man has a right to go his own way. Much of the plot derives from various efforts to force Prewitt to go out for the regimental boxing squad; having blinded a friend in the ring, he refuses.

Warden is cynical, sardonic, and magnificently skilled in his trade of soldiering. He and Prewitt are in continual conflict and yet have a deep bond – they are both career soldiers, thirty-year men, for whom the regular army is the heart and blood of life. They are committed to yet hate the army; they are both proud and afraid of it; it supports them and threatens to emasculate them. Both men are in love: Warden with his captain's wife, Karen Holmes, and Prewitt with a prostitute, Alma Schmidt.

Jones's army is a haven of caste, privilege, favoritism, politics, and arbitrary authority. The authority is vested in officers to whom its exercise generally means little, but to enlisted men it means the difference between a good life and an intolerable one. In his notes for the novel Jones writes that he should "*show a man caught by the army*. Prewitt. He is forced in by economic forces and once in cannot escape without sacrificing his self-respect and integrity, which he refuses to do." The "main channel of the book," Jones goes on, is Prewitt's attempt to save his pride in himself as he is "gradually forced by external, irrational forces and his own inflexible honor into becoming a criminal." Prewitt's ambition – to assert his integrity at all costs – is admirable, but it implies a prideful belief, familiar from classical tragedy, that a man can determine his own destiny.

What Jones terms the "arid hopelessness" of the enlisted man's life is caused by the hierarchy of authority, which destroys the individuality of subordinates; the favoritism which induces a renunciation of integrity; the lack of women other than prostitutes; the lack of money; and the utter lack of intimate friendship. Warden subsists in such an environment by holding the center; he knows that the army runs on its first sergeants, not its officers or its lesser enlisted men. He is an efficiency expert who loves running the company. He understands Prewitt's idealism, but he lives in the real world of illusionless cynicism; he knows the rules and appears to live by them. "I think," Jones wrote in a letter to B. W. Griffith, Jr. (13 June 1954), "that had Prewitt lived, and continued to live, he would eventually become a Warden."

From Here to Eternity offers a rich variety of minor characters, of whom Private Maggio, a close friend of Prewitt, is perhaps most noteworthy. Despite his suffering in the post stockade, Maggio, who epitomizes the proletarian underdog, dramatizes the possibility that the outsider can successfully conspire to outwit the army as he feigns insanity to gain a Section 8 discharge. Sgt. Fatso Judson, who tortures Maggio and is eventually killed by Prewitt, exemplifies power exercised without moral or ethical check. High up the chain of command is an intellectual malefactor, the totalitarian General Slater, who takes on Captain Holmes as a protégé. Together the three embody the old army's corruption.

From Here to Eternity is magnificently funny at times, profoundly sad at others, occasionally lyrical, and consistently authentic in its depiction of institutional life. The novel exemplifies, as George Garrett

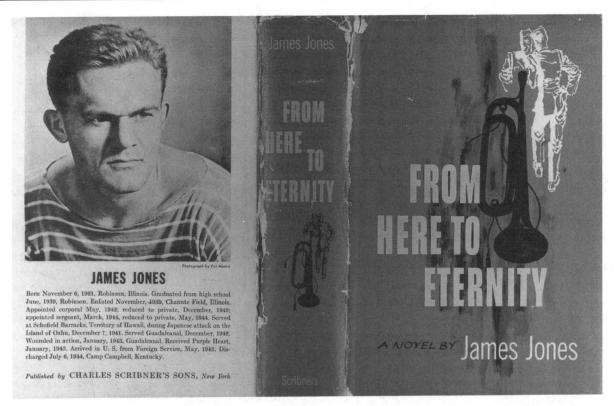

JAMES JONES

Born November 6, 1921, Robinson, Illinois. Graduated from high school June, 1939, Robinson. Enlisted November, 1939, Chanute Field, Illinois. Appointed corporal May, 1942; reduced to private, December, 1943; appointed sergeant, March, 1944, reduced to private, May, 1944. Served at Schofield Barracks, Territory of Hawaii, during Japanese attack on the Island of Oahu, December 7, 1941. Served Guadalcanal, December, 1942. Wounded in action, January, 1943, Guadalcanal. Received Purple Heart, January, 1943. Arrived in U. S. from Foreign Service, May, 1943. Discharged July 6, 1944, Camp Campbell, Kentucky.

Published by CHARLES SCRIBNER'S SONS, New York

Dust jacket for Jones's first novel, which concerns regular army enlisted men in Hawaii during the days leading up to the Japanese attack on Pearl Harbor

puts it, the "successful marriage of the concerns of serious fiction with the pleasures of popular fiction." At 861 pages it is a sizable book, but the pace is unflagging, the reader effortlessly carried forward by the novel's remarkable narrative drive. The characters are people about whom the reader soon comes to care, and with rare exceptions Jones does not attempt to make them overtly symbolic or to denigrate them. Given his experience as an enlisted man and his proletarian sympathies, it is not surprising that in his notes on Captain Holmes the author writes that he has "neither space nor material to show intimately a *good* officer," and indeed there are none in any of Jones's books before *Viet Journal* (1974), in which a general emerges as a hero.

It is often observed, with some justice, that Jones's portrayal of women tends to be one-dimensional and unsympathetic. Karen Holmes, however, is a notable exception and altogether a remarkable portrait, one that provides evidence of Jones's ability to cross gender and class lines as he depicts Karen's passionately and persuasively expressing and defining herself to her lover, Warden.

One manifestation of the authenticity of *From Here to Eternity* is apparent in the author's copious use of obscenity and profanity; another is the shock-

ing brutality commonplace in the operation of the stockade. Many contemporary reviewers took strong exception to both. As a stylist, Jones is notably uneven; on average his prose is direct and workmanlike, but he can be awkward and pretentious. Readers with Jamesian tastes understandably find him a trial.

Jones was thirty when *From Here to Eternity* was published. It remained the measure of his work for the rest of his career, and, since he never achieved a comparable critical and commercial success, in middle age he came to have ambivalent feelings about his celebrated first novel. Yet, as his onetime friend and constant competitor, the never-modest Norman Mailer, concedes in *Advertisements for Myself* (1959), "I felt then and can still say now that *From Here to Eternity* has been the best American novel since the war."

From Here to Eternity made Jones a well-paid celebrity, and he maintained that role for the rest of his life. With profits from his best-selling novel and the sale of film rights Jones helped Harry and Lowney Handy establish a writers' colony and build a house in Marshall, Illinois; he continued to live there during the writing of *Some Came Running* (1957) and built his first house just off the colony grounds, near Lowney Handy's cottage. Jones's eventual falling-out with his mentor was occasioned in part by her stern discipline, his growing reputation, and finally by his whirlwind romance and marriage in 1957 to Gloria Mosolino, a glamorous New Yorker.

Even more than most first novels, *From Here to Eternity* proved to be a hard act to follow. The need at least to equal, if not indeed to surpass, that celebrated work imposed a terrible burden on the author. Although *Some Came Running* is an enormously ambitious novel, and although it was a considerable commercial success, it was widely accounted an artistic failure, even a disaster. As early as 1953 Jones identified what remains the novel's major shortcoming when he wrote in a letter to Burroughs Mitchell (31 July 1953), "I should be leaving more unsaid, to be handled by the imagination." In the novel Jones talks endlessly about his ideas but does not effectively dramatize them.

Some Came Running depicts the impact of World War II and encroaching modernity on the provincial rigidities of Parkman, Illinois – a small, claustrophobic, middle-American town not unlike Jones's place of birth – between 1947 and 1950. The future of the American dream is made to seem dark as the narrative emphasizes parallels with the decline of ancient Rome. The return of native son Dave Hirsch – black sheep, struggling writer, and veteran – opens Jones's engagement with two thematic concerns. The first is the glorification of the lower classes – honest and individualistic, salt of the earth – whom Dave prefers to the respectable, hypocritical townspeople, personified by his older brother Frank. The second theme is the nature of artistic activity, whose articulation is largely left to a local literary virgin, Gwen French, whom Dave lusts after but never wins. Other characters of consequence include 'Bama Dillert, a restless professional gambler who becomes Dave's best friend; Ginnie Moorehouse, an unappealing, uneducated, promiscuous factory worker whom Dave eventually marries; and Jane Staley, a triumphantly dirty old woman, grandmother of Frank Hirsch's secretary-mistress.

Few reviewers of the novel failed to exclaim over its remarkable length of 1,266 pages – 130 more than Leo Tolstoy's *War and Peace* (1863–1869) – and certainly no one has ever wished it longer. In many reviews Jones was charged with reprehensible morality, sophomoric thinking, and subliterary prose. Charles Rolo, in the *Atlantic* (January 1958), found Jones's style "plodding, clumsy and repetitious; it has drabness as dispiriting as the 'eats' on the counter of a sleazy beanery." Edmund Fuller, in the *Chicago Tribune* (12 January 1958), advised that "if you like the grossest promiscuity, the most callous adultery, aggressive vulgarity, shoddy and befuddled philosophy, 'Some Came Running' is your book." J. A. Burns, in *Library Journal* (January 1958), substantially concurred, indicting the novel as "a 1200 page orgy of sex, self-pity and sloppy prose" and warning that "it will be a long time before the reader will forget the hours lost plowing through Jones's murky writing." The *Kirkus* (1 November 1957) reviewer summed up such negative views of the novel: "It has nothing – repeat nothing – to recommend it."

In a more balanced assessment Gene Baro, in the *New York Herald Tribune Book Review* (12 January 1958), judged Jones to be "a peculiarly provoking writer" because his genuine powers were undermined by carelessness and lack of discipline. Thus "an excellent eye and ear are consistently evident but a sense of selection is not." In the *New York Times* (12 January 1958) Dempsey expressed "disappointment" but added that *Some Came Running* is still "in places, a work of stunning and even prodigal talents." In his insightful evaluation Dempsey observed that the novel "disappoints chiefly because it is far too long for what it has to say, because of the immaturity of its attitudes, and finally, because its intellectual intentions (one might better say pretensions) are never made entirely plausible."

There can be no argument in regard to the excessive length of *Some Came Running;* Jones apparently was not well served by his editors. Dempsey's reference to the immaturity of the novel's attitudes raises the question of whose attitudes are expressed. The novel is cast in the omniscient point of view, allowing investigation of all the characters' thoughts, yet – contrary to common misapprehension – none of the characters should be assumed to speak for the author. Such confusion of author and character was doubtless prompted in part by Jones's development in *Some Came Running* of what he called "colloquial forms." This term refers to the extensive use of the vernacular – free and easy American English – beyond the words and thoughts of the characters to much of the narrative itself, so that the narrator sometimes sounds like the characters: that is, possessed of the characters' own linguistic and intellectual capacities and limitations.

In a 1959 *Paris Review* interview Jones explained that a classic style in writing tends to remove the reader one level from the immediacy of the experience: "For any normal reader, I think a colloquial style makes him feel more as though he is within the action, instead of just reading about it."

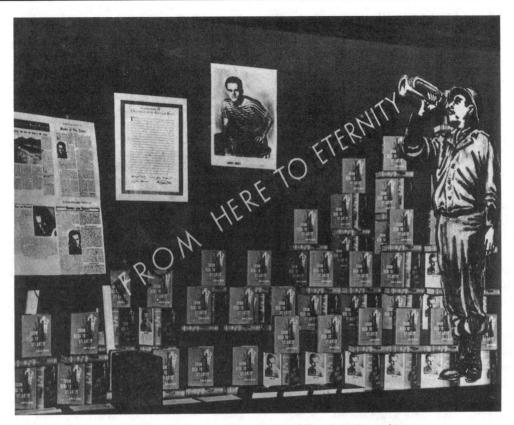

Scribners bookstore window display of Jones's 1951 novel

For many readers of *Some Came Running,* however, the practical consequence of Jones's experiment was their conclusion that the narrator was endorsing the characters' words and thoughts, however imprecise, repetitive, and vulgar they might be. Confronting such semiliterate narrative passages, some readers understandably concluded as well that Jones did not know how to write.

The intellectual intentions (or pretensions) of the novel are not made entirely plausible, as Dempsey pointed out, nor very clear. Jones's characterization seems principally responsible for these problems. Thus there is Gwen's theory that all art, literary and otherwise, comes from the artist's personal agony, which is primarily evidenced in unhappy love affairs. To Dave, this observation comes as a revelation, yet the theory is ludicrous on its face, and its spokeswoman is neither admirable nor believable. The characterization of 'Bama raises similar problems. A member of that Parkman underclass that Jones glorifies, 'Bama is a self-made expert on practically everything, holding forth at inordinate length on such varied topics as sex, gambling, wallpapering, driving, drinking, the Civil War, and the true nature of southerners. At times he seems

cast as the novel's real hero, a stylish cynic (like Warden in *From Here to Eternity*) who intuitively works the angles because he has the artist's sensibility without the artist's need to express it. But like Gwen, he is boring and impossible to take seriously. Dave personifies the Jonesian version of the writer's dilemma – the need for both self-exposure and self-protection. Writing, with its self-conscious discipline and detachment, is antithetical to the naturalness and sincerity Dave seeks. Yet he is simply not adequate to the articulation of these and other related ideas.

It must be said that Jones does do some things at least well enough to make the reader realize how uneven the novel is. He is persuasive in his representation of the boondocks; he convincingly establishes the cultural claustrophobia of small-town life and the quirks of personality that sometimes go with it. His rendering of aimless young men and women endlessly hanging around in cheap bars where uninterrupted guzzling produces maudlin confessions, sudden fights, desperate pairings, and profound despair by closing time is assuredly a true account. And when, to cite but one domestic instance, Dave visits his brother's house for dinner,

Jones gets all the details exactly right – from the powerful Manhattans to the enormous frozen steaks to the loud, whirring noise of the much-admired new dishwasher.

Jones – newly separated from the Handys and the writers' colony, newly married to Mosolino – left the United States in 1958 and settled in Paris. Although the Joneses made frequent visits to the United States, often staying a summer, they continued to live in Paris until 1974. The effect on his work of such voluntary exile has been much debated. It has been said that he cut himself off from his roots and his material, that he did not understand the French and never mastered the language, and that his expensive, highly social lifestyle militated against artistic dedication. All that can be said with certainty is that, during his years on the Ile Saint-Louis, Jones produced some of his best and worst fiction. *The Pistol* belongs in the former category.

Looking back over eight years to the publication of *The Pistol,* Jones recalled in a *Paris Review* interview that the book was "an experiment in writing a deliberately symbolic little novella" and that it was "okay, for an easy job, an easy out." In fact *The Pistol* is a virtuoso performance, both in its narrative content and in the success of those techniques with which Jones experimented. The novella recounts the ordeal of nineteen-year-old Pfc. Richard Mast in retaining possession of a government-issue .45 pistol, which, like Jones, he was wearing when the Japanese attack on Pearl Harbor occurred. In the course of several months the pistol becomes for Mast – and for all the other men who try to take it from him by force or fraud – what each man must have, that which will secure him happiness, safety, and salvation.

The very inevitability of five men losing what they most desire might produce on the part of the author an attitude either of involved compassion or detached irony. Mast is initially presented with a certain sympathy, as Jones is intent on indicating why the pistol is so important to him and why returning it to the supply room is such a disturbing prospect. Throughout much of the novella, however, Mast is the butt of rather heavy irony. But, at the end, after authority – in the form of Private Musso from the supply room – routinely reclaims the pistol, the distraught Mast wonders whether it was all for naught, and O'Brien, one of the men who had stolen it back, shouts, "You got no right! It ain't fair! You got no right to do that to us!" Then "in the violence of his emotion he threw his head back and yelled it at the top of his lungs, so that in

an odd way, while he was shaking his fist after the carrier [containing Musso] O'Brien himself, his teeth bared, was staring fiercely upward at the sky, as he went on shouting." Here irony departs the scene as O'Brien protests his human fate to the author of everything.

One is fully prepared, with a Jones novel, to see the little man, the average enlisted man, crushed by authority, as indeed happens when the prize is withdrawn. The primary focus, however, is on internecine struggle, and Jones makes clear that the fraud and violence these men practice on one another is not solely the product of corrupting institutions, the army, or authority from whatever source, but of human nature itself. One could well argue, despite Mast's desperate endurance and O'Brien's anguished cry, that authority saves these men from each other. Contrarily, authority – because of its often-bungling inconsistency – can be construed not as a merely threatening presence but even as an enemy.

Each of the five men who attempt to take Mast's pistol is, as Jones recalled in the *Paris Review* interview, "deliberately symbolic of the various aspects of humanity." Each is distinct from the others, yet the pistol has essentially the same meaning to all of them. Each man passionately rejects the moral validity of another's need; the ego is king. In the mind of each man is an image of his own destruction: a Japanese major about to cleave him with a samurai sword.

Three of the five men actually succeed in getting the pistol away from Mast, and each of them, once in possession of it, adopts Mast's "outraged righteousness" as someone else stakes his moral claim on the pistol. These, then, are the constants of human nature: each man single-mindedly pursues his own salvation and to this end will perpetrate any cruelty, however ridiculous or outrageous. Each man establishes his own moral ascendancy: it is *right* that he should have the pistol, *wrong* that anyone else should. It may seem that the only prospect that can establish some measure of community is the hope that they can take from someone or that some outside force, authority, may intervene and carry off the prize. One may also argue, as James R. Giles does in *James Jones* (1981), that "the gradual revelation that each seeker of the pistol has a common fantasy of extinction and views the weapon as a talisman of salvation indicates a potential for communion."

Particularly as one thinks of the two predecessors to *The Pistol,* it is apparent that the novella differs notably from Jones's novels; it is based on a few relatively simple ideas developed soundly and with marked economy. The writing is disciplined, and the book is terse and compact without being excessively schematic. The central symbol, the .45, is not static but evolves consistently and coherently. The sequence of incidents – the acts in Mast's drama – introduces characters who, though they may seem at first repetitious, are in fact distinct from each other. In reading *The Pistol* one has the impression, belying the usual sense of the term *experiment,* that the author knew exactly what he was doing. That the result is neither skeletal allegory nor a truncated version of the big, densely detailed novel he elsewhere favored testifies to his mastery of a hitherto alien genre.

Jones wrote two kinds of novels – one about war, the other about being a writer. The first kind is commonly contained, intense, and resonant; the second is usually diffuse, self-important, and despairing. *The Thin Red Line* is arguably the best of the war novels and indeed of all Jones's work. It is fully equal in its fashion to the World War II fiction of any of his most accomplished contemporaries – John Horne Burns's *The Gallery* (1947), James Gould Cozzens's *Guard of Honor* (1948), Mailer's *The Naked and the Dead* (1948), and Joseph Heller's *Catch-22* (1961). The critical response to *The Thin Red Line,* as to *The Pistol* three years earlier, was strongly favorable.

The Thin Red Line recounts the experiences of an infantry unit, C-for-Charlie Company, from its arrival at Guadalcanal, through two battles, to the end of that campaign. As the novel closes, C Company is training for an amphibious landing on the next of a seemingly endless string of Pacific islands occupied by the Japanese. Both the terrain and the events in the novel closely resemble those Jones's F-for-Fox Company encountered in 1943. The similarities, down to the smallest details, are sufficient, as Garrett points out in *James Jones* (1984), to "give the book almost the quality of a nonfiction documentary." For example, on Guadalcanal an unarmed Jones killed a Japanese soldier and was later (28 January 1943) wounded, experiences ascribed to two different characters in the novel. Reliving the nightmarish horrors of the campaign in order to get them down on paper proved so difficult for Jones, as Frank MacShane recounts in *Into Eternity: The Life of James Jones, American Writer* (1985), that "sometimes he would break down and weep while he was writing."

Although *The Thin Red Line* is an independent, self-sustaining work, it benefits from being read in the context of the author's World War II trilogy.

French poster for the 1953 film version of From Here to Eternity, which won eight Academy Awards

Many key people in the company, given different names but preserving general characteristics, survive through two or all three volumes. Thus Welsh (*The Thin Red Line*) has his antecedent in Warden (*From Here to Eternity*) and his successor in Winch (*Whistle*). Even more striking, Winch's fate back in the United States is anticipated – one might say produced – by Welsh's experiences on Guadalcanal. Similarly, Prewitt (*From Here to Eternity*) evolves into Witt (*The Thin Red Line*), who grows into Prell (*Whistle*). Thus Prewitt's romantic individualism is converted into Witt's implacable stubbornness, which in turn blossoms into Prell's Medal of Honor–winning heroism. Another trio incorporates Stark (*From Here to Eternity*), who becomes Storm (*The Thin Red Line*), who becomes Strange (*Whistle*).

The Thin Red Line offers a cast of more than eighty named characters, of whom thirty are clearly developed as individuals; however, C Company itself emerges as the composite hero. For that hero's delineation the narrative technique seems ideal: Jones employs an omniscient narrator and a succession of focal characters' insights in order to provide both an overall perspective on the action and a substantial assortment of individual views. *The Thin*

Red Line depicts no villains among the American officers or the Japanese. The enemies, in fact, are given full marks; although sick, dirty, starving, and badly outnumbered, they fight hard and well and are no more savage than the American troopers.

Jones's style in the novel is flat, taut, objective, and – in its liberal use of obscenity and profanity in both dialogue and narrative – an altogether accurate representation of American men at war. Although the novel, at 495 pages, is considerably shorter than Jones's first two, during the writing he worried about its length. He told his editor that "every ounce of cutting that can be done to it will be all to the good." In its relative brevity, consistent tightness of focus, and confident dependence on the power of implication, *The Thin Red Line* much more resembles *The Pistol* than *Some Came Running*.

The Thin Red Line is an intense, brutal book that demonstrates that the army is made up of infinitely replaceable parts, men and equipment alike. Men as links, as objects – as against their feelings – is Jones's subject matter. All who enter the army are consumed, their places filled with identical pieces, which are in turn consumed.

On the beaches and in the jungle Jones's GIs discover that there really is no such thing as rational cause and effect in human affairs, except insofar as people insist on seeing it. They live in a chance world where luck, good or bad, is the only discernible reality. In a soldier's evolution the experience of the tedium of modern technological war and its insane confusion enforces, at least conditionally, an acceptance of anonymity. Individualism yields to group cooperation. Men worry about courage and their capacity for heroism, but the truth is that both are mainly impulses stemming from a fear of others' adverse opinions.

The officers in the novel perform somewhat better than might be expected. If the class as a whole is ineffectual and corrupt, C Company's enlisted men witness some apparent exceptions to the rule. And the army, despite its terrible institutional inhumanity, induces feelings of camaraderie, pride, and even joy. It is apparent, as MacShane remarks, that "*The Thin Red Line* is . . . a natural extension of the mixed feelings of love and hate that lay behind the writing of *From Here to Eternity*."

Among the key characters in *The Thin Red Line* are the first commander of Company C, Captain Stein; the top noncommissioned officer, First Sergeant Welsh; the original company clerk, Corporal Fife; a former officer, Private Bell; and an occasional member of the company, Private Witt. Stein – an intelligent, humane citizen-soldier who works as

a lawyer in peacetime – proves to be well intentioned but ineffectual; he is not a West Pointer and is subject to endemic institutional anti-Semitism. The battalion commander, a WASP patrician whom Stein has antagonized, judges him lacking as an infantry officer, relieves him of command, and ships him back to Washington.

Welsh is a one-answer man who believes that war (and most of human history) is about the acquisition or defense of property. He has come to accept his own anonymity fully, recognizing the inconsequence of his or anyone else's life or death. A recruiting-poster veteran of twelve years' service, he is professionally gifted and profoundly cynical. He is master of the consciously theatrical act, whether suddenly exploding at a speechless subordinate or tossing grenades as if they were footballs. He looks after his people, often without their knowing it, but by the novel's end he is beginning to lose his self-possession, a loss that in *Whistle* eventuates in the insanity of his successor, Winch.

Fife, a partly autobiographical character, is idealistic, uncertain, overwhelmed by Welsh, and advised by Stein – who judges him intelligent but immature – to apply for a commission in an administrative branch. In a typical instance of Jonesian irony, Stein ends up in an administrative branch. Fife is convinced at times that he is a hopeless coward, at others that he is invulnerable and can cope with anything. Plagued by the same ankle injury that incapacitated Jones on Guadalcanal, Fife is finally evacuated after experiencing a last example of the benign despotism of his first sergeant (Welsh so insults him that he cannot stay) and the perfect arbitrariness of other powers (a doctor who had berated him for cowardice now conspires to get him off the island).

As a former officer, Bell is a special case. He is a good man, a skilled soldier, and the novel's resident intellectual – the most overt, insistent, and comprehensive thinker in the cast. He reflects on his evolution as a soldier, on the role of officers, and on the phenomena of anonymity, bravery, and combat numbness. Considerable poignance is added to Bell's characterization by his failure (or unwillingness) to understand what is soon apparent to the reader – that his young wife back home is cuckolding him.

Witt is an indomitable exponent of anti-institutionalism; his individualism approaches anarchism. He will give body and soul to his friends, but he will not serve under officers of whom he does not approve, a determination that accounts for his habitual comings and goings. He is a wonder-

Dust jacket for Jones's second novel, which the Chicago Tribune *recommended for readers who "like the grossest promiscuity, the most callous adultery, aggressive vulgarity, shoddy and befuddled philosophy"*

fully accomplished soldier and a man of principle, but in comparison with his predecessor, Prewitt, Witt is so primitive that he could not sustain a larger role in the novel.

In *The Thin Red Line* Jones develops the theme of a universal blankness to any assertion of human will introduced in *From Here to Eternity*. Jones does not analyze the overpowering injustice of the world, something that the characters cannot stomach, understand, explain, or change. Instead, the narrator is virtually indistinguishable from the characters, remaining throughout close and sympathetic to their every word and thought, whether it be Stein's suffering profound, unwarranted humiliation or Fife's being undone by the certainty of his abysmal cowardice and prospective death or Bell's resisting the import of the latest letter from home.

William Styron, a close friend of Jones, remarks in his foreword to *To Reach Eternity: The Letters of James Jones* (1989) that "Jim wrote some exceedingly inferior work during his Paris years." As principal instance he cites *Go to the Widow-Maker* (1967), which he describes as "a chaotic novel of immeasurable length, filled with plywood characters, implausible dialogue, and thick wedges of plain atrocious writing." Relenting briefly, Styron concedes that "there were, to be sure, some spectacular

underwater scenes and moments of descriptive power almost like the Jones of *Eternity*. But in general the work was a disappointment, lacking both grace and cohesion." Styron's judgment is widely shared and generally well founded.

Contrary opinions were expressed, however, most notably perhaps that of another friend, critic and literary historian Maxwell Geismar (quoted on the novel's dust jacket), who held that Jones "stands alone in our literary annals as a writer of army life and war fiction. In *Go to the Widow-Maker,* however, he has also demonstrated his ability to create a memorable novel of ordinary civilian life, of human relationships which are both typical and strange, of love and passion and pathology." Geismar concludes that Jones "has turned out to be an astute and probing psychologist of the human soul as well as a radical critic of his society."

Geismar's commentary certainly identifies what Jones wished to accomplish in *Go to the Widow-Maker* – to demonstrate after the success of *From Here to Eternity, The Pistol,* and *The Thin Red Line* and the failure of *Some Came Running* that he could indeed write a "memorable novel of ordinary civilian life," that he could treat "love and passion and pathology" insightfully and movingly, and that he was both a "probing psychologist" and a "radical critic."

Jones, however, habitually gets in his own way, fails to control the medium, and ends up being merely relentless. He tries and tries but gets nowhere, just as the principal characters are tiresomely obsessive and their itinerary – that is, the plot – notably repetitive. As the hero, Ron Grant, remarks, "In the end it was difficult, after a while, to see a reef or a beach or a coco palm that did not resemble generally the remembered aggregate of all the other reefs and coco palms one had seen."

In *Go to the Widow-Maker* Jones undertakes to preserve the strengths and minimize the weaknesses of his earlier works and to capitalize on new opportunities. Thus again in this roman à clef he works close to life, transmuting recently assimilated material. He also reengages major themes – for instance, the anguish men have over their maleness, the nature of courage, the certainty of mortality, and the right relation between men and women – and creates vivid actions (diving, spearfishing, sailing) apt for their dramatization. Jones understood these activities well from long practice, and he was intimately familiar with the exotic Caribbean settings.

Many of the male characters in *Go to the Widow-Maker* have served earlier in the military, and male camaraderie is a major motif. For social commentary Jones situates his hero, a world-renowned playwright with midwestern roots, among the moneyed, sophisticated denizens of New York, Houston, and Jamaica. In order to achieve interaction of characters and evolution of plot, he organizes his cast in a succession of unstable adulterous triangles. In order to dramatize the individual perspectives of a large cast, he employs a third-person point of view within which he focalizes different characters in successive chapters. What appeared to be a formula for success, however, produced – as Styron observed – a substantial disappointment.

The most notable deficiency in the novel is the quality of the writing. Jones wanted supple, colloquial American English appropriate for both narrative and dialogue, but he produced language that is too often inept, imprecise, and sloppy. Only when recounting scenes underwater does he write with clarity and grace. Such neologisms as "electrocutionee," "Hemingwayize," and "despairfully" display the limit of his stylistic inventiveness.

In part Jones writes an apologia, but he also means for the characters to be representative figures as well as individuals. Thus Ron Grant is – as the reader is frequently reminded – a major playwright, an artist of the first importance, and the legitimate

successor to Eugene O'Neill. This is what the reader is told, but one is never shown any convincing evidence of his intelligence, awareness, sensitivity, or even his experience in the theater. When Jones alleges Grant's enduring curiosity about human motivation, he so mangles the language as to make Grant seem absurd; thus, in a grotesquely mixed metaphor, the reader is told that Grant "wants to know what makes the wellsprings of human character tick."

As if he might persuade the reader of his hero's superiority through other characters' extravagant testimony, Jones causes them to avow that Grant is "built like a Greek god" (his wife), that he is "a pretty rare type" (Al Bonham), and that he is "an almost perfect human being" (Jim Grointon). Though Jones intended all the characters to be humanly imperfect, he must be said to have outdone himself with Grant, who has little to recommend him. Despite his boxer's shoulders and bravery below the waves, Grant is a passive man who dislikes argument and suffers from a "terrible inferiority complex" and a "rejection syndrome." He believes himself oversexed, he drinks to excess so as to tolerate himself and others, and he is an unhappy, untalented recruit in the Jonesian war between the sexes dramatized in the novel.

Lucia (Lucky) Vivendi Grant owes as much to Gloria Mosolino Jones as Ron Grant does to the author, but she is also presented as an embodiment of the sexually liberated new woman of the 1960s. However, she emerges as less a symbolic character than a caricature, a James Bond fantasy playgirl. Jones writes that "her figure was enough to drive men mad," and she claims to have had sexual relations with more than four hundred (presumably happy) men. On her honeymoon in the Caribbean she carries high-powered binoculars to observe the size and shape of local fishermen's penises. "Sometimes," she says halfway through the novel, "I think that the whole of the United States is totally and completely sexually sick, sick to the danger point." This is offered as a serious observation, which the promiscuity of the speaker might be thought to validate, but the reader will have long since dismissed Lucky as one of those "plywood" characters of whom Styron speaks.

At one time or another all of the principal male characters are accused of being homosexual by female characters; thus Lucky says she hates all these men in love with other men. The males typically counter with allegations of whorishness and lesbianism. The men, who are said to lack confidence, are fervidly misogynistic, conceding, in Bonham's words, that "we need women and hate them for it." Women appear to know the tricks of making men appear morally wrong and inspiring guilt, anger, and frustration in them.

Lucky articulates a view of male/female roles that is generally subscribed to in the novel when she reflects that "it was right and proper for men not to want to get married, and for women to want to marry them, that was life, women *were* nest-builders, men *were* rovers." Jim Grointon – one of Grant's heroes, who has also perhaps cuckolded him – seems wholly in agreement when he asserts, "Men like to kill fish and game . . . and women usually like them for it." Ron adds, smiling ominously, "And, sometimes, they like to kill each other," to which Grointon agrees. "That's what it is to be a man," he says. "That's what a man needs to feel he is a man." Lucky concludes the scene by conceding, "Of course you're absolutely right."

Jones's model for *Go to the Widow-Maker,* Ernest Hemingway's "The Short Happy Life of Francis Macomber" (*The Fifth Column and the First Forty-Nine Stories,* 1938), is less criticized, however, than emulated and climactically altered. Ron learns the values of the diving and spearfishing fraternity from two handsome, highly successful "white hunters" (Jones's phrase) and is observed by his sexually practiced spouse who, angry with him, promises that she will cuckold him. However, Ron – after being battered in a hopelessly one-sided contest by a more powerful antagonist – is awarded what Francis is denied: a happily-ever-after conclusion.

The Ice-Cream Headache and Other Stories (1968) is one of Jones's better – yet probably least known and certainly most underrated – books. Of the thirteen stories, written between 1947 and 1967, several are first-rate, yet none is included in current American literature or short-fiction anthologies, which are ready gauges of academic recognition. Even in his earliest apprentice work Jones is surprisingly adept at shaping characterization, controlling narrative, and focusing thematic concerns – abilities not always apparent in his novels. At his best he is certainly good enough to make one wish that his ambition and the literary circumstances of the time had led or enabled him to pursue short fiction further.

In his candid introduction to *The Ice-Cream Headache* Jones explains why he did not continue writing in the short-story genre. He was primarily committed to the novel, and he had trouble getting stories published (at least before the success of *From Here to Eternity*) and could not live on the income from short fiction. Furthermore, he could not write anything outspoken about sexuality and expect to

Dust jacket for Jones's 1959 novella, in which six men struggle for possession of a stolen army weapon

see it in print in any reputable magazine. Among the many affirmative reviews of *The Ice-Cream Headache,* Sara Blackburn's in the *Nation* (17 June 1968) is perhaps the most incisive. She observed that the stories "are anything but dated, and the variety of experiences they convey results not only in very moving fiction but, cumulatively, in a compact social history of what it was like for Mr. Jones's generation to grow up, to go to war, marry, and generally, to become people in America."

The best of the stories do indeed hold up well, engaging a substantial variety of subjects and themes. Jones's accounts of midwestern childhood in particular – founded on family alienation, possessive mothers, and male masochism – are frequently poignant. Some of the stories remind the reader of his early masters: Sherwood Anderson, Stephen Crane, William Faulkner, James Joyce, and Hemingway. As Blackburn astutely remarks, *The Ice-Cream Headache* provides a "compact social history," with Jones conceiving of himself – rather like John

Dos Passos, whose work he admired – as reporter, historian, and social commentator.

Through the course of the stories, which are all exemplary of mainstream realism, the reader follows a young male – he is called John Slade in some of the stories – from approximately age eight to age thirty-five. From the 1930s to the 1960s the stories span his life from childhood through adolescence into manhood, out of school and into the army, from the Midwest to the South Pacific, from peace to war and back to postwar America, and into marriage and out. To readers of his World War II trilogy it comes as no surprise that Jones is from the outset a master of the enlisted man's life and the experience of combat. To readers of *Some Came Running,* however, it is remarkable to discover the psychological acuity and narrative economy of most of his midwestern stories.

As is true of many young short-story writers, Jones's work is profoundly autobiographical, from ethos to naturalistic detail, drawing on his formative years in Robinson, Illinois. As he states in his introduction, he was beginning "to write well, in my own voice and my own way." Jones singles out an overlong, slice-of-life narrative, "None Sing So Wildly," as being "as near to a real autobiographical story as I've ever come." That story is also representative because it exemplifies both "[his] own way" and the substantial influence of another writer, in this instance Hemingway.

In "None Sing So Wildly," which at times reads like an excised chapter from *Some Came Running,* Sylvanus Merrick, the generic young Jones male, is engaged in what Count Mippipopoulos of Hemingway's *The Sun Also Rises* (1926) calls "learning the values." Sylvanus, sounding much like Jake Barnes in *The Sun Also Rises,* comes regretfully to acknowledge that "you paid for everything in this world." That lesson at least partially learned, Sylvanus takes leave of his fiancée, Norma Fry, the generic young Jones female, thereby suffering (to invoke another Hemingway title) the end of something.

Among the most commendable of Jones's stories are "The Way It Is," "Greater Love," "The Valentine," and "Just like the Girl," the last of which being his best. The title "The Way It Is" embodies several enduring verities in Jones's fictional world: that money is power; that power makes the rules and defines truth; and that, against the odds, it becomes a good man to assert his own values and resist power. The scene is Kaneohe Bay, near Makapuu Point, familiar from both *From Here to Eternity* and *The Pistol.* The time is three weeks after the bombing of Pearl Harbor, and the good man is Cpl. John Slade, member of a road guard that has just stopped a suspicious person, whom Slade recognizes as a longtime island resident. Exercising the power of money and position, the man – once released with apologies – soon has the road guard disbanded and the officers in charge reprimanded, all for doing their duty. Again, as Slade remarks, "That's the way it is."

Slade, it must be said, knows too much and too overtly articulates the author's perspective; he is too pleased with himself, too easily superior to both his dull and idealistic comrades to be wholly sympathetic. The road guard is situated on the windward side of the island; this location perhaps legitimizes the inclusion of no fewer than twenty-five references to the strong wind blowing, the symbolic import of which is most pointed in Slade's assertion that he "liked to sit there at night alone, defying the wind." He realizes, however, that "a man could do it only so long."

"Greater Love" focuses on another corporal, Quentin Thatcher, who at Guadalcanal evolves from an idealistic rear-area company clerk whose principal concern is his brother's safety to a traumatized infantryman. He is last viewed looking for more Japanese soldiers to kill, his initiation benevolently presided over by a first sergeant reminiscent of Warden and Welsh. The biblical allusion of the title ("Greater love has no man than this, that a man lay down his life for his friends") is developed through three sets of brothers – Quentin and Shelby Thatcher, Al and Vic Zwermann, and the Martuscellis, one of whom, Joe, sourly says, "I'm glad my brother is in Africa," at which a man named Gorman growls, "I'm gladder yet . . . I ain't got one." On graves-registration duty, Al digs up Vic's recently buried body and is temporarily unbalanced by the experience. Later Quentin, in the heat of combat, sees his brother fall but imagines in his deranged state that Shelby is lying down to rest, and Quentin is both incensed and embarrassed at his brother's cowardice. The first sergeant at Quentin's side best exemplifies the responsibilities of war brotherhood – staying alive so as to kill.

"The Valentine" again features John Slade, now twelve and powerfully smitten with a girl "whose lovely beautiful name was Margaret Simpson" and for whom he buys an expensive Valentine box of candy. The reader knows almost at once that John is fated to crushing disappointment, that Margaret will prove cold and unresponsive. Suspense inheres not in how the story will come out but

Dust jacket for Jones's 1962 novel, an account of an army infantry unit during the Guadalcanal campaign of
World War II

rather in the precise nature of the awful details and in how John will take his humiliation. In situation, characterization, and language the story recalls Joyce's "Araby" (*Dubliners*, 1914).

"Just like the Girl" (that married dear old Dad) is a chilling, autobiographically derived tale that Jones, as he recounts in his introduction, "once showed . . . to a newspaper editor in my hometown . . . who had known and admired my mother. The strange, guilty, upset, almost disbelieving look on his face when he handed it back, which seemed to say: 'Even if it's true, why *do* it?' was worth to me all the effort I put into writing it." "Just like the Girl" is a classic indictment of the bad mother, a woman who is hypocritical, self-serving, frigid, manipulative, and possessive, who imposes guilt, self-pity, and self-hatred on her younger son and sets him against his father and older brother. It is difficult not to feel complete sympathy for such a victimized child; only the boy's disinclination (or inability) to recognize the pain and inherent decency of his inarticulate alcoholic father may limit the reader's engagement.

Jones did not think of himself as a short-story writer; it was for him a secondary form, complementary and to a substantial degree anticipatory to the novel. After *The Ice-Cream Headache,* in the last

nine years of his life, he published no more stories. Eleven of the thirteen stories in the collection are about home or the army; the best ones concern the pangs of childhood and draw on small-town news and gossip. In the less successful stories the structure and proportion are generally at fault.

In a letter (19 January 1972) to the American scholar R. W. Stallman that Jones wrote after the storm of critical abuse of his novel *The Merry Month of May* (1971) had dissipated somewhat, Jones remarks, "It may interest you to know that it was written deliberately in the genre of *The Sun Also Rises* and *The Great Gatsby,* a deliberate attempt to try to use the virtues of that form and to update it." It is Hemingway's novel that seems the more apt analogy, given its world-weary, essentially passive narrator-observer and his account of American expatriate life in Paris. That account becomes a qualitative study of varying degrees of sexual frustration and spiritual maturity, projected against a background of boredom and malaise that is everywhere implicitly condemned. Among the unutilized virtues of *The Sun Also Rises,* however, is Jake Barnes's commitment to "learning the values"; that is, in Jones's novel neither Jonathan James Hartley III, the cynical, ambivalent narrator-observer, nor any other character learns any values that people are encouraged or even allowed to admire. Indeed it is difficult to identify anyone likable in *The Merry Month of May,* much less anyone about whom the reader can feel, as Nick Carraway does about Gatsby in F. Scott Fitzgerald's 1925 novel, that he or she is "worth the whole damn bunch put together."

As his ostensibly wellborn name is meant to suggest, Jonathan James Hartley III is a narrator-protagonist unlike any of his predecessors (or successors) in Jones's canon. At forty-seven he is a failed poet, novelist, and husband. As editor of *The Two Islands Review* he is purportedly an intelligent, cultivated, well-read, and reflective man. "Low-keyed sexually," he is "best friend" of the Gallagher family and is blessed with little to do and all the time in the world to do it. He hates to be disturbed during his leisurely morning ritual of shaving, bathing, dining, and reading. His editorial duties are notably undemanding. He is witness to two revolutions of the 1960s – one political and one sexual – both of which he says he finds exciting, but neither of which he really understands or takes seriously. He regards the students as children, their would-be revolution a childish expression of sexual immaturity.

Although many things happen in *The Merry Month of May* – with periodic touring of a riot zone, observing of police, dropping in at student-revolutionary headquarters, dining at the Brasserie Lipp, and drinking at the Gallaghers' – the plot is desultory and disconnected, cause and effect left unclear. As if he had a street map at his elbow, Jones pays close attention to the routes by which his characters traverse Paris, but he does not succeed in making the city an exciting, living force in the novel, as Hemingway does in both *The Sun Also Rises* and *A Moveable Feast* (1964). Because Jones's narrator does not pretend to know France or the French, it is necessary that Jones introduce – almost halfway through the novel and to the reader's considerable surprise – Hartley's mistress, whose function is to explain to him (and to the reader) not only what is going on but also what is to be expected.

Observing with helpless horror the disintegration of the Gallagher family (Harry, Louisa, Hill, and McKenna) takes up most of Hartley's time and energy. Harry – a former marine, successful screenwriter, and self-proclaimed "fighting liberal" – was questioned by the House Un-American Activities Committee and is now living in comfortable exile in an apartment closely resembling the author's own on the Ile Saint-Louis. He is "a very highly sexed individual," habitually unfaithful to his wife, and much attracted to the idea and practice of sexual threesomes (two women, one man) and oral sex.

Of the student revolutionaries – including his son, Hill – Harry complains, "They don't even want to utilize our knowledge and experience to help them." From the other side of the generation gap Hill countercomplains, "They've never let me do anything on my own." Hill, who is studying sociology and cinema at the Sorbonne, is naive, idealistic, and incompetent as a filmmaker. He is no match for his practiced, cynical father either in ideological debate or in contention for the favors of Samantha Everton, a young, equally practiced, bisexual black woman who undertakes to seduce all adult members of the Gallagher family. Samantha may figure as an updated version of Hemingway's Brett Ashley. Harry and Samantha end up in Israel by way of Rome. Louisa – after an abortive effort to seduce the narrator, thereby striking back at her absent husband, and a failed suicide attempt – is left brain damaged. Hill, preyed on by counterculturalists, takes up residence in a cave in Spain; and McKenna, the "delightful" goddaughter of the narrator, is taken in by a family friend.

Despite Jones's best efforts, however, Hartley remains a bland presence; Jones's depiction of politics in theory and practice is never engaging; and a major concern, the investigation of American sexual maladjustment, is rendered in psychologically primitive terms. For good reasons the critical majority voted firmly against *The Merry Month of May,* finding it puzzling, offensive, and inept. In *Newsweek* (15 February 1971) Geoffrey Wolff concluded that "Jones writes so badly that his offenses constitute as great a crime against nature as against literature." The failure of the novel had a lasting effect. As Giles observes, "It is unfortunate that *Go to the Widow-Maker* and *The Merry Month of May* were the last two serious novels during Jones's lifetime. Their failures have much to do with the critical neglect of his best work at the time of his death." Fortunately, Jones returned to his World War II trilogy in *Whistle.*

In 1970, his fiftieth year, Jones experienced his first attack of congestive heart failure, the condition that killed him seven years later. Frank (Lobo) Davies, the hard-boiled hero of the author's only mystery novel, *A Touch of Danger* (1973), most clearly reflects the author's unease with the passage of time and the work still undone. *A Touch of Danger* began as a film script titled "Hippy Murders," which Jones, in need of money, reworked into a novel and sold to Doubleday for $250,000. Although the novel proved harder to write than Jones had anticipated, both he and the publisher were sufficiently pleased with the result to promise, on the dust jacket, that the novel's hero "will be heard from again," a promise that in fact did not bear fruit. As mystery-adventure fiction in the tradition of Raymond Chandler, Dashiell Hammett, and Ian Fleming, *A Touch of Danger* has much to recommend it. If the achievement of the novel seems not to accord with Jones's description of it in a letter to Helen Meyer (23 August 1972) as a work of "high literary merit," it is nonetheless well conceived, with good structure and pacing and exemplary plotting. It is, as reviewers noted, the work of a pro.

A Touch of Danger is perhaps most interesting as Davies responds, not always with equanimity, to a variety of cultural issues of the late 1960s and early 1970s. On the Greek island of Tsatsos, Davies, who is feeling his age at fifty, investigates two murders that illustrate the destructive extremes of the sexual revolution and the drug culture among the predominantly young, mostly American expatriate population. Although he is vulnerable to charges of misogyny and resentment of the young, he often agrees in principle to the resistance of the young to constituted authority. His queries may be better informed, but he too questions authority, particularly that based on class and money. For reasons both practical and principled, he opposes the war in Vietnam and extends conditional approval to draft dodging.

A major concern for Davies is his fear of being fifty, his resistance to aging: he will not go gently. For this condition the best anodyne proves to be his attachment to two women. One is his lover – elegant, charming, sexy, and approximately his contemporary. In her he sees, studies, and criticizes his own alarm; he appraises her resistance, accounting her vain, foolish, and brave. The other woman, metaphorically his daughter, is a young counterculturalist who evokes in him both carnal and paternal responses, of which the latter comes to dominate. Unlikely as it seems for such a worldly man, events on Tsatsos comprise Davies's first European adventure. He finds, in time-honored American fashion, that Europe is an older, richer, magically attractive, and yet somehow corrupted culture.

In 1973 Jones went on assignment to Vietnam for the *New York Times Magazine*. *Viet Journal*, a narrative of his one-month visit, recounts the last days of American involvement there. The book consists of seventy-nine often vivid, bountifully detailed sections, each averaging three to four pages. They are followed by a nostalgic epilogue in which Jones, "bearing witness," returns to Hawaii after an absence of thirty-one years.

Though Jones counts himself unbiased, indeed "cynical about both sides," he emphasizes Commu-

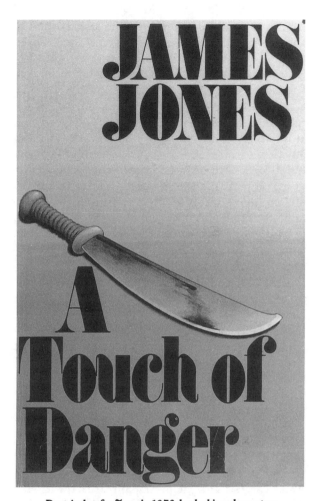

Dust jacket for Jones's 1973 book, his only mystery

nist savagery and duplicity as well as the fatuity of such liberal-intellectual antiwar ideologues as Mary McCarthy and Frances Fitzgerald. The former Private Jones, now fifty-two, is most often in the company of high-ranking officers, an "apprentice" in their "arrogant corporation." He seems usually at ease and generally admiring with these men of power, and one of them, Gen. Mike Healy, emerges as the book's hero.

The action of the narrative rises to and declines after the author's participation in an unarmed helicopter-resupply run to Dak Pek, an isolated Montagnard base surrounded by Vietcong. Jones travels widely (unaccountably, there is no map), less as a working journalist than as an intermediate-grade celebrity. He is at pains to represent the sights, sounds, and smells of the country accurately but makes no pretense of understanding either Vietnam or the Vietnamese. He assimilates information, official and unofficial, and tries to convey something of the cost of the war, of America's blunders and naiveté. He appreciates good "New Army" American soldiering – relishes the camaraderie of Cuban cigars, high-stakes poker games, and shared danger – but back in Hawaii he is "only animally grateful" and wholly undisturbed by his social conscience.

Of the sketches in *Viet Journal* "Hawaiian Recall" is the longest, best focused, most deeply felt, and most clearly related to Jones's other work. The conjunction of now and then, of being fifty-two and twenty-one, of celebrity and anonymity, of being able to buy anything in the shops and having to borrow fifty cents for a cab, is affecting, as are both the uncertainty at this point of who had done what – Jones, Prewitt, Mast, somebody else – and the unspoken awareness that he will never come back here again.

In 1974 the Jones family, with daughter Kaylie (born 1960) and son Jamie (born 1961), at last returned to the United States. Before buying a Long Island farmhouse, which was to be his last home, Jones briefly taught creative writing at Miami International University, taking advantage of free time in order to write. It was the only period during his married life in which he had a salary and lived on it. To help eliminate his debts he composed the text for a picture book of World War II graphic art, most of it American. *WW II: A Chronicle of Soldiering* (1975) was the result – the last book Jones lived to complete. Its subtitle indicates both the focus of the volume (the experience of the average, anonymous American GI) and the principal reason for its substantial success (the nature of the narrative, which is personal and autobiographical rather than scholarly and all-inclusive).

"Military men," Jones writes in *WW II,* "always like it better, and feel more comfortable, if they can talk or write about the war on a purely professional level, without taking up in detail all the social, religious, political, ethical, and psychological factors which also go into giving a particular war its particular peculiar character." He goes on to state, "Military men always find it cleaner not to go into all that other stuff very deeply. But somebody always does have to go into it if a war – all war – is to be understood at all." In *WW II,* as in his military fiction, it is precisely Jones's intention to "go into all that other stuff " so that the reader may better understand the experience of war.

History, Jones believes, is usually written by the upper classes for the upper classes, one consequence of which is that the lower classes, who fill up the enlisted ranks, cannot find their experiences recorded, much less honored, in print. Jones was born into a family that in his grandparents' or great-

grandparents' generation was accounted upper class but that by Jones's enlistment in 1939 was working class. He writes that his postwar career moved him "back in among the upper classes by reason of a certain success as a writer." Certainly he is appreciative of commanders' problems, of the strategic talents of a "vainglorious" old campaigner such as Gen. Douglas MacArthur. He notes further that MacArthur "could never be accused of 'wasting' his men carelessly or thoughtlessly."

Jones is principally concerned, however, with sketching what he calls the evolution of a soldier, a major theme as well in his military fiction. In brief, Jones's representative enlisted man is initially awed by the historical moment of the war's beginning and wonders whether he will survive. The training he receives, which he experiences as a depersonalized harassment, deprives him of his sense of individuality while it gives him a sense of competence. To know and accept beforehand that he is dead, that he is fated not to make it, enables him to become what Jones calls a "professional," expert in his work and loving it, with "combat numbness" being the condition of the well-tempered veteran. The prospect of the war's end reinstills hope, a painful process likened to a frozen foot's thawing. The soldier finally passes through "de-evolution," gradual reintegration into civilian life.

The simple, flexible format of *WW II* – a succession of short essays linked by chronology, topic, setting, and the author's personality – recalls that of *Viet Journal.* Not surprising, Jones's commentary on the Pacific theater of war is better than that of the European theater; in his narrative of the latter he is sometimes reduced to laboring through "I wonder what it would have been like" scenarios. For descriptions of the Pacific theater – *his* war – and the home front, he turns to good effect to that same body of personal experience that informs his four long military fictions and some of his short stories. Thus his historical account of the prewar army draws on both *From Here to Eternity* and *The Pistol,* as does *Viet Journal.* Jones's recollections of combat on Guadalcanal are dramatized in part through excerpts from *The Thin Red Line.* Similarly, "Hospital" (*WW II*) incorporates material from *Whistle,* at the time his work in progress.

Throughout *WW II* Jones asserts "the distressing complexity and puzzling diffusion of war" and its "terrifying impersonality" and nowhere neglects the truth of Gen. William T. Sherman's observation that war is hell. Telling the whole truth, however, also requires citation of "the greatest cliche of them all," quoted from an unnamed friend who confided that "I hated it. But I wouldn't have missed it for anything. I'm just glad I didn't miss it."

Jones did not live to complete his last novel. He died in Southampton on 9 May 1977. His friend Willie Morris set down the final three and a half chapters of *Whistle,* reconstructed from the author's own thoughts and language, based on conversations and tape recordings. *Whistle* concludes Jones's World War II trilogy; it brings home four wounded survivors of the infantry company featured in the two earlier volumes.

Returning stateside on a hospital ship in 1943, 1st Sgt. Mart Winch, Mess Sgt. John Strange, and Pvt. Bobby Prell, along with nonregular army Sgt. Marion Landers, suffer less from their wounds than from what Jones in *WW II* calls the "de-evolution of a soldier" – a mixture of survival guilt, fear of recovery and return to combat, and resentment of the "nice soft people" who are so profitably running the home front. Their fellow citizens, they discover, are devoted to family, jobs, homes, investments, and other material benefits of victory.

While *Whistle* is not a wholly satisfying novel, it often speaks eloquently to the reader and is clearly better in all respects than the fiction Jones had written in the fifteen years since *The Thin Red Line.* There are several reasons for such striking artistic recuperation. One is the subject matter, of which he was past master. With three of the four veterans turning to suicide and one lapsing into insanity, the story is bleak and tragic, yet not altogether unrelieved. Although the novel is frustratingly inconsistent, it displays substantial energy, vitality, humor, and richness of observed detail.

Jones has evolved a prose style that appears to be awkward, even slovenly on occasion, but Jones is so direct in his way of seeing the world that his style contributes its own moral force to the narrative. Jones is also capable of dramatizing, as perhaps no other writer of his own or succeeding generations has been, the simultaneous sense of terror and release that comes from knowing that one must die in combat. This sense haunts the four heroes of *Whistle,* and being redeemed from their fate proves even more destructive than fulfilling it. In many ways, too, the novel addresses itself to contemporary postwar America, notably the altered relationship between men and women.

One of Jones's major concerns throughout the novel is oral sex, particularly cunnilingus. Most of the women with whom the recuperating soldiers party in Luxor, the location of Kilrainey Army General Hospital, are defined by their interest in it. Strange's wife, Mary Lou, leaves him for another

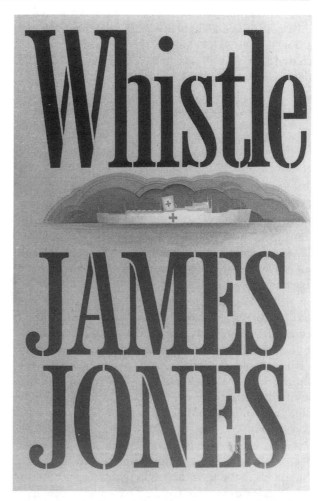

Dust jacket for Jones's final novel, which was finished by his friend Willie Morris after Jones's death

man largely because of his lack of interest in it. When Strange finally tries it with another woman and discovers that he likes it, he worries endlessly that he is a "pervert" for doing so. The characters perform it repeatedly and graphically; they even wonder at its reported illegality in thirty-six of the forty-eight states and seriously analyze the reasons for its prohibition.

Asked why American men generally do not like to perform cunnilingus, Winch explains:

> I suppose it's our American religious training. American Christianity. Sex is all scrambled up in our religion. Evil, dirty, filthy. Guilt. It shouldn't be. It's all very primitive. Medieval. But it's all tied in with our puritanism.

Such attention to oral sex principally reflects an acknowledgment of women's liberation from the role of passive sexual partner. Several times it is stated as fact that only by oral stimulation can a woman truly experience orgasm, and this belief in turn constitutes a challenge to the old army way of seeing things. It challenges the view of women as chattel that an old, admired West Pointer, Colonel (later General) Stevens, expresses to Prell:

> We men. We men like to have our good times. But we don't like to have to pay up for it. We are supposed to look after women, and take care of them. Protect them. They need that from us. Our whole civilization is based on that.

Finally Stevens's view threatens the concomitant view that the only true source of love and companionship is to be found in male society. As much as Jones's heroes are haunted by nightmares of soldiers who have died because of or for them, they are terrified at the loss of a male-bonded society.

For Winch, Strange, Prell, and Landers the old company had been home, family, and hope of continuance, yet, even as they reach the hospital in a "half-unmanned state," the company has already disintegrated, is already history. For each man the three others are what remain of his "real life." From civilian life, moreover, they are impossibly alienated; as Landers testifies, "There's no after the war. Not for me."

To emphasize this point, each man has what seems to be a chance for a new life, of which Landers's is the most elaborately developed. Subsequent to his desertion, Landers, aided by a local girl, goes to Barleyville, Tennessee, to be received by the girl's father, the local sheriff. Within a few weeks it becomes apparent that Landers, if he chooses, may have a new home, job, family, wife, and the protection of the local law. "It was," Jones writes, "a munificent offer, in its way. Almost unbelievable." Citing "too many things that had not been resolved," however, Landers returns to the army, is saved from a general court-martial by Winch, and is given an honorable medical discharge. At last "a free man able to go anywhere he pleased to go," he walks directly in front of a car while still on post. For him, as for the others, there is no escape.

Of the four characters Winch is the most fully developed, Prell the least so. His legs shattered by Japanese machine-gun bullets, Prell is the group's designated hero, winner of the Medal of Honor. He is a romantic, self-destructive figure, reduced in the second half of the novel to subordinate status, too much – some readers may feel – a pathetic victim. He contends with pain, the surgeons' decision to amputate his legs, the nightmare of his squad's last patrol, and his sense that he does not truly merit the Medal of Honor. He feels guilty about failing Strange and Landers. His marriage to Della Mae Kinkaid is a farce, and his assignment as a war bond–selling celebrity makes him a minor vaudevillian. Finally he procures his own death in a barroom brawl.

At first Winch seems wonderfully energetic, knowing, sardonic, and self-possessed, but the reader soon discovers that he is seriously ill with congestive heart disease (from which Jones suffered) and that he is too tired any longer to be the man on whom everyone else depends. Yet no other role is tolerable. His admiration for Strange, who he believes "really did not give a damn about anything," suggests his own increasingly apparent vulnerability. Master of army politics and skillful manipulator of officers though he is, he finally cannot save his people from themselves. He arranges a "perfect sinecure" for himself at Second Army Headquarters and acquires a lover exactly half his age, but the job is no help and the relationship is doomed. As his nightmare grows more oppressive, his always-precarious sanity breaks down, and he is last heard screaming from a prison ward, "Get them out of here, goddam it, get them out of here."

John (Mother) Strange and Landers both seem to be inconsistently portrayed. Strange, as his nickname suggests, is thought to care for his people: he is never happier than when cooking for his company in the field. But, if Winch is to be believed, in reality Strange cares about nothing and no one, finally not even himself. Strange's obsessive concern with oral sex dominates his characterization and makes him seem almost freakish. He is, it seems, a victim of the revolution in sexual mores in which women, beginning with his unfaithful wife, are seen as the enemy. He commits suicide because he cannot bear to see recapitulated in Europe the horrors of war already familiar to him from the Pacific.

Landers is the youngest, best educated (a "college man"), and most articulate of the four. From the time of his wounding he develops an "outside feeling" that becomes finally a sense of utter detachment from his species. He suffers from profound depression, loneliness, nightmares, guilt, and a rage that precipitates frequent fistfights. By the time of his death he has become certifiably sociopathic. Though his idealism is briefly resuscitated by his commitment to his company commander, Lieutenant Prevor, a victim of anti-Semitism, it becomes apparent that Landers cannot live in or out of the army: "What he wanted was to creep into somebody's arms, and be held."

In the postmodern era it has become easy to discount Jones and the eleven books that make up and not just because of their rank;

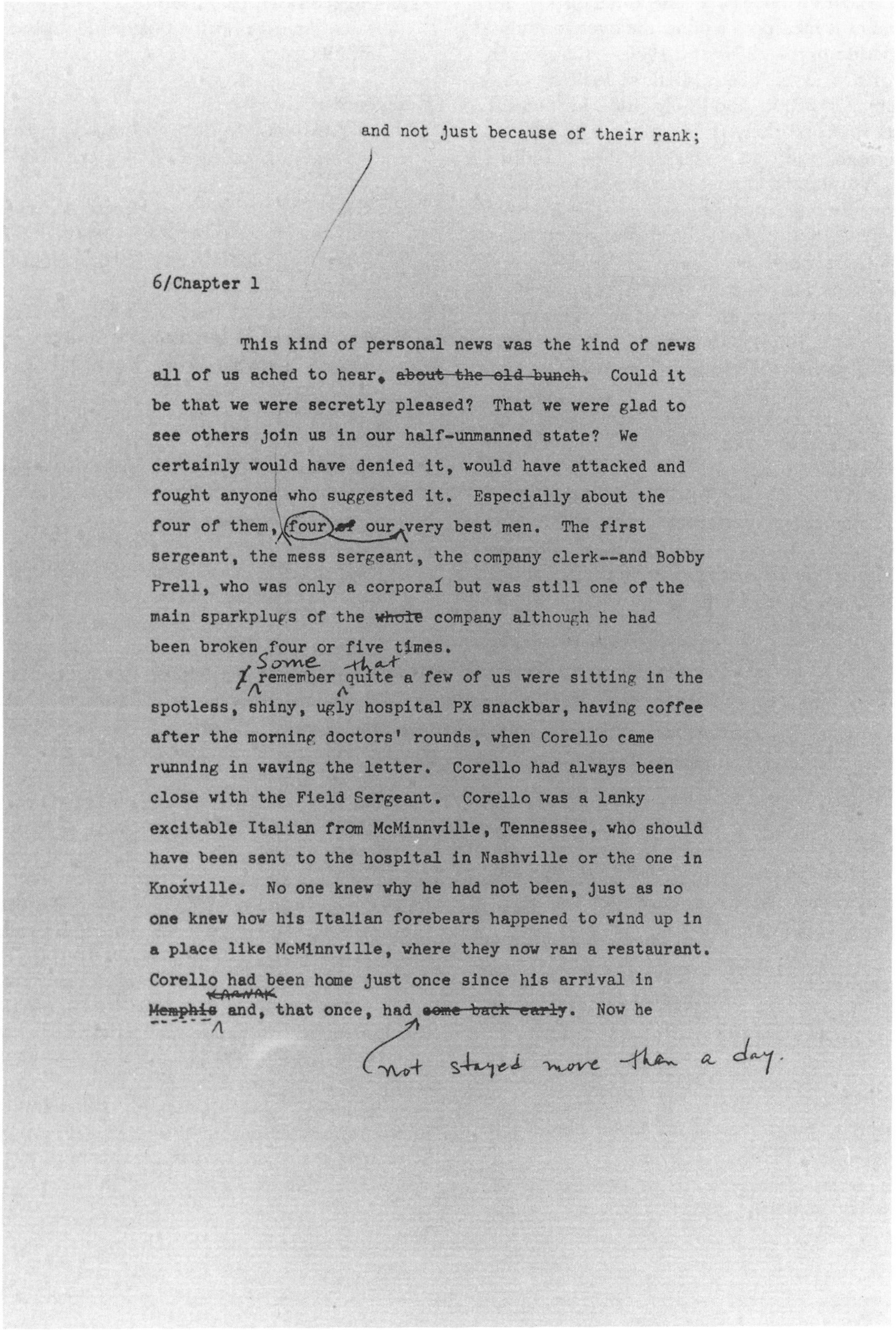

6/Chapter 1

This kind of personal news was the kind of news
all of us ached to hear, ~~about the old bunch.~~ Could it
be that we were secretly pleased? That we were glad to
see others join us in our half-unmanned state? We
certainly would have denied it, would have attacked and
fought anyone who suggested it. Especially about the
four of them, (four) of our very best men. The first
sergeant, the mess sergeant, the company clerk--and Bobby
Prell, who was only a corporal but was still one of the
main sparkplugs of the ~~whole~~ company although he had
been broken four or five times.
        I remember *Some that* quite a few of us were sitting in the
spotless, shiny, ugly hospital PX snackbar, having coffee
after the morning doctors' rounds, when Corello came
running in waving the letter. Corello had always been
close with the Field Sergeant. Corello was a lanky
excitable Italian from McMinnville, Tennessee, who should
have been sent to the hospital in Nashville or the one in
Knoxville. No one knew why he had not been, just as no
one knew how his Italian forebears happened to wind up in
a place like McMinnville, where they now ran a restaurant.
Corello had been home just once since his arrival in
~~Memphis~~ *KARNAK* and, that once, had ~~come back early.~~ Now he

not stayed more than a day.

Page from the typescript for Whistle, *with Jones's corrections (from* Whistle: A Work in Progress, *1974)* most of his lifework. This case intensifies if his achievement is measured against the overtly sophisticated fiction of the 1950s and 1960s – the sleeker, more worldly novels of Saul Bellow, William Gaddis, Thomas Pynchon, and Philip Roth. In such calculations Jones is likely to be counted as another old-fashioned, traditional, macho realist, of limited interest. A standard annual source of information regarding academic attention, *American Literary Scholarship,* reveals that the last recorded essay on Jones appeared in Italy in 1988.

Yet Jones has not gone unread, unstudied, or unadmired since his death. As a writer of army life and war fiction, Jones is unsurpassed in American literature. It is Jones – to quote from *WW II* – who takes up "in detail all the social, religious, political, ethical, and psychological factors" that enable his readers to understand the particular character of World War II and that give his fiction much of its substance. As social critic, historian, reporter, and, above all, storyteller, Jones shows himself to limited advantage in his novels of civilian life, though as a short-story writer he deserves to be rediscovered. Throughout his career he displayed an original and uneven, though often powerful and utterly honest, talent.

Letters:

To Reach Eternity: The Letters of James Jones, edited by George Hendrick, foreword by William Styron (New York: Random House, 1989).

Interview:

Writers at Work: The Paris Review Interviews, Third Series, edited by Malcolm Cowley (New York: Viking, 1967), pp. 231–250.

Bibliography:

John R. Hopkins, *James Jones: A Checklist* (Detroit: Gale Research, 1974).

Biographies:

Willie Morris, *James Jones: A Friendship* (New York: Doubleday, 1978);

George Garrett, *James Jones* (New York: Harcourt Brace Jovanovich, 1984);

Frank MacShane, *Into Eternity: The Life of James Jones, American Writer* (Boston: Houghton Mifflin, 1985).

References:

Richard P. Adams, "A Second Look at *From Here to Eternity*," *College English,* 17 (January 1965): 205–210;

Saul Bellow, "Some Notes on Recent American Fiction," in *The American Novel Since World War II,* edited by Marcus Klein (Greenwich, Conn.: Fawcett, 1965), pp. 159–174;

Maxwell Geismar, "James Jones: And the American War Novel," in his *American Moderns: From Rebellion to Conformity* (New York: Hill & Wang, 1958), pp. 225–238;

James R. Giles, *James Jones* (Boston: G. K. Hall, 1981);

Ihab Hassan, *Radical Innocence: Studies in the Contemporary American Novel* (Princeton, N.J.: Princeton University Press, 1961);

Peter G. Jones, *War and the Novelist: Appraising the American War Novel* (Columbia: University of Missouri Press, 1976);

Norman Mailer, *Advertisements for Myself* (New York: Putnam, 1959);

Allen Shepherd, " 'A Deliberately Symbolic Little Novella': James Jones's *The Pistol*," *South Dakota Review,* 10 (Spring 1972): 111–129;

Edmund Volpe, "James Jones – Norman Mailer," in *Contemporary American Novelists,* edited by Harry T. Moore (Carbondale: Southern Illinois University Press, 1964), pp. 106–119.

Papers:

Jones's papers and manuscripts are in the Beinecke Library, Yale University; the Harry Ransom Humanities Research Center, University of Texas at Austin; and the Firestone Library, Princeton University. The manuscript of *From Here to Eternity* is at the University of Illinois Libraries, Urbana. The Handy Writers' Colony Collection in the Sangamon State University Library Archives (Springfield, Illinois) holds eighteen James Jones boxes as well as photographs, the author-corrected galley proofs of *From Here to Eternity,* and the manuscript of Jones's unpublished novel, "They Shall Inherit the Laughter."

William Kennedy

(16 January 1928 -)

Edward C. Reilly
Arkansas State University

See also the Kennedy entry in *DLB Yearbook: 1985.*

BOOKS: *The Ink Truck* (New York: Dial, 1969; London: Macdonald, 1970);

Legs (New York: Coward-McCann, 1975; London: Cape, 1976);

Billy Phelan's Greatest Game (New York: Viking, 1978);

Ironweed (New York: Viking, 1983; Middlesex, U.K.: Penguin, 1983);

O Albany! Improbable City of Political Wizards, Fearless Ethnics, Spectacular Aristocrats, Splendid Nobodies and Underrated Scoundrels (New York: Viking, 1983);

Charlie Malarkey and the Belly-Button Machine, by Kennedy and Brendan Kennedy (New York: Atlantic Monthly, 1986; London: Cape, 1987);

Quinn's Book (New York: Viking, 1988; London: Cape, 1988);

The Making of Ironweed (New York: Viking, 1988);

Very Old Bones (New York: Viking, 1992; London: Penguin, 1992);

Riding the Yellow Trolley Car (New York: Viking, 1993);

Charlie Malarkey and the Singing Moose, by Kennedy and Brendan Kennedy (New York: Viking, 1994).

MOTION PICTURES: *The Cotton Club,* screenplay by Kennedy and Francis Ford Coppola, Orion, 1984;

Ironweed, Tri-Star, 1987.

SELECTED PERIODICAL PUBLICATIONS – UNCOLLECTED:

FICTION

"The Concept of Being Twenty-Two," *San Juan Review,* 1 (June 1964): 18–20, 27–29;

"Figgy Blue," *San Juan Review,* 3 (February 1966): 36–38;

"The Secrets of Creative Love," *Harper's,* 267 (July 1983): 54–58;

William Kennedy, 1987 (photograph by Thomas Victor)

"An Exchange of Gifts," *Glens Falls Review,* 3 (1985/1986): 7–9;

"Dinner at the Phelans," *Weber Studies,* 10 (Winter 1993): 7–20.

NONFICTION

"The Yellow Trolley Car in Barcelona and Other Visions: A Profile of Gabriel García Márquez," *Atlantic Monthly,* 231 (January 1973): 50–59;

"The Quest for Heliotrope," *Atlantic Monthly,* 233 (May 1974): 53–60;

"Getting It All, Saving It All: Some Notes by an Extremist," New York State Governor's Conference on Libraries, 1978;

"If Saul Bellow Doesn't Have a True Word to Say, He Keeps His Mouth Shut," *Esquire,* 92 (February 1982): 48–50, 52, 54;

"William Kennedy's Cotton Club Stomp," *Vanity Fair,* 47 (November 1984): 42–48, 116–118;

"How Winning the Pulitzer Prize Has Changed One Writer's Life," *Life,* 8 (January 1985): 156–157;

"My Life in the Fast Lane," *Esquire,* 105 (June 1986): 59–60;

"Be Reasonable – Unless You're a Writer," *New York Times Book Review,* 25 January 1987, p. 3;

"(Re) Creating *Ironweed,*" *American Film,* 13 (January/February 1988): 18–25;

"Carlos Fuentes: Dreaming of History," *Review of Contemporary Fiction,* 8 (Summer 1988): 234–237;

"Writers and Their Songs," *Michigan Quarterly Review,* 29 (Summer 1990): 393–405; reprinted as "Why It Took So Long," *New York Times Book Review,* 20 May 1990, pp. 1, 32–34;

"Two Grandfathers," *Life,* 16 (February 1993): 86–87.

In 1984 William Kennedy told Terrence Petty that between the publication of *The Ink Truck* (1969), *Legs* (1975), and *Billy Phelan's Greatest Game* (1978) he and his family "lived on credit and promises to pay. It was a good life, and we had a lot of fun. But we never had an extra nickel." Then, when *Ironweed* (1983) was rejected by thirteen publishers – including Viking, its eventual publisher – Kennedy's future seemed even bleaker, until Saul Bellow admonished Viking for not publishing *Ironweed* and even prophesied that this novel would be both a commercial and a literary success. Not only was *Ironweed* a financial boon for Viking, but it also became Kennedy's leprechaun's gold in that it won both the 1983 National Book Critics Circle Award for fiction and the Pulitzer Prize for fiction.

Kennedy's other novels were republished in 1983. On his fifty-fifth birthday he received a $264,000 grant from the John D. and Catherine T. MacArthur Foundation; he used part of that money to establish the Writers Institute in Albany. He co-authored the screenplay for *The Cotton Club* (1984) with Francis Ford Coppola, and the screen rights for *Legs, Billy Phelan's Greatest Game,* and *Ironweed* were sold. The film version of *Ironweed* premiered in Albany in 1987. After struggling in obscurity, Kennedy has become a major voice in contemporary American letters, and he rightfully deserves such recognition.

William Kennedy was born in Albany, New York, on 16 January 1928 to William Joseph and Mary Elizabeth McDonald Kennedy, whose Irish ancestors had settled in North Albany several generations before. Kennedy was reared in North Albany, a predominantly Irish-Catholic neighborhood, often called the North End or Limerick. He attended Public School 20, was an altar boy at Sacred Heart Church, and even aspired to the priesthood. In *O Albany!* (1983), however, he emphasizes that his religious aspirations lasted until about the seventh grade, when he began drawing cartoons, printing his own newspaper, and was "fixated on the world of print."

Still, his Irish-Catholic roots were and are deep, even though he admits that he refused to sing "Too-ra-loo-ra-loo-ra," a traditional Irish lullaby, and walked out of mass "during narrowback sermons" when he was a young man. But he finally realized that "I thought myself free, and found out that not only wasn't I free, I was fettered to all of it." In North Albany, Kennedy was also introduced to Irish-Democratic politics, most notably the United States' first Irish-Democratic political machine, which was organized and perpetuated by Daniel Peter O'Connell, whom Kennedy fictionalizes in *Billy Phelan's Greatest Game* as political boss Patsy McCall. In addition, "Big Jim" Carroll, Kennedy's great-grandfather, was an influential political leader in Albany's Ninth Ward; William Kennedy, Sr., was a deputy sheriff who worked the polls and took young Kennedy to political rallies. Similarly, on his mother's side, his uncles Coop and Jim McDonald were political appointees. As Kennedy emphasizes in *O Albany!,* "I can think of half a dozen more family ties to the city or county payrolls."

Having developed a love for journalism when he was in the seventh grade, Kennedy worked on his high-school newspaper at Christian Brothers Academy; became executive editor for the Siena College newspaper (the *Siena News,* later changed to the *Indian*); and worked for the *Post Star* in Glens Falls, New York, as sports editor and columnist. After he was drafted into the army in 1950, Kennedy became a journalist for the Fourth Division's newspaper in Europe. After his discharge in 1952 he worked for the Albany *Times-Union* until 1956, and then he accepted a position on the *Puerto Rico World Journal,* only to see it go under after nine months. Kennedy moved to Miami, worked as a reporter for the *Miami Herald,* returned to Puerto Rico in 1957 to write fiction, and in 1959 became the founding managing editor for the *San Juan Star.* As Kennedy told Tom Smith in 1993, "I had a good time for two years and then I quit, which was my swan song as a full-time journalist. I realized after those years as managing editor, which was as high as I ever aspired, I wanted to return to fiction."

When he returned to Albany in 1963 to care for his ailing father, Kennedy worked again for the *Times-Union,* at the same time writing a series of articles about Albany that served as the genesis for *O Albany!* From 1972 to 1975 Kennedy reviewed books for *Life, Look,* the *New Republic, Saturday Review,* and the *New York Times.* He contributed thirty-seven reviews to the *National Observer* from 1964 to 1972. Because he is so busy with his creative writing projects, he rarely reviews books anymore. Although he told Michael Robertson that journalism is a "great training ground" and that "no bailbondsman, no lawyer, no politician, no bartender, no actor can enter the variety of worlds that a journalist can," he emphasized that "writing novels is what I'm supposed to do in this world."

However, Kennedy's sojourn in Puerto Rico significantly changed his destiny. He married Ana Daisy (Dana) Segarra, whom he praises in *O Albany!* for making him "as happy as any writer can ever expect to be" and "who is very good at putting together superior children ... without losing her talent for making unbearably good cognac chicken and running a business and teaching dance and managing our precarious finances in a way that kept us out of the debtor's prison." Kennedy also enrolled in Bellow's creative-writing class at the University of Puerto Rico at Río Piedras. In 1983 Kennedy told Joseph Barbato that Bellow was "very, very encouraging" and confirmed Kennedy's belief that "I had something to say."

Kennedy had eagerly left Albany in search of his muse and thought Puerto Rico would be the catalyst. Indeed it was, but with an ironic twist. After trying to write stories about Puerto Rico — but failing because he felt like a tourist and could not write convincingly about the island and its people — he finally discovered his literary turf when he began poring over picture histories of Albany from 1842, 1867, and 1899. As he told Larry McCaffery and Sinda Gregory in 1984, he began writing about Albany, and the "transition was extraordinary. I found myself ranging through sixty years of the history of the family, the Phelan family. . . . I found that by focusing on these people and locations something happened to my imagination that freed me to invent readily. . . . It became magical." Indeed, he dedicated *O Albany!* to "people who used to think they hated the place where they grew up, and then took a second look."

In "Albany as a State of Mind," the first essay in *O Albany!,* Kennedy identifies his fictional landscape and purpose:

> I write this book not as a booster of Albany, which I am, nor as an apologist for the city, which I sometimes am, but rather a person whose imagination has become fused with a single place, and in that place finds all the elements that a man needs for the life of the soul. . . . It is the task of this and other books I have written, and

hope to write, to peer into the heart of this always-shifting past, to be there when it ceases to be what it was, when it becomes what it must become under scrutiny, when it turns so magically, so inevitably, from then into now.

In Kennedy's novels and in *O Albany!* and *Riding the Yellow Trolley Car* (1993), Albany becomes his historical and fictional corner of the world. Not only is the city the setting for his fiction, but those influences and experiences that are part of Kennedy's own matrix also figure prominently in his works: the North End; Catholicism; Irishness; Democratic politics; Albany's Nighttown; journalism; and the world of bums, gangsters, gambling, sports and swells; and show business. In his early novels Kennedy's is a primarily male-oriented world. He remarked to Kay Bonnetti that "you didn't *see* women in that society ... tables for ladies, back entrances, that's the way it was." In "My Life in the Fast Lane" (*O Albany!*) Kennedy describes the Knights of Columbus, a Catholic men's fraternal organization, as a place where "women came ... only for parties, dances and bingo; club life excluded them otherwise." His early novels feature strong male characters; strong female characters only begin to emerge with Annie Phelan and Helen Archer.

Although each stands by itself, Kennedy's novels are interconnected not only through setting but also through historical facts and incidents, characters, and plot details. For instance, characters such as Jack Diamond and Francis Phelan may be the major focus in a particular novel but secondary characters in another work. Similarly, Charlie Boy McCall's kidnapping is a major incident in *Billy Phelan's Greatest Game* but secondary in *Ironweed.* With its 1800s setting, characters, family genealogies, and historical facts and incidents, *Quinn's Book* (1988) ties in with the novels that precede it and with *Very Old Bones* (1992), which fleshes out more details about the Phelans. Because of these deliberate interconnections, Kennedy calls his novels "a cycle," an idea he emphasizes in Edward C. Reilly's *William Kennedy* (1991): "I had been thinking about my books being interconnected and had arrived at the word 'cycle' because it was open-ended. It would never be just a trilogy, or a septology or any particular number until I was finished writing forever."

Kennedy's characters, who hail from Irish-Catholic lower- or middle-class backgrounds, achieve various levels of social and economic success. Daniel Quinn and Emmett Daugherty are self-made men; John the Brawn becomes successful

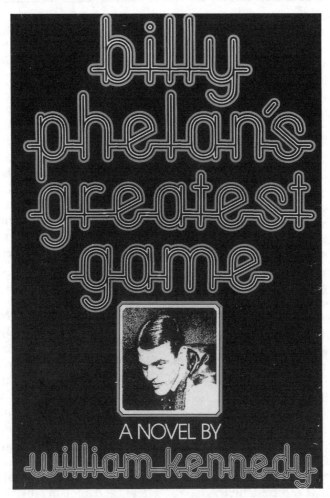

Dust jacket for Kennedy's 1978 novel, about a gambler in Albany, New York, during the 1930s

through entrepreneurial opportunities and boxing, Magdalena Colón and Maud Fallon through show business. Legs Diamond's success comes through criminal activities, the McCalls through political machinations, Billy Phelan's through pool hustling in Albany's Nighttown, and Peter Phelan's through his artwork. One of Kennedy's major themes is regeneration, and thus his protagonists usually fall before they are regenerated. For instance, Bailey is ousted from the Newspaper Guild and descends into the State Library's subterranean stacks, Diamond's criminal empire collapses, Billy Phelan falls from McCall grace, Francis Phelan and Helen Archer endure bumdom, Quinn undergoes painful Civil War experiences, and Orson Purcell plunges into madness. Concomitantly, Kennedy calls his protagonists "warriors" who strive to become "something valuable in life," who "sustain a serious attitude toward survival." Like Francis Phelan, they must learn that the "trick was to live, to beat the bastards,

survive the mob and the fateful chaos, and show them what a man can do to set things right, once he sets his mind to it."

The Ink Truck, Kennedy's first novel, is loosely based on a 1964 strike at the *Times-Union,* but the facts of the strike are transformed into fiction. As the novel opens, the strike has dragged on for a year — the actual strike lasted eighteen days — and most of the Newspaper Guild members have either capitulated or have been wooed back to work by the various absurd, and often nefarious, schemes that Stanley, the newspaper's manager, concocts. For example, he promises raises, but, when most of the financially strained workers return, he cuts their pay. He offers all-expenses-paid vacations at the newspaper's Florida resort, and many of the winter-weary strikers accept the offer. He organizes a "series of Granny strip shows" to lure the workers past age sixty-five; and he hires Queen Putzina's Gypsies to spy on, and even to stand silent watch outside, strikers' homes. As a result, only Bailey, Irma, Rosenthal, and Jarvis remain active in the strike, but Jarvis capitulates, and Irma and Rosenthal totter on the brink of defection.

Bailey presages Kennedy's later Irish-Catholic protagonists who, through chance or circumstances, live on the edge, who fall before they rise, and who live by a code of conduct that dictates that a person must do whatever necessary to reestablish purpose and meaning in his life. Bailey is clubbed by company goons, kidnapped by Putzina's Gypsies, sexually tempted by Miss Blue, and offered an odious deal by Stanley; Bailey's defiance, therefore, forces him to live on the edge. His metaphorical fall occurs when he descends into the State Library's subterranean stacks where, during a surrealistic return to 1832 Albany and a conversation with the Voice, he is regenerated. He is, as Joseph Campbell (*The Hero with a Thousand Faces*) says in one of the novel's prefatory quotations, "dismembered totally and, then reborn." When he emerges from the stacks, he resumes solitary picketing augmented by a hunger strike and finally succeeds in sabotaging a company ink truck. He is again clubbed by company guards, but his triumph is evident in his "soundless, utterly private, internal but inescapably joyous giggle." His heroic code of conduct is implied in his idea that "trouble, if it doesn't kill you, strengthens you," an idea similar to Francis Phelan's comment about doing "what a man can do to set things right, once he sets his mind to it."

In the author's note for the 1984 edition of *The Ink Truck* Kennedy asserts, "All that needs saying is that this is not a book about an anonymous city, but about Albany, N.Y., and a few of its dynamics during two centuries." However, Kennedy told McCaffery and Gregory that, although "Albany's never mentioned in *The Ink Truck,* I feel I have the same streets, and the same newspaper . . . the same characters running saloons, the same traditional figures existing in the history of this mythical city I'm inhabiting in my imagination." Although *The Ink Truck* is set in Albany and references are made to the cholera epidemic, Goat Hill, Cabbageville, Fobie's bar, and the newspaper that is the *Times-Union,* Kennedy does not convincingly establish the city's sense of place, something he does successfully in his later novels.

The Ink Truck received both critical praise and rejection. In *Best Sellers* (15 October 1969) E. A. Dooley wrote that the novel's action is "too jumpy" and that, while Kennedy is a "skilled weaver of words," he should concentrate on "straight picturesque writing rather than on mystifying fantasy." In the *New Statesman* (14 August 1970), Stanley Reyn-

olds observed that the novel "has the look of something typed in dull moments around the newspaper office," that "one feels Mr. Kennedy was unfortunate to have had the free time to finish his 'comic masterpiece,' " but that Kennedy "has something to say about the way American society crushes idealism." On the other hand, in *Library Journal* (1 February 1970) Dorothy Curley remarked that Kennedy's "aims and characters are sympathetic" and recommended *The Ink Truck* as an "intriguing first novel." Shane Stevens's review in the *Washington Post* (5 October 1969) praised the novel as "inventive, circular, and multi-layered," with characters "as real as they are symbolic, the scenes as much reality as fantasy." Stevens concluded that "Kennedy has been able to confine his wickedly surrealist imagination within a well-told tale. The result is a Dantean journey through the hells of existence."

When *The Ink Truck* was republished after the success of *Ironweed,* critics noted that Kennedy's first novel foreshadowed his succeeding works. In the *New Republic* (15 October 1984) Anne Tyler commented that *The Ink Truck* is a "finger-exercise for the Albany cycle." In the *National Review* (9 August 1985) Loxley Nichols claimed that the novel contains many elements that have come to make up Kennedy's fictional landscape – a "predominantly Irish (American) world of unsuspected heroes, lost causes, and errant pookas." Joel Conarroe in the *New York Times Book Review* (30 September 1984) contended that the novel establishes "numerous thematic links with the later books" and indicates an "energetic but as yet undisciplined artist working his way somewhat clumsily to the flexible style that would become his trademark."

In *Understanding William Kennedy* (1991), J. K. Van Dover writes that "many of Kennedy's characteristic virtues as a writer are already evident in *The Ink Truck* . . . but they are not, it must be admitted, prevalent. Having read the later Albany novels, one can identify seminal themes and techniques in *The Ink Truck* but the reader who came first upon *The Ink Truck* could hardly predict the later Albany novels." In *William Kennedy,* Reilly, while admitting the novel has some "minor stylistic flaws," contends that *The Ink Truck* should be analyzed within the spectrum of 1960s literature: "Kennedy did precisely what he said he was going to do – he wrote about the 1960s. As a book about this turbulent decade, *The Ink Truck* is just as chilling as *One Flew Over the Cuckoo's Nest,* just as absurd as *Catch-22,* and just as experimental in its techniques as any of the avant garde works of the era."

Although Kennedy told Bonnetti that *The Ink Truck* is a "willful leap into surrealism," he abandons surrealism in his later novels, especially *Legs:* "I felt I couldn't go on writing this hyperbolic comedy which is always six inches off the ground. I needed to be grounded in reality. *Legs* is a consequence of that." Kennedy's second novel focuses on the life of John T. Diamond, alias Legs Diamond, one of the flamboyant killers who galvanized the events of the Roaring Twenties, the age of the gangster. Neither born nor raised in Albany, Diamond nevertheless has ties to the city: he supplies Albany's speakeasies with bootleg whiskey and beer; has dealings with Albany's Oley brothers' gang; parties at the Kenmore Hotel's Rain-Bo Room; recovers at Albany Hospital from the Aratoga Inn assassination attempt; hires Albany lawyer Daniel H. Prior to defend him during the Grover Parks kidnapping case; and is murdered at about 5:30 A.M. on 18 December 1931 in Laura Wood's rooming house at 67 Dove Street, a house that Kennedy now owns.

In 1985 Kennedy remarked to David Thomson that when he began *Legs* it was not going to be about Diamond. "He was just going to be a character," Kennedy said, adding, "I looked at our morgue at the paper. Holy Christ! The things that had happened to him." Kennedy began researching his materials, spent a "small fortune Xeroxing newspapers," discovered many contradictory facts, and so decided to "reinvent" Diamond as a "brand new fictional character." Kennedy also said that he would not become bogged down again with extensive research because it interferes with the creative process. While historically factual, the "daily specifics of Jack, his wife, Alice, and his girl friend Marion ('Kiki') Roberts . . . are products of one man's imagination," writes Kennedy in *O Albany!*

In reinventing Diamond, Kennedy gives him human dimensions because, as he said to Margaret Croyden, "I don't think of gangsters as animals beyond redemption, or inarticulate, or that they have no soul. . . . The people that live this kind of life are human beings like you and me. People did love Legs Diamond." Kennedy emphasizes Diamond's personality in various scenes, such as his buying Marcus Gorman, his lawyer, a forty-nine-cent paperweight, his dancing the Charleston with Kiki Roberts at Mike Brady's Top O' The Mountain House, and his attending mass and carrying his rosary. At the same time, however, Kennedy juxtaposes Diamond's human side with his cobralike tendencies, which are evident in the killings he either commits himself or orders his shooters to do. As Kennedy states in *O Albany!*, "[Diamond's] cru-

elty pervades my book." Moreover, in reinventing Diamond, Kennedy also wanted to explain why Diamond "was so revered" and why "people courted his presence" — an idea Kennedy underscores in the novel's epigraph: "People like killers. And if one feels sympathy for the victims it's by way of thanking them for letting themselves be killed."

Kennedy wrote *Legs* over a period of six years, during which he tried various structural techniques, including writing a novel about a movie being made of Diamond's life, but he says, "The cameraman kept getting in the way of the story." He also tried to tell the story in a surrealistic fashion, as a chronological narrative composed of an accumulation of voices, and as a detailed account of Diamond's last day of life. None of these worked. After Kennedy read Henry James's notes on writing a novel, the focus for the story became apparent:

> Marcus Gorman became the narrator and that was necessary. I found out that I could not have all the multiple voices and make it work. I had to have somebody collating all this. Maybe Henry James turned me around. I was reading his marvelous prefaces and notes on the novel, and he was talking about the importance of an intelligent narrator and I realized this is what I needed. So I began. It just fell into place then and I also found a dramatic focus to build to a climax of his life which was the torturing of the trucker, Clem Streeter.

Legs actually concentrates on Diamond's fall as his criminal empire crumbles after the Hotsy Totsy Club gun battle. As Gorman says, "The crest of his life collapsed with the Hotsy shooting," as well as all Diamond had been "building to for most of a decade — his beer and booze operations, the labor racketeering . . . his protection of crooked bucketshops . . . his connections with the dope market." Other plot details emphasize Diamond's fall and waning gangster power: Charlie Northrup spits beer at him; Diamond is barred from Europe and Philadelphia; Gorman cannot bribe Warren Van Dusen during one of Diamond's trials; New York's governor, Franklin D. Roosevelt, wants Diamond tried and imprisoned; the four assassination attempts on Diamond take their physical and mental tolls; Diamond's trusted henchmen are either killed or imprisoned; Diamond's trials for kidnapping and torturing Clem Streeter in 1931 (historically the Grover Parks kidnapping); and finally Diamond's murder in the Dove Street rooming house.

Diamond is also another of Kennedy's warrior heroes who establishes purpose and meaning in his life through a sharply defined code of conduct that is more deadly because the gangster world dictates its terms: never inform, never reveal assassins, and always retaliate in kind. Diamond lives on the edge as he often pits himself against neophyte shooters aspiring to underworld legend; rival, cold-blooded mobsters; and local, state, and federal police. The constant in Diamond's characterization is his will to survive as he renews "his vulnerability to punishment, death, and damnation." Unlike the earthly regenerations that Kennedy's other heroes achieve, Diamond's regeneration occurs when he is murdered and reborn into myth, or, as Kennedy told McCaffery and Gregory, "The whole thrust of the last scene had to do with Legs being reborn into this life as legend, then a mythic figure, a figure in American history who will be with us a long time to come. . . . That's one of the things I was driving at in *Legs,* that sense of the gangster myth, the idea that Legs was moving into mythic status after his life on earth."

Diamond's becoming an American myth is also evident in the novel's plot – when, in the opening section, forty-three years after Diamond's death, Gorman, Flossie, Tipper Kelley, and Packy Delaney meet in the Kenmore Hotel's Rain-Bo Room to reminisce about Diamond; when the American and foreign newspapers embellish his crimes and legends; and when Gorman calls him the "dude of all gangsters, the most active brain in the New York underworld," and "one of the truly new American Irishmen of his day . . . shaping the dream that you could grow up in America and shoot your way to glory and riches." Diamond's mythical image transcends the final "historical image" – Diamond's corpse "clad in underwear, flat-assed out in bed, broke and alone."

In addition to being a credible narrator, Gorman plays two other roles in *Legs.* First, when Diamond falls and his gangster world crumbles, Gorman experiences his own moral collapse as his life becomes inextricably entwined with Diamond's. Gorman first accepts six quarts of bootleg scotch from Diamond in exchange for wrangling an Albany County pistol permit, and then Gorman accepts Diamond's invitation to Sunday dinner. Gorman is enervated by his contact with Diamond, who is "alive" in a way that he is not. Gorman's further involvement and moral decay are evident when he sails to Europe with Diamond "against all sane judgment"; when he wears Diamond's money belt, which contains Jimmy Biondo's money; and when he fabricates fifteen witnesses to testify at Diamond's first Troy trial and concocts the nun story during the second trial. Symbolically, the extent of Gorman's fall becomes evident when he meets a

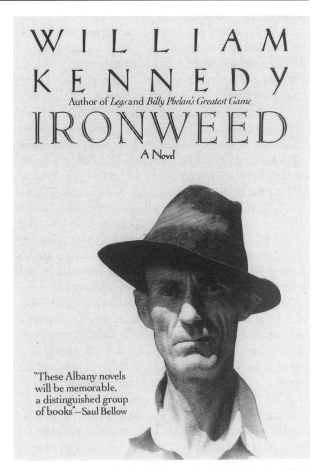

Dust jacket for Kennedy's Pulitzer Prize–winning novel, which he adapted for a 1987 film starring Meryl Streep and Jack Nicholson

woman in the ship's bar, coaxes her back to his cabin, and subjects her to what he calls a "quasi-rape."

Gorman's attraction to Diamond not only further underscores the novel's epigraph but also parallels both Alice's and Kiki's fascination. Alice says, "Don't tell me I should've married somebody pure and holy. They would've bored the ass off me years ago. After all, I didn't marry a priest, Jesus. I married a thief." Even Kiki says her life "started going someplace, someplace weird and good," when she met Diamond. Moreover, Gorman's, Alice's, and Kiki's interest in Diamond is mirrored in the newspapermen's attraction to him and in the people who want his autograph, who want their picture taken with him. Many women want to have affairs with him, or, as Kiki says, "We go out, me and Jack, out to the best places with the best people, rich people, I mean, society people, famous people like politicians and actors and they fall all over us. They all want to make sex with us and kiss us and love us."

As Kennedy stated to Susan Agrest, "To write about Diamond I had to respect someone who was a mean, cruel son-of-a-bitch. Yet he fascinated America. My role was to find out why he was so revered. Why people treated him like Lindbergh and Al Jolson. Why people courted his presence."

In concentrating on Diamond's Albany years, 1930 and 1931, and in choosing Gorman, a native Albanian, as narrator, Kennedy creates a more detailed sense of place in *Legs* than he does in *The Ink Truck*. There are specific references to such Albany landmarks as the Elks Club, the Knights of Columbus Hall, the Rain-Bo Room, Union Station, North Albany, and Sacred Heart Church; and to such streets as Broadway, North Pearl, North Second, Genesee, and Erie. Furthermore, in *Billy Phelan's Greatest Game* and *Ironweed* Kennedy emphasizes the cycle in his Albany novels by establishing interconnections with *Legs* through characters such as Gorman, who appears in the two later novels; through the stories George Quinn and Morrie Berman tell about Diamond in *Billy Phelan's Greatest Game*; and through the fact that Berman and Diamond partied together. There is also a reference to Diamond in *Very Old Bones*.

Early reviews of *Legs* were generally more favorable than those of *The Ink Truck*. Bruce Allen (*Library Journal,* 1 May 1975) faulted *Legs* because it reads like a "made-for-TV book" and because Kennedy never questions Gorman's "mindless life-force worship" of Diamond. L. J. Davis (*Washington Post Book World,* 18 May 1975) wrote that *Legs,* while a "good book but not a great one," is what a "novel is supposed to be: a mirror walking down the road of man, and it deserves our closest and most serious attention." In a review about crime novels Peter S. Prescott (*Newsweek,* 23 June 1975) identified the major thrust of *Legs:* "Kennedy means to prove our peculiar American habit of reviling gangsters while pressing them for autographs."

As with *The Ink Truck,* later reviewers and critics could evaluate *Legs,* after it was republished, in terms of Kennedy's other works. Nichols notes: "Albany not only gives Kennedy place, but it also gives him subject, and through subject he acquires time, the 1930s, a period to which he adhered in his last two novels." Dean Flower (*Hudson Review,* Summer 1983) claimed that *Legs* was better than *Billy Phelan's Greatest Game:* "*Legs* is a shade more convincing, not because Kennedy dramatizes an historic figure . . . but because he is created for us by Marcus Gorman and because Gorman pieces the story together from memories. Twice distanced, the speakeasies and gangsters and fast talk seem im-

mediate and legendary with Irish-Catholic Albany as a microcosm of the thirties." In *William Kennedy* Reilly states that, in comparison with *The Ink Truck, Legs* denotes Kennedy's maturing literary skills in that it is "more tightly structured, contains a more detailed sense of place, and foreshadows Kennedy's later works." Similarly, Van Dover believes that in *Legs* Kennedy "began to exploit the essential matter of his fiction: the concrete realities of Albany" and that *Legs* presages Kennedy's eventual focusing the "action upon native Albanians."

The political theme and background for *Billy Phelan's Greatest Game,* Kennedy's third novel, came from his involvement with Irish-Democratic politics and from his series for the *Times-Union* about Mayor Erastus Corning and the O'Connells, articles for which he interviewed Daniel Peter O'Connell. While admitting in *O Albany!* that some good resulted from the O'Connells' political control – "the job, the perpetuation of the job, the dole when there was no job, the loan when there was no dole, the security of the neighborhood" – he adds that the power the O'Connells "held was so pervasive that you often didn't even know it existed until you contravened it. Then God help you, poor soul. Cast into outer darkness." Kennedy told Bonnetti that *Billy Phelan's Greatest Game* is a "political novel . . . about the *power* of a few politicians to control everybody's life, right down to the lowly hustler on the street who only wants to play pool and cards, and they can lock him out of every bar in town just by putting the word out."

In the novel the few politicians are the fictional McCalls (based on the O'Connells), who include Patsy, the patron; Matt, the lawyer; and Benjamin ("Bindy"), the boss of Albany's Nighttown. To contravene the McCalls' power is to suffer the consequences. They put the "word" out on Georgie Fox, who, after living like a mole for two years, leaps off the Hawk Street viaduct, and who "was dead long before he hit the pavement, sucked dry by Bindy's order." After showing up drunk at a political rally and being chastised by Patsy McCall, Jigger Bigley quits his job and moves to Cleveland. When Edward Daugherty sues the Albany *Sentinel* for printing a story about his scandalous affair with Melissa Spencer, the McCalls "saw to it that the judge in the case was attuned to the local realities, saw to it also that a hand-picked jury gave proper consideration to Patsy's former Colonie Street neighbor." Furthermore, the *Sentinel* closes after the McCalls force readers to cancel their subscriptions en masse and also quintuple the newspaper's taxes.

Coinciding with the novel's political theme, the plot's major conflict results when Charlie Boy

McCall is kidnapped (based on John O'Connell, Jr.'s, 1933 kidnapping). Because they suspect Morrie Berman, the McCalls ask Billy to spy on Morrie, Billy's close friend and sometime financial backer in bowling, pool, and card games. The McCalls promise Billy "one hell of a future in this town.... For a starter we clear up your debt with Martin Daugherty. And you never worry about anything again. Your family the same." Billy refuses, falls from McCall grace, and is locked out of Albany's Nighttown world.

A major metaphor in *Billy Phelan's Greatest Game* involves games, a concept Kennedy underscored in the McCaffery and Gregory interview: "Just about every form of game you can imagine is being played out in that book. But that notion of play, the way people live life as a game, has always been valuable to me." Martin Daugherty plays psychic games with himself, Melissa Spencer plays a sexual game with Martin Daugherty to get his father's ledger, and Angie Velez feigns pregnancy to win Billy. Charlie Boy McCall's kidnapping is a game; and gambling, pimping, and life are all games played by certain rules. In all the games he plays Billy is a winner: he beats Scotty Streck at bowling and Lemon Lewis at cards, and he wins in the game with the McCalls. As Martin Daugherty writes in his newspaper article, Billy is a "gamester who accepted the rules and played by them, but who also played above them."

As do Bailey and Diamond, Billy Phelan develops his own stylized code of conduct, one forged and polished in the sludge of Albany's Nighttown world and neither tarnished nor sullied by such a life. Angie Velez pinpoints Billy's code when, after her pregnancy ploy, she tells him, " 'You're such a life-bringer, Billy. You're the real man for me, but you're the wrong clay.... You can't be molded. Sex won't do it and money won't.' " The depth of Billy's code becomes evident when he refuses to kowtow to the McCalls' request that he spy on Morrie. Furthermore, Billy's fall from grace and his rise also typify Kennedy's warrior heroes. Although his regeneration may depend on a deus ex machina (Martin Daugherty's second newspaper article), Billy remains true to his code despite being locked out of every bar in town. Significantly, he neither leaves town like Jigger Bigley nor kills himself like Georgie Fox. Ultimately, Billy's greatest game is neither his 299 score in bowling nor the other contests he handles so well, but rather his being exonerated by the McCalls and his remaining true to his code despite life's forces. He does indeed play by and above the rules.

Martin Daugherty, the novel's secondary focus, also falls before he can reestablish purpose and meaning in his life. His descent occurs after his first sexual debauch with Melissa Spencer, his father's mistress. Because she wants Edward Daugherty's ledger from February 1908 to April 1909 in order to promote her acting and movie career, she lures Martin to her Hampton Hotel room and seduces him, after which he sells her the ledger for eight hundred dollars, is filled with self-loathing, and imagines himself covered with "simonical stink." His debauch becomes his "psychic downfall" as he both loses his gift of foresight and experiences a stasis that is further compounded because Peter, his fourteen-year-old son, has decided to study for the priesthood. Martin rails at the priests for having stolen Peter away, and *stolen* interconnects with Charlie Boy, who has been stolen by his kidnappers, except that the kidnapping could have a more tragic outcome.

Ironically, Martin Daugherty's regeneration occurs ten years later when he sees Melissa in *The Flaming Corsage* and again makes love to her. As he makes love to her this time, however, he finally understands his father's affair with Melissa and thus forgives him. Significantly, too, Martin understands his own "psychic mendacity, for trying to persuade himself he had other than venereal reasons for jingling everybody's favorite triangle." Martin can now forgive and even begin to love himself. Consequently, he reconciles himself to Peter's decision to be a priest, and he chastises the McCalls' treatment of Billy in a newspaper article.

Another central theme in *Billy Phelan's Greatest Game* is the father/son relationships. In fact, Martin's relationship with Peter mirrors other father/son bonds: Billy and Francis Phelan, Martin and Edward Daugherty, Bindy and Charlie Boy McCall, and Jake and Morrie Berman. Moreover, when Francis abandons home and family, Martin assumes a paternal role in Billy's life. For example, he takes Billy to a hospital to have his smashed finger stitched, he watches Billy mature, and he metaphorically defends Billy in the newspaper article. Various forces often separate the father from the son: Francis's flight after fatally dropping his son, Edward Daugherty's encroaching senility, Charlie Boy's kidnapping, Morrie Berman's quasi-underworld life and connections, and Billy's being a pariah in Nighttown. Yet there are reconciliations: Francis returns home, Charlie Boy is ransomed, Jake hires Marcus Gorman to defend Morrie, Martin defends Billy with the article, and Martin reconciles himself to Peter's priestly vocation.

Kennedy writes in the preface to *Billy Phelan's Greatest Game* that Albany "exists in the real world"

William Kennedy against the backdrop of the new and the old: the South Mall in the foreground and the State Capitol at the rear.

ISBN 0-670-52067-X

Dust jacket for Kennedy's 1983 collection of essays about the history of his hometown

but that "there are no authentically real people in these pages." The novel indeed evokes a more detailed sense of place than either *The Ink Truck* or *Legs,* a sense highlighted especially by the political theme and the concrete rendering of Albany's Nighttown world of bright lights; characters; hotels; restaurants; bars; and bowling, pool, and card games. In addition, Kennedy's cycle-novel theory becomes more evident in the conscious interconnections between *Legs* and *Billy Phelan's Greatest Game* in terms of characters as well as in historical and fictional incidents.

Billy Phelan's Greatest Game was not as successful as *The Ink Truck* and *Legs;* only thirty-five hundred copies were sold. Kennedy told Bonnetti that his second novel was "badly publicized and cheaply publicized too. It was scandalous the way they treated that book. I was an absolute innocent and let it all happen. They treated it like a Mafia book, as if that were the way to go." Early reviews were not positive. In *Commonweal* (13 October 1978) Philip Corwin criticized the novel because of its "repugnant characters" and because of Kennedy's "invoking a feeling of time" instead of "conveying a message." In *Library Journal* (1 June 1978) Jack Oakley claimed that Martin Daugherty's "mind excursions into religion, philosophy, and the past" distract the

reader and that both Billy and Martin lack Diamond's "vitality and charm." Similarly, in *Newsweek* (8 May 1978) Prescott faulted the novel for its dull plot and lack of unity and plot progression.

After it was republished, later reviewers generally praised *Billy Phelan's Greatest Game.* Doris Grumbach (*Saturday Review,* 29 April 1978) pointed out its "comic spirit," "wonderful language," detailed sense of place — Kennedy "knows every bar, store, bowling alley, pool hall, and whore house" — and its "entire *Decameron* of anecdotes, memories, and details of small lives." Nichols writes that *Billy Phelan's Greatest Game* is a "transition": "In *Legs* a single character acts upon and thus creates Albany, whereas in this third novel the place itself molds and ultimately identifies the character. As in *Legs* its plot is built on an excerpt of Albany's history, but there the nonfictional element provides context rather than focus, and instead of one central figure there are two." In *William Kennedy* Reilly writes that *Billy Phelan's Greatest Game* conveys a more "detailed sense of Albany and its history which interconnects with and complements the novel's plot, setting, characterization, and theme." Claiming that the novel came from Kennedy's unpublished play "The Angels and the Sparrows," Van Dover writes that in

Legs Kennedy "began to exploit the essential matter of his fiction: the concrete realities of Albany," but in his later novels Kennedy focuses the action on "native Albanians," and *Billy Phelan's Greatest Game* "establishes this new orientation."

"While I was writing *Billy Phelan,*" Kennedy told Reilly, "I had already decided . . . I wanted to give Francis his own book." *Ironweed* is indeed Francis Phelan's book. However, the *Ironweed* manuscript had an odyssey from publisher to publisher. With rejection after rejection Kennedy thought that "nobody was going to buy it," even though he felt it was his "best book." Publishing anomalies haunted the *Ironweed* manuscript. One major editor wrote, "Nobody has ever written better on this subject matter, but I just can't publish another novel that won't make any money." E. P. Dutton editor Henry Robbins looked forward to reading the manuscript and adding Kennedy to Dutton's list, but Robbins died of a heart attack, and Kennedy lost his champion at Dutton. In talking with Croyden, Tom Smith, one of the "four good men" to whom Kennedy dedicated *Ironweed,* aptly summarized those bleak times:

> This was a man who felt deeply rejected . . . but he had an energetic stubbornness which is at the bottom of all his characters. Some other guy would just give it all up. But he continued to write. . . . In his mind, he was like one of his characters, a bum, a literary bum. . . . But through it all, he would climb up there and just plug away.

During this bleak period Kennedy interviewed Bellow, who, according to Kennedy, "had just read *Billy Phelan* for the first time and it was on the basis of reading this book and not *Ironweed* that he wrote the letter to Cork Smith that changed my life."

In *Ironweed* Francis Phelan returns to Albany in 1938 after fleeing for twenty-two years because he accidentally and fatally dropped Gerald, his thirteen-day-old son, while changing his diaper. Although he comes back primarily to earn some easy money by voting as many times as possible at five dollars a vote, his return is his regeneration because he makes peace with the ghosts of his past, among them Harold Allen, Aldo Campione, Rowdy Dick Doolan, and especially Gerald. During his hiatus Francis's life spirals downward until he becomes a bum, a "social maggot, streetside slug." Moreover, as his scarred face and hands attest, his life is filled with violence and death. That violence will be part of his life is suggested when he accidentally kills Harold Allen during the 1901 trolley strike and first flees Albany.

During Francis's years on the bum, police shoot Campione as Francis tries to help him into a freight car. When Doolan attacks Francis with a meat cleaver, Francis kills him by bashing his head against a Chicago bridge abutment, and when civic-minded American Legionnaires raid a hobo jungle, Francis kills one of them in self-defense. The dead and dying are so much a part of Francis's life that he realizes, "Bodies in alleys, bodies in gutters, bodies anywhere, were part of his eternal landscape: a physical litany of the dead."

That Francis's return to Albany is to be his redemption is evident, first of all, in the novel's prefatory quotation from Dante's *Purgatorio* (completed circa 1321): "To course o'er better waters now hoists sail the little bark . . . leaving behind her a sea so cruel." Metaphorically, the "sea so cruel" is hell, and Francis's hell has been his bumdom. Second, like Dante's ascent from hell's pit, the novel opens as Francis rides "up the winding road of Saint Agnes Cemetery," where he will not only visit Gerald's grave for the first time but, more important, where he will be compelled "to perform his final acts of expiation" – not for Gerald's accidental death, but "for abandoning the family":

> You will not know, the child silently said, what these acts are until you have performed them all. And after you have performed them you will not understand that they were expiatory any more than you have understood all the other expiation that has kept you in prolonged humiliation. Then, when these final acts are complete, you will stop trying to die because of me.

Francis's final expiatory acts occur when he goes home and humbly confesses his sins to Annie, his wife: " 'Jesus Christ, Annie, I missed everybody and everything, but I ain't worth a goddamn in the world and never was. . . . I'm so goddamned sorry. . . . It's nothin' to what I did to you and the kids. I can't make it up.' " Although he leaves this earthly paradise and spends the night in the hobo jungle where he kills the raider, he returns home and seeks "sanctuary under the holy Phelan eaves."

In comparison with Bailey, Diamond, and Billy, Francis Phelan is the epitome of Kennedy's warrior heroes, and, more significant, Francis's struggle for redemption is solitary, without a Marcus Gorman to put incidents into mythical dimensions or a Martin Daugherty to write an exonerative letter. Concomitantly, in his bumdom Francis falls further and experiences more humiliating degradations, such as sleeping in weeds or hobo jungles and begging on the streets. In a 1993 interview with Smith, Kennedy emphasized Francis's fallen state:

"I mean the physical, psychic, and moral odds against him are staggering. He must strive constantly to stay alive physically, psychically, psychologically, sexually, professionally as a baseball player, and emotionally as a family member. He's always challenged at every level you could imagine a man being challenged at, and he survives." And his spirit is resilient, or, as he says on one occasion: " 'Ain't a whole hell of a lot of me left, but I ain't gone entirely. Be god-diddley-damned if I'm gonna roll over and die.' " His determination to live provides him with his stylized code: "The trick was to live, to beat the bastards, survive the mob and that fateful chaos, and show them all what a man can do to set things right, once he sets his mind to it." In this sense Francis personifies an ironweed plant, which is noted for the toughness of its stem, an idea Kennedy emphasizes with the novel's other prefatory quotation, from John James Audubon's *Field Guide to North American Wildflowers.*

Another notable difference between Kennedy's first three novels and *Ironweed* is that both Annie Phelan and Helen Archer emerge as strong female characters, also personifying the ironweed's tough stem. Parallels exist, in fact, between the two women: both are staunch Catholics, both lose children fathered by Francis (Annie loses Gerald, and Helen miscarries), and both love Francis. Helen's love is apparent when she decides to separate herself from Francis so that he can return home: "She admits she is leaving Francis . . . the way the King of England abdicated for the woman he loved. . . . If Francis could become a beggar out of love, why can't Helen abdicate for the same reason?" Annie's love is evident because she never tells anyone that Francis accidentally dropped Gerald, because she has kept Francis's belongings in the attic trunk, and because, when he does return home, she welcomes him and "opened the door wide." If Francis personifies an ironweed plant, so, too, do Annie and Helen.

While there are technical links between *Legs* and *Billy Phelan's Greatest Game* and between *Legs* and *Ironweed,* the strongest interconnections are between *Billy Phelan's Greatest Game* and *Ironweed.* Not only do these two novels end on the same day, but in *Billy Phelan's Greatest Game* Billy learns that Francis dropped Gerald and invites Francis home; Francis also learns that Annie has never told anyone about the accident. Later, when Billy tells Peg and his mother what he has learned, Annie pours out her grief and compassion. In fact, Kennedy told Peter J. Quinn: "*Billy Phelan* and *Ironweed* end on the same day, and they do that only because having cre-

ated the dynamics of Billy meeting his father, the logical thing when I dealt with Francis was to see him in those post-confrontational days with Billy. . . . Francis wouldn't go home until he knew that Annie had never condemned him or blamed him. So first comes the two things: the invitation from Billy and the knowledge about Annie." Furthermore, in *Billy Phelan's Greatest Game* Martin Daugherty tells Billy about Francis's first flight from Albany during the 1901 trolley strike, a flight in which both Martin and Patsy McCall figure prominently. As reviewers and critics have noted, these interconnections augment both Kennedy's sense of place and his cycle-novel theory.

Kennedy believes that *Ironweed* is the best of his first four novels, and critics agree. In his *New Republic* (14 February 1983) review William H. Pritchard claimed that *Ironweed* is the "best" of Kennedy's novels and "should bring this original and invigorating novelist to the attention of many new readers, especially since it is written in a language that is vital throughout." In *Time* (24 January 1983) Paul Gray praised the novel's characterizations and plot, mentioned that *Legs* and *Billy Phelan's Greatest Game* were being republished, and then stated: "Those who wish to watch a geography of the imagination take shape should read all three and then pray for more." The most perceptive review of *Ironweed* was Prescott's in *Newsweek* (31 January 1983): "William Kennedy has written good fiction before, which has largely gone unnoticed. This novel . . . should place him among the best of our current American novelists. In its refusal to sentimentality, its freshness of language and the originality with which its author approaches scenes well worn before his arrival, *Ironweed* has a sense of permanence about it."

O Albany! evolved from a series of articles Kennedy wrote for the *Times-Union,* and he said he had "always wanted to reprint those essays because I felt they had permanent value to a lot of people for Albany." When Susanne Dumbleton and Anne Older started Albany's Washington Park Press, they decided to publish these essays, but, as Kennedy realized, "Twenty years had elapsed and a lot of things had changed including my prose style, and I couldn't abide most of them, and obviously I had to do a lot more reporting." With the exception of three essays – "The Romance of the Oriflamme," "The Democrats Convene," and "Capitol Hill: A Visit with the Pruyn Family" – the other essays "were done from scratch," said Kennedy, "and those old newspaper articles became merely raw material for the new chapters."

Although they need not be read to understand Kennedy's fiction, the *O Albany!* essays augment the

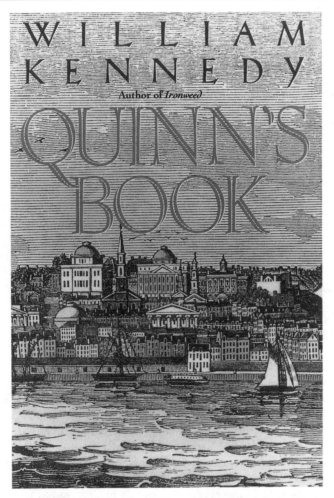

*Dust jacket for Kennedy's 1988 novel, set in Albany during the
years 1849 to 1864*

reader's understanding of the works. Especially valuable are the pieces that supply biographical information about Kennedy's family and his formative experiences: "Albany as a State of Mind," "Legacy from a Lady," "North Albany: Crucible for a Childhood," "Debts and Butterings," and "Albany as a Pair of Suspenders and a Movie." Essays that illuminate the fictional elements include, for *Legs,* "Prohibition: It Can't Happen Here" and "The Death of Legs Diamond"; for *Billy Phelan's Greatest Game* and *Ironweed,* "The Democrats Convene, or, One Man's Family," "The Bowery: Cabbages, Plucks, and Bloodsuckers," "Sports and Swells," and "They Bury the Boss, Dan Ex-Machina."

Some of the *O Albany!* essays – such as "The Romance of the Oriflamme," "Arbor Hill: Yesterday's Arcadia," and "The Gut: Our Boulevard of Bluest Dreams" – are about beginnings and endings, or falls and resurrections. Kennedy's sense of humor becomes especially apparent in "Prohibition:

It Can't Happen Here," where he recalls a "miracle" in which several barrels of whiskey were confiscated and stored in Central Avenue's Fifth Precinct: "Overnight ... inside the police station every barrel's contents had turned to water."

In *Library Journal* (December 1983) James W. Oberly underscored the significance of *O Albany!* in that the book is composed "in part" of the "nonfictional stories" that Kennedy creates in his novels. Thomas Fleming (*New York Times Book Review,* 1 January 1984) pointed out that *O Albany!* "recalls how many reincarnations Albany and the rest of America has undergone in the 370 years since a handful of Dutchmen sailed up the Hudson to open a trading post. ... So many flourishings, fadings, deaths and rebirths. Albany has been counted out a dozen times. ... Each time it has returned to improbable life." Van Dover writes that *O Albany!* "provides a very personal survey of the history, topography, and sociology of the place which has inspired all of

Kennedy's fiction. . . . And the spirit with which Kennedy approached *O Albany!* is the same as that with which he approached his fiction." Bill Beuttler states that *O Albany!* "gave Kennedy's fiction the rootedness it had been missing. The result: the richest continuing fictional exploration of an American place since Faulkner's Yoknapatawpha County." Kennedy informed Beuttler:

> Something had to happen to transform you, to make you like your history, you know? I mean, once you like it, then you can go back and find it again, which is what happened to me. . . . That's why I dedicated *O Albany!* to "people who used to think they hated the place where they grew up, and then took a second look." And loved it, whatever. That was a true thing.

Kennedy's comment about going back and finding his history – and Albany's too – applies to *Quinn's Book,* the genesis for which, he told Kim Heron, began when he talked with his father: "My father was endlessly full of small details about his life, his neighborhood, working in the foundry. I thought about how important it all was to him – of the long-dead past being so vivid and wanting to communicate it to me." After working all summer in 1977 and producing a "novel's worth of notes that were all dead in the water," he threw away what he had done and wrote "*Ironweed* or *O Albany!* or something." He eventually resumed work on *Quinn's Book,* which concerns the Quinns, Daughertys, and Katrina's ancestors. In a 1985 interview with Quinn, Kennedy discussed the setting and time frame: "Albany is still going to be Albany, but I'm going backward now to discover patterns that anticipate the twentieth century present. It's a preconsciousness I'm working on now." His "going backward" coincides with the novel's fifteen-year time frame, from 1849 to 1864, a more expansive span than in his previous novels.

The novel's main plot involves Daniel Quinn (an ancestor of George and Danny Quinn in *Billy Phelan's Greatest Game, Ironweed,* and *Very Old Bones*), who has emigrated from Ireland to Albany with his parents and sisters and who is orphaned when his father, mother, and a sister die during the 1849 cholera epidemic. Quinn is first apprenticed to Masterson, a tyrannical Erie Canal boatmaster whom he flees, and then to John the Brawn McGee, another canaller. In the winter of 1849 Quinn and McGee row out on the ice-clogged Hudson to rescue Magdalena Colón and her niece, Maud Lucinda Fallon, also an orphan. After her harrowing escape from the river, Maud makes Quinn promise that he will someday "steal" her away. Thus his promise

becomes his quest, and the Quinn/Maud love story becomes the heart of the plot and the rites of passage for both characters.

In the hero-meets-heroine tradition, however, various forces separate the lovers and prolong the metaphorical kidnapping. John the Brawn abandons the sleeping Quinn on the canal bank, Maud mysteriously disappears when they are reunited in Saratoga, Quinn haughtily spurns her in 1858, the Civil War begins, and Quinn becomes a war correspondent for the *Albany Chronicle.* In the novel's concluding section, "Saratoga August 1864," Quinn and Maud are reunited, and their love is rekindled at Hillegond's mansion, where they first kissed and where Quinn promised to kidnap Maud – "this mansion, which Maud ever since had known as a place where the miracle of love rises gloriously out of death, relinquishes its scars, and moves on to the next order of fulfillment."

In typical Kennedy fashion both Quinn and Maud fall before they can rise and progress "to the next order of fulfillment." Quinn's fall begins when he is initiated into the human barbarity of the novel's first two sections. His descent reaches its lowest point when he witnesses the Civil War and the New York Draft Riots, and when he hears about Hillegond's murder. His rise begins when he writes Magdalena's notice of proximate death, "an act of faith, not reason," and his final transcendence occurs in his love for Maud. Maud's fall results from her desire for social fame and fortune, in quest of which she performs the Mazeppa act, climbing "barebacked, perhaps barebuttocked and bare busted . . . those Albany platforms to scandalously glamorous international heights." Like Quinn's saving grace, hers comes in her decision to marry Quinn.

In the novel's last section Quinn watches the carriages moving toward the new Saratoga Springs racetrack and realizes that the procession is an "American motley" and a "moving mosaic," all going forward "at inch-pace progress." Symbolically, the "American motley" and "moving mosaic" refer to the many characters who enter and exit the plot and become small mosaic stones in the history of both Albany and the United States. The Staats family, for instance, personifies the early Dutch settlers who arrived at Fort Orange in 1638 and who began their family fortune through fur trading and then mercantilism. Magdalena achieves her success through show business and marrying well; the Toddy Ryan family typifies the plight of the Famine Irish; Joshua's family history is one of slavery and emancipation; and Lyman Fitzgibbon's history traces his rise through shrewd investments in banks, insurance, railroads, and land to become one of Albany's richest and most honored men. John the Brawn McGee is another American success story; he rises from canaller, to champion boxer, to bar proprietor (of the Blue Heaven bar in Albany's lumber district, an establishment eventually operated by Big Jim Carroll, Kennedy's great-grandfather), and finally to a principal stockholder in Saratoga Springs's new racetrack. Each character's microhistory becomes, therefore, a part of those events that ultimately shape Albany's ethnic neighborhoods, commerce, industry, and future generations. In addition, Kennedy contends that "everything that's happened in the country . . . all happened here" in Albany, and so, by extension, each character's microhistory reflects a macrohistory of the United States.

Quinn's Book opens with two cataclysms – the flood resulting from an exploding iceberg and the fire resulting from the flood. As Kennedy said in a 1989 interview with Reilly, "But there's nothing that hasn't been vividly documented in history including the cataclysms in the beginning of the book. They're taken from history. Maybe I've amalgamated them and made them happen on top of one another in ways that history . . . or Mother Nature had not seen fit to do, but I'm not being false to possibility." Symbolically, the novel's opening cataclysms suggest those upheavals that will affect the nation's and Albany's history as well as the characters' lives: the 1832 and 1849 cholera epidemics, the arrival and treatment of the Famine Irish, the battle between the Hills and the Creeks (two of Albany's ethnic factions), slavery and the Underground Railroad, the draft riots, and the Civil War. Just as the characters will transcend those forces and events in their lives, so too will Albany and the United States move at "inch-pace" progress toward the "next order of fulfillment."

As Kennedy stated in the Reilly interview, *Quinn's Book* "goes back to 1849 and beyond. There are allusions to the whole city, its history under the patroons, taking the genealogy of one Dutch family and moving it forward from the time of the Revolution and up to the time of pre–Civil War." In this sense, then, *Quinn's Book* is just as integral a part of Kennedy's Albany cycle as are the other novels. At the same time, Kennedy augments and enhances the historical and fictional backgrounds of his other novels – and the *O Albany!* essays as well – through various interconnections.

Quinn's Book received mixed reviews. Most critics – among them John Leggett in the *Washington*

Post (8 May 1988), Frederic Koppel in the *Memphis Commercial Appeal* (29 May 1988), and Walter Kirn in *Connoisseur* (July 1988) – faulted the novel for being crammed too full of details that hamper character and plot development. While praising the book for its "ferociously charming prose that seems to have altogether too much fun by itself," Prescott (*Newsweek*, 9 May 1988) echoed Leggett's, Koppel's, and Kirn's criticism:

> In *Quinn's Book* Kennedy forgets that legendary figures need to rise from the real world; the writer who begins with the miraculous ends with hot air. Too bad, because when Kennedy lets his adjectives and metaphors rest for a moment, he can write a moving scene in which Irish immigrants who have failed in New York board a train for the West. Nothing in this book makes us doubt his ability – only, this once, his judgment.

On the other hand, while faulting the novel for "its weight of history" that sacrifices "narrative drive and cohesion to the historical sidelights" and for its "ersatz 19th century idiom that often rings false," T. Coraghessan Boyle (*New York Times Book Review*, 22 May 1988) concluded, "*Quinn's Book* is a revelation. Large-minded, ardent, alive on every page with its author's passion for his place and the events that made it, it is a novel to savor." *Publishers Weekly* (14 March 1988) praised Kennedy for his "bold departure that (finally) made him famous," an insight Paul Gray (*Time*, 16 May 1988) shared, stating that *Quinn's Book* "successfully captures" America's "dazzling paradoxical panorama. . . . In the past Kennedy has excelled at revealing the dignity hidden within mean, pinched lives. This time he gives his characters plenty of elbowroom and lets them move forward toward folly or heroism. But the end result is the same: a novel that is both engrossing and eerily profound." Van Dover writes that "in the context of the Albany cycle *Quinn's Book* is unquestionably a major achievement. It adds crucial new dimensions to Kennedy's portrayal of the paradigmatic Irish-American experience of America . . . the characters and themes of Kennedy's next novel will surely be drawn from those already established in the Albany cycle."

That Kennedy draws characters and themes "from those already established in the Albany cycle" is apparent in *Very Old Bones*. If *Quinn's Book* returns to the past to flesh out the history of both Albany and the characters, then *Very Old Bones* moves forward, to the 1950s, to detail further the lives and fates of the Phelans. As Kennedy remarked to Beuttler about *Very Old Bones*, "Francis comes back and Billy Phelan comes back. . . . So in

Kennedy beside the graves of two people whose lives he fictionalized for his Albany novels
(photograph by Mariana Cook)

a sense, it's a climactic work in the Albany novels — for the Phelan family." Moreover, *Very Old Bones* is a complex and profound novel because of what Kennedy accomplishes in the plot. As evident in the family-tree diagrams that form the novel's endpapers, *Very Old Bones* flashes back from the 1950s to 1813 and thus includes the lives and fates of Malachi and Lizzie (née Cronin) McIlhenny as well as Michael and Kathryn (née McIlhenny) Phelan and their children — Francis, Sarah, Charles ("Chick"), Peter, Julia, Mary ("Molly"), and Thomas. The family's curse and secret sin result when Malachi, a Catholic religious fanatic, attempts to exorcise Lizzie but only succeeds in brutally killing her.

The protagonist-narrator, Orson Purcell, is the bastard son of Peter Phelan and Claire Purcell. As the novel opens on Saturday, 26 July 1958, thirty-four-year-old Orson is living in the Phelan house with Peter, his seventy-one-year-old father, whose precarious health results from a serious heart condition. On this day and with Orson's help, Peter has arranged a Phelan family gathering to "redirect everybody's life." Besides ridding the house of clut-

ter, Orson's main task is to ensure that Billy Phelan will attend the gathering, since Billy has not visited the house because of the way Sarah treated Francis, his father. Orson's memoir flashes back to reveal not only his own life but also what has happened in the Phelan family.

Orson recalls, for example, that he first met the Phelans in 1934, when Peter took him to Albany for Kathryn Phelan's funeral. During that visit Peter uses the four-hundred-dollar profit from selling one of his paintings to buy three chandeliers that will bring electric lighting to the Phelans' dimly lit house. During the first visit Orson says, "I liked Albany, liked the relatives, especially my Aunt Molly, who became my nurse after I went crazy for the second time, and I liked Billy, who always tried to tell the truth about himself." Orson's further ties to Albany and the Phelans are evident in that he went to college in Albany before and after World War II, had dinner with the Phelans on various occasions, and thus "slowly" got "to know this ancestral place and its inhabitants: the Phelans and the McIlhennys, their loves, their work, their disasters."

Orson's memoir – which he began five years before the novel opens, at Saratoga's Grand View Lake House – illuminates the truth he has learned about the Phelan family:

> I came to see how disaster does not always enter the house with thunder, high winds, and a splitting of the earth. Sometimes it burrows under the foundation and, like a field mouse on tiptoe, and at its own deliberate speed, gnaws away the entire substructure. One needs time to see this happening, of course, and eventually I had plenty of that.

Orson's insight also parallels Peter Phelan's understanding about his family and its history, but, whereas Orson's insight comes about through his writing the memoir, Peter's comes through his paintings – most notably his Itinerant series, which pays homage to Francis Phelan, and the Malachi suite, about the Phelan ancestors, Malachi and Lizzie. Or, as Orson indicates, Peter's "work already had an effect on the moral history of the family, and would continue to do so through the inevitable retellings of the story associated with the paintings; and these retellings would surely provide an enduring antidote to the poison Malachi had injected into the world. The work would stand also as a corrective to the long-held image of Kathryn in the family's communal mind."

Like Kennedy's other protagonists, Orson must fall before he can redeem himself. His first descent into madness occurs when, after serving in World War II and remaining in the reserves, he is activated during the Korean conflict and is sent to Germany. There he meets and eventually marries Giselle Marais, whom he impresses during their courtship by taking her to expensive restaurants and on exorbitantly pricey vacations. To finance his courtship he cheats at cards and becomes involved with Meister Geld, a German black marketer and currency speculator. When the military police arrest Orson, he plunges into madness and severely bites himself in five places while proclaiming he is the new Jesus, ironically in front of the patrons at Fritz's Garden of Eden. Orson's first plunge into madness occurs because he is a bastard and because he has accomplished nothing significant in his life. He receives a medical discharge and is sent back to New York, where he lives with Peter Phelan in a Greenwich Village flat. Orson's second plunge into madness occurs when Giselle rejoins him after her six-month stint as a photographer for *Paris Match*. During this second fall Orson forges checks, fraudulently uses another person's business cards, and almost drinks himself to death in Meriwether

McBeth's apartment, where Giselle and Peter find him and decide to take him to Albany because, as Giselle says, " 'You obviously can't live in this city.' "

When Giselle becomes too restless in Albany, she leaves to pursue her career as a *Life* magazine photographer, and, as Orson recalls, "It fell to Molly to oversee my reentry into the human race. An instrument of angelic mercy, she soothed my psychic wounds with gentleness." Ironically, Molly realizes that Orson cannot recover fully in the Phelan house, so she talks to Alice Shugrue and arranges for him to live and work as a handyman at Saratoga's Grand View Lake House. Its name is symbolic. There Orson begins his memoir about himself and the Phelans, a task through which he finally understands the tragedies and strengths of the Phelan family. His dark vision about himself and the Phelans has been replaced by a grander view, a more affirmative outlook on life and the world.

Regarding Orson Purcell as the narrator, Kennedy told Smith: "That's an evolutionary event. I started to tell it through Daniel Quinn who, in a certain sense, being the son of George Quinn and Peg, was somewhat akin to myself. And I couldn't make that work. I felt that that was artificial. I was full of constraint. I find it very difficult to invent out of my personal life." Instead, Kennedy said Orson became an amalgamation of characteristics that Kennedy had discovered in some of his own acquaintances:

> And that's in a certain way what I did when I found Orson. Orson was able to go crazy and be outlandish and have experiences that were really very, very far afield of my own. His World War II experiences, his whole experience with the Nazis in Germany, was very much different from what I was ever involved in. But I knew about people who had comparable experiences, and I was able to fuse all that.

And, in comparing *Quinn's Book* and *Very Old Bones*, Kennedy emphasized that "Quinn was looking back from an advanced age to his childhood and young manhood, whereas Orson is looking, not only at himself, but at everybody, and put into some profound family focus, what really was the underpinning behavior of this peculiar family."

In addition to the details about the death of and wake for Kathryn Phelan, Orson's memoir recounts the fates of the other Phelans. In 1910 Julia dies at age twenty-two. Thomas, born an idiot, becomes the cause of his mother's final frigidity. Sixty-three years old, he is brought home by Albany policemen for lifting up Letty Buckley's skirt with his cane in imitation of Charlie Chaplin. When

Thomas's self-righteous and indignant sister Sarah beats him on his naked buttocks with the edge of a two-foot ruler, she severely damages his spine. Although this injury sporadically immobilizes him, he returns to his job as a sweeper at the filtration plant. In 1956 the pain strikes him, and he collapses, rolls into one of the filtering pools, and drowns. When Chick learns about Thomas's spine, he telephones Evelyn Hurley, whom he has been courting for seventeen years. He proposes marriage, gives his two weeks' notice at the *Times-Union,* and moves to Miami with Evelyn, never to return.

When Molly comes back after spending Labor Day 1954 weekend at Saratoga's Grand View Lake House with Thomas, Sarah's health has suddenly declined in a way, writes Orson, that "seemed uncharacteristically abrupt. We all thought she would struggle more vigorously against the cabal of forces that had beset her, but . . . all her strength and will centered on the downward rush to death." On 17 November 1954 – what would have been her mother's ninety-fourth birthday – Sarah dies. In 1943 Francis Phelan dies of a heart attack while coaching third base for the Albany Senators baseball team.

Annie Phelan is alive but senile; she resides with the Quinns. Agnes Dempsey, Billy Phelan's girlfriend, is Annie's live-in nurse. Fifty-one-year-old Billy also lives with the Quinns, but he has fallen on hard times because Broadway and its bars, betting rooms, pool halls, and card games are all closing down, or, as he confesses to Orson, " 'I never could hold a job. I never knew how to do nothin'. I couldn't even stay in the army. I got eye trouble and they sent me home after eight months. . . . I could always get a buck around Broadway but now there ain't no Broadway.' " Yet, as he does in *Billy Phelan's Greatest Game,* Billy still lives by his stylized code of honor, and he is still resilient.

Molly secretly marries Walter Mangan, whom she meets and falls in love with at the Grand View Lake House. Although Walter is killed in a car crash and their child, whom Molly buries in the Phelan cellar, is stillborn, Molly survives her fits of melancholy and depression – her fall into darkness – and reestablishes purpose and meaning in her life by first nursing the injured Thomas and then caring for Orson after his second plunge into madness. Despite his age and heart condition, Peter dedicates himself to his art and manages to transcend the pall hanging over the Phelan family and house.

In an episode reminiscent of the frolic at the conclusion of *Quinn's Book, Very Old Bones* ends af-

firmatively with the family gathering on 26 July 1958, during which they feast on roast lamb, Sarah's mint jelly, new peas, and mashed potatoes, all prepared in the Phelan kitchen. Before the meal, however, Roger Dailey, Peter's lawyer, reads Peter's will, in which he bequeaths his money to Chick, Molly, Billy, and Peg. Peter names Orson as executor of his estate, acknowledges that Orson is his "true and only son," and asks him to change his legal name to Orson Michael Phelan. According to Orson, Peter's artwork and bequests were creative and a "form of atonement after contemplating what wreckage was left in the wake of the behavior of the males in the family: Malachi's lunacy, Michael's mindless martyring of Sarah, Francis's absence of so many years, the imploding Chick, Peter's own behavior as son, husband, father: in sum, a pattern of abdication, or flight, or exile, with the women left behind to pick up the pieces of fractured life." Other suggestions of affirmation in the novel's conclusion are that Giselle is pregnant, young Danny Quinn is going to marry, and George Quinn has asked Patsy McCall for a job.

Kennedy remarked that the original working title of the novel was *Old Bones,* but then he added *Very.* As he explained to Smith – who asked, "Why *Very Old Bones?*" – "Well, the story of Malachi, and the dredging up of that skeleton in the family closet, so to speak, I felt that was one element of bones. There were other bones. There were the mastodon bones . . . also Billy's broken leg, Tommy's chipped backbone, and Peter's arthritic hips, and the corpse of the infant in the cellar." By extension, "old bones" are also evident when Orson writes about disasters that burrow "under the foundation" and gnaw "away at the entire substructure" of the Phelan house. These "very old bones" are the foundation of the Phelan family, whose members must transcend them in order to establish purpose and meaning in their lives. And all of them eventually do.

In establishing Albany as a sense of place, *Very Old Bones* is just as strong as, if not stronger than, *Billy Phelan's Greatest Game* and *Ironweed. Very Old Bones,* however, is set in the 1950s, when the Albany of the last three decades was changing rapidly, and change is always a major theme in Kennedy's works. Not only are the politicians closing down the gambling, but other significant events also occur. The North Albany Filtration Plant is being demolished, and The Wheelbarrow – the saloon operated by Iron Joe Farrell, Annie's father – now houses the truckers' union: "Trucking companies had replaced the lumber yards as the commerce along Erie Boulevard, the filled-in bed of the old canal." Louie's poolroom is closed; Sport Schindler's, once a Broadway hot spot, is now a "haven for the aging population of Broadway"; and at Becker's Tavern no one notices the 1932 photographic mural of the men with the gold stars on their chests. More important, Colonie Street is changing. For example, blacks are moving in, "creating a new world order, displacing the old Irish and Germans," and even Patsy McCall and his wife are moving out after forty-four years on Colonie Street.

Very Old Bones also reinforces Kennedy's Albany-cycle novels not only by interconnecting places such as those mentioned above but also through events in the Phelans' lives. In both Billy Phelan's Greatest Game and Ironweed, for example, Francis and Billy row down Broadway during the 1913 flood to pick up Peter at Keeler's Hotel for Men Only and take him to Union Station to board a train for New York City. Very Old Bones details why Peter left the Phelan house after a fight with his mother and Sarah about the Daughertys, Edward and Katrina, whom his mother and sister call "a family of filth . . . an evil man . . . a low woman . . . a vile slut . . . a corrupter of innocents." Moreover, additional details about Francis Phelan's life unfold. When Sarah tells the whole family about Francis's affair with Katrina Daugherty and he calls Sarah a " 'bitch . . . you stinkin' little sister bitch,' " Kathryn Phelan knocks Francis into the china cabinet. When Francis returns for his mother's funeral in 1934, Sarah shuns him and will not let him stay: " 'He's not part of this family and hasn't been for over thirty years. Feed him if you like, but that's all he gets out of us.' " At the 1958 family gathering Billy supplies the last bit of information about his father's life. Francis came back in 1942, when Billy was drafted, and, even though Francis lived at Hoffman's Hotel near the ballpark, he "stayed close" to Annie until he died of the heart attack while coaching third base.

As with Kennedy's other novels, Very Old Bones had its detractors and acclaimers. In the Christian Science Monitor (12 May 1992) Merle Rubin said that the novel "promises more than it delivers" and that its main weaknesses are its "stereotyped characters" and the "self-important, pseudo-aesthetic posturing of it all." In the Memphis Commercial Appeal (28 June 1992) Donald La Badie wrote that Very Old Bones reads as if it were written "because it was time to publish again" and that Orson is a "flat, derivative character whose life lacks the urgency needed to carry the narrative." La Badie adds that, while the opening of the grave of Molly's stillborn child does

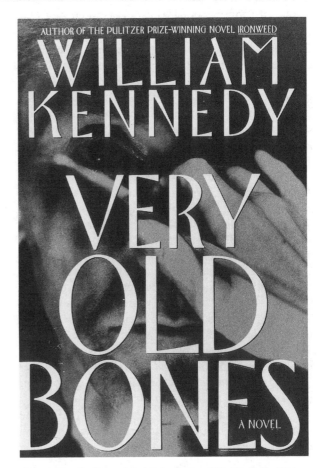

Dust jacket for Kennedy's 1992 novel, which details the history of an Albany family from 1813 through the 1950s

produce a "kind of Greek catharsis," this "finale is so unrelated to the quality of the preceding action, it can't rescue a weak book." In the Times Literary Supplement (21 August 1992) John Sutherland claimed that the novel's form is "not entirely successful," that the "interior monologue encourages flights of artificially literary writing," and that the reader "misses the racy dialogue and picaresque adventures which propel Ironweed."

In Commonweal (22 May 1992) – while claiming that Very Old Bones contains the "scrabble wit, verbal grace, and classicism" of all of Kennedy's works – Paul Elie, a native Albanian, faulted the novel because it "lacks the significant form of Kennedy's previous books; and it is hard not to wonder if its pastiche structure reflects not so much an Albany Irishman's response to the ghosts of his past as the successful novelist's response to the busy schedule of his present." On the other hand, in the New York Times Book Review (10 May 1992) Maureen Howard praised the novel as a "grand leap, the very best of William Kennedy's work so far." In Library Journal

(1 March 1992) Michael Rogers recommended *Very Old Bones:* "Though not a genuine masterpiece like *Ironweed* . . . this book is still moving, sometimes bleak and difficult but often humorous, much like the Phelans themselves. The Phelans can claim a place beside O'Neill's Tyrones and Steinbeck's Joads as one of the premier families of American literature who endure and . . . prevail. If you think great books are no longer being written, reading William Kennedy will change your mind."

In 1993 Kennedy was elected to the American Academy of Arts and Letters. That year he also completed a three-act play, "The Angels and the Sparrows" (the first act is his "Dinner at the Phelans" [1993], somewhat changed). Both plays are taken from *Very Old Bones.* Capitol Repertory Company, an Albany theater group, has received a one-hundred-thousand-dollar grant to produce a play co-authored by Kennedy and Romulus Linney. This play will be based on Kennedy's work and his knowledge of Albany. Kennedy and his only son, Brendan, have collaborated on two children's books, *Charlie Malarkey and the Belly-Button Machine* (1986) and *Charlie Malarkey and the Singing Moose* (1994).

When Smith asked Kennedy whether he would exhaust his Albany-cycle material if he lived to be 150 years old, Kennedy replied:

> I think I have an awful lot of books in my head. . . . If I lived to be 150, which is not that far away, it's only 86 years, I have maybe five books right at this moment that I could begin to focus on. There's always five out there somehow. Because the more I go, the more I learn about these various moments in history, and then more and more people demand attention. I mean, Quinn in *Quinn's Book* is an incomplete character. Whatever happened to him? Well, I'm going to have to figure that out sooner or later. Whatever happened to Maud? Where did George Quinn come from? Where did Danny Quinn come from? Six novels. I forgot about Puerto Rico. Somewhere I've got to do Puerto Rico, but I don't know how, and I'll probably be as transient about it as I was in the treatment of Germany . . . I have a political novel about Dan O'Connell, the old Albany political boss and all of that crowd.

And so Kennedy is indeed alive, well (even with two new artificial hip joints), and still writing. He is presently focusing on a novel about the making of *The Flaming Corsage,* the play mentioned in *Billy Phelan's Greatest Game,* and the beginning of America's silent-movie era. He is also contemplating a novel about race and religion in the 1960s. Then, of course, he could continue to write about the Phelans, the Quinns, the Daughertys, and Albany – in all of which, as he affirms in *O Albany!,* Kennedy "finds all the elements that a man ever needs for the life of the soul."

Interviews:

Irene Stokvis, "First Novelists: Twenty-Five New Writers – Fall 1969 – Discuss Their First Published Novels," *Library Journal,* 94 (1 October 1969): 3475;

Joseph Barbato, "*PW* Interviews William Kennedy," *Publishers Weekly,* 224 (9 December 1983): 52–53;

Larry McCaffery and Sinda Gregory, "An Interview with William Kennedy," *Fiction International,* 15, no. 1 (1984): 157–159; reprinted in *Alive and Writing: Interviews with American Authors of the 1980s* (Chicago: University of Illinois Press, 1987), pp. 151–174;

Kay Bonnetti, "William Kennedy: An Interview," *Missouri Review,* 8, no. 2 (1985): 71–86;

David Thomson, "The Man Has Legs: William Kennedy Interviewed," *Film Comment,* 21 (March–April 1985): 54–59;

Peter J. Quinn, "William Kennedy: An Interview," *Recorder: A Journal of the American Irish Historical Society,* 1 (Winter 1985): 65–81;

Patrick Farrelly, "Francis Phelan Goes Hollywood," *Irish America* (November 1987): 25–29, 51;

Kim Heron, "The Responsibility of Carrying the Dead," *New York Times Book Review,* 22 May 1988, p. 4;

Stephan Salisbury, "William Kennedy's Moveable Feast," *Philadelphia Inquirer,* 31 July 1988, pp. 36, 38, 43;

Edward C. Reilly, "On an Averill Park Afternoon with William Kennedy," *South Carolina Review,* 21 (Spring 1989): 11–24;

Douglas R. Allen and Mona Simpson, "The Art of Fiction CXI – William Kennedy," *Paris Review,* 31 (Fall 1989): 35–59;

Tom Smith, "Very Bountiful Bones: An Interview with William Kennedy," *Weber Studies,* 10 (Winter 1993): 21–44;

Don Williams, "William Kennedy: An Interview by Don Williams," *Poets & Writers,* 22 (March/April 1994): 42–49.

Bibliography:

Edward C. Reilly, "A William Kennedy Bibliography," *Bulletin of Bibliography,* 48 (June 1991): 61–74.

References:

John Affleck, "Novelist William Kennedy Is Back on Turf," *Jonesboro* (Arkansas) *Sun,* 26 April 1992, p. B15;

Susan Agrest, "Tough Guy with a Golden Touch," *Hudson Valley Magazine* (July 1987): 42–49, 72;

Douglas Bauer, "Talking with William Kennedy," *Washington Book World,* 13 (16 January 1983): 6;

Bill Beuttler, "O Albany," *American Way,* 26 (1 January 1993): 60–66, 85–87;

David Black, "The Fusion of Past and Present in William Kennedy's *Ironweed,*" *Critique,* 27 (Spring 1986): 177–184;

Peter P. Clarke, "Classical Myth in William Kennedy's *Ironweed,*" *Critique,* 27 (Spring 1986): 167–176;

Geneva Collins, "Novel Blends Styles: Author Idolizes William Faulkner," *Jonesboro Sun,* 24 July 1988, p. C3;

Margaret Croyden, "The Sudden Fame of William Kennedy," *New York Times Magazine,* 26 August 1984, pp. 33, 43, 52–53, 57, 59, 64, 68, 70, 73;

Claudio Edinger, *The Making of Ironweed* (New York: Penguin, 1988);

Robert Gibb, "The Life of the Soul: William Kennedy, Magical Realist," Ph.D. dissertation, Lehigh University, 1986;

Paul F. Griffin, "The Moral Implications of Annie Phelan's Jello," *San Jose Studies,* 14 (1988): 85–95;

Griffin, "Susan Sontag, Francis Phelan, and the Moral Implications of Photographs," *Midwest Quarterly,* 29 (1988): 194–202;

George W. Hunt, "William Kennedy's Albany Trilogy," *America,* 150 (19 May 1984): 373–375;

Hunt and Peter Quinn, "William Kennedy's Albany," *America,* 150 (17 March 1984): 189–191;

Richard Jameson, "It Is, Too, Good," *Film Comment,* 21 (March–April 1985): 51–53;

Elaine Kendall, "Albany Is His Kind of Community: James Joyce Has Dublin; Author Kennedy Has NY Capitol," *Los Angeles Times,* 10 February 1984, V: 12–13;

Dardis McNamee, "The Making of *Ironweed,*" *Capitol Region Magazine,* 3 (December 1987): 44–50;

"Men's Libraries: Five Passionate Collectors Invite You to Browse," *Gentleman's Quarterly,* 58 (January 1988): 154–159;

Daniel Martin Murtaugh, "Fathers and Their Sons: William Kennedy's Hero-Transgressors," *Commonweal,* 116 (19 May 1989): 298–302;

Loxley F. Nichols, "William Kennedy Comes of Age," *National Review,* 37 (9 August 1985): 46–48;

Terrence Petty, "Once Ignored, Kennedy's Now a Writer Besieged," *Times-Picayune* (New Orleans), 6 May 1984, III: 11;

Peter S. Prescott and Agrest, "Having the Time of His Life," *Newsweek,* 103 (6 February 1984): 78–79;

Kit Rachlis, "It's About Time, Part I: Kennedy and the Week That Was," *Boston Phoenix,* 24 May 1983, pp. 1–2;

Rachlis, "It's About Time, Part II: Kennedy and the Years That Were," *Boston Phoenix,* 31 May 1983, pp. 2–3;

Edward C. Reilly, "Dante's *Purgatorio* and Kennedy's *Ironweed:* Journeys to Redemption," *Notes on Contemporary Literature,* 17 (May 1987): 5–8;

Reilly, "The Pigeons and Circular Flight in Kennedy's *Ironweed,*" *Notes on Contemporary Literature,* 16 (March 1986): 8;

Reilly, *William Kennedy* (Boston: Twayne, 1991);

Reilly, "William Kennedy's Albany Trilogy: Cutting Through the Sludge," *Publications of the Arkansas Philological Association,* 12 (Spring 1986): 43–55;

Michael Robertson, "The Reporter as Novelist: The Case of William Kennedy," *Columbia Journalism Review,* 24 (January–February 1986): 49–50, 52;

Michael Ryan, "The Making of *Ironweed,*" *People,* 29 (18 January 1988): 84–87;

Alvin P. Sanoff, "A Novelist's Need to Go Home Again," *U.S. News & World Report,* 104 (20 June 1988): 66;

R. Z. Sheppard, "A Winning Rebel with a Lost Cause," *Time,* 124 (1 October 1984): 79–80;

Curt Suplee, "The Bard of Albany: Novelist William Kennedy and His Spurt of Success," *Washington Post,* 28 December 1983, pp. B1, B9;

William Tierce, "William Kennedy's Odyssey: The Travels of Francis Phelan," *Classical and Modern Literature,* 8 (Summer 1988): 247–263;

J. K. Van Dover, *Understanding William Kennedy* (Columbia: University of South Carolina Press, 1991);

Stephen Whittaker, "The Lawyer as Narrator in William Kennedy's *Legs,*" *Legal Studies Forum,* 9, no. 2 (1985): 157–164.

Stephen King

(21 September 1947 –   )

Carol A. Senf
Georgia Institute of Technology

See also the King entry in *DLB Yearbook: 1980*.

BOOKS: *Carrie* (Garden City, N.Y.: Doubleday, 1974; London: New English Library, 1977);

'Salem's Lot (Garden City, N.Y.: Doubleday, 1975; London: New English Library, 1976);

Rage, as Richard Bachman (New York: New American Library/Signet, 1977);

The Shining (Garden City, N.Y.: Doubleday, 1977; London: New English Library, 1977);

The Stand (Garden City, N.Y.: Doubleday, 1978; London: New English Library, 1979); revised and enlarged as *The Stand: The Complete and Uncut Edition* (Garden City, N.Y.: Doubleday, 1990);

Night Shift (Garden City, N.Y.: Doubleday, 1978; London: New English Library, 1978);

The Dead Zone (New York: Viking, 1979; London: Macdonald & Jane's, 1979);

The Long Walk, as Bachman (New York: New American Library, 1979);

Firestarter (New York: Viking, 1980; London: Macdonald Futura, 1980);

Cujo (New York: Viking, 1981; London: Macdonald, 1982);

Danse Macabre (New York: Random House, 1981; London: Macdonald, 1981);

Roadwork, as Bachman (New York: New American Library/Signet, 1981);

Stephen King's Creepshow (New York: New American Library, 1982);

The Dark Tower: The Gunslinger (West Kingston, R.I.: Donald M. Grant, 1982);

Different Seasons (New York: Viking, 1982; London: Macdonald, 1982);

The Running Man, as Bachman (New York: New American Library/Signet, 1982; London: New English Library, 1983);

Christine (New York: Viking, 1983; London: Hodder & Stoughton, 1983);

Stephen King

Cycle of the Werewolf (Westland, Mich.: Land of Enchantment, 1983); revised and enlarged as *Silver Bullet* (New York: Signet, 1985);

Pet Sematary (Garden City, N.Y.: Doubleday, 1983; London: Hodder & Stoughton, 1983);

The Eyes of the Dragon (Bangor, Maine: Philtrum Press, 1984; revised and enlarged edition, New York: Viking, 1987; London: Macdonald, 1987);

The Talisman, by King and Peter Straub (New York: Viking, 1984; New York: Putnam, 1984);

Thinner, as Bachman (New York: New American Library, 1984; London: New English Library, 1985);

The Bachman Books (New York: New American Library, 1985);

Skeleton Crew (New York: Putnam, 1985; London: Macdonald, 1985);

IT (New York: Viking, 1986; London: Hodder, 1986);

The Dark Tower II: The Drawing of the Three (West Kingston, R.I.: Donald M. Grant, 1987);

Misery (New York: Viking, 1987; London: Hodder, 1987);

The Tommyknockers (New York: Putnam, 1987; London: New English Library, 1989);

The Dark Half (New York: Viking, 1989; London: Hodder, 1989);

Dolan's Cadillac (Northridge, Cal.: Lord John Press, 1989);

My Pretty Pony (New York: Whitney Museum, 1989; New York: Knopf, 1989);

Four Past Midnight (New York: Viking, 1990; London: Hodder, 1990);

The Dark Tower III: The Wastelands (Hampton Falls, N.H.: Donald M. Grant, 1991);

Needful Things (New York: Viking, 1991; London: Hodder, 1991);

Gerald's Game (New York: Viking, 1992; London: Hodder, 1992);

Dolores Claiborne (New York: Viking, 1993; London: Hodder, 1993);

Nightmares and Dreamscapes (New York: Viking, 1993).

MOTION PICTURES: *Creepshow,* Warner Bros., 1982;

Cat's Eye, M-G-M/United Artists, 1985;

Stephen King's Silver Bullet, Paramount, 1985;

Maximum Overdrive, written and directed by King, De Laurentiis, 1986;

Pet Sematary, Paramount, 1989;

Stephen King's Sleepwalkers, Columbia, 1992.

TELEVISION: "Sorry, Right Number," *Tales from the Darkside,* 20 November 1987;

Stephen King's Golden Years, 16 July to 22 August 1991;

Stephen King's The Stand, 8, 9, 11, and 12 May 1994.

RECORDINGS: *The Dark Tower: The Gunslinger,* cassette read by King, NAL, 1988;

The Dark Tower II: The Drawing of the Three, cassette read by King, NAL, 1989;

The Dark Tower III: The Wastelands, cassette read by King, Penguin, 1991;

Needful Things, cassette read by King, Penguin, 1991.

Stephen King has written twenty-six novels (including five under the pen name Richard Bachman), five collections of short fiction, one book of criticism, six screenplays, and other short works. According to Stephen J. Spignesi in *The Shape Under the Sheet: The Complete Stephen King Encyclopedia* (1991), which details King's work up to 1990, King is best known as a best-selling novelist: "Of the top twenty-five *Publishers Weekly* fiction best-sellers of the eighties, Stephen King had seven titles on the list: *The Dark Half, The Tommyknockers, IT, Misery, The Talisman, The Eyes of the Dragon,* and *Skeleton Crew.* The twenty-five titles on the list sold a combined total of 25,889,924 copies. Of that total, 7,269,929 — or twenty-eight percent — were Stephen King titles." However, while he earned his reputation as a writer of genre fiction, especially of horror and fantasy, and remains identified as such, many of King's recent novels might be classified as mainstream fiction. Some of his works include material that links him to such local-color and regional writers as Sherwood Anderson, Eudora Welty, and Mary E. Wilkins Freeman. Perhaps even more important than his work within various traditions is that he has mapped out new areas in American literature by combining supernatural horror with careful analysis of small-town life and by mingling sword-and-sorcery fantasy with science fiction.

Born in Portland, Maine, on 21 September 1947, King is the second son of Donald Edwin King, a master mariner in the U.S. Merchant Marine, and Nellie Ruth Pillsbury King. His father abandoned the family when King was two, and King remembers nothing of him except for finding a box of his books (paperbacks from the 1940s, including a sampler of stories from *Weird Tales* magazine and stories by H. P. Lovecraft) in 1959 or 1960, an experience he relates in *Danse Macabre* (1981). King's mother was more influential, reading to him and later encouraging him to submit his manuscripts to publishers. She died of cancer in 1973, before King was recognized as a writer. He has dedicated two books to her, including *Dolores Claiborne* (1993).

King, his mother, and his older brother, David Victor, lived with relatives in Durham, Maine; Malden, Massachusetts; Chicago; West De Pere, Wisconsin; Stratford, Connecticut; and Fort

Wayne, Indiana. Nellie Ruth King, whom King describes in *Danse Macabre* as a "talented pianist and a woman with a great and sometimes eccentric sense of humor," kept the family together by working at a succession of low-paying jobs. In 1958 the family moved to Durham, Maine (later fictionalized as Castle Rock, Maine), to care for her parents. King finished elementary school in a one-room building in Durham and attended high school in nearby Lisbon Falls. He gained his first experience as a professional writer while still in high school, covering high-school sports for the *Lisbon Enterprise.* In 1965 he published his first story, "I Was a Teenage Grave Robber," in *Comics Review,* a fan magazine, and wrote his first novel-length manuscript, "The Aftermath," about life after an atomic-bomb explosion.

King received a scholarship to the University of Maine at Orono. He majored in English and minored in speech; wrote a column, "King's Garbage Truck," for the *Maine Campus,* the student newspaper; and participated in student politics and the antiwar movement. During this period he also published the first fiction for which he was paid, "The Glass Floor," in *Startling Mystery Stories* (Fall 1967). While still an undergraduate, King taught a seminar, Popular Literature and Culture, after criticizing the English department's traditional approach to literature. He graduated in 1970 and, unable to find a teaching job, pumped gas and worked in a laundry, experiences he later incorporated into his fiction.

On 2 January 1971 King married Tabitha Jane Spruce, whom he had met in college. King writes fondly of her in "Why I Was Bachman," the introduction to *The Bachman Books* (1985): "The only important thing I ever did in my life for a conscious reason was to ask Tabitha Spruce ... if she would marry me." Also a novelist, Tabitha King has written *Small World* (1981), *Caretakers* (1983), *The Trap* (1985), *Pearl* (1988), and *One on One* (1993). King speaks warmly of their marriage and has dedicated five books to her as well as books to each of their children – Naomi Rachel King, Joseph Hillstrom King, and Owen Phillip King. The family resides at 47 West Broadway, Bangor, Maine.

Before the sale of the paperback rights to *Carrie* (1974) to the New American Library in 1973 allowed him to become a full-time writer, King taught at the Hampden Academy in Hampden, Maine. In 1978 he was writer in residence and instructor at the University of Maine at Orono. Both because of a course he taught there and because Bill Thompson, who edited King's

first five books at Doubleday, invited him to write about the horror genre, King produced *Danse Macabre,* which analyzes horror in literature, film, and other popular culture.

King is identified as a writer of horror fiction primarily because the first three novels he published under his own name were in that genre; ten later books, along with all his screenplays, fall into that genre. Moreover, some of his nonfictional works, including *Danse Macabre* and a 1973 essay, "The Horror Writer and the Ten Bears," reveal his familiarity with that tradition. The essay describes his personal fears in ascending order of importance – fear *for* someone else, fear of others, fear of death, fear of insects, fear of closed-in places, fear of rats, fear of snakes, fear of deformity, fear of "squishy" things, and fear of the dark – and readers can find evidence of his personal apprehensions in works other than his horror fiction.

Readers can also detect his awareness of traditional horror literature, especially in his early works. For example, *'Salem's Lot* (1975) reveals what happens when a vampire moves to a small Maine town, and *Cycle of the Werewolf* (1983) also transports a traditional monster to contemporary America. Both *The Shining* (1977) and *The Talisman* (1984), which was written in collaboration with Peter Straub, feature haunted houses, while *Pet Sematary* (1983) is centered on the Native American legend of the Wendigo (a flesh-devouring natural spirit) as well as the more general fear of ghosts returning to haunt their former loved ones. *Needful Things* (1991) features the devil, and *IT* (1986) incorporates traditional monsters, including the vampire, the werewolf, and the alien.

In addition to horror novels King has written science fiction, although not the kind of "hard" science fiction associated with Robert A. Heinlein. *The Tommyknockers* (1987) reveals what happens when residents of a small town find a spaceship; *IT* presents a decidedly malevolent alien. Both *The Stand* (1978) and *Firestarter* (1980) examine what happens when science rages out of control. *Christine* (1983) presents a scenario in which a machine gains power.

Other works by King might be classified as fantasy. *The Talisman,* an epic-quest romance, pits a boy named Jack Sawyer against dark, ominous forces. The object of Jack's quest is a mysterious talisman, his mother's only hope to survive cancer. Obviously influenced by Mark Twain's *The Adventures of Tom Sawyer* (1876) and *The Adventures of Huckleberry Finn* (1885), *The Talisman* explores the world of childhood as well as the genre of epic fantasy.

King (right) signing a copy of Pet Sematary, *3 December 1983 (Gannett)*

The Dark Tower trilogy, which King promises will ultimately number seven or eight volumes, combines elements of science fiction, the Western, and fantasy, and *The Eyes of the Dragon* (1984), often mistaken for a children's story, resembles J. R. R. Tolkien's *The Lord of the Rings* (1954–1955).

Several of King's novels defy classification, among them *Christine* – whose chief character may be a demon, a vampire, or a technological fantasy – and *Cujo* (1981), which seems to be mainstream though it contains elements of fantasy and horror. In addition, King – who came to political awareness during the Vietnam War era and named his older son Joseph Hillstrom King after Joe Hill, a Swedish-American union organizer and hero of radical labor – often combines political analysis with horror to create a new genre that might be termed political horror. *The Stand, Firestarter,* and *The Dead Zone* (1979) all suggest that the government is more horrifying than any supernatural monster.

King has also written six psychological novels: *Dolores Claiborne, Misery* (1987), *Gerald's Game* (1992), *Rage* (1977), *The Long Walk* (1979), and *Roadwork* (1981) – the latter three as Richard Bachman. *Misery* focuses on the novelist Paul Sheldon and the deranged Annie Wilkes, Sheldon's number

one fan. *Gerald's Game* and *Dolores Claiborne* deal with women as outsiders. Like *The Shining,* both novels expose the seamy underside of seemingly normal families and the horrors of child abuse. In the three Bachman books ordinary people must confront more than they can endure. In *Rage,* for example, a teenager shoots two teachers and holds his fellow students hostage. *Roadwork* features a middle-aged man whose job and home are threatened by the construction of a new highway. *The Long Walk,* which takes place in the near future, examines one hundred young men who enter a race knowing that the winner will receive a prize but all the losers will die. Despite their sometimes extreme situations and future settings, these novels can be described as mainstream literature rather than horror, science fiction, or fantasy.

King keeps returning to such subjects as growing up in the 1950s, life in small towns, the devastating impact of politics on ordinary human beings, technology in modern life, childhood (especially in *Carrie, Cujo,* and *IT*), and parenthood (especially in *The Shining, Cujo, Pet Sematary,* and *The Dark Half,* 1989). Moreover, *Misery* and *The Dark Half* explore writing and the powerful relationships that writers have with their fans. Regardless of their subjects,

King's novels display a strong moral bent, a sympathy for working people and residents of small towns, and a sensitivity to the often extreme cruelty of the ordinary world.

Although many of King's novels stem from his personal experiences as a boy growing up in Maine, as a working man with too many debts and too few opportunities, as a parent, and ultimately as a writer whose fame occasionally overwhelms him, others examine the lives of young women growing up in the United States. This trend begins with his first novel, *Carrie,* and continues to the recent *Dolores Claiborne.* In between are *The Stand,* in which one major character is a pregnant adolescent; *Firestarter,* whose main character is a girl with the mental ability to set fires; *Cujo,* whose heroine and her son are trapped in her broken-down Pinto by a rabid Saint Bernard; and *Gerald's Game,* whose protagonist, handcuffed to the bedposts by her aging husband, must face her past as a sexually abused child and a future without her husband. *The Shining* presents a mother who is willing to fight to save her son's life; the group of heroic children in *IT* includes one girl; and female characters in *Needful Things* and *Dolores Claiborne* face disturbing truths about themselves. Although many of King's earlier works are limited to a focus on women who are strong in their traditional maternal role, King seems to be moving to a full exploration of feminine consciousness and everything that lies behind women's public personas.

King is a compulsive writer who works 362 days a year. The exceptions are his birthday, Christmas, and the Fourth of July. Furthermore, although critics generally describe him as a storyteller rather than a craftsman, he has scrapped entire novels that failed to meet his standards. King wrote the basic story for *Carrie,* his first published novel, during summer 1972 but discarded it until Tabitha King rescued it from the trash can and encouraged him to continue. The result was a twenty-five-thousand-word story, too long to be a short story and too short to be a novel until King adopted the strategy – used by John Dos Passos in *U.S.A.* (1938) and by Bram Stoker in *Dracula* (1897) – of supplementing the main narrative with documentation from a variety of publications. In *Carrie* this technique provides both length and a neutral perspective on the horrifying main story, producing what Douglas E. Winter describes as King's "most eccentric" novel. Combining traditional narrative with newspaper clippings, letters, and other documentation presents a "cacophony of perspectives on an otherwise brief and simplistic story."

King sent the manuscript to William Thompson at Doubleday, and Thompson asked him to rewrite the last section. The popularity of Ira Levin's *Rosemary's Baby* (1967), William Peter Blatty's *The Exorcist* (1971), and Thomas Tryon's *The Other* (1971) had generated interest in horror fiction among publishers. Some reviewers of *Carrie* appreciated the horror of the title character's life and death, while others bemoaned the violence in the novel. The hardcover edition sold a modest thirteen thousand copies, but the paperback edition, published in April 1975, initially sold more than a million copies. In 1976 – when *'Salem's Lot* was published in paperback and a paperback edition of *Carrie* was released in conjunction with Brian De Palma's film adaptation – King became a best-selling author. The two paperback editions of *Carrie* sold more than 3.5 million copies.

King's first novel shares characteristics with much of his following fiction. In addition to its emphasis on horror and the supernatural, *Carrie* reveals King's concern with adolescence and his empathy with women. The novel examines female power, for Carrie gains her telekinetic abilities with her first menstruation, as well as women's roles within the community. Carrie's mother is particularly hateful; religious fundamentalism causes her to deny her sexuality and to insist that Carrie also repress her womanliness.

Carrie, however, does more than explore stereotypes; it is a compelling character study of a persecuted teenager who finally uses her powers to turn the table on her persecutors. The result is a violent explosion that destroys the mother who had taught her self-hatred and the high-school peers who had made her a scapegoat. The novel pits the individual against the group. King reveals the intensity of the pressure to belong – even when the group is clearly immoral or hostile – for it affects all the attractive characters in the novel, such as the popular Susan Snell and Tommy Ross as well as Carrie White. King returns to the theme of the individual besieged by the community in his later fiction, perhaps most strongly in *The Tommyknockers.*

King wrote *'Salem's Lot,* his second published novel, in 1973. Originally titled "Second Coming" and written just after he had sold *Carrie* to Doubleday, *'Salem's Lot* also examines conformity and community forces. In fact, the idea for the novel came from a conversation about community. King, his wife, and their friend Chris Chesley wondered what might happen if Dracula returned to contemporary America. Rooted in an awareness of Stoker's classic novel, *'Salem's Lot* is, like *Dracula,* concerned with the vampire as a physical embodiment of whatever traits human beings fear most. Stoker, for example, emphasizes Dracula's primitive nature and the fact that he comes from the mysterious East; King, on the other hand, reveals that the vampire is one's neighbor or one's friend. Stoker's ordinary characters are confronted with a figure of immense supernatural power, but King is more interested in examining ordinary small-town characters and exposing the evil in them, a topic he pursues in such novels as *The Tommyknockers* and *Needful Things.* *'Salem's Lot* explores the power of goodness, for the novelist Ben Mears and the child Mark Petrie escape the conflagration that destroys their community and spend their lives tracking down and annihilating the vampires in their midst.

While *'Salem's Lot* sold a respectable twenty-six thousand copies in hardcover, the paperback edition topped the *New York Times* best-seller list. In "Why I Was Bachman" King explains that his publishers thought he was saturating the market, a situation that prompted him to adopt a pseudonym. This introduction also provides background on *Rage,* his third published novel, begun in 1966 when he was a senior in high school. He reworked it during his junior year in college and finished it in 1971. Primarily a first-person narrative, *Rage* involves a high-school boy, Charlie Decker, who brings a gun to school, kills two teachers, and holds his classmates hostage for a day. Like *The Shining, Roadwork,* and *Misery,* the novel is a study of madness. Chapter 1 begins with Charlie's referring to "the time I started to lose my mind," and both he and fellow classmate Ted Jones wind up in the state mental hospital.

Despite its careful look at two people who are diagnosed as insane, *Rage* is also a story of adolescence, especially of adolescence during the Vietnam War era. Charlie distrusts his father and other authority figures, whom King presents as either corrupt or drunk with power. Charlie's father – who has made a career out of the navy, ending up as a recruiter – is a dull man who bullies Charlie and his mother. Recognized by *Publishers Weekly* (25 July 1977) as the work of a fledgling writer, *Rage* received relatively little critical attention, and King explains that none of the Bachman books sold well because they were published without fanfare.

The Shining, King's third novel published under his own name, was his longest to that date and would have been longer if he had not accepted his editor's request to remove its prologue, "Before the Play," and original epilogue, "After the Play." Sell-

ing fifty thousand copies in hardback and 2.3 million in paperback, it was the first King book to hit the *New York Times* best-seller list for hardcover fiction. Like *'Salem's Lot, The Shining* reveals King's awareness of the horror tradition. The setting, the Overlook Hotel, which is closed for the winter, resembles both a Gothic castle and a haunted house. King imprints his own brand of horror on the traditional horror story, for *The Shining* combines monstrous and horrifying images (such as topiary animals that suddenly come to life, corridors that fill with blood, and elevators that begin moving autonomously) with the human drama of the Torrance family.

Jack Torrance is a recovering alcoholic, and his job at the Overlook is his last chance to establish himself as a writer and to renew his relationship with his wife, Wendy, and their five-year-old son, Danny, a psychic receptor who can see the paranormal world. Jack's weaknesses make it easy for evil forces at the Overlook to influence him and to use him to try to channel Danny's extraordinary powers. Despite these supernatural elements and the Gothic backdrop, the novel emphasizes the human drama – Jack's love for his family, his alcoholism, and his potential for abuse; Wendy's discovery of her strength; and Danny's growth.

King wrote *The Shining* after moving his family to Colorado in summer 1974 for an extended vacation. There he began a novel, "The House on Value Street," loosely based on the February 1974 kidnapping of newspaper heiress Patty Hearst. A chance stay at a grand old hotel on the day before it closed for the winter convinced King that he had the ideal setting for a horror story.

King's fifth novel, *The Stand,* is different from *The Shining.* While the earlier novel focuses on a single family, *The Stand* deals with the entire human race. In Colorado, King became haunted by news of a biological-warfare chemical spill in Utah that nearly endangered Salt Lake City, and he returned to an idea he explores in "Night Surf " (*Night Shift,* 1978), in which a horrific virus destroys the world's population. Described by Winter in *Stephen King: The Art of Darkness* (1986) as "the first of several highly successful novels that transcended the horror genre and that also explicitly grappled with sociopolitical themes," *The Stand* is an epic quest fantasy that begins when an experimental biological weapon escapes from a secret military installation to destroy most of the human population and concludes when an atomic bomb destroys almost everyone who had survived the flu. Although it resembles other epic fantasies, *The Stand* has a distinctly Amer-

*Dust jacket for King's 1986 novel, about a shape-shifting creature
that dwells in the sewers of a small Maine town and kills children*

ican slant and features uniquely American characters who cross the United States seeking other survivors. Many of them represent positive aspects of American heritage: Stu Redman, a Texas blue-collar worker, is the protagonist and a type of American Adam; Fran Goldsmith, a pregnant Maine college student and ultimately the mother of the first postflu baby, is his Eve. The two are joined by the mute Nick Andros, a self-educated orphan; Tom Cullen, a retarded Oklahoma man; and Glen Bateman, a New Hampshire sociology professor.

Opposing these characters are several negative figures of Americana, most notably Randall Flagg (the Dark Man) and Donald Merwin Elbert (the Trashcan Man, whose pyromania is matched by his instinctive technical wizardry). Since both characters use technology to manipulate people, they reinforce King's notion that science may unleash horrors that human beings cannot control, an idea he

continues to explore in *The Talisman, Firestarter, Roadwork,* and *The Tommyknockers. The Stand,* however, is more than a sociopolitical analysis, for it also examines good and evil on an elemental level. Evil becomes identified with Flagg, a dark, faceless man, and with Las Vegas, whereas good is associated with an old black woman, Mother Abagail, an earth mother who offers sanctuary to those who join her in Boulder.

The Stand received generally positive reviews, but neither readers nor reviewers knew that King deleted approximately four hundred manuscript pages from the final draft in order to keep the book's retail price down. King restored these pages in *The Stand: The Complete and Uncut Edition* (1990).

If *The Stand* includes elements of fantasy, King's next novel, *The Dead Zone,* is realistic, and the lives of its limited cast of characters are realistic despite its central premise that the protagonist can see the past or future of people and objects by touching them. Aside from his paranormal ability, John Smith is a modern Everyman. At the beginning of the novel he is a twenty-two-year-old high-school English teacher in love with Sarah Bracknell, another teacher. Returning home one evening he has an automobile accident and spends four years in a coma. When he awakes, Sarah is married; his mother has become a religious fanatic; and the landscape of American culture and politics has changed so much that he has a hard time adjusting: "The world had changed more resoundingly than he would have believed possible in so short a time. He felt out of step and out of tune." John tries to live a normal life but cannot avoid his destiny: he identifies the Castle Rock strangler, warns Chuck Chatsworth that lightning will strike the building where his class is holding its senior party, and finally attempts to assassinate Greg Stillson, a candidate for political office whose handshake reveals both madness and corruption and the fact that he will one day become president of the United States.

Written in 1976 and 1977, *The Dead Zone* – King's first novel after leaving Doubleday for Viking – sold 175,000 copies its first year, indicating that King's novels appealed to readers of mainstream fiction. King confessed that writing *The Stand* had taken so much out of him that he was not able to complete another novel for a while, though he worked on two that he never published, "Welcome to Clearwater" and "The Corner," as well as *The Dead Zone* and *Firestarter.* The two successful novels share many similarities, including an awareness of politics. After coming out of his coma, John Smith must come to terms with such national issues as Watergate, Vietnam, and President Richard Nixon's resignation at the same time he copes with his personal problems.

Unlike *The Dead Zone,* King's second novel as Bachman, *The Long Walk,* appeared without fanfare. Like *Rage,* it was among the five novels King wrote before *Carrie,* and, like *Rage,* it sold poorly. Conceived as King hitchhiked home during his freshman year in college and written the same year, *The Long Walk* is set in a futuristic United States, which has become a military dictatorship. While King's fiction often explores politics, this work emphasizes character. The Long Walk of the title is a contest in which one hundred boys must walk south from northern Maine until only one remains. Those who falter receive three warnings before being shot; the single survivor receives The Prize from the Major, who apparently designed the contest and who represents authority in the novel. As the walk proceeds, sixteen-year-old Ray Garraty, both the survivor and

the novel's central consciousness, and his companions are stripped of everything but their individual identities. Thus it is possible to read their walk or journey as a metaphor for life itself.

Several members of the English department at the University of Maine – Burton Hatlen, Jim Bishop, Edward Holmes, and Carroll Terrell – read the manuscript enthusiastically. Encouraged by them, King submitted it to the Bennett Cerf/Random House first-novel competition. Receiving a form rejection letter, King put the work aside though he continued to like its story. In "Why I Was Bachman" he describes it as "pretty good" because it's "nothing but story," though he confesses that both it and *Rage* are full of "windy psychological preachments."

King wrote *Firestarter* at the same time as *The Dead Zone* when, after abandoning two novels, he wondered whether he had fallen into self-parody. *Firestarter* examines themes explored in *Carrie* and *The Shining,* though Charlie McGee has greater control over her psychic talent and her opponent is the U.S. government. Its Department of Scientific Intelligence (The Shop) had given her parents an experimental drug when they were college students. A total of twelve students participated in the experiment; two have died, two have become insane, five have committed suicide, and two have married and produced a child with pyrokinetic power, the mental ability to set fires. (The twelfth student was unaffected by the experiment.) Hearing of Charlie's power, The Shop kills her mother and drives her and her father underground; much of the novel focuses on their attempts to elude the government and its agencies. In fact, the afterword to the paperback edition reminds readers of government intervention in their lives: "The U.S. government, or agencies thereof, has indeed administered potentially dangerous drugs to unwitting subjects on more than one occasion."

By emphasizing government's power over individuals, the afterword links the reader to the characters, who, despite their extraordinary abilities, face the same difficulties King's ordinary readers face – financial worries, fear of betrayal by loved ones, and worries about their children. Andy McGee had participated in the experimental program because he was a poor scholarship student. His daughter, Charlie, supposedly modeled on King's daughter, is a normal seven-year-old who loves her father and wants to do the right thing. Only when she is pressured to save herself and her father from capture and death does she unleash her destructive powers. King polished the final draft while teaching two literature courses and two creative-writing seminars at the University of Maine at Orono. *Firestarter* sold 285,000 copies its first year, 110,000 copies more than *The Dead Zone* the previous year.

If *Firestarter* is rooted in ordinary human experience, then *Cujo* is even more solidly rooted in ordinary life. Written in 1977, it anticipates the unrelenting naturalism of King's most recent fiction and may well be his most pessimistic novel. Set in Castle Rock, the novel focuses on two families – the middle-class Trentons (Donna, Vic, and Tad) and the working-class Cambers (Joe, Charity, and Brett) – and emphasizes similarities in the two unhappy marriages. Donna has a brief affair with Steve Kemp, a failed poet who vandalizes her home when she ends their affair. Charity comes to despise Joe for not wanting something better for their son, a subject to which King returns in *Dolores Claiborne*.

The plot links the two families when Donna takes her car to Joe's garage and discovers that Cujo, the Cambers's rabid Saint Bernard, has already killed Joe. Trapped in the Pinto for three July days, she watches Tad suffer before she escapes and kills Cujo with Brett's baseball bat. Her heroic efforts come too late for Tad, however, for he dies during her struggle.

Although King is now uncomfortable with the pessimism of *Cujo*, he regards *Roadwork*, his third novel as Bachman, as one of his least successful works. In "Why I Was Bachman" he explains his evaluation by saying that he wrote it to make sense of his mother's painful death and that "it tries so hard to be good and to find some answers to the conundrum of human pain." Written between *'Salem's Lot* and *The Shining* as an effort to produce a "straight" novel, *Roadwork* presents relentless realism after the fashion of Theodore Dreiser and Frank Norris. The story of Barton George Dawes, *Roadwork* is set in winter 1973, the period when King's mother was dying, and contains other biographical elements. Dawes, as King had once done, works in an industrial laundry; and he is also trying to make sense of death after his son's demise from a brain tumor.

Roadwork continues King's emphasis on politics. A highway extension threatens Dawes with the loss of both his house and his job. King connects those material losses with the loss of something larger when Dawes contemplates that the country has changed during his lifetime through the Kent State massacre, the assassinations of John and Robert Kennedy and Martin Luther King, the Vietnam War, and the energy crisis. The novel concludes when Dawes, whose wife has filed for divorce, confronts the police in a gunfight and commits suicide

by blowing up his house, an act that is a negation rather than a meaningful protest. In fact, Dawes contrasts his plan with the political protest over the Vietnam War, and several characters use the term *roadwork* to describe meaningless labor. The message that life has no meaning is reinforced in the epilogue, which describes "Roadwork," a documentary made after Dawes's death that examined "the necessity – or lack of it – for the 784 extension" and pointed out that building the road "had nothing to do with traffic patterns or commuter convenience or anything else of such a practical sort. The municipality had to build so many miles of road per year or begin losing federal money on all interstate construction."

The Dark Tower: The Gunslinger (1982) has a checkered history. Conceived while King was in college and written over a twelve-year period, the five installments were published in the *Magazine of Fantasy and Science Fiction* in 1980 and 1981 and collected in a first edition of ten thousand hardback copies and a limited edition of five hundred copies signed by King and illustrator Michael Whelan. To pacify King's fans, the publisher brought out a second edition of ten thousand copies. Ultimately the first volume of *The Dark Tower* – whose final form, King notes, will consist of twenty-five interlocking short stories – was published in several trade editions and a set of cassettes read by King.

Inspired by Robert Browning's "Childe Roland to the Dark Tower Came" (*The Ring and the Book*, 1868–1869), *The Dark Tower: The Gunslinger* is set in a postapocalypse wasteland that resembles the setting of *The Stand* and parts of *The Talisman*. Roland, the last gunslinger, searches for the Tower and meets huddled remnants of humanity as well as other, less-than-human creatures. King does not say what is responsible for the devastation, though Roland occasionally sees relics from the present, especially "machines that usually didn't work ... and which sometimes ate the men when they did." Unlike *The Stand*, *Firestarter*, and *The Talisman*, which focus on the dangers of science and technology, *The Dark Tower: The Gunslinger* emphasizes Roland's quest.

The fourth Bachman book, *The Running Man*, shares several obvious characteristics with *The Long Walk*. Both use a deadly game show as a metaphor for human life; and both take place in the future when the problems that confront contemporary America have reached a crisis. *The Running Man* is a darker novel, for King adds pollution and diseases caused by pollution, overcrowding, and hostility between races and classes to the impersonal big government, poverty, and unemploy-

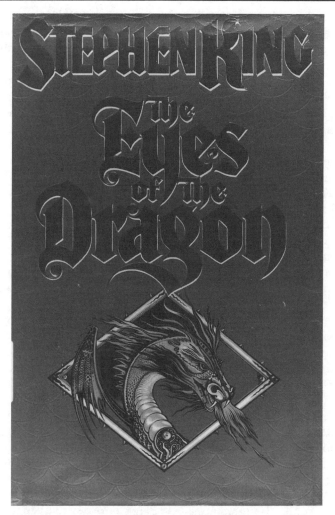

*Dust jacket for the revised and enlarged 1987 edition of King's
1984 fantasy about two children, a prince, and an evil magician*

ment featured in *The Long Walk*. Moreover, *The Running Man* shows how government manipulates people, for it uses television to keep them from asking questions and even issues library cards only to people with a guaranteed income. *The Running Man* was written in 1971, when King was still teaching during the day, writing at night, and receiving rejection letters (in fact, it received King's third rejection in a row from Doubleday). The concerns over money and the general hopelessness that King apparently felt during the period are evident in the novel, which focuses on Ben Richards, who has been blacklisted and is therefore unable to find employment. When his daughter falls ill and his wife turns to prostitution to earn money, he decides to risk his life at the Games to get medicine. The rest of the novel involves his struggle to survive.

Reviewers ignored *The Running Man,* though it was made into a 1987 film starring Arnold Schwarzenegger. In "Why I Was Bachman" King explains that the novel was "written in a period of seventy-two hours and published with virtually no changes," describing it as "nothing but story." However, while its story line is strong, *The Running Man* is also a compelling psychological profile of an interesting character as well as an astute analysis of what the United States could become — a country where class warfare is so rife that people are eager to hunt down and kill the animal they perceive in Ben Richards. By filtering the world through Richards's consciousness, King encourages the reader to identify with Richards's intelligent criticism of the world and also presents the intelligent, individualistic Richards as an anachronism. Thus the reader is not surprised at the conclusion when Richards, learning that his wife and child are dead and that he is fatally wounded, crashes a hijacked plane into the Games Building, destroying it and all the corrupt individuals within.

King began *Christine* in summer 1978 as a short story about a teenage boy and a car whose odometer runs backward. As the car goes backward, the boy gets younger and younger. However, the short story blossomed into a horror novel about America's love affair with automobiles. The main character is a misfit, Arnie Cunningham, who buys a broken-down 1958 Plymouth Fury from Roland LeBay and names it Christine. The story quickly takes on sinister overtones, for the car has miraculous powers. Furthermore – as in several short stories in *Night Shift,* in which machines destroy their human creators, and as in *The Stand* and *Firestarter,* in which technological products assume lives of their own – Christine possesses Arnie, destroys the people around him, and finally destroys Arnie himself.

Christine also exposes the dark side of the 1950s, a period often sentimentally portrayed in such films as *American Graffiti* (1973) and in such television series as *Happy Days.* The central character in the television series was named Richie Cunningham, and he and his friends congregated at a diner named Arnold's. By 1978 people were less optimistic, and *Christine,* which is told by one of Arnie's friends fours years after the events in the story occur, suggests a loss of innocence. Not only does the narrator, now grown up and a teacher, reflect on adolescent problems; but he also examines a period when America's love affair with technological products, especially gas-guzzling muscle cars, had begun to sour.

King initially thought that *Pet Sematary,* written while he was writer in residence at the University of Maine at Orono, was too horrifying to publish. He completed a first draft in May 1979 and put it away until a contractual dispute with his former hardcover publisher, Doubleday, led him to rewrite it in 1982. King had earlier signed an agreement that Doubleday would pay him an annual sum of fifty thousand dollars. In order to get out of that contract, King offered Doubleday *Pet Sematary,* which sold 657,000 copies its first year even though King did virtually no promotion on its behalf.

What made *Pet Sematary* so painful to King was its proximity to real life. While writer in residence he rented a house that bordered a major truck route. In the woods behind the house, neighborhood children had created an informal pet cemetery where they buried the dogs and cats killed on the road. King became further aware of the cemetery when his daughter's cat was killed. In addition, his youngest child, Owen, ran out into the road. Although the boy was unharmed, King began to brood over the death of a child.

Despite the book's painful subject, reviewers praised it as a work that transcended the traditional horror genre. Indeed, although *Pet Sematary* includes familiar horror elements, it also grapples with death, the last and most mundane horror facing human beings. Furthermore, the novel examines the particular horror of death for people such as the protagonist, Louis Creed, who has no spiritual resources to help him cope with it.

King wrote *The Eyes of the Dragon* for his daughter, Naomi Rachel, who does not like horror novels, and Peter Straub's son Ben. King includes as characters a heroic girl named Naomi Reechul and an equally heroic boy named Ben Staad, the best friend of Prince Peter, the main character. The story centers on King Roland; his sons, Peter and Thomas; and the evil magician Flagg. Because Flagg, actually a demon in disguise, wants a king whom he can dominate, he poisons Roland and makes it look as though Peter is responsible. With Peter imprisoned, Flagg can control the younger and weaker Thomas and ultimately produce the anarchy that he desires. In fact, Thomas, who sees Flagg give the poisoned wine to his father, lacks the courage to tell the truth until five years later, when Peter escapes from prison. At the end Peter is crowned king, and Thomas goes on a quest to find Flagg in order to avenge his father's death and to atone for his sin against his brother.

Originally conceived as a children's story, *The Eyes of the Dragon* nonetheless addresses issues that King examines elsewhere. For example, Flagg, who appears as the Dark Man in *The Stand,* represents evil in this work as well. The courageous young people in *The Eyes of the Dragon* finally confront him, although they succeed only in driving him away rather than destroying him. In *IT* a group of young people succeeds in destroying the evil force.

King completed a first draft of *The Eyes of the Dragon* (originally titled "The Napkins") in late 1983 at much the same time that he completed first drafts of *The Talisman* and *The Tommyknockers.* The book, which was designed by Michael Alpert and illustrated by Kenny Ray Linkous, was originally published as a true limited edition, unavailable in any other form, by King's own specialty press, Philtrum Press. The print run was 250 red-numbered copies for private distribution and 1,000 black-numbered copies for sale by lottery. Advertisements in *Fantasy Newsletter, Locus,* and *F&SF* announced that the book would cost $120 and that interested people should send in their names. If more than a thousand people were interested, there would be a lottery. Two thousand people responded. In 1987 Viking brought out a hardback edition with new illustrations by David Palladini, and these also appear in the paperback edition.

The Talisman is King's only full-length collaborative work. Written with Straub, the project was initiated in 1977, the year the two writers met in London and became friends. However, commitments to existing projects meant that they could not begin writing until 1980, when Straub moved to Connecticut. During a brief period together in 1981, King and Straub developed an outline for the book, a step unusual for King. Writing began in 1982, and the two exchanged pages electronically between word processors. Each writer worked on the manuscript until he came to a convenient stopping point and then sent his installment to the other. Meeting during Thanksgiving 1982, King and Straub streamlined the manuscript for publication.

Although both King and Straub are known as writers of horror, The Talisman more clearly resembles The Eyes of the Dragon than it does Straub's Julia (1975) or King's Pet Sematary. As Carroll F. Terrell observes, The Talisman resembles such famous literary quests as the search for the Holy Grail and Jason's search for the Golden Fleece. Jack Sawyer, the main character, is sometimes called Jason. Like the mythic hero, Jack can accomplish his goals only after completing the quest.

The Talisman is also a peculiarly American epic fantasy that resembles The Adventures of Huckleberry Finn as much as it does The Lord of the Rings. Twelve-year-old Jack moves to New Hampshire with his mother, a former movie actress who is afflicted with cancer and is manipulated financially by Morgan Sloat, the novel's villain. Jack learns from Speedy Parker, an aging black man who serves as his mentor, that he must head for the Territories, a parallel world, to seek the Talisman, which will save his mother's life. Unlike the United States in 1981, the Territories is an agrarian world whose bible is The Book of Good Farming. Jack learns to "flip" back and forth between worlds and is joined by several friends – Wolf from the Territories and Richard Sloat, his childhood friend from California – as he crosses the United States and its Territories equivalent. Facing imprisonment and ambush by evil forces, Jack ultimately finds the Talisman and rescues both his mother and his mother's "Twinner," or correspondent self in the Territories.

As epic fantasy The Talisman works well. Moreover, it continues several familiar King themes. Like IT, The Talisman features courageous children. Like Firestarter and The Stand, it questions what people have done to the American landscape. Not only do Jack and his friends face evil human characters both in the United States and in the Territories (one particularly devastated place is The Blasted Lands, which seem to have been destroyed by nuclear fallout), but they also realize the impact of technology on the American landscape. Winter comments on the novel's serious message: Laura DeLoessian, Queen of the Territories, is also the earth. (Winter argues that the name comes from the German word loess, which means "of the earth.") Rescuing the Talisman and destroying Morgan Sloat, Jack initiates the healing process that will cleanse his mother, the queen, and the land. Predictably, The Talisman received mixed reviews, for neither reviewers nor fans knew what to make of a work that combines the strengths of such different novelists writing in a form for which they were unknown.

Thinner (1984), the most recent Bachman book, is the only one that can be classified as a horror novel. Originally a short story that grew to novel length, Thinner sold relatively well (twenty-eight thousand hardcover copies, according to King in "Why I Was Bachman") even before King confessed to being Bachman. Thinner tells what happens when Billy Halleck, a successful man who is respected by his peers and loved by his family, accidentally kills an old Gypsy woman. Because Halleck is socially prominent, Police Chief Duncan Hopley fails to investigate the accident, and Judge Cary Rossington lets him off. The dead woman's father curses the three men, and King examines the effect of the curse on these individuals. Rossington and Hopley commit suicide, but Halleck learns what it means to be hated and feared. A character study of a man facing imminent death, Thinner also examines the relationship between the despised Gypsies and the affluent residents of Fairview. Trying to find the Gypsies to convince them to remove the curse, Halleck recognizes them as a marginalized group: " 'Sure we need the Gypsies. . . . Because if you don't have someone to run out of town once in a while, how are you going to know you yourself belong there?' " The original title, "Gypsy Pie," suggests that the political message was important to King.

According to King's note at the end of IT, he began the novel in 1981 and finished it in 1985. Like most of his novels, IT received mixed reviews, many of them commenting on its length – 1,138

*Dust jacket for the 1987 King novel that was the basis for a
popular 1990 movie starring James Caan and Kathy Bates*

pages – as well as on other excesses. Some critics, however, praised King's poignant presentation of growing up in a small town. *IT* is the latest King novel to deal with childhood, for his subsequent novels focus more specifically on adult problems. King, the same age as the novel's main characters, often notes that adults see the world differently than children. As a result, only children and a few adults with strong memories of childhood see the monster and combat it. Significantly, the novel that took almost four years to write and left him temporarily unable to complete any other is dedicated to his children, who "taught me how to be free."

IT is a transitional work in other ways, for it is also the latest King novel to deal with traditional monsters. Told through multiple viewpoints in two different times – 1958 and 1985 – *IT* features six adults who return to the town where they grew up to destroy the monstrous IT, a killer of children. The monster was originally from outer space, an

idea King explores again in *The Tommyknockers*. IT inhabits the sewers of Derry, Maine (a community based on Bangor), and appears to children as various monsters, including Frankenstein's creature, the werewolf, the vampire, the Creature from the Black Lagoon, and something known by a variety of names that can read people's minds and assume the shape of the thing they most fear.

IT focuses on other evils, for the monster is also the spirit of Derry, a city seemingly oblivious to the violence in its midst and to a variety of human evils – homophobia, racism, and the abuse of women, children, and members of minority groups. In addition, King examines individual human evil as he does in *Misery*. For example, Henry Bowers, who is committed to Juniper Hill, an institution for the criminally insane, is a bully long before IT uses him to persecute the members of the Losers Club and long before he kills his father. King examines the cycle of abuse in the dysfunctional Bowers family, for Butch Bowers is responsible for making his son a bully. Butch is also a victim, however, for his experiences during World War II have left him an emotional cripple and unfit father.

IT also explores themes common to King's other novels. If King's early novels tend to focus on childhood, novels in his second period – including *Misery, The Tommyknockers,* and *The Dark Half* – often focus on writers. In fact, *IT* features two writers: Bill Denbrough is a writer of best-selling horror novels, and Michael Hanlon, the town librarian, writes a history of the community and discovers its cycle of violence before he calls his childhood friends back home. In later novels King continues to explore the special power that authors have. He also continues to explore real social horrors. For example, much of his later fiction has a kind of gritty realism and deals with the horrors found in newspapers and government reports – kidnapping in *Misery,* nuclear contamination in *The Tommyknockers,* and child abuse and wife abuse in *Gerald's Game* and *Dolores Claiborne.*

The Dark Tower II: The Drawing of the Three (1987) is clearly a novel rather than a series of interrelated short stories. Featuring Roland and his quest for the Tower, *The Drawing of the Three* picks up seven hours after the first installment left off. The realm of this second installment is even more clearly a fantasy world, with doors that open into the United States at certain historical moments. Through these doors Roland connects with three individuals who help him with his quest. He meets the first, Eddie Dean, in 1987 and saves him from a drug bust and a Mafia hit. He meets the second in 1964 and discovers that two personalities, Detta Walker and Odetta Holmes, inhabit a single schizophrenic being. Finally he meets Jack Mort, who had pushed Odetta in front of a train in 1959 and is therefore responsible for her dual personality and the loss of her legs. While the gunslinger brings Eddie and Odetta/Detta back to his world, Roland has Mort jump in front of another train, an action that unites Detta and Odetta into a third personality, Susannah Dean.

Like a typical quest adventure, *The Drawing of the Three* places the characters in adventures that help them discover who they are. However, many topical references suggest that King is equally concerned with post–World War II American culture. Through Eddie's life he examines the drug culture and other problems faced by Vietnam veterans, for Eddie's brother Henry served in Vietnam and became an addict after returning state-

side. With Detta/Odetta King examines what it is like to be African-American in white America. The novel includes references to the early civil rights movement, since the wealthy Odetta Holmes has just returned from Oxford, Mississippi, in 1964 when Roland brings her back to his world. Although Odetta is the daughter of a man who made a fortune in dental technologies, Detta Walker, her alter ego, reveals insights into another aspect of the African-American experience. A foul-mouthed ghetto woman, she hates all white people; King suggests that only love and sacrifice in the white community (Roland and Eddie) and the destruction of that community's violent members (Jack Mort) can cure that division.

The Drawing of the Three was initially published in a small print run of 30,000 copies in its trade edition and 850 copies in a deluxe edition, which was numbered and signed by King and artist Phil Hale. In the afterword King admits to being haunted by the characters, "Roland most of all," and projects that the Dark Tower series will eventually include seven books.

Many consider *Misery,* written in 1984 and originally intended as a Bachman book, King's best novel. Its stark, often depressing realism resembles the naturalism of the Bachman novels and reveals King's high-school and college interest in British and American naturalists – Thomas Hardy, Dreiser, and Norris. As in *IT,* which combines supernatural horror with the horror of ordinary human life, *Misery* reveals that the life of ordinary human beings is horrifying even without the intervention of supernatural monsters. The novel focuses on two characters in a remote Colorado farmhouse. One, the romance novelist Paul Sheldon, believes that his readers and his publisher have forced him to produce potboilers about Misery Chastain. Wanting to be a "serious" novelist, Sheldon feels trapped. While celebrating the completion of a serious novel, *Fast Cars,* he skids off the road during a snowstorm only to be literally trapped by Annie Wilkes, his number one fan.

Wilkes is a uniquely human monster. A psychopath who has killed her father, husband, and college roommate, she is a registered nurse who has moved from hospital to hospital, killing patients until her well-publicized trial forces her retirement to the farmhouse where she takes Sheldon. Not only is she Sheldon's jailer and fan, but she also serves as a literary critic, forcing him to burn the manuscript of *Fast Cars* and to write another novel about Misery. Equally horrifying, she keeps Sheldon dependent on drugs, chops off his foot with a hatchet when he attempts to escape, and threatens to kill him. In fact, Sheldon realizes that she will kill him when his novel is completed. *Misery* examines the writer's creative power, for Sheldon's desire to create keeps him alive in spite of truly adverse conditions and ultimately makes him strong enough to overcome Wilkes and return to his life as a writer.

Misery, which is both shorter and more tightly plotted than most of King's novels, received enthusiastic reviews, for which King credits his editor's advice. After the publication of *Misery,* however, King has often had to explain that he does not see fans as Annie Wilkeses. His warm relationship with his thousands of fans is evident at book signings and other public appearances.

With *The Tommyknockers* King once again returns to horror, although this novel might also be considered science fiction, for the monsters are spirits of a long-dead alien species whose spaceship crashed in Haven, Maine, twenty-five thousand years ago and became buried in a forested region. When Bobbi Anderson stumbles over an unburied portion of the ship and starts to dig it up, the residents are possessed by the spirits of this alien species and start to become like them, a process that several describe as becoming "new and improved." This resemblance is physical, mental, and emotional, for they become violent and irascible and know instinctively how to modify or "improve" existing mechanical objects.

King, whose novels often reveal apprehensions about technology, points out the horrifying negative side of these improvements. The aliens are not especially creative, and they are totally amoral. Instead of using DC converters, they use living creatures to power their contraptions. Thus whatever they create is ultimately exploitative. As Winter observes, *The Tommyknockers* satirizes the "pragmatic side of science fiction, which seemingly worships the technological solution over human emotion."

The novel asks readers to examine that old science-fiction question of confronting an alien species and also to examine existing technology, for the main character, Jim Gardener, an alcoholic poet, has protested the nuclear power movement in the United States, along with the power that business and government have over the lives of ordinary citizens. Thus *The Tommyknockers* examines corruption on both the individual and community levels. Gardener, through whose mind the reader sees many of the events in the novel, often links the Tommyknockers, his name for the aliens, to the police, the government, and employees of various power companies.

If *The Tommyknockers* criticizes America's love affair with technology and power of all types, it also celebrates ordinary humanity, especially the human ability to love. Although Gardener has failed at everything and had contemplated suicide before returning to help Anderson, he saves humanity in his dying moments by piloting the spaceship away from earth. Gardener also rescues a child, David Brown, who had been sent away to a distant planet, and the novel concludes with David and his older brother curled up together in bed. While *The Tommyknockers* does not focus on children as King's earlier fiction does, it ends on a note of love – Gardener's love for the human race and Hilly Brown's love for his younger brother. *The Tommyknockers* thus becomes a celebration of ordinary humanity in the manner of *IT.*

King completed the rough draft of *The Tommyknockers* in 1983, at the same time he was working on *The Talisman* and *The Eyes of the Dragon,* and finished it in 1987. Unlike *Misery,* which King admits benefited from his editor's advice, *The Tommyknockers* suffers because King did not listen carefully enough to such advice. If King's self-criticism is harsh, critics were even harsher, observing that the book lacks originality and that its characters are cartoonish.

The Dark Half, which King wrote between November 1987 and March 1989, examines the relationship between a writer and his pen name. King admits that he started to wonder whether the alter ego he had created in Bachman would stay dead. The novel presents the doppelgänger motif that appears in Edgar Allan Poe's "William Wilson" (1839) and Joseph Conrad's *The Secret Sharer* (1910). Because the two beings in *The Dark Half* – Thad Beaumont and George Stark – are so different, it also resembles Robert Louis Stevenson's *Strange Case of Dr. Jekyll and Mr. Hyde* (1886), which King discusses in *Danse Macabre* as a work about the duality of human nature published three decades before Sigmund Freud's theories of the divided consciousness. King stresses that Stevenson's monster focuses on the subhuman characteristics of human beings; the alter ego or pen name in *The Dark Half* is totally amoral and will do anything necessary to survive and – equally important – continue to write, an aspect of the novel that reveals the importance of the creative process.

The novel also explores twinship, for Beaumont has neurosurgery as a child to remove the vestigial remains of a twin. When he and his wife cre-

King's house in Bangor, Maine

ate a pen name, George Stark, who writes vastly different novels from those of Beaumont himself, King suggests that they resurrect the pen name as a physical presence who murders Beaumont's literary friends and attempts to dominate Beaumont and his family. Beaumont ultimately destroys his alter ego, though the novel reveals a great deal about the unconscious forces that people try to repress. Along with *Misery* and "Secret Window, Secret Garden," a short work in *Different Seasons* (1982), *The Dark Half* also explores the writer's psyche and the power of the creative process. Although King often features writers in his works, he had never emphasized the writing process to the degree that he does in these three works. *Publishers Weekly* (1 September 1990) noted the similarity between *Misery* and *The Dark Half,* "among the best of his voluminous work," but remarked that this "new King thriller is so wondrously frightening that mesmerized readers won't be able to fault the master for reusing a premise."

The Dark Tower III: The Wastelands (1991) was originally published by Donald M. Grant in two separate editions: a trade edition of forty thousand copies and a numbered edition of twelve hundred copies signed by King and artist Ned Dameron. It picks up where the second installment leaves off, with Roland, Eddie, and Susannah still seeking the Tower. They are joined by the child Jake, whom Roland abandons in the first volume, an act that continues to haunt the gunslinger. Furthermore, the interplay between Roland's world, which had "moved on," and Jake's world provides insights into contemporary problems. King emphasizes these similarities when the group encounters Shardik, a two-thousand-year-old cyborg in the shape of a bear, and when they come to Lud, a city destroyed in a civil war several hundred years earlier and currently inhabited by descendants of the two opposing sides. Outside the city lie the Waste Lands, the result of the same war that had destroyed the city and turned many people into mutants; Susannah and Eddie suspect that nuclear weapons were responsible. Inside the city lies Blaine, a monorail that the group hopes will take them to the Tower.

Like several of his earlier novels, *The Wastelands* reveals King's apprehensions about technology and government. For example, Shardik and his accompanying small mechanical creatures have gone mad; Blaine, undoubtedly the craziest machine of all, destroys Lud and its inhabitants and threatens Roland and his friends with death if they fail to tell him a riddle that he cannot guess. At this point the volume ends, though the author's note assures readers that the "business of Blaine the Mono will be resolved" and promises more information about Roland's background and the heroic world that has produced him.

The Wastelands received mixed reviews. Usually receptive to King's works, *Publishers Weekly* (8 November 1991) objected to its cliff-hanger ending. More positive was *Locus,* the trade journal for the science-fiction field. Its reviewer noted the novel's peculiar blend of science fiction and fantasy, observing that the Dark Tower series differs radically from what is expected of King – the horror story, set in everyday America, in which extraordinary things happen to ordinary people.

In *Needful Things* King destroys Castle Rock, the town where he set six previous works – *Cujo;* "Mrs. Todd's Shortcut," "Uncle Otto's Truck," and "Gramma" in *Skeleton Crew* (1985); *The Dark Half;* and "The Sun Dog" in *Four Past Midnight* (1990) – and which he mentions in *The Dead Zone* and *IT.* According to George Beahm's *The Stephen King Story* (1992), King could have continued to write about Castle Rock but chose to destroy it because, feeling overly comfortable there, he decided it was time to move on: " 'On the one hand, it was a welcoming place to write about. But there is a downside to that. You become complacent; you begin to accept boundaries; the familiarity of the place discourages risks. So I am burning my bridges and destroying the town. . . . It's sad but it had to be done.' "

Beahm reveals the inspiration for the novel – an image of a boy throwing mud at sheets. King also explained that he wanted to write about obsession and compulsion because these behaviors are condoned in the United States. These simple beginnings resulted in a work that demonstrates its American origins, for it is a late-twentieth-century version of Mark Twain's *The Mysterious Stranger* (1916) or his *The Man That Corrupted Hadleyburg* (1900), in which the devil comes to a community and corrupts most of its residents. *Time* (11 November 1991) reviewer Stefan Kanfer described the narrator of *Needful Things* as a stage manager in the manner of the narrator in Thornton Wilder's *Our Town* (1938).

In *Needful Things* King once again combines the supernatural with naturalistic details, for Leland Gaunt, the devil, reads minds to determine what people need most and uses this knowledge to gain their souls. Gaunt differs from traditional devils, for he is more interested in his own amusement than in souls. Still, because he resembles the devil in many classic works, several characters – including Brian Rusk, the child with whom the story begins; Polly Chalmers; and Sheriff Alan Pangborn, who also appears in *The Dark Half* – recognize him, though not

before his evil tricks and the existing conflicts of residents destroy Castle Rock. Ironically, the conflict between Baptists and Catholics is largely responsible for involving the entire community in a literal battle. It is almost as if King were saying that organized religion is poorly equipped to deal with evil in its midst.

Needful Things, with its large cast of characters and reliance on the supernatural, resembles such early King works as *The Stand, IT,* and *The Tommyknockers,* though the folksy narrator who begins and closes the novel asks readers to examine small-town life and ordinary human problems. The novel received mixed reviews: *Publishers Weekly* (25 July 1991) found much to like, but the *New York Times Book Review* (29 September 1991) and the *Washington Post* (29 September 1991) were critical. In fact, the *Post* review, which emphasized King's popularity and the amoral message of the novel, prompted King to write a letter to the editor (17 November 1991) defending himself, his novel, and his readers.

It is difficult to discuss *Gerald's Game* and *Dolores Claiborne* separately because both feature strong women characters who are concerned with sexual abuse of children, both depict important scenes during a 1963 eclipse, and each work refers to occurrences in the other. There are reasons for the connections. Having finished *The Wastelands,* King planned to take a break from writing over the summer before tackling *Dolores Claiborne,* the novel scheduled for fall 1992. Falling asleep on an airplane, though, he came up with the idea for *Gerald's Game,* which he describes as being "like an unplanned pregnancy."

Although *Gerald's Game* contains horrifying details, including a character who is a thief, murderer, ghoul, and necrophile, most of the novel is a psychological profile of a middle-aged woman, Jessie Burlingame. Her husband has died after handcuffing her to the bed at their summer home, and Jessie must face her life, including the memory that her father had sexually abused her, and her fears alone. Since these fears include an intruder in the house and a stray dog that devours parts of her husband's corpse, *Gerald's Game* continues in the naturalistic vein of *Misery* and the Bachman books. Furthermore, it continues an interest, begun in *Carrie* and continued through many of King's novels, in women as outsiders. Dedicated to his wife and five other women in her family, *Gerald's Game* is the novel that most clearly reveals King's concern with women and women's issues. *Dolores Claiborne,* which he dedicated to his mother and which features the voice of a single woman character, continues the exploration of this interest.

Critical response to *Gerald's Game* was mixed. *Publishers Weekly* (25 May 1992) hailed it as "one of the best-written stories King has ever published" but objected to its "sheer bad taste." *Time* (13 July 1992) described it as "the old Helpless Woman in the Haunted House number, but refreshed by a combination King has rarely used before: subtle plotting and acute psychological insight."

Although *Dolores Claiborne* features an older woman, it is concerned with issues that face all women. The novel has a single speaking voice, almost as though the mature woman has come into her own. Accused of murdering her husband twenty years earlier and her employer earlier that week, Dolores addresses two local policemen and a woman stenographer. In the process she reveals a great deal about growing up as a poor woman, though the plot line suggests that her wealthy employer had faced similar problems, most notably a drunken, abusive husband. In the end she confesses that she has done everything for love – love of her daughter, whose father had sexually abused her, and love of her employer.

Unlike *Gerald's Game*, *Dolores Claiborne* includes few of the horrifying scenes for which King is known. He seems to be moving away from the supernatural horror that catapulted him to fame and into mainstream fiction that explores the psychology of ordinary people placed in extreme circumstances. Still primarily a storyteller rather than a conscious craftsman, he nonetheless continues to develop rather than to mine familiar material, and he is not afraid to take risks by venturing into areas that are new to him and his readers. King has taken horror literature out of the closet and has injected new life into familiar genres – initially horror, but more recently fantasy, science fiction, and the Western. He is not afraid to mix those genres in fresh ways to produce novels that examine contemporary American culture.

Immensely popular, King can expect practically anything he writes to be a hit with his fans, who continue to demand his novels and short stories and the movies that are inevitably made from them. He is not yet a favorite with academics or literary critics, partly because they still regard him as "Bestsellasaurus Rex," as Beahm notes in *The Stephen King Story,* and partly because even his most tightly constructed works can be uneven. As he has admitted on many occasions, he recognizes terror and horror as finer emotions but is not ashamed to "go for the gross out"; even his best novels include occasional gratuitous violence and gore. However, he is gaining acceptance in the scholarly commu-

nity: two critical analyses of his works have been published by university presses, and the *MLA Bibliography* includes articles on King every year.

As King has mentioned in several interviews, he is not at a loss for more stories, including a baseball novel. He is also thinking about writing a novel about Jonestown and one about an evangelist – subjects that tie in with his interest in religious figures. Whatever he does in the future, King has already shown that he is willing to branch out in new directions and to scrap existing projects when more interesting ideas occur to him. He has promised to continue The Dark Tower series. Moreover, certain works, including *'Salem's Lot* and *The Eyes of the Dragon,* seem to require sequels. One thing is certain: as long as he is able, King will continue to write.

Interviews:

Tim Underwood and Chuck Miller, eds., *Bare Bones: Conversations on Terror with Stephen King* (New York: McGraw-Hill, 1987);

Don Herron, ed., *Feast of Fear: Conversations with Stephen King* (Lancaster, Pa.: Underwood-Miller, 1989).

Bibliographies:

Michael R. Collings, *The Annotated Guide to Stephen King: A Primary and Secondary Bibliography of the Works of America's Premier Horror Writer* (Mercer Island, Wash.: Starmont House, 1987);

Tim Murphy, *In the Darkest Night: A Student's Guide to Stephen King* (Mercer Island, Wash.: Starmont House, 1992).

Biography:

George Beahm, *The Stephen King Story* (Kansas City, Mo.: Andrews & McMeel, 1992).

References:

George Beahm, *The Stephen King Companion* (Kansas City, Mo.: Andrews & McMeel, 1989);

Tyson Blue, *The Unseen King* (Mercer Island, Wash.: Starmont House, 1989);

Michael R. Collings, *The Many Facets of Stephen King* (Mercer Island, Wash.: Starmont House, 1985);

Collings, *Stephen King as Richard Bachman* (Mercer Island, Wash.: Starmont House, 1985);

Collings, *The Stephen King Phenomenon* (Mercer Island, Wash.: Starmont House, 1987);

Don Herron, ed., *Reign of Fear: Fiction and Film of Stephen King* (Lancaster, Pa.: Underwood-Miller, 1988);

Gary Hoppenstand and Ray B. Browne, eds., *The Gothic World of Stephen King: Landscape of Nightmares* (Bowling Green, Ohio: Bowling Green State University Popular Press, 1987);

Tony Magistrale, *Landscape of Fear: Stephen King's American Gothic* (Bowling Green, Ohio: Bowling Green State University Popular Press, 1988);

Magistrale, *The Moral Voyages of Stephen King* (Mercer Island, Wash.: Starmont House, 1989);

Joseph Reino, *Stephen King: The First Decade, "Carrie" to "Pet Sematary"* (Boston: Twayne, 1988);

Darrell Schweitzer, *Discovering Stephen King* (Mercer Island, Wash.: Starmont House, 1985);

Stephen J. Spignesi, *The Shape Under the Sheet: The Complete Stephen King Encyclopedia* (Chicago: Popular Culture, Ink., 1991);

Carroll F. Terrell, *Stephen King: Man and Artist* (Orono, Maine: Northern Lights, 1991);

Tim Underwood and Chuck Miller, eds., *Fear Itself: The Horror Fiction of Stephen King* (New York: Signet, 1982);

Underwood and Miller, eds., *Kingdom of Fear: The World of Stephen King* (New York: NAL/Plume Trade Paperback, 1986);

Douglas E. Winter, *Stephen King: The Art of Darkness* (New York: Signet, 1986);

Edward J. Zagorski, *Teacher's Manual: Novels of Stephen King* (New York: New American Library, 1981).

Papers:

Most of King's papers are held in the special collections of the Fogler Library at his alma mater, the University of Maine at Orono. Included are drafts and galleys for *Carrie, 'Salem's Lot, The Dead Zone, The Stand, The Shining, Night Shift, Firestarter, Cujo, Pet Sematary, Christine, Skeleton Crew,* and *The Talisman.* Also housed at the University of Maine at Orono are the manuscripts for several of King's early novels, all unpublished – "The Aftermath," "Blaze," "Second Coming" (the first of three drafts of *'Salem's Lot*), and "Sword in the Darkness" – and correspondence that includes letters from fans, press material, and letters from friends.

Ross Lockridge, Jr.

(25 April 1914 – 6 March 1948)

Donald J. Greiner
University of South Carolina

See also the Lockridge entry in *DLB Yearbook: 1980*.

BOOK: *Raintree County* (New York: Houghton Mifflin, 1948; London: Macdonald, 1949).

The tragedy occurred more than four decades ago, but the suicide of Ross Lockridge, Jr., continues to echo through informed discussions about contemporary American fiction. What, the initiated reader wonders, might the author of *Raintree County* (1948) have contributed not only to American literature but also to the genre of fiction following the stunning achievement of his only novel? Would he have weathered the curious combination of clamor and glory that swirls around the gifted young novelist with a major success and then have moved on to make his mark as a respected artist of an enduring canon? Or would he have gone the route of countless other successful beginners and given way to the hoopla – to the approval and applause, to the checks and contracts – and written a series of books that failed to measure up to the standards of the initial breakthrough? These queries are, of course, forever moot, for Lockridge killed himself two months after the publication of his masterpiece. Thus the question that subsumes all the others about him is *why?*

To speculate about the answer is to consider that mass neurosis known as the American dream. The story has a familiar ring to it: the dream consumes the dreamer, and the fall from grace occurs. What is puzzling about the history of *Raintree County* is that Lockridge's all-American hero, John Wickliff Shawnessy, survives with his epic unwritten but his dreams intact, while Lockridge found himself with a masterpiece completed but his dreams in disarray.

His association with his fictional dreamer is so close that speculation about the suicide unfortunately often overshadows discussions of the novel. Published on 5 January 1948 to reviews that John Leggett, Lockridge's "unauthorized" biographer, describes as having "a prominence and profusion

that is no longer seen," *Raintree County* remains a curio of contemporary American literature. Its current status – admired but not read – is baffling when one considers that *Raintree County* had a widespread prepublicity campaign, that it won the coveted M-G-M award of $150,000 for movie rights and the resulting publicity, that by March 1948 it was the number one best-seller in the country, that Howard Mumford Jones saluted it in the *Saturday Review of Literature* (3 January 1948) as marking "the end of a long slump in American fiction," and that it occasionally appears on lists that name the best American novels since World War II.

Perhaps Lockridge himself feared the silence after the cheering stopped. Born in Bloomington, Indiana, he grew up in the heart of the country and first announced his ambition to write a great American novel while a student at Indiana University from 1931 to 1935. (He was graduated summa cum laude and was elected to Phi Beta Kappa.) His father had introduced him to family and local myths as well as to national history, and Lockridge became intrigued by the life of his maternal grandfather, John Wesley Shockley. The echoes of Shockley in the fictional Shawnessy are even more apparent when one realizes that "Seth Twigs," the grandfather's newspaper pseudonym, is the same name Lockridge assigned to Shawnessy's backwoods "reporter." Apparently suspecting, like Shawnessy, that his family was illegitimately descended from Thomas Carlyle, Lockridge looked for continuity in local myths and formulated his idea of the quest for the golden rain tree while researching the history of Robert Owen's nineteenth-century social experiment, New Harmony. But, although he was a brilliant student, renowned for his memory and his achievement of earning the highest grade average in the history of Indiana University, Lockridge feared the specter of failure.

It is not at all outrageous to suggest that the sudden flash of success and the subsequent plunge into despair that Lockridge suffered were trans-

Ross Lockridge, Jr.

posed to the character of Shawnessy in an attempt to exorcise the fear. But Shawnessy remains a man of the middle while his creator felt the scorch of the extremes. For, despite attraction to the American dream and confidence in his own creative genius, Lockridge strove to accomplish more for fear of achieving less. His obsession to be the best took concrete form when he decided to be an author.

According to Leggett, Lockridge's first plan to write a novel about his Indiana family went nowhere. Abandoning the project in 1938, he began an epic poem, "The Dream of the Flesh of Iron." The unpublished poem is unavailable to the public, but it is the forerunner of *Raintree County* because the sensitive, every-American hero seeks the meaning of his country in the guise of a beautiful woman. When the dream girl eludes the dreamer, he discovers that the quest alone has meaning. From the little that is known about this unpublished poem, two

points are significant. First, by 1940 Lockridge had completed the germ of the unconsummated love that adds such poignancy and despair to *Raintree County,* the story of what would become Shawnessy's courtship of Nell Gaither. More important, it seems, Lockridge realized that the American dreamer always fails in his quest. Few would insist that he foresaw personal disillusionment at this point in his life, but for the purposes of his writing he understood how the glorious dreams and deeds that he gave his fictional counterpart would be forever unfulfilled. The contrast between Lockridge's own confidence and the mood of defeat in the poem is not only startling but also prophetic when one has the advantage of hindsight.

By December 1940 Lockridge, then a graduate student at Harvard University, had completed four hundred typed pages of "The Dream of the Flesh of Iron." Unapologetic about his aspirations, he submitted the epic to Houghton Mifflin in February 1941. It was promptly rejected. Shelving the typescript with his confidence still intact, he immediately began writing the novel that would earn him wealth and fame. The ordeal of composition took six years.

Unfortunately, the task devoured his strength. Attracted to the structure of James Joyce's *Ulysses* (1922), the lyricism of Thomas Wolfe's *Look Homeward, Angel* (1929), Thomas Mann's descriptions of a shattered culture, and the unusual transitions between historical moments in D. W. Griffith's film *Intolerance* (1916) and Orson Welles's *Citizen Kane* (1941), Lockridge learned how to set his novel during a single day (4 July 1892) and still unite dream sequences and the literal histories of nineteenth-century America, Indiana, and the Shockley family. He confidently stated his goal: to write "the first real representation of the American culture in fiction." Significantly, Shawnessy has the same plan. Earning his living by teaching at Simmons College (1941–1945) in Boston, Lockridge once scrapped a two-thousand-page rough draft and began anew. The final draft, which was submitted to Houghton Mifflin as "The Riddle of Raintree County" on 24 April 1946, contained six hundred thousand words, weighed twenty pounds, and had taken his wife, Verniece, eighteen months to type.

Although he seemed entirely certain the novel would be the masterpiece many critics have judged it to be, the tension between confidence and fear of failure apparently began to stretch to unbearable lengths following the submission of the manuscript to Houghton Mifflin. Lockridge entered a period of unsettling highs and lows that ended with his suicide. Outwardly, he exuded confidence. Not only did he reject an offer to serialize parts of the novel in *Ladies' Home Journal* because he wanted *Raintree County* to be published in one piece, but he also took the extraordinary step of flooding the Houghton Mifflin offices with letters of advice about how to publicize the book. Leggett notes that he even wrote to editor Dorothy Hillyer, "It will be talked about, written about, and read, read, read!"

The truth is that his judgment was correct. The irony is that behind the show of confidence lurked the shadow of failure that had nagged him all along. Too much of his spirit had gone into *Raintree County,* and he found that he could neither let it go without directing the entire publication process nor smooth the rough edges without giving rein to his doubts. His revisions became compulsive. Awaiting publication, he tried and failed to begin a new novel. His emotional difficulties were diagnosed as paranoia, and he endured a series of shock treatments. Perhaps the saddest sign of his breakdown was the list of rules he drew up in the hope of regaining his balance and discipline. Leggett reports that the first rule was to forget *Raintree County:* "I should exclude it from my thoughts or, if I think of it at all, simply pick it up and read one of the optimistic 'sweet' parts." But nothing worked. The novel had exhausted him. On 6 March 1948, two months after the publication of his great book, Lockridge drove his new Kaiser into the garage, locked the door, switched on the engine, and died from carbon monoxide inhalation.

No one knows the answer to why Lockridge killed himself, but Leggett speculates that Lockridge was plagued by the bitch goddess to which American authors seem peculiarly vulnerable. Another possible answer is the suggestion that Lockridge's faith in his novel amounted to an idealism that could not withstand the impact of the practical decisions to revise the manuscript. But the most acceptable answer may come from the close relationship between Lockridge and Shawnessy, in which the author recognized in his fictional hero a similar spirit-draining dilemma: well-founded confidence challenged by unexpected doubt.

Shawnessy never considers suicide to be the way out of the dilemma; indeed, at the end of this long novel (1,066 published pages), he returns home with his dreams still beckoning, having parried a series of verbal thrusts from his attractive, yet cynical, alter ego, Jerusalem Webster Stiles. But, now in his fifties, Shawnessy has not completed the glorious epic with which he has been tinkering for thirty years, his tale "of a man's days on the breast of the land," and the reader knows he never will. The similarity between author and character spotlights the irony, and Lockridge undoubtedly saw his tragedy in these lines from the end of *Raintree County:* "Make way, make way for the Hero of Raintree County! His victory is not in consummations but in quests!" Both men stop short of the laurel crown, but Shawnessy stumbles homeward with his "great fair dream" still intact. Now, more than four decades after the suicide, one wonders if in consummating his own dream Lockridge consumed himself. The quest was all.

Even the reviews of *Raintree County* exacerbated Lockridge's sense of success tainted by failure. Ecstatic praise from such commentators as Jones, James Hilton, and Charles Lee was tempered by attacks from M. P. Corcoran and Hamilton Basso. Published while Lockridge was near mental collapse, the negative reviews, especially those that

Dust jacket for Lockridge's only novel, a Civil War–era epic set in a mythical Indiana county

accused him of moral laxity and "rank obscenity," exaggerated his own doubts. He was so worried, for example, about his parents' reactions to the descriptions of Nell's nakedness and Susanna's scarred breasts that he feared the book's appearance in Bloomington.

The point is that Lockridge suffered puritan pangs of guilt and that he gave Shawnessy the same moral twinges. Apparently, Shawnessy is the man Lockridge wished to be, the passionate artist who dreams a masterpiece but never completes the task. But that predicament would also have been intolerable, for Lockridge realized that his hero's unfinished epic has the taint of failure. Trapped between consummation and quest, between a flawed creation and the obsession to create, both men missed the goal. The primary difference is that Shawnessy holds the golden ideal in sight because his guilt can be absorbed in the privacy of his lyrical dreams.

Lockridge could not do the same once he delivered his typescript to the publisher, for his visions became public when he attributed them to his fictional hero.

No better illustration of Lockridge's dilemma can be found than the dust jacket and map that he drew for the novel. Glanced at hastily, the jacket shows the shape of the county. Looked at a second time, the jacket outlines a reclining nude female, with hills for breasts and a tributary of the Shawmucky River flowing between her legs to her genitals. Just as symbolic is the map of the county that Lockridge placed opposite the title page. The Shawmucky, the river of life, flows toward both Lake Paradise and the Great Swamp, and the feminine curves near the townships of Mount Pleasant and Summit point toward the town of Climax. Reading with the dust jacket and map in mind, one soon realizes that Shawnessy's pursuit of the ideal

America is wrapped up in the temptations of sexual intercourse. Apprehensive about moral censure, Lockridge nevertheless explicitly identifies his hero's quest with the map: "He was certain that in the pattern of its lines and letters this map contained the answer to the old conundrum of his life in Raintree County.... With a feeling suspended between erotic hunger and intellectual curiosity, he looked for the young woman."

Lockridge uses the sexual allusions consciously when he suggests that Shawnessy associates the glory of America as a Garden of Eden with the mysteries of sexuality: "The two were always colliding with each other as Mr. Shawnessy went his ritual way through conversations and thoroughfares, and mr. shawnessy carried on his eternal vagabondage through a vast reserve of memories and dreams.... It was clearly the whim of mr. shawnessy to prepare a naked woman on the stone slab in the Post Office, but it was Mr. Shawnessy who timidly asked for a newspaper, trying his best to adapt himself and his puritan conscience to the bizarre world of his twin."

Unlike his creator, however, Shawnessy does not question his union of sexuality and idealism to the point of self-doubt. He feels guilty, for example, when he is stunned while watching Nell Gaither swim nude in the Shawmucky, but he easily merges his guilt with his idealization of her as a goddess. A similar guilt looms when he romps with Southern belle Susanna Drake beside the same river, but, even though her beautiful, though scarred, breasts signal both her own dissolution and that of America in the Civil War, he neutralizes the guilt by marrying her. Later, he dodges an invitation from actress Laura Golden to enter her secret bedroom. And finally, now a middle-aged husband to someone other than Nell or Susanna, he shrinks from the public while turning the pages of a pirated history of Raintree County in search of nude drawings. The implications are shattering to the dreamer: his vision of the goddess recedes farther the older he gets or the faster he pursues it. Married to a good but hardly awe-inspiring woman half his age, Shawnessy discovers that he is left with not Nell's naked beauty to shape his dream but only the rumor of nude drawings to fire his curiosity.

Professor Jerusalem Webster Stiles nevertheless hints that Shawnessy successfully finds his heritage and his future in the sexually suggestive map, and that thus Shawnessy fulfills his destiny as both creator and preserver of the American dream. As a final gesture of homage and farewell, the professor traces in smoke the letters *JWS,* which, when swirled by the wind, take the shape of the Shawmucky River on the map. Lockridge yearned for the same identification with America, but one continues to wonder about the motive he assigns to the professor's gesture. Possessing the same initials, the professor is clearly the dark side of Shawnessy's questing innocence, a cynical counterbalance to the believer in never-ending possibilities and golden days. Shawnessy may need Stiles because the mentor forces the pupil to defend his faith in the quest, but Stiles, for all his wit and charm, is nevertheless associated with the devil. Journalist, urban, and promiscuous where Shawnessy is poet, rural, and monogamous, Stiles believes as fervently in his cynicism as Shawnessy does in his dreams.

The professor's gesture may thus be suspect, as Lockridge no doubt knew. Showing his dexterity by carving the initials *JWS* backward in the smoke so that they are easily identified by his pupil, Stiles may indeed be celebrating the battered but still-searching hero. But, recalling that *JWS* are also the professor's initials, one wonders if Stiles is playing his final cynical trump, revealing to Shawnessy that the hero's unfinished epic and unfulfilled quest are noble, but useless, relics of an America long past, worth no more in the post–Civil War era than initials fading away in the darkness and gloom.

Lockridge, of course, created these negative implications, and he knew readers would understand that Shawnessy's dreams are tarnished by incompleteness. Pushing himself for six years to fashion an ideal American hero who epitomizes his own aspirations for the nation, he could not fail to note the negative side of his own hopefulness when the hero stops short of the goal. The ironic dilemma is that Shawnessy must leave forever incomplete the grand myth of the nation because the country itself never fulfills its promise. Shaping his lyricism in the relative innocence of antebellum America, he discovers that his vision no longer speaks to the realities of slavery, war, and urban squalor. The sickening purge of the national conscience by the bloodshed of the Civil War sullies both the dreamer and his dream. Thus Shawnessy's inability to complete his epic suggests America's failure to meet its potential. When Shawnessy turns from Laura and the city to return home to Indiana and the land, he finds, to his sorrow and Lockridge's, not Nell beside the river but trains upon the earth.

Yet to say that Shawnessy must leave his myth incomplete is not to dismiss the suggestion that he is also culpable, as Lockridge undoubtedly realized. Irony and failure dog his life as much as love and promise glorify it. The reader understands, even if

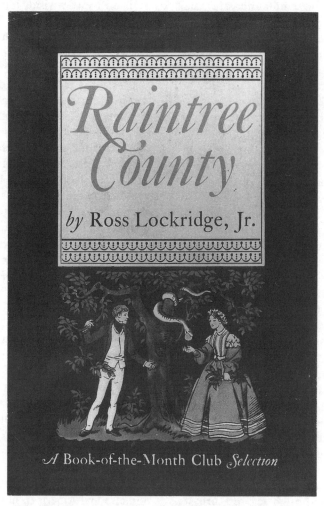

Dust jacket for the 1948 Riverside Press edition of Lockridge's novel

Shawnessy does not, that he makes the wrong choice time after time. While a young man, for example, he refuses to trek down the Great National Road to the alluring West, despite the beckoning of its call and the symbolism of the road's presence through the center of the county. He never consummates his love for Nell, the personification of America's lovely potential, giving himself instead to the scarred Susanna, to the still-beautiful but grievously flawed nation. Worse, when Susanna collapses in madness with the onslaught of fratricide and war, Shawnessy enlists in the Union army and thus loses his second chance with Nell. Finally, after the war, he marries a woman half his age and turns his back on the city, where the new, albeit less glorious, America will have to build its future out of the horror of blood and smoke. No one who cares about America's perpetual falls from grace can fail to feel the pathos of these questions in the novel:

"Was this the Union they had hammered out ringing on the forge of Battle? Was this the Raintree County of which Johnny Shawnessy had intended to become the hero?" The answer to both, unfortunately, for Shawnessy and Lockridge, is yes and no: yes, because disastrous choices blurred the vision and ruined the country; no, because for many Americans the dream will never die. Shawnessy can accept the paradox; Lockridge could not.

Shawnessy fails because he refuses to change with his country. Yet his heroism lies in his refusal, for he sings not of consummation but of quest. If Shawnessy repudiates the professor's cynicism; if, even in the defeats of middle age, he insists on shaping the legend of his life "by a myth of homecoming and a myth of resurrection," Lockridge was not as sure. Wanting to believe as he voiced his vision, he could not believe when he completed his novel. Too many of his doubts surfaced in his fictional hero, and too much of his confidence seeped away when realities did not square with dreams. If one censures Shawnessy even as one praises him, one knows that Lockridge deserves the same.

Lockridge's suicide was a stunning blow to American literature. The pathos is that during the writing of *Raintree County* he apparently tried but failed to exorcise the threats to his once-pervasive confidence. Unable to finish his epic, Shawnessy finds a measure of success – he refuses to abandon his dream. Lockridge was not as lucky. He suspected that in completing his masterpiece he had compromised his vision. One can only read *Raintree County* and regret the loss of what his continued presence and writing might have offered to the spiritual life of the nation – a sense of creation, a story, an ever-expanding hope.

Biography:

Laurence Lockridge, *Shade of the Raintree: The Life and Death of Ross Lockridge, Jr., Author of "Raintree County"* (New York: Viking, 1994).

References:

Joseph L. Blotner, "*Raintree County* Revisited," *Western Humanities Review,* 10 (Winter 1956): 57–64;

Delia Clarke, "*Raintree County:* Psychological Symbolism, Archetype, and Myth," *Thoth,* 11 (Fall 1970): 31–39;

Lawrence J. Dessner, "Value in Popular Fiction: The Case of *Raintree County,*" *Junction,* 1 (Spring 1973): 147–152;

Fred Erisman, "*Raintree County* and the Power of Place," *Markham Review,* 8 (Winter 1979): 36–40;

Park Dixon Goist, "Habits of the Heart in *Raintree County,*" *MidAmerica,* 13 (1986): 94–106;

Donald J. Greiner, "Ross Lockridge and the Tragedy of *Raintree County,*" *Critique,* 20 (April 1979): 51–63;

John Leggett, *Ross and Tom: Two American Tragedies* (New York: Simon & Schuster, 1974);

Boyd Litzinger, "Mythmaking in America: 'The Great Stone Face' and *Raintree County,*" *Tennessee Studies in Literature,* 8 (1963): 81–84;

Leonard Lutwack, "*Raintree County* and the Epicising Poet in American Fiction," *Ball State University Forum,* 13 (Winter 1972): 14–28;

Gerald C. Nemanic, "Ross Lockridge, *Raintree County,* and the Epic of Iron," *MidAmerica,* 2 (1975): 35–46;

Delia Clarke Temes, "The American Epic Tradition and *Raintree County,*" Ph.D. dissertation, Syracuse University, 1974;

Ray Lewis White, "*Raintree County* and the Critics of '48," *MidAmerica,* 11 (1984): 149–170.

Papers:

The major collections of Lockridge's papers are at the Lilly Library, Indiana University, and at the Houghton Library, Harvard University.

Cormac McCarthy
(20 July 1933 –)

Dianne C. Luce
Midlands Technical College

See also the McCarthy entry in *DLB 6: American Novelists Since World War II, Second Series.*

BOOKS: *The Orchard Keeper* (New York: Random House, 1965; London: Deutsch, 1966);

Outer Dark (New York: Random House, 1968; London: Deutsch, 1970);

Child of God (New York: Random House, 1974; London: Chatto & Windus, 1975);

Suttree (New York: Random House, 1979; London: Chatto & Windus, 1980);

Blood Meridian or The Evening Redness in the West (New York: Random House, 1985; London: Picador/Pan, 1989);

All the Pretty Horses (New York: Knopf, 1992; London: Picador, 1993);

The Stonemason: A Play in Five Acts (Hopewell, N.J.: Ecco, 1994);

The Crossing (New York: Knopf, 1994).

TELEVISION: *The Gardener's Son,* Rip/Filmhaus (for PBS *Visions* series), January 1977.

SELECTED PERIODICAL PUBLICATIONS – UNCOLLECTED: "Wake for Susan," as C. J. McCarthy, Jr., *Phoenix* (October 1959): 3–6;

"A Drowning Incident," as C. J. McCarthy, *Phoenix* (March 1960): 3–4.

Cormac McCarthy, circa 1979 (photograph by Dan Moore)

In the three decades leading to his sixtieth birthday, Cormac McCarthy produced six novels and a screenplay that are stunning in their originality and craftsmanship. Though McCarthy has been loath to court attention, especially in the academic arena, and slow to receive it, he has never truly gone without recognition, receiving the admiration – even the championship – of such contemporary American writers as Shelby Foote, Ralph Ellison, Annie Dillard, Larry Brown, Lee Smith, Saul Bellow, Robert Coles, and Madison Smartt Bell. McCarthy has also gathered nearly a dozen significant literary fellowships and awards. In 1988 Vereen M. Bell published the first book assessing McCarthy's works, calling him "our best unknown major writer by many measures." Since then the first six of McCarthy's novels have been published in paperback, and two more book-length studies of his works have appeared. An increasing number of scholars are writing dissertations or theses on McCarthy, and in 1993 the first national McCarthy conference was held at Bellarmine College in Louisville, Kentucky.

McCarthy's novels have grown out of his experiences in and reading about Tennessee, Texas, and Mexico. Centering on spiritual nomads — male characters who are, with varying degrees of consciousness, engaged in quests or antiquests — his plots climax in epiphanies or antiepiphanies and occasionally in apocalypse. The metaphysical themes of McCarthy's books emerge out of his loving attention to the natural world and the world of human tools, crafts, and action. Thomas D. Young, Jr., observes that, "in all Cormac McCarthy's work, nature is itself the principal presence." Several critics have noticed that in McCarthy's world animal forms (and even the landscape itself) seem to watch people — witnesses to their folly and brutality or to their rare heroism. McCarthy is a master of tone and language (one reviewer has said that the English language is the real hero of all McCarthy's books), and his novels are symphonic orchestrations of the tragic, grotesque, lyrical, and comic.

Born in Providence, Rhode Island, on 20 July 1933, McCarthy moved with his parents to the Knoxville, Tennessee, area at age four. He is the third child and oldest son of Charles Joseph and Gladys McGrail McCarthy; Cormac's two younger brothers and younger sister were born in Knoxville. He was named Charles Joseph McCarthy, Jr., after his father, a Yale-educated lawyer who worked as counsel for the Tennessee Valley Authority. The senior McCarthy also served as special assistant to the attorney general in the U.S. Justice Department, Washington, D.C., in 1938 and 1939. The McCarthys lived in a large frame house outside Knoxville. In the country surroundings McCarthy hunted, fished, and rode horses belonging to friends. He also came into contact with the country people about whom he writes; he told interviewer Richard B. Woodward, "We were considered rich because all the people around us were living in one- or two-room shacks."

McCarthy was raised as a Roman Catholic; he attended parochial schools, which he hated ("I felt early on I wasn't going to be a respectable citizen," he told Woodward). But he was keenly interested in everything he observed around him: "I remember in grammar school the teacher asked if anyone had any hobbies. I was the only one with any hobbies, and I had every hobby there was. . . . Name anything, no matter how esoteric, I had found it and dabbled in it."

After graduating from Catholic High School in Knoxville, McCarthy attended the University of Tennessee as a liberal-arts major for the 1951–1952 academic year and then devoted a year to wandering and working at odd jobs. He spent the next four years (1953–1957) in the U.S. Air Force — two of them in Alaska, where he began an intensive self-designed reading program. In spring 1957 he returned to the university, where he eventually enrolled in Robert Daniel's course in fiction writing. Based on his work in this course, McCarthy was chosen by the English department to receive the Ingram-Merrill Award for creative writing in the 1959–1960 academic year. The university's literary magazine, the *Phoenix,* published two of his short stories — "Wake for Susan" (1959) and "A Drowning Incident" (1960) — the first of his known fiction. While at the university he began work on what became his first and fourth novels (*The Orchard Keeper,* 1965, and *Suttree,* 1979) and perhaps his second (*Outer Dark,* 1968) as well. After the 1960 summer term he left the university without a degree in order to pursue a writing career. McCarthy still harbors a distaste for organized instruction: "Teaching writing is a hustle," he told Woodward.

Though *The Orchard Keeper* is deeply anchored in McCarthy's home state of Tennessee, he composed it on the move, working on it in Sevier County, Tennessee; Asheville, North Carolina; and Chicago. On 3 January 1961 McCarthy married Lee Holleman, a fellow student from the University of Tennessee, who later became a poet. (Her first volume of poems, *Desire's Door,* was published in 1991.) They moved to Chicago, where he worked on *The Orchard Keeper* while he was employed part-time in an auto-parts warehouse. Although they had a son, Cullen, the marriage was short-lived, and they divorced before McCarthy finished his first book. McCarthy sent his manuscript to Random House, where it came under the wing of Albert Erskine, McCarthy's editor for the next twenty years. It was published on 5 May 1965.

Technically ambitious for a first novel, *The Orchard Keeper* centers on young John Wesley Rattner and his coming into manhood in the isolation of the east Tennessee mountains. The novel is composed of three main narrative strands, and John Wesley's is the last to be introduced. The others center on his two mentors, the men who teach him mostly by precept and example. The first is Marion Sylder, a young bootlegger who kills John Wesley's vicious father in self-defense, hiding the body in an insecticide pit in an abandoned peach orchard. This incident occurs in 1934, when John Wesley is six. The second mentor is the orchard keeper, old Arthur Ownby, who discovers the corpse and keeps watch over it for seven years, until he feels its soul is at rest. Neither knows the other or the identity of the dead man, and neither meets John Wesley until 1940.

The novel is developed chronologically, from 1934 to 1941, with most of the action following the course of seasons from fall through spring in the year 1940–1941 and with a prologue and final episodes set in 1948; but it is built of discrete episodes focusing on the various characters, with little exposition to clarify the relation in time among these incidents. Italicized passages present flashbacks to earlier events, most of these representing the reflective stream of consciousness of a major character.

Through its three major characters the novel explores the relationship between the individual integrity and independence achievable in the remote and primitive natural world of the mountains and the often mindless strictures imposed by the advance of urban technology and bureaus. From the outset of his career McCarthy thus announces his deep skepticism about the human capacity for progress. The urban, institutional mechanization of human interaction is represented in such inflexible legal codes as the taxation of liquor and by a government-erected tank atop a mountain. This structure so offends Ownby that he shoots an *x* on its surface to protest its encroachment on his natural environment. The *x* as the Greek letter *chi* also represents the old man's rejection of this "great silver ikon, fat and bald and sinister" that would replace the old human verities, whether Christian or pre-Christian.

Such structures of civilization make outlaws of Sylder and Ownby – both, by contrast with the icon's keepers, "genial, unofficial, and awake" – though each is possessed of more generosity, fairmindedness, and discipline than the local constable and thug, Jefferson Gifford, or his inept tagalong, Legwater, who requires seven shots to execute a stray dog he has wounded with the first. Near the end of the novel both of John Wesley's surrogate fathers are incarcerated by the machinery of the new order. Sylder is jailed and beaten by Gifford; Ownby is locked up for an indeterminate period in a mental hospital.

John Wesley's grief for his friends leads him in turn to reject the new order of the modern world and to become a different man from the one his father had been. By internalizing the values of Uncle Ather (Ownby) he becomes the keeper of the orchard – at least in memory. There is nothing sentimental about the boy. He has lived in poverty in the natural world of fecundity and decay, helping himself to its resources when he could use them, teaching himself to be a hunter and trapper. His repudia-

tion of the world of bureaucracy and commerce occurs in the context of his sportsman's experience. He finds an ailing sparrow hawk that he first tries to nurse back to health; but when it dies he takes it to the county courthouse to collect a hawk bounty. Months later, after the arrests of his mentors, John Wesley returns to the courthouse to buy the bird back in a rejection of the purposes of the world of courts and laws. But he is further horrified to learn that the bird has been burned, "somehow figuring still that they must be kept, must have some value or use commensurate with a dollar other than the fact of their demise."

The fate of the sparrow hawk reinforces the lesson of Sylder and Ownby: "And thow people in jail and beat up on em. . . . And old men in the crazy house." In a final gesture of repudiation John Wesley thrusts the money onto the counter and leaves. When he returns to the region seven years later, the change has been accomplished completely: "No avatar, no scion, no vestige of that people remains. On the lips of the strange race that now dwells there their names are myth, legend, dust."

The corpse of Kenneth Rattner – which decays over seven years and is finally unwittingly set afire by John Wesley and his boyhood friends – functions as an analogue for the race of John Wesley's fathers. After seven years Ownby tells the authorities about the corpse, and the ashes are sifted by Legwater, who hopes to find the platinum plate reputed to have been in its skull – another bounty. His disappointment in locating nothing of value in the ashes leads him to kill Ownby's aged hound in a final demonstration of man's devotion to waste and death. When he returns to Red Branch at age twenty-one, John Wesley is an anachronism, a ghost of an earlier age. But he has inherited from Ownby the role of orchard keeper – the guardian of old ways and values – and this fate is not tragic.

Several reviewers of *The Orchard Keeper* saw in it great promise for even better work to come, and many lauded the evocative quality of its prose style. Arthur Edelstein (*National Observer*, 5 July 1965) admired McCarthy's "fusion of concreteness and metaphorical suggestiveness," a hallmark of his later work as well. Walter Sullivan (*Sewanee Review*, Autumn 1965) found McCarthy's language "magnificent, full of energy and sharp detail and the sounds and smells of God's creation." But many reviewers, even while noting the power of his language, stated that it was inconsistent, excessive, or overly indebted to William Faulkner and, less frequently, James Joyce. Sullivan responded that "such impressions are fleeting and prove to be false. McCarthy is like nobody so much as he is like all the writers who have gone before him and had sense enough to see in the land a source of human salvation." Reviewers were divided about whether the difficulties presented by the book's structure and narrative ambiguities were worth the reader's effort. And the objectivity with which McCarthy renders his characters caused some reviewers to miss the deep-running consciousness out of which the main characters act.

But the reception was largely positive, and Erskine likely brought *The Orchard Keeper* to the attention of the William Faulkner Foundation, which awarded the book its 1965 prize for the best first novel by an American. One of the three judges who made the selection was poet and Hollins College creative-writing teacher R. H. W. Dillard, who stated that "Cormac McCarthy is a young writer of dark vision who has been able in *The Orchard Keeper* to transmute that vision into an art which is strong and vital for all its darkness. . . . His is a powerful novel."

Later scholarly commentary has continued to focus on the ways in which *The Orchard Keeper* confounds the expectations of its readers and on the illusion – created by McCarthy's devotion to "objective" description of the physical context in which his characters find themselves – that his characters have no inner life. But those critics who have undertaken the most extended study of *The Orchard Keeper,* such as David Paul Ragan and William J. Schafer, have expressed appreciation for its complexity of structure and vision. Schafer finds in it evidence that "a mystery of existence which fascinates McCarthy is the resonance of human deeds – how a single act of good or evil radiates and affects the entire human community." In "Values and Structure in *The Orchard Keeper*" (*Perspectives on Cormac McCarthy,* 1993), Ragan argues, "When disintegrating cultural values are understood as informing not only McCarthy's themes but his narrative method . . . the episodes reveal a fully controlled, deliberately structured examination of the intrinsic human need to order, or at least to interpret, the world of nature and to understand the motivations of men."

When *The Orchard Keeper* was published, McCarthy had already been awarded a fellowship by the American Academy of Arts and Letters for a year of travel abroad. He embarked for Ireland by way of England on the *Sylvania* in summer 1965 with a rough draft of his second novel. En route he met a young singer and ballet dancer, Anne DeLisle – of Hamble, near Southampton in Hampshire, En-

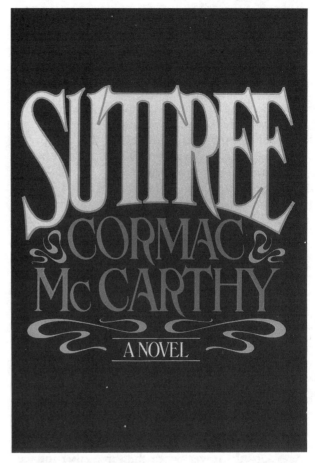

Dust jacket for McCarthy's 1979 novel, which is set primarily in a seamy section of Knoxville, Tennessee, during the early 1950s

gland – who was employed as an entertainer on the ship. They were married on 14 May 1966. With additional support from a Rockefeller Foundation grant (1966–1968), the pair traveled in Europe for two more years, spending long periods in London, Paris, and on the island of Ibiza in the Balearics, often in the company of novelist Leslie Garrett. Anne recalled, "That was a time when Ebiza [*sic*] was all writers and musicians and it really was a bohemian time and . . . it was like people were trying to recapture a feeling of '20s Paris with Hemingway."

McCarthy revised *Outer Dark* three or four times during this period. The novel was finished in Spain before he and his wife returned to the United States in December 1967 to live in Rockford, Tennessee, near Knoxville. Anne told an interviewer, "We lived in a little house for $50 a month, a little pig farm. Just outrageous." They settled into their new home just as McCarthy's parents were pulling up stakes. In 1968 McCarthy's father retired from the Tennessee Valley Authority, and he and Mc-Carthy's mother moved to Washington, D.C., where he went into a private law partnership.

Outer Dark was published in September 1968. The plot of *The Orchard Keeper* is basically simple, but its episodic development makes for more complexity in form. In *The Orchard Keeper* McCarthy employs a mythic technique so infused with naturalistic detail that the possibilities for mythic interpretation are scarcely apparent until near the end, when the design in the fabric suddenly becomes clear. *Outer Dark* is similar in structure to McCarthy's first novel, but it is much sparser. Its allegorical nature is made apparent in its opening – a prologue that introduces three mysterious figures who roam the landscape:

> *THEY CRESTED OUT on the bluff in the late afternoon sun with their shadows long on the sawgrass and burnt sedge, moving single file and slowly high above the river and with something of its own implacability . . . and then dropping under the crest of the hill into a fold of blue shadow with light touching them about the head in spurious sanctity until they had gone on for such a time as saw the sun down altogether and they moved in shadow altogether which suited them very well.*

The movements of these emissaries of darkness are reported in isolated italicized passages until fifty pages into the novel, when the three enter into its main action, scourging the environs of Culla Holme, the main character, who wanders the land. Ultimately their path twice converges with his, and they profoundly affect his fate.

In *The Orchard Keeper* the main characters are placed in an identifiable geographical region so remote as to be historically beyond the reach of civil law. The characters in *Outer Dark*, Culla Holme and his sister Rinthy, have taken up a life in the mountains in an ahistorical dreamscape of the outer darkness that bears topographical and cultural similarities to the rural American South. They are four miles from the nearest store and outside any human community – in such isolation that they might seem beyond the reach of any custom, common law, or moral law regulating the relations of human beings. Guilty of incest, Culla has moved them here to avoid exposure, and their story opens as Rinthy goes into labor and delivers their son. Guilt-ridden, Culla leaves the infant to perish in the woods and tells Rinthy it died at birth. The baby is taken up by a grotesque tinker, himself an outcast of human society; and Rinthy, intuiting these circumstances with a "willingness to disbelief" in the death of her baby, sets off to find the tinker and claim her child.

Culla in turn wanders in search of Rinthy – or so he tells those who ask.

The title of the novel comes from Matthew 8:9–12 and is an allusion to Christ's prediction that the faithless will be cast out to wander in outer darkness. The different fates of Culla and Rinthy, who share equally in their original sin, are parables of the fates of the faithful and the lost. Rinthy's faith is almost a biological process. The mere thought of her baby, or any suggestion that she is close to finding it, causes her milk to flow, and in her months of searching her milk never dries up. She is treated with relative kindness by the strangers she meets, even when they sense her sin. Her steadiness of purpose, her willingness to take responsibility for her child, and her quiet self-acceptance typically exempt her from harsh moral judgment. She is a natural creature like the doe, to which she is often compared. Yet she wanders in pain, repeatedly encountering families with varying configurations of children, living or dead.

Culla's wandering is much harsher and full of threat. Followed or anticipated in his travels by the dark figures who dispense death and violence wherever they go and who seem to predetermine some of his acts, Culla is greeted with suspicion and judgment by the people he meets, often being accused of the crimes committed by the three "foot soldiers of the apocalypse," as Schafer calls them. The distrust of the people he meets seems to arise from their instinctive recognition of his state of sin. Indeed, the narrative faintly implicates Culla in the dark figures' crimes, and, though he is unaware of any connection between them and himself, he repeatedly acquiesces in the guilt of which he is suspected, fleeing rather than answering people's accusations.

Culla's guilt is not so much the incest for which he feels overwhelming shame, but the very state of his soul – his lack of faith and grace – which seems both his sin and his punishment. Culla claims to be seeking, but in fact he makes no inquiry, follows no lead that might bring him to Rinthy. In his soul sickness he avoids human ties, just as he has discarded his own son. The world he wanders is a spiritual wasteland, a limbo, in which all beings partake of the satanic, perhaps most when they judge one another.

The lack of distinction between the satanic and their victims is most remarkably exemplified when Culla encounters a group of drovers with an immense herd of hogs. The devilish nature of all hogs – those with cloven hooves and those without – is established in Culla's conversation with one of the drovers, a talkative man who is later carried over a river bluff to his death when the demon hogs stampede. The drovers howl in satanic despair at this disaster yet are shown to contribute to it "as if they were no true swineherds but disciples of darkness got among these charges to herd them to their doom." Subsequently they blame Culla for the event, and, at the instigation of a diabolic parson who arrives "fending flies," they drive him to follow the hogs over the bluff to escape hanging. Culla is ostensibly a victim, but by jumping he identifies himself with the demon hogs. As a blind disciple of darkness he becomes a victim of darkness.

Though he travels the same terrain as Rinthy and though his history is nearly identical to hers, Culla is brought to a different end because of his spiritual blindness. He tells one of his acquaintances that his father taught him that a man makes his own luck. The contrast between Culla's and Rinthy's fates reinforces the notion that Culla's world of darkness is of his own choosing, his own making. Rinthy also suffers, as any living creature must. She finds the tinker, but he refuses to give her the child, judging in his own bitterness that she is not fit to have it. She never understands what has happened to her, nor why. But her seeking is itself a kind of salvation, and finally she is released from her quest and sleeps, whereas Culla continues to wander. Called to answer for several crimes, Culla is invariably found guilty by his human and allegorical inquisitors, both real and dreamed. Rinthy is found guilty only once, by the outcast tinker.

The ultimate scene of judgment, however, is brought about by the three dark emissaries in a repulsive version of divine retribution. Culla finds them in the tinker's camp, where they have hanged the tinker (apparently claiming their own) and are in custody of the child. In emblem of his divided nature and of the opposed natures of his parents, the boy is scarred over one half of his body and blind in one eye. With every word and action infused with threat, the leader of the three challenges Culla to own the child, much as Solomon used the threat of murder to determine the mother of the disputed infant. Culla denies his kinship to the boy, and the bearded "prophet" cuts the child's throat and delivers him up to the cannibalistic enjoyment of one of his fellows.

Yet this climactic judgment against Culla brings him no closer to spiritual atonement. The final scene finds him several years later, still wandering. He watches a blind man progressing toward a swamp, with no insight of the relevance of such an image to himself: "He wondered where the blind man was going and did he know how the road ended. Someone should tell a blind man before setting him out that way."

Reviews of *Outer Dark* were even more sharply divided than those of *The Orchard Keeper*. Some critics gave it short shrift, complaining of its murky Gothicism, inconsistent tone, and flamboyant prose. Neither book was appreciated by British reviewers. But several American writers – Guy Davenport, Robert Coles, and John William Corrington among them – agreed that *Outer Dark* was superior even to *The Orchard Keeper* and admired the virtuosity of McCarthy's prose styles: the vernacular and the elevated. In a long, meditative, and highly serious review-essay, Coles (*New Yorker,* 22 March 1969) commented on the intersection of style and matter: "The reader . . . is rewarded with an astonishing range of language – slow-paced and heavy or delightfully light, relaxed or intense, perfectly plain or thoroughly intricate. Eternal principles mix company with the details of everyday, pastoral life – always under some apocalyptic cloud, though." These reviewers compared the book's treatment of fate to Greek tragedy, its treatment of the horrific to Isak Dinesen's Gothic tales. Addressing the inner life of McCarthy's characters, Coles wrote: "[McCarthy] can bring about emotions in both his characters and his readers without making a whole showy business out of the effort."

Recent critics have tended to give more attention to McCarthy's later, bigger books, but Edwin T. Arnold, one of the earliest and most appreciative of McCarthy scholars, has seen in *Outer Dark* a paradigm for the moral vision that informs all of McCarthy's later work. Answering Bell's assessment that *Outer Dark* is "as brutally nihilistic as any serious novel written in this century in this unnihilistic country," Arnold argues that in this novel, as in the others, "There is . . . always the possibility of grace and redemption . . . although that redemption may require more of his characters than they are ultimately willing to give" because "sins must be named and owned before they can be forgiven." Arnold builds on Schafer, demonstrating the novel's use of biblical themes set forth in Matthew, 1 Corinthians, and Revelation.

In 1969 McCarthy received a Guggenheim Fellowship for fiction writing. While living on such grants he continued work on *Suttree,* which he had begun in the early 1960s, but he again spelled himself on this big project by writing a shorter book that probably had its inception in 1965. *Child of God* (1974) is based on an actual murder case in the Knoxville area, and the novel dates the death of the main character and the recovery of his victims' bodies in April 1965. Possibly McCarthy had been

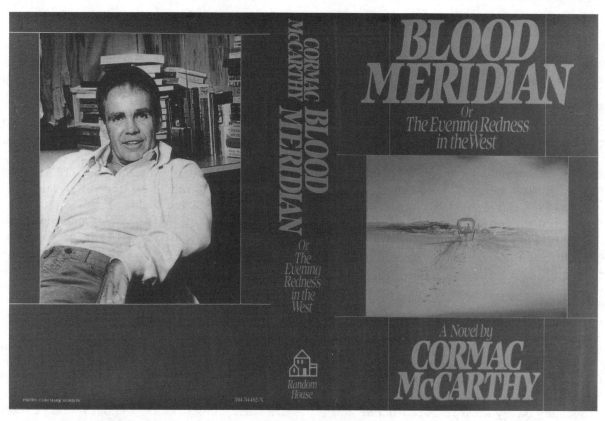

Dust jacket for McCarthy's 1985 novel, in which a bounty hunter and his gang pursue Apache Indians in the Southwest and Mexico in 1849 and 1850

reading newspaper accounts and talking with locals about this case just before he departed for Europe that summer. He was known to be working on *Child of God* in October 1968, and he and Anne were talking about going to Mexico and back to Europe when it was completed.

Lester Ballard, the central character in *Child of God,* is another outcast and outlaw, one alienated from human society and from anything else that might nurture the human soul within him. He is a child of God, "much like yourself perhaps," the narrator remarks. Yet what Ballard endures and what he does are outside the experience of McCarthy's implied reader. The novel chronicles the process of Ballard's alienation and consequent abandonment of any of the standards that typically govern human behavior. Its opening scene introduces the dominant theme of dispossession, as Ballard's small farm is auctioned for nonpayment of taxes. When he protests, brandishing a rifle, he is felled from behind with the blunt side of an ax.

In one of several scenes in which Ballard's neighbors in Sevier County, Tennessee, recall events of his childhood and youth, one among them concludes that Ballard was never quite right after being hit with the ax. But these brief scenes of idle community dialogue – the source of a region's legends – stand in opposition to the novel's third-person narrative of the twenty-seventh year of Ballard's life. Ballard's neighbors mean to account for his behavior, but their explanations are only partial ones. In recalling his mother's abandoning him and his father, his father's subsequent suicide, Lester's matter-of-fact report of that event in the nearby store, or his bullying behavior toward other children, the members of his community provide important background information, but they draw conclusions that do not fit the larger pattern as it is shown to the reader.

Ballard at twenty-seven is a man with almost nothing – no family, no home, no profession, and no acceptance within the community. He is divested of all but his basic human needs, his raging anger, and his ability to shoot a rifle with deadly accuracy. After his property is sold, a neighbor allows him the use of an abandoned cabin, and Ballard seeks a way of living even as his range of choices becomes more and more constricted.

Ballard's predicament is dramatized in terms of his human needs not only for a home and shelter but also for sexual contact. Considered peculiar, he finds it nearly impossible to approach the women he knows. They rebuff him not because they are chaste, nor because they are less crude than he, but because he is in some way marked as a pariah. As his parents and the law have dispossessed him of what he considers his by right, so the women he approaches deny him both sexual outlet and intimacy. This process of denial reaches a culmination when Ballard discovers a whore sleeping by the roadside; she has been abandoned wearing only a thin nightgown. He wakes her to ask whether she is cold, only to be attacked, vilified, accused of rape, and temporarily jailed.

Given his status as social outcast, Ballard does what he can to satisfy his sexual urge. In an inexorable progression of events that bear a horrifyingly logical relationship to one another, Ballard relieves his sexual frustration first by spying on a couple parked at a turnaround on a mountain road and masturbating on their car fender; then by taking home the body of a young woman who has died there of carbon-monoxide poisoning so that he can possess her sexually; and finally — after his borrowed house and the woman's corpse burn — by killing people in order to possess them. He becomes a necrophiliac by apparent necessity. Ballard has an instinctive understanding of his first murder victim's idiot child (another child of God), who chews off the legs of a robin because "he wanted it to where it couldn't run off."

When his borrowed house and the first corpse burn, Ballard retreats to a cave in the mountains, living more and more like an animal yet still a child of God with his all-too-human perversions. Denied the society of the living, Ballard peoples his cave with the dead. Suspect and pursued, he struggles to preserve his life and belongings, dimly aware that he has become alien even from himself, dressing in women's clothing and scalps and wondering at night of what stuff he is made.

But, unlike Culla Holme, who is doomed to perpetual blindness, Ballard has brief, intermittent glimmerings of what has happened to him, and these insights bring an end to his life as an outlaw. The process of dispossession does not end (he ultimately loses his arm, his freedom, and his life), but Ballard seems finally to accept it. Spring brings a consciousness of soul sickness, and Ballard dreams of his death. In a desperate culmination of his self-destructive rage, Ballard tries to kill the man who had bought his home at auction, but his victim shoots back, blasting away Ballard's arm. A mob takes him from the hospital and forces him to lead them to his victims' corpses, but he eludes them in the caverns. After three days of wandering underground, lost himself, he emerges; and, after a startling vision of a little boy's face in the window of a church bus — a face he feels is his own — he returns to the hospital, where he says he belongs.

Though the story of Lester Ballard seems a case study in depravity, and though the progression of events from cause to effect seems inevitable and logical, the emphasis of this novel is not entirely on the psychological motivation of a psychopathic character. *Child of God* is the most overt example of McCarthy's practice of depicting his characters' motivations as they arise from that locus in the mind where psyche and spirit intersect. In fact, to a degree even more pronounced than in *Outer Dark,* this novel insists upon both the mystery of Ballard's fate and the fact that he is not inherently different from his neighbors. The suggestions of Sevier County residents that Ballard was born different, that he was always beyond the pale, and that his family had bad blood ignore his essential humanity and the community's bloody and corrupt history and thus emphasize the inadequacy of explanations for the violence and aberrations that so delineate human experience.

When Ballard, pursued, tries to cross a flood-swollen creek, the narrator comments, "He could not swim, but how would you drown him? His wrath seemed to buoy him up. Some halt in the way of things seems to work here." Rejecting what the reader "could say" — that "he's sustained by his fellow men, like you. . . . A race that gives suck to the maimed and the crazed, that wants their wrong blood in its history and will have it" — he falls back on the question: "How then is he borne up? Or rather, why will not these waters take him?"

The horror of *Child of God* is that McCarthy insists that Ballard is not far removed from the reader — an example of what can so readily go wrong with a child of God. In a set piece that serves as a kind of parable of Ballard's and of everyman's life, Ballard takes an ax to a blacksmith for sharpening, whereupon the smith delivers a discourse on the proper dressing of an ax. Lecturing as he works, he eulogizes attention to detail and careful provision of the proper conditions for fine, strong steel that will hold a sharp edge. The tool must be fashioned for its function from start to finish: "Do the least part of it wrong," the smith concludes, "and ye'd just as well to do it all wrong."

The implication is that the Craftsman is to blame for the flawed creation that Ballard is.

Through inattention or indifference – or perhaps by design – such children of God come to be. Earlier, and more pointedly, the smith says, "Some people will poke around at somethin else and leave the tool they're heatin to perdition but the proper thing is to fetch her out the minute she shows the color of grace." Ballard is, until the end, without grace. "Were there darker provinces of night he would have found them," the narrator says. Dispossessed of his earthly parents, he seems dispossessed of God the Father as well. He is an outcast child, unable to establish ties with the human family or to find guidance from outside himself. As such, he – like Culla – wanders in outer darkness, loving death rather than life.

The reviews of *Child of God* were mixed. While most of the negative reviewers conceded that the novel was compelling and that its prose was lean and beautiful, they complained that Ballard was not sufficiently explained or motivated and the book lacked moral sophistication and universal vision. In the *New York Times Book Review* (13 January 1974) Richard P. Brickner chafed at McCarthy's "hostility toward the reader," and several reviewers were hard-pressed to come to terms with McCarthy's narrative stance. The more positive reviews were generous in their praise, and McCarthy's third novel received more extended, informed discussions from its American reviewers than had his previous two. Some critics, such as Doris Grumbach and Coles, praised McCarthy's tragic sense; Coles (*New Yorker,* 26 August 1974) found that "McCarthy resembles the ancient Greek dramatists and medieval moralists – a strange, incompatible mixture," concluding that "he is a novelist of religious feeling who appears to subscribe to no creed but who cannot stop wondering in the most passionate and honest way what gives life meaning." Coles felt that McCarthy asked no compassion for his character, while Anatole Broyard (*New York Times,* 5 December 1973) marveled at the way in which the writer prompted his readers to care about the warped, loveless Ballard. Broyard pinpointed the strengths of McCarthy's prose style in its "risky eloquence, intricate rhythms and dead-to-rights accuracy."

In a mixed review (*Commonweal,* 29 March 1974) Robert Leiter placed the novel within the context of McCarthy's earlier books: "Lester is all there is to *Child of God,* and for all his mystery he is not enough. The novel is thinner, less full-bodied than either *The Orchard Keeper* or *Outer Dark;* this has little to do with length." Subsequent assessments of *Child of God* have not been inconsistent with Leiter's view. While most critics see the novel as fully successful on its own terms, it is regarded as a smaller, less ambitious work, interesting in its own right but also for its pronounced links with McCarthy's later, more ambitious treatment of the murderous history of humankind in *Blood Meridian or The Evening Redness in the West* (1985).

Although the *Knoxville News-Sentinel* carried stories during the 1960s and 1970s about McCarthy's books, awards, and travels, sometimes eliciting brief statements from him, he was already arranging his life to preserve his time and energy for his writing. To the dismay of his wife, he was willing to live simply and rustically and was reluctant to supplement their income by lecturing. She told Woodward, "Someone would call up and offer him $2,000 to come speak at a university about his books. And he would tell them that everything he had to say was there on the page. So we would eat beans for another week." To Williams she said, "He didn't carry insurance. He was such a rebel that he didn't live the same kind of life anybody else on earth lived." During most of the 1970s they lived in a refurbished barn in Louisville, Tennessee. McCarthy did the masonry work himself, constructing a stone chimney and room and salvaging bricks from the James Agee house, which was being demolished for urban renewal. They lived on grants and the income Anne gathered from operating a dance studio.

McCarthy's privacy became increasingly important to him. He had agreed to be listed in *Who's Who* as late as the 1972–1973 edition; after that he allowed no further entries. And he declined to be interviewed. In 1990 his brother Dennis observed, "It's almost like superstition. . . . He's afraid he'll ruin whatever he has going if he talks. I think there's a lot to be said for pushing your books. But then he's been able to write all these years. Sales have not been all that great, but he's been able to do it. I very much respect his sense of privacy."

According to Anne, an emotional separation developed between her and McCarthy around 1974, though they did not separate until 1976, nor divorce until 1980. But there were times when McCarthy was away from Knoxville working on his writing projects. He may have made his first extended trip to El Paso, Texas, as early as 1974. In 1975 he wrote *The Gardener's Son* for the *Visions* series of original television dramas on public television. He collaborated on the project with film director Richard Pearce, who was interested in making a film based on a historical event and who asked McCarthy to write the television play about a murder committed in 1876 in the textile village of Granite-

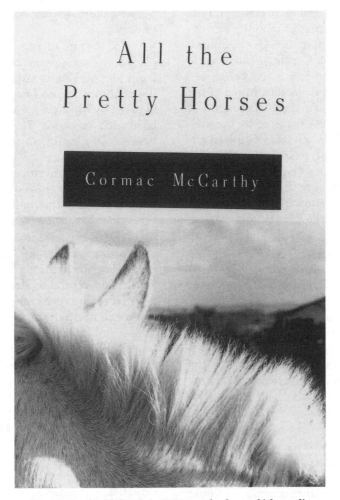

Dust jacket for McCarthy's 1992 novel, about which novelist
Madison Smartt Bell wrote, "McCarthy's vision is deeper than
Larry McMurtry's and, in its own way, darker than
Mark Twain's"

ville, South Carolina. They did much of the historical research together, and McCarthy was involved in the making of the film as well. He appears in it in a brief, nonspeaking role as one of the mill company's stockholders.

McCarthy's story of Robert McEvoy – the crippled son of a laboring family who murders the scion of the Gregg family, owners of the mill – is, like his novels, dark and complex. McCarthy said of McEvoy, "The kid was a natural rebel, probably just a troublemaker in real life. But in our film he has a certain nobility. He stands up and says, 'No, this is intolerable and I want to do something about it!'" The teleplay has affinities with *The Orchard Keeper* in its exploration of the diminished sense of responsibility toward one's brothers that follows in the wake of commercial and technological progress. The tragic nobility with which McCarthy's teleplay invests Robert McEvoy resides in his conquering

the soul sickness that dominates him in order to face his unjust hanging with acceptance and dignity. The program was first aired in January 1977.

Though McCarthy's involvement with *The Gardener's Son* took him away from the Knoxville area for at least part of 1975, he was continuing to work on *Suttree*. On New Year's Eve he told Anne that he would be leaving her, and he departed for El Paso in January. There he began *Blood Meridian,* another big project, which was not published for nearly ten years.

February 1979 brought the culmination of McCarthy's twenty years' work on *Suttree*. This big, ambitious book again focuses on a single misfit character who suffers from a kind of soul sickness. It employs some of the themes and techniques of the two novels that precede it but with a much richer texture and on a much larger canvas. In *Suttree* McCarthy moves from the rural mountain settings of his earlier novels into the city of Knoxville, but his main character has a wide range of mobility and experience. There are scenes in the Great Smoky Mountains; Asheville, North Carolina; Gatlinburg, Tennessee; and other places in eastern Tennessee as well as in various parts of Knoxville. Much of the action is centered in the McAnally Flats section of Knoxville – a seamy district inhabited by the substrata of the black and white residents of the city, a half mile from the river where Cornelius (Buddy) Suttree lives in a houseboat. Whereas community life is sketched in broad strokes in McCarthy's earlier novels, in *Suttree* the community of drunks and derelicts among whom Suttree lives is finely articulated. Dozens of McAnally Flats inhabitants are introduced, and of these a good number emerge as fully conceived characters.

Suttree is a young man from a prominent Knoxville family who – like McCarthy himself – attended Catholic schools and then the University of Tennessee. While there Suttree met a girl from a small mountain town, married her, had a son with her, and then abandoned her, retreating to the riverfront in Knoxville, where he makes a meager living as a fisherman in the filthy Tennessee River – the "cloaca maxima" of the city – and occasionally, despite better intentions, gets drunk with the inhabitants of McAnally Flats.

The novel relates the events of Suttree's life from October 1950, when he is in the workhouse, until spring 1955, when he leaves the city. Opening in summer 1951, its structure is predominantly chronological except for the major dislocation in time in which the novel's second most important character – Gene Harrogate, Suttree's "little buddy" – is introduced and his life is brought into confluence with Suttree's in the workhouse. Throughout, McCarthy employs a flexible third-person narration that often takes on the diction and perspective of its subject to merge almost without seam into a first-person point of view. The narration fluctuates smoothly from objective, to central, to first-person perspectives, providing some of the intimate acquaintance with the main character that interior monologue might, without ever seeming to report anything but the experience of the character. Inner obsessions are projected into the external world, and inner experience, such as dreaming, is undifferentiated from external, sensory experience. The technique perfectly dramatizes what McCarthy uses the contrasting experiences of Culla and Rinthy Holme in *Outer Dark* to illustrate: that the world one experiences is of one's own making and that the outer world one experiences is as much a projection of one's state of mind and soul as is the inner world of dreams.

In its state of ruin Suttree's city is often perceived as a wasteland. Suttree himself is a refugee from life, especially from family life and from the life of commerce and professional achievement advocated by his father. Half in pursuit of death, half in morbid fear of it, Suttree in fact feels that he is twinned with death, since his twin brother was stillborn. He suffers, the narrator observes, a "subtle obsession with uniqueness," and part of his rejection of his family is his compulsive denial of the genetic repetition among family members – the very repetition that makes life possible.

Dreading both death and life Suttree has withdrawn, but neither life nor death will leave him alone. His decaying environment is teeming with animal and vegetable life reclaiming the ruins of the city. His impoverished friends, all of whom have fewer intellectual and physical resources than he does, continually touch his humanity, drawing him into familial relations, involving him in their lives and their pain. And, because he cannot divorce himself from life, Suttree is constantly confronted with death. In grim succession his son dies, then a young girl with whom he shares a mock-pastoral love affair in one of the episodes set outside of Knoxville, and then a series of his friends from McAnally Flats.

Suttree's sensibilities, both physical and emotional, are constantly harrowed. His head is battered by a drunk wielding an electric floor buffer, by a boat thief slinging rocks, and by exposure to alcohol of inferior quality. He witnesses other men's pain, is coerced into helping a friend submerge the corpse of his father six months dead, and descends into the sewers under the city to find Harrogate, whose mindless opportunism has led him nearly to kill himself by dynamiting a sewage restraining wall, imagining it leads to a bank vault.

Intelligent, often admirable, and even sane by the standards of this novel, Suttree is yet another wanderer in outer darkness, prey to soul sickness. The metaphoric implications of existence in the wasteland of McAnally Flats are most explicitly stated in reference to Harrogate's wandering in the underground tunnels: "He began to suspect some dimensional displacement in these descents to the underworld, some disparity unaccountable between the above and the below." The nadir of Suttree's course occurs when he becomes involved with a whore who carries on unspecified but very lucrative dealings in successive towns in neighboring states. Suttree takes an apartment in Knoxville with her, holding the money she sends and gradually allowing her to support him. But he is unable to respond to the debased humanity in her or to understand why, finally, she falls into a drunken rage, kicking the car she has provided him and shredding the money that is the basis of their relationship.

Unlike Culla Holme, however, Suttree is at last redeemed. A near-fatal encounter with typhoid fever provides a final challenge to his life and sanity. In the last of a series of hallucinations and dreams, Suttree faces his own death, stands self-accused of squandering his life, and wakes affirming life as process and his own uniqueness. Returning to his houseboat, he finds a corpse in his bed, a body somehow identified with himself; but he is able to face it calmly and then to leave the waste of McAnally Flats. The brief final section of the novel suggests the changed quality of his experience in quick strokes: a blond waterboy offers him a drink and a passing car stops to offer him a ride, though he has asked for neither. The novel ends with Suttree's recognition of the agents of darkness that had dominated him:

> Somewhere in the gray wood by the river is the huntsman and in the brooming corn and in the castellated press of cities. His work lies all wheres and his hounds tire not. I have seen them in a dream, slaverous and wild and their eyes crazed with ravening for souls in this world. Fly them.

Suttree provoked a new wave of reviewers' complaints about McCarthy's choice of horrific and grotesque materials and his "Thesauritis," although most critics praised his ear for dialect. Even Sullivan (*Sewanee Review*, April 1979), who had praised McCarthy's earlier work, found in *Suttree* a "limited use of an enormous talent": amorphous structure, lack of resolution, and overwriting. But Davenport (*National Review*, 16 March 1979), anticipating these charges, defended the book: "Critics have sniped at McCarthy's studied prose rhythms and unfamiliar words, not seeing the need he has of them. He must summon his world before our eyes in all its richness and exactness of shape, because that is all he is summoning." He added, "Though it seems to ramble from jail to river to alley, its structure is as tight as the strings on a guitar." In an impassioned defense of the novel provoked by a negative review in the *Memphis Press-Scimitar*, Shelby Foote (17 February 1979) pointed out the resolution provided in "Suttree's redemption" and wrote, "I cannot see how anyone . . . can avoid the deep-rocking belly laughs I found on almost every page of this evocative and highly poetic examination of what is admit-

tedly the bottom stratum of our society." Others praised the book's humor as well, and Jim Crace, reviewing the British edition for the *New Statesman* (2 May 1980), commented, "Compared to [*Suttree*] much of the current British fiction seems insipid and self-consciously discursive."

Despite these appreciative assessments, *Suttree* received surprisingly little serious attention from reviewers – perhaps because the book is too complex, too difficult to yield to a quick read. As much or more than McCarthy's earlier books, it seems to have been, initially, a succès d'estime. Even the *New York Times Book Review* (18 February 1979) assessment by novelist Jerome Charyn was relatively brief and noncommittal, and that by Broyard (*New York Times*, 20 January 1979), while admiring the book's depiction of hell as local color, consisted mostly of plot summary and long quotations.

Since the middle 1980s, however, *Suttree* has elicited several article-length studies, most of them focusing on Suttree's obsession with death and his progress toward redemption, and the novel is now regarded as the pinnacle of McCarthy's work with his Tennessee materials. Thomas D. Young, Jr., has found that "the assertion of the ultimate integrity and sufficiency of the self and of the value of a human community based on an affiliation of such selves is what *Suttree* – and McCarthy's fiction in general – comes to affirm." Increasingly there seems to be a recognition that – with its interior monologues of Suttree's hallucinations and dream states and even waking states – this novel is McCarthy's most explicit portrait of the tumultuous inner life of his main characters.

In the decade between *Suttree* and *Blood Meridian*, McCarthy continued to live in spartan simplicity: he stayed in rented rooms and, like Suttree, gave up alcohol. While writing *Blood Meridian*, he traced the path of its nomadic characters, researching the geography, topography, and life – wild and civil – of its southwestern settings as well as the history and the Spanish language. With a home base in El Paso, where he had at least a vault for his manuscripts and an attorney friend to receive his mail, he worked on the book in Arizona, Mexico, Texas, and Santa Fe. McCarthy told photographer Mark Morrow, "I just decide to go to a place, take a room, and write." In 1981, when McCarthy learned that he had been awarded a MacArthur Foundation "genius grant" of $236,000 over five years, he was staying in a Knoxville motel. The following year he bought a small cottage in El Paso – "a distinctly Andalusian structure of white-washed stone with black iron grilles over the windows," according to Robert

Draper in *Texas Monthly* – and began renovations. McCarthy finished *Blood Meridian* in a motel room on Kingston Pike in Knoxville, not far from one of his early childhood homes. It was published in March 1985.

"There's no such thing as life without bloodshed," McCarthy told Woodward. "I think the notion that the species can be improved in some way, that everyone could live in harmony, is a really dangerous idea. Those who are afflicted with this notion are the first ones to give up their souls, their freedom. Your desire that it be that way will enslave you and make your life vacuous." This observation is an apt gloss on *Blood Meridian,* a deeply researched historical novel tracing the scalp-hunting expeditions waged by bounty hunter John Joel Glanton and his gang against the Apache Indians in Mexico and the American Southwest in 1849 and 1850.

The novel follows the life of a nameless "kid" – loosely based on Samuel Chamberlain as he describes his adventures in *My Confession* (1956), but not precisely a historical character – from the day he leaves his home and alcoholic father in rural Tennessee at age fourteen until his death in 1878 at forty-three. Ignorant, penniless, and already with "a taste for mindless violence," the kid drifts to Memphis, Saint Louis, and New Orleans, where he brawls with "men from lands so far and queer that standing over them where they lie bleeding in the mud he feels mankind itself vindicated." After the kid crosses the Mississippi River and heads west into Texas, the narrator announces, "Only now is the child finally divested of all that he has been. His origins are become remote as is his destiny and not again in all the world's turning will there be terrains so wild and barbarous to try whether the stuff of creation may be shaped to man's will or whether his own heart is not another kind of clay."

The plot of *Blood Meridian* is in some ways a more fully articulated reworking of that of *Outer Dark,* with the kid retracing the spiritual wandering of Culla Holme while apparently answering some of the basic compulsions of Lester Ballard. Divested of family and nearly all material possessions, the kid passes up the opportunity to join a group of working cowhands, instead finding sustenance and companions first in a band of military irregulars organized by Captain William White to wrest Sonora from the Mexicans – "a race of degenerates," White claims, "a people manifestly incapable of governing themselves" – and then, when White's unit is destroyed by Comanche Indians, in Glanton's gang, hired by the Mexican government to scalp Indians.

Under the direction of the mad Glanton and his familiar, the Mephistophelian Judge Holden, the gang wages an escalating racial war against all "niggers" – Indian or Mexican – and becomes hunted by the Mexican army until it takes control of the Yuma ferry on the Colorado River to rob and kill the argonauts and other westward pilgrims who must cross there. The gang is finally decimated by the Yuma Indians, whom they have cheated.

For much of the book, while Glanton is alive and the gang is pursuing his mad bloodletting, the kid is absorbed into the communal life of the gang – like Ishmael, who follows his own mad captain in Herman Melville's *Moby-Dick* (1851), virtually disappearing into the narrative. After he joins Glanton, the kid's presence is seldom felt in the novel's narrative voice, and, though he is witness to and participant in the horrendous deeds of the gang, his particular acts of violence are not detailed. His individual life becomes real to the reader (and perhaps to himself) only in the few scenes in which he becomes separated out by his own choices or by those of the judge.

He differentiates himself when he commits gestures of compassion toward his ruthless companions: he would draw an arrow from his wounded ally Juan Miguel, but Glanton intervenes and puts a bullet through the Mexican's head. The kid alone volunteers to push clear the arrow lodged in the leg of another companion, David Brown, but when he has succeeded, the "expriest" Tobin hisses, "Fool. . . . Dont you know he'd of took you with him? He'd of took you, boy. Like a bride to the altar." The kid's fleeting and rare impulses toward sympathy are inspired by sentimentality and are quickly admonished. They come from no abiding commitment to life. One of the novel's epigraphs, from Paul Valéry, aptly comments, "Your acts of pity and cruelty are absurd, committed with no calm, as if they were irresistible. Finally, you fear blood more and more. Blood and time." The kid's compassion is as absurd as that of his friend Toadvine, who, to ransom them from a Mexican prison, has volunteered them both as Indian killers, but who is outraged when the judge murders and scalps a young Indian boy Holden has preserved from one of their massacres only a few days earlier.

It becomes increasingly clear that the kid's acts are little of his own determination: that he, like the others, has accepted a pact with the diabolical judge who has appeared out of nowhere to save Glanton's gang from Indians and who holds them all on a tether, mystifying them with learned discourse and obfuscating "sermons" delivered around

McCarthy, circa 1992 (photograph by Marion Ettlinger)

their campfires. In one of the last of these sermons, he casts a coin that "must have been fastened to some subtle lead" into the dark beyond the firelight, catching it on its return to his hand: "The arc of circling bodies is determined by the length of their tether, said the judge. Moons, coins, men."

As if to test and temper his commitment to the life of the darkness, the kid – only apparently by chance – is elected by lottery to stay behind the gang to execute the wounded Shelby rather than leave him to the mercies of the Sonoran cavalry. Here the kid is left alone, resolved back into his individuality to make a choice for compassion or cruelty or any kind of responsible action. But he evades responsibility for Shelby's fate, offering to leave him alive if that is Shelby's preference, but declining actively to assist him by giving him a gun. He has no answer to Shelby's question, "You're no better than [Glanton]. Are you?" His gesture of offering Shelby the choice of life is again absurd; Shelby's choice is predetermined by his terror of death, and, as the kid leaves him, Elias's troops are fast approaching. Nor does the kid take this oppor-

tunity to free himself from his bond to Glanton and the judge. Pursued by Elias and separated from the gang for several days, he arduously tracks them down and rejoins them.

After Glanton's death the plot is less structured by historical event, and the narrative perspective focuses more consistently on the kid. Once more he is given latitude to break away from the judge's power. Stalked by the judge in the desert west of the Yuma ferry, the kid is urged by Tobin to shoot Holden – a strange invocation because all along Tobin has tutored the kid on the demonic nature of the judge. But, when the kid has the judge in his sights, he fails to act. "Ye'll get no such a chance as that again," says Tobin, and, as if he has fulfilled his role, the "expriest" disappears from the novel soon thereafter.

The kid is arrested when he reaches San Diego. Jailed, "he began to speak with a strange urgency of things few men have seen in a lifetime and his jailers said that his mind had come uncottered by the acts of blood in which he had participated." In a dream or hallucination reminiscent of Suttree's, he is visited by the judge, who asserts the kid's responsibility for the destruction at the Yuma ferry (the kid had not been in the encampment at the time), accusing him of imperfect devotion to the life of the darkness:

> You came forward . . . to take part in a work. But you were a witness against yourself. You sat in judgement on your own deeds. You put your own allowances before the judgements of history and you broke with the body of which you were pledged a part and poisoned it in all its enterprise.

The kid counters, "It was you. . . . You were the one." The dream encounter dramatizes the interiority of outer dark. It is both the kid's self-accusation and his denial of responsibility, and like Culla Holme he continues to wander, neither fully committed to the life of carnage to which he has been initiated nor redeemed.

After several years of guiding pilgrims to the West, during which he makes a few aborted gestures of penitence or atonement, the kid – now in 1878 "the man" – is challenged to own his part in the deeds of the scalp hunters by another kid, Elrod, one of the "violent children orphaned by war." Provoking the man, perhaps out of jealousy for his violent deeds, Elrod expresses disdainful disbelief in the man's story of how he came to own the scapular of mummified human ears that he wears ambiguously, as souvenir or penance. When Elrod stalks the man at night, he is lying in wait, and he kills the boy.

A few days later, coming to the end of the tether allowed him, his path converges with that of the judge in a saloon in Fort Griffin, where the man claims to have come for drink and whores. Deeply afraid despite his denial, he avoids the judge's eyes, but the judge seeks him out, calling him "the last of the true" and saying, "Drink up. This night thy soul may be required of thee." In a reflection of the Faust legend, later that night the man as by necessity delivers himself up to the judge, who awaits him in the outhouse: "The judge was seated upon the closet. He was naked and he rose up smiling and gathered him in his arms against his immense and terrible flesh and shot the wooden barlatch home behind him."

The final image in the novel proper is of the judge dancing in celebration of his triumph: "He dances in light and in shadow and he is a great favorite. He never sleeps, the judge. He is dancing, dancing. He says that he will never die." A one-paragraph epilogue that stands outside the narrative frame of the novel comments on those who search and those who do not and posits an alternative to the kid, a man who, unlike others, is able to progress over the plain, "*striking the fire out of the rock which God has put there.*"

Probably because its chronicle of man's capacity for mindless violence is so unrelenting, *Blood Meridian* was not extensively reviewed, and those reviewers who stayed with the book but were confused by McCarthy's objectivity often were hard-pressed to identify its moral vision. Sullivan (*Sewanee Review,* Fall 1985), a longtime follower of McCarthy's career, professed difficulty, interpreting the novel as a "celebration of rapacity." At the same time, Sullivan admitted, "[McCarthy] comprehends evil in all its dimensions, and this makes him a prophet. Visit his blasted landscapes, read the dark hearts of his people, and get a view of the world in which we live." Both Sullivan and Terence Moran in the *New Republic* (6 May 1985) complained that the novel is sometimes boring. Moran savaged the book for its "hyperbolic violence, strained surrealism," and the judge's "pseudo-philosophic palaver," narrowly missing McCarthy's point when he declared that McCarthy's Holden is "The Man Who Never Shuts Up" and added, "He may also be the devil." Sullivan was kinder but writes, "His eye for terrain is too good: his catalogues of fauna and flora and geologic contour can be tiresome."

Yet the book had several glowing reviews, some by readers in the West who were new to McCarthy's work. They recognized that *Blood Meridian* is a revisionist historical novel that parodies the romantic popular Westerns of the nineteenth and twentieth centuries. Even Moran admired this trait and agreed with more appreciative readers who noticed McCarthy's imbuing his allegorical landscape with a kind of sentience: "McCarthy's landscape is his real protagonist, looming over the kid's story like some perverse deity or idiot narrator." Several reviewers defended the brutality of McCarthy's fictional materials and argued for placing him in the contexts of Fyodor Dostoyevsky, Melville, and Joseph Conrad, or John Milton and William Shakespeare. Interestingly, complaints about McCarthy's use of language were not forthcoming.

In a retrospective on the 1980s for the *Bloomsbury Review* (January–February 1990) Gregory McNamee wrote that in that decade, "Cormac McCarthy's *Blood Meridian* . . . one of the truly great American novels, saw print, was immediately forgotten, and achieved cult status in the space of a little more than a year." This seems a fair statement. In an *American Heritage* (October 1992) feature listing contemporary writers' favorite historical novels, *Blood Meridian* was nominated by both Annie Dillard and Foote. The book has indeed won new readers for McCarthy; regarded as his most challenging work to date, *Blood Meridian* is becoming his most studied by academic critics.

John Emil Sepich has undertaken exhaustive identification of McCarthy's historical sources in a book and several related articles, and there have been studies of the philosophical themes in *Blood Meridian*. At the first national McCarthy conference, three separate sessions were devoted to this novel. *Blood Meridian* is seen by many as a culmination of McCarthy's career-long concern with humankind's dark history and with its feeble contention against spiritual wilderness.

Since moving to the Southwest in 1976, McCarthy has completed or drafted at least three novels in addition to *Blood Meridian*; a stage play, *The Stonemason* (1994); and at least one screenplay. When *All the Pretty Horses* was published in April 1992, his publisher announced that it was to be part 1 of "The Border Trilogy." The third volume was written more than ten years earlier as a screenplay, which Pearce was interested in directing if a producer could be found. According to Woodward its plot centers on John Grady Cole, also the protagonist of *All the Pretty Horses,* and concerns his love for a young Mexican prostitute. This may or may not be the same screenplay described by a friend as "a comparison between Sodom and Gomorrah with El Paso and Juarez." It is uncertain when the second volume, *The Crossing* (1994), had its inception, although McCarthy was working on it when Woodward interviewed him in March 1992, and it is doubtful that McCarthy himself conceived of the books as a trilogy in any usual sense.

The Stonemason was written in the late 1980s. It was to have been presented by the Arena Stage in Washington, D.C., in fall 1992, and McCarthy spent some time there that summer, participating in readings by a cast of actors and making revisions. But the production was postponed and then canceled. However, the play was published in April 1994 by Ecco Press. It concerns a family of black stonemasons in Louisville, Kentucky, in the 1970s and represents McCarthy's most extended treatment of the values of craftsmanship.

In *All the Pretty Horses* McCarthy returns to the kind of protagonist he first explored in John Wesley Rattner in *The Orchard Keeper* – the young boy who represents an older way of life and values, the boy who, as McCarthy said of Billy Parham (*The Crossing*) in *Esquire* (July 1993), "is likely becoming

something of an extinct species himself." The novel's young hero, John Grady Cole, at fifteen "sat a horse not only as if he'd been born to it which he was but as if were he begot by malice or mischance into some queer land where horses never were he would have found them anyway. Would have known that there was something missing for the world to be right or he right in it and would have set forth to wander wherever it was needed for as long as it took until he came upon one and he would have known that that was what he sought and it would have been." When John Grady's grandfather dies, his mother sells the ranch that he considers his birthright, and John Grady is left in something of the position of Lester Ballard.

But this boy, though young, is of sturdier character than either Ballard or the kid in *Blood Meridian*. *All the Pretty Horses* reads like an alternative to the spiritual wilderness that inhabits these earlier characters even while it brings John Grady dangerously close to succumbing to "the wildness within." Rather than accepting his loss, John Grady sets out on horseback for Mexico in hopes of finding a new ranch, talking his less resolute friend, Lacey Rawlins, into accompanying him. On the way they are joined by a younger boy who is traveling under the alias of Jimmy Blevins (borrowed from a radio evangelist), who rides a magnificent horse he has probably stolen and who proves to shoot a pistol with deadly accuracy. Reminiscent of Gene Harrogate in *Suttree,* Jimmy is amoral, unlovable, ridiculous, and yet somehow pathetic. He appears mysteriously, like an agent of the fall, and, though the boys are separated from him in the idyllic middle portions of the book, he resurfaces like a bad conscience.

Irrationally afraid of lightning, Jimmy loses his horse, clothes, and pistol in a thunderstorm; later the boys see the horse in the small village of Encantadas and help Jimmy to steal him back. Pursued, they decide to split up. John Grady and Rawlins secure jobs as hands on a large, prosperous cattle ranch where John Grady so impresses the owner, Don Hector, with his knowledge of horses that he is made trainer. He rides on the campo with Don Hector's daughter Alejandra and falls in love with her. But his youthful denial of the capacity for evil in himself and others and his reluctance to face what is, rather than insist on what should be, cost him this newfound paradise as well. He lies to the Don when asked if he and Rawlins have come into Mexico alone; and he ignores the charge to protect Alejandra's reputation given him by her great-aunt, the dueña Alfonsa, allowing Alejandra to use him as an agent of her rebellion against her aunt. They ride out together at night, making love at the lagoon where they swim, an experience John Grady finds "sweeter for the larceny of time and flesh, sweeter for the betrayal."

But John Grady discovers through experience what Alfonsa will later explain to him: "The world is quite ruthless in selecting between the dream and the reality, even where we will not. Between the wish and the thing the world lies waiting." Don Hector discovers his betrayal and turns him and Rawlins over to the corrupt agents of law in Encantadas, where they are jailed with Jimmy Blevins, who has returned to the village for his pistol and has killed a man. En route to their ordeal in prison at Saltillo, the captain marches Jimmy out into the campo and executes him. Then John Grady and Rawlins must defend their own lives in the prison, and they are ransomed by Alfonsa in a secular moment of grace after John Grady has successfully stood the test of reality by killing the young *cuchillero* (knife man) hired to assassinate him.

Life is not through testing and tempering John Grady, however. His experiences continue to batter him as relentlessly as Suttree's do him. John Grady returns to the ranch to demand an explanation of Alfonsa, who graciously speaks to him honestly and at length of her own history and Mexico's, of responsibility and courage, and of desire and loss. Through his conversations with Alfonsa and later with Alejandra, he comes to accept that because of their shared denial and irresponsibility he has lost Alejandra, though he still only dimly sees that her loss has been at least as great as his. He spends one night drunkenly wallowing in his shame and grief, then recovers himself.

Returning to Encantadas to reclaim the American horses, he finds within himself a renewed integrity with which to face down life's pain, putting into action another of Alfonsa's lessons: "That all courage was a form of constancy. That it was always himself that the coward abandoned first." He retrieves the horses and makes good his escape from Encantadas by taking the captain hostage, receiving a bullet wound in the thigh at the same time. Having cauterized the wound with a red-hot pistol barrel and having decided not to let the corrupt captain die, he is relieved of his "loathesome charge" by the abrupt appearance of some "men of the country" in another moment of grace. He returns to Texas having regained no paradise but having learned a new love for the world and acceptance of himself that are based in reality rather than wishes. He will remain a wanderer, but of a kind different from Culla

Holme, Lester Ballard, or the kid. John Grady's figurative older brothers among McCarthy's protagonists are John Wesley Rattner and Cornelius Suttree; the other three are these characters' dark twins, their shadows.

Readers have found mythic analogues to John Grady's descent into Mexico in Genesis, Dante, and the Orpheus myth. There are also parallels to the chivalric-romance tradition in the novel's romantic quest and the various tests, trials, and ordeals with which the young knight is challenged. Though the novel's ending is bittersweet, it represents McCarthy's most direct statement of the positive values his other novels affirm more obliquely by their lack of positive exemplars.

With this novel, deemed to be more accessible to the general reader than McCarthy's earlier books, his publisher orchestrated an avalanche of publicity. The book went into many printings in hardcover and paperback and in its first year was on the *New York Times* best-seller list for twenty-one weeks, selling more than one hundred thousand copies. It won the National Book Award and the National Book Critics Circle Award and was a close contender for the Pulitzer Prize. As a favor to his agent and publisher, McCarthy agreed to a single interview, which was published in the *New York Times Magazine*.

All the Pretty Horses was extensively reviewed in the usual forums for literary reviews and in general-readership periodicals as well. Unfortunately many of these reviews, while positive and while certainly contributing to the advertising and sales of the novel, appear to have been prompted by a bandwagon mentality. Among them there were no more thoughtful treatments than McCarthy's earlier books had received from fewer reviewers. The book was praised as an engaging adventure tale, a coming-of-age novel comparable to Mark Twain's *The Adventures of Huckleberry Finn* (1884), though its protagonist was often criticized for being unbelievably accomplished with horses and the chessboard, incredibly resourceful and stoic in the face of adversity. And there was disagreement about the success with which McCarthy handled the stock materials of his adolescent lovers. Denis Donaghue, in the *New York Review of Books* (24 June 1993), wrote, "I can only think that McCarthy, who has appeared to be able to imagine anything, can't bring himself to imagine the forms of civil life. . . . He is not good with village Romeos and Juliets or indeed with any lives that have entered upon communities, cultural interests, attended by customs, proprieties, and laws."

Other admirers of McCarthy were troubled by the book's affirmative vision and conventional plot and could not immediately reconcile it with the hauntedness of his earlier work – particularly *Blood Meridian,* which *All the Pretty Horses* in many ways counterpoints. Eyal Amiran (*American Book Review,* February–March 1993), for instance, queried: "How does one reconcile its pitilessly predigested plot with its lyrical language and with McCarthy's proven depth?" Amiran suggested that McCarthy was yet again attempting "to push the formula of plot – the possible – to its limit." Gail Caldwell (*Boston Globe,* 3 May 1992) observed that "while 'All the Pretty Horses' propels itself by standard plot devices – those of intrigue, romance and moral reckoning – its central resource is the underground, near-mythic tale that runs throughout."

Novelist Madison Smartt Bell (*New York Times Book Review,* 17 May 1992) wrote, "In the hands of some other writer, this material might make for a combination of 'Lonesome Dove' and 'Huckleberry Finn,' but Mr. McCarthy's vision is deeper than Larry McMurtry's and, in its own way, darker than Mark Twain's. Along with the manifold felicities of his writing goes a serious concern with the nature of God (if God exists) and, almost obsessively, the nature of something most readers have assumed to be evil." Still others found thematic continuities with McCarthy's earlier works. Bruce Allen (*World & I,* September 1992) stated that *All the Pretty Horses* is consistent with "McCarthy's uncompromising vision of human experience as continuous exposure to mortal danger" but noted that in the novel, "beneath the coiled dangers lurking everywhere on its surface, Cormac McCarthy's world trembles with possibility and promise. God may be out there, and we had better keep looking."

The Crossing, published as volume two of the Border Trilogy, has strong affinities of theme, plot, and setting with *All the Pretty Horses,* but it does not continue the story of John Grady Cole. Rather, it focuses on another sixteen-year-old, Billy Parham, who lives with his family on a cattle ranch in New Mexico in the years just before World War II. Billy succeeds in trapping a live wolf that has crossed the border from Mexico and is killing his father's cattle. Leading it toward home on a rope behind his horse, he realizes he cannot take it there and sets off for Mexico to release it. This is the first of three round-trip journeys he makes into Mexico, each of which is a confrontation with injustice, mortality, his own limitations, and the novel's pivotal problem of one's having survived in a world that destroys what one

loves. The wolf is taken from Billy and placed in a pit to fight dogs to the death.

Billy returns to New Mexico to find that his parents have been murdered by Indian vagabonds, and he and his fourteen-year-old brother Boyd venture into Mexico on a mission of revenge. After Boyd's bravado makes him a hero, he leaves Billy with a young Mexican girl they have rescued from would-be rapists. Billy searches for them fruitlessly and returns to the United States to find his country at war and to learn that he is ineligible to serve because of a heart murmur. At age nineteen he returns to Mexico, learns that Boyd has been killed, and recovers Boyd's bones. Though he succeeds in this last endeavor, the novel ends with the juxtaposition of Billy's utter aloneness and the rising of "the right and godmade sun . . . once again, for all and without distinction."

The Crossing is punctuated with stories told to Billy by Indians, Mormons, Gypsies, Mexican peasants, and fortune-tellers. These tales oracularly predict his future or, in recounting at length others' struggles to accommodate their unspeakable losses, comment indirectly on Billy's painful experiences. *The Crossing* is likely to be more a critical than popular success; it is philosophically challenging, darker than *All the Pretty Horses* and infused with McCarthy's soaring and delving prose.

McCarthy is increasingly acknowledged as a consummate stylist and a deeply serious writer whose work comes out of a unique personal vision influenced by a panoply of great authors (scholarly exploration of the sources of his philosophical thought has lagged behind the identification of his historical sources). The 1990s should see the completion of his Border Trilogy and perhaps more efforts in dramatic forms. Vigorously working and as vitally interested as ever in all that he observes around him, McCarthy promises to remain productive.

Interviews:

Richard B. Woodward, "Cormac McCarthy's Venomous Fiction," *New York Times Magazine,* 19 April 1992, pp. 28–31ff.;

Garry Wallace, "Meeting McCarthy," *Southern Quarterly,* 30 (Summer 1992): 134–139.

Bibliography:

Dianne C. Luce, "Cormac McCarthy: A Bibliography," in *Perspectives on Cormac McCarthy,* edited by Edwin T. Arnold and Luce (Jackson: University Press of Mississippi, 1993), pp. 199–206.

References:

Edwin T. Arnold and Dianne C. Luce, eds., *Perspectives on Cormac McCarthy* (Jackson: University Press of Mississippi, 1993);

Andrew Bartlett, "From Voyeurism to Archaeology: Cormac McCarthy's *Child of God*," *Southern Literary Journal*, 24 (Fall 1991): 3–15;

Vereen M. Bell, *The Achievement of Cormac McCarthy* (Baton Rouge: Louisiana State University Press, 1988);

John Ditsky, "Further into Darkness: The Novels of Cormac McCarthy," *Hollins Critic*, 18 April 1981, pp. 1–11;

Robert Draper, "The Invisible Man," *Texas Monthly* (July 1992): 42–46;

John Lewis Longley, Jr., "Suttree and the Metaphysics of Death," *Southern Literary Journal*, 17 (Spring 1985): 79–90;

Mark Morrow, "Cormac McCarthy," in his *Images of the Southern Writer* (Athens: University of Georgia Press, 1985), pp. 52–53;

William J. Schafer, "Cormac McCarthy: The Hard Wages of Original Sin," *Appalachian Journal*, 4 (Winter 1977): 105–119;

John Emil Sepich, "A 'bloody dark pastryman': Cormac McCarthy's Recipe for Gunpowder and Historical Fiction in *Blood Meridian*," *Mississippi Quarterly*, 46 (Fall 1993): 547–563;

Sepich, "The Dance of History in Cormac McCarthy's *Blood Meridian*," *Southern Literary Journal*, 24 (Fall 1991): 16–31;

Sepich, *Notes on Blood Meridian* (Louisville, Ky.: Bellarmine College Press, 1993);

Frank W. Shelton, "Suttree and Suicide," *Southern Quarterly*, 29 (Fall 1990): 71–83;

William Christopher Spencer, "The Extremities of Cormac McCarthy: The Major Character Types," Ph.D. dissertation, University of Tennessee, 1993;

Don Williams, "Annie De Lisle: Cormac McCarthy's Ex-wife Prefers to Recall the Romance," *News-Sentinel* (Knoxville, Tenn.), 10 June 1990, pp. E1–E2;

Williams, "Cormac McCarthy: Knoxville's Most Famous Contemporary Writer Prefers His Anonymity," *News-Sentinel* (Knoxville, Tenn.), 10 June 1990, pp. E1–E2;

Terri Witek, " 'He's Hell When He's Well': Cormac McCarthy's Rhyming Dictions," *Shenandoah*, 41 (Fall 1991): 51–66;

Thomas D. Young, Jr., "Cormac McCarthy and the Geology of Being," Ph.D. dissertation, Miami University, 1990.

Papers:

A copy of the shooting script for *The Gardener's Son* is in the Richard Inman Pearce papers at the University of South Carolina's South Caroliniana Library in Columbia. Small holdings of McCarthy's letters are in the Southwestern Writers Collection at Southwest Texas State University, San Marcos, and in the Southern Historical Collection at the University of North Carolina at Chapel Hill.

Larry McMurtry

(3 June 1936 –   )

John Gerlach
Cleveland State University

See also the McMurtry entries in *DLB 2: American Novelists Since World War II, First Series; DLB Yearbook: 1980;* and *DLB Yearbook: 1987.*

BOOKS: *Horseman, Pass By* (New York: Harper, 1961); republished as *Hud* (New York: Popular Library, 1963; London: Sphere, 1971);

Leaving Cheyenne (New York: Harper & Row, 1963; London: Sphere, 1972);

The Last Picture Show (New York: Dial, 1966; London: Sphere, 1972);

In a Narrow Grave: Essays on Texas (Austin: Encino Press, 1968);

Moving On (New York: Simon & Schuster, 1970; London: Weidenfeld & Nicolson, 1971);

All My Friends Are Going to Be Strangers (New York: Simon & Schuster, 1972; London: Secker & Warburg, 1973);

Terms of Endearment (New York: Simon & Schuster, 1975; London: W. H. Allen, 1977);

Somebody's Darling (New York: Simon & Schuster, 1978);

Cadillac Jack (New York: Simon & Schuster, 1982; London: W. H. Allen, 1986);

The Desert Rose (New York: Simon & Schuster, 1983; London: W. H. Allen, 1985);

Lonesome Dove (New York: Simon & Schuster, 1985; London: Pan, 1986);

Film Flam: Essays on Hollywood (New York: Simon & Schuster, 1987);

Texasville (New York: Simon & Schuster, 1987; London: Sidgwick & Jackson, 1987);

Anything for Billy (New York: Simon & Schuster, 1988; London: Collins, 1989);

Some Can Whistle (New York: Simon & Schuster, 1989; London: Century, 1990);

Buffalo Girls (New York: Simon & Schuster, 1990; London: Century, 1991);

Evening Star (New York: Simon & Schuster, 1992);

Streets of Laredo (New York: Simon & Schuster, 1993; London: Orion, 1993).

Larry McMurtry (photograph by Lee Marmon)

MOTION PICTURE: *The Last Picture Show,* by McMurtry and Peter Bogdanovich, Columbia, 1971.

SELECTED PERIODICAL PUBLICATION –
UNCOLLECTED: "Ever a Bridegroom: Reflections on the Failure of Texas Literature," *Texas Observer* (13 October 1981): pp. 1, 8–19.

Larry McMurtry has been known to sport a sweatshirt bearing the inscription *Minor Regional Novelist,* a statement that could be read as self-flagellation, mocking self-irony, realistic self-appraisal, or an attempt (like Hester Prynne's) to embroider shame into a badge of triumph. In writing about his own region McMurtry has been writing about myth and the modern condition, about the uneasy fit between a faded heroic past and the constricting demands of the present. He has been ambivalent about both the past and present, as he states in "Take My Saddle from the Wall: A Valediction" (*In a Narrow Grave: Essays on Texas*, 1968): "I am critical of the past, yet attracted to it; and though I am even more critical of the present I am also quite clearly attracted to it."

Born 3 June 1936 in Wichita Falls, Texas, to William Jefferson McMurtry and Hazel Ruth McIver McMurtry, Larry McMurtry was educated in his home state, receiving a B.A. from North Texas State University in 1958 and an M.A. from Rice University in 1960. He married Josephine Ballard on 15 July 1959; they divorced in 1966. He has one son, James Lawrence. A Stegner Fellowship enabled McMurtry to do further graduate work at Stanford University after which he returned to Texas to teach creative writing at Rice from 1963 to 1969, with time off for a Guggenheim Fellowship in 1964. Since then he has left the academic world, and he lives off and on in Texas and Arizona. He owns a rare-book store, Booked Up, in Washington, D.C. Since 1969 he has been more inclined to think and write about Texas at a considerable distance. He has served as president of the American P.E.N. Center in an era when it has primarily drawn public attention for its $750-per-plate fund-raisers.

Critics have traced several themes in McMurtry's works, ranging from initiation (like Sonny's in *The Last Picture Show*, 1966), to the breakup of marriage (most notably in *Moving On*, 1970, and *All My Friends Are Going to Be Strangers*, 1972), to the alienating effect of modern civilization (*Texasville*, 1987). Certainly two other themes – the need for place (as well as the stultifying effect place might have on character) and the enduring power of the myth of the West – have clearly been central to McMurtry's work.

As a child, McMurtry, the son and grandson of Texas cattle ranchers, absorbed a sense of the grandeur of the past along with a nostalgia for its loss. The energy, self-reliance, and hardiness of the pioneer era no longer seem relevant to the twentieth century. As Christopher Baker puts it, "McMurtry's novels record the dilemmas of those who must live in the moral and emotional vacuum left after the death of this age of exuberance."

In McMurtry's first novel, *Horseman, Pass By* (1961), Homer Bannon stands for the values of the past against the materialistic, selfish desires of his stepson Hud, in whom, as Tom Pilkington observes, the "aggressive self-sufficiency of the frontier has been transformed into simple-minded viciousness." The central event – the discovery of hoof-and-mouth disease among cattle on Homer's ranch – develops inexorably toward the destruction of the cattle and with them Homer's will to live. The story is narrated by Homer's grandson, Lonnie, who is clearly in the tradition of Huck Finn, discerning much – but not all – of the falseness around him, unwilling to corrupt himself. Lonnie's narrative voice can be heard in his comments on Homer's funeral:

> They had put paint on him, like a woman wears, red paint. I could see it on his cheeks, and caked around his mouth. I could see slick oil on his hair, and some sticky stuff like honey around his eyes. I wished I could have buried him like he died; he was better that way.

In the course of living through his grandfather's ordeal, Lonnie rejects his earlier desire to leave the ranch. He also rejects Hud, who wants to unload the diseased cattle on any buyer he can find, and Jesse, a floating forty-year-old cowboy who has been everything and missed everything. Ultimately Lonnie elects to stay on the land, "looking at the green grass on the ground and watching the white clouds ease into the sky from the South," in acceptance of his responsibilities to the land and his friends. Beneath these affirmations stirs an unsettling attraction to Halmea, the black helper on the Bannon ranch. He desires her partly as lover, partly as mother. The tenderness, lack of fulfillment, and separation caused by differences in age and race trace out the beginning of what becomes an essential theme in McMurtry's later works: people's needs do not match their circumstances.

The film adaptation of *Horseman, Pass By* – *Hud* (1963), starring Paul Newman as the title character – shifts the values of the story, making Homer more sententious and Hud more sympathetic, blurring a nostalgia for old Western ways in the novel, which even McMurtry has come to disparage as part of a young man's oversimplified view of the world, a "sentimental first novel." But to some, particularly Kerry Ahearn ("More D'Urban: The Texas Novels of Larry McMurtry," 1989), the book is more honest than the film version.

The second novel of what has been called the Thalia trilogy (novels set in or around Thalia, a mythical town based on McMurtry's own Archer City) is *Leaving Cheyenne* (1963), the title of which comes from an old Western song, "Goodbye, Old

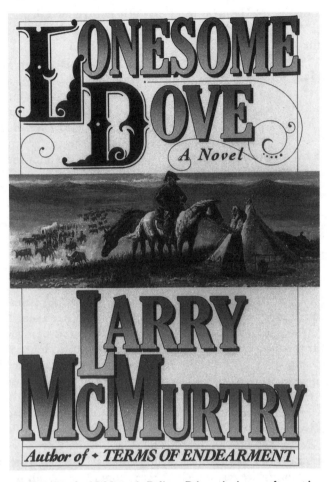

*Dust jacket for McMurtry's Pulitzer Prize–winning novel, an epic
Western about a trail drive from Texas to Montana*

Paint." McMurtry's ambivalence about the American West plays out here through the choices Molly must make between Gideon, a rancher, and Johnny, a cowboy. She chooses neither, marrying instead a third man, Eddie, an abusive oil-rig worker. Instead of having children by Eddie, she has one son by Gideon and one by Johnny, and both sons die in World War II. The story is related by three narrators – first by Gideon, who tells of the group of young adults; then by Molly, who narrates the middle period, during which she raises the children and attends to all three of the men; and finally by Johnny, who as an old man tells of Gideon's death.

In the third novel from this group, *The Last Picture Show,* the glorious Western past is embodied in Sam the Lion – a former rancher and rodeo rider, once Lois Farrow's lover and now one of the many failed parent substitutes in Thalia – and in the Westerns that Thalia teenagers watch at the local movie house. The central focus is on three teenagers: Sonny, his friend Duane, and Jacy Far-

row, a girl they both desire. As in *Leaving Cheyenne,* neither boy can keep the girl for himself, and the girl seems always about to slip into the hands of another rival. The pursuits of a similar group of characters in *Leaving Cheyenne* gave them a certain nobility, fully developed over time. The characters in *The Last Picture Show,* however, are amusingly diminished by their comic sexual-initiation rituals – Jacy by her activities at a swimming party and later in a motel with Duane, and Duane and Sonny by their frustrating visit to a whorehouse in Mexico.

Their stumbling ascent to maturity runs parallel to the revelation of the past relationship between Jacy's mother and Sam the Lion, who is a father figure for Sonny and Duane. Her affair with Sam is now only a memory. After Sam dies, Thalia rushes to extinction: the movie house closes; Duane goes off to war in Korea; and retarded Billy, in despair at the closing of the movie house, puts on two eye patches and is run over by a truck.

The relationship of Lonnie to Halmea in *Horseman, Pass By* resembles Sonny's affair with Ruth Popper, the wife of the high-school coach. Temporarily leaving her for Jacy, Sonny returns after a brief experience with Jacy's mother, who remarks, "Your mother and I sat next to one another in the first grade. . . . We graduated together. I sure didn't expect to sleep with her son. That's small town life for you." As Sonny is reconciled to Ruth, who is also old enough to be his mother, it is clear that love is sad, impossible, and sweet in its contrasts and absurdities.

The Last Picture Show is "lovingly dedicated" to McMurtry's hometown, but the dedication is ironic: as Charles Peavy (1967) points out, the book deflates such small-town icons as the beauty queen (Jacy) and the coach (Herman Popper). In Ahearn's words the book deflates all of human existence, revealing three aspects of futility: "human sexuality, the absence of community and family, and the illusory nature of friendship." As Baker explains, Sonny cannot shake nostalgia for the past and he cannot leave Thalia, though it has no value for him.

The Last Picture Show commanded more attention than McMurtry's earlier works. To many readers the incest, sodomy, homosexuality, and assorted sexual exhibitions were offensive, but to W. T. Jack in the *New York Times Book Review* (13 November 1966), "McMurtry is an alchemist who converts the basest metals to gold." Pilkington, however, contends that the book wobbles between "realism, satire, and poison-pen caricature." The 1971 film adaptation of the novel – starring Timothy Bottoms, Jeff Bridges, Ben Johnson, Cloris Leachman, Cybill Shepherd, Ellen Burstyn, and Eileen Brennan – by writer-director Peter Bogdanovich (McMurtry helped with the screenplay) offered, as Peavy puts it, a "more sympathetic portrait of McMurtry's hometown novel." McMurtry has since regretted his treatment of the town, noting that his attitude "represented a failure of generosity for which I blame no one but myself."

By 1969 McMurtry was ready for a change. He had been divorced in 1966, a subject on which he remained silent in interviews, but divorce figures prominently in his succeeding novels. He moved to Washington, D.C., in 1969, taught creative-writing courses at George Mason and American universities, but concluded that he was not needed for teaching – "most of the kids that are really going to write will go ahead and do it anyway." Instead he capitalized on his interest in book collecting and went into partnership to operate a rare-book store, Booked Up. Books had been his only escape in his youth in Archer City; he had worked as a book scout while at Stanford and later with a Houston firm, The Bookworm.

During his stay in Washington he completed *Moving On* and the two succeeding novels. These three novels concern marriage and Texans moving toward the urban experience. In the introduction to *In a Narrow Grave* McMurtry notes: "As the cowboys leave the range and learn to accommodate themselves to the suburbs, defeats that are tragic in quality must occur and may be recorded." For many critics these novels – designated as the Houston Trilogy in Clay Reynolds's collection *Taking Stock: A Larry McMurtry Casebook* (1989) – are not always successful. Ernestine P. Sewell believes that in the trilogy McMurtry has lost a sense of place, of voices tied to place, and that he adopts a loose, unstructured narrative form as a consequence of his focus on "rootless, restless, directionless, city folk." McMurtry has been sensitive to his change of theme and has resented being remembered only for the Thalia group. Pilkington's explanation of McMurtry's rejection is that, once he had moved on to new topics, he did not like hearing people ask him to return to old themes, for that made him feel "like his best work was behind him."

Western myth in *Moving On* shrinks to dalliance and to Jim Carpenter's interest in photographing rodeos. The marriage of Jim and Patsy Carpenter is about to end, but not before it is tested by and compared to the relationship of Pete and Boots, a May-December couple; of rich Eleanor Guthrie and world-champion cowboy Sonny Shanks, who has his girls in the converted hearse in which he lives; of Bill Duffin, a cynical professor of modern literature who has published eight books, and his wife Lee, the campus Cassandra; and of Clara Clark, a "California Girl" playing at being a graduate student, and her graduate-student boyfriend, Hank Malory.

The setting moves through the same kind of random sequence. After several hundred pages of rodeo locations, it shifts to graduate school at Rice, as McMurtry draws on his experience there. McMurtry further risks losing the reader's attention by endless talk: Patsy speaks at times with a sharp tongue, as does her friend Emma Horton, but then none of the characters consistently speaks with distinction over the course of 794 pages. Jim is portrayed through his hobbies – photography, linguistics, and then graduate school. There are countless sexual arousals, somewhat fewer consummations, fragments of popular songs, references to dozens of books and authors, and meals with comments on the freshness of the salad or the gristle in the steak. In his *New York Times* review, "*Moving On,* and On . . . and On" (10 June 1970), John Leonard commented, "It's a little like turning on the radio and leaving it on for years."

And yet by the final quarter of the book, "Summer's Lease," the accumulation of material begins to take hold. Jim finds out about Patsy's affair with Hank; she wishes to break it off but does so in a most jagged, continuously backsliding way. In time she breaks from Jim as well, with an equally prolonged assortment of vague reconciliations and indirections. Emma's husband Flap tries to commit suicide and fails. Emma's comment, "I knew the minute I started going with him years ago that I'd never get rid of him and I just couldn't believe he would die," gives some indication of McMurtry's purpose. This world of unshakable banality cannot be represented with the normal economies of fiction.

All My Friends Are Going to Be Strangers, the second novel of the Houston trilogy, concerns Danny Deck, who has published one novel and is working on a second, and who feels trapped in a hopeless marriage. During pregnancy his wife turns from him to a blind man downstairs. Danny drifts from one adventure to another, trying to live with a kind, talented cartoonist named Jill, who is not interested in sex. McMurtry draws on his family tradition of the West only to satirize it. Uncle L, based on McMurtry's Uncle Johnny, is a rancher who parodies Homer Bannon. Uncle L sleeps in a bedroll behind his luxurious ranch house; digs postholes indiscriminately; keeps a menagerie, including a camel, instead of cattle; and has three Mexican helpers, each named Pierre.

After leaving him Danny drowns the manuscript of his second novel, and possibly even himself, in the Rio Grande; there is no way to return to a mythical Western past to sustain a meaningful life. Barbara Granzow sees *All My Friends Are Going to Be Strangers* as McMurtry's attempt to show the Western writer coming to terms with the literary establishment – Danny's Western values "inhibit yet sustain him." In drowning his book Danny shows that "everything that has happened to him has been simply what he deserved, the price for his rejection of Texas." *All My Friends Are Going to Be Strangers* is not without its defenders: Jim Harrison (*New York Times Book Review,* 19 March 1972) praised it, noting that McMurtry has a "comic genius" and a "sense of construction and proper velocity that always saves him."

In *Terms of Endearment* (1975), the third novel of the Houston trilogy, the Western past is mini-mized to the person of the cowboy Vernon Dalhart, one of Aurora Greenway's suitors. Aurora, Emma Horton's mother and a widow originally from Boston, has settled in Houston. She ought to be intolerable: she corrects the grammar of her friends, exploits her suitors, and calls her daughter to say, "I was thinking you might want to wish me good night." But Aurora is likable because she loves life and can turn a phrase: she says of two of her suitors, "The brutal fact is that they're both old, short, and afraid of me. If I stacked them one on top of the other they might be tall enough, but they'd still be afraid of me."

The last quarter of the book deals with Emma, who is dying of cancer, and it peacefully terminates that long-suffering victim of this and the previous novel, *Moving On.* Christopher Lehmann-Haupt praised the book in the *New York Times* (22 October 1975), stating that "one laughs at the slapstick, one weeps at the maudlin, and one likes all of McMurtry's characters, no matter how delicately or broadly they are drawn." But for Ahearn, Aurora has given up taking life seriously, and "the philosophy of taking nothing seriously seems to guide even McMurtry, who creates superficial characters only to condescend to them." The 1983 film version of *Terms of Endearment* – with Shirley MacLaine as Aurora, Jack Nicholson as Gerrit Breedlove (a conflation of Aurora's various suitors), Debra Winger as Emma, and Jeff Daniels as Emma's husband Flap – simplifies the storyline and effaces most of Aurora's foolery in favor of a more conventional romance. Nevertheless, the film garnered critical and popular acclaim as well as five Academy Awards, including best picture.

McMurtry's next three novels – *Somebody's Darling* (1978), *Cadillac Jack* (1982), and *The Desert Rose* (1983) – have been characterized as the "trash trilogy." As Mark Busby explains, these books are about displaced characters searching the trash of Hollywood, Washington, D.C., and Las Vegas. They have not appealed much to critics, have not been made into movies, and, except for *The Desert Rose,* are not highly regarded by McMurtry himself. Hollywood, Washington, and Las Vegas are probably the most placeless places McMurtry could have picked, tissues of myth and disappointment. He has passed time in each city – in Hollywood as a screenwriter, in Washington with his bookstore, and in Las Vegas to do a prospective screenplay on a showgirl. But living in these cities, as McMurtry has confessed, did not really entitle him to imagine that the sense of language he had captured really gave him clues about the places.

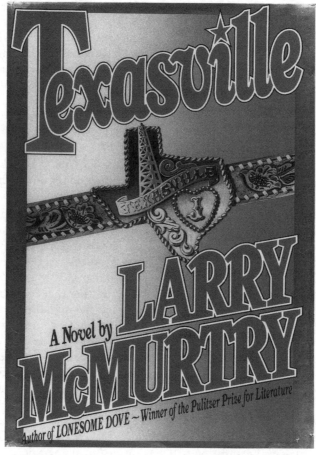

Dust jacket for McMurtry's 1987 sequel to The Last Picture Show *(1966)*

Looking back on *Somebody's Darling,* McMurtry has been particularly aware of having run out of steam. He split telling the story of Jill Peel, a fugitive from *All My Friends Are Going to Be Strangers,* into three sections told by Joe Percy, an old scriptwriter; Owen Oarson, a Texan; and Jill herself. McMurtry has confessed that he had waited too long to return to Jill and that his interest in her had flagged.

Cadillac Jack has its own Texan, former rodeo rider Jack McGriff. Here, the only yardstick by which to measure an unknown place is still a Texan, one that many critics have seen as a stand-in for McMurtry himself, with antique hunting replacing McMurtry's penchant for book collecting. McMurtry, like his character, shares a passion for cross-country collecting in a Cadillac. Bereft of place, Cadillac Jack makes car-phone calls to former wives and current girlfriends. Washington itself hardly seems a real place, peopled as it is by folk with such strange names as Pencil Penrose and Dunscombe Cotswinkle. Jonathan Yardley of the

Washington Post (13 October 1982) noted that "the city as it emerges is a mere caricature." Cadillac Jack is rootless and discontented; but, as Busby points out, instead of scorning him McMurtry satirizes the world with which Jack collides. Janice Stout contends the novel does not work because McMurtry pushed "the basic idea too far. Too many bits and pieces are picked up and passed along; they mount up like piles of stuff in a mammoth garage sale."

The Desert Rose was a turning point, a project that renewed McMurtry's interest in writing. Originally begun as a screenplay – a break from working on what would become *Lonesome Dove* (1985) – it turned into a novel. Even the title implies renewal despite desolation and suggests something emerging from nothing, from a place of absence. The rose in this case is Harmony, an aging Las Vegas showgirl who can maintain confidence and optimism despite the loss of her job, despite a boyfriend who not only wrecks her car and leaves her but also steals her insurance checks. Her daughter Pepper does get a husband and her mother's job, but the reader sympathizes with Harmony.

The Desert Rose is one of McMurtry's stylistic experiments, and for a while the contorted syntax of Harmony's consciousness satisfies the reader with its novelty, but ultimately the device does not allow enough variation to sustain interest. Some critics, such as Charles Adams (*Western American Literature,* 1985) and Keith Mano (*National Review,* 25 November 1983), have faulted the book for McMurtry's choice of limiting himself to the narrow range of language and perception of these characters, but Emily Benedek has praised him for finally being "capable of writing about the modern West without being derailed by ghosts or stylistic artifice."

In a 1981 essay, "Ever a Bridegroom: Reflections on the Failure of Texas Literature," McMurtry shovels a little more dirt on his fellow Texas writers – the triumvirate of J. Frank Dobie, Roy Bedichek, and Walter Prescott Webb – whom he had already buried in his youthful essay "Southwestern Literature?" (*In a Narrow Grave*). In "Ever a Bridegroom" he states that in 1969 he had thought "the death of the cowboy and the ending of the rural way of life had been lamented sufficiently, and there was really no more that needed to be said about it," but by 1981 he had found that many of his readers still wanted him to write *Leaving Cheyenne* again. However, he did not want to be trapped in "shallow, self-repetitive literature" that failed to "do justice to the complexities of life in the state."

What could be more shallow and shopworn than writing another trail-drive novel? And yet that is exactly what McMurtry did in *Lonesome Dove.* In part he must have had an eye on the movie rights – nothing like a blockbuster to shore up one's career and provide the income and leisure to write what one wants. But, more likely, McMurtry may have thought it was possible to go back and write a good trail-drive novel and to do it in a way that transcended formula. Seeds of that possibility sprout even in "Ever a Bridegroom," in which he notes that Robert Flynn's trail-drive novel, *North to Yesterday* (1967), was a "world-class idea," but Flynn's powers "weren't adequate to the visionary tragicomedy that would have done justice to it." In writing his own version of the past, McMurtry found one way to go beyond his ambivalence about the myth of the West.

Stereotypes abound in *Lonesome Dove,* and these have been duly noted by critics. The book features two archetypal former Texas Ranger comrades – the silent workaholic Woodrow Call, no

more able to admit human emotion on the sea of the prairie than Ahab, and the endlessly loquacious Augustus McCrae. Don Graham traces McMurtry's stock traditions not only to other trail-drive novels and narrative accounts but also to films and television, with the improbability of bringing a whore along prefigured in *Red River* (1948), the subplot of Roscoe derived from Chester of *Gunsmoke,* and the models for Call and Gus established in John Wayne and Jimmy Stewart. Reynolds cites minor infractions of plausibility – by the time Call brings back Gus's coffin, Kansas seems populated as it was in the 1880s, not the 1870s; chance meetings of characters from the various threads of the plot strain credulity, while subplots overwhelm the main plot; and McMurtry sometimes loses control of the narrative voice, mixing his own with the vernacular. Stout observes how McMurtry twice confounds the reader's expectations without making "significant the fact that he does not fulfill them," first by having Call desire to keep going straight into Canada instead of stopping at the intended destination of Montana, thus implying that the goal is just being on the road. Then, by having Call go back to Texas to bury Gus, McMurtry seems to indicate a return to roots, but those roots are not there when Call arrives.

Whatever its flaws, readers have responded favorably to *Lonesome Dove,* and it won the Pulitzer Prize for fiction in 1986. As McMurtry has pointed out, readers respond to its nineteenth-century frame "because they want the 19th century back. It offers readers an alternative to the complexities of the 20th century." For all its defects, this big novel satisfies in small ways as well as grand ones. Although McMurtry has low regard for Texas writers who fritter away their talents on bucolic description, he sends Gus out early to cook breakfast so that he can see the sunrise: "The eastern sky was red as coals in a forge." McMurtry also produces many good lines, for example: "This town was a two-bit town when we came here and it looks to me like it's lost about fifteen cents since then." He writes bang-up descriptions of stampedes and river crossings, and he creates characters who are wonderful sparring partners. Gus working the prostitute Lorena for a fifty-dollar "poke" is matched by her own toying with him.

Comic scenes are followed by high drama, such as the abduction of Lorena by the comanchero Blue Duck, and the edge of suspense and adventure gives ensuing comic scenes a darker edge. One is never certain when comedy may turn dark or an adventure may become light. Masterful scenes in such subplots as Elmira's acceptance of the faithful, oxlike, smelly buffalo-hunter Big Zwey as a husband, tinged as it is with the edge of both threat and protection, are comic foils to Gus's courtship of both Lorena and Clara, a soap opera considerably more interesting than the fate of the cattle drive. By smoothly handling an absorbing set of major characters and carefully controlling pace and tone, McMurtry brings an old convention to life.

A natural source for film or television, *Lonesome Dove* was adapted for an eight-hour miniseries in 1989. Robert Duvall starred as Gus; a Texan, Tommy Lee Jones, as Call; Anjelica Houston played Clara; and Danny Glover portrayed Deets. This production was the most popular miniseries since 1984, something of a surprise given the low estate of the Western as a genre. Steve Fore accounts for this popularity by considering it a "cultural document of the late Reagan era," noting that adherence to earlier conventions of the Western "marks it as a 'return to traditionalism' in keeping with Reaganite ideology's willful conflation of history with myth in its rereading of America's past."

McMurtry's novels have clustered in patterns of threes – the Thalia trilogy, the Houston trilogy, and the trash trilogy. In the six novels starting with *Lonesome Dove*, McMurtry alternates two different settings, the West of the past and the Texas of the present. The two types are not wholly distinct, for the techniques and themes of the Western find their way into the contemporary Texas stories. Past and present begin to fuse, and the theme of the fictiveness of fact begins to predominate.

The Western past in *Texasville*, a reprise of *The Last Picture Show*, has shrunken to the grotesque. The myth of the Old West surfaces only twice, first in the form of a log doghouse shaped like a frontier fort, a structure that Duane fitfully blasts with a pistol while sitting by the pool outside his mansion, and second in the preparation for the centennial, which loosely scaffolds this sprawling, nearly formless book. The centennial itself degenerates into a pageant (with Duane and Jacy as Adam and Eve), a tumbleweed stampede, and an egg fight.

The West is now the East – jogging, tennis, and video stores have invaded Texas. Duane is trying to cope with the oil glut, massive debt, and too many women. Familiar characters from *The Last Picture Show* swim through, as when Jacy Farrow, now a jungle queen in Italian movies, surfaces in a pond to which Duane retreats to escape from his troubles. Sonny is now the mayor, but he suffers from bouts of amnesia. Love is entangled in amorous confusion – both Duane and his druggie son Dickie are pursuing Mrs. Marlow and Mrs. Nolan. About all

that endures is the friendship between Duane and his wife Karla, which manages to survive all their open and weary affairs.

As Louise Erdrich notes, *Texasville* is not a satisfying sequel: "In *The Last Picture Show*, the quest for love was not only for sex, but sex linked to tenderness and mystery, to love. In *Texasville* sex is just sex. It happens everywhere and often." One of McMurtry's main talents is mixing a large assemblage of characters, but here the mix is too easy, and there is no resistance against the comedy, just quick shuffling of various sexual permutations. The 1991 film version, like *The Last Picture Show* directed by Bogdanovich and including several members of the original cast, was hardly more warmly received than the novel. *Rolling Stone* (18 April 1991) referred to it as a fiasco and challenged the viewer to "recognize or empathize" with any of the characters.

McMurtry then returned to the past, but the West in *Anything for Billy* (1988) is much different from the West in *Lonesome Dove*. The filter through which the West is seen here is the narrator Ben Sippy, "a famous dime novelist not tight with my adjectives." His characters' names, such as Orson Oxx, Man of Iron, echo those of McMurtry's characters – in this case, Owen Oarson, from *Somebody's Darling*. Billy the Kid is inescapably the focus of the reader's attentions – Billy with his superstitions, his shortcomings as a gunman (he is more of a blaster than a marksman), and his brutality (he will kill anyone – a friend of his sidekick, a man bearing a flag of truce, a wandering Indian boy). The point, as Reynolds puts it, is that Billy is "so concerned with living up to the legend that has developed around his name that he consciously tries to become the outlaw he is supposed to be, ultimately with horrible success."

But, just as F. Scott Fitzgerald's *The Great Gatsby* (1925) is as much about the narrator Nick Carraway as it is about Jay Gatsby, *Anything for Billy* is also about Ben Sippy. Everyone in the West seems to be reading his books – Will Isinglass, who seems to own most of Texas and wants Billy out of it, Lady Cecilie Snow, who wants Ben for strange sexual power games – every one but Billy and Indians such as Bloody Feather, who would probably read him if they could read at all. The scenes with Ben are among the most memorable – particularly Cecilie's seduction of him – told in the short two- or three-page chapters McMurtry employs throughout the book with the precision and economy of stanzas in a ballad.

McMurtry uses the presence of Ben as a successful exercise in metafiction, distancing the reader yet involving the reader in its creation, seducing the

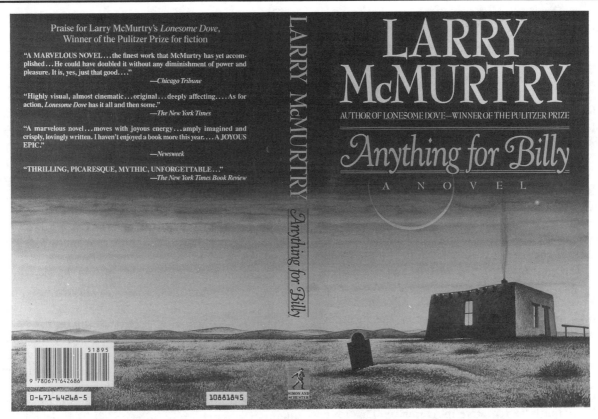

Dust jacket for McMurtry's 1988 novel, in which the central character is outlaw Billy the Kid

reader into its illusion. Few scenes in fiction are more comically horrifying than Mesty Woolah's disembowelment of Wild Jerry. Riding up on his camel, the seven-foot African undoes the braggart Wild Jerry with a scimitar, sliding under the camel like a Comanche.

Characters such as Mesty Woolah and the wild woman Katie Garza, Billy's lover and assassin, are fictitious, but the actual life of Billy the Kid, a slippery matter in itself, plays through in curious fashion. Even those only vaguely familiar with Billy's legend will realize McMurtry has twisted matters by having Katie rather than Pat Garrett kill Billy. (Ben of course has an explanation for that.) Garrett himself does not appear, but, as Reynolds points out, his role is taken by Tully Roebuck. Incidents parallel to those attached to Billy, such as the battle at Skunkwater Flats, echo an actual shootout at Stinking Springs.

Through Ben's perception, however, the reader comes to terms, insofar as one can, with the West and myth. Ben has gone west to see what he has been mythicizing. He discovers something as concocted as fiction itself, a world in which few of the gunfighters "managed to shoot the right people, and even fewer got to die gloriously in a shoot-out with a

peer." Ben does not parody or deflate myth but instead allows the reader to see how myth dominates the lives of those who live it, how it both nourishes and entraps. That is another resolution to the ambivalence McMurtry has felt toward the myth of the West: he is drawn to it, disappointed by it, but cannot escape it; and that personal reaction may well be a mirror of America's reaction as a nation.

In *Some Can Whistle* (1989) McMurtry resurrects Danny Deck, the novelist who drowned his manuscript (but clearly not himself) in the Rio Grande at the end of *All My Friends Are Going to Be Strangers* and in whose mansion, Los Dolores, in Thalia Jacy stays in *Texasville*. Danny seems like another autobiographical surrogate, a sort of parody of the reclusive McMurtry himself, a modern Ben Sippy. In the now-middle-aged Danny, McMurtry can explore the dichotomies of his own fiction and presumably his own experience. Danny struggles with the opposition of art high (the novel) and low (the television series *Al & Sal,* which leads to wealth and fame) and with the nurturing and the chaos of family versus the need for solitude.

Themes merge into one another, with the purpose of solitude being to allow the writing of a novel, and with family and fame both fulfilling one's innermost wishes for the expression of self while threatening death to the self. The connections to early novels other than *All My Friends Are Going to Be Strangers* seem clear – Danny is as notorious as the dime novelist Ben Sippy, and the autobiographical connections between *Al & Sal* and the miniseries made from *Lonesome Dove* seem clear enough. Danny could be considered McMurtry's attempt to deal with the fact that a shy man has been granted his secret wish and his secret dread: fame.

The family/solitude theme is dominant, and it works itself out in the presence of T. R., the daughter whom Danny had to abandon at her birth at the end of *All My Friends Are Going to Be Strangers*. She reappears as a twenty-two-year-old woman at the beginning of the novel, calling him on the phone to ask, "Are you my stinkin' Daddy?" She is a classic gold digger, but she brings an honesty and urgency in her search for the bedrock of fatherhood, just as Danny himself is discovering a purity and strength of family feeling that he does not know in any other human connection. Especially in the light of the generational lines over which the spark of sex is likely to leap in Thalia (from *The Last Picture Show* to *Texasville*), the love between father and daughter seems virtually redemptive in its purity. This love provides Danny with the fulfillment he always seems to avoid by distancing Jeannie Vertus, a film director (a Jill Peel figure), who warns Danny how lonely he will be if he fails to realize he had a "perfectly nice woman available . . . [and] did absolutely nothing about it."

But the price of this fulfilling fantasy between father and daughter is that it must vanish. Earl Dee – the father of Bo, the first of T. R.'s two children – escapes from jail to murder T. R. Also murdered are Godwin, whose lust for his homosexual pickups and whose goatish inclination toward T. R. represent all that a father figure should not be, and Buddy, the security guard and former love of long-suffering Gladys, Danny's noncooking cook and housekeeper. This parable about fatherhood – in which what has been so senselessly lost for so long has now been magically restored (a kind of *Winter's Tale*) – descends into killings as brutal and sudden as the violence in *Anything for Billy*. Thalia has become a Western. Perhaps even more grotesque, in the last portion of the novel McMurtry keeps inventing T. R. surrogates whom Danny tries to put through college. They include Melinda, a fat girl who had sex with a deputy in order to allow Earl Dee to escape, and Jesse, T. R.'s daughter, who makes whirlwind tours through filmmaking, anthro-

pology, and world-class universities in the quick fast-forward that concludes the novel.

Barbara Kingsolver (*New York Times Book Review*, 22 October 1989) observes that McMurtry's final flurry is "hard to follow and emotionally disengaged, like a rushed catch-up at a class reunion," but thinks this "tagged-on anticlimax" serves to prove "that Danny will never acquire his daughter's virtuosity for living." Lehmann-Haupt (*New York Times*, 16 October 1989) remarks that *Some Can Whistle* is a crowded novel in which "characters not only press one another, they also assault the reader's sensibilities and threaten to suffocate us with their boisterous demands." Even so, he believes the book has a "uniquely amusing yet wistful flavor."

Ultimately the theme of blasted wishes begins to ring sentimental, especially in Danny's recall of T. R.: "It was as if she had risen unexpectedly from the dark sea of time, walked with me on the beach for a few bright moments, and had then gone quietly back to the long waters." What is essentially most memorable about this novel is not this schmaltz but T. R.; Godwin, fouling his way through airports; and Danny, flashing his passport and Cannes credentials at a deputy in order to get T. R. into jail to see her boyfriend Muddy (Jesse's father), and then discovering that T. R. is planning a jailbreak. Fathering is a universal mythos, and McMurtry is able to touch its chords as ably as he plays on the trail-drive motif in *Lonesome Dove*.

Having already revisited one western legend in Billy the Kid, McMurtry turns to another, Calamity Jane, in *Buffalo Girls* (1990). The two buffalo girls who come out to play in this case are the madam, Dora Du Fran, and Calamity, whose letters to her daughter, Janey (supposedly fathered by Wild Bill Hickok), frame this tale. The story threads its way through Buffalo Bill Cody's attempt to assemble a crew of oldtimers to put on his Wild West Show for Queen Victoria, producing a kind of pageant similar to the centennial planned in *Texasville*. Like most of McMurtry's novels, this one depicts the end of an era, dominated by the superannuated – such as Calamity, forever drunk and falling off her horse, and Jim Ragg and Bartle Bone, a rag-and-bone pair who have outlived their quests – as well as by entrepreneurs such as Cody who profit from exploiting legendary figures of the West.

Familiar themes recur: friendship is portrayed in the relationship of Dora Du Fran to the sexually ambiguous Calamity, along with the relationship of the silent, beaver-struck Jim Ragg (he finally finds beaver in the London Zoo) to the ever-talkative

Bartle Bone, recalling the relationship between one-track Woodrow Call and the philosopher Augustus McCrae in *Lonesome Dove*. The sad state of marriage is reworked in the melancholy love of Dora Du Fran for T. Blue, each married to someone else. The giant Ogden Prideaux seems a reprise of Big Zwey from *Lonesome Dove,* one of the endless stream of McMurtry males duped by wiser, opportunistic women, a theme also repeated in the little English waif Pansy's predatory treatment of Bartle.

Viewed from a strictly structural perspective, *Buffalo Girls* collapses once the London trip is over two-thirds of the way through the novel, but no one reads McMurtry for plot and efficiency anyway; one has to savor the dawdle. The final revelation that Calamity is probably a hermaphrodite and that she has imagined Janey, closes the novel with convenience rather than conviction. Like the writers he most favors · ıck Kerouac, Miguel de Cervantes, and, to a lesser extent, Charles Dickens and William Makepeace Thackeray – McMurtry needs to be appreciated not for point but for progression, for wonderful incidents and recollections, such as the strange tale of why the Indian No Ears killed his beautiful wife Sun in the Face, or of how Pansy's brother Ben, an advocate of murdering old ladies, is in fact done in by the first lady he tries to victimize.

McMurtry's revision of history is sometimes less satisfying. He twists historical figures such as Sitting Bull through the meat grinder of his comic imagination, turning the man the *Reader's Encyclopedia of the American West* (1977) characterizes as "a loving father and a brave defender, always affable in manner, devoutly religious, and a prophet with much honor" into an archetypal dirty old man who squeezes white women when they ask for his autograph, wants to arrange a hunting party to kill animals in the London Zoo, and tries to blow smoke through No Ear's earholes.

The most compelling character, however, is No Ears himself – McMurtry's fictional creation. No Ears lost his ears to the white man as a child. He tried to sew on wolf ears as a young man, and he has acquired a dozen wax ears from a London wax museum. No Ears is the innocent perceiver of a new world, of whales in the ocean and the strange creatures in the London Zoo. His keen olfactory sense – he can even smell death coming – serves McMurtry well as the author kills off one character after another to close his tale. No Ears, hoping to pass along his wisdom to his tribe – like a Joseph Campbell figure sharing the fruits of his hero quest upon his return – finds no one who will listen to him, and the young braves steal twenty-three of his twenty-

four wax ears. It is a wistful, comic tale with the "folksy immediacy of a family album," as reviewer Michiko Kakutami observed in the *New York Times* (16 October 1990).

In *Evening Star* (1992) McMurtry returns to the other pole of his work, Texas of the present, to track down Aurora Greenway, now in her seventies. After Emma's death from cancer at the end of *Terms of Endearment,* Aurora felt responsible for Emma's three children, and in *Evening Star* they are grown – grown crazy. Tommie is in prison for killing his girlfriend. Teddy is married and a father, precariously recovering from a mental breakdown and barely tolerated by a wife who sees "nothing wrong with wanting a little girl nooky in the morning and a little boy nooky at night." He works at a 7–11 in a neighborhood blistered by shootings and robberies. The third child, Melanie, is pregnant, father uncertain.

Aurora, virtually in the same position as Calamity Jane, is summing up a lifetime, tempted to begin a Proustian recall of every day of her past. In bed with the now-impotent General Scott, who adds clothes for sleeping to compensate for poor circulation, she quips, "Either I'm holding hands with a glove or I'm being fondled by an icy claw. It's very disappointing that this is how life ends."

But, of all the characters McMurtry has selected in various novels to confront the ravages of time, Aurora is the most combative. While nursing along the general, she both torments and pursues Pascal (her Frenchman of the crooked penis), Jerry Bruckner (her self-declared psychiatrist), and, finally, one of two Greek brothers she stumbles upon after Jerry is killed by the jealous boyfriend of his fifteen-year-old tamale-stand conquest, Juanita. In all her pursuits Aurora is speech itself, the human voice creating and commanding in the darkness: she is never at a loss for an answer, even when there is no question.

The novel itself thematizes both speech and the evasion of communication – Bump, Teddy's son, begins to talk at a much later age than he should, and Tommie is occupied in prison with creating a secret code designed to frustrate the psychiatrists who examine him. Even when a stroke robs her of speech, Aurora survives by writing imperious commands on a legal pad. She will remain forever memorable as seen and heard at the end by her great-grandson Henry, who is too young to recognize that the lovely sound that she uses to speak to him is in fact a deafening CD of the Brahms Requiem selected to accompany her own death.

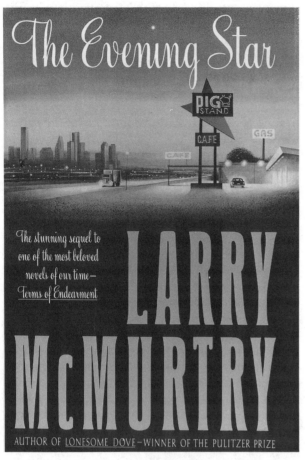

Dust jacket for McMurtry's 1992 novel, which involves many of the characters from Terms of Endearment *(1975)*

McMurtry has been prolific, writing fifteen novels since 1961, some of considerable length. He disdains such stylists as William Goyen, whose "prose gathers so much attention to itself that virtually none is left for his characters," and he disdains writers who settle for a career of only one or two novels. He has claimed to work through three drafts of each of his novels, and he claims not to have reread his books after they are published. He states that he does not care what critics think of his work, sounding at times like a perpetual adolescent: "Essentially I have had 30 years of writing my books and having a nice time and not much caring about what people thought of them." And yet in "Ever a Bridegroom" he magisterially surveys the field of Texas writing and finds it entirely lacking in intensity and significance, without reflection or a sense of direction. McMurtry certainly is not an economical or even a careful novelist: it is sometimes difficult to understand the function of a particular scene in *Evening Star,* why must Aurora get a speeding ticket for running a stop on her way to see her psychiatrist,

Jerry? Why must the end of Melanie's relationship with a boyfriend the reader has hardly met feature a brutal argument over anal sex?

Despite these defects, which sometimes seem the flow of a writer indulged for writing too much, McMurtry is still a compelling storyteller. As Kakutami put it in a *New York Times* review (12 May 1992) of *Evening Star,* "His quick, eager sympathy for his characters, his uncanny ability to zip in and out of all their minds and his effortless narrative inventiveness all combine to create a story that's as emotionally involving as it is entertaining." This capacity to "zip in and out" is a product of his rapid shifts in point of view. McMurtry declines the suspense of limited omniscience and simply tells the reader all one wants to know about everyone involved in a scene. What the reader finds out is sometimes hardly fine perception — more often it reveals boredom, weakness, or massive uncertainty. Generally the shifts are successful, as with the move to the great-grandson at the end of *Evening Star.* Here the distancing of emotion created by the child's view provides the appropriate restraint of understatement for a strongly emotional scene.

Above all McMurtry loves the dazzle of rapid diffusion. Jerry, the psychiatrist in *Evening Star,* uncomfortably explains to Patsy Carpenter (whose sexual overtures have overwhelmed him) why he feels enmeshed within Aurora's sexual attentions. At the same time, he recalls his tall, toothy waitress companion, Lalani, and his desire to leave Houston altogether with Juanita, and he also tries to ignore Patsy's daughter Katie floating topless in the pool outside Patsy's window. This scene is quintessential McMurtry.

In McMurtry's novels characters proliferate like weeds, only to be chopped down quickly. A character such as the resourceful Janey — an orphan who lopes along with July Johnson's deputy, Roscoe, in *Lonesome Dove* — is not clever enough to defend herself from the vicious Blue Duck. Even main characters are bloodily dispatched, such as T. R. in *Some Can Whistle,* or more slowly wasted, as with Emma's cancer in *Terms of Endearment,* as if McMurtry preferred the pathos of loss over the more demanding challenge of lifetime confrontations. Ahearn noted this pattern after McMurtry's first six novels, observing that they have "a tendency to dodge the responsibility of developing serious themes they introduce." Long-term relationships almost by definition lead to dead relationships, as with the coma of Bob, Clara's husband in *Lonesome Dove,* or the general trailing into impotence in *Evening Star.*

McMurtry's most recent novel, *Streets of Laredo* (1993), is a reprise of *Lonesome Dove*, written after McMurtry had recovered from quadruple-bypass surgery. In a 1993 *Newsweek* interview with Malcolm Jones he noted that writing it "was a little like taking dictation," as if the book were "faxed" to him by his "former self." It reads that way, too, like something written on autopilot. Page by page it has the feel of an epic, with incidents proliferating into byways of suspense, loving detail, and sudden insights into a character's pain and fortitude, but it spirals mindlessly on its way.

The plot is driven by Woodrow Call's search for Joey Garza, a train robber with a telescopic German rifle, a deadly aim, and a bright-eyed compulsion for torture. The subplot simply duplicates the same theme, with a secondary search for Mox Mox the manburner. The book has the feel of a baroque romance or of the succeeding installments of James Fenimore Cooper's Leatherstocking tales, with old characters met once more and each action festooned by the memory of past deeds. Pea Eye is remembered for his naked trek through Cheyenne country; even the crazy cook Bol wants one more go at the past. Events seem to be generated out of correspondence to incidents from *Lonesome Dove* – Call saves his life by sacrificing a battered leg, where Augustus had earlier died for wanting to keep his. Throughout, characters wander about a landscape not much more specific and identifiable than Cooper's prairie.

The real center of the book is the women – Maria, Joey's mother, and Lorena, now a schoolteacher married to Pea Eye. The men are not good for much more than feeble conversation, the absorption of lead and the exuding of blood during battle, and a pervasive longing for the comforts of domesticity. Some of the wives of Call's entourage expire after their men leave, but Lorena and Maria endure, tracking down their men with considerably more success than the men can hunt up Joey or Mox Mox. Maria in particular stands out, with her four husbands, idiot son, and blind daughter, not to mention her oldest mental case, Joey. Maria's thought ultimately reveals the most valuable nugget in the book: "Maria didn't know why men resented the very women who gave them the most pleasure, and gave it generously. It was foolish, very foolish, of men to resent the good that came from women." Nobody really expects a sequel to match its predecessor, and in that sense nobody can be disappointed with *Streets of Laredo*. As Noel Perrin (*New York Times Book Review*, 25 July 1993) puts it, "It turns out that the person who can write the best parody of Larry McMurtry is Larry McMurtry."

"Being a writer and a Texan is an amusing fate," McMurtry declares in *In a Narrow Grave*, especially when one is a "regionalist from an unpopular region." But perhaps the emphasis on the sweatshirt motto should not be on the *minor* or the *regional* but on the problem of being a *novelist* in twentieth-century America. By his own admission he has been influenced by the great nineteenth-century British novelists who aimed for laughter and tears, who wanted to instruct, reprove, or uplift. But McMurtry has attempted to continue this tradition in a century tortured by alienation and uncertainty, an age more likely to fracture fictions than to honor them. Furthermore, to be part of the West, yet not wholly satisfied with it, creates uneasy alliances: who is more critical of a Westerner than an Easterner? Does McMurtry really want to classify himself with Easterners? Cadillac Jack does not.

Cadillac Jack may be the ultimate metaphor for twentieth-century America's view of itself: there is a whole country out there and a big Cadillac to see it in, but no place to call home. In that sense Texas may be an excellent regional synecdoche for all of America: as Hamlin Hill points out, "The essential Texan is blood kin to modern man." McMurtry – finding himself at the strange intersection of a complex European tradition of fiction and troubled contemporary America – has given a comical, elegiac view of America past and present.

Interviews:

Doris Grumbach, "Talking with McMurtry," *Washingtonian* (June 1976): 119–120ff.;

Patrick Bennett, "Larry McMurtry: Thalia, Houston, and Hollywood," in his *Talking With Texas Writers: Twelve Interviews* (College Station: Texas A & M University Press, 1980), pp. 15–36;

Malcolm Jones, "The Ghost Writer at Home on the Range – *Streets of Laredo*," *Newsweek*, 122 (2 August 1993): 52–53.

Bibliographies:

Charles D. Peavy, "A Larry McMurtry Bibliography," *Western American Literature*, 3 (Fall 1968): 235–248;

Charles Williams, "Bibliography," in *Taking Stock: A Larry McMurtry Casebook*, edited by Clay Reynolds (Dallas: Southern Methodist University Press, 1989), pp. 409–444.

References:

Kerry Ahearn, "Larry McMurtry," in *Fifty Western Writers: A Bio-bibliographical Sourcebook*, edited by Fred Erisman and Richard Etulain (Westport, Conn.: Greenwood Press, 1982), pp. 280–290;

Ahearn, "More D'Urban: The Texas Novels of Larry McMurtry," in *Taking Stock: A Larry McMurtry Casebook,* edited by Clay Reynolds (Dallas: Southern Methodist University Press, 1989), pp. 206–227;

Christopher Baker, "The Death of the Frontier in the Novels of Larry McMurtry," in *Taking Stock: A Larry McMurtry Casebook,* pp. 164–172;

Emily Benedek, "An Author Recaptures His Voice," in *Taking Stock: A Larry McMurtry Casebook,* pp. 288–291;

Mark Busby, "Leaving Texas: The Trash Trilogy," in *Taking Stock: A Larry McMurtry Casebook,* pp. 259–268;

Alan F. Crooks, "Larry McMurtry – A Writer in Transition: An Essay-Review," *Western American Literature,* 7 (Summer 1972): 151–155;

Kenneth W. Davis, "The Themes of Initiation in the Works of Larry McMurtry and Tom Mayer," *Arlington Quarterly,* 2 (Winter 1969–1970): 29–43;

Louise Erdrich, "Why Is that Man Tired?," in *Taking Stock: A Larry McMurtry Casebook,* pp. 338–341;

James K. Folsom, "*Shane* and *Hud:* Two Stories in Search of a Medium," *Western Humanities Review,* 24 (Autumn 1970): 359–372;

Steve Fore, "The Same Old Others: The Western, *Lonesome Dove,* and the Lingering Difficulty of Difference," *Velvet Light Trap,* 27 (Spring 1991): 49–62:

John Gerlach, "*The Last Picture Show* and One More Adaptation," *Literature/Film Quarterly,* 1 (April 1973): 161–166;

Don Graham, "*Lonesome Dove:* Butch and Sundance Go on a Cattle-drive," in *Taking Stock: A Larry McMurtry Casebook,* pp. 311–316;

Barbara Granzow, "The Western Writer: A Study of Larry McMurtry's *All My Friends Are Going to Be Strangers,*" in *Taking Stock: A Larry McMurtry Casebook,* pp. 242–258;

Hamlin Hill, "Summing Up," in *Taking Stock: A Larry McMurtry Casebook,* pp. 397–407;

Thomas Landess, *Larry McMurtry,* (Austin: Steck-Vaughn, 1969);

Lera Patrick Tyler Lich, *Larry McMurtry's Texas: Evolution of the Myth* (Austin: Eakin, 1987);

Raymond L. Neinstein, *The Ghost Country: A Study of the Novels of Larry McMurtry* (Berkeley: Creative Arts, 1976);

Charles Peavy, "Coming of Age in Texas: The Novels of Larry McMurtry," *Western American Literature,* 4 (Fall 1969): 171–188;

Peavy, *Larry McMurtry* (Boston: Twayne, 1977);

Peavy, "Larry McMurtry and Black Humor: A Note on *The Last Picture Show,*" *Western American Literature,* 2 (Fall 1967): 223–227;

Raymond C. Phillips, Jr., "The Ranch as Place and Symbol in the Novels of Larry McMurtry," *South Dakota Review,* 13 (Summer 1975): 27–47;

Tom Pilkington, "Doing Without: The Thalia Trilogy," in *Taking Stock: A Larry McMurtry Casebook,* pp. 113–127;

Clay Reynolds, "Back Trailing to Glory: *Lonesome Dove* and the Novels of Larry McMurtry," in *Taking Stock: A Larry McMurtry Casebook,* pp. 327–334;

Ernestine P. Sewell, "Moving On: The Houston Trilogy," in *Taking Stock: A Larry McMurtry Casebook,* pp. 193–204;

Janis Stout, "Cadillac Larry Rides Again: McMurtry and the Song of the Open Road," *Western American Literature,* 24 (November 1989): 243–251.

Papers:

The University of Houston has the typescripts of *The Last Picture Show, Leaving Cheyenne,* and shorter published works; the manuscripts of two unpublished novels and an unpublished screenplay; and other miscellaneous manuscript materials.

Sue Miller

(29 November 1943 –)

Brenda Daly
Iowa State University

and

Susan L. Woods
Iowa State University

BOOKS: *The Good Mother* (New York: Harper &
  Row, 1986; London: Gollancz, 1986);
Inventing the Abbotts (New York: Harper & Row,
  1987; London: Gollancz, 1987);
Family Pictures (New York: HarperCollins, 1990;
  London: Gollancz, 1990);
For Love (New York: HarperCollins, 1993; London:
  Doubleday, 1993).

SELECTED PERIODICAL PUBLICATIONS –
UNCOLLECTED: "Given Names," *North American
  Review,* 266 (September 1981): 12–17;
"Leaving Home," *Atlantic,* 249 (June 1982): 67–72;
"Tyler and Brina," *Atlantic,* 255 (May 1985): 59–63;
"The Lover of Women," *Mademoiselle,* 92 (March
  1986): 148;
"Calling," *Boston Globe Magazine,* 6 July 1986, p. 1;
"The Moms of Summer," *Life,* 14 (August 1991):
  87.

Since the publication of her first novel, *The
Good Mother* (1986), Sue Miller has been highly acclaimed for her authentic depictions of conflicts arising from changing roles and expectations in middle-
class American families. Like Miller herself, the female protagonists of her three novels have all been
divorced, and all either have children or, in one instance, are about to give birth. Critics often praise
Miller's exceptional ability to portray children,
most of whom are afflicted in some way by the conflicts of their parents – conflicts that sometimes lead
to divorce and remarriage. She is also noted for her
ability to probe the complex psychological and
moral conflicts that arise not only between husbands and wives but also between different generations of a family.

In a 1986 interview Miller told Rosemary Herbert that she attributes this moral questioning, which

Sue Miller (photograph © Jerry Bauer)

she calls "the homiletic turn" in her fiction, to the
fact that her family has been "ecclesiastical on both
sides for generations." Part of the impulse to write
her first novel, Miller explained to Herbert, came
from her objection to novels that implied that life
after divorce is always positive: "I have been di-

vorced, and that wasn't my experience or the experience of anyone else I knew." Investigations of family relationships in Miller's novels often span three generations, usually reaching back at least to the 1950s. Because the family has been the subject of political conflict since the 1950s, it is not surprising that Miller has been both criticized and praised for her focus on domestic spaces.

Born on 29 November 1943, Miller grew up on Harper Avenue in an integrated Chicago neighborhood; her second novel, *Family Pictures* (1990), is set on that street. Her mother was Judith Beach Nichols, and her father, James Hastings Nichols, is an ordained minister who taught church history at the University of Chicago Divinity School and Princeton Theological Seminary before retiring. Both of Miller's grandfathers were also Protestant clergymen, one Presbyterian and one Congregational. Reflecting on her extended family and its influence on her writing, Miller told Herbert that she has inherited strong ideals about right and wrong. She is thankful to be "shaped" by these values, to "know clearly what [she] feels and thinks about things." According to Miller, "the ability to see moral patterns in your life and all around you gives you not only a sense of what is wrong, it also gives you a sense of beauty." Such beauty is evident in her writing.

Miller entered Radcliffe College at age sixteen, earning a B.A. in English literature in 1964. She also received a master's degree in early childhood education from Harvard University; a master's degree in creative writing from Boston University; and a master's degree in English education from Wesleyan University in Connecticut. Soon after graduating from Radcliffe, Miller married her first husband, a medical student who later became a psychiatrist, and worked in a variety of positions, including high-school teacher, waitress, model, and researcher. The couple divorced in the early 1970s, three years after the birth of their son, Ben. Miller worked for the next eight years as a day-care teacher, an experience she claims has been invaluable to her writing.

Miller chose to leave the field of early childhood care in order to develop her writing skills. In 1979 she was awarded a creative-writing fellowship at Boston University. She and author Doug Bauer, whom she married in the mid 1980s, make their home in Boston. She is currently working as a writer and has given up teaching creative writing at Boston-area colleges. "I did it for a while," she told *People* magazine in 1993, but finally "the sense of freshness was gone." Miller received an honorable

mention from the Pushcart Press in 1984 for her short stories and a National Book Critics Circle Award nomination in 1991 for *Family Pictures*. She has also received a Guggenheim Fellowship, the Bunting Institute Fellowship from Radcliffe College, and a grant from the Massachusetts Artists Foundation.

The Good Mother, which Miller developed from a short story she published in the *North American Review* (September 1981), centers on the struggles of Anna Dunlap, the recently divorced mother of four-year-old Molly. Free from a passionless marriage to her first husband, Brian, Anna meets and falls in love with Leo, an artist who gives her emotional and sexual fulfillment. Anna soon finds that what the law views as "life without limits" exacts a terrible price: she loses custody of her daughter. As *The Good Mother* illustrates, Miller objects to those "post-feminist novels which suggested that all you need to do is shed your husband and then you enter this glorious new life of accomplishment and ease."

The book opens with Anna and Molly moving into their new home. The quiet scenes in which mother and daughter share moments of their daily lives – eating breakfast or ice-cream cones – are drawn with great skill. In the *New York Times Book Review* (27 April 1986) Linda Wolfe praised Miller for her "skillful rendition of the ordinary, particularly the commonplaces of motherhood. . . . No one has done it better." Molly's character is extremely believable, and the dialogue between her and Anna is particularly touching. Miller told Herbert that her keen observations of children can be attributed to her experiences as a day-care teacher: "People are very revealing to a day care person and talk to you a lot. It was an opportunity, unparalleled in any other kind of work, to learn about communication in a special sense. The teacher had to understand from signals, from gestures, what children were really thinking about. This trained me in observation."

Because *The Good Mother* has such striking authenticity, some readers might wonder to what degree the work is autobiographical. While Miller stated to Herbert that "there is a sense remotely in which the larger family is like mine, in that it is a very achieving, very accomplished family," there is little in the book that she has personally experienced: "The events in [Anna's] life, outside of being divorced and a single mother living in Cambridge, are nothing that I've experienced, thank God."

Beyond the realism of her characters and her skillful use of dialogue, Miller has been praised for her ability to write about sexual encounters, a talent

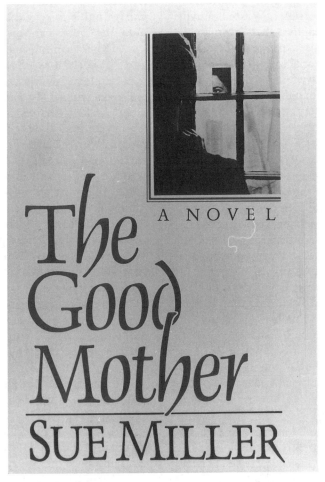

Dust jacket for Miller's first novel, which concerns a divorced woman who loses her daughter in a bitter custody battle

necessary in a novel that, at least according to some reviewers, pits maternal and erotic love. Miller, however, told Polly LaBarre that she views this interpretation of the novel as a "misreading." In fact, Miller's depiction of the relationship between Anna and Leo is complex, portraying a love based on more than good sex. Leo is, for example, a sensitive, thoughtful parent to Molly. Both Anna and Leo, who spend a good deal of time with Molly, are affectionate and attentive toward the child.

However, after Leo allows Molly, who has wandered in while he is taking a shower, to see and touch his nude body, Anna's former husband hires a lawyer and accuses her of "sexual irregularities with a minor child." Brian is obviously motivated not only by concern for his daughter but also by a desire to retaliate against a woman who has, prior to seeking a divorce, criticized his sexual performance. Brian manipulates the law to exact revenge, and Anna pays a terrible price: she loses custody of

Molly. Under these circumstances, in order to have some contact with her daughter, Anna must move to another city and, as a result, give up her relationship with Leo.

However, it is also possible to interpret Anna's willingness to give up Leo as, to some degree, self-punishing, and this behavior – which is presumed to be submissive and even masochistic – angers those readers who desire a more liberated protagonist and a more positive outcome. For example, some feminists interpret Anna's giving up Leo as a gesture to the courts that she is willing to be the good mother once again and accuse Miller of calling for the maternal sacrifice of erotic love. As Roberta White argues, feminist readers may never be satisfied with the character of Anna because of her lack of achievement and assertiveness.

Miller told LaBarre that she "felt singularly called to task by feminist reviewers of *The Good Mother:* The heroine wasn't heroic enough. . . . But, on the other hand, I don't know many people who are heroic in that way." However, White believes that part of the novel's strength is that "even a passive person like Anna, confused and of modest aspirations, can realize her potential for wisdom, depth, and grace," a grace bestowed through the "constancy of her love for her daughter." White interprets Anna's choice not to stay with Leo as a "mark of new strength – not aggressiveness but quiet strength."

Miller's second book, *Inventing the Abbotts* (1987), is a collection of stories. As in her novels, many of the stories portray the conflicts of families and social class and the complexities of growing up, along with the conflicts between sexual relationships and parenting, between divorce and remarriage. The narrator of the title story analyzes his brother Jacey's obsessive involvement throughout his adolescence with three daughters from a family, the Abbotts, with more social standing than theirs. When Mrs. Abbott suggests that Jacey is trying "to marry *up*," the narrator, offended by the remark, asks, "Why do you assume that for him to have married one of you would be to marry up?" This story, as well as the perspective of a mature mother in "Leaving Home," anticipates themes in Miller's third novel, *For Love* (1993).

Other stories – such as "Appropriate Affect," "Expensive Gifts," and "The Birds and the Bees" – portray problems central in *The Good Mother*. For example, like Anna's grandmother in *The Good Mother*, the usually submissive Franny in "Appropriate Affect" finally rebels against her husband; following a stroke, she suddenly reveals her discontent with her husband Henry. "The. Nasty. Man," she says to a startled daughter. After years of silence Franny confronts Henry with her knowledge that he was "Fuck-ing Mrs. Sheffield," a nurse hired to help her following the delivery of each of her four daughters. In an ending that is a bit too neat, Franny returns from the hospital where, upon her arrival, the family applauds her years of performing – with "appropriate affect" – as a wife and mother.

The sexual education of an adolescent girl, which is also a theme in Miller's first two novels, is depicted in "The Birds and the Bees." Like Anna in *The Good Mother*, Ginny is the daughter of a father who "married up" and a mother who never got used to Chicago. Although Ginny's mother has given her a pamphlet about sex, her real education begins when she and a friend encounter an exhibitionist. The adolescent girl in "What Ernest Says" has a similarly rude sexual beginning. Following her initiation by Ernest – the young African-American who

sits behind her and whispers, "*cock, pussy, suck, eat*" – she is unable to repeat the words of her first Communion, "Take, eat, this is my body."

Other stories in the collection, such as "Slides" and "Travel," use photography to illustrate how men employ cameras to establish distance and control over women. In *Family Pictures* Miller applies a more complex rhetoric of photography to dramatize the psychological development of a female photographer, Nina Eberhardt. One of the most powerful stories in the collection, "The Quality of Life," achieves its haunting effect by juxtaposing two scenes that portray blows to a son's face – the first following the announcement of his parents' divorce, the second during a visit to his father's new family. A son also experiences pain in *Family Pictures*, not only because of his parents' separation but also because of his mother's decision to keep her autistic son at home.

One of the most striking features of *Family Pictures* is its narrative technique – its fluidly familial point of view. Although anchored in Nina Eberhardt's perspective, the novel shifts its angle of vision to explore the perspectives of her parents, David and Lainey, as well as those of other family members. As in most families, everyone sees things a little differently. The Eberhardts live in a Chicago suburb through the 1950s and 1960s. The silent presence of their autistic son, Randall, exerts a powerful influence on the entire family.

Among the children, Randall's influence is felt most by those closest in age to him, Mack and Nina. As Miller has noted, reviewers picked up most on the mother/daughter relationship, but the novel explores a wide range of family relationships. However, for some women readers, as Brenda Daly notes, the most central relationship is between Nina and her mother, even though the relationship between Mack and his parents is also well developed. According to Daly one "radical innovation" in this novel is that it "opens a space from which the mother, who has long been silenced in both fictional and psychoanalytic narratives, may finally speak and claim her own subjectivity."

Daly focuses in particular on Miller's use of the rhetoric of photography to depict a daughter's development from early adolescence, at which time she prefers her father, into a mature woman who finally comes to respect her mother: "Each time references to photographs or Freud surface in the novel, and usually they occur together, they indicate an important moment in Nina's maturation." However, Miller analyzes Freud's view of the family not only through her narrative technique but also by

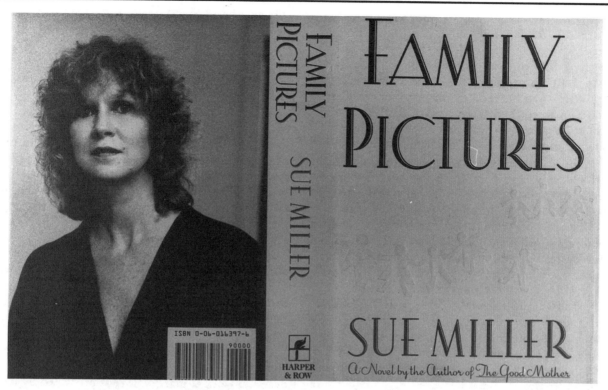

Dust jacket for Miller's 1990 novel, which focuses on a family in which one of the children is autistic

portraying David's and Lainey's preferences for different rhetorics – David's as psychoanalytic, Lainey's as "pre-Freudian" unorthodox spirituality.

Family Pictures effectively presents an unusually wide range of characters and relationships, including those between husband and wife, father and son, and father and daughters, as well as those between siblings, particularly Mack and Nina. Lainey's father is an ordained minister, and she has inherited religious values that conflict with those of her psychiatrist husband. Miller, who told LaBarre that she considered calling the novel "Perfection," explained that "Randall is an extreme example of a destructive factor who suddenly fractures the idea of the unified myth." For many reasons – including their inability to decide on how to care for Randall – David moves out, leaving the care of the family to Lainey. Before and after they finally divorce, the Eberhardts argue about whose fault the "fracture" is.

In order to write *Family Pictures,* Miller researched families with physically and emotionally disabled children. She chose to portray David as a Freudian analyst who accepts Bruno Bettelheim's view that mothers are to blame for autism. Characteristic of husbands of that period, David assumes that in order to protect his family, he should take

control. Lainey resists her husband by keeping Randall at home, a decision with effects that are most damaging to Mack, the eldest son. Out of resistance to his father, Mack refuses to see a psychiatrist, but Nina benefits from working with one; hence the novel provides a well-balanced critique of Freudian theory and practice.

In the *New York Times Book Review* (21 April 1990) Jane Smiley described *Family Pictures* as a "virtuoso" novel that depicts domestic spaces – kitchen, dining room, and bedrooms – in a manner "as spacious and encompassing as any respected American novel, a work whose cumulative insight blossoms into wisdom and whose steady focus on a single family reveals much of what there is to know about the American middle class in the middle of our century." However, in a review for *Mother Jones* (July–August 1990), Valerie Miner criticized the novel for its lack of social engagement, especially "the way it buys into current rhetoric about the family." Some reviewers also described *Family Pictures* as too weighted with detail despite the fact that Miller cut about one hundred pages from the novel.

Miller's next novel, *For Love,* is a psychological drama that opens with the death of an au pair named Jessica – a scene imagined by the narrator, forty-four-year-old Lottie Gardner. Jessica's death, which occurs during a summer in which Lottie has returned to the family home in Cambridge, Massachusetts, becomes the occasion for Lottie to examine the ethics of love. With the help of her son, Ryan, Lottie is preparing the house for sale following the death of her mother. Since Lottie's brother, Cameron Reed, had taken care of their alcoholic mother for years, she feels an obligation to help despite her anger toward her neglectful mother.

She also needs an excuse to separate from her husband, Jack, and their already-troubled new marriage. Inevitably, the return to her old neighborhood on Farmington Street forces Lottie to confront unresolved issues from her past, including her childhood relationship with a neighbor, Elizabeth Harbour Butterfield, who once had a passionate affair with Lottie's brother. Elizabeth, whose marriage is also troubled, has returned to Cambridge as well. During the summer she renews her passionate affair with Cameron, while Lottie acts as audience to the romance. During the almost two months in which Lottie cleans out and paints her mother's house with the help of Ryan, a college senior, she reflects on the varieties of love.

A writer for women's magazines, Lottie specializes in pieces that explain medical issues, but she has decided to write a series of articles that will examine the medicalization of terms used to discuss emotions, the first of which will focus on love. She does not have to go far to research the topic. By way of parallel plots the novel contrasts the small joys and heartaches of the marital love of Lottie and Jack with Cameron's renewed romantic obsession for Elizabeth. The lovers once lived on the same street, but they are from different social classes. Elizabeth, the daughter of an anthropology professor, grew up in a disciplined family in a large Victorian house, while Cameron, the son of a small-time embezzler, grew up with an alcoholic mother in a small house with old, fake-brick asphalt siding.

Lottie reexperiences these differences in class through Elizabeth's careless and cruel flirtation with Cameron. Elizabeth, who is also insensitive to Lottie, calls her "Char" even though Lottie's struggle to redefine herself is perceptible in the changes she marks with changes in her name, from Char to Charlotte to Lottie. Despite these shifting appellations, however, Lottie discovers that she has not completely escaped her past. For example, because she does not feel at home in her upper-middle-class husband's house, she has redecorated only two rooms in what had been Jack's home with his former wife: the housekeeper's room, which she now uses as a study; and a bedroom for Ryan. Cameron

also has scars from childhood. Fueled by his desire for upper-class status, his love for Elizabeth is obsessive and destructive. In fact, he accidentally kills the au pair, who is waiting in the driveway to intercept him, when he insists on seeing Elizabeth after she has phoned to tell him their affair is over.

Lottie discovers her love for Jack is troubled not only by class conflicts but also by her desire for the "high" of an illicit relationship. Lottie had such a relationship with Jack during his wife's long illness, but he has been in mourning for most of their brief marriage; this complication, along with her stepdaughter's antagonism, has caused an estrangement between them. Lottie finds herself excited by the thought of separating from Jack and, at moments, even more excited by the "blank slate" of possibility should she divorce him. When Jack visits her in Cambridge, conflicts emerge. She still prefers the excitement of her former illicit romance with Jack, but Jack prefers the sunshine of their marriage.

Despite these unresolved conflicts, there is reason to hope that the marriage will survive. Lottie's desire to work at married love is prompted by Jessica's death and what she regards as her brother's romantic egocentricity, which results in his apparent indifference to the young woman's death. Before Jessica's death Lottie defends the emotional "excess" of romantic love; afterward, however, she views Cameron's obsession with Elizabeth as similar to his devotion to their mother: both relationships satisfy his need to define himself as "noble," but neither has much to do with the actual needs of the women involved. Moreover, though each woman has been abusive to Cameron, he does not allow himself to feel anger.

Because her brother is so closed off, Lottie understands that she will never truly know him; at the same time, she is relieved to recognize their differences at last. A major difference is that, in his obsession for Elizabeth, Cameron shows no concern about Jessica's family. The process of cleaning out her mother's house has helped Lottie sort out her emotions. Though painful, like the recurring toothache she suffers, this emotional housecleaning enables Lottie to avoid her brother's self-destructive romanticism and return to what is at least potentially a good marriage.

In the *New York Times Book Review* (11 April 1993) Ron Carlson wrote that Miller "maps the emotional terrain carefully, precisely, graphically" in *For Love*. He describes her great gift as offering the reader "*new* terms, *new* possibilities," not in "the realm of the happily-ever-after or the merely occa-

*Dust jacket for Miller's 1993 novel, in which a woman confronts
the unresolved relationships of her past during
a stay at her mother's home*

sional happily-ever-after, but somewhere in between, where so many real lives are lived." However, in the *Women's Review of Books* (July 1993), Gail Pool criticized the novel for failing to overcome the "air of melodrama" imparted in the prologue, pointing out that only Lottie, who cannot carry the novel alone, is a fully drawn character. Pool argued that the reader does not learn enough about either Elizabeth or Cameron, in part because the novel lacks ironic detachment. On the other hand, a critical response to Elizabeth and Cameron's love affair depends on the reader's seeing them almost exclusively through Lottie's eyes.

Although Miller believes her novels have not received serious critical attention – she told Mickey Pearlman that there has been a "lack of metaphoric discussion of *The Good Mother* and of *Family Pictures* too" – this situation has begun to change. Reviewers and literary critics have begun to analyze Miller's complex art: her ability at character development; her skill with dialogue and setting; her effec-

tive use of imagery, especially photographic images; and her innovative narrative techniques, such as variations in point of view. However, Miller told Pearlman that she is "very interested in the reader of the book, in touching people, and less interested in . . . experiments with language. I am careful about such things, but I don't think that is my particular gift; I'm a storyteller in an unfashionable way, and that's my interest."

In fact, as Miller explained to Pearlman, *The Good Mother* represents an attempt "to master . . . the notion of plot," while in *Family Pictures* "there were other things I wanted to master. In some sense I was turning away from plot and wanted to move, in the third person, among a whole group of characters." *For Love* is a different kind of experiment. As in *Family Pictures,* a daughter is both the narrator and a character in the drama, but in *For Love* the narrative focuses on a brother, Cameron. By making Lottie a writer, however, Miller manages to rewrite the typical romance story from the perspective of a woman who – unlike Gustave Flaubert's Emma Bovary or Leo Tolstoy's Anna Karenina – is capable of change.

Miller also told Pearlman that she objects to the critical discussion of "women writers as women, rather than as literary people concerned with painful, truthful images," in part because this approach prevents men from reading women's writing. Miller says that men as well as women should learn to understand how women writers are using their experiences metaphorically. Some of Miller's contemporaries have also resisted the category "woman writer," but one wonders why the label should continue to be perceived as denigrating when many of the best contemporary novels, including those of Sue Miller, are being written by women.

Interviews:

Lori Miller, "The Novelist Hangs Around," *New York Times Book Review,* 27 April 1986, p. 40;

Rosemary Herbert, "Sue Miller," *Publishers Weekly* (2 May 1986): 60–61;

Marilyn Stasio, "Fiction's Fresh New Wave," *Cosmopolitan,* 202 (March 1987): 288;

Polly LaBarre, "Sue Miller: Re-exploring the Territory of the Home," in *In the Vernacular: Interviews at Yale with Sculptors of Culture,* edited by Melissa E. Biggs (Jefferson, N.C.: McFarland, 1991), pp. 169–177;

Susan Toepfer, "Talking with . . . Sue Miller: Off to Radcliffe at a Tender Age," *People,* 39 (26 April 1993): 33;

Mickey Pearlman, *Listen to Their Voices: Twenty Interviews with Women Who Write* (New York: Norton, 1993), pp. 162–171.

References:

Brenda Daly, "The Rhetoric of Photography in Sue Miller's *Family Pictures," WILLA,* 1 (Fall 1992): 20–25;

Dawn Ann Drzal, "Casualties of the Feminine Mystique," *Antioch,* 46 (Fall 1988): 450–461;

Roberta White, "Anna's Quotidian Love: Sue Miller's *The Good Mother,*" in *Mother Puzzles: Daughters and Mothers in Contemporary American Life,* edited by Mickey Pearlman (New York: Greenwood Press, 1989), pp. 11–22;

Toby Silverman Zinman, "The Good Old Days in *The Good Mother,*" *Modern Fiction Studies,* 34 (Autumn 1988): 405–412.

N. Scott Momaday

(27 February 1934 –)

Alan R. Velie
Oklahoma University

BOOKS: *The Journey of Tai-Me* (Santa Barbara, Cal.: Privately printed, 1967);

House Made of Dawn (New York: Harper & Row, 1968; London: Gollancz, 1969);

The Way to Rainy Mountain (Albuquerque: University of New Mexico Press, 1969);

Colorado: Summer, Fall, Winter, Spring (New York: Rand McNally, 1973);

Angle of Geese and Other Poems (Boston: Godine, 1974);

The Colors of Night (San Francisco: Arion Press, 1976);

The Gourd Dancer (New York & London: Harper & Row, 1976);

The Names: A Memoir (New York: Harper & Row, 1977);

The Ancient Child (New York: Doubleday, 1989);

In the Presence of the Sun: Stories and Poems, 1961–1991 (New York: St. Martin's Press, 1992).

PLAY PRODUCTION: *The Indolent Boys,* Syracuse, New York, Syracuse Stage, February 1994.

OTHER: *The Complete Poems of Frederick Goddard Tuckerman,* edited by Momaday (New York: Oxford University Press, 1965).

N. Scott Momaday is the dean of American Indian authors. (Indians, especially in Oklahoma and the Southwest, use the term *Indian.* Academics are the ones who chiefly use *Native American.*) Momaday's novel *House Made of Dawn* (1968) began the renaissance in American Indian literature. He is the author of another novel, two memoirs, and four volumes of poems. He is also well known as an artist whose paintings and drawings have been exhibited widely throughout the West. His honors include the Academy of American Poets Prize in 1962 for "The Bear" (collected in *Angle of Geese and Other Poems,* 1974); the Pulitzer Prize for fiction in 1969 for *House Made of Dawn;* the Western Heritage Award in 1974 for *Colorado: Summer, Fall, Winter, Spring* (1973); the Premio Litterario Internazionale Mondelo, Italy's highest literary prize, in 1979; the Distinguished Service Award

from the Western Literature Association in 1983; the Native American Literature Prize in 1989, and the Returning the Gift Lifetime Achievement Award in 1992.

N. Scott Momaday was born on 27 February 1934 at the Kiowa and Comanche Indian Hospital at Lawton, Oklahoma. His birth certificate records him as Novarro Scotte Mammedatty, the original family surname; his father, Al Momaday, adopted the present spelling shortly afterward. According to the records of the Bureau of Indian Affairs, Momaday is "7/8 Indian Blood." In actuality his father was Kiowa, with perhaps a French-Canadian ancestor as well as some Mexican blood, acquired when, as Momaday puts it, "the Kiowas . . . stole people as well as horses in their heydey." His mother, Mayme Natachee, had only one Indian ancestor, a Cherokee great-grandmother. However faint her Indian heritage was genetically, Natachee conceived of herself as Indian and after high school enrolled in Haskell Institute, an Indian school in Lawrence, Kansas. In *The Names: A Memoir* (1977) Momaday writes of her:

> She began to see herself as an Indian. That dim native heritage became a fascination and a cause for her, inasmuch, perhaps, as it enabled her to assume an attitude of defiance, an attitude which she assumed with particular style and satisfaction; it became her. She imagined who she was. This act of the imagination was, I believe, among the most important events of my mother's early life, as later the same essential act was to be among the most important of my own.

Momaday returns frequently in his writings to the theme of identity as an existential act of imagination. Although he writes at length in *The Names* about his southern Anglo forebears, he told Matthias Schubnell that he "thinks of himself as an Indian." Momaday added that it was in doing research on Kiowa history and culture that he "acquired an identity; it is an Indian identity, as far as I am concerned." He has also written of his keen sense of being different from Indians, who occasionally appear as the hostile other in his imaginings. This complex set of attitudes

159

N. Scott Momaday hand coloring one of his etchings (Sun Valley Center for the Arts and Humanities, Sun Valley, Idaho)

toward cultural identity is at the heart of Moma-day's fiction.

Al Momaday and Natachee Scott were married in 1933 and moved to Mountain View, Oklahoma, to live with Al's family. The Mammedattys did not take well to the bride, whom they viewed as an outsider, so the couple moved to the desert Southwest, where their son grew up. From 1936 to 1943 the Momadays lived among the Navajo on the reservation at Shiprock, New Mexico, and then in Tuba City and San Carlos, Arizona. For three years they lived in Hobbs, New Mexico, and in 1946 moved to the Jemez Pueblo in New Mexico, the "last best home of [his] childhood."

At Jemez, Momaday's parents taught at the day school, and, although the family grew close to the people of the pueblo, they remained outsiders not allowed to participate in sacred ceremonies. In general New Mexico Indians are inclined to con-sider Indians from Oklahoma as not "really In-dian," especially if they are employed in professions Pueblo Indians consider "white" — teaching, public health, or government work. This contributed to Momaday's ambivalence about his ethnic identity.

While growing up Momaday attended Indian and parochial schools in New Mexico, but he was not satisfied with them. In an interview with Charles

Woodard he described the nuns who taught him as "the worst teachers I've ever had," stating that they discouraged learning about Indian culture. Having "run out of schools" in New Mexico, Momaday spent his final year of high school at a military school in Virginia, where he won a prize in decla-mation — an indication of one of his most impress-ive talents, his oratorical ability. Momaday uses his sonorous bass as a fine instrument in reading his prose and verse.

At age eighteen Momaday matriculated at the University of New Mexico. In 1956 he left for a year to study law at the University of Virginia, where he met William Faulkner, whose influence on Momaday may be noticed in the style of his novels as well as in the theme of his poem "The Bear." Momaday returned to New Mexico to graduate in 1958 with a B.A. in political science.

After college Momaday taught for a year at Dulce School on the Jicarilla Apache Reservation, where he wrote poetry in his spare time. Although he has achieved more fame as a novelist — and perhaps even as an artist — than as a poet, it is important to note that Momaday was a poet first. The lyrical nature of his prose owes a great deal to his work with verse forms. (It is also worth noting that while it is uncommon for most novelists to be successful as poets, it is the rule rather than the exception for Indian writers. James Welch, Gerald Vizenor, Leslie Marmon Silko, Louise Erdrich, Simon Ortiz, and Linda Hogan have published both poetry and fiction.)

During his year at Dulce in 1959, Momaday married Gaye Mangold. They have three daughters: Cael, Jill, and Brit. While at Dulce, Momaday won a creative-writing scholarship to Stanford University, matriculating in fall 1959. He was selected for the scholarship by the poet and critic Yvor Winters, who had long been interested in Indian poetry. Winters and Wallace Stegner became important teachers for Momaday. Winters, in fact, more or less adopted Momaday, persuading him to remain at Stanford for his Ph.D. After Momaday left Stanford, Winters told other students anecdotes about him — as he did about all his publishing writers — sometimes focusing on size and strength in Momaday's case. Winters had done some boxing in his youth and had great respect for physical power.

Winters had a strong influence on Momaday's verse, especially the early work. Among Winters's favorite poets were those he designated postsymbolist — those for whom "the sharp sensory detail contained in a poem or passage is of such a nature that the detail is charged with meaning without our being told of the meaning explicitly." Typical of Momaday's postsymbolist verse is "Angle of Geese" (*Angle of Geese and Other Poems*):

How shall we adorn
Recognition with our speech? –
    Now the dead firstborn
Will lag in the wake of words.

Custom intervenes;
We are civil, something more:
    More than language means,
The mute presence mulls and marks.

Almost of a mind,
We take measure of the loss;
    I am slow to find
The mere margin of repose.

And one November
It was longer in the watch,
    As if forever,
Of the huge ancestral goose.

So much symmetry!
Like the pale angle of time
    And eternity.
The great shape labored and fell.

Quit of hope and hurt,

It held a motionless gaze,
    Wide of time, alert,
On the dark distant flurry.

The poem describes two events: the death of a friend's child and the death of a goose that a fellow hunter shot on a hunting trip Momaday took as a teenager. In the first section the poet ponders the adequate response to the death of the child. Speech – the customary remarks – seems inadequate. As Momaday uses it, "civil" implies the contrast between Anglo reticence and repression of grief and the lamentation of Kiowa acts of mourning, disfigurement, and keening the tremolo (wailing in a vibrato fashion). In the second section Momaday uses the image of the dying goose to broach a metaphysical point. The goose, here "huge" and "eternal," an archetype, in its death transcends the limits of time for eternity.

In "The Bear" Momaday uses the depiction of Old Ben in Faulkner's story "The Bear" (*Go Down, Moses, and Other Stories,* 1942) much the way William Shakespeare appropriated Plutarch's description of Cleopatra's barge:

What ruse of vision,
escarping the wall of leaves,
    rending indecision
into countless surfaces,

would cull and color
his somnolence, whose old age
    has outworn valor,
all but the fact of courage?

Seen, he does not come,
move, but seems forever there,
    dimensionless, dumb,
in the windless noon's hot glare.

More scarred than others
these years since the trap maimed him,
    pain slants his withers,
drawing up the crooked limb.

Then he is gone, whole,
without urgency, from sight,
    as buzzards control
imperceptibly, their flight.

In Faulkner's story Old Ben stood "immobile, fixed in the green and windless noon's hot dappling ... dimensionless against the dappled obscurity." The style of Momaday's poem owes a great deal to Winters in its solemn tone, its formal and abstract diction, its heavy use of polysyllabic Latinate words, and its occasional plain-style brilliance of

Momaday's parents, Al and Natachee Momaday, 1933 (courtesy of N. Scott Momaday)

statement and image. Momaday's early poems sometimes exhibit a formality – a stateliness – that can be powerful, but on occasion ponderous.

Although he wrote a great deal of poetry at Stanford, the first book Momaday published was a work of scholarship – an edition (1965) of the poems of Frederick Goddard Tuckerman that grew out of Momaday's doctoral dissertation. Neither Winters's nor Momaday's efforts established Tuckerman as a major poet, but Tuckerman had an effect on Momaday's work. Schubnell points out areas of similarities between the poets:

> Like Tuckerman, Momaday is something of an amateur naturalist, capable of describing and naming minute details in the natural world. Second, Momaday, like Tuckerman, exerts the power of his imagination on the landscape in order to re-create its past and repopulate it with its vanished inhabitants. And third, some of Momaday's work reflects a view of nature not dissimilar from Tuckerman's in that it suggests the ultimate inscrutability and potential evil in the physical world.

Perhaps the poem that best shows Tuckerman's influence is "Before an Old Painting of the Crucifixion" (*Angle of Geese*), written while Momaday was at Stanford. According to Schubnell the theme, the "existential position of human life in an indifferent

universe," may be attributed to Momaday's reading of Tuckerman's ode "The Cricket" (*Poems,* 1860).

After Stanford, Momaday joined the English faculty at the University of California, Santa Barbara, where he designed a course in American Indian studies, which included an examination of the Indian oral tradition. In preparing for the course Momaday compiled a collection of traditional Kiowa narratives that he published privately in 1967 as *The Journey of Tai-Me.* Tai-me is the sacred Sun Dance doll of the Kiowa tribe. It is kept in a rawhide bundle and has not been displayed since the Sun Dance of 1888. Momaday had the privilege of viewing the bundle and, in an interview with Lee Abbott, described the experience as "one of the most intensely religious feelings" he had ever known. Momaday told Schubnell:

> From the time I stood before the *Tai-me issikia* I knew a certain restlessness. I felt I had come to know something about myself I had never known before. I became more keenly aware of myself as someone who had walked through time and in whose blood there is something inestimably old and undying. It was as if I had remembered something that had happened two hundred years ago.

This experience was extremely important to Momaday in writing *The Journey of Tai-Me,* which he later expanded into *The Way to Rainy Mountain* (1969). It figures as well in both his novels, *House Made of Dawn* and *The Ancient Child* (1989).

House Made of Dawn, Momaday's first literary success, is also his masterpiece. He originally planned the book as a series of poems, but Stegner helped him reconceive the work first as stories, then as a novel. The book centers around Abel, an Indian veteran who returns to a Pueblo reservation in New Mexico after World War II. Momaday calls the town (obviously based on Jemez) Walatowa, its original Indian name, and refers to the tribe as Tanoan, the language group to which the Jemez belong. Abel – who is drunk when the reader first encounters him – is highly reminiscent of Ira Hayes, the Pima Marine who became famous when he helped raise the flag on Iwo Jima but who could not readjust to life on the reservation and died of exposure while drunk. Hayes is the subject of the film *The Outsider* (1961), which was advertised as the story of a man who "could die for his country, but not live in it." Johnny Cash's "Ballad of Ira Hayes" – which, like the film, makes a strong statement of social protest – is composed in a trite, sentimental folk idiom. Momaday's story and hero are far more complex.

Abel is not simply torn between traditional Indian and mainstream American culture. Because he is illegitimate – his father apparently was Navajo – Abel was an outsider among the Jemez before he left for the army, as he remains after his return. Abel's name links him to the biblical figure in Genesis, especially since Momaday never gives him a last name. Critics usually identify Cain in the novel as white society, but the biblical Abel was assaulted by his brother, and in the novel Abel's brother Indians do him the most damage.

At the climax of the first section of the novel, Abel murders an albino Jemez who has humiliated him at a traditional ceremony. Momaday uses the term *white man* to describe the albino, and the murder is rendered in sexual terms – a sort of macabre double entendre – which make it appear that, if one Indian is literally murdering another, the white man is symbolically raping the Indian:

> Abel waited. The white man raised his arms, as if to embrace him. . . . Then he closed his hands upon Abel and drew him close. Abel heard the strange excitement of the white man's breath, and the quick, uneven blowing at his ear, and felt the blue shivering lips upon him, felt even the scales of the lips and the hot slippery point of the tongue. . . . He withdrew the knife and thrust again lower, deep into the groin.

Abel is convicted for his crime, and, after he serves an eight-year sentence, the government relocates him in Los Angeles, where he meets the Reverend John Big Bluff Tosamah, a Kiowa who runs a storefront Indian church. Tosamah, who detests Abel for being a "longhair" – an unassimilated Indian who is looked down upon by whites and is therefore a discredit to his race – bears a remarkable resemblance to Momaday. Both are large, bulky Kiowa men with booming voices, and Tosamah's life story is Momaday's own – the narrative that he turns into the prologue of *The Way to Rainy Mountain*.

It is something of a surprise to find in a novel by an Indian author about an Indian victim that one of the victim's worst oppressors is a character based on the author himself. The figure of Tosamah, more of a caricature than a self-portrait, reveals Momaday's ambivalence toward his cultural identity. It is also important to recall that Indians are not simply one people but that each tribe is a separate ethnic group. Kiowa and Pueblos are less closely related ethnically than are French and Germans, but they have as long a history of warfare and hatred. Columbus lumped Indians together as one people, and most Americans have been oblivi-

ous to distinctions, but Momaday grew up at Jemez feeling different from the Indians indigenous to the place.

Abel almost dies when he is severely beaten by a sadistic Hispanic policeman. He is nursed to health by his friend Benally, apparently a distant relative of Abel's father, who teaches Abel the Navajo prayer song "House Made of Dawn." When Abel recovers, he returns to Jemez as his grandfather is dying. He buries his grandfather in the traditional Jemez way and then participates in a ritual race for good hunting and harvests – a race his grandfather had won years before. As Abel runs, he sings "House Made of Dawn." In singing the Navajo song while performing the Jemez ritual, Abel integrates the disparate parts of his heritage. The book ends on a positive note; for the first time in his life Abel is whole.

Momaday's achievement in *House Made of Dawn* is significant. He was able to employ the rhythms and imagery of his verse in creating a prose style that is both lyrical and powerful. It is no mean achievement to make the self-destructive, alcoholic Abel a sympathetic and complex character, or to portray the dusty pueblo of Jemez as a beautiful and exotic place. The most memorable character is Tosamah – the self-ordained Priest of the Sun – the peyote road man and minister of the gospel. Tosamah's sermon on the Book of John delivers but also parodies Momaday's ideas about the sacredness of language and the different ways it is used by whites and Indians:

> "In the beginning was the Word. . . . " And, man, right then and there he should have stopped . . . old John was a white man, and the white man has his ways. . . . He talks about the Word. He talks through it and around it. He builds upon it with syllables, with prefixes and suffixes, and hyphens and accents. He adds and divides and multiplies the Word. And in all of this he subtracts the Truth.

An important aspect of the novel is Momaday's depiction of Walatowa as a blend of cultures. The original Tanoan civilization first absorbed Hispanic Catholic culture and after the Gadsden Purchase became part of English-speaking America. Through the use of an old friar's diary Momaday shows how in the 1880s Catholicism and traditional Tanoan religion had not yet blended: Fray Nicolai thinks of Abel's grandfather as a devil worshiper because he takes part in dances in the village kiva, the underground chamber used for ceremonies of the old tribal religion, the Katsina Cult. However, by the 1940s the priest who serves the village takes

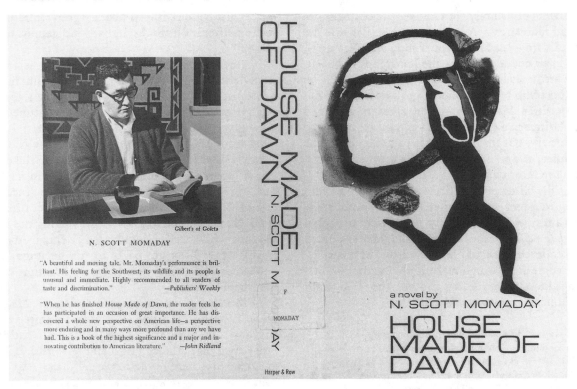

Dust jacket for Momaday's Pulitzer Prize–winning novel, which concerns the personal and cultural turmoil of an Indian veteran of World War II

tourists to see the traditional Tanoan dances, which have been incorporated as part of the celebration of the village's patron saint, Santiago. The legend of the saint is a combination of a hagiography, with its traditional miracles, and a trickster tale, the dominant Indian genre.

Santiago is a Spanish form of Saint James, the apostle whose day is celebrated 25 July. In Tanoan tradition Santiago becomes a Pueblo culture hero who travels into Mexico, where he obtains a magic rooster that, when sacrificed, provides the plants and animals on which the Tanoans depend. The story of a culture hero who uses trickery or magic to aid his people is a staple of Indian mythology throughout North America. It is not uncommon for Mesoamericans to give saints a local origin and story; San Simón of highlands Maya Guatemala, for instance, is another such figure described in local legends.

Momaday received instant celebrity for *House Made of Dawn*. The Pulitzer jury for fiction heralded "the arrival on the American literary scene of a matured, sophisticated literary artist from the original Americans." The success of the novel and the favorable critical reception of *The Way to Rainy Mountain* kicked off the American Indian literary renaissance, as publishers began to seek Indian writers. Before

House Made of Dawn six Indian authors had published a total of nine novels. By the early 1990s more than thirty Indians had published novels, and more than a hundred had published verse.

Momaday's next book, *The Way to Rainy Mountain* combines narratives from *The Journey of Tai-Me* and *House Made of Dawn* with a good deal of new material. From *The Journey of Tai-Me* Momaday took the traditional oral tales he had collected – stories of the origin, triumphs, and travails of the Kiowa; from *House Made of Dawn* he took Tosamah's autobiographical narrative, which he had published separately in slightly different form in the *Reporter* (26 January 1967). Throughout his career, to a far greater extent than other writers, Momaday has made a habit of reusing the same material. Other writers often repeat themes or symbols; Momaday employs the same events and stories over and over.

The Way to Rainy Mountain, which is illustrated by Momaday's father, is a series of fragments, a literary collage composed of poems, essays, myths, historical notes, and personal anecdotes. It is unified by its theme: the emergence, development, and decline of the Kiowa culture. In this autobiographical memoir and impressionistic history of the Kiowa, Momaday retraces the journey that the tribe made from their ancestral territory in the northern Rocky Mountains to their present home on the plains of Oklahoma.

In the prologue Momaday sets the upbeat tone of the work: he will not ignore the crushing defeats that the Kiowa suffered at the hands of the whites, what he calls the "mean and ordinary agonies of human history," but he will not dwell on them. Instead he will pay the bulk of his attention to "the time of great adventure and nobility and fulfillment." Momaday emphasizes the transformation of the Kiowa, "the last culture to evolve in North America," as they acquired the Sun Dance religion from the Crows and the horse from the whites. These things dramatically changed the way the Kiowa lived and conceived of themselves, but Momaday's point is that change did not happen to the Kiowa; they changed themselves. He views culture the way he does personality, as a matter of existential decision: "In the course of that long migration they had come of age as a people. They had conceived a good idea of themselves; they had dared to imagine who they were."

They were "a lordly and dangerous society of fighters and thieves, hunters and priests of the sun." In the introduction Momaday appropriates the narrative that Tosamah delivers in *House Made of Dawn*. Momaday discusses his links to the Kiowa legacy by telling of his grandmother, Aho, who was born when "the Kiowas were living that last great moment of their history." He retraces his pilgrimage from Devils Tower in the Black Hills to Rainy Mountain Ceremony in Oklahoma, where Aho is buried.

The bulk of *The Way to Rainy Mountain* consists of a series of short narratives written in three different voices. First comes a myth or legend, then a historical or anthropological note, and finally a personal anecdote. The three narratives develop variations on a theme, depicting related events from different perspectives. For instance, a narrative on buffalo starts with the myth of a buffalo with horns of steel, killed by a Kiowa warrior. The tone is lofty and bardic, clearly the tale of a culture hero:

> There was a strange thing, a buffalo with horns of steel. One day a man came upon it in the plain, just there where once upon a time four trees stood close together. The man and the buffalo began to fight. . . . The buffalo went away and turned, spreading its hooves, and the man drew the arrow to his bow. His aim was true and the arrow struck deep into the soft flesh of the hoof. The great bull shuddered and fell, and its steel horns flashed once in the sun.

The historical passage is a pathetic vignette describing the last Kiowa buffalo hunt: two old men mounted on workhorses chase down a feeble old buffalo bull while the townspeople of Carnegie, Oklahoma, watch in amusement. The personal anecdote tells how Momaday and his father were pursued by a buffalo cow while walking in a game preserve. The tone is upbeat: "I think we had not been in any real danger. But the spring morning was deep and beautiful and our hearts were beating fast and we knew just then what it was to be alive."

A narrative on the Kiowa treatment of women shows three different viewpoints. The mythic one begins, "Bad women are thrown away" and illustrates why with the story of a treacherous wife. The historical section states that the lives of Kiowa women were hard, whether they were bad or not. It tells the tale of a wife who was stolen from her husband and then made to suffer for it. The personal passage concerns Momaday's great-great-grandmother, Kau-au-ointy, a Mexican captive who "would not play the part of a Kiowa woman." She rose from slavery to be a tribal leader.

The Way to Rainy Mountain concludes with an elegiac epilogue:

> But indeed the golden age of the Kiowas had been short lived, ninety or a hundred years say, from about 1740. The culture would persist for a while in decline, until about 1875, but then it would be gone, and there would be very little material evidence that it had ever been. Yet it is within reach of memory still, though tenuously now, and moreover it is even defined in a remarkably rich and living verbal tradition which demands to be preserved for its own sake.

The Way to Rainy Mountain, a monument to the Kiowa oral tradition, does a great deal to preserve the memory of Kiowa culture.

In 1976 Momaday published his second book of verse, *The Gourd Dancer*. The first part reprints *Angle of Geese;* the second part, "The Gourd Dancer," includes prose poems based on Indian themes; the third part, "Anywhere Is a Street into the Night," depicts scenes from Momaday's 1974 trip to Russia. In "The Gourd Dancer" Momaday largely abandons the Latinate diction and syllabic verse of his earlier poetry, moving to a sort of verse that approaches prose. The title poem is a series of sketches of Momaday's grandfather, Mammedatty:

> Someone spoke his name, Mammedatty, in which his essence was and is. It was a serious matter that his name should be spoken there in the circle, among the many people, and he was thoughtful, full of wonder, and aware of himself and his name.

Momaday as a boy (courtesy of N. Scott Momaday)

The most impressive poem in the collection is "The Colors of Night," which Momaday published separately through a small press the same year. The poem is also a series of sketches, what Momaday describes as "quintessential novels." The first describes Setangya, the Kiowa chief who carried the bones of his slain son with him wherever he went. Momaday retells the story in *The Ancient Child*. The last of the sketches involves a woman whose long hair was able to hide her from Age. In "Anywhere Is a Street into the Night" Momaday returns to more formal verse forms. "Abstract: Old Woman in a Room" consists of couplets:

> Here is no place of easy consequence
> But where you come to reckon recompense.
> And here the vacancy in which are met
> The vague contingencies of your regret.

"Krasnopresnenskaya Station" is a chronicle of Momaday's feelings of isolation and alienation in Russia:

> I sit at the window. I wonder
> that they keep so, to themselves,

in their trains, in the deep streets.
I have no prospects here.

In *The Names* Momaday returns to autobiography – a memoir of his childhood. He reexamines some favorite themes: the sacred nature of the land and of language, and the relationship of language to being. In explaining the title Momaday told Charles Woodard: "Because it's an autobiographical narrative, the great principle of selection in the book is the principle in naming . . . a sacred business. . . . When you name something you confer being on it at the same time. . . . Language is essentially a process of naming." Momaday draws from many sources in depicting his early years. Schubnell traces the influence of Isak Dinesen's *Out of Africa* (1937) in Momaday's lyrical evocation of landscapes and of James Joyce's *Portrait of the Artist as a Young Man* (1914–1915) in the young Momaday's development of an awareness of language. There are also echoes of Faulkner and Marcel Proust.

A major theme of *The Names* is Momaday's development of a sense of what makes up Indianness and in what ways he is part of an Indian heritage. When he was a child in grade school, a teacher asked him about being Indian. He replied:

> Oh I feel so dumb I can't answer all those questions I don't know how to be a Kiowa Indian my grandmother lives in a house it's like your house Miss Marshall . . . only it doesn't have lights and light switches and the toilet is outside . . . but that isn't what makes it Indian its my grandma the way she is she looks her hair in braids the clothes somehow . . . wait I know why it's an Indian house because there are pictures of Indians on the walls photographs of people with long braids and buckskin dresses . . . yes that's it and there is Indian stuff all around blankets and shawls . . . and everyone there acts like an Indian, everyone even me and my dad when we're there we eat meat and everyone talks Kiowa and the old people wear Indian clothes well those dresses dark blue and braids and hats and there is laughing Indians laugh a lot . . . and they sing oh yes they love to sing.

Although Momaday developed a sense of ethnicity on his visits to Oklahoma, his feelings were highly ambivalent. He often fantasized about killing an ugly Indian he called Big Knife. At Jemez, the place he not only loves but to which he also feels a mystic attachment, his relationship to the local Indians was also complicated. As the child of the people who ran the day school, he was respected and admired by the Jemez, but he certainly was not one of them. Although he and his parents were honored guests at many festivals, there were sacred occasions on which the Jemez posted guards on the roads and kept all who were not members of the tribe out of the village. At these times the Momadays kept "to our reservation of the day school."

Nonetheless Momaday developed a mystical bond with Jemez, an attitude J. K. Wright has called geopiety – "a broad range of emotional bonds between man and his terrestrial home." The term may seem inflated, but Momaday's attachment to Jemez – and to other places that have been important in his life – which developed out of traditional Kiowa attitudes to their lands, greatly transcends the sentimental attachment many Americans feel toward their hometowns: "A part of my life happened to take place in Jemez. I existed in that landscape, and part of my existence was indivisible with it. I placed my shadow there in the hills, my voice in the wind that ran there, in those old mornings and afternoons and evenings."

In *The Names* Momaday describes in full many of the events that made their way in modified form into *House Made of Dawn*: the feast of San Diego, the chicken pull, the race for good hunting and harvests, and the killing of the goose, which also provides the subject of "Angle of Geese." An important topic in *The Names* is horsemanship, Momaday's and that of others. One vignette features a Navajo girl who embarrasses a group of Jemez horsemen by picking a dollar off the ground while riding at full gallop (Momaday uses the story again in *The Ancient Child*). Other tales involve Momaday's prowess at racing his roan against all comers, having to invent handicaps in order to get anyone to go against him.

To Momaday riding was an "exercise of the mind," a phrase he uses when writing about Billy the Kid in *The Ancient Child*. But riding was more than a physical activity; it triggered Momaday's imagination:

On the back of my horse I had a different view of the world. I could see more of it, how it reached away beyond all the horizons I had ever seen; and yet it was more concentrated in its appearance, too, and more accessible to my mind, my imagination. My mind loomed upon the farthest edges of the earth, where I could feel the full force of the planet whirling into space.

Riding was also a matter of ethnic tradition: "I am a Kiowa ... therefore there is in me, as there is in the Tartars, an old sacred notion of the horse." *The Names* ends with a dramatic incident in which Momaday almost fell to his death. The event changed the way he views the world and marks the end of his childhood.

After *The Names* Momaday published nothing for twelve years. In 1978 he married Reina Heitzer, a Bavarian woman he met while lecturing in Germany. They have a daughter, Lore. In 1981 he accepted the position he still holds, Regents Professor of the Humanities at the University of Arizona. During the early 1980s Momaday worked sporadically on *The Ancient Child* but spent a great deal of his time on his painting. Indians in general, and the Kiowa in particular, have a long tradition of painting. Before contact with whites, the Kiowa painted on their tepees and produced illustrated calendars called winter counts. In the 1920s Oscar Jacobsen brought a group of young Indians who became known as the Kiowa Five to the School of Art at the University of Oklahoma, where they began careers in painting that brought them notice throughout the United States and Europe. Al Momaday's artwork developed out of the tradition of the Kiowa Five, painting such traditional tribal subjects as peyote figures and buffalo hunters.

Momaday has written about Indian aesthetics. In the essay "A Garment of Brightness" (*The Names*) he states:

There is a remarkable aesthetic perception in the Indian world, I believe, a sense of beauty, of proportion and design.... An Indian child, by virtue of his whole experience, hereditary as well as environmental, sees the world in terms of this aesthetic sense.... The practical result of this vision one finds in the extraordinary variety and achievement of Indian art. At its best, it is an expression that is at once universal and unique, the essence of abstraction and the abstraction of essences.

During the 1970s Momaday became more conscious of the correspondences between painting and writing. As Woodard writes, "About that time, Momaday's writing, which had always been dramatically pictorial, began to contain more explicit verbal connections between painting and prose. He was beginning to integrate the mediums through which he could create angles of vision."

Momaday's first exhibition, at the University of North Dakota Art Galleries in 1979, was a collection of paintings of Indian war shields. He describes them as being like "coats of arms, but they're more personal." At that time he planned a book about shields, a "collection of very short stories – quintessential stories" to accompany illustrations of the shields. The work was published in a signed, limited edition by the Rydal Press of Santa Fe in 1991 and was reprinted in *In the Presence of the Sun* (1992).

Momaday also did a series of paintings on Indian dolls, which are not playthings; they are usu-

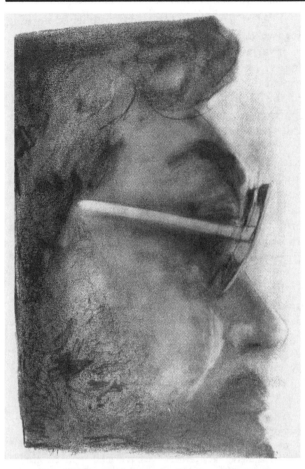

Self-portrait, 1976 (courtesy of N. Scott Momaday)

ally shamanistic images or fetishes. In the Southwest dolls represent kachinas, or spirits, and are ubiquitous in the homes of Indians. Momaday is attracted by the power he believes they radiate. Perhaps his most impressive paintings are the watercolor series on Billy the Kid. The painting of L. G. Murphy, Billy's jailer, is actually a self-portrait; Murphy's build may be slight, but his face is unmistakably Momaday's.

Twenty-one years after the publication of *House Made of Dawn*, Momaday brought out another novel, *The Ancient Child*. In it he returns to some favorite subjects: the nature of Indianness, the aesthetics of painting, and the life and death of Billy the Kid. Momaday's ambivalence about his ethnic identity is revealed is the two protagonists: Locke Setman, a painter of Kiowa descent, and Grey, a young, mixed-blood (Kiowa and Navajo) woman who calls herself the Mayor of Bote, Oklahoma. *Bote* is the Kiowa word for the innards of a cow or buffalo, a dish the Kiowa prefer raw.

Set, as Locke is called, initially knows little of his Kiowa heritage. His parents died young, and he

was raised in San Francisco by a white philosophy professor. Set has become a nationally renowned artist whose paintings are shown in galleries in New York and Paris. On a trip to Oklahoma to attend the funeral of a relative, Set meets Grey, who gives him a medicine bundle, a collection of sacred objects that the tribe venerates; it begins to exert a strange power over him. Set returns to San Francisco but becomes increasingly disenchanted with his life. Although he is in love with a beautiful, talented woman and has achieved great success with his painting, under the supernatural influence of the medicine bundle he becomes more and more dissatisfied until he finally has a nervous breakdown. When he recovers, he leaves San Francisco to live with Grey. In his desire to enter her Indian world he completely subjugates himself to her. What has seemed like a realistic, if occasionally strange, novel then shifts abruptly to a wholly different sort of narrative. At the climax of the book Grey performs a ritual that turns Set into a bear.

The Ancient Child combines the conventions of the modern novel with the Kiowa myth of Tsoai, the story of a boy who changes into a bear and chases his sisters up a tree. The sisters become the stars of the Big Dipper; the tree becomes Tsoai, Devils Tower. Momaday has been fascinated with the story, and the figure of the bear, throughout his life. He told Woodard:

> My Kiowa name, Tsoai-talee, means "Rock Tree Boy," and it is, of course, associated immediately with the rock tree, what is now called Devils Tower. It is the sacred place in Kiowa tradition, and it is the place where the boy turned into a bear. I identify with that boy. I have for many years.

The use of mythology to add a symbolic dimension to a novel is of course nothing new, nor is the act of metamorphosis. What Momaday is doing, however, is fundamentally different from what Franz Kafka or Joyce did. He is not using symbolism or allegory; he is writing about a different plane of reality. He remarked to Woodard:

> I am a bear. I do have this capacity to become a bear. The bear sometimes takes me over ... after the end of the [myth], the bear remains and the boy remains and they come together now and then ... probably in every generation there is a reincarnation of the bear – the boy bear. And I feel that I am such a reincarnation, and I am very curious about it.

Set is the Kiowa word for bear; "Setman" is obviously "bear-man." Momaday also includes other myths in

The Ancient Child. Set is also the Egyptian god of the desert, regarded as the embodiment of evil. When Locke turns into the bear – in the New Mexico desert – he feels the power of evil within him. Locke's childhood nickname is "Loki," the Nordic shapeshifter.

An important character in *The Ancient Child* is Billy the Kid, Grey's fantasy lover. Momaday has long been fascinated with the outlaw. In 1973 he wrote a series of columns for the *Santa Fe New Mexican* in which he described his imaginary adventures with Billy. He later wrote a series of poems to go with the prose sketches, but, although he circulated the manuscript among friends, he has not published it. In *The Ancient Child* he gives his fantasies to Grey, adding a few amorous interludes.

Among other things *The Ancient Child* is a chronicle of the West; with the introduction of Billy, Momaday is able to depict a cowboy along with the Indians. Momaday's Billy is a mysterious figure who represents what was best and worst about the frontier. He kills without remorse and yet is capable of great kindness. He is chivalric toward women, not only Grey but also a nun, Sister Blandina. Resourceful and courageous, he is loyal to his friends. The historical Billy, William Bonney, began his career as an outlaw by killing three Indians, but Momaday never mentions that, though of course he knows it. His Billy is more victim than villain. Witness to the cruel death of his mother, Billy is later abused by a sadistic jailer and killed by the treacherous Pat Garrett. Momaday's Billy is thus more sinned against than sinning. In a way Billy is like the bear; there is a power of evil in him, but mostly he is just wild and free.

Momaday's latest book, *In the Presence of the Sun,* is a collection of poems and the short prose pieces he calls stories. Many of the poems were published in *Angle of Geese* and *The Gourd Dancer,* but he adds twenty-seven new works. The volume also features sixty of his drawings. *In the Presence of the Sun* includes the original sketches and poems about Billy the Kid that Momaday reworked for *The Ancient Child.* Momaday reappropriates Billy, excising Grey from the account. Billy is once again Momaday's sidekick.

There are sixteen stories and sketches of shields, along with an essay explaining the importance of shields to Kiowa warriors. According to Momaday, "The Plains shield reflects the character of the Plains culture. . . . It evidences a nomadic society and a warrior ideal . . . the shields are meditations that make a round of life." He gives capsulized histories of the shields and the men that carried them into battle.

The new poems in the volume reflect a new side of Momaday; they have little of the solemnity of his

Self-portrait as a bear, 1987 (courtesy of N. Scott Momaday)

early verse and are marked by a biting wit. He begins the collection with some epigrams:

The Death of Beauty

She died a beauty of repute,
Her other virtues in dispute.

On Chastity

Here lies a lady sweet and chaste.
Here lies the matter: chaste makes waste.

"At Risk" begins, "I played at words. / It was a long season." Perhaps the best poem of the lot is "The Great Fillmore Street Buffalo Drive," a surrealistic depiction of a herd of bison stampeding from Pacific Heights to the ocean.

In February 1994 Momaday's first play, *The Indolent Boys,* premiered at the Syracuse Stage. According to Mel Gussow, the play "deals with three Kiowa youths who ran away from a United States Government school in 1891 and froze to death on the trek home. . . . Momaday counterpoints Indian tradition with the enforced colonialism of government and school officials, and makes evocative use of ritual and storytelling techniques."

As he enters his sixties, Momaday is at the height of his powers. A complex figure, he takes as much pride in being a member of the Kiowa Gourd Dance Society as he does in being a fellow of the American Academy of Arts and Sciences. It is fitting that he began the American Indian renaissance, for he is truly a Renaissance man. Painter, poet, novelist, professor, he is also a cook of distinction and a wonderful raconteur. Perhaps most important of all, he is a bear.

Interviews:

"Discussion: The Man Made of Words," in *Indian Voices: The First Convocation of American Indian Scholars,* edited by Rupert Costo (San Francisco: Indian Historian Press, 1970), pp. 62–84;

Lee Abbott, "An Interview with N. Scott Momaday," *Puerto Del Sol,* 12 (1973): 21–38;

Lawrence Evers, "A Conversation with N. Scott Momaday," *Sun Tracks: An American Indian Literary Magazine,* 2 (1976): 18–21;

Gretchen Bataille, "An Interview with N. Scott Momaday – April 16, 1977," *Iowa English Bulletin,* 29 (1979): 28–32;

Bataille, "Interview with N. Scott Momaday – April 11, 1979," *Newsletter of the Association for the Study of American Indian Literature,* new series 4 (1980): 1–3;

Joseph Bruchac, "N. Scott Momaday: An Interview by Joseph Bruchac," *American Poetry Review,* 13 (July–August 1984): 13–18;

"Shouting at the Machine: An Interview with N. Scott Momaday," *Persona* (Spring 1984): 24–44;

Charles Woodard, *Ancestral Voice: Conversations with N. Scott Momaday* (Lincoln: University of Nebraska Press, 1989);

Laura Coltelli, "N. Scott Momaday," in *Winged Words: American Indian Writers Speak* (Lincoln: University of Nebraska Press, 1990), pp. 89–102.

References:

Robert Berner, "N. Scott Momaday: Beyond Rainy Mountain," *American Indian Culture and Research Journal,* 3, no. 1 (1979): 57–67;

Mel Gussow, "Director Shakes Up Syracuse Stage," *New York Times,* 24 February 1994, pp. C13, C18;

Kenneth Lincoln, "Word Senders: Black Elk and N. Scott Momaday," in *Native American Renaissance* (Berkeley: University of California Press, 1983), pp. 82–121;

Louis Owens, "Acts of Imagination: The Novels of N. Scott Momaday," in *Other Destinies: Understanding the American Indian Novel* (Norman: University of Oklahoma Press, 1992), pp. 90–127;

Matthias Schubnell, *N. Scott Momaday: The Cultural and Literary Background* (Norman: University of Oklahoma Press, 1985);

Alan R. Velie, "*House Made of Dawn:* Nobody's Protest Novel," in *Four American Indian Literary Masters* (Norman: University of Oklahoma Press, 1982), pp. 51–64;

Yvor Winters, *The Function of Criticism* (Denver: Alan Swallow, 1957);

J. K. Wright, "Notes on Early American Geopiety," in his *Human Nature in Geography* (Cambridge, Mass.: Harvard University Press, 1961), p. 251.

Toni Morrison

(18 February 1931 –)

Denise Heinze
Western Carolina University

See also the Morrison entries in *DLB 6: American Novelists Since World War II, Second Series; DLB 33: Afro-American Fiction Writers After 1955;* and *DLB Yearbook: 1981.*

BOOKS: *The Bluest Eye* (New York: Holt, Rinehart & Winston, 1970; London: Chatto & Windus, 1979);

Sula (New York: Plume, 1973; London: Allen Lane, 1974);

Song of Solomon (New York: Knopf, 1977; London: Chatto & Windus, 1978);

Tar Baby (New York: Knopf, 1981; London: Chatto & Windus, 1981);

Beloved (New York: Knopf, 1987; London: Chatto & Windus, 1987);

Jazz (New York: Knopf, 1992; London: Chatto & Windus, 1992);

Playing in the Dark: Whiteness and the Literary Imagination (Cambridge, Mass.: Harvard University Press, 1992).

PLAY PRODUCTION: *Dreaming Emmett*, Albany, New York, 4 January 1986.

OTHER: *The Black Book*, compiled by Middleton Harris, edited by Morrison (New York: Random House, 1974);

"Rootedness: The Ancestor as Foundation," in *Black Women Writers (1950–1980): A Critical Evaluation*, edited by Mari Evans (Garden City, N.Y.: Doubleday, 1984), pp. 339–345;

Race-ing, Justice, En-gendering Power: Essays on Anita Hill, Clarence Thomas and the Construction of Social Reality, edited, with an introduction, by Morrison (New York: Pantheon, 1992).

SELECTED PERIODICAL PUBLICATIONS – UNCOLLECTED: "What the Black Woman Thinks About Women's Lib," *New York Times Magazine*, 22 August 1971, pp. 14–15, 63–64, 66;

Toni Morrison, circa 1981 (photograph by Thomas Victor)

"Cooking Out," *New York Times Book Review*, 10 June 1973, pp. 4, 12;

"Behind the Making of the Black Book," *Black World*, 23 (February 1974): 86–90;

"Rediscovering Black History," *New York Times Magazine*, 11 August 1974, pp. 14, 16, 18, 20, 22, 24;

"Reading," *Mademoiselle*, 81 (May 1975): 14;

"A Slow Walk of Trees (as Grandmother Would Say) Hopeless (as Grandfather Would Say)," *New York Times Magazine*, 4 July 1976, pp. 104, 150, 152, 160, 162, 164;

"Memory, Creation, and Writing," *Thought*, 59 (December 1984): 385–390;

"Unspeakable Things Unspoken: The Afro-American Presence in American Literature," *Michigan Quarterly Review*, 28 (Winter 1989): 1–34.

Toni Morrison became a novelist for the ages when she was awarded the 1993 Nobel Prize for literature. Only the eighth woman and the first black to win the prize, Morrison expressed surprise and delight at receiving the honor and displayed an impetuous generosity:

> I was thrilled that my mother is still alive and can share this with me. And I can claim representation in so many areas. I'm a Midwesterner, and everyone in Ohio is excited. I'm also a New Yorker, and a New Jerseyan, and an American, plus I'm an African-American, and a woman. I know it seems like I'm spreading like algae when I put it this way, but I'd like to think of the prize being distributed to these regions and nations and races.

Morrison's image of herself as a literary organism whose creative force is fed by all that has encompassed her is reflected in her fiction, a combination of prose and poetry so lyrical and evocative that it often transcends the narrative of African-Americans that she presents, exhorting all her readers to share in and accept responsibility for the creative act they are witnessing. In her Nobel Prize acceptance speech Morrison told a story in which the roles of storyteller and listener eventually elide one another so that both are involved in fiction making. "How lovely it is," the storyteller concludes, "this thing we have done – together."

In describing Morrison's work the Nobel Committee of the Swedish Academy stated: "She delves into the language itself, a language she wants to liberate from the fetters of race. And she addresses us with the luster of poetry." For Morrison it is the language that, as she said in her acceptance speech, "may be the measure of our lives," and as such it must not be a language that oppresses or manipulates, "the policing languages of mastery," but that can "limn the actual, imagined and possible lives of its speaker, readers, writers." It must be free of the arrogance of absolute definition. "Its force, its felicity is in its reach toward the ineffable."

Morrison has become one of the literary elite even though, since she is an African-American and a female, her writings are often a challenge to the canon of predominantly white-male American writing. Morrison's remarkable accomplishment is summed up by Henry Louis Gates, Jr.: "Just two centuries ago, the African-American literary tradition was born in slave narratives. Now our greatest writer has won the Nobel Prize." The fact that Morrison has received the most prestigious of writing awards serves not only to expand the literary criteria for greatness but has also initiated discussion about the evolving nature of American literature.

Morrison was born Chloe Anthony Wofford in Lorain, Ohio, the second of four children raised in a family that had endured economic and social adversity. Morrison's maternal grandparents, Ardelia and John Solomon Willis, were sharecroppers in Greenville, Alabama, having lost their land at the turn of the century. In 1912 her grandparents decided to head north to escape the hopeless debt of sharecropping and the fear of racism, which posed the threat of sexual violation to their pubescent daughters. They traveled to Kentucky, where Morrison's grandfather worked in a coal mine and her mother was a laundress. But they left abruptly when their daughters came home from school one day, having taught the white teacher how to do long division. In search of a better education for their children, Morrison's grandparents eventually settled in Lorain.

While growing up during the Depression, Morrison witnessed the struggles of her father, George Wofford, who had migrated from Georgia, and mother, Ramah Willis Wofford, to support their family. George Wofford often worked many jobs at a time – a shipyard welder, car washer, steel-mill welder, and construction worker – while Ramah Wofford, Morrison revealed in an interview with Nellie McKay, "took 'humiliating jobs' in order to send Morrison money regularly while she was in college and graduate school." Her parents' willingness to take on hard and sometimes demeaning work was coupled with a distinct unwillingness to relinquish their own sense of value and humanity. Morrison's father was meticulous in his work, writing his name in the side of the ship whenever he welded a perfect seam. Her mother at one point wrote a letter of protest to President Franklin D. Roosevelt when her family received unfit government-sponsored flour.

While Morrison's parents grappled with economic hardship, they also struggled to retain their sense of worth in an oppressive white world. Their early experiences with racism shaped their respective views of white people. Morrison's father was, in her words, a racist; she told Jean Strouse that, as a child in Georgia, he received "shocking impressions of adult white people." Morrison's mother held out hope for the white race to improve, but her father was convinced that whites were never to be trusted or believed. He once threw a white man out of his home, believing the visitor planned to molest his daughters. Both parents had reservations about the potential for the white race and thus taught their children to rely on themselves and the black community rather than the vagaries of a larger society whose worth to them was highly suspect.

Morrison did not suffer the effects of racism early on because she was the only black in her first-grade class and the only one who could read. However, she told Bonnie Angelo that her innocence was soon shattered:

I remember in the fifth grade a smart little boy who had just arrived and didn't speak any English. He sat next to me. I read well, and I taught him to read just by doing it. I remember the moment he found out that I was black — a nigger. It took him six months; he was told. And that's the moment when he belonged, that was his entrance. Every immigrant knew he would not come as the very bottom. He had to come above at least one group — and that was us.

Morrison confronted other incidents of racism, but her parents' emphasis on the value of African-Americans as a people, of their family as an inviolable unit, and of themselves as individuals was no doubt the psychological foundation that sustained and nurtured her. Her father was convinced that blacks were superior to whites, a belief that deeply influenced Morrison. At age thirteen, when she complained about the mean white family whose house she cleaned, her father told her she did not live with them, but "here. So you go do your work, get your money and come on home." Morrison did not adopt her father's racism, but she always knew, she remarked in an interview with Charlie Rose (Public Broadcasting System, 7 May 1993), "I had the moral high ground all my life."

Though deprived of monetary resources in a hostile world, Morrison's family and community held a remarkable wealth of music, storytelling, the supernatural, and black language — major influences on Morrison and her writings. Morrison woke up to the sound of her mother's voice, singing both at home and for the church choir. But music, Morrison said in the Rose interview, "was not entertainment for us" but more a means of detecting her mother's moods. It acted as a support system. Though her family could not read music, they could reproduce the music they heard. Other forms of support included storytelling that involved every member of the family. After adults told stories, they invited the children to do the same. Morrison considered this part as important, if not more important, than listening to the stories.

Though there were few books in her house, Morrison learned early the importance of reading. Her grandfather was a figure of awe and respect to her because, with the help of his sister, he had taught himself to read. Morrison was encouraged to read and did so voraciously, including a wide range of world literature. She told Strouse:

Those books were not written for a little black girl in Lorain, Ohio, but they were so magnificently done that I got them anyway — they spoke directly to me out of their own specificity. I wasn't thinking of writing then — I wanted to be a dancer like Maria Tallchief — but when I wrote my first novel years later, I wanted to capture that same specificity about the nature and feeling of the culture I grew up in.

Though Morrison did not read literature by black women writers until adulthood, she told Gloria Naylor that her affinity with them, which critics have identified, is evidence that "the world as perceived by black women at certain times does exist."

That world was often rife with the supernatural. When asked by Mel Watkins whether she believed in ghosts, Morrison replied, "Yes. Do you believe in germs? It's part of our heritage." Morrison stated that her family was "intimate with the supernatural," her parents often telling exciting and terrifying ghost stories that the children were encouraged to repeat. Dreams were a constituent of reality — her grandmother even played the numbers with the use of a dream book — and ghostly apparitions were not considered astonishing. Without the belief in the supernatural, Morrison remarked to Valerie Smith, "I would have been dependent on so-called scientific data to explain hopelessly unscientific things and also I would have relied on information that even subsequent objectivity has proved to be fraudulent." Her novels, too, would have been bereft of their unique blend of fantasy and reality, myth and history, folklore and legend. So intertwined are the supernatural and empirical reality in Morrison's novels that the seen and the unseen often elide one another.

After high school Morrison attended Howard University; her dream was to be a teacher. She majored in English and minored in the classics, and she changed her name to Toni — because people had trouble pronouncing Chloe. She soon became disenchanted with Howard and the importance students placed on marriage, fashion, socializing, and chic. She joined the Howard University Players, thus getting an opportunity to travel in the South, to experience its history and geography, and to relive her grandparents' harrowing flight from poverty and racism. Morrison graduated from Howard in 1953 and then enrolled in graduate school at Cornell University.

Morrison's rich history of family and community filters directly into her novels, a progression of works that begins by addressing the black family and then broadens to the black community, regions of the United States, foreign lands and alien cul-

*Dust jacket for Morrison's 1973 novel, in which, Morrison says, the title
character is "willing to risk in her imagination a lot of things and pay
the price and also go astray"*

tures, history, and reality. In her novels Morrison celebrates the rich heritage and language of the black community and the values it struggles to maintain in a predominantly white society whose own value system, she finds, has lost its collective way. Morrison's thematic consistency is refigured in each novel so that her canon constitutes a progressive troping of her own works. Each novel is an original and refreshing revoicing of her previous concerns with the black community and family. She experiments almost relentlessly with language, with narrative forms, and with fictive reality in an endeavor to redefine the African-American experience not as marginal or peripheral, but as American.

Morrison received her master's degree from Cornell in 1955. She wrote her thesis on the theme of suicide in the works of Virginia Woolf and Wil-

liam Faulkner. She then taught English at Texas Southern University in Houston for two years, beginning a teaching career that she proudly continues to this day. According to Smith, Morrison has taught at "Yale, Bard, the State University of New York at Purchase, and the State University of New York at Albany. Since 1988 she has held the Robert F. Goheen Professorship of the Humanities at Princeton University."

In 1957 Morrison, then an English instructor at Howard, began to meet and influence young men who became prominent in the 1960s, among them Amiri Baraka, Andrew Young, and Claude Brown. She taught Stokely Carmichael in one of her classes; she told Strouse that he was " 'the kind of student you always want in a class – smart, perceptive, funny and a bit of a rogue.' " Morrison stayed at

Howard from 1957 to 1964, leaving because she did not have the Ph.D. necessary for tenure.

Two major events marked her period of teaching at Howard. She began to write, and she married Harold Morrison, a Jamaican architect. During her marriage Morrison joined a writer's group at Howard, composing a story that grew into her first novel, *The Bluest Eye* (1970), about a little girl who longs for blue eyes. With her writing career only in its infancy, her marriage ended around 1964, leaving Morrison with two sons, Harold Ford and Slade Kevin. Though reticent about her marriage and reluctant even to discuss its actual date, she does refer to cultural differences and a feeling of personal bankruptcy: "It was as though I had nothing left but my imagination. I had no will, no judgment, no perspective, no power, no authority, no self — just this brutal sense of irony, melancholy and a trembling respect for words."

After her divorce Morrison lived with her parents in Lorain for a year and a half and then accepted an editorial position with a textbook subsidiary at Random House in Syracuse, New York. Her mother expressed dismay that Morrison was a single parent without other family there — a difficult, isolated condition for anyone, but especially for African-Americans, who to a great extent rely on extended family and community for well-being in an indifferent, if not inhospitable, world. Morrison talked to Rose about raising children alone: "It was terrible. Very hard. Awful." She added, "You need everybody [to raise a child]." For Morrison writing helped fill the void of family, husband, and, to a great extent, self. She remarked to Naylor: "But I was really in a corner. And whatever was being threatened by the circumstances in which I found myself, alone with two children in a town where I didn't know anybody, I knew that I would not deliver to my children a parent that was of no use to them. So I was thrown back on, luckily, the only thing I could depend on, my own resources."

While in Syracuse, Morrison continued work on *The Bluest Eye* as a way to find her place in a world where she felt she no longer belonged. She told Naylor that writing the novel became a process of reclamation:

And I began to do it. I began to pick up scraps of things that I had seen or felt, or didn't see or didn't feel, but imagined. And speculated about and wondered about. And I fell in love with myself. I reclaimed myself and the world . . . I named it. I described it. I listed it. I identified it. I recreated it. And having done that, at least, then the books belonged in the world.

An editor read the partly completed manuscript and suggested she finish it. It was rejected many times before Holt, Rinehart and Winston published *The Bluest Eye* in 1970.

The Bluest Eye is a wrenching account of how the Western notion of idealized beauty and its penchant for blue eyes and blond hair turn self-esteem in the black community into self-loathing. The novel reveals the destructive potential of a standard of beauty that places value on the way people look rather than on their intrinsic worth. This condition is manifested in the character of Pecola Breedlove, a young black girl on the verge of womanhood, who longs for blue eyes as an avenue to prettiness and, hence, love. Her desire for the impossible would be less pathetic given the unconditional love and support of family and community. However, her mother, suffering from her own belief in the ugliness of her family, ignores her, while her drunken father's twisted attempt at loving his daughter turns into rape. The community watches but does nothing as Pecola gives birth to a baby that dies and as she then lapses into an insanity in which she is finally possessed of the bluest eyes.

Pecola's tragedy is the ultimate expression of an entire community infected with distorted notions of worth. Most of the characters in the novel suffer different degrees of victimization at the hands of a society that confuses whiteness with virtue. Morrison shows that blacks in a white society often have learned to identify against themselves, as Judith Fetterly would say, by adopting the racist attitudes that dehumanize them. The prime example of this tendency is Pecola's mother, Pauline Breedlove, who, convinced of her own ugliness, retreats to a movie theater and images of white beauty she vicariously experiences. She prefers the quiet order and tidiness of the white people's houses she cleans to the confusion of her own ragtag storefront home. Pecola's blackness is a constant reminder to Pauline of her own inability to approximate the ideal of white beauty. As a result, she simply ignores her daughter rather than sustain her.

Pecola's father, Cholly, has learned that his blackness is a sign of absence and exclusion. He is abandoned by his mother and father as an infant. In his first act of lovemaking he is surprised by white hunters, who force him to complete the act. Though he is initially capable of investing Pauline with a sense of her own beauty, he is divested of his authority by the overwhelming influence of white society. Powerless to empower, Cholly resorts to drunkenness, and eventually to rape, in a demented effort to convince Pecola that she is lovable.

The Bluest Eye is flooded with characters whose humanity has been diminished as a consequence of their blackness, a signifier of lack to white society, their own community, and even themselves. Most disturbing in the novel are the light-skinned blacks who distance themselves from their black heritage in an exercise of same-race hatred. As Maureen Peal's actions illustrate, black children are taught early to assume a superiority based on the lightness of their skin. Maureen, the "high-yellow dream" who has "lynch ropes for hair," deals Pecola the ultimate insult: "I *am* cute! And you ugly! Black and ugly black e mos."

Another light-skinned character, Geraldine, attempts literally to scrub the blackness from her life and that of her son, Junior. When she finds Pecola in her home, she unleashes a rage on her simply because she cannot tolerate the relative darkness of her skin. The ultimate manifestation of self-hatred and same-race hatred is Soaphead Church, who was taught "to separate [himself] in body, mind and spirit from all that suggested Africa." He is so twisted by an obsession with whiteness and cleanliness that he resorts to molesting little girls rather than engage in a mature sexual relationship.

As in most of her novels, in the *The Bluest Eye* Morrison presents ways of surviving in a world suffused with psychic pain and suffering. The MacTeers represent a black family who, though struggling for its economic life, has not been divested of its humanity. Blessed with a hardworking father and a dutiful mother, the MacTeers nevertheless are profoundly affected by the difficult conditions of their lives. In Mrs. MacTeer is a "misery colored by the greens and blues in her voice." Her life, marked by poverty and a bitter climate, shapes her sometimes-harsh treatment of her children, Claudia and Frieda.

But love, not money, is the motivating force in the MacTeer household, and it is that which sustains them. Mrs. MacTeer is capable, as Claudia recalls, of music, warm laughter, and an abiding love: "Love, thick and dark as Alaga syrup, eased up into that cracked window. I could smell it – taste it . . . everywhere in the house." Even more remarkable than the love in the MacTeer household is their willingness to extend it into the community. They take in Pecola for a brief time, increasing the burden on an already strapped existence. Mrs. MacTeer becomes the moral authority in the novel in her condemnation of the Breedloves and their irresponsible treatment of Pecola. " 'Folks,' " she says, " 'just dump they children off on you and go

on 'bout they business. . . . What kind of something is that?' "

The domestic blues of the MacTeer family and the general gloominess of the novel are offset by the world of the prostitutes China, Poland, and Miss Marie. Though they exist outside society, despised and reviled, they create an atmosphere of jocularity and freshness that momentarily brightens the darkness of the novel. Pecola takes refuge in this world because the prostitutes remain unaffected by the standards of a culture that has already rejected them. They are, therefore, oblivious to Pecola's ugliness and dirt, and they treat her with genuine warmth and affection. Pecola is so content in an environment of laughter and unconditional love that she wonders, "Were they real?" Still, the whorehouse provides only a brief respite from the reality of Pecola's world. The prostitutes, like the other members of the community, cannot or do not take responsibility for Pecola's life.

Pecola's insanity, in which she convinces herself that she possesses blue eyes, is an ironic reversal of a society that considers itself sane in its valorization of physical features. If Pecola's raison d'être revolves around the color of her skin and her eyes, she must imagine herself into existence in order to survive. While her survival is perceived as craziness, it is the only alternative given her treatment as a black person. Pecola's insanity, then, is a manifestation of corrupt societal values and an indictment of the human beings who perpetuate them. The consequences of reducing human worth to the limited criteria of physical beauty are insanity, death, and sterility. Claudia realizes that, as a young black girl, she is an endangered species from which "no green was going to spring." The soil is " 'bad,' " she says, " 'for certain kinds of flowers.' "

Reviews of *The Bluest Eye* were generally encouraging, though at times reserved in their praise. Many reviewers recognized a brilliant novelist in the making, emphasizing the beauty of her prose, her authentic dialogue, and her insight into black life. But they also criticized what they saw as an excess and abuse of those same qualities. In the *New York Times* (13 November 1970) John Leonard provided the most enthusiastic appraisal of *The Bluest Eye,* characterizing Morrison's prose as "so precise, so faithful to speech and so charged with pain and wonder that the novel becomes poetry." Several reviewers were less laudatory, criticizing her for what L. E. Sissman in the *New Yorker* called "an occasional error of fact or judgment" or what Haskel Frankel (*New York Times Book Review,* 1 November 1970) saw as "fuzziness born of flights of poetic imagery."

But even reviewers most critical of Morrison's first novel sensed her potential. The *Choice* reviewer stated that *The Bluest Eye* may not be the "best first novel ever published; it is, however, a sympathetic and moving portrayal of human beings . . . and for this alone it deserves to be read." Sissman concluded that, in spite of Morrison's penchant for "an occasion false or bombastic line," none of it matters "beside her real and greatly promising achievement." Frankel conceded that, though Morrison "has gotten lost in her construction," she is a writer "to seek out and encourage."

In the late 1960s and early 1970s Morrison's career as a writer paralleled her increasing prominence in the publishing world and as one of the cultural elite of the black community. She left Syracuse to become a senior editor at Random House in New York City. There, she established herself as a mentor for such aspiring African-American women writers as Toni Cade Bambara, Gayl Jones, and Angela Davis. Bambara told Strouse that Morrison is "a superb editor" whose judgment she trusts "absolutely." In the same article Young remarked that "Toni had done more to encourage and publish other black writers than anyone I know." Morrison also supported the publication of important works on black history, including *The Black Book* (1974), which she edited. Morrison was called on increasingly in the early 1970s to review books, especially for the *New York Times Book Review,* for which she critiqued twenty-eight books from 1971 to 1972. In 1971 she also wrote an article, "What the Black Woman Thinks About Women's Lib," for the *New York Times Magazine.*

The idea for Morrison's second novel, *Sula* (1973), came months after she finished *The Bluest Eye*. In her conversation with Naylor she stated:

> And so after I finished that book I was in some despair because several months passed and I didn't have another idea. And then I got to thinking about this girl, this woman. If it wasn't unconventional, she didn't want it. She was willing to risk in her imagination a lot of things and pay the price and also go astray. It wasn't as though she was this fantastic power who didn't have a flaw in her character. I wanted to throw her relationship with another woman into relief. Those two women – that too is us, those two desires, to have your adventure *and* safety. So I just cut it up.

In *Sula* Morrison focuses on the friendship of the two women she imagined. Nel represents the traditional roles of wife and mother in a patriarchal society, and Sula rejects those roles in favor of a life that is separate from family and community. They

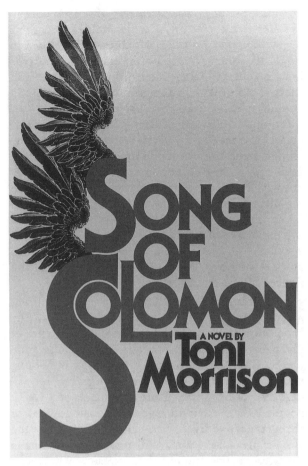

Dust jacket for Morrison's third novel, her first to feature a male protagonist

are inseparable as childhood friends, sharing a complicity in the death of a young boy Sula accidentally lets slip into a raging river. Eventually Sula leaves the community, only to return in search of her friend and any of Nel's life experiences she may have missed, including Nel's husband, Jude, with whom she has an affair.

As children, Nel and Sula are exposed to the unique, often bizarre configuration of their town and the people who inhabit it. Bottom is a black hilltop community that overlooks the white valley town of Medallion. In Bottom the residents are often as topsy-turvy as the topographically misleading name of the town indicates. Shadrack is a mad World War I veteran who celebrates National Suicide Day. Sula's mother, Eva, has sacrificed her leg for the economic security of disability payments, while Nel's mother, Helene Wright, has assimilated white, patriarchal ways even though her own mother is a Creole whore. Death through fire, drowning, disease, and madness becomes the fate of Bottom residents – a fictional apocalypse both frightening and confusing in its implications.

In *Sula,* as in *The Bluest Eye,* Morrison continues her denunciation of white values and their negative impact on the black community. *Sula* is a novel of contrasts, ironic reversals, and mirror images reflected in the fates of her characters and their community. Bottom and Medallion exist in an uneasy social stasis because they represent two often-opposite ways of living. Medallion generates commerce and industry, while Bottom, excluded from the economic benefits of the valley town, concentrates its efforts on family and community. Bottom residents struggle with the shifting plates of their stability. The notion of nuclear family as ideal undergoes a strong challenge from the existence of Eva's household. Reality is balanced by the ever-present supernatural. Women's roles – the novel's focus – are scrutinized in the figures of Nel and Sula.

Bottom and Medallion, as top and bottom, generate an opposition that frames the story. The geography emphasizes the contending ideologies of the two communities. Medallion represents commerce, whereas Bottom is a community of people, not an aggregation of houses surrounding a business district. However, Bottom residents and valley people look to each other for the missing pieces of their respective lives. The valley people envy the simple pleasures of the hill people, who engage freely in creative and artistic expression, whether in the form of laughter, singing, playing the banjo, donning a flowered dress, or high stepping. The hill people release the joy of life absent in Medallion, where residents wistfully long for an existence less rigidly defined by dollars and cents.

But the longing of the valley people blinds them to the pain of the Bottom residents, who struggle simply to survive. Having no choice in their setting and divorced from the mainstream, the people of Bottom must create an identity and a purpose that must necessarily include an identification with a culture that shuns them and a heritage that threatens to escape them. In the midst of this confusion Bottom residents are influenced by the same value system that generated Medallion. They embrace a tunnel project as their way out of poverty but are symbolically and literally crushed by it. The deaths of the tunnel victims initiate the death of a community that eventually assimilates into Medallion. Bottom residents turn to the valley, and, "just like that, [whites] had changed their minds and . . . now they wanted a hilltop house." In *Sula* Bottom and the valley, rather than melding and resolving the dialectic of their inhabitants' lives, simply switch places in a circular fashion.

The fate of Bottom is shared by many of its residents. The strong Eva, who creates a haven of her home by including all walks of life, goes mad after burning her drug-addicted son to death and watching as her daughter Hannah is also consumed by flames. Though her home is an alternative to the restrictive, stultifying atmosphere of Helene Wright's house, it cannot isolate itself from the externalities of racism and oppression that infect it. Sula becomes the town pariah whose evil presence is evidenced in several omens. In an effort to understand an unrelenting reality, Bottom residents invoke the supernatural to explain the phenomenon of a woman who does not and will not succumb to traditional gender roles. Nel finally appreciates the nature and function of her friend, but only after Sula dies. Finally, Bottom residents attempt to destroy a tunnel that once promised economic security, but they end up being destroyed by it. The community of Bottom, which possesses so much potential as an alternative to a white world struggling to find its spiritual center, ends up burying itself in physical and spiritual death. There is no synthesis for this fictional world, only "circles and circles of sorrow."

With the publication of *Sula* Morrison's importance as a writer was established. The novel received more critical and popular attention than *The Bluest Eye* and was excerpted in *Redbook,* selected as an alternate for the Book-of-the-Month Club, and nominated for the 1975 National Book Award in fiction. Reviewers of *Sula* both praised and condemned Morrison's prose poetry, narrative construction, and moral and ethical vision of black life. The positive reviews, such as Jerry Bryant's in the *Nation* (6 July 1974), cited the beauty of her language and her originality. Both *Booklist* (15 March 1974) and *Choice* (March 1974) commended *Sula* for its authenticity and craftsmanship.

Other reviewers, however, criticized *Sula* for what they perceived to be a lack of careful craftsmanship. The *Times Literary Supplement* (4 October 1974) called the plot "contrived," and Christopher Lehmann-Haupt in the *New York Times* (7 January 1974) complained that Morrison's scenes seem "written from scratch" and that her prose poetry, in an attempt to avoid clichés, ends up "call[ing] them to mind." Lehmann-Haupt stated that the novel suffers from a lack of objectivity, and Sara Blackburn in the *New York Times Book Review* (30 December 1973) complained of a "narrowness" and "refusal to brim over into the world outside its provincial setting." In response to these observations the *Black World* (June 1974) reviewer commented that angry responses to *Sula* were a "ripping hostility" to Morrison's "excellence and skill."

Morrison's third novel, *Song of Solomon* (1977), expands beyond the time and place of her first two books, moving from North to South and from present to past in an endeavor to uncover and rediscover the personal history of an African-American family. *Song of Solomon* is, in some ways, a fictionalized venture of another project in which Morrison was involved, *The Black Book,* a scrapbook of African-American history published soon after *Sula.* In *Song of Solomon* Morrison for the first time uses a male protagonist, Milkman, to undergo a rite of passage — not from innocence to experience but from one history to another, one culture to another, and one value system to another. He undergoes a ritual immersion into the South and his own history in an attempt to understand himself and his culture.

As in *The Bluest Eye* and *Sula,* the black community in *Song of Solomon* struggles with a double consciousness that can wreak havoc on their lives. Not willing to give up the distinctive quality of their African-American culture, they are nevertheless pressured or lured into a desire for assimilation that in this novel takes the shape of land ownership, a crucial aspect of African-American history because it constitutes physical and legal evidence of a history and tradition. Perhaps for this reason many of the characters in *Song of Solomon* adopt the appropriative, rather than the custodial, view of the land.

Milkman's father, Macon, is a money-grubbing landlord who exploits his own community for profit; Guitar Baines is obsessive in his desire for the money, land, and even blood of those who have oppressed him. While appropriation characterizes the motives of Macon Dead and Guitar Baines, it can be seen earlier in Macon's grandfather, a separatist who attempts to create a private paradise and, hence, a measure of autonomy. Yet his land, Lincoln's Heaven, is also stripped from him, and he is murdered. The exception to the destructive policies of appropriation is Pilate, for whom land is not an entity to be owned. It simply *is.* She envisions herself as a temporary custodian of the land, which itself is eternal and thus independent of the generations of people who will lay claim to it. Freed from the obsession of appropriation, Pilate can channel her energies into human relationships and eventually into the community.

Milkman must find his way through the turnstiles of this double vision, as Ralph Ellison calls it, to create a sense of self that does not yet exist. To reach this point he embarks on a traditionally male mythic journey that Morrison implies is an extremely clumsy approach to the obvious. Milkman travels to Pennsylvania in search of gold for his selfish purposes, but he acquires an education that takes him south through Danville and then Shalimar. In Danville he becomes reacquainted with his grandfather's history of proud landownership. Since his death, however, the community has limped along, clinging to tradition but lacking the vitality to generate any. This inertia motivates Milkman to the wrong action. His desire for gold becomes a form of revenge on the people who murdered his grandfather.

Once he arrives in Shalimar, Milkman's transformation begins. He is confronted by a town that boasts no commerce, transportation, or government. Invisible even on a map, Shalimar does not exist on the level of civilization. In this sequestered setting Milkman undergoes a series of initiations that strip him of his cultural indoctrinations. Eventually he is led to the myth of flight, which is a catalyst for his symbolic and literal leap out of ignorance into the knowledge of his past and himself. It is also a leap into confrontation with yet another distorted value system — represented by Guitar's blood lust — that could end up destroying the African-American community.

Though Milkman's fate is in question and Pilate, one of Morrison's most enduring characters, dies at the end of the novel, *Song of Solomon* represents a significant departure from Morrison's first two novels in that celebration and hope eclipse despondency and utter despair. The novel is often an expression of joy — especially in Pilate's household, with the "three women singing in the candlelight," and, later, in Milkman's discovery of the myth of Shalimar. *Song of Solomon* suggests that, through history, African-Americans can begin to make sense of their lives in the context of being American. With knowledge comes connection and a sense of responsibility, a process that Pilate initiates with her arrival in Southside and that she is able to pass on to Milkman before her death. But Morrison, always a reserved optimist, leaves sufficient doubt about what Milkman will be able to accomplish as a way of reminding readers that the resolution to hundreds of years of oppression will be a long, painful journey.

Mitigating the reality of Southside is a Morrison trademark, the use of the supernatural. In *Song of Solomon* she indulges in myth, fantasy, and the supernatural as a form of transcendence for her African-American characters. While she dabbles in the supernatural in both *The Bluest Eye* and *Sula,* in *Song of Solomon* she further blurs the lines between mimesis

Dust jacket for Morrison's 1981 novel, in which she employs myth, ghosts, and evil in a Caribbean island setting

and fantasy. In this novel Morrison uses myth as a device that mitigates the dichotomy of being black in white society. Myth, as used in *Song of Solomon,* is not only a metaphor but also a course of action that, as it muddies the distinction between spiritual and physical flight, provides fuel for the collective imagination. Fantasy also figures heavily in *Song of Solomon.* Pilate can talk to her dead father, Ruth's watermark does grow each day, and Solomon and Milkman can fly. By casually mingling the real and the bizarre, Morrison negotiates the chasm between reality and fantasy so that the impossible becomes the inevitable.

Song of Solomon was both a popular and critical success, establishing Morrison as one of America's most important novelists. The novel became a paperback best-seller, with 570,000 copies in print in 1979. *Song of Solomon* was a Book-of-the-Month Club main selection, the first novel by an African-American so chosen since Richard Wright's *Native Son* (1940). Morrison's success and recognition led to her 1980 appointment by President Jimmy Carter to the National Council on the Arts. In 1981 she was elected to the American Academy and Institute of Arts and Letters.

Reviews of *Song of Solomon* were generally enthusiastic and appreciative of the depth and richness of Morrison's art, with its mixture of reality and fantasy and its strikingly original use of language. Susan Lardner in the *New Yorker* (7 November 1977) considered Morrison "a genuine rhapsode," while Linda Kuehl in the *Saturday Review* (17 September 1977) called Morrison a "romantic revolutionary" whose new novel is "the vision of an original, eccentric, inventive imagination." Several reviewers remarked on Morrison's growth as a writer. On the front page of the *New York Times Book Review* (11 September 1977) Reynolds Price stated that in *Song of Solomon* "the depths of the younger work are still evident, but now they thrust outward, into wider fields." Angela Wigan in *Time* (12 September 1977) observed that *Song of Solomon* is in what Morrison herself described as the fifth stage of African-American writing, "an artistic vision that encompasses both a private and a national heritage."

Some reviewers praised Morrison for her moral sensibility. In the *Nation* (19 November 1977) Earl Frederick called Morrison "appealingly old fashioned" in her vision of "love as an abiding need, and dignity and desperation as inseparable aspects of individual existence." The *World Literature Today* (Summer 1978) reviewer compared Morrison to Karl Marx "because her novel turns upside down many of the established social, moral and cultural beliefs that the Western world has inherited from the Judeo-Christian and Greco-Roman traditions." Some criticism was muted and centered on Morrison's choice of a man as her protagonist. Vivian Gornick in the *Village Voice* (29 August 1977) stated that the "source of artistic trouble in *Song of Solomon* resided in Morrison's choice of Milkman as protagonist – instead of with one of the women in the book."

In *Tar Baby* (1981) Morrison no longer focuses exclusively on the black family and community, setting her novel in the Caribbean and thus incorporating several different cultures, including the island natives, Philadelphia Negroes, and Western imperialists, all of whom are mutually dependent on one another but who are alienated from any sense of community. With this hodgepodge of people comes a conflicting set of values that struggle for an impossible hegemony in a riot of interdependency. Therese, Gideon, and Alme Estee as well as Ondine, Sydney, and Jadine rely on the beneficence of the white Streets for their livelihood, as Valerian and Margaret Street rely on them for their service and devotion.

The occupants of the house engage in a subtle warfare in which subterfuge, subversion, and emotional blackmail are employed to gain some measure of control. In the Street household the dependents gain power and control within the system but do not free themselves from it. All are essentially codependents of the addictive system that has minimalized their lives. Yet they cannot live without it, for to do so would require total self-reliance, a concept too frightening for them to consider. Only Son continues to be a human being capable of spiritual, emotional, and intellectual growth. And, as a male, he signals a departure from Morrison's earlier conceptions of woman as spiritual healer and as separate from society at large.

The social fabric in *Tar Baby* is multifaceted and highly complex. Filled with inter- and intraracial conflict as well as class and gender conflict, the Isle de Chevaliers is a microcosm of modern society. As in *Song of Solomon* these conflicts involve the real and imagined ownership of the island, a tendency that includes both a physical and spiritual preoccupation with the land. Both cultures lay claim to a symbolic geography: the white imperialists justify occupation by their commercial interests and the belief that a hundred French cavaliers haunt the island; the natives claim custodianship of the island by virtue of their presence and the myth of the shipwrecked blind slaves.

This difference in the mythic beliefs and land ownership informs the relationship of all the characters – to each other and to the communities in which they live. Valerian's sense of security is directly linked to ownership of his plantation. Even his last name, Street, suggests a manipulation of nature into municipality. As servants to Valerian, Sydney and Ondine are appendages to his system and thus have no affinity or connection to the land. Jadine sees the world as a global mall, a consumer's paradise that is hers for the taking.

Son retains a mythic notion of community in Eloe; but, in spite of Son's attempts to romanticize it, Eloe lacks direction and purpose. Finally, it is Therese, the island native, who sees land as something one must work with and not against, in cooperation and dependency. The natives are convinced that they will remain through a string of occupations; thus, their values represent the custodial rather than the appropriative view of the land. This sense of the relationship between the land and people becomes the metaphor for community in contradistinction to the Street occupation and is the essential value that Therese wishes to impart to Son.

In *Tar Baby* Morrison again relies on myth, ghosts, and evil, intensifying their mystical qualities by placing them in the isolated setting of a Caribbean island. Morrison invokes the supernatural as a way to fend off a reality in which whites are set against blacks, women against men, culture against primitivism, and civilization against nature. Morrison challenges these dualities by creating an atmosphere in which the island itself is sentient, competing myths on the island proliferate, and several characters experience psychic occurrences.

The Isle de Chevalier is cluttered with spirits and myths that should inevitably minimize individual differences but instead tend to intensify them. Given a more complete perspective of alternative realities, individuals should be able to release themselves from their own limited vision and open up to creative solutions. If Jadine and Son, Valerian and Son, Ondine and Jadine, and Margaret and Michael cannot solve their problems it is because they do not possess total knowledge. Morrison provides her characters with that missing information by way of the supernatural, although they may not always be able to interpret it adequately. At the end of the novel Son appears to embark on a journey that is a rebirth of sorts, but, as is often the case in Morrison's novels, considerable doubt exists as to whether or not Son will be able to reacquaint himself with his "ancient properties."

Tar Baby met with considerable advance publicity, as publication coincided with a cover story on Morrison in *Newsweek*. However, reviewers expressed a measure of ambivalence about the novel, especially in terms of Morrison's thematic intent. Wilfrid Sheed in the *Atlantic Monthly* (April 1981) commented, "We have experienced Morrison, half at her very best and the other half presumably having fun, dabbling in something new – white light comedy – with only sporadic success. And there's no harm in any of that." Less conciliatory, David Dubal in the *Hudson Review* (Autumn 1981) characterized her "response to both the personal and cultural crisis of the book . . . perplexing, if not confused." Brina Caplan in the *Nation* (2 May 1981) stated that *Tar Baby* suffers because it is "a novel of ideas set in the white world." Nicholas Shrimpton in the *New Statesman* (23 October 1981) called *Tar Baby* "a seriously overweight novel."

More positive reviews zeroed in on Morrison's "vast curiosity," "her terrible honesty," and what Maureen Howard in the *New Republic* (21 March 1981) admitted is a "pleasure I associate with the best kind of reading." Some reviewers, including Selden Rodman in the *National Review* (26 June 1981) commented on the negative portrayal of white characters in the novel, continuing a pattern of critique that appears to hold Morrison accountable for her depiction of fictional characters and worlds in ways that other writers have not been. She has been chastised for her narrow vision of black life in *The Bluest Eye* and *Sula,* her lack of strong male characters, her selection of a male hero in *Song of Solomon,* her exclusion of white characters, and her characterization of white people. Evaluation of Morrison's powerful art often appears colored by the political agendas of her constituents.

In *Beloved* (1987) Morrison embraces the supernatural as perhaps the ideal vehicle for the investigation of slavery, an institution so incomprehensible that Morrison suggests that most Americans would like to bury it, since it is the historical reminder of a national disgrace. Morrison delayed the writing of this novel because she anticipated the pain of recovery and confrontation. She told Elizabeth Kastor, "I had forgotten that when I started the book, I was very frightened. . . . It was an unwillingness and a terror of going into an area for which you have no preparation. It's a commitment of three or four years to living inside – because you do try to enter that life." In spite of "this terrible reluctance about dwelling on that era," Morrison informed Angelo that she went ahead with the writing of the book because "I was trying to make it a personal experience."

Beloved is based on the true story of the slave Margaret Garner, who murdered her own child rather than return her to slavery. In the novel the slave woman, Sethe, escapes to freedom in the North, where she lives with her remaining children. Morrison altered the true story, she told Marsha Darling, in that Garner was not tried for murder:

> She was tried for a *real* crime, which was running away – although the abolitionists were trying very hard to get her tried for murder because they wanted the Fugitive Slave Law to be unconstitutional. They did not want her tried on those grounds, so they tried to switch it to murder as a kind of success story. They thought that they could make it impossible for Ohio, as a free state, to acknowledge the right of a slave-owner to come get those people. In fact, the sanctuary movement now is exactly the same. But they all went back to Boone County and apparently the man who took them back – the man she was going to kill herself and her children to get away from – he sold her down river, which was as bad as being separated from each other. But apparently the boat hit a sandbar or something, and she fell or jumped with her daughter, her baby, into the water. It is not clear whether she fell or jumped, but they rescued her and I guess she went on down to New Orleans and I don't know.

Morrison informed Darling that she did not do much research on Garner because "I wanted to invent her life, which is a way of saying I wanted to be accessible to anything the characters had to say about it. Recording her life as lived would not interest me, and would not make me available to anything that might be pertinent." The metaphor for Morrison's reluctance for mimesis is the configuration of Beloved – part ghost, zombie, devil, and memory. Morrison reveals Beloved in tantalizing degrees until she is manifested as a full-blooded person. Like a childhood trauma Beloved comes back in snatches until finally her history is retold, a discovery process shared by Morrison, her characters, and the readers as the primary step to collective spiritual recovery.

Beloved is a purging of the guilt of the American psyche, and it acts as a historical precedent to and psychological referent for the rage of the oppressed in Morrison's other books. Sethe's slave status involves total loss of freedom and humanity and serves as the origin of all subsequent forms of oppression endured by Morrison's other characters and the motivation for their violent reactions to them. In *The Bluest Eye* Cholly's response to racial oppression is the rape of his own daughter. In *Sula* oppression caused by war turns Eva's Plum into a drug addict, forcing her to euthanatize him. Sexual oppression in *Tar Baby* drives Margaret to burn little holes in her baby. All these acts testify profoundly to the legacy of an institution so evil that it affords a mother no alternative for her children but death.

Reviewers, sensing that they were witnessing a literary phenomenon, lavished *Beloved* with praise. *Publishers Weekly* (17 July 1987) called it a milestone in the chronicling of the black experience in America, while Merle Rubin in the *Christian Science Monitor* (5 October 1987) said it is "a stunning book and lasting achievement [that] transforms the sorrows of history into the luminous truth of art." Leonard (*Los Angeles Times Book Review*, 30 August 1987) stated that, without *Beloved*, "our imagination of the nation's self has a hole in it big enough to die from." He felt *Beloved* "belongs on the highest shelf of American literature, even if half a dozen canonized white boys have to be elbowed off." Walter Clemons in *Newsweek* (28 September 1987) declared, "I think we have a masterpiece on our hands here." Not all reviews were positive, however. Stanley Crouch in the *New Republic* (19 October 1987) saw *Beloved* as "the failure of feeling that is sentimentality." He accused Morrison of "almost always [losing] control" and of not resisting "the temptation of the trite or the sentimental." Michiko Kakutani in the *New York Times* (2 September 1987) wrote, "There is a contemporaneous quality to time past and time present as well as a sense that the lines between reality and fiction, truth and memory, have become inextricably blurred."

Beloved earned the Pulitzer Prize, an award that had been denied another great writer, James Baldwin. In an effort to prevent the glaring oversight that Baldwin suffered and to secure Morrison's place in literary history, many African-American writers had published a tribute to Morrison in the *New York Times Book Review* (24 January 1988), "Black Writers in Praise of Toni Morrison," that states in part: "We find your life work ever building to a monument of vision and discovery and trust." The writers argued that, "despite the international stature of Toni Morrison, she has yet to receive the national recognition that her five major works of fiction entirely deserve: she has yet to receive the keystone honors of the National Book Award or the Pulitzer Prize. We, the undersigned black critics and black writers, here assert ourselves against such oversight and harmful whimsy."

Jazz (1992), Morrison's sixth novel, is based on a photograph in James Van DerZee's *Harlem*

Book of the Dead (1978) that shows, according to Leonard in the *Nation* (25 May 1992), "the body of a young girl, shot at a party by a jealous boyfriend, who died refusing to identify her assailant." Morrison told Rose that she wished to investigate "the question" of male/female passion, hence the story of Joe, a middle-aged cosmetic salesman; his childless wife Violet; and the teenage Dorcas, with whom Joe has an affair and whom he shoots when he is jilted for a younger lover. While *Jazz* may have begun with the issue of male/female passion, it ends as a fictive re-creation of two parallel narratives set during major historical events in African-American history – Reconstruction and the Jazz Age.

Morrison weaves together the story of Joe, Violet, and Dorcas with the history of their predecessors True Belle, Violet's grandmother; Vera Louise, a wealthy white woman; and Golden Gray, her mulatto son. True Belle serves as caretaker of Vera Louise and Golden Gray. The respective stories are so intricately linked that Golden Gray at one point rescues Wild, Joe's crazed mother, while she is pregnant with him. Though Joe's and Violet's histories intersect at this moment, they never attempt to integrate into their troubled lives the significance of their pasts.

The initiative that Joe and Violet lack in recovering their personal histories is more than compensated for by the narrator, who possesses a surfeit of curiosity, taking great pains to reimagine both stories. An enigmatic presence in the book, the narrator possesses a feminine, African-American voice. At first arrogant in her ability to present the truth, the narrator eventually undergoes a rite of passage perhaps more subtle, but no less profound, than that of Milkman. The narrator begins by trying to "figure out [her characters'] plans, their reasonings, long before they do." In spite of the narrator's efforts, the narration follows a path of its own, independent of the will of the narrator. The narrator has judged inaccurately that Joe will repeat the act of violence that took Dorcas's life. When Joe instead reconciles with Violet, the narrator chastises his/her inability to present the truth: "I have been careless and stupid and it infuriates me to discover (again) how unreliable I am." In a self-reflective moment the narrator questions the authority of authorship. Thus what is ultimately at stake in *Jazz* is the process of reclamation and arrival at truth.

In *Jazz* Morrison continues her investigation of the debilitating impact of history on black families. In this novel she does not focus on slavery, but on its legacy to a generation removed in time but not place from its grasp. The unrelenting, destruc-

Dust jacket for Morrison's Pulitzer Prize–winning 1987 novel, about which the Newsweek *reviewer declared, "I think we have a masterpiece on our hands here"*

tive influence of racism and oppression on the black family is manifested in *Jazz* by the almost-total absence of the black family. Even Morrison's mothers, previously incomparable in their strength and endurance, succumb to the social, economic, and political forces of history. Joe, Violet, and Dorcas lose their mothers to insanity, suicide, and murder. Their deaths are directly attributable to institutionalized racism.

Considered little more than chattel to the dominant culture, women probably endured unspeakable abuse. Rose Dear, abandoned by a husband who is denied the economic opportunity to support his family, jumped to her death in a well rather than face homelessness and starvation. Dorcas's parents were innocent victims of the East Saint Louis riots. With no father or mother to form their identities and to succor them, Joe, Violet, and Dorcas are left to be raised by kindly friends or relatives, all of whom themselves are disconnected in various ways from family and community.

For many of the characters in the novel, the absence of family is replaced by the ever-present city. Morrison attempts to reconstruct the complex set of factors that brought black people to the city in the first place as well as those factors that compelled

them to stay. She told Rose that one of the goals she tried to accomplish in *Jazz* was "[to] recall . . . what it was like when people went to the city, when the city was the place to go." Morrison cited economic opportunity and social equality as primary reasons for flight, but, while initially "running from want and violence," black people, Morrison shows, sought more than a safe job and a secure environment, amenities even the city could not guarantee.

Perhaps most important for black people, the city represented indifference. A community of steel and concrete more than of people, the city protects black people from constant scrutiny, from the ever-present, appropriating glare of a racist society that defines and shapes their identity. Separated by the enormity of the city from the "Look," black people can reclaim the freedom of self-definition that is tied to their anonymity: "There, in a city, they are not so much new as themselves: their stronger, riskier selves."

Jazz was published simultaneously with Morrison's *Playing in the Dark: Whiteness and the Literary Imagination,* a scholarly work based on three lectures she gave at Harvard University. According to the *Chronicle of Higher Education* (22 April 1992), the publisher, Harvard University Press, decided to print twenty-five thousand first-run copies of this book instead of the traditional fifteen hundred. Harvard University Press's confidence in a scholarly work is clearly indicative of Morrison's stature as, David Gates wrote (*Newsweek,* 27 April 1992), "the last classic American writer, squarely in the tradition of Poe, Melville, Twain and Faulkner." Reviews of *Jazz* praised Morrison's language and intricate plot construction but tended to admonish her use of an unreliable narrator. Leonard in the *Nation* (25 May 1992) called *Jazz* a "brand-new star" in Morrison's "constellation of humming spheres." Jane Smiley in *Vogue* (May 1992) stated that Morrison's style "is commanding and seductive at the same time."

Less complimentary reviews included Edna O'Brien's in the *New York Times* (5 April 1992), which stated that *Jazz* lacks an "emotional nexus" so that "what remains are the bold arresting strokes of a poster and not the cold astonishment of a painting." Ann Hulbert in the *New Republic* (18 May 1992) complained that Morrison's narrative strategy undermines her authority as author: "Morrison has charged her narrator with the duty to avoid the weakness that she herself has acknowledged – an inclination to romanticize black lives." Hulbert concluded that "her relentless vigilance, rather than issuing in creative sympathy, leads her toward the double dead end of indicting other writers for failures of vision and apologizing for her own." Focusing less on the narrator, Gates characterized Morrison's narration as "metafictional shenanigans" that nevertheless "hardly affect the experience of reading *Jazz*."

Morrison is one of the great living American writers; her goal has been, as Rose said, "to redefine how African-American experience fits into the American experience." In the Rose interview Morrison suggested that "if you study the culture and art of African-Americans you are not studying a regional or minor culture. What you are studying is American." In her six novels she has re-created for America the energy, passion, and dynamic of African-American culture with an originality and a depth that are unsurpassed. In the pages of her novels readers themselves emerge in the complexity of African-American families, their communities, the history and geography that they are rediscovering, the reality that they must often transcend in order to survive, and the inexhaustible capacity for love that motivates, sustains, and strengthens them. The encounter with Morrison's characters – with the language and the sheer humanity that suffuse her works – becomes an embrace of a long-unrecognized aspect of America and its citizens.

Morrison's concern in *Jazz* with the responsibility of the artist and the possibility or impossibility of presenting truth through language exhibits the range of her career-long experimentation in novel writing. Morrison has successfully invoked, among other literary movements, naturalism, magical realism, high modernism, historical revisionism, and postmodernism in an endeavor to get at the very essence of her subject matter. Morrison takes increasing risks with language, narrative construction, and most of the contrivances of literary convention in order to communicate the most profound secrets of the human heart. She told Rose that when a young black man at a Princeton lecture asked her who she wrote for, she replied: "I want to write for people like me, which is to say black people, curious people, demanding people . . . people who can't be faked, people who don't need to be patronized, people who have very, very high criteria."

Morrison's experimentation with the novel coincides with her ever-increasing thematic concerns. As if constricted by the necessary closure of a novel, Morrison expands the consciousness of each successive novel without leaving behind the burning issues that mark her previous ones. Thus family, community, and the love they provide or deny are a constant in her canon. History, geography, and eventually myth, fable, and the supernatural are gradually implemented to illuminate the nature of those families and communities. Morrison's first two novels, *The Bluest Eye* and *Sula,* are spatially and chronologically limited, though *Sula* introduces World War I as a historical backdrop. *Song of Solomon* moves in time and place from present to past and from North to South, while *Tar Baby* is set outside the continental United States on an island where past and present frequently intermingle. *Beloved* is a historical novel that concerns Reconstruction, yet it implies ahistoricity in the amazing figure of Beloved. *Jazz* integrates historical eras and moves to the city, all the while disavowing its own efficacy to reproduce either time or place.

But time and place only partially reflect Morrison's desire for circumference – Emily Dickinson's term for the endeavor to comprehend totality. Morrison always begins with a different question and then finds the characters to manifest it. The questions and the characters change dramatically in each novel. In *The Bluest Eye* sexual abuse and idealized beauty afflict a little black girl, while in *Sula* Morrison chooses two adult black women to illustrate the nature of sexual freedom and moral responsibility. In *Song of Solomon* a black male undergoes the recovery of personal history, and in *Tar Baby* another black male is a source of spiritual renewal. In *Beloved* a ghost symbolizes the horror of slavery, and in *Jazz* an even-less-visible presence admits failure in understanding the nature of male/female passion. But such a summary is reductive and does little to convey the myriad other themes and characters Morrison invokes. She uses children and adults, men and women, blacks and whites, haints, and a metaphysical metafiction to give voice to the shimmering essence of humanity.

Ultimately in *Jazz* Morrison questions her ability to answer the very issues she raises, extending the responsibility of her own novel writing to her readers. Morrison's narrator at the end of *Jazz* invokes his/her readership to "Make me. Remake me." Morrison thereby sends an invitation to her readers to become a part of that struggle to comprehend totality that will continue to spur her genius.

Interviews:

Mel Watkins, "Talk with Toni Morrison," *New York Times Book Review,* 11 September 1977, pp. 48, 50;

Robert B. Stepto, " 'Intimate Things in Place': A Conversation with Toni Morrison," *Massachusetts Review,* 18 (Autumn 1977): 473–489;

Jane Bakerman, "The Seams Can't Show: An Interview with Toni Morrison," *Black American Literature Forum,* 12 (Summer 1978): 56–60;

Bettye J. Parker, "Complexity: Toni Morrison's Women – An Interview Essay," in *Sturdy Black Bridges: Visions of Black Women in Literature,* edited by Roseann P. Bell and others (Garden City, N.Y.: Doubleday, 1979), pp. 251–257;

Thomas LeClair, " 'The Language Must Not Sweat,' " *New Republic,* 184 (21 March 1981): 25–29;

Nellie Y. McKay, "An Interview with Toni Morrison," *Contemporary Literature,* 24 (Winter 1983): 413–429;

Claudia Tate, "Toni Morrison," in *Black Women Writers at Work,* edited by Tate (New York: Continuum, 1983), pp. 117–131;

Gloria Naylor, "A Conversation," *Southern Review,* new series 21 (July 1985): 567–593;

Bessie W. Jones, "An Interview with Toni Morrison," in *The World of Toni Morrison,* edited by Jones and Audrey L. Vison (Dubuque, Iowa: Kendall/Hunt, 1985), p. 135;

Marsha Darling, "In the Realm of Responsibility: A Conversation with Toni Morrison," *Women's Review of Books,* 5 (March 1988): 5–6;

Christina Davis, "Interview with Toni Morrison," *Presence Africaine,* 145 (1988): 141–150;

Bonnie Angelo, "The Pain of Being Black," *Time,* 133 (22 May 1989): 120–122.

Bibliographies:

Curtis Martin, "A Bibliography of Writings by Toni Morrison," in *Contemporary American Women Writers: Narrative Strategies,* edited by Catherine Rainwater and William J. Scheick (Lexington: University Press of Kentucky, 1985), pp. 205–207;

Harriet Alexander, "Toni Morrison: An Annotated Bibliography of Critical Articles and Essays, 1975–1984," *College Language Association Journal,* 33 (September 1989): 81–93.

References:

Michael Awkward, *Inspiriting Influences: Tradition, Revision, and Afro-American Women's Novels* (New York: Columbia University Press, 1989);

Susan L. Blake, "Folklore and Community in *Song of Solomon,*" *MELUS,* 7 (Fall 1980): 77–82;

Diane Kim Bowman, "Flying High: The American Icarus in Morrison, Roth, and Updike," *Perspectives on Contemporary Literature,* 8 (1982): 10–17;

Joanne Braxton, *Wild Women in the Whirlwind: Afro-American Culture and the Contemporary Literary Renaissance* (New Brunswick, N. J.: Rutgers University Press, 1990);

Barbara Christian, *Black Women Novelists: The Development of a Tradition, 1892–1976* (Westport, Conn.: Greenwood Press, 1980);

Norris Clark, "Flying Black: Toni Morrison's *The Bluest Eye, Sula* and *Song of Solomon,*" *Minority Voices,* 4 (Fall 1980): 51–63;

James W. Coleman, "Beyond the Reach of Love and Caring: Black Life in Toni Morrison's *Song of Solomon,*" *Obsidian,* 2 (Winter 1986): 151–161;

David Cowart, "Faulkner and Joyce in Morrison's *Song of Solomon,*" *American Literature,* 62 (March 1980): 87–100;

Jacqueline de Weever, "The Inverted World of Toni Morrison's *The Bluest Eye* and *Sula,*" *College Language Association Journal,* 22 (June 1979): 402–414;

Leslie A. Harris, "Myth as Structure in Toni Morrison's *Song of Solomon,*" *MELUS,* 7 (Fall 1980): 69–76;

Trudier Harris, *Fiction and Folklore: The Novels of Toni Morrison* (Knoxville: University of Tennessee Press, 1991);

Denise Heinze, *The Dilemma of "Double-Consciousness":
Toni Morrison's Novels* (Athens: University of
Georgia Press, 1993);

Karla Holloway and Stephanie Dematrakopoulos,
*New Dimensions of Spirituality: A Biracial and Bi-
cultural Reading of the Novels of Toni Morrison*
(New York: Greenwood Press, 1987);

Lauren Lepow, "Paradise Lost and Found: Dualism
and Edenic Myth in Toni Morrison's *Tar Baby*,"
Contemporary Literature, 28, no. 3 (1987): 364–
377;

Nellie Y. McKay, ed., *Critical Essays on Toni Morrison*
(Boston: G. K. Hall, 1988);

Chikwenye Okonjo Ogunyemi, "Order and Disorder in Toni Morrison's *The Bluest Eye*," *Critique,*
19, no. 1 (1977): 112–120;

Terry Otten, *The Crime of Innocence in the Fiction of
Toni Morrison* (Columbia: University of Missouri Press, 1989);

Harry Reed, "Toni Morrison, *Song of Solomon* and
Black Cultural Nationalism," *Centennial Review,* 32 (Winter 1988): 50–64;

Philip Royster, "Milkman's Flying: The Scapegoat
Transcended in Toni Morrison's *Song of Solomon*," *CLA Journal,* 24 (June 1981): 419–440;

Wilfrid Samuels, "Liminality and the Search for Self
in Toni Morrison's *Song of Solomon*," *Minority
Voices,* 5 (Spring–Fall 1981): 59–68;

Jean Strouse, "Toni Morrison's Black Magic," *Newsweek,* 97 (30 March 1981): 52–57;

Claudia Tate, ed., *Black Women Writers at Work* (New
York: Continuum, 1983);

Susan Willis, *Specifying: Black Women Writing the
American Experience* (Madison: University of
Wisconsin Press, 1987).

Willard Motley

(14 July 1909 – 4 March 1965)

Robert E. Fleming
University of New Mexico

See also the Motley entry in *DLB 76: Afro-American Writers, 1940–1955.*

BOOKS: *Knock on Any Door* (New York & London: Appleton-Century, 1947; London: Collins, 1948);

We Fished All Night (New York: Appleton-Century-Crofts, 1951);

Let No Man Write My Epitaph (New York: Random House, 1958; London: Longmans, 1959);

Let Noon Be Fair (New York: Putnam, 1966; London: Longmans, 1966).

Edition: *The Diaries of Willard Motley,* edited by Jerome Klinkowitz (Ames: Iowa State University Press, 1979).

OTHER: "The Almost White Boy," in *Soon, One Morning: New Writing by American Negroes,* edited by Herbert Hill (New York: Knopf, 1963), pp. 389–402.

Willard Motley, circa 1945

During Willard Motley's lifetime the brief biographies of him that were printed in newspapers or on the dust jackets of his best-selling novels presented him as a writer who had clawed his way up from the proletariat. The jacket of *Let Noon Be Fair* (1966), for example, listed his previous occupations as migrant laborer, ranch hand, cook, shipping clerk, and photographer and mentioned that he had served a jail sentence for vagrancy in Cheyenne, Wyoming. In truth, despite his sincere interest in the have-nots of American society, Motley was the product of a middle-class black home in the integrated Englewood district of Chicago's South Side.

The son of Florence Motley, Willard Motley was born on 14 July 1909 and grew up under the illusion that his grandparents were his father and mother. These parental surrogates provided strong role models. Archibald Motley, Sr., a Pullman porter, stood for moral and financial responsibility, subjects over which he clashed with Willard as the boy was growing up. Mary Motley, known as Mae

to her family and friends, was a strong woman with deep moral and religious convictions. Another formative influence was Willard's uncle Archibald, Jr., a successful painter, who demonstrated that an African-American could achieve recognition in the arts.

Motley began his literary career at age thirteen, when a short story he had published on the children's page of the *Chicago Defender* won him the chance to write his own weekly column in that African-American newspaper, under the pen name "Bud Billiken." He wrote columns ranging from mere amusement for children to think pieces on subjects such as poverty and racial pride from 9

December 1922 through 5 July 1924. At Englewood High School he was active on the newspaper and yearbook staffs.

Graduating in 1929, Motley wanted to attend the University of Wisconsin to pursue a career as a writer but was unable to do so. Instead the road became his university as he took a bicycle trip to New York City and two automobile trips to the West Coast. The short fiction he submitted to popular magazines during the 1930s was returned to him with form rejection slips, but by the end of the decade he was publishing occasional travel articles. More-literary sketches by Motley appeared in *Hull-House Magazine,* a journal he helped edit at the famous settlement house founded by Jane Addams in 1889. Both his nonfiction and fiction emphasized the social consciousness that he had learned from Mae Motley and further developed by his experiences on the road.

Motley's work with *Hull-House Magazine* exposed him to the literature that he would otherwise have encountered at the university. His fellow editors William P. Schenk and Alexander Saxton prescribed a reading list ranging from the classics to the works of modernist authors such as Ernest Hemingway and John Dos Passos. By 1940 Motley had personally encountered some successful authors. After submitting a story to him, he met Jack Conroy, a successful proletarian novelist (*The Disinherited,* 1933) who edited the leftist periodical the *Anvil.* Motley worked with Richard Wright, Margaret Walker, Nelson Algren, Meridel Le Sueur, and Arna Bontemps on the Works Progress Administration Federal Writers' Project.

By the beginning of 1941 Motley felt that he had made a start on his literary career. He had published a dozen articles and stories, although most had appeared in obscure magazines. More important, he had decided on the subject of his first novel and was hard at work on it. *Knock on Any Door* (1947) is an exposé of the penal system, especially as it deals with young offenders. The novel centers on a youth who was the subject of Motley's sketch "The Boy" (*Ohio Motorist,* August 1938). Motley also drew on his acquaintance with another juvenile delinquent and on his research into the case of the youthful murderer of four people, Bernard Sawicki, whose trial Motley attended in 1941.

Based on these case histories as well as fact-finding visits to the Saint Charles, Illinois, School for Boys and the Cook County Jail, *Knock on Any Door* mixes sociology with art. Motley views poverty as the source of crime and the penal system as a contributing factor in the creation of habitual criminals. Because they frequently inhabit the bottom rungs of the economic ladder, immigrants are most susceptible to being drawn into crime.

The first prototype of the character Nick Romano was Mexican-American and the second and third were Polish-American. The son of an Italian immigrant, Nick is happy and blameless while his father owns a small business. When Nick's father loses the store during the Depression, the family moves to a poor section of Denver, where Nick begins to associate with tough boys who encourage him to commit petty crimes. In reform school Nick is brutalized both by guards and fellow inmates. By the time he is released and the family moves to Chicago, Nick is ready for the lessons he will learn from skid row – how to rob drunks and commit armed robbery. From his first imprisonment (at age fourteen) until his execution in the electric chair at age twenty-one, Nick is caught up in a web of circumstances from which he cannot escape.

Unlike a social scientist studying the same material, Motley informs his story with a great deal of sentiment. His diaries (1979) suggest the depth of his emotional commitment to his characters, based on actual people whom he had known well. For example, on the night he wrote the passage about Nick's execution, he cried as if a real person had died. Motley further removes the novel from the realm of social science by employing the idiom of his characters in his narration.

Although Motley had trouble finding a publisher for *Knock on Any Door,* it was an immediate popular success, selling 47,000 copies in its first three weeks in print. By 1950 350,000 copies had been sold. It was condensed in *Omnibook Magazine* (October 1947) and presented in comic-strip form by the King Features Syndicate (15 December 1947 – 20 January 1948). *Look* magazine (30 September 1947) ran a photo feature juxtaposing passages from the novel with photographs of people from the poverty-stricken neighborhood where Motley had lived during much of its composition. In June 1949 *Color* magazine featured Motley – along with such black authors as Wright, W. E. B. DuBois, and Langston Hughes – in a feature titled "America's Top Negro Authors." In 1949 the movie version of *Knock on Any Door* – with John Derek as Nick and Humphrey Bogart as his attorney – was released by Columbia Pictures.

Critics were favorably impressed with the novel. Orville Prescott, in the *New York Times* (5 May 1947), commented, "No abler recruit has joined the extreme naturalist school of fiction in a long time than Mr. Motley. The grim effectiveness of his soci-

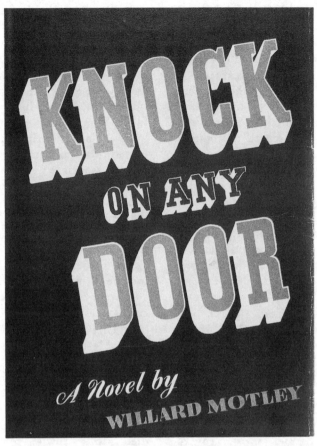

*Dust jacket for Motley's first novel, which is primarily concerned
with the effects of the penal system on young offenders*

ological reporting is beyond question and the narrative pace of his storytelling is superior to nine of ten naturalistic novels." Reviews in the *Atlantic Monthly* (July 1947), *Harper's* (July 1947), and *Saturday Review* (24 May 1947) compared *Knock on Any Door* favorably with Wright's *Native Son* (1940), and black critics welcomed the "raceless novel" as a trendsetter demonstrating that African-American novelists could treat nonracial material successfully. Critics of the 1950s, such as Walter Rideout and Blanche Gelfant, considered *Knock on Any Door* one of the major naturalistic works of its decade, Rideout listing it as one of the ten best radical novels of the 1940s. Later critics, however, have been less enthusiastic. Robert A. Bone suggests in *The Negro Novel in America* that Motley's book is derivative of Wright's *Native Son*.

Motley followed up his first book with a more technically sophisticated but less successful novel, *We Fished All Night* (1951). In this work Motley, a conscientious objector during World War II, attempts to capture the negative aftermath of the war in a panoramic novel that treats the breakdown of an older order in society. To do so he fashions three representative men who embody the ills of the postwar world.

Don Lockwood, born Chet Kosinski, is an actor in more ways than one. Involved in amateur theater before the war, the hedonistic Lockwood loses a leg in action, returns to Chicago as a war hero, and trades the stage for the wider arena of Chicago politics. Although his personality and reputation earn him a secure place in the political machine, by the end of the novel he has become disillusioned with his postwar calling. He realizes that he is being used by political boss Tom McCarren, and he regrets being unable to live up to the standards of his closest wartime friend, who died in battle.

A second major character, Aaron Levin, is a budding poet whose talent is destroyed by the war. Drafted into the army, Aaron has a nervous breakdown and deserts his unit, which is then completely wiped out by the Germans. After his court-martial and dishonorable discharge, he returns to Chicago, attempting to find some faith by which to live. After rejecting his father's Judaism, he experiments with

Catholicism and communism. When all these creeds fail him, Aaron retreats to the illusion that he is a great poet. He wanders the streets of Chicago like a Sherwood Anderson grotesque, writing his "poems" on scraps of paper.

The third victim of the war is Jim Norris, a well-adjusted, popular labor organizer in a major Chicago corporation. Unlike the other two protagonists, the patriotic Norris enlisted in the army, but he too comes back scarred by his wartime experiences. He can no longer believe in the union to which he was so strongly committed before the war. His mental disorders are indicated by sexual symptoms: first he is unable to make love to his wife, and later he finds himself irresistibly drawn to young girls who remind him of a fourteen-year-old French prostitute he encountered during the war. After being accused of the rape of an even younger girl, the tormented Jim is struck and killed by a policeman while leading a strike for the union in which he has lost all faith.

The plot and themes of *We Fished All Night* evolved out of Motley's outlines for two projected novels, and the resulting book became unwieldy in its lack of focus. Although the war and its results are the main theme of the novel, Motley also criticizes corruption in Chicago politics, examines the conflict between capital and organized labor, explodes the myth of America as a melting pot, and laments the decline of the writer in America at mid-century.

Sincere as Motley is in his antiwar sentiments, his attempts to blame World War II for the disorders of his three protagonists ring hollow. Don is a crude opportunist, even before the war, willing to exploit his family and the women who are attracted by his handsome face. His postwar manipulation of the political system is made easier by his being a visibly wounded veteran, but his character is so flawed that he probably would have come to a similar end if he had not gone to war. Similarly, Aaron is thoroughly maladjusted before he enters the army, and the strain of combat simply exacerbates an existing nervous condition. Even Jim, the all-American boy, eventually remembers that his sexual maladjustment began not with his visit to an underage French prostitute, but with his mother's punishment after she caught him playing doctor with his sister.

If Motley fails to convince the reader with his attack on war, he is more successful with his secondary themes. The Don Lockwood plot is an effective exposé of Chicago's infamous political machine: fueled by kickbacks and bribes, the politicians stuff ballot boxes, buy votes, and destroy bal-

lots in precincts where the vote is running against them. The police are in league with their illegally elected superiors, enforcing the machine's election practices rather than the law. When the time comes to pay back wealthy contributors, the fraudulent politicians grant contracts to their firms or dispatch police to break strikes at their places of business.

The theme treating the battle between capital and labor is undermined by Motley's oversimplification of the two forces. He sets up Emerson Bradley, president of the Haines Company, as a totally corrupt character who exploits his workers both economically and sexually. From his appearance to his habit of having young page girls "come to his office and entertain him in an unusual way," Bradley is the embodiment of evil. His company foists shoddy goods on unsuspecting consumers while treating employees as serfs. Meanwhile a propaganda film, *The Happy Worker,* is shown to an unwilling audience of employees. Set against Bradley is Jim Norris, whose faith in the cause of labor is as painfully unconvincing as the depiction of his antagonist. Yet in the final confrontation between strikers and police Motley creates a powerful scene and awakens sympathy for the strikers.

Motley was one of the first writers to question the notion of America as a melting pot. Immigrants such as Don's Polish grandfather or Aaron's father are not assimilated. Americans who have been in the country longer discriminate against them, and Aaron's father faces the additional stigma of being Jewish. Even as the country mobilizes against Adolf Hitler, a persistent anti-Semitism flourishes in Chicago. Motley also touches on racism directed at black people, although he dropped the idea of using Dave Wilson, an African-American, as one of the major characters.

The treatment of Aaron as misunderstood writer is less successful than the other two themes. While it is easy to respond to Aaron's boyish desire to become a writer (and to discern in his story some autobiographical elements), Aaron is drafted before he has an opportunity to develop his talent, if indeed he has one. Motley had a story to tell about the treatment suffered by a sincere writer at the hands of editors and about the effects of commercial pressure on twentieth-century American novelists, but he did not achieve it in his creation of Aaron. Nevertheless, the theme of the rejected artist, writing only for himself, has a certain appeal.

Reviewers understandably believed that *We Fished All Night* was a disappointing book from the author of *Knock on Any Door.* Although *We Fished All Night* was reviewed in the *New York Times* (16 No-

Jack Conroy, Nelson Algren, Emmett Dedmon, and Willard Motley, circa 1948

vember 1951), Prescott wrote that it was "not even minor league material compared with its predecessor" and called the effort "strictly amateur." While Prescott liked some sections of the book for their "relentless realism" and "sharply accurate glimpses of . . . various minority groups," he felt that these scattered passages could not redeem the bad writing in most of the work. Altogether, Prescott accurately viewed *We Fished All Night* as "the raw material for a novel" rather than a finished work of art.

Most critics were far less balanced in their reviews. Writing for *Commonweal* (11 January 1952), Frank Getlein called *We Fished All Night* "worthless," pointing to its intellectual oversimplification and its repetition. Reviewing the novel for the *Nation* (29 December 1951), Harvey Swados also attacked the book on intellectual grounds and objected to Don Lockwood as a cliché. In *Saturday Review* (8 December 1951) James Gray termed the book a failure, in spite of its "earnestness," because it did not "reach the mind or the heart." Only in Chicago did the book get positive reviews, and then probably more for reasons of pride in Motley as a local

writer. Robert Cromie recommended the book to readers of the *Chicago Tribune* (25 November 1951) by reminding them of Motley's previous success with *Knock on Any Door*. In the *Chicago Daily News* (21 November 1951) Van Allen Bradley called the novel a "curious admixture of strength and weakness" but said that in some ways it was "a better novel than 'Knock on Any Door.' " In spite of its ambition, *We Fished All Night* is not the equal of *Knock on Any Door*. Motley's praiseworthy attempt to grow as a novelist and produce a panoramic epic novel of the postwar period falls short. Its characters are not as well realized as Nick Romano, and the social issues it treats are oversimplified.

Soon after completing his second novel, Motley took a trip to Mexico. He bought a house near Mexico City in 1952 and lived there with an adopted son, Sergio Lopez, for the rest of his life. Although he had left his native Chicago, Motley was still concerned about its social problems, and his next novel continued to chronicle the city. As in *We Fished All Night* he attempts to employ several major characters and weave together multiple plots in *Let No Man Write My Epitaph* (1958), in which he returns to the family of his most memorable character, Nick Romano.

Let No Man Write My Epitaph treats the lives of Nick, Jr., the illegitimate son of Nick Romano and Nellie Watkins, and Nick's brother Louie, who was a baby at the time of Nick's execution. Like *Knock on Any Door,* Motley's third novel has a strong social thesis, attacking the narcotics problem in Chicago. In addition, Motley ventures for the first time into a serious and sustained examination of racial prejudice, on which he had merely touched in his two previous novels.

Nellie Watkins is a waitress who appears in the latter part of *Knock on Any Door. Let No Man Write My Epitaph* reveals that she was pregnant when she took the stand in Nick's defense. After his execution she gave birth to a child whom she named Nick Romano, Jr. Although she must raise Nick, Jr., in a tough lower-class neighborhood, Nellie attempts to bring him up carefully. Unfortunately the strains of single parenthood and overwork lead her into alcoholism, narcotics addiction, and sexual exploitation by her drug pusher, Frankie Ramponi. Nellie is helped in her child rearing by a group of self-appointed "uncles" who watch over Nick and, when he too becomes addicted to heroin, rescue him by sending him for a cure.

Louie Romano looks and sounds much like his older brother and is well on his way to a similar fate, taking part in gang activities and petty crimes. He is saved from a probable execution himself after his Aunt Rosa tells him the long-suppressed story of his brother's death in the electric chair. Louie is redeemed by this sobering news and by his love for Judy, a beautiful black woman. Judy and Louie face considerable prejudice for their interracial love affair, allowing Motley to expose racism as he had encountered it in Chicago. Although their love story is never resolved in the novel, Motley made notes for a third Romano book in which Judy and Louie would have married.

As in *Knock on Any Door* Motley emphasizes the importance of environment. Both Louie and Nick, Jr., are protected by their families from the heritage of Nick, Sr., but a hostile environment wins out and corrupts both of them. However, this time Motley relieves the tragedy of his theme by the introduction of Nick's "uncles," a Dickensian collection of colorful, often humorous characters, such as Judge Sullivan, an alcoholic whose elegant manners and language nevertheless help him to serve as a role model. The sentimentality of the scenes in which these minor characters appear weakens the effect of the tragic strands of the plot and detracts from the

unity of the novel. More successful are Motley's minor black characters, who range from the middle-class inhabitants of Judy's world to the denizens of the lower depths where black and white addicts democratically share needles.

Let No Man Write My Epitaph met with a mixed reaction. The hardbound Random House edition sold so slowly that in 1963 the publisher rewrote its contract with Motley, giving him a 10 percent royalty on sales rather than 15 percent. When the book was published as a Signet paperback, it failed to earn back Motley's advance within its first five years in print. On the other hand, the novel attracted enough attention that, two years after its publication, Columbia Pictures used it as the basis for a movie starring James Darren, Shelley Winters, Ricardo Montalban, Ella Fitzgerald, and Burl Ives. The screenplay sensationalized the gritty narcotics plot and emphasized the humorous nature of the supporting cast.

Literary reviewers were less impressed with *Let No Man Write My Epitaph* than was Hollywood. In the *New York Times Book Review* (10 August 1958) David Dempsey compared Motley's Chicago unfavorably to the city as portrayed by Algren, Saul Bellow, and James T. Farrell and barely mentioned *Knock on Any Door*. Algren wrote in the *Nation* (16 August 1958) that Motley's treatment of narcotics addiction – the subject of Algren's masterpiece, *The Man with the Golden Arm* (1949) – lacked authenticity. The anonymous reviewer for *Time* (11 August 1958) gave Motley credit for his reporting but faulted his perceived inability to transform his observations into art. Only Granville Hicks, writing for the *Saturday Review* (9 August 1958), saw strengths balancing the weaknesses. Hicks observed that, in spite of its shortcomings, *Let No Man Write My Epitaph* demonstrated the continuing viability of literary naturalism.

Setting aside his interest in Chicago, Motley expressed his affection for his adopted country, Mexico, in a lengthy nonfiction manuscript, "My House Is Your House," for which he was not able to find a publisher. He placed four chapters of the work, covering topics from food to prostitution, with *Rogue* (August, October, and December 1964; August 1965), a Chicago men's magazine. Since Motley's death a fifth chapter, a reflection on racism in the United States, has been published in *Minority Voices* (Spring 1978).

When he returned to fiction, Motley began a panoramic study of a Mexican town that becomes a popular resort. *Let Noon Be Fair* (1966) is a thesis novel that seeks to demonstrate that the United

States exploits Mexico. Internally, the country is crippled by the Catholic church, corruption, and a predatory upper class. Motley traces the decline of his fictional town, Las Casas – based on Puerto Vallarta – from a homey fishing village to a spoiled watering hole of the rich and famous. Along the way the inhabitants lose their land, their language, and their integrity. At the urging of his new publisher, Putnam, Motley emphasized the sexual exploitation of the Mexican people in an attempt to commercialize the book. Mexican boys are seduced by middle-aged American women or by aging homosexuals. Because Motley died two weeks after completing the draft manuscript of *Let Noon Be Fair,* he did not participate in the final editing of the novel.

The reviews of *Let Noon Be Fair* were uniformly negative. Motley's old friend Conroy attempted in an essay in the *Chicago Daily News* (26 February 1966) to explain away the failure by suggesting that *Let Noon Be Fair* was not the Mexican novel that Motley had wished to write. Motley, he asserted, had been typecast as a sensationalistic author and had been persuaded to write his last novel to order by a publisher interested in cashing in on a sexy best-seller. Although the *New York Times* gave the book two reviews, one in the newspaper and one in the *New York Times Book Review,* both were unfavorable. Charles Poore in the daily *Times* (24 February 1966) criticized the novel for its "stubborn emphasis on orgies," and Alexander Coleman in the *New York Times Book Review* (27 February 1966) contrasted it with one of D. H. Lawrence's vastly superior books on Mexico, *The Plumed Serpent* (1926). José Donoso in the *Saturday Review* (12 March 1966) appreciated Motley's intention to write an exposé on the corruption of Mexico but found the result "an empty carcass of the panoramic novel."

Motley died of intestinal gangrene in a Mexico City hospital on 4 March 1965. The *New York Times* (5 March 1965) obituary quoted his son, Sergio, as stating that Motley had always been proud of his strength – he had been known as the "little iron man" when he played high-school football – and hated to see doctors. But Motley's poverty was probably more of a contributing factor to his death. For some time he had been leading a precarious existence. His royalties from American publishers had been attached by the IRS because of a tax dispute, and Motley often had to live on small royalty checks from foreign editions of his works. His literary reputation, which had been so high after the publication of his first novel, suf-

fered from two factors – the decline of interest in naturalistic fiction and the rise of African-American authors who addressed black life more directly than he did.

Interest in Motley underwent a modest revival in the 1970s, partly as a result of the opening up to scholars of a large collection of his manuscripts. A biographical-critical study appeared in 1978, and an edition of Motley's diaries from the years before the publication of *Knock on Any Door* was brought out in 1979. Motley is likely to retain his place in literary history as one of the best practitioners of the "raceless novel" movement of the 1940s and 1950s, a movement that includes such other prominent African-American novelists as James Baldwin, Chester Himes, Zora Neale Hurston, Ann Petry, and Wright. *Knock on Any Door* stands as one of the last great naturalistic American novels.

References:

Craig S. Abbott, "Versions of a Best-Seller: Motley's *Knock on Any Door,*" *Papers of the Bibliographical Society of America,* 81 (1987): 175–185;

Abbott and Kay Van Mol, "The Willard Motley Papers at NIU," *Resources for American Literary Study,* 7 (Spring 1977): 3–26;

Robert A. Bone, *The Negro Novel in America,* revised edition (New Haven: Yale University Press, 1965), pp. 178–180;

Robert E. Fleming, "The First Nick Romano: The Origins of *Knock on Any Door,*" in *Mid America II* (East Lansing, Mich.: Midwestern Press, 1975), pp. 80–87;

Fleming, *Willard Motley* (Boston: Twayne, 1978);

Fleming, "The Willard Motley Nobody Knows: Reflections on Racism in 'My House Is Your House,'" *Minority Voices,* 2 (Spring 1978): 1–10;

James R. Giles, "Willard Motley's Concept of 'Style' and 'Material': Some Comments Based Upon the Motley Collection at the University of Wisconsin," *Studies in Black Literature,* 4 (Spring 1973): 4–6;

Giles and Jerome Klinkowitz, "The Emergence of Willard Motley in Black American Literature," *Negro American Literature Forum,* 6 (Summer 1972): 31–34;

Giles and N. Jill Weyant, "The Short Fiction of Willard Motley," *Negro American Literature Forum,* 9 (Spring 1975): 3–10;

M. E. Grenander, "Criminal Responsibility in *Native Son* and *Knock on Any Door*," *American Literature,* 49 (May 1977): 221–233;

Thomas D. Jarrett, "Sociology and Imagery in a Great American Novel," *English Journal,* 38 (November 1949): 518–520;

Klinkowitz, Giles, and John T. O'Brien, "The Willard Motley Papers at the University of Wisconsin," *Resources for American Literary Study,* 2 (Autumn 1972): 218–273;

Klinkowitz and Karen Wood, "The Making and Unmaking of *Knock on Any Door*," *Proof,* 3 (1973): 121–137;

Ann Rayson, "Prototypes for Nick Romano of *Knock on Any Door*," *Negro American Literature Forum,* 8 (Fall 1974): 248–251;

Walter Rideout, *The Radical Novel in the United States, 1900–1954* (Cambridge, Mass.: Harvard University Press, 1965);

Alfred Weissgarber, "Willard Motley and the Sociological Novel," *Studi Americani,* 7 (1961): 299–309;

Weyant, "Lyrical Experimentation in Willard Motley's Mexican Novel: *Let Noon Be Fair*," *Negro American Literature Forum,* 10 (Spring 1976): 95–99;

Weyant, "Willard Motley's Pivotal Novel: *Let No Man Write My Epitaph*," *Black American Literature Forum,* 11 (Summer 1977): 56–61;

Charles Wood, "The Adventure Manuscript: New Light on Willard Motley's Naturalism," *Negro American Literature Forum,* 6 (Summer 1972): 35–38.

Papers:

The largest holding of Motley's papers is the Motley Collection in the library of Northern Illinois University, DeKalb. It consists of letters, notes, clippings, journals, and early manuscripts of *Knock on Any Door, We Fished All Night,* and *Let Noon Be Fair* as well as unpublished manuscripts of short stories and "My House Is Your House." The Motley Collection in the library of the University of Wisconsin – Madison, contains letters, notes, clippings, and some manuscripts. The Beinecke Library at Yale University has most of the typescript of *Knock on Any Door,* consisting of 1,078 pages (the first 87 pages are missing).

Leslie Marmon Silko

(5 March 1948 –   )

William M. Clements
Arkansas State University

BOOKS: *Laguna Woman: Poems by Leslie Silko* (Greenfield Center, N.Y.: Greenfield Review Press, 1974);
Ceremony (New York: Viking, 1977);
Storyteller (New York: Seaver, 1981);
Almanac of the Dead: A Novel (New York & London: Simon & Schuster, 1991);
Sacred Water (Tucson: Flood Plain Press, 1993).

OTHER: "The Man to Send Rain Clouds," "Yellow Woman," "Tony's Story," "Uncle Tony's Goat," "A Geronimo Story," "Bravura," and "From Humaweepi the Warrior Priest," in *The Man to Send Rain Clouds: Contemporary Stories by American Indians,* edited by Kenneth Rosen (New York: Viking, 1974), pp. 3–8, 33–45, 69–78, 93–100, 128–144, 149–154, 161–168;
"Language and Literature from a Pueblo Indian Perspective," in *English Literature: Opening Up the Canon,* edited by Leslie A. Fiedler and Houston A. Baker, Jr. (Baltimore: Johns Hopkins University Press, 1981), pp. 54–72.

SELECTED PERIODICAL PUBLICATIONS – UNCOLLECTED: "An Old-Time Indian Attack Conducted in Two Parts," *Yardbird Reader,* 5 (1976): 77–84;
"Landscape, History, and the Pueblo Imagination," *Antaeus,* 51 (1986): 83–94.

Leslie Marmon Silko (photograph by Gus Nitsche)

Even before the publication of her novel *Ceremony* (1977), Leslie Marmon Silko had become recognized as one of the preeminent figures in what Kenneth Lincoln calls the Native American Renaissance – the literary movement that began in the late 1960s among American Indian writers who draw on their tribal verbal art heritages to inform their poetry, fiction, and nonfiction. In the early 1970s Silko was perhaps this movement's most prominent writer of short fiction, and she had also published some highly regarded poems. *Ceremony* confirmed her position among contemporary Native American writers, and subsequent books, especially *Storyteller* (1981), have not disappointed her readers. Though not as favorably received as her earlier works, Silko's most recent novel, *Almanac of the Dead* (1991), continues to develop some of the themes that have characterized her poetry and fiction.

Leslie Marmon Silko was born 5 March 1948 in Albuquerque, New Mexico, and grew up in Old Laguna, a pueblo some forty miles to the west. Her mixed-blood lineage reflects both the tensions and the strengths that have affected life at this community since at least the late nineteenth century – forces of continuity and adaptability that figure into Silko's fiction. In 1868 Walter G. Marmon came from Ohio to Laguna to survey the pueblo boundary. He remained in the community, becoming a government schoolteacher in 1871. The following year his brother, Robert G. Marmon, Silko's great-grandfather, settled at Laguna as a surveyor and trader. His second wife was Marie Anaya, a Laguna, who had attended the Indian boarding school in Carlisle, Pennsylvania. She later lived next door to Silko, who called her Grandma A'mooh, providing the future novelist with an important link to traditional Laguna ways.

Both Walter and Robert Marmon served terms as pueblo governor during the 1870s, when the three-hundred-year-old synthesis of traditional Laguna spirituality and Roman Catholicism was facing challenges from Protestant missionaries. As Protestants, the Marmons were agents of change and were partially responsible for the destruction of the pueblo's largest kivas (sites of traditional worship activities) and for undercutting the Catholic influence. Some Laguna traditionalists even abandoned the pueblo at the time, creating a spiritual vacuum that remained until some ceremonies began to be revived in the mid twentieth century.

The ability of the Marmons – recent Euramerican arrivals who attained political power in the pueblo – to influence community affairs, religious and secular, reflected the general adaptability of Laguna culture. The pueblo's location on a major route west – one that later became U.S. Highway 66 – probably affected its receptivity to external influences, including that of the Marmons. The presence of Anglo ranchers in the area beginning in the mid 1800s and the discovery of uranium on pueblo lands a century later also ensured that contact with the mainstreams of Euramerican culture would contribute to Laguna affairs.

At the same time, though, traditional ways have endured, and, despite her ancestors' negative impact on some aspects of Laguna tradition, Silko became aware of her American Indian heritage during her childhood. In addition to Grandma A'mooh, an important figure in conveying Laguna culture to Silko was Susie Reyes Marmon, the wife of her grandfather Henry Marmon's brother. Having attended both Carlisle Indian School and Dickinson College, Aunt Susie taught school at Laguna during the 1920s but remained committed to the community's oral tradition, which she passed on to Silko.

Among other family members who particularly influenced Silko were Henry Marmon, whose aspirations to design automobiles were stifled by early-twentieth-century preconceptions about the career possibilities open to Native Americans; Francesca Stagner Marmon (Grandma Lillie, Henry Marmon's wife), whose mother had given over Francesca's rearing to a Navajo woman; and Silko's father, Lee H. Marmon, a highly regarded photographer whose work appears in *Storyteller*. The most important lesson they provided Silko was their emphasis on the forces of continuity and adaptability in Laguna traditional culture – forces their position in Laguna society and that of their Marmon ancestors have demonstrated.

Silko began her formal education at the local Bureau of Indian Affairs School. After the fifth grade she moved to Catholic schools in Albuquerque, where she also later attended the University of New Mexico, receiving a B.A. in English in 1969. She then began law school in a program designed to provide Native Americans with Indian lawyers. Silko taught two years at Navajo Community College in Tsaile, Arizona, and spent another two years in Ketchikan, Alaska, where *Ceremony* was written. She taught at the University of New Mexico and then at the University of Arizona. In 1981 Silko received a five-year MacArthur Foundation grant, which provided her with the opportunity to work on *Almanac of the Dead*. She has also received a National Endowment for the Humanities Grant in order to make films based on Laguna oral traditions. Silko has been divorced twice and has two sons, Robert William Chapman and Cazimir Silko.

The predominant, recurring themes in Silko's writing derive in large part from her family background and her ancestors' participation in community affairs, as well as from the continuing nature of Laguna interaction with Euramerican culture. For while Silko consistently draws on Laguna tradition, especially its storytelling, she recognizes that the tradition's dynamism is an essential component of its strength. Instead of focusing on a nostalgic past when Laguna ways were unaffected by Euramerican contact – a situation that, in fact, has not existed at the pueblo for several centuries – Silko shows how the Laguna heritage can and must adapt to the twentieth century. While Laguna culture remains distinct and viable, it does so through its flexibility and ability to incorporate and shape outside influences. Just as Laguna society had incorporated the Marmon family, so the rituals, customs, patterns of storytelling, and other aspects of culture have survived by adapting to and exploiting the modern world.

Silko's first important publication was the short story "The Man to Send Rain Clouds," written while she was a student at the University of New Mexico and published in the *New Mexico Quarterly* (Winter–Spring 1969). Stemming, like much of her work, from an actual incident at Laguna, the story treats the tensions between the Catholic Church and Laguna religious tradition. Though they rely primarily on traditional approaches in their funeral preparations, relatives of a deceased Laguna elder manage to involve the parish priest in the ceremony. While he realizes that sprinkling holy water on the old man's grave does not have the significance for the mourners that he would wish, the priest performs the ritual anyway. According to Laguna belief, the act encourages the dead man's spirit to return in the form of rain clouds to water the arid New Mexico landscape.

The integration of compartmentalized Native American and Euramerican religious forms and values that informs this story parallels the family and community contexts in which Silko grew up. As her first published work, the story anticipates one of the important themes that has dominated her poetry and fiction: the necessity for adaptability in the presence of cultural dynamism. Her most successful works have continued to demonstrate how people from Laguna, and occasionally from other Native American communities, are able to retain the values inculcated by their heritages while incorporating and exploiting a Euramerican culture that may be dominant only in appearance.

When Kenneth Rosen edited a 1974 anthology of short fiction by contemporary American Indian writers, he used the title of Silko's story as the main title for his book. *The Man to Send Rain Clouds* includes six other pieces by Silko, whose stories comprise about one third of the anthology. The most widely known and artistically successful of these are "Yellow Woman," which updates a Laguna tradition about the abduction of mortal women by spiritual beings; "Tony's Story," in which a young Laguna boy perceives an abusive highway patrolman in terms of traditional Pueblo witchcraft beliefs and responds accordingly to the officer's brutality; "Uncle Tony's Goat," an account of the misadventures of a misanthropic barnyard animal similar to stories Silko had heard from her relatives at Laguna; and "A Geronimo Story," in which the Laguna Regulars — a group of scouts who accompany a contingent of the U.S. Cavalry — pursues an Apache warrior, turning the outing into a holiday. In all these stories Silko's ties to her cultural heritage are foregrounded, but she clearly recognizes — in fact, celebrates — the ways in which that heritage has successively adjusted to the nineteenth and twentieth centuries.

When Rosen's anthology brought Silko's short fiction to general attention in 1974, it was one among three important events of that year in Silko's career. Another was the publication of *Laguna Woman,* a collection of her poetry. Like her short stories, Silko's poems reflect her roots in Laguna culture and the landscape of the Southwest. They also reiterate her theme of the adaptability and dynamism of Native American traditions. A poem exemplifying this theme is "Toe'osh: A Laguna Coyote Story," which she dedicates to Simon Ortiz, a writer from nearby Ácoma Pueblo. The poem unifies a series of eight sketchy stories, some from oral tradition, dealing with Coyote the Trickster and others and showing how modern Lagunas and other Native Americans have outsmarted Euramericans by drawing on devices similar to those used by the mythic figure. Other poems recall experiences in the mountains and canyons of western New Mexico and emphasize the spiritual associations that many of the region's landmarks continue to have for Lagunas and other American Indians of the region.

Also in 1974 Silko's short story "Lullaby" was published in both the *Chicago Review* and *Yardbird Reader.* The story treats an elderly Navajo couple who live near Laguna, portraying their conflicts with Euramerican authority. However, instead of absolutely condemning the latter, Silko shows that some of the tension arises from differences in cultural values, which neither the Navajos nor the Euramericans fully understand. Though the story ends with the death of the old man, it also reaffirms life and the potency of tradition as his widow sings a lullaby she had learned from her grandmother. "Lullaby" was selected for inclusion in *The Best American Short Stories of 1975.*

In 1976 Silko published a brief, but important, essay in *Yardbird Reader.* In "An Old-Time Indian Attack Conducted in Two Parts" she articulates the frustration that many Native Americans had been experiencing over the appropriation of their traditions by non-Indian writers. Criticizing literary works such as *Laughing Boy* (a 1929 novel about Navajo life by New Englander Oliver La Farge), the novels of William Eastlake, and the poetry of Jerome Rothenberg and Gary Snyder (whose Pulitzer Prize–winning *Turtle Island* [1974] merits the entire second part of Silko's attack), she identifies two implicitly racist assumptions that permit such works to be produced. One of these assumptions holds that Euramerican cultural superiority allows them to master the essence of Native American worldviews so effectively that they can write from an Indian point of view. The other racist assumption refers to the belief that oral materials gathered from Native American storytellers and singers and published by ethnologists have become public property, which Euramerican writers can revise and present as they choose. Essentially a critique of what Geary Hobson calls "white shamanism," Silko's piece was a timely reminder that imperialism remained vital, even if it was now directed at American Indian art rather than land and economic resources.

Silko's early poems and short stories have received considerable attention, several of the latter (especially "The Man to Send Rain Clouds" and "Lullaby") being included in anthologies of contemporary American literature and women's writing as well as collections focusing exclusively on the work of American Indian authors. But an important artistic milestone for Silko – and, in fact, a landmark in the Native American Renaissance – was the publication of *Ceremony*. Her first novel, *Ceremony* has been republished in paperback several times and is one of the most widely known works by a Native American writer. Similar in plot to *House Made of Dawn* (1968) – a novel by Kiowa author N. Scott Momaday set at Jemez Pueblo, not far from Laguna – Silko's narrative concerns the attempts by a Laguna veteran of World War II to come to terms with a variety of conflicts rooted in his mixed-blood background, his wartime experiences, and the changing culture of Laguna in the late 1940s.

Written during a two-year residence in Alaska, the longest period that Silko has spent away from the Southwest, *Ceremony* represents a significant achievement. Silko skillfully interweaves poetic renderings of Laguna mythology with the story of Tayo, the novel's protagonist, to show the ways in which the values and forces represented in her tribal oral heritage continue to figure even in the highly acculturated pueblo of the mid twentieth century. Tayo comes to terms with his sense of alienation and guilt by recognizing how values that have been central to Laguna culture for generations continue – albeit with necessary changes and adaptations – to provide a way of defining his place in the world. He experiences healing by becoming one with myth. Tayo's alienation – a psychological and spiritual state similar to that of many characters in the works of contemporary American Indian novelists – stems originally from his mixed-blood status, a condition that isolates him from both mainstream Euramerican and Laguna cultures; he is a "breed," according to the terminology used by many Native Americans.

Born of a now-dead Laguna mother who had lived as a prostitute in Gallup, New Mexico, and a Euramerican father, he has grown up in the family of his mother's sister (Auntie), a self-righteous woman who will not let Tayo forget his mixed-blood genealogy. Others in the household include Tayo's grandmother, who still adheres to traditional Laguna ways; Josiah, his uncle and Auntie's brother, whose dreams of wealth through raising range cattle also reflect a continuing commitment to tradition; and Rocky, his cousin and Auntie's son, who has become devoted to mainstream Euramerican values during his schooling in nearby Albuquerque. From Auntie's perspective Rocky represents the family's future, and she consistently stresses Tayo's subservient status to her own son. Silko shows this attitude through Auntie's allowing Tayo to become involved in Josiah's cattle-raising schemes, an old-fashioned pursuit that Auntie would deem inappropriate for the progressive Rocky.

Despite Auntie's attitudes Tayo and Rocky are devoted friends who join the military together and are ultimately sent to the Philippines. There Rocky dies, and Tayo returns to Laguna after the war with a load of guilt that stems from a variety of sources: his failure to protect Rocky, even though Auntie had admonished him that this was his responsibility; the death of Josiah, which occurs while Tayo is away, and the loss of his cattle herd, which has wandered away; the sins of his mother, which Auntie will not let him forget; and the drought plaguing the New Mexico desert, a situation Tayo feels he has caused by trying to pray away the soaking, tropical precipitation of the Philippine rain forest. Moreover, Tayo suffers from his awareness of the loss of traditional values at Laguna, attributed to the apparent outside force of witchery.

Silko's identification of these sources of Tayo's guilt suggests the complexity of contextual factors that inform the novel. Not only does the "survivor guilt" recognized by modern psychology contribute to Tayo's condition, but traditional Laguna beliefs about the interrelatedness of all life and nature also affect his sense of responsibility for the ills that are afflicting his family and the entire countryside. Silko also portrays some of the ways that American Indians have frequently dealt with guilt arising from such sources and with the alienation brought on by the loss of their traditional cultures from Euramerican influences. Tayo's contemporaries, other Lagunas who have returned to the pueblo after military service, react to these problems by engaging in a round of drinking, violence, promiscuity, and boasting about the martial and sexual conquests that they achieved while in uniform. Though Tayo is tempted to join them in using these means to escape from his guilt and alienation, he does not fully yield to them.

He has not, however, received much help from conventional healing methods, either those of the Euramerican world to which he was subjected in veterans' hospitals after returning from the Philippines or those of the traditional Laguna practices embodied in a medicine man named Ku'oosh, whom his grandmother arranges for him to see. Healing begins for Tayo only when he contacts Betonie, a part-Navajo healer who lives near Gallup in a dwelling furnished with materials from both Native American and Euramerican cultures. Like Tayo a breed who has experienced life outside the tribal environment, Betonie understands the necessity of change. But he stresses that change means adaptation, not rejection of the past.

This important theme of the novel, one that recurs throughout Silko's work, finds expression both in the failed healing methods – the Euramerican approach, which takes no notice of the Laguna heritage, and Ku'oosh's traditional approach, which remains trapped in a static past – and in the ultimate success of Betonie's prescription. For Betonie recommends that Tayo recommit himself to Laguna values, as embodied in timeless mythology, while recognizing that life in the twentieth century offers new challenges and rewards.

Betonie's emphasis on the significance of myth reinforces another important theme in *Ceremony* and Silko's other works – the importance of stories and storytelling. The account of Tayo's healing, which comprises the book's second half, involves his enacting the traditional sacred story that Silko interweaves throughout the novel. Tayo returns to sacred time, the setting for myth, by ascending Mount Taylor, a landmark of spiritual significance for Lagunas and most other Native peoples of western New Mexico. There he finds Josiah's lost cattle and comes into contact with Tseh, a woman whose love for Tayo and obvious ties with the sacredness of nature contribute to his restoration. Renewed and reharmonized with the cosmos, Tayo descends from the holy mountain with the fundamentals of spiritual health restored.

The novel's climactic scene occurs at an abandoned uranium mine where Tayo has hidden to escape from his former friends, the other war veterans, who are now seeking to kill him. They seem to represent the loss of values at Laguna; they seem to be the witches. As Tayo watches in horror, they torture and kill one of their number, and he feels bound to try to stop them. But he senses that such an act would be self-destructive, that the witchery that appears to be embodied in others actually lurks within himself, waiting for the opportunity to emerge, and that the recommitment to holiness that he has made on Mount Taylor through living in myth requires him not to participate in their violence. The novel ends with Tayo's revealing to Laguna elders the lesson he has learned. His grandmother comments that what has occurred represents a timeless pattern, rooted in tradition and updated only to take into account contemporary specifics.

The achievement of *Ceremony* in emphasizing the enduring powers of restoration in an American Indian heritage, especially the role of storytelling that artists such as Silko continue, brought the novel generally favorable reviews. Though some reviewers sniped at the book's occasional verbosity and loss of precise focus, comparing it disadvantageously to Silko's tightly structured short stories, even these critics, for the most part, admired the novel's narrative power and its iteration of the continuing significance of Native culture. *Ceremony* also clearly established Silko as one of the most important figures in the Native American literary Renaissance, second only perhaps to Momaday, whose *House Made of Dawn* won the Pulitzer Prize for fiction in 1969. A significant body of critical scholarship regarding *Ceremony* has appeared since 1977, most of which has placed it within the traditions of Native American storytelling, of which Silko views her work as an extension.

Silko's growing prominence received a further boost from the publication of *Storyteller*. Impossible to categorize in terms of conventional Euramerican literary genres, this book affirms the role of the storyteller as preserver of cultural values, as contributor to communal and individual spiritual health, and as definer of the cosmos. Though rooted clearly in Silko's Laguna experience (some critics, in fact, have considered autobiography to be the most appropriate generic designation of *Storyteller*), the themes of the book transcend the particulars of time and place. In fact, she dedicates it to "the storytellers as far back as memory goes and to the telling which continues and through which they all live and we with them." One of Silko's purposes in *Storyteller* is to stress the continuity of her literary work with the oral tradition that she had absorbed from Grandma Am'ooh, Aunt Susie, and others at Laguna during the 1950s. Verbal and photographic portraits of both these ancestors – and of many other members of Silko's family – appear in the book, for it is a work that focuses specifically on her family heritage and on the Laguna oral literary heritage as well as more generally on the process of storytelling in a variety of media.

Storyteller brings together much of Silko's previously published work, both short fiction from

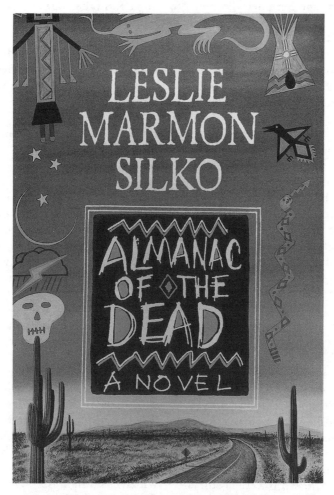

*Dust jacket for Silko's 1991 novel, in which the discovery of
apocalyptic prophecies underscores the theme of a unified tribal
movement to control North America*

Rosen's anthology and elsewhere and poems from *Laguna Woman*. The book also includes nonfictional vignettes of her life at Laguna and some poems and short stories written since *The Man to Send Rain Clouds* and *Laguna Woman*. The title story, originally published in *Puerto del Sol* (Fall 1975) reflects the themes of the entire work – those already familiar to readers of Silko's poetry and fiction.

Set in Alaska – and consequently Silko's only major work of fiction without a Southwestern setting – "Storyteller" deals with an orphaned Inuit girl who lives with an elderly couple. After the old woman dies, Euramerican oil drillers living in a nearby community sexually exploit the girl, but she eventually lures the village storekeeper, who is responsible for her parents' death, onto the ice of a frozen river, where he breaks through and drowns. Meanwhile, the old man with whom she continues to live is telling a story about a polar bear's relentless stalking of a hunter in the snow- and ice-covered wilderness. Concurrently, the implacable cold of the Arctic winter is gradually overpowering the futile attempts by "civilization" to deal with the harsh environment. Clearly, the girl's revenge assumes mythic or legendary form as it parallels the actions of the bear in the old man's story. Though a product of a seemingly moribund culture, the story continues to exert a force on the present. And that story is founded in the seasonal cycle, the polar bear's destruction of the hunter being just as inevitable as the coming of winter cold.

Though it brings together pieces, many of which were published separately in their original incarnations, *Storyteller* is far more than a "collected works" volume. As she does with traditional myth and her own narrative in *Ceremony*, Silko creates an integrated whole in *Storyteller* by interweaving retellings of stories from the Laguna oral heritage with family stories, photographs, and her poetry and fiction. She has cited the example of John Cage's *A Year from Monday* (1967) as a parallel for her arrangement. All the material in *Storyteller* works together to demonstrate continuity and change.

Silko's short story "Yellow Woman," for example, is juxtaposed with presentations of traditional legends of abductions of women by spiritual beings, thus showing that these legends have retained their vitality. Her short story "Uncle Tony's Goat" parallels accounts of legendary roosters about which her family told tales, and it thus becomes an extension of the heritage of family storytelling with which Silko grew up. The trickster figure Coyote, from Laguna and other tribal traditions, has modern relatives who appear in Silko's poetry as well as in the figure of the Laguna womanizer who tricks some Hopi women into letting him feel their thighs in the short story "Coyote Holds a Full House in His Hand."

While the theme of continuity and change may be evident in the individual pieces, it is shown with utmost clarity through the ways in which Silko forges the interconnections among various forms, genres, and media. Moreover, she clearly sees herself as a representative of the archetypal figure of the book's title. Like Grandma Am'ooh and Aunt Susie, like the generations of verbal artists who have performed myths and legends of Coyote and Yellow Woman, like her father (whose photographs appear in the volume), Silko herself is a tribal storyteller who extends an oral tradition into a modern medium, written English. She reinforces this point in "Language and Literature from a Pueblo Indian Perspective," a talk she delivered to the English Institute in 1979 and which was published in 1981.

Though not as widely read as *Ceremony, Storyteller* received an equally positive response from reviewers, many of whom, though, were unsure what to make of the book. Generic categorization has continued to be a concern of some commentators, but others have addressed such matters as how the book's structure and its successful use of various media contribute to Silko's celebration of the continuing role of storytelling in Laguna life and in other contexts.

A useful companion piece to both *Ceremony* and *Storyteller* is Silko's essay "Landscape, History, and the Pueblo Imagination" (1986). An overview of some important components of Pueblo thought, the essay provides essential information on storytelling and on the way in which place figures into oral tradition. Silko stresses the centrality of story to Pueblo experience, relating how people at La-

guna and other pueblos perceive themselves as part of a continuing story that begins with their primordial ancestors' emergence from the fourth world into this world. Acknowledging this perception is what restores Tayo to health in *Ceremony*. In the essay Silko also shows how specific features of the terrain inform storytelling. Knowledge of the landscape and the communal processes of oral narration, which her work especially in *Storyteller* continues, reinforce one another.

Anne Wright's edition of letters exchanged between her husband, poet James Wright, and Silko between 1978 and 1980 was published in 1986. *The Delicacy and Strength of Lace* presents an epistolary friendship that began when James Wright, who had met Silko briefly when she gave a reading in Michigan, wrote to express his appreciation for *Ceremony*. Silko responded to his gracious letter, and for the next couple of years they wrote one another regularly. Silko was putting *Storyteller* together at the time, so some insights into what lies behind this book emerge from the correspondence. But she also treats personal concerns – her life in the Tucson mountains and the loss of a child-custody case, for example – and the older Wright served somewhat as a mentor, both professionally and personally. The correspondence ends with Wright's death in March 1980, a couple of months after Silko visited him in a New York City hospital, only the second time the two met face-to-face. The letters, some of which contain material that Silko uses in *Storyteller*, document mutual warmth and respect between two artists who forged a personal relationship based initially on their shared artistry.

Some of Silko's readers expressed disappointment in *Almanac of the Dead*, written partially under the auspices of the five-year MacArthur Foundation grant she received in 1981 but not published until a decade later. A sprawling novel of more than seven hundred pages, *Almanac of the Dead* provided Silko with challenges she had not dealt with previously – particularly the management of literally dozens of characters and the projection of strident ethnic militancy – without losing a sense of aesthetic purpose. Though she may not have been totally successful in meeting either of these challenges, the book has many interesting, compelling features, especially its delineation of individual characters and the scenes and episodes set in Tucson, where Silko lived during most of the book's composition.

The title *Almanac of the Dead* refers to a set of notebooks bequeathed in the nineteenth century to Yoeme, a Yaqui Indian. One of her granddaughters, Lecha, a television talk show psychic now living in a heavily guarded compound near Tucson, wants to decipher these notebooks, which contain traditional Native American history and apocalyptic prophecies of a unified movement of tribal peoples designed to resume their control of North America. She attempts to do so with the help of Seese, who has come to Tucson from San Diego, California, in hopes that Lecha's psychic powers can locate her kidnapped child.

The scenes in the Tucson compound, which also affords a base for drug- and gun-smuggling operations, provide only one setting for the action in this complex novel. Another major center of plot development in the book is Tuxtla Gutiérrez, in Chiapas, the southernmost and most Indian state in Mexico, where Menardo Panson, a mestizo who has made a fortune through the drug and gun trades, lives in lavish, repressive splendor. Menardo serves as foil to a revolutionary army that is being organized in central Mexico to march northward to reclaim tribal lands, part of the apocalypse foretold in Yoeme's notebooks.

These principal narrative threads – the deciphering of Yoeme's notebooks and the preparations of the revolutionary army – take place against a panorama of other plot lines and imagery that stress a recurrent point: North America as dominated by Euramericans has become a place of consummate corruption, but it will ultimately be retaken by the tribal peoples from whom it was stolen. Consequently, Silko presents an encyclopedic portrayal of perversions, mostly sexual and violent in nature, to illustrate what Euramerican influence has produced: child pornography, bestiality, and drug abuse, to name only a few. Even those Native American characters who have been corrupted by Euramerican influences commit these sins. But it is all to end soon as the age-old prophecies in the Almanac of the Dead work themselves out so that tribal values may be reasserted.

Both the bleakness and the radical hope depicted in the novel find expression in Sterling, the principal Laguna character. When the reader first encounters him, Sterling is working as a gardener at Lecha's compound after having been exiled from Laguna for revealing sacred secrets to outsiders. He has experienced the corrupting influence of Euramerican values. Before the novel has ended, though, Sterling becomes reintegrated with the sacred forces of his ancestral heritage. His sense of traditional values is restored as he awaits the inevitable apocalypse, but only by rejecting the influences that have tainted him.

Read against Ceremony and many of Silko's other works, which view cultural blending as a force that strengthens rather than debilitates, the emphasis in Almanac of the Dead on the virtually inevitable corruption that stems from Native contact with Euramerican ways and the necessity of rejecting those ways to recapture true spirituality seems jarring. At the same time, though, there are continuities among this novel and Silko's earlier works. A significant example is the emphasis on traditional story as a paradigm for contemporary and future behavior. The Indians in Mexico and the Southwest who are setting the stage for tribal recovery of the North American continent are, like Tayo in Ceremony, following the patterns of mythology, particularly as sacred stories have been preserved in Yoeme's notebooks. Traditional patterns and motifs involving heroic twinship and serpent power, for example, inform the impending resurgence of tribal peoples.

Some critics probably responded negatively to Almanac of the Dead because of its graphic brutality and bitter tone. Others got beyond these features and suggested that, while the book has many scenes, episodes, and descriptions of real power, they often become buried in many less successful sections. Silko's use of so many characters in so many different settings (mostly in the Southwest and Mexico yet actually stretching from South America to Alaska) seems to generate confusion. Many of the plotlines remain unresolved and produce loose ends with little overt relevance to the novel's central themes. But Silko's reason for including so much in the novel may be to reinforce the imagery of Euramerican perversity. For many readers the result, though, is loss of focus. While Almanac of the Dead has been reviewed in many major periodicals, it has not yet received much attention from scholarly commentators, a situation that will surely change as they begin to assess this novel's place in the body of Silko's work.

The most recent addition to that corpus is Sacred Water (1993), a collection of autobiographical vignettes relating to experience (her own, her family's, Laguna society's, and Native Americans') with water in the arid Southwest. Like Storyteller, this book exploits visual as well as written images as Silko juxtaposes on facing pages verbal pictures with relevant graphic designs. Moreover, Silko has assumed control of the physical production of this book, which is published under her own imprint, Flood Plain Press, and she assembles, numbers, and binds every copy by hand.

Although it is too early to assess the general impact of Sacred Water or, in fact, Almanac of the Dead on the direction that Silko's work is taking (she has a two-book contract with Simon and Schuster), it remains obvious that her poetry and prose – both fiction and nonfiction – represent some of the most stimulating writing produced by a Native American author in the late twentieth century. And even without the ethnic label Silko's work deserves the attention of readers who wish to explore the ways in which a literary tradition, emerging from orally performed verbal art, has maintained its ties to that art while utilizing many of the devices of written literature. Silko's principal achievement is the novel *Ceremony,* but to single out that or any of her other works ignores the thematic and methodological continuities that recur throughout her poetry, short fiction, nonfiction, and novels.

Letters:

The Delicacy and Strength of Lace: Letters Between Leslie Marmon Silko and James Wright, edited by Anne Wright (Saint Paul, Minn.: Graywolf Press, 1986).

Interviews:

Lawrence J. Evers and Dennis W. Carr, "A Conversation with Leslie Marmon Silko," *Sun Tracks: An American Indian Literary Magazine,* 3 (Fall 1976): 28–33;

James Fitzgerald and John Hudak, "Leslie Silko: Storyteller," *Persona* (1980): 21–38;

Dexter Fisher, "Stories and Their Tellers: A Conversation with Leslie Marmon Silko," in *The Third Woman: Minority Women Writers of the United States* (Boston: Houghton Mifflin, 1980), pp. 18–23;

Elaine Jahner, "The Novel and Oral Tradition: An Interview with Leslie Marmon Silko," *Book Forum,* 5, no. 3 (1981): 383–388;

Per Seyersted, "Two Interviews with Leslie Marmon Silko," *American Studies in Scandinavia,* 13 (1981): 17–33;

Kim Barnes, "A Leslie Marmon Silko Interview," *Journal of Ethnic Studies,* 13, no. 4 (1986): 83–105;

Laura Coltelli, "Leslie Marmon Silko," in *Winged Words: American Indian Writers Speak* (Lincoln: University of Nebraska Press, 1990), pp. 135–153.

References:

Paula Gunn Allen, "The Feminine Landscape of Leslie Marmon Silko's *Ceremony,*" in *Studies in American Indian Literature,* edited by Allen (New York: Modern Language Association, 1983), pp. 127–133;

Judith A. Antell, "Momaday, Welch, and Silko: Expressing the Feminine Principle through Male Alienation," *American Indian Quarterly,* 12, no. 3 (1988): 213–220;

Peter G. Beidler, "Animals and Theme in *Ceremony,*" *American Indian Quarterly,* 5, no. 1 (1979): 13–18;

Robert C. Bell, "Circular Design in *Ceremony,*" *American Indian Quarterly,* 5, no. 1 (1979): 47–62;

Edith Blicksilver, "Traditionalism vs. Modernity: Leslie Silko on American Indian Women," *Southwest Review,* 64, no. 2 (1979): 149–160;

Linda Danielson, "*Storyteller:* Grandmother's Spider Web," *Journal of the Southwest,* 30, no. 3 (1988): 325–355;

Danielson, "The Storytellers in *Storyteller,*" *Studies in American Indian Literatures,* 1, no. 2 (1989): 21–31;

Elizabeth N. Evasdaughter, "Leslie Marmon Silko's *Ceremony:* Healing Ethnic Hatred by Mixed Breed Laughter," *MELUS,* 15, no. 1 (1988): 83–95;

Reyes Garcia, "Senses of Place in *Ceremony,*" *MELUS,* 10, no. 4 (1983): 37–48;

Bernard A. Hirsch, "'The Telling Which Continues': Oral Tradition and the Written Word in Leslie Marmon Silko's *Storyteller,*" *American Indian Quarterly,* 12, no. 1 (1988): 1–26;

Geary Hobson, "The Rise of the White Shaman as a New Version of Cultural Imperialism," in *The Remembered Earth: An Anthology of Contemporary Native American Literature,* edited by Hobson (Albuquerque: University of New Mexico Press, 1980), pp. 100–108;

Dennis Hoilman, "'A World Made of Stories': An Interpretation of Leslie Silko's *Ceremony,*" *South Dakota Review,* 17, no. 4 (1979): 54–66;

Elaine Jahner, "An Act of Attention: Event Structure in *Ceremony,*" *American Indian Quarterly,* 5, no. 1 (1979): 37–46;

Arnold Krupat, "The Dialogic of Silko's *Storyteller,*" in *Narrative Chance: Postmodern Discourse on Native American Indian Literatures,* edited by Gerald A. Vizenor (Albuquerque: University of New Mexico Press, 1989), pp. 69–90;

Toby C. S. Langen, "*Storyteller* as Hopi Basket," *Studies in American Indian Literatures,* 5, no. 1 (1993): 7–24;

Charles A. Larson, *American Indian Fiction* (Albuquerque: University of New Mexico Press, 1978), pp. 150–161;

Kenneth Lincoln, *Native American Renaissance* (Berkeley: University of California Press, 1983), pp. 222–250;

Paul H. Lorenz, "The Other Story of Leslie Marmon Silko's 'Storyteller,' " *South Central Review,* 8, no. 4 (1991): 59–75;

Ambrose Lucero, "For the People: Leslie Silko's *Storyteller,*" *Minority Voices,* 5, no. 1–2 (1981): 1–10;

Kathleen Manley, "Leslie Marmon Silko's Use of Color in *Ceremony,*" *Southern Folklore,* 46, no. 2 (1989): 133–146;

Mary McBride, "Shelter of Refuge: The Art of Mimesis in Leslie Marmon Silko's 'Lullaby,' " *Wicazo Sa Review,* 3, no. 2 (1987): 15–17;

Carol Mitchell, "*Ceremony* as Ritual," *American Indian Quarterly,* 5 (1979): 27–35;

Robert M. Nelson, "He Said/She Said: Writing Oral Tradition in John Gunn's 'Ko-pot Ka-nat' and Leslie Silko's *Storyteller,*" *Studies in American Indian Literatures,* 5, no. 1 (1993): 31–50;

Nelson, "Place and Vision: The Function of Landscape in *Ceremony,*" *Journal of the Southwest,* 30, no. 3 (1988): 281–316;

William Oandasan, "A Familiar Love Component of Love in *Ceremony,*" in *Critical Perspectives on Native American Fiction,* edited by Richard F. Fleck (Washington, D.C.: Three Continents Press, 1993), pp. 240–245;

Gretchen Ronnow, "Tayo, Death, and Desire: A Lacanian Reading of *Ceremony,*" in *Narrative Chance: Postmodern Discourse on Native American Indian Literatures,* edited by Vizenor (Albuquerque: University of New Mexico Press, 1989), pp. 55–68;

A. LaVonne Ruoff, "Ritual and Renewal: Keres Traditions in the Short Fiction of Leslie Silko," *MELUS,* 5, no. 4 (1978): 2–17;

James Ruppert, "The Reader's Lessons in *Ceremony,*" *Arizona Quarterly,* 44, no. 1 (1988): 78–85;

B. A. St. Andrews, "Healing the Witchery: Medicine in Silko's *Ceremony,*" *Arizona Quarterly,* 44, no. 1 (1988): 86–94;

Susan J. Scarberry, "Memory as Medicine: The Power of Recollection in *Ceremony,*" *American Indian Quarterly,* 5, no. 1 (1979): 19–26;

Per Seyersted, *Leslie Marmon Silko* (Boise, Idaho: Boise State University Press, 1980);

Mary Slowik, "Henry James, Meet Spider Woman: A Study of Narrative Form in Leslie Silko's *Ceremony,*" *North Dakota Quarterly,* 57, no. 2 (1989): 104–120;

Edith Swan, "Healing via the Sunwise Cycle in Silko's *Ceremony,*" *American Indian Quarterly,* 12, no. 4 (1988): 313–328;

Swan, "Laguna Symbolic Geography and Silko's *Ceremony,*" *American Indian Quarterly,* 12, no. 3 (1988): 229–249;

Joan Thompson, "Yellow Woman, Old and New: Oral Tradition and Leslie Marmon Silko's *Ceremony,*" *Wicazo Sa Review,* 5, no. 2 (1989): 22–25;

C. W. Truesdale, "Tradition and Ceremony: Leslie Marmon Silko as an American Novelist," *North Dakota Quarterly,* 59, no. 4 (1991): 200–208;

Alan R. Velie, *Four American Indian Literary Masters: N. Scott Momaday, James Welch, Leslie Marmon Silko, and Gerald Vizenor* (Norman: University of Oklahoma Press, 1982);

Norma Wilson, "Outlook for Survival," *Denver Quarterly,* 14, no. 4 (1980): 22–30;

Hertha Dawn Wong, *Sending My Heart Back Across the Years: Tradition and Innovation in Native American Autobiography* (New York: Oxford University Press, 1992), pp. 186–196.

Lee Smith

(1 November 1944 –   )

John D. Kalb
Salisbury State University

See also the Smith entry in *DLB Yearbook: 1983*.

BOOKS: *The Last Day the Dogbushes Bloomed* (New
York: Harper & Row, 1968);
Something in the Wind (New York: Harper & Row,
1971);
Fancy Strut (New York: Harper & Row, 1973);
Black Mountain Breakdown (New York: Putnam,
1980);
Cakewalk (New York: Putnam, 1981);
Oral History (New York: Putnam, 1983; London:
Pan, 1989);
Family Linen (New York: Putnam, 1985);
Fair and Tender Ladies (New York: Putnam, 1988;
London: Macmillan, 1989);
Bob, a Dog (Chapel Hill, N.C.: Mud Puppy Press,
1988);
Me and My Baby View the Eclipse (New York: Putnam,
1990);
The Devil's Dream (New York: Putnam, 1992).

Lee Smith (photograph by John Rosenthal)

Much of Lee Smith's fiction entails experiments
in narrative voice and structure. Her protagonists
often suffer some traumatic and dramatic past event
with which they must wrestle in order for them to understand their present and prepare themselves for
their future. Smith's storytelling involves a pronounced affection for her characters and the challenges they face, a strong sense of place (particularly
in those works set in and around Smith's Appalachian
home ground of Buchanan County, Virginia), and a
concern with the roles women serve and make for
themselves if they are to survive in this world. In her
best works she also incorporates the folklore and storytelling of the southwestern Virginia natives, having
carefully researched her postage stamp of soil.

Smith was born on 1 November 1944 to Ernest
Lee Smith and Virginia Elizabeth Marshall Smith in
the small mining town of Grundy, Virginia, where her
father ran the dime store. Although an only child, she
had a large extended family, from her paternal grandfather, who was the county treasurer for forty years,

to a variety of aunts, uncles, and cousins. Still, she
spent much of her childhood reading, creating imaginary playmates, and writing stories. In a 1980 interview with Mark Scandling she recalls writing a
"wonderful book," "Jane Russell and Adlai Stevenson Go West in a Covered Wagon," on her
mother's stationery when she was eight years old.
"And that's all they did – they went west in a
wagon and eventually became Mormons." In 1961
she left the mountains of southwestern Virginia to
attend Saint Catherine's School in Richmond, and
following her graduation in 1963 she enrolled in
Hollins College, where she studied creative writing
under the guidance of Louis Rubin, whom Smith
credits as a major influence.

Smith's first novel, *The Last Day the Dogbushes Bloomed* (1968), written while she was attending Hollins, earned her a Book-of-the-Month Club Writing Fellowship. In this first-person narrative Susan Tobey retells the events of her ninth summer. Although these events occurred several years earlier, the narrative voice maintains the language and diction of the preadolescent Susan. As this crucial summer marks Susan's introduction to the often cruel realities of the world outside her innocent childhood sphere, the dogbushes – named two summers before for a dog she found under them and a place in which she often hides – will, by the end of the season, fail to offer her the protection she has sought among them. About midway through the novel Susan sits beneath the dogbushes and feels, by turns, "like a woman of the world" and "like I was two." Her head feels "too little for all the things I was putting into it." She gradually becomes aware that she will need to forget the things of childhood in order to make room in her head for the "new stuff" of this summer's experiences.

The Last Day the Dogbushes Bloomed is reminiscent of Carson McCullers's coming-of-age novella, *The Member of the Wedding* (1946), especially in the relationship the young Susan has with the black housekeeper-cook Elsie Mae, who, like Berenice in McCullers's work, often offers more guidance and comfort than the other adults in the household. Susan's storybook notions color her view of the world, as she envisions her home as the castle, her mother as the Queen, her sister Betty as the Princess, and Elsie Mae as the Handmaid. The intrusions of two outsiders – as well as a flood and the death of Frank, a man who tends the Tobeys' yard – shape the summer's events. In addition, a man she designates the Baron steals the Queen from Daddy, and Eugene, a disturbed boy visiting the neighborhood from the city, introduces Susan and her friends to sex in a particularly ugly and brutal way.

Although Smith was offered a writing fellowship at Columbia University after receiving her bachelor's degree in English, she chose instead to marry poet James Seay, whom she met at a poetry reading at Hollins, in 1967. Smith and Seay moved to Tuscaloosa, Alabama, where she became a reporter and features writer for the *Tuscaloosa News* and wrote *Something in the Wind* (1971). In this novel Smith provides a compelling psychological study of a young woman's numbing year's experiences following the death of her childhood sweetheart.

Another first-person narrative, *Something in the Wind* opens with seventeen-year-old Brooke Kincaid's return to River Bend, Virginia, from St.

Dominique's, a private girl's school in Richmond, for the funeral of Charles Hughes. She does not know what to make of this loss: "Charles had made my mind and if he was really dead like everybody was saying, then I didn't know what would go on in my head." When Brooke returns to school for the remaining weeks before graduation, she is dumbfounded and annoyed by the attention thrust upon her by friends and strangers alike. Oddly, she is the only one who understands "perfectly" the pattern that the graduating seniors form, under the guidance of the headmistress, in shifting motion on the grass: "'I think the idea is kaleidoscopic,' I said. And I couldn't understand how it was that I could understand the graduation figure, but I couldn't understand most other things in the world." The kaleidoscopic image appears twice more in the course of the novel and serves to underscore the fragmentation of Brooke's psyche. This psychological disintegration leads Brooke, a graduate about to go "into the world," to select a "life plan": "I would imitate everybody until everything became second nature . . . and I wouldn't have to bother to imitate any more, I would simply *be*." In the fall she goes off to an unnamed university in North Carolina, protected by her credo: "Do what you will with Brooke's body . . . but please stay out of her mind." With this detached third-person perspective on her activities, she soon loses her virginity to Bob Griffin, whom she calls Houston.

One image – similar in some regards to Sylvia Plath's bell jar – that Smith uses to underscore Brooke's cool remoteness and her desire to control her environment is a large paperweight, a glass-enclosed, snow-covered village, that Brooke purchases: "I knew without even touching it, what would happen if you turned it upside down. You could make a snowstorm." Later, when the relationship with Houston comes to its inevitable end, she threatens to "turn everything upside down and make it snow." Yet her world is already upside down and seems beyond her control.

Following the breakup with Houston and a disastrous first quarter of college, Brooke begins to sleep with other young men, telling each that she is a virgin. Bentley T. Hooks does not take her claim seriously, but, after he does things to Brooke "that nobody else had ever done," he is shocked and angered to discover blood on the sheets. Until now, she has been impenetrable in both body and mind. Predictably, for the remainder of the novel, Brooke has a few cathartic experiences through which others – and eventually she – become "real."

Perhaps the most unfortunate element of *Something in the Wind* is the unexplained, allegedly super-

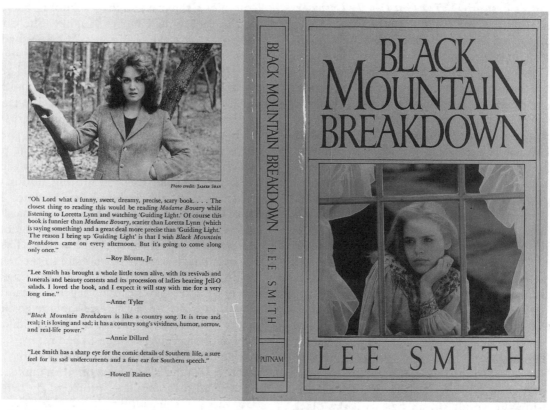

Dust jacket for Smith's 1980 novel, a tragicomic exploration of a girl's emergence into womanhood in an Appalachian county of Virginia

natural events that eventually lead to her breakup with Bentley and that seem contrary to Brooke's need to develop the conscious will and self-control to advance to the next step of her healing. This deus ex machina of alluded-to inexplicable events – perhaps somehow made manifest by Bentley's evil nature or from the combination of both characters' dual natures (the "something in the wind" of the title, taken from a line in William Shakespeare's *The Comedy of Errors* [performed 1594], a play of mistaken and imposed identities) – intrudes on the realism of the rest of Brooke's struggles.

Both *The Last Day the Dogbushes Bloomed* and *Something in the Wind* have their first-novel weaknesses, most notably the tunnel-vision perspective of their narrators, to whom all other characters remain flatly defined. In interviews Smith has criticized her early writings as "typical first-writer things," admitted that the completion of her second novel became a race with the impending birth of her second son, and said she "was writing about all kinds of things I didn't know anything about." Even the locations of events, like the characters, have an undeveloped, undefined quality. However, the notion of women being defined by others – particularly men – as suf-

fered by Brooke, is a thematic issue to which Smith returns in subsequent novels and stories.

With *Fancy Strut* (1973) Smith moves her characters to the town of Speed, Alabama, which is celebrating its 1965 sesquicentennial, for a comic novel inspired by her coverage of Tuscaloosa's 150th anniversary for the city's newspaper in the late 1960s. She utilizes third-person narration, which, unlike the claustrophobic narration in her two previous novels, affords her the opportunity to delve more deeply into her characters and the complexity, irony, and humor of their attitudes and situations. The title is taken from a majorette maneuver in the prestigious Susan Arch Finlay Memorial Marching Contest, and the novel's chapters switch the point of view from one character to another, allowing a variety of characters to "strut their stuff" in what might best be compared to a soap opera.

Fancy Strut relies on a panorama of subplots, from that of a racist and frightened iconoclast, Miss Iona, who wishes 150 years had not changed Speed one iota, to that of adolescent Bevo Cartwright, whose "love" for one of the majorettes leads him to set fire to the stage at the Sesquicentennial Queen pageant. Speed is a small southern town wrenched into the twentieth century, caught between its hoped-for image and its troubled realities of racism, infidelity, hypocrisy, violence, and commercialism. The attempt to put Speed on the map via the anniversary festivities has both comic and tragic consequences.

Smith put Alabama behind her when her husband joined the creative-writing faculty at the University of North Carolina at Chapel Hill in 1974. In the years that followed Smith taught at Carolina Friends School, Duke University, and the University of North Carolina at Chapel Hill, eventually accepting a full-time appointment in creative writing at North Carolina State University in Raleigh in 1981. She continued to juggle her writing with the demands of her regular job and raising her two sons, Josh and Page.

Black Mountain Breakdown (1980) marks Smith's return, through her writing, to Appalachian Buchanan County and to more serious subjects. For the first time she artfully mingles the comic with the tragic. Crystal Spangler has been traumatized by an event in her youth, as had Brooke in *Something in the Wind;* however, Crystal does not recall the ordeal until much later in her life, when the recollection comes at the expense of her sanity. For this novel, set in Black Rock, Virginia, Smith expanded on a previously published short story, "Paralyzed: A True Story" (*Southern Exposure,* Spring 1977).

Even at age twelve Crystal, according to her best friend, Agnes McClanahan, "seems to lack something, some hard thing inside that Agnes and Babe [Agnes's little sister] were born with." Crystal's mother, Lorene, hopes to make something of her attractive daughter in order to make up for her failure with the two older boys and her own failure in marrying Grant Spangler, an emphysematous alcoholic who occupies the darkened front room of their home. Soon Crystal is in high school, making the cheerleading squad and dating its handsome star, Roger Lee Combs, yet she is attracted to the dangerous Mack Stiltner. She and Roger are an attractive couple, and, in Lorene's view of the world, appearances are what matter.

While on a visit to her great-aunt's in Dry Fork, Crystal is raped by her father's retarded younger brother, Devere, who resembles her father. This rape is not revealed to the reader until near the end of the novel, since Crystal's conscious mind blocks it from her. However, the next day she comes home to discover her father dead in the front room. At the funeral Crystal "feels empty as light, somewhere outside herself," and in the weeks to come she breaks up with Roger, calls Mack, and begins, like Brooke, dating "anybody."

Crystal drifts through the subsequent years, driven by her mother to compete in beauty pageants and guided by various young men to their beds and backseats. It is "only when she's with boys that she feels pretty, or popular, or fun. In the way they talk to her and act around her, Crystal can see what they think of her, and then that's the way she is." On the one hand, Crystal, as her name suggests, is a transparent object that others color to their liking. On the other hand, like Black Mountain itself, she is "impenetrable," until one day when she sees a young boy who reminds her of Devere, and her world and self shatter.

During the seven years between the publication of *Fancy Strut* and *Black Mountain Breakdown,* Smith – in addition to reworking the original draft of the latter, which Harper and Row had rejected – published short stories in various periodicals and popular magazines. These and other stories were published in *Cakewalk* (1981). Two stories first published in *Carolina Quarterly* – "Mrs. Darcy Meets the Blue-Eyed Stranger at the Beach" and "Between the Lines" – received O. Henry awards in 1979 and 1981, respectively.

"Mrs. Darcy Meets the Blue-Eyed Stranger at the Beach" concerns a recently widowed grandmother whose adult daughters do not know what to do with her now that she has lost interest in living. Mrs. Darcy does not cook or keep house as she had in the past and seems without direction or ambition. All of Smith's sympathy in this story goes to Mrs. Darcy, a woman who is identified only by her roles, and not to her children and grandchildren. All that her daughters want is for the problem to be taken care of somehow, and in effect it will be by the end of the story. They wonder whether a suitable period of mourning has passed, but, like many widows, Mrs. Darcy no longer has a life in which to be interested. She has been a wife, a mother, and a grandmother, and now it seems there is little for her to do. However, her hands have been blessed with the mysterious power of healing, and by the end of the story she is ready for her "date" with the blue-eyed stranger – the peacefulness of death.

"Between the Lines" is the name of the column Joline B. Newhouse of Salt Lick writes fortnightly for the *Greenville Herald* about the events in her small community, intended to uplift her readers. However, the most important aspect of her column is what she communicates indirectly, "between the lines." At first Joline may seem a bit of a snippy, opinionated woman, but this slice-of-life story, cov-

*Dust jacket for Smith's 1983 novel, which portrays three
generations of a family in rural Virginia*

ering a single day and night in her life, reveals the between-the-lines sadness and joy she and her family have had over the years and her compassion for others, even when she does not show it. Life goes on between the lines of "this pain and loving, mystery and loss."

Most of the other stories in *Cakewalk* also concern women trying to get over or through troubling life situations and events. The collection is marked by experiments in point of view, tense, and form. "The Seven Deadly Sins" and "Horses" feature more craft than content, and "Not Pictured," a male-narrated story, seems less satisfying than many of the others. The best stories, such as "All the Days of Our Lives," in which a soap opera seems more real than Helen Long's life, depict women attempting to unravel the mysteries of life, love, and marriage and hoping for "another chance, another love, another world."

Smith's first four novels and her experiments in short fiction served her well as preparation for her next three novels, which are her best. *Oral History* (1983), *Family Linen* (1985), and *Fair and Tender Ladies* (1988) show Smith's storyteller's sense of character, voice, place, style, and structure, something only hinted at in her earlier works.

Oral History reveals Smith at a plateau of both form and content as she mines Buchanan County for its folklore, characters, and voices. At the time of the novel's composition Smith's marriage was beginning to unravel, eventually ending in divorce in 1982. On occasional returns to Grundy, seeking some breathing space, she discovered progress was altering her remote hometown. She began tape-recording the old people's conversations and doing research. She also met a girl who was taping the noises of a haunted house for an oral-history project. That girl became the subject of a short story, "Oral History," and the two halves of that story became the bookends for the novel's storytellers, who explain the history of that haunted house and the family who lived there.

Oral History consists of seven first-person oral narratives and one first-person written narrative interspersed among four pieces told by third-person narrators who are sometimes omniscient and sometimes limited to a single perspective. The resulting tale spans three generations, capturing the spirit, vitality, and dashed hopes of the cursed (or merely unlucky) Cantrell family. Ironically, most of what is revealed in the novel's five sections remains undisclosed to naive Jennifer Bingham of Abingdon, Virginia, although she will get an A in oral history for taping the haunting sounds in the now-abandoned Cantrell homestead. This haunting drove Ora Mae and Little Luther Wade – who she mistakenly thinks are her grandparents – to move in with their son's family. But the real haunting is revealed to the reader, not Jennifer, in the passages of oral and written history that fill the space between her narrow frame of text.

Jennifer records her impressions of her experiences with her kin in a notebook, another portion of first-person narration, ruminating that "one feels that the true benefits of this trip may derive not from what is recorded by the tape now spinning in that empty room above me, but from my new knowledge of my heritage and a new appreciation of these colorful, interesting folk. My *roots*." "One" might expect this, but Jennifer leaves as she has arrived, in ignorance. She casts aside the "cheap, half broken" beads she finds, not knowing they belonged to her grandmother. She thinks her cousin Al (who she supposes is her uncle) and his wife, Debra, have been carpeting their van, when carpet is not at all what was getting "laid." And her romanticized notions of these people mirror the idealized illusions of her maternal grandfather, Richard Burlage.

Oral History is antiromantic. The reader is nearly seduced by Burlage's romanticized notions of Dory – whose sexual desire and experience he finds "a kind of purity" and with whom he "made love as no mortals have ever made love before" – yet these are self-deceptions and delusions. The photograph he takes of Dory ten years later, blurred and indistinct, indicates the way in which he and his granddaughter leave these remote mountains with little understanding of what really occurred there. Smith portrays her characters without sentimentality, setting them forth, often in their own words, in realistic fashion with devastating accuracy, yet with her characteristic compassion and sympathy.

Oral History was well received, earning the Sir Walter Raleigh Award for Fiction (1983) and the North Carolina Award for Fiction (1984). In 1985 Smith was promoted to associate professor at North Carolina State, married syndicated columnist Harold B. Crowther, Jr., published *Family Linen,* and was honored with a Lee Smith Festival at Emory and Henry College. With *Family Linen* Smith fashions another family-history novel, this time blended with the genres of the psychological novel and murder mystery. In *Family Linen,* as in *Oral History,* the multiple-perspective narration reveals more to the reader than to any of the characters.

While the murderer in the novel may be revealed by its end, the motive for this crime is explained in Nettie's narrative. Much dirty linen of this sort is revealed to the reader alone. However, the four siblings – brought together by the death of the family matriarch, Elizabeth, and their subsequent attempts to unravel the mysterious memory of the eldest daughter, Sybill – discover another sort of family linen, the fabric that connects "this odd gaggle of disparate family teetering here on the brink of the past" to one another despite their differences and conflicts, infidelities and ignorances.

Smith's narrative structure underscores the reformation of this family community. Another alternating blend of first- and third-person, single-character-perspective chapters eventually gives way to third-person, multiple-character-perspective chapters when the family ironically comes together as they descend on Elizabeth's house with the intent to divide her possessions and when the family reunites once again in unexpected ways for the wedding of a member of the next generation.

For her next novel Smith set upon a risky venture – fashioning an epistolary novel consisting solely of letters (some sent, some merely written) from a single female character. As *Oral History* seems to bring Smith's apprenticeship writings to a new level of insight, clarity, and style, *Fair and Tender Ladies* serves as an enormous leap forward in its depiction of nearly a century of change and growth in the remote area of Sugar Fork, Virginia, and in its development of the authorial voice of the remarkable Ivy Rowe. Smith took her inspiration for her most vital, rich, and rewarding novel to date from a packet of letters written by a woman to her sister, a treasure she purchased at a flea market for seventy-five cents. Through Ivy's letters to a variety of respondents and nonrespondents, Smith painstakingly chronicles the twofold evolution of Ivy as a woman and a writer. While a single point of view results in a narrow tunnel image in Smith's early novels, here the scope is expansive.

Even in her first letter – to a hoped-for pen pal – the naive child Ivy proclaims her desire to be

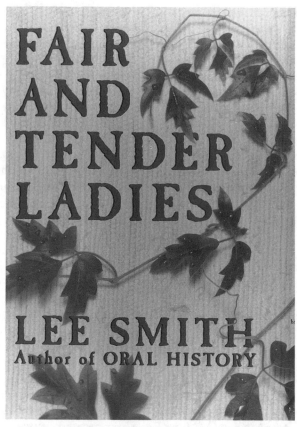

Dust jacket for Smith's 1988 epistolary novel, inspired by a packet of letters she purchased at a flea market

a writer: "It is what I love the bestest in this world." Born at the turn of the century, Ivy is prevented from pursuing her education and writing career by the harsh realities of living and loving in Sugar Fork and the nearby boomtowns of Majestic and Diamond Fork. The death of her father, a teenage pregnancy, and the death of her mother conspire to make Ivy's dream of leaving the region to pursue an education impossible. But, as she continues her correspondence, she is able to put form, shape, and substance to her life experiences. By the end of the novel, when she destroys the bulk of her letters to her lost sister, Silvaney, she finally realizes that the letters themselves had no meaning, but "it was the writing of them, that signified." The creative act, the process itself, gave Ivy's life its meaning and context.

While her daughter, Joli, manages to pursue the intellectual life denied Ivy, and Ivy enjoys living through her daughter, Ivy never realizes, as the reader does, that she has written herself into being, into substance, and rises above her many hardships into a woman of legendary, mythic proportions, a woman whose observations show humor, grace,

compassion, and forgiveness. Because the world is not particularly fair, the women in this novel who survive their life situations most effectively – Ivy; Ivy's sisters, Beulah and Ethel; and the boarding-house mistress, Geneva Hunt – lack the luxury of being tender. They must be strong and tough. In contrast with the epistolary novels of the eighteenth century – the authors of which might agree with Ivy's brother, a preacher named Garney, that she is "a whore and an abomination" – *Fair and Tender Ladies* celebrates women who find empowerment through unconventional means.

Fair and Tender Ladies remains a hard act to follow. Smith's second collection of short fiction, *Me and My Baby View the Eclipse* (1990), offers nine stories. Eight of them deal with traumas (eclipses) – divorce ("Bob, a Dog," the 1991 P.E.N./Faulkner Award–winning "Mom," "Life on the Moon," "The Interpretation of Dreams"), imminent family disintegration as a young girl matures ("Tongues of Fire," "Dreamers"), death ("Intensive Care"), and an illicit love affair fated to end ("Me and My Baby View the Eclipse") – that force change on Smith's characters. "Desire on Domino Island" offers a humorous glimpse of an author's difficulty in writing a formulaic romance novel filled with flat characters and contrived situations.

The title story is the best of the lot, told with characteristic humor and compassion in a swift, concise fashion. Sharon Shaw will end her unexpected affair with Raymond Stewart and return her attention to her husband and children, but Raymond has "shown her things" she might not have otherwise had the courage or wisdom to see. "Bob, a Dog," previously printed in a 1988 limited-edition single volume, depicts a woman deserted by her husband. Cheryl is warned by friends not to "make any big decisions," but indecisiveness plagues her as she drifts through life. Even the dog her son brings home one day easily takes over, growing and howling in the way Cheryl perhaps wishes she could. Once she becomes decisive about what to do concerning the dog, Bob – just as June will need to take "one small step" in order to make sense of her "Life on the Moon" – she is able to contemplate other choices that are hers to make.

In an interview with Edwin T. Arnold eight years before the publication of *The Devil's Dream* (1992), Smith drew some comparisons between the modernization and commercialization she saw in Buchanan County and chronicled in *Oral History* and similar commercialism in country music: "The whole history of Appalachia, just as the whole history of country music, has been one of exploitation, of the land, of the whatever, and I think if you are going to try to faithfully observe that, write something that pretends to depict that kind of life, then that is what happens." These parallels may explain why she turned her attention to the country-music industry – the commercialized, permed, and blow-dried bastard offspring of the traditional bluegrass of Appalachia.

The Devil's Dream has the sprawling, multigenerational scope of *Oral History* and *Fair and Tender Ladies* and the multiple-perspective narration of *Oral History* and *Family Linen*. *The Devil's Dream* is flanked at the beginning and end (similar to the structure of *Oral History*) by the italicized story of the reunion of the musical Bailey family in Opryland for a historic, final recording session with their most famous progeny, country star Katie Cocker. The intervening chapters chronicle about 150 years of this musical family. Dedicated to "all the real country artists," *The Devil's Dream* is the first novel Smith has written with music as its major subtext. While songs and musicians have often figured prominently in her fiction – for example, the fiddle tune "The Devil's Dream" serves as musical accom-

paniment in the opening pages of *Black Mountain Breakdown,* and eight lines of the song "Fair and Tender Ladies" form the epigraph for *Oral History* – this novel marks her first effort to focus exclusively on a family's musical heritage, with invented and traditional songs serving as the undertext for the novel.

"The Devil's Dream," which might be called the title track, suggests the way the Baileys, like the Cantrells before them, are cursed. God-fearing patriarch Moses Bailey warned his son, Jeremiah, that "the fiddle is a instrument of the Devil," but the temptation of music was too much for Jeremiah and the succeeding generations to resist. In a similar fashion the Nashville music machine requires a certain surrender of the soul, suggested even in the move of the Grand Old Opry from the Ryman Auditorium to Opryland. As Katie Cocker remarks, "There was something like a *church* about the Opry in those days when it was still at the Ryman Auditorium – why, shoot, the Ryman used to *be* a church." The Christmas reunion at Opryland seems worlds away from that hauntingly beautiful fiddle, singing out across Lone Bald Mountain those many years ago.

Much of the oral history of these characters is fascinating, but *The Devil's Dream* does not come together as effectively as the three previous novels do. Perhaps some of this lack of coalescence stems from the family members' failure to harmonize except in music and song. Even at the reunion many still harbor petty jealousies. They put a good face on things for the country-music press covering the event, but the reader knows their fractious history, which is filled with rancor, animosity, and divisiveness. Because of the span of the narrative's events and the self-centered focus of many of the participants, it is difficult to care much about these people. This family's dirty linen remains too much the stuff of Opryland gossip.

Critics of Smith's writings often address the sorts of questions she poses about the conflicts between low- and highbrow art and about the intellectual's often-acute failure as artist in a world in which beauticians and cake bakers succeed in the art of living. Lucinda H. MacKethan was among the first to consider Smith's work seriously, focusing on the first four novels and the *Cakewalk* stories, which she argues share a central thematic issue of "the value of balance," in which characters must choose "between or balancing the ordinary and the mysterious." MacKethan sees *Fancy Strut* and *Black Mountain Breakdown* as technically and artistically achieving "a balance of effects, particularly in their choices of tone, point of view, and texture."

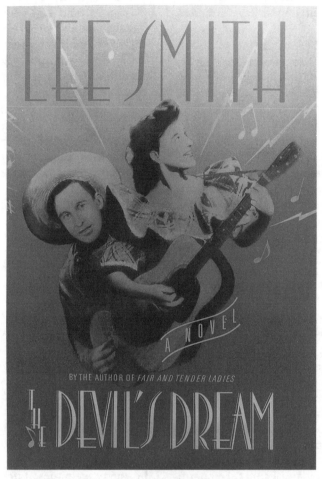

*Dust jacket for Smith's 1992 novel, which chronicles 150 years of
a musical Appalachian family*

In "The World of Lee Smith" Anne Goodwyn Jones, a friend of Smith and an unabashed fan of her writings, also looks at the first five books, providing concise overviews of Smith's offerings and the observation that, in Smith's world, the "low" artist fares much better than the intellectual. Jones concludes that Smith "writes from and about an extremely rigid traditional system . . . and she tells us what she hears. What she hears is the sometimes heroic, sometimes comic, sometimes sneaky and petty ways in which Southern women and men try to salvage a sense of self within a system that tries to define that self for them."

In a later overview – one that encompasses this first phase of writings, the second phase of *Oral History* and *Family Linen,* and the final phase of *Fair and Tender Ladies* – Katherine Kearns discovers "a steady progression . . . from the female character as self-perceived artistic product to the female character as artist." Kearns characterizes *Fancy Strut,* for in-

stance, "as a manifesto on self-conscious art and self-claimed artists" and "a comic deflation of 'art.'" In the earlier works "women with artistic and intellectual leanings so unsex themselves that they generate an antithesis, the freely sensual 'fallen' woman." Artistic pursuits are risky ventures, and Kearns sees Ivy Rowe as articulating "the dilemma of the artist torn between the need for autonomy and the demands of family and community" and as the character through which "Smith bespeaks her own growing confidence in the mutually regenerative powers of life and art."

Harriette C. Buchanan covers the works through *Family Linen,* finding the connecting links among them in their portrayal of "women faced with a world for which they are unprepared . . . [and] have little idea of where to look for guidance, because their families and communities provide so little in the way of honest or genuinely nurturing support." She finds Smith's characters' lives tragic, but the "telling is extremely funny," and she notes that the specificity of time and place in the later works have afforded Smith's storytelling additional "depth and breadth."

Dorothy Combs Hill's *Lee Smith* (1992), the first book-length study of the author, covers the works through *Me and My Baby View the Eclipse*. In Hill's analysis, Smith "redresses . . . the terrible cultural wound inflicted on creative women that keeps them from understanding themselves and even denies them any access to themselves." She sees Smith as an acutely imaginative artist who reinvents "powerful goddess figures eclipsed by patriarchy." In addition to a careful presentation of the literary biography, Hill offers provocative insights into the mythic female underpinnings of Smith's fiction, which she concludes "searches for the intersection between sex and sanctity and the intersection between wildness and domesticity. [Smith] is interested in the authentic female self and the authentic artistic self, which in her fiction are found in authentic relationship and authentic language."

Among the critics who deal with individual works, Parks Lanier, Jr., views *Black Mountain Breakdown* as a "psychological thriller" and "skillful psychological novel" in which physical spaces underscore Crystal's psychic state until the novel's end, when the bright lights of her environment are unable to penetrate the "dark spider's parlor" of her mind. John D. Kalb focuses on the debilitating impact of Roger Lee Combs's verbal and physical manipulations on Crystal's already tenuous psychological state.

Of Smith's novels *Oral History* has generated the most critical attention, with the Winter 1986 issue of *Iron Mountain Review* offering three views of her narrative achievement, all focusing on the conflict between the written and the spoken word. Ben Jennings finds the distance between the "contemporary middle-class world view" and Appalachia reflected in Jennifer's "self-conscious and contrived" language. The "world of the Appalachian hollow" inherent in Granny Younger's oral speech underscores Jennifer's failure to fathom the mystery of her ancestry. Anne Goodwyn Jones's essay cites the frequency of "ora" and "or" included in characters' names – Ora Mae, Dory, Orvil, Morris – and attempts to uncover the connections among three thematic concepts – speaking (oratory), sexuality (orifice and adore), and prophecy (oracle) – all of which are damaged or destroyed "with the penetration of the dominant culture" into this mountain hollow.

With a similar focus on the outsiders Jennifer and Richard Burlage and their written texts, Frank Soos notes both characters' failure to unravel the mystery. He points to Granny's invitation and "challenge to us readers, to us outsiders" to enter and accept a mystical world at variance with "our own system of truth." Suzanne W. Jones also focuses on the language of the insiders and outsiders, the former allowing readers the knowledge that "Smith's Hoot Owl Holler resonates with meaning that it does not have for the outsiders of the novel."

Rosalind B. Reilly takes a different approach to *Oral History,* with a comparison between the creator of fiction (the storyteller) and the dreamer. She sees the wind "associated with a preverbal, prenarrative power which arouses the imagination, stirring up dreams as it stirs up the landscape, a power very close, perhaps, to the creative 'inspiration' or breath of the author." She also finds the wind a seductive force, particularly on Richard, and associates the spell on a pair of gold earrings with the spell of dreams. For Reilly, Sally's "good humored" narrative awakens the reader to a world of "new dreams," but she finds the future portrayed in the epilogue "fantastically mundane."

Corinne Dale's study of the language in *Oral History* also focuses on Sally. Dale contrasts the patriarchal linguistic and sexual anxiety of Jennifer and Richard's written discourse with the "genuine feeling and authentic language" inherent in Sally's narrative, which she characterizes as "the most positive voice in the novel, partly because she can accept the limitations of her symbolic language without accepting limitations on experiences." Since the publication of *Oral History,* Smith's storytelling skills have finally generated the sort of serious attention a writer of her ability deserves. Unlike the Appalachian area of her origins, her fictional landscape has just begun to be mined.

Interviews:

Mark Scandling, "Staying in Touch with the Real World," *Carolina Quarterly,* 32 (Winter 1980): 51–57;

Edwin T. Arnold, "An Interview with Lee Smith," *Appalachian Journal,* 11 (Spring 1984): 240–254;

Michelle Lodge, "PW Interviews: Lee Smith," *Publishers Weekly,* 228 (20 September 1985): 110–111;

Pat Arnow, "Lee Smith: An Interview," *Now and Then,* 6 (Summer 1989): 24–27;

Virginia A. Smith, "On Regionalism, Women's Writing, and Writing as a Woman: A Conversation with Lee Smith," *Southern Review,* 26 (Autumn 1990): 784–795;

Dorothy Combs Hill, "An Interview with Lee Smith," *Southern Quarterly,* 28 (Winter 1990): 5–19.

References:

Harriette C. Buchanan, "Lee Smith: The Storyteller's Voice," in *Southern Women Writers: The New Generation,* edited by Tonette Bond Inge (Tuscaloosa: University of Alabama Press, 1990), pp. 324–345;

Corinne Dale, "The Power of Language in Lee Smith's *Oral History,*" *Southern Quarterly,* 28 (Winter 1990): 21–34;

Dorothy Combs Hill, *Lee Smith* (New York: Twayne, 1992);

Ben Jennings, "Language and Reality in Lee Smith's *Oral History,*" *Iron Mountain Review,* 3 (Winter 1986): 10–14;

Anne Goodwyn Jones, "The Orality of *Oral History,*" *Iron Mountain Review,* 3 (Winter 1986): 15–19;

Jones, "The World of Lee Smith," in *Women Writers of the Contemporary South,* edited by Peggy Whitman Prenshaw (Jackson: University Press of Mississippi, 1984), pp. 249–272;

Suzanne W. Jones, "City Folks in Hoot Owl Holler: Narrative Strategy in Lee Smith's *Oral History,*" *Southern Literary Journal,* 20 (Fall 1987): 101–112;

John D. Kalb, "The Second 'Rape' of Crystal Spangler," *Southern Literary Journal,* 21 (Fall 1988): 23–30;

Katherine Kearns, "From Shadow to Substance: The Empowerment of the Artist Figure in Lee Smith's Fiction," in *Writing the Woman Artist: Essays on Poetics, Politics, and Portraiture,* edited by Suzanne W. Jones (Philadelphia: University of Pennsylvania Press, 1991), pp. 175–195;

Parks Lanier, Jr., "Psychic Space in Lee Smith's *Black Mountain Breakdown,*" in *The Poetics of Appalachian Space,* edited by Lanier (Knoxville: University of Tennessee Press, 1991), pp. 58–66;

Lucinda H. MacKethan, "Artists and Beauticians: Balance in Lee Smith's Fiction," *Southern Literary Journal,* 15 (Fall 1982): 3–14;

Rosalind B. Reilly, "*Oral History:* The Enchanted Circle of Narrative and Dream," *Southern Literary Journal,* 23 (Fall 1990): 79–92;

Frank Soos, "Insiders and Outsiders: Point of View in Lee Smith's *Oral History,*" *Iron Mountain Review,* 3 (Winter 1986): 20–24.

William Styron

(11 June 1925 –)

Philip W. Leon

The Citadel

See also the Styron entries in *DLB 2: American Novelists Since World War II, First Series* and *DLB Yearbook: 1980.*

BOOKS: *Lie Down in Darkness* (Indianapolis: Bobbs-Merrill, 1951; London: Hamish Hamilton, 1952);

The Long March (New York: Random House, 1956; London: Hamish Hamilton, 1962);

Set This House on Fire (New York: Random House, 1960; London: Hamish Hamilton, 1961);

The Confessions of Nat Turner (New York: Random House, 1967; London: Cape, 1968);

In the Clap Shack (New York: Random House, 1973);

Sophie's Choice (New York: Random House, 1979; London: Panthera, 1979);

This Quiet Dust and Other Writings (New York: Random House, 1982);

Darkness Visible: A Memoir of Madness (New York: Random House, 1990; London: Cape, 1991);

A Tidewater Morning: Three Tales from Youth (New York: Random House, 1993).

PLAY PRODUCTION: *In the Clap Shack,* New Haven, Conn., Yale Repertory Theatre, 15 December 1972.

OTHER: Joan Barthel, *A Death in Canaan,* introduction by Styron (New York: Dutton, 1976);

Florence Aadland, *The Big Love,* introduction by Styron (New York: Warner, 1986);

George Hendrick, ed., *To Reach Eternity: The Letters of James Jones,* introduction by Styron (New York: Random House, 1989);

Mariana Cook, *Fathers and Daughters,* introduction by Styron (New York: Chronicle, 1994).

SELECTED PERIODICAL PUBLICATIONS – UNCOLLECTED:

FICTION

"The McCabes," *Paris Review,* 6 (Autumn–Winter 1960): 12–28;

William Styron, 1993 (photograph © Peter Simon)

"Marriott, the Marine," *Esquire,* 76 (September 1971): 100–104, 196, 198, 200, 202, 204, 207, 208, 210;

"Dead!," by Styron and John Phillips, *Esquire,* 65 (December 1973): 161–168, 264, 266, 270, 274, 277, 278, 280, 282, 286, 288, 290;

"The Seduction of Leslie," *Esquire,* 86 (September 1976): 92–97;

"My Life as a Publisher," *Esquire,* 89 (March 1978): 71–79.

NONFICTION

"Letter to an Editor," *Paris Review,* 1 (Spring 1953): 9–13;

"The Prevalence of Wonders," *Nation,* 176 (2 May 1953): 370–371;

"The Paris Review," *Harper's Bazaar,* 87 (August 1953): 122, 173;

"If You Write for Television . . . ," *New Republic,* 140 (6 April 1959): 16;

"Mrs. Aadland's Little Girl, Beverly," *Esquire,* 56 (November 1961): 142, 189–191;

"The Death-in-Life of Benjamin Reid," *Esquire,* 57 (February 1962): 114, 141–145;

"As He Lay Dead, A Bitter Grief," *Life,* 53 (20 July 1962): 39–42;

"Aftermath of Benjamin Reid," *Esquire,* 58 (November 1962): 79, 81, 158, 160, 164;

"Two Writers Talk It Over," *Esquire,* 60 (July 1963): 57–59;

"Truth and Nat Turner: An Exchange – William Styron Replies," *Nation,* 206 (22 April 1968): 544–547;

"The Shade of Thomas Wolfe," *Harper's,* 236 (April 1968): 96–104;

"Oldest America," *McCall's,* 95 (July 1968): 94, 123;

"My Generation," *Esquire,* 70 (October 1968): 123–124;

"On Creativity," *Playboy,* 15 (December 1968): 138;

"The Uses of History in Fiction," *Southern Literary Journal,* 1 (Spring 1969): 57–90;

"Kuznetsov's Confession," *New York Times,* 14 September 1969, IV: 13;

"A Friend's Farewell to James Jones," *New York,* 10 (6 June 1977): 40–41;

" 'Race Is the Plague of Civilization': An Author's View," *U.S. News & World Report,* 88 (28 January 1980): 65–66;

"Almost a Rhodes Scholar: A Personal Reminiscence," *South Atlantic Bulletin,* 45 (May 1980): 1–7;

"A Literary Friendship," *Esquire,* 111 (April 1989): 154–155, 158, 160, 162, 164, 165;

"Nat Turner Revisited," *American Heritage,* 43 (October 1992): 64–73;

"Profits and Pills: Prozac Days, Halcion Nights," *Nation,* 256 (4 January 1993): 1, 18, 20, 21;

"The Enduring Metaphors of Auschwitz and Hiroshima," *Newsweek,* 121 (11 January 1993): 28–29.

William Styron's first novel, *Lie Down in Darkness* (1951), placed him in the vanguard of promising young American authors of the post–World War II era, along with such writers as J. D. Salinger, Norman Mailer, Saul Bellow, John Updike, Joseph Heller, and Philip Roth. While some of those writers have been more prolific than Styron and are perhaps better known to a general readership, none surpasses Styron in his ambitious themes, his wonderfully crafted style, or his intelligently drawn characters. Ironically, Styron's greater public recognition results from his recent appearances on magazine-format television shows, discussing his successful emergence from depression. His nonfiction account of his descent into depression, *Darkness Visible: A Memoir of Madness* (1990) – the title of which is drawn from John Milton's *Paradise Lost* (1667) – bears a perhaps subconscious similarity to the title of his first novel.

All of Styron's novels probe into the realms of darkness. Captain Mannix of *The Long March* (1956) limps painfully and defiantly on a forced road march, excoriated verbally and physically by an unbending military authority. Cass Kinsolving's nightmare of alcoholism in *Set This House on Fire* (1960), an underrated novel of despair and violence, closely parallels Styron's later battle with depression. The psychologically tormented title character of *The Confessions of Nat Turner* (1967) mounts an ill-fated rebellion against his white masters in 1831 Virginia. In *Sophie's Choice* (1979) the title character's escalatingly horrible choices haunt her and eventually shock the narrator, Stingo, who seeks expiation from his own demons through the telling of Sophie's story.

William Styron was born in Newport News, Virginia, on 11 June 1925. His father, William Clark Styron, was an engineer at the Newport News shipyard. His mother, Pauline Margaret Abraham Styron, died when Styron was thirteen. An energetic youth, he was sent to Christchurch, an Episcopal preparatory school in Virginia. At Davidson College – a scholastically demanding Presbyterian college near Charlotte, North Carolina – he studied with other young southern men, receiving a traditional education grounded in the classics and overlaid with a proper Protestant sense of hard work and discipline.

World War II was raging, and Styron enlisted in the Marine Corps, which sent him to Duke University in the V–12 officer-training program. There he took writing classes with William Blackburn prior to receiving an officer's commission. Styron served honorably in the Pacific theater toward the end of the war, but he was spared the heaviest part of the fighting by the nuclear annihilation of Hiroshima and Nagasaki. His participation in World War II, and as a reservist recalled during the Korean War, lies at the core of several of his published and unpublished works. The best known of these, *The Long March,* renders in excruciatingly realistic detail the agony of recently activated Marine reservists on a stateside forced road march. A lesser-known work, the play *In the Clap Shack* (1973), uses humor to reveal Styron's deep mistrust and dislike of the military.

Styron spent 1946 in Italy, helping with the recovery from the war and gathering background for *Set This House on Fire*. The following year he returned to Duke, graduated, and went to New York City. The only regular job Styron has ever held was a short, unhappy stint as a copy editor and book-jacket blurb writer for McGraw-Hill publishers. There Styron resolved to give himself full-time to the writing he knew he was capable of producing. In a mad moment he showed up at the staid publishing firm wearing his old Marine cap and a seersucker suit. His audacity in sailing paper airplanes and in floating soap bubbles from the windows of the McGraw-Hill building sealed the end of his career — at least at that end of the publishing industry.

Financed by his father, Styron enrolled in the New School for Social Research to study writing with Hiram Haydn. He began *Lie Down in Darkness,* which concerns a girl from Virginia who commits suicide in New York City by leaping from the top floor of a tenement. Many critics regard *Lie Down in Darkness* as the best first novel ever produced by an American. Certainly for a writer so young Styron showed unusual maturity and craftsmanship in his fiction.

Styron's customary slow pace of composition, writing and rewriting only two to three pages a day, was quickened by his recall to active duty with the Marine Corps to serve in Korea. He handed over the manuscript of *Lie Down in Darkness* just before he reported to Camp Lejeune, North Carolina. He never went to Korea, obtaining a release from service because of an eye ailment. Almost as though he wanted to dissociate himself from the government that attempted to return him to fighting, Styron left for Europe.

In France, Styron cofounded the *Paris Review* with Peter Matthiessen and George Plimpton. While so many of the little magazines have failed, this one has flourished and remains a prestigious outlet for fiction and poetry. Styron and his literary set had no illusions about their relationship to another band of expatriates — Ernest Hemingway, F. Scott Fitzgerald, John Dos Passos, and others. Styron's generation of writers clearly followed the group Gertrude Stein labeled the Lost Generation. In *Lie Down in Darkness* Peyton Loftis says her father's generation was not lost. Rather, they were losing the next generation — that is, Styron's.

Styron is enormously popular in France. *Lie Down in Darkness* was named to the *Agrégation,* the reading list for French universities, for 1973–1974. Styron was the only living American author on the list; Nathaniel Hawthorne and Edgar Allan Poe were the only other Americans named that year. Styron's writings, particularly *Set This House on Fire,* are amenable to the French *nouveau roman* (new novel) genre.

Styron returned to the United States in 1953. He met Rose Burgunder at Johns Hopkins University, and a short time later that year they were married in Rome. She is the best critic of Styron's works in progress and helps maintain his ties to the *Paris Review* through her work as a contributing poetry editor. Rose Styron often speaks on behalf of Amnesty International, an organization that seeks the liberation of political prisoners and relief for victims of human-rights violations worldwide. The Styrons have four grown children: Susanna, Paola, Thomas, and Alexandra. William and Rose Styron reside in a large farmhouse in Roxbury, Connecticut, and spend summers at their home on Martha's Vineyard, Massachusetts.

While Styron has mused that he may someday return to his native South, he is firmly settled in the North, his ties to Yale University being particularly strong through his friendship with the late Robert Penn Warren. Styron was named a fellow of Silliman College at Yale in 1964, and in 1972 the Yale Repertory Theatre staged his play, *In the Clap Shack.* The recipient of many prizes and awards, Styron has a firm place among modern American writers. *Lie Down in Darkness* was a candidate for the Pulitzer Prize and won the Prix de Rome of the American Academy of Arts and Letters. He was named in 1963 to the board of directors of the Inter-American Foundation of the Arts and in 1970 to the editorial board of the *American Scholar.* That same year he was the recipient of the William Dean Howells Medal of the American Academy of Arts and Letters. In October 1993 President Bill Clinton awarded Styron the National Medal of the Arts at the White House for "outstanding contributions to the cultural life of the nation."

The most notable of Styron's literary honors is the 1967 Pulitzer Prize for *The Confessions of Nat Turner,* a work that brought him both hostile fire and great admiration from the academic community. He has received honorary doctorates from Wilberforce University, Duke University, the New School for Social Research, and Tufts University. In 1976 he received the University Union Award for Distinction in Literature from the University of

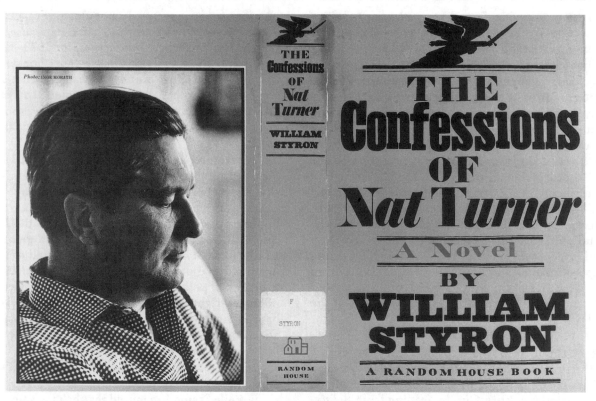

Dust jacket for Styron's Pulitzer Prize–winning novel, a controversial account of the leader of an 1831 slave insurrection in Virginia

South Carolina, an award previously given to Robert Penn Warren, Robert Lowell, and Archibald MacLeish.

Styron's books are as popular in the former Soviet Union as they are in France. He has said that he feels at home in both places because of the friendly reception given his work. However, he amended this position when he stirred up a minor tempest in 1969 by commenting on the defection of Anatoly Kuznetsov from the Soviet Union, saying that the author's actions could endanger other dissidents still in that country. Styron had to clarify his statement in order not to be interpreted as advocating the docile acceptance of the lot of Soviet writers, artists, and intellectuals. He said he deplored Kuznetsov's "precipitate haste" in denouncing the Soviet Union in such a way as to endanger other writers. Styron also said he found the oppression so unbearable on a three-week trip to Moscow that "he became desperate to get out again."

Styron again became involved in the cause of Soviet writers in 1972, when he joined Bellow, Mailer, Herbert Mitgang, Malcolm Cowley, Bernard Malamud, Louis Auchincloss, Lionel Trilling, and Rex Stout in sending a letter to Soviet leader Nikolay Podgorny, urging him to restore funda-

mental human rights to Soviet Jews. The writers particularly wanted to see the restoration of cultural and educational opportunities that were being denied. While Styron is not Jewish, he does not hesitate to enter struggles of this sort. Styron's fiction and public utterances display his firm stance for human rights.

For instance, Styron testified in court that he saw Chicago police beat demonstrators in Lincoln Park during the 1968 Democratic Convention. As a pro–Eugene McCarthy alternate delegate to the convention, Styron witnessed the brutality inflicted on young people protesting the Vietnam War. Styron and his neighbor Arthur Miller often join forces on social issues. When a teacher in Roxbury was suspended for refusing to say the Pledge of Allegiance with her class, Styron and Miller, along with two dozen local residents, signed a statement protesting the suspension. Styron is not anti-American; he supports the civil liberties guaranteed by the uniquely American system.

In 1961 Styron became involved in prison reform through the case of Benjamin Reid, a black man who faced certain death in the electric chair until Styron led a crusade to have his sentence commuted to life imprisonment. Sadly, Styron had to dissociate himself from Reid's cause when Reid escaped from a work crew and went on a rampage of violence shortly before he was due for parole. There can be little doubt that the irony was not lost on Styron that Reid, like Styron's Nat Turner, rebelled violently in the face of kindness. Though Styron could hardly condone Reid's behavior, he could appreciate the forces that drove him to his abortive attempt to be free: a prison – or slave – system cannot be benevolent. Much of the hostile criticism from black intellectuals toward *The Confessions of Nat Turner* springs from Styron's attempt at a psychological portrait showing Turner as a proud black man who comes to resent the favors shown him by his white masters.

Styron's experience with legal issues was not soured by his disappointment with Reid. In 1975 he joined Miller and director Mike Nichols in establishing a defense fund for an eighteen-year-old convicted in 1973 for the manslaughter of his mother in Canaan, Connecticut, near Styron's home. Miller noticed some discrepancies in the case, concluding that the boy was psychologically incapable of committing the crime, and Styron and Nichols joined the cause. They hired a new lawyer and secured coverage of the story in the *New York Times*. Because of their influence the investigation was reopened, another suspect was arrested, and the boy was cleared. Joan Barthel's *A Death in Canaan* (1976) details the case; Styron wrote the introduction to her book.

Styron became involved in examining the motivations behind the Nazi concentration camps, in which millions of Jews and non-Jews were slaughtered. His interest stemmed in part from research for his enormously successful novel *Sophie's Choice*. Following a tour of Auschwitz, Styron called the Holocaust "awesomely central to our present-day consciousness."

Letters to the editors of such publications as the *New York Times* and the *New York Review of Books* continue to provide Styron a forum for his public stand on controversial issues. Appalled at the suppression of the freedom of expression and information through the deaths of more than a dozen Turkish journalists in 1992-1993, Styron – along with his wife Rose, Miller, and such writers as Edward Albee, E. L. Doctorow, Toni Morrison, Harold Pinter, and Kurt Vonnegut – wrote a letter (13 May 1993) to the *New York Review of Books*. They called on the Turkish government to "demonstrate its commitment" to human rights by aggressively investigating the deaths and instituting procedures to protect journalists in their efforts to impart information.

Styron's public willingness to concern himself with commitments of time and money to the oppressed, the victimized, and the downtrodden finds expression in his novels. The forms of oppression may vary, but in each major work there is the recurring theme of individuals who struggle and usually fail. Peyton Loftis of *Lie Down in Darkness* and Sophie of *Sophie's Choice* commit suicide. Nat Turner dooms himself and other slaves to execution for embarking on their impossible mission to overcome their white masters. Captain Mannix of *The Long March* surrenders his will and admits his inability to be anything other than a small cog in the massive military machine. Cass Kinsolving of *Set This House on Fire* finds a measure of peace by merely "choosing to exist" rather than killing himself and by "considering the good" in himself following his utter debasement at the hands of the diabolically manipulative Mason Flagg.

Time present in *Lie Down in Darkness* reveals Milton Loftis, accompanied by his mistress, Dolly Bonner, awaiting the arrival of the body of his daughter Peyton at Port Warwick, Virginia, from New York City. Through flashbacks consisting of interior monologues the reader sees events from various points of view, which, taken together, show the circumstances that prompted Peyton to propel herself from the roof of a Harlem tenement. The reader sees into the lives of Milton, his wife Helen, and the Reverend Carey Carr, on whom Helen depends for spiritual succor as Milton does on Dolly for his physical needs. Peyton's older sister Maudie is hopelessly enfeebled physically and mentally, a source of constant guilt for her parents. In this family unit Styron places Peyton, a vivacious, outgoing girl characterized by scenes of light, parties, and overflowing happiness. The novel's discontinuous time shifts and various points of view reveal the reason for Peyton's suicide.

Styron shows Milton as shadowy, murky, and confused – his frequent, prolonged spells of drunkenness and his hangovers symbolizing his indecisive personality. Milton "despised his father. The old man had given him too much." Milton's father arranged a commission for him during World War II, and he partied away the war on Governor's Island in the New York harbor. But Milton, repeating his father's mistakes, gives Peyton everything she desires, smothering her with an affection strongly hinting at incestuous desire. Milton's boozing has rendered his legal practice ineffectual, and he depends on Helen's inheritance from her father. His life represents a strange mixture, a blending of paradoxes. An army captain with no military merit, he is wealthy, but from his wife's money; he is married yet separated.

Helen, too, is the product of her father, a professional military man. Colonel Peyton's men called him "Blood and Jesus Peyton," obviously modeled after "Old Blood and Guts" Patton of World War II fame. Helen confides to Carr that her parents were both "strict and severe with me." She tells him how religious her father was and recalls how handsome he appeared "swaggering off in his jodhpurs and riding crop, and I thought he was just like God." Her father's favorite horse was a silver gelding named Champ. Styron's powerful images of Colonel Peyton's strict religiosity and emasculated horse depict Helen's father as a formidable shaper of her values, endowing her with the capacity for a vicious sexual frigidity toward Milton. With her keen sense of right and wrong she suffers through Milton's affair with Dolly and the suspected incestuous relationship between Milton and Peyton.

One of Styron's most complex minor characters is Carr, rector of Saint Mark's Protestant Episcopal Church, who wants more than anything to "attain a complete vision of God." Carr takes Helen's suffering as his own burden and counsels her for a period of six years. He thinks "despairingly of his God who, he had prayed, would reveal Himself finally this year and preferably before Advent." Helen smugly feels that she knows God and prides herself on the firmness of her religious commitment, while Carr, unsure of his sincerity and righteousness, sees that he lacks the ability to correct Helen's shortcomings or to deal with his own. Helen is doomed to remain as she is – cold, inflexible, and imperfect herself yet demanding perfection from others.

While each character searches for something missing, the reader wonders about Peyton's death, the causes for which are revealed through the succession of narrative viewpoints. Peyton, like Milton and Helen, feels lost. She blames Helen for Milton's misery. Peyton's passionate relationship with college man Dick Cartwright parodies the sexless relationship of her parents. When Peyton and Dick make love, she realizes that sex itself does not ensure happiness. Following one such encounter with Dick, Peyton says their generation is "lost." She leaves the conformity of Sweet Briar College – which Styron presents as a sort of holding pen for females expected to meet and marry a Kappa Alpha from the University of Virginia – and joins the bohemian society of New York's Greenwich Village. At a party she meets and falls in love with Harry Miller, a Jewish artist. Their marriage takes

place at the Loftis home in Port Warwick, and Milton becomes insanely jealous when he sees Harry kiss Peyton. Drinking heavily, Milton loses control and kisses Peyton "in front of everyone, much more than a father." This crucial scene foretells the inevitable dissolution of all the relationships. Both Harry and Helen witness Milton's attempt to supplant Harry as Peyton's lover.

Styron's handling of Peyton's descent into madness and suicide is a tour de force – a long, nightmarish interior monologue that recalls images of light and dark, flightless birds, artificially induced happiness through alcohol, and empty religious platitudes. Peyton's infidelities with several men, ostensibly to punish Harry for what she imagines are infidelities on his part, finally force him to leave her. In an alien place without friends or family, she goes mad. In a series of carefully layered symbols Styron shows her climbing the stairs of a Harlem tenement. At every landing moths flutter crazily about naked light bulbs. She removes all her clothes and is "naked, clean, if sweating, just as I had come." Like the moth that flies to its death at the light bulb, Peyton, now a "wingless bird," flies to her death by plunging to the street below. She lies down in darkness through the irreversible act of suicide, but at least she has acted. Milton, Helen, Dolly, and Carr remain bewildered, unforgiving, lustful, and shallow. Their valueless world is the true darkness of society.

While in Paris, Styron wrote *The Long March,* a novella about the futility of struggling against overwhelming forces. The work is based on an actual incident at Camp Lejeune. Styron makes clear that he has no love for the military and feels that military life corrupts people through its pressures to conform and to submit to authority. The book has three principal characters: Colonel Templeton, a regular Marine; Lieutenant Culver, a reserve officer who speaks for Styron; and Captain Mannix, another reservist who rebels against the authority of Colonel Templeton. Much of the story is related through Culver's thoughts as he watches the struggle between Mannix and Templeton.

Templeton, the battalion commander, orders a thirty-six-mile road march at night in order to test the combat effectiveness of his unit, composed largely of soft reservists recalled to duty. Mannix – who hates himself for remaining in the reserves and who hates the marines for subjecting him to degrading experiences – rebels, but his is a rebellion in reverse. Instead of refusing to lead his men he becomes cruelly insistent that they all finish the long march in order to spite the colonel, who expects them to fall

James Jones and Styron, early 1970s

out. Culver's thoughts tell the reader that Mannix's rebellion is futile and ironically tragic, for in determining to finish the march Mannix does precisely what Templeton wants him to do. *The Long March* represents an intensely personal statement of Styron's antimilitary, antiwar feelings. He believes that American involvement in World War II was justified, and he is proud of his service in the Pacific, but his recall to duty sparked the antimilitarism that has been consistent to the present.

The Long March begins with a ghastly scene of eight young Marines killed by a "short" mortar round while the unit is on bivouac. This scene of carnage sets the tone of the stupidity of waste that pervades the novel. Templeton, symbolizing the Marine Corps, takes no responsibility for the accidental deaths of the young marines. When informed of the accident, Templeton, with a gesture similar to that of Pontius Pilate at the trial of Christ, wipes his hands clean, assuming none of the blame. His name suggests that he is a priest in the military "cult," and he represents the system – innocent of a specific crime but culpable because he perpetuates the system that caused the incident.

Mannix is the "Nix-man," the hero who will fail because of the overwhelming forces he opposes, but he will fail gloriously. Culver, though he sympathizes with Mannix, abnegates his individuality; he acquiesces, becoming an unwilling convert to Templeton's religion. He stumbles "behind the Colonel,

like a ewe who follows the slaughterhouse ram, dumb and undoubting." Culver finishes the march, but only out of personal pride, not out of rebellion or spite. He is essentially a coward – afraid of what the enlisted men will think of him, and what he will think of himself, if he does not finish the march. Templeton is not personally evil; the system he represents is evil because it robs people of their freedom and individuality.

The story of the march is not that of Mannix as Moses leading his men on an exodus away from bondage and slavery; it is an excursion in the night that takes them deeper and deeper into the system. As the men fall by the side of the road from heat, exhaustion, and blisters, they in effect acknowledge that they are unable to meet and conquer the corps; it is too big, too impersonal, too uncaring. Mannix fails to realize that he becomes to his men just as uncaring as Templeton. Mannix does not care about them as individuals. He wants his company to finish the march so that he can prove something to Templeton, but Mannix's men have to suffer under his harangues just as Mannix has to suffer under Templeton's domination.

When Templeton orders Mannix to ride in on one of the trucks because he has been crippled by a nail pushing through his boot, Mannix explodes and commits an unacceptable act of insubordination for which he will receive a court-martial. Templeton promises that Mannix will be sent to Korea – that is, hell. Culver, Styron's spokesman, experiences deepening gloom as he attempts to make sense of Mannix's futile rebellion, which has caused his men to hate him and which results in judicial punishment. Mannix painfully finishes the march, but he does not triumph. *The Long March* shows that, though the human will may be ultimately defeated, the indomitable spirit will at least attempt to overcome the challenges of each individual's "long march."

Set This House on Fire is a lengthy, complex novel with an intricate narrative structure. There are, in fact, two narrators: Peter Leverett and Cass Kinsolving. As the novel opens, Peter Leverett (Styron may have consciously sustained the initials of Peyton Loftis), a Virginia-born New York lawyer, goes to Charleston, South Carolina, to visit Cass. Peter and Cass had been in Sambuco, Italy, at the same time, and both men knew Mason Flagg, the third principal character. Peter feels haunted by the experience of Mason's apparent suicide in Sambuco and seeks out Cass to learn what he can of the circumstances that led to Mason's death. In the first half of the book Peter tells Cass of the days when he knew Mason at prep school and in New York, establishing the character of Mason as despicable, unscrupulous, and lascivious. Cass takes over the narration for the second half, although Peter ostensibly is still the narrator of the entire work. Styron has been faulted for this dual narrative structure, but much of the artistry of the novel depends on this juxtaposition of points of view.

Cass admits that he killed Mason in Sambuco and goes on to tell Peter why he did so. But to do that he must recall events in his life that occurred long before he met Mason in Italy. He relates various stories of his life as a struggling painter in Paris and later in Rome. There are other stories that go back to his days as a young man in North Carolina and Virginia. In Sambuco, where the central action occurs, Cass falls in love with Francesca, a peasant girl who works for Mason. A wealthy man, Mason has a mysterious power over him that involves supplying liquor for the alcoholic Cass, food for Cass's wife Poppy and their four children, and American drugs from the U.S. Army PX in Salerno for Francesca's dying father, Michele.

When Mason feels that Cass is about to escape from his bondage, he rapes Francesca, who alone offers Cass a sense of stability and purpose, and she dies a short time later. Cass, thinking Mason has killed Francesca, stalks him like an animal in pursuit of its prey, traps him on a cliff overlooking the town, and tosses his body off the cliff after smashing his skull with a rock. Actually Francesca was killed by Saverio, a retarded peasant who meant her no harm. Luigi, a police corporal and Cass's friend, alters the clues of the case when he discovers that Cass has killed Mason; the case is ruled a murder-suicide with Mason, not Saverio, designated as Francesca's murderer. Peter returns to New York, Cass to South Carolina; two years after the events in Sambuco, the two men meet in Charleston to exchange their versions of what took place.

Styron said that he would never attempt another novel as ambitious as this one, though critics may see just as much complexity, if not more, in his psychological portraits of Nat Turner and Sophie Zawistowska. *Set This House on Fire* could be called Styron's "European" novel, not simply because it has a European setting, but because of its *nouveau roman* elements. Existential novels depend on a series of scenes or moments, each intense in its own way, which taken in their totality, rather than in a linear progression leading to a climactic moment, reveal the novel's essential truth. Thus, when Styron takes the reader into the past lives of Peter and Cass, both of whom narrate learning experiences and shaping events from their youth, the reader sees the psychological motivations that result in Mason's death.

Cass's decision to exist is not a choice of the present moment apart from all that has gone before; his decision is unalterably enmeshed with his significant earlier experiences. The novel suggests that the way to exist in the modern world – the way to maintain one's sense of individuality – is to deal directly with the problem of evil in the world, here symbolized by Mason. Cass's soul is the particular house that is set on fire, though the other characters must also endure Mason's various forms of evil. Peter and Cass gradually learn that they are not so dissimilar from Mason or from each other. Peter, a lawyer, wants a sense of propriety, of things being right in the world. At one point in the story a hillbilly song, "What's the Matter with This World?," booms out over Mason's villa in Sambuco. Like Cass, the unproductive artist who plays the hillbilly record, people sometimes stumble – drunken, confused, or infatuated – hoping to attain high goals.

Mason represents evil and sin in myriad ways: pathological lying, adultery, salacious obsession with pornography, cunning extortion, and rape. Because Peter and Cass are involved with Mason, they are involved with his evil and see in him the frightening capacity for unspeakable depravity in themselves. If one cannot extinguish evil in the world, perhaps one can only try to be good and confront evil. When Luigi says he will not imprison Cass, he frees him to consider the good in himself — to go forward and live in the world, to exist, to be.

Near the end of *Set This House on Fire* Cass and Peter try to explain to each other the reasons they think motivated Mason to rape the beautiful peasant girl Francesca. Cass says he thinks Mason was a man who found release from his unfulfilled desire through violence. Cass's explanation of Mason's violence could serve as an explanation for Nat Turner's leading his fellow slaves in an insurrection against their white masters in Virginia. *The Confessions of Nat Turner* develops the historical Nat Turner into a fictional character driven by uncontrollable desires and emotions; the only way he can deal with those emotions is to channel them into a violent rebellion against the system that enslaves him.

Much of the novel's artistry has been obscured because of the controversy surrounding Styron's right to adapt a historical personage for fictional purposes. Many articles, and even entire books, have been written on that single aspect of the novel. The controversy stems from the inability of some critics to recognize that creativity and imagination far outweigh historical accuracy in a work of fiction. Styron insists that his novel is "an essay of the imagination." The opposition to it indicates the profundity of the emotions with which Styron imbues his character; in this psychological domain Nat becomes an artistically drawn character of fiction.

As a slave, Styron's Nat is automatically limited in certain human freedoms. But, as a privileged house servant, Nat is granted many more advantages than most other slaves. Under a kind master, Samuel Turner, Nat learns to read and write, which is forbidden by law. He learns mathematics; he recites Scripture committed to memory under the tutelage of the Turner women; and he becomes a carpenter whose skills are the envy of many of the white plantation owners. But Nat's upbringing is marred by several incidents that intensify his feelings of isolation. Styron constructs a complex sex life for Nat. The only direct sexual contact with another human being in Nat's life is a homosexual encounter with a young slave. In his dreams he makes love to various white women, and one in particular becomes the object of these fantasies. Margaret Whitehead, the only victim Nat personally kills during the insurrection, occupies his thoughts even as he is led away to the gallows.

Nat's sex life is one aspect of his total psyche — his total being — that Styron creates. Styron does not, however, simply construct a sexual misfit, as

some critics charge. Rather, Nat's sexual problems indicate a greater deficiency: his incompleteness as a human being. Styron must show Nat as a human being, not as just another nameless human chattel in the dehumanizing slave system. To do this Styron has to give him emotions — love, hate, envy, compassion. Through Nat's confessions the reader learns the drives (not just the sexual drives), the passions, and the human needs that cause him alternately to hate his fellow blacks and his white masters, to lust after white women, and to be deeply religious, even as he plans mass murder. In short, the reader learns all the private thoughts that prove Nat to be a psychologically complex man. That he is black by birth but white by training and acculturation causes his psychological imbalance. The novel shows how a man who is denied his manhood all his life can be driven to reject society's values and strike out at that society in order to assert his humanity.

Marse Samuel educates Nat to such a degree that he is more literate than most of the poor whites in the county, people who are most often seen drinking, cursing, and being generally crude in the market in Jerusalem, Virginia, on Saturday mornings. Nat knows he is better than these evil, godless men who are separated from the poverty and ignobility of slavery only because of their skin color. The incongruity of their relative freedom causes deep resentment in Nat. But Marse Samuel has such faith in his ability to survive as a free man that he arranges for Nat, following his release from bondage, to be apprenticed to a contractor in Richmond, where he can work as a skilled carpenter.

Marse Samuel's plantation, like so many of that region, is failing economically because the tobacco crops have depleted the soil. Forced to liquidate his assets in order to make his fortune again in the Deep South, he sells most of his slaves but arranges for Nat to pass temporarily into ownership of the Reverend Eppes, a severe, zealous, and maniacal Baptist preacher who is to provide for Nat's needs until final arrangements can be made with the Richmond contractor. Marse Samuel never communicates with Nat or Eppes again, thus ending Nat's hopes for his promised freedom. Nat suffers a brutal existence as Eppes's chattel, particularly stupefying in its crudity and degradation after the elegance and sophistication of the Turner plantation. Nat comes to know hard work and, more important, for the first time comes to know what it means to be black and a slave.

Nat passes from master to master, each in turn exploiting his abilities and making a profit from his

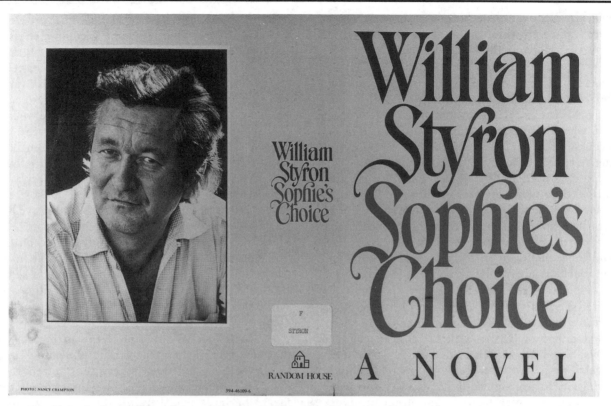

William
Styron
Sophie's
Choice

F
STYRON

RANDOM HOUSE

William
Styron
Sophie's
Choice
A NOVEL

PHOTO: NANCY CRAMPTON

394-46109-6

Dust jacket for Styron's 1979 Holocaust novel, in which the title character struggles with her guilt over sending one of her children to death

labors while denying him the respect, friendship, and dignity which are due a man. As the whites betray him, Nat's loyalty shifts to his fellow slaves, whom he once scorned but who now share his predicament. Nat learns to speak the dialect of the field hands, using levels of articulation appropriate to his audience. Nat's bilingual ability demonstrates his cultural dichotomy. The slaves are Nat's peers in a legal sense, but it is the inhuman inflexibility of the slave laws that prevents him from achieving his individual potential in human affairs. Nat knows he is not on the same level with the other slaves, and this knowledge produces a deepening sense of isolation.

After Nat learns to read, he daily pores over his Bible, a gift from Marse Samuel, and becomes fanatic in his religious beliefs. Nat baptizes both black and white supplicants and later uses his knowledge of Scripture and his power as a speaker to enlist the impressionable slaves in his cause. Ironically, just as the Reverend Richard Whitehead quotes Scripture to the slaves on Mission Sunday as proof of the propriety of their bondage and the holy requirement of their subservience, so Nat manipulates appropriate passages of Old Testament prophecy to justify his insurrection against the whites.

Nat labors for ten years as a slave to Thomas Moore of Southampton County, adopting a "hound-like obedience" while he plans his insurrection. When Will and Sam, two slaves who later join Nat's army, are forced to fight like animals for the entertainment of poor whites in the town's market, Nat decides that the whites "would perish by my design and at my hands." He receives a vision in the forest that he interprets as a mission from God to destroy the whites of the county. His religious zealotry becomes infused with a suppressed sexuality. He suffers a series of sexual fantasies about white women, beginning with Miss Emmeline Turner, whom Nat sees making love with her cousin; with Mrs. Ridley, whose confusion on hearing unintelligible slave dialect causes Nat to want to possess her violently on the spot; and with Margaret Whitehead, the young belle of the county.

Thomas Gray, the white lawyer who records Nat's confessions, asks him early in the novel why he killed only one person, Margaret Whitehead, in the course of the insurrection in which sixty whites die. Nat tries to avoid answering, but Gray persists. The entire narrative is an effort by Nat to reason out his motives for the insurrection and his feeble participation once the insurrection begins. His reluctance to answer Gray's insistent questions about Margaret indicates her importance in Nat's undertaking. His feelings toward the seemingly pure and kind Margaret become a collage of mingled physical lust, spiritual love, and destructive rapaciousness.

At one moment Nat views Margaret as an angel, as he once viewed Miss Emmeline. At another moment Nat's desires for Margaret are blunted by guilt and remorse, just as he feels after fantasizing about Mrs. Ridley. And at still another moment Nat greedily lusts after Margaret, wishing to devour her without any feelings of guilt. When Nat drives Margaret to church in a buggy, she babbles innocently about some poetry she has written about "Christian love" and slavery. Nat begins to feel confusion, something akin to hatred, toward Margaret. He wants no sympathy from her; he wants simple human friendship and respect. Margaret's sympathy, however well intentioned, becomes a source of distrust as despicable to Nat as Marse Samuel's paternalistic kindness years before. Margaret's sympathy for Nat emasculates him, and his pent-up rage explodes in insurrection.

When the rebellion gets under way, Nat leads his men from house to house, destroying all the whites along the way. He attempts to strike killing blows in several instances, but in most he is either unable or unwilling to do so. Other slave participants have to dispatch the victims on these occasions, and the men begin to doubt Nat's ability to lead. When the slaves arrive at Mrs. Whitehead's plantation, the crazed, murderous Will taunts Nat into killing Margaret. Nat pursues Margaret across a field: "*Ah, how I want her,* I thought, and unsheathed my sword." Styron's use of this obvious phallic symbol indicates that Nat's pursuit of Margaret combines both hate and love. He desires her sexually but wishes to kill her. He stabs her twice, wounding her. When she pleads for mercy, Nat recalls the erotic moans of Miss Emmeline, who urges her lover to sexual consummation with cries of "mercy."

When Margaret dies from Nat's wounds, he loses his desire to continue the insurrection. The act of murdering Margaret dispels all his lifelong frustration of being black in a white world. Her death releases him from his suffering, for, in asserting his masculinity in a symbolic rape, he not only affirms his own manhood but achieves vengeance for the defilement and abuse of all the whites who have held him in bondage. The insurrection changes his status from chattel to human being.

There is much about this powerful novel of slavery to commend it to readers interested in the uses of history in fiction in general and to readers of Styron's work in particular. While articles about the controversy surrounding Styron's use of the first person to re-create a fictional character out of a black cultural hero often become pointlessly strident, legitimate questions of the limits of art and imagination arise. But no amount of articles attacking Styron's creative license can obscure his creative use of the canvas of American slavery to depict his consistent theme of the victimization of powerless people by others.

Styron's fifth novel, *Sophie's Choice,* depicts the theme of group victimization – of both Jews and non-Jews in the Nazi death camps. The similarity between coffles of American slaves taken away to baleful servitude in the Deep South and Europeans herded onto cattle cars for shipment to the death camps is obvious. Less obvious is Styron's consistency in relating *Sophie's Choice* to *Set This House on Fire.* Peter Leverett says to Cass Kinsolving, "Deep down and for reasons I couldn't fathom, he had his own private riddles to solve and untangle. And just as I thought that he could clear up my oppressive mysteries, so he saw in me the key to his own." Similarly, in *Sophie's Choice* Stingo comes to understand guilt in its poisonous extremity when he learns of Sophie's unbearably miserable life.

Again and again Sophie, a Polish Catholic, speaks of her guilt – a guilt rooted primarily in the loss of her children and in her unsuccessful efforts to save them. The reader sees her demented Jewish lover, Nathan Landau, alternating between tenderness and abuse, increasing her guilt by asking her how she, a Gentile, could live through Auschwitz when so many others, particularly Jews, were gassed. The reader witnesses her torment through the narration of Stingo, a southern WASP, at a further remove from the firsthand experience of the Jews. Styron has said that, in order to convey the true horror of the death camps, his main character had to be non-Jewish; if she had been Jewish, readers would have simply accepted Sophie's story as that of yet another victim of the Holocaust – and Styron might have invited the wrath of actual survivors. In making Sophie a non-Jew, Styron opens up the possibility of a shared humanity through a shared guilt.

Stingo, a Styronic persona, reflects the naiveté of America regarding the Holocaust. As he hears of the significant moments of Sophie's life – the day her husband and father were killed, the day she was arrested, and the day she chose which of her two children would live – he remembers where he was and what he was doing. His life, vapid and carefree, mocks Sophie's suffering. He indirectly experiences the suffering and guilt that she experiences directly; her suffering, filtered through his adolescent insouciance, magnifies his guilt. Having heard her story,

Stingo must make her a part of his life as well. Sophie's narration, a counterpoint to Stingo's first-person narration, provides a balance between his lusty humor and her inutterable despair.

Stingo's sexual inexperience is shown through such amusing scenes as his frustrated gropings with Leslie Lapidus. In contrast Styron presents the sadomasochistic eroticism of Sophie and her lover, Nathan. Stingo's innocent view of sex yields to Sophie's blending of sex with violence. There are other scenes with a sexual leitmotiv. When Sophie and her children, a son and daughter, disembark from the train at Auschwitz, she is confronted by Jemand von Niemand, the camp doctor, who tells her she should sleep with him. He then forces her on the spot to choose which one of her children will live. That fateful choice haunts her memory and produces her largest measure of guilt.

Later, in confused dreams, she imagines having sex with this same camp doctor. In another scene, on a packed Brooklyn subway, with Sophie crushed between "rubbery torsos and slick perspiring arms," a stranger probes Sophie's private parts with his finger: "A straightforward, conventional rape would have done less violation to her spirit and identity." This subway scene suggests the trains stuffed with unfortunate souls on their way to Auschwitz, Treblinka, or Buchenwald. The massive Nazi war machine collectively rapes the death-camp inmates in a terrifyingly dehumanizing totality, and Sophie is assaulted by a single anonymous thug.

Stingo envies Sophie and Nathan as they make passionate, noisy love in the room above him. But they commit suicide with poison in this same bed. Stingo says, "Wasn't there some inexpressible meaning in the fact that my entire experience of Sophie and Nathan was circumscribed by a bed, from the moment — which now seemed centuries past — when I first heard them above me in the glorious circus of their lovemaking to the final tableau of that same bed, whose image would stay with me until dotage or my own death erased it from my mind?"

Styron understands that death and love have been archetypally entwined in literature. Nathan, Sophie's lover, becomes her executioner. The Nazis could not kill her, but her lover-torturer could. The self-destructive violence of their relationship leads the reader back to the brutality of Auschwitz, where Sophie was consumed with trying to survive. Having lived through that special horror, she finds in her new life in America the demonic Nathan, who elicits from her such an insurmountable, unsurvivable measure of guilt that she must join him in sui-

cide. Stingo survives to tell his story. In the final scene of the novel, following Sophie's funeral, he goes to Coney Island, a place of carnal pleasure. He sleeps on the beach and awakes the next morning covered with sand placed on him by children – a symbolic burial. His resurrection on this "excellent and fair" morning forces him back into the world of responsibility.

While his fiction can stand alone on its merits, Styron readily discusses his work in interviews, and his extensive nonfiction publications often complement his novels. In 1982 he published *This Quiet Dust and Other Writings,* a collection of some of his nonfictional prose, only a small percentage of his prodigious output. In this volume Styron shares his thoughts on such subjects as racial tension, prisons, capital punishment, other writers, the craft of writing, the South, military service, and adolescence. Readers of Styron's novels will profit from this collection. For instance, to understand *The Long March* and the play *In the Clap Shack* more fully, it is instructive to hear the nonfictional voice of Styron, the former marine, reflecting on the worth of the individual despite his subjugation to the monolithic military system. Styron's review (*New York Review of Books,* 14 May 1964) of Douglas MacArthur's *Reminiscences* (1964) is characteristically blunt: "The world that MacArthur thrills to makes most of his fellow Americans choke with horror." His articles on other writers are of interest to readers of William Faulkner, Robert Penn Warren, and James Jones. Styron's eulogy at Jones's funeral was an eloquent expression of love both for Jones and for their profession.

Darkness Visible is Styron's account of his descent into depression, which began around 1985. Styron's memoir of his debilitating battle with depression (first published in a briefer version in *Vanity Fair,* December 1989) brought him a new readership — fellow sufferers, medical doctors, counselors, and pharmacologists. He appeared on television talk shows and newsmagazine-format programs to discuss his triumph over the disease. Parts of *Darkness Visible* recall images from his novels. Styron deals with the self-destructive aspects of depression: "Death . . . was now a daily presence, blowing over me in cold gusts. I had not conceived precisely how my end would come. In short, I was still keeping the idea of suicide at bay. But plainly the possibility was around the corner, and I would soon meet it face to face." In a similar tone Cass Kinsolving tells Peter Leverett, "I didn't know anything at all. I was *half* a person, trapped by terror, trapped by booze, trapped by self. I was a regular ambulating biologi-

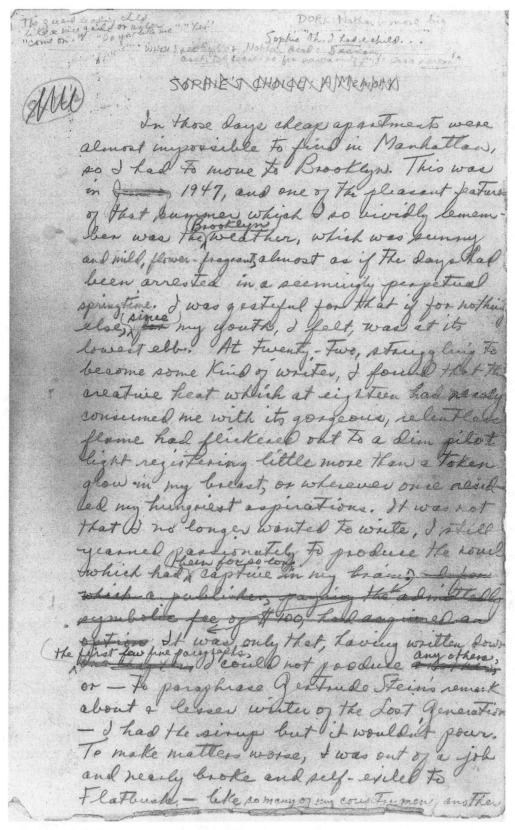

First page of the manuscript for Sophie's Choice *(courtesy of Duke University; by permission of William Styron)*

cal disaster, a bag full of corruption held together by one single poisonous thought – and that was to destroy myself in the most agonizing way there was."

Forms of suicide abound in Styron's fiction. Peyton Loftis leaps to her death from the top of a building. Nathan and Sophie take sodium cyanide. Captain Mannix dooms himself by committing an intolerable act of insubordination, guaranteeing himself a place on the next troopship to the combat zone. Nat Turner enters into a futile rebellion that results in his capture and execution. Cass Kinsolving, speaking of the despicable Mason Flagg, sums up the agony of Styron's characters, who have "one of the most agonizing things that can afflict a man, this raging constant desire with no outlet, a starvation with no chance of fulfillment, which must fever and shake and torment a man until he can only find a release in violence."

Styron's latest book, *A Tidewater Morning: Three Tales from Youth* (1993), collects three stories previously published in *Esquire* over a ten-year period including the time of Styron's depression. These stories represent an intensely autobiographical retrospective for Styron, including such defining memories of his life as his active duty with the marines in the South Pacific ("Love Day"), recollections of black people from his youth who were old enough to have been former slaves ("Shadrach"), and the death of his mother ("A Tidewater Morning").

Styron's fictional persona in this collection, Paul Whitehurst, narrates the three stories, remembering his youth and the people who shaped him. In the South Pacific, eager to go into combat, Paul (whose name doubtless derives from Styron's mother's name, Pauline) must endure the mindless leadership of Lt. Col. "Happy" Halloran: "He was 101 percent Marine Corps – member of a fellowship of knights, professor of a faith, a way of life to which he had consecrated himself as fiercely as any guardian of the Grail." During one of Halloran's endless stories Paul drifts back to a scene fifteen years earlier when his father, an engineer at the local shipyard, berates Paul's mother for her failure to accept the reality of war. His father predicts the war with Japan, in which Paul now finds himself aboard a ship awaiting an invasion of Okinawa. Swaggeringly concealing his fear and talking enthusiastically about "getting into action," Paul becomes physically ill with relief when he learns that the unit's mission has been changed and they will return to Saipan and safety.

"Shadrach" recalls Paul's "tenth summer on earth, in the year 1935" when he meets an allegori-

cally ancient black man: "Shadrach appeared then. We somehow sensed his presence, looked up, and found him there. We had not heard him approach; he had come as silently and portentously as if he had been lowered on some celestial apparatus operated by unseen hands." Ninety-nine-year-old Shadrach returns from Alabama to his native Virginia, where he had been sold before the Civil War. He comes home to die on Dabney land, now owned by the threadbare bootlegger Vernon Dabney, descendant of a once-proud planter family. At first only Paul understands Shadrach's Negro dialect, "muddied by the crippled cadences of senility," and he translates for Vernon Dabney – a symbolic and literarily satisfying image of Styron's efforts in *The Confessions of Nat Turner* to translate fictionally the dehumanizing slave system, with its blacks and whites living not just separately but horribly unequally as well. Paul "understands" Shadrach, mirroring Styron's understanding of his character Nat.

In "A Tidewater Morning" Paul's mother is suffering an agonizing death from cancer. Paul's father, Jeff Whitehurst, consumed with grief, berates the Rev. Dr. Taliaferro and his wife, who have come to offer spiritual succor: "In the incomprehensibility of my wife's agony I have found a terrible answer of sorts. If there is a God he cares nothing for humankind. I will not believe in such a God! If such a God exists, then I abominate him!" In *Set This House on Fire* Luigi voices a similar outrage over the death of his brother during the war: "I did not believe in a God who could create a universe in which it would be possible for a single innocent child to suffer like that." And in *Sophie's Choice* Stingo, trying to make sense of Sophie's death, asks himself, "At Auschwitz, tell me, where was God?" He answers himself, "Where was man?"

Styron's intelligently crafted fiction, written in an age of anxiety, occupies a place of significant achievement among post–World War II authors – a generation of writers who were the first to deal forthrightly with such issues as the finality of war in the nuclear age, racial inequality, and injustice in its various forms. Styron sensitively explores complex themes of contemporary social responsibility, consistently confronting the inherent corruption of the powerful over the powerless.

Interview:

James L. W. West III, ed., *Conversations with William Styron* (Jackson, Miss.: University Press of Mississippi, 1985).

Bibliographies:

James L. W. West III, *William Styron: A Descriptive Bibliography* (Boston: G. K. Hall, 1977);

Jackson Bryer and Mary Beth Hatem, *William Styron: A Reference Guide* (Boston: G. K. Hall, 1978);

Philip W. Leon, *William Styron: An Annotated Bibliography of Criticism* (Westport, Conn.: Greenwood Press, 1978).

References:

Arthur D. Casciato and James L. W. West III, eds., *Critical Essays on William Styron* (Boston: G. K. Hall, 1982);

John H. Clark and others, *William Styron's Nat Turner: Ten Black Writers Respond* (Boston: Beacon Press, 1968);

John K. Crane, *The Root of All Evil: The Thematic Unity of William Styron's Fiction* (Columbia: University of South Carolina Press, 1984);

John B. Duff and Peter M. Mitchell, eds., *The Nat Turner Story: The Historical Event and the Modern Controversy* (New York: Harper & Row, 1971);

Robert H. Fossum, *William Styron: A Critical Essay* (Grand Rapids, Mich.: Erdmans, 1968);

Michael Kreyling, "Speakable and Unspeakable in Styron's *Sophie's Choice*," *Southern Review,* 20 (Summer 1984): 546–561;

Richard G. Law, "The Reach of Fiction: Narrative Technique in Styron's *Sophie's Choice*," *Southern Literary Journal,* 23 (Fall 1990): 45–65;

Philip W. Leon, "*The Lost Boy* and a Lost Girl," *Southern Literary Journal,* 9 (Fall 1976): 61–69;

Barbara T. Lupack, "The Politics of Gender: William Styron's *Sophie's Choice*," *Connecticut Review,* 14 (Fall 1992): 1–8;

Robert K. Morris and Irving Malin, eds., *The Achievement of William Styron* (Athens: University of Georgia Press, 1981);

Judith Ruderman, *William Styron* (New York: Ungar, 1987);

Albert E. Stone, *The Return of Nat Turner: History, Literature, and Cultural Politics in Sixties America* (Athens: University of Georgia Press, 1992).

Papers:

The main repository for Styron's papers – including student writings, unpublished short stories, and correspondence – is the Rare Books Room, Perkins Library, Duke University. The Library of Congress also has a few holdings.

Anne Tyler

(25 October 1941 –)

Caren J. Town
Georgia Southern University

See also the Tyler entries in *DLB 6: American Novelists Since World War II, Second Series* and *DLB Yearbook: 1982.*

BOOKS: *If Morning Ever Comes* (New York: Knopf, 1964; London: Chatto & Windus, 1965);

The Tin Can Tree (New York: Knopf, 1965; London: Macmillan, 1966);

A Slipping-Down Life (New York: Knopf, 1970; London: Severn House, 1983);

The Clock Winder (New York: Knopf, 1972; London: Chatto & Windus, 1973);

Celestial Navigation (New York: Knopf, 1974; London: Chatto & Windus, 1975);

Searching for Caleb (New York: Knopf, 1976; London: Chatto & Windus, 1976);

Earthly Possessions (New York: Knopf, 1977; London: Chatto & Windus, 1977);

Morgan's Passing (New York: Knopf, 1980; London: Chatto & Windus, 1980);

Dinner at the Homesick Restaurant (New York: Knopf, 1982; London: Chatto & Windus, 1982);

The Accidental Tourist (New York: Knopf, 1985; London: Chatto & Windus, 1985);

Breathing Lessons (New York: Knopf, 1988; London: Chatto & Windus, 1989);

Saint Maybe (New York: Knopf, 1991).

OTHER: "Still Just Writing," in *The Writer and Her Work: Contemporary Women Writers Reflect on Their Art and Situation,* edited by Janet Sternburg (New York: Norton, 1980), pp. 3–16.

SELECTED PERIODICAL PUBLICATIONS – UNCOLLECTED:

FICTION

"Laura," *Archive,* 71 (March 1959): 36–37;

"Lights on the River," *Archive,* 72 (October 1959): 5–6;

"The Bridge," *Archive,* 72 (March 1960): 10–15;

"I Never Saw Morning," *Archive,* 73 (April 1961): 11–14;

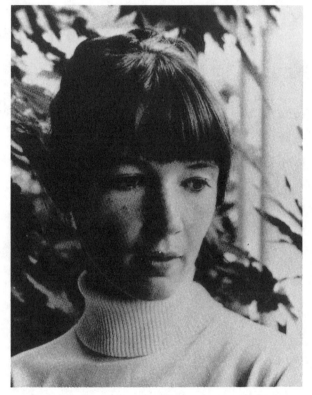

Anne Tyler, circa 1974 (photograph by Jeannie Allen)

"The Baltimore Birth Certificate," *The Critic: A Catholic Review of Books and the Arts,* 21 (February–March 1963): 41–45;

"I Play Kings," *Seventeen,* 22 (August 1963): 338–341;

"The Street of Bugles," *Saturday Evening Post,* 236 (30 November 1963): 64–66;

"Nobody Answers the Door," *Antioch Review,* 24 (Fall 1964): 379–386;

"Dry Water," *Southern Review,* 1 (April 1965): 259–291;

"I'm Not Going to Ask You Again," *Harper's,* 231 (September 1965): 88–98;

"The Saints in Caesar's Household," *Archive,* 79 (September 1966): 18–21;

"As the Earth Gets Old," *New Yorker*, 42 (29 October 1966): 60–64;

"Two People and a Clock on the Wall," *New Yorker*, 42 (19 November 1966): 207–208;

"The Genuine Fur Eyelashes," *Mademoiselle*, 69 (January 1967): 102–103, 136–138;

"The Tea-Machine," *Southern Review*, 3 (January 1967): 171–179;

"The Feather Behind the Rock," *New Yorker*, 43 (12 August 1967): 26–30;

"A Flaw in the Crust of the Earth," *Reporter*, 37 (2 November 1967): 43–46;

"Who Would Want a Little Boy?," *Ladies Home Journal*, 85 (May 1968): 132–133, 156–158;

"The Common Courtesies," *McCall's*, 95 (June 1968): 62–63, 115–116;

"With All Flags Flying," *Redbook*, 137 (June 1971): 88–89, 136–139, 140;

"Outside," *Southern Review*, 7 (Autumn 1971): 1130–1144;

"The Bride in the Boatyard," *McCall's*, 99 (June 1972): 92–93;

"Respect," *Mademoiselle*, 75 (June 1972): 146;

"A Misstep of the Mind," *Seventeen*, 31 (October 1972): 118ff.;

"Spending," *Shenandoah*, 24 (Winter 1973): 58–68;

"The Base-Metal Egg," *Southern Review*, 9 (Summer 1973): 682–686;

"Neutral Ground," *Family Circle*, 85 (November 1974): 36ff.;

"Half-Truths and Semi-Miracles," *Cosmopolitan*, 177 (December 1974): 264ff.;

"A Knack for Languages," *New Yorker*, 50 (13 January 1975): 32–37;

"The Artificial Family," *Southern Review*, 11 (Summer 1975): 615–621;

"The Geologist's Maid," *New Yorker*, 51 (28 July 1975): 29–33;

"Some Sign That I Ever Made You Happy," *McCall's*, 103 (October 1975): 90, 124–133;

"Your Place Is Empty," *New Yorker*, 52 (22 November 1976): 45–54;

"Holding Things Together," *New Yorker*, 52 (24 January 1977): 30–35;

"Average Waves in Unprotected Waters," *New Yorker*, 53 (28 February 1977): 32–36;

"Under the Bosom Tree," *Archive*, 89 (Spring 1977): 72–77;

"Foot-Footing On," *Mademoiselle*, 83 (November 1977): 82ff.;

"Uncle Ahmad," *Quest/77*, 1 (November/December 1977): 76–82;

"Linguistics," *Washington Post Magazine*, 12 November 1978, pp. 38ff.;

"Laps," *Parents' Magazine*, 56 (August 1981): 66–70;

"The Country Cook," *Harper's*, 264 (March 1982): 54–62;

"Teenage Wasteland," *Seventeen*, 42 (November 1983): 144–148;

"Rerun," *New Yorker*, 64 (4 July 1988): 20–32.

NONFICTION

"Youth Talks About Youth: 'Will This Seem Ridiculous?,' " *Vogue*, 145 (1 February 1965): 85, 206;

"Olives Out of a Bottle," *Archive*, 87 (Spring 1975): 70–90;

"Because I Want More Than One Life," *Washington Post*, 15 August 1976, pp. G1, G7;

"Trouble in the Boys' Club: The Trials of Marvin Mandel," *New Republic*, 177 (30 July 1977): 16–19;

"Chocolates in the Afternoon and Other Temptations of a Novelist," *Washington Post Book World*, 4 December 1977, p. 3;

"Writers' Writers: Gabriel García Márquez," *New York Times Book Review*, 4 December 1977, p. 70;

"My Summer," *New York Times Book Review*, 4 June 1978, pp. 35–36;

"Please Don't Call It Persia," *New York Times Book Review*, 18 February 1979, pp. 3, 34–36;

"The Fine, Full World of Eudora Welty," *Washington Star*, 26 October 1980, p. D1;

"A Visit with Eudora Welty," *New York Times Book Review*, 2 November 1980, pp. 33–34;

"Why I Still Treasure 'The Little House,' " *New York Times Book Review*, 9 November 1986, p. 56.

"The real heroes to me in my books," Anne Tyler told Marguerite Michaels, "are first the ones who manage to endure and second the ones who somehow are able to grant other people the privacy of the space around them and yet still produce some warmth." Tyler herself has managed to endure — producing twelve novels in thirty years — while demanding space around her (she steadfastly refuses teaching appointments, lectures, readings, and most interviews). Her frequently warm, often shy characters have endured in the minds of her readers as well, creating an enthusiastic following for this private Baltimore writer.

The daughter of chemist Lloyd Parry Tyler and social worker Phyllis Mahon Tyler, Anne Tyler was born on 25 October 1941 in Minneapolis, Minnesota. From there the family moved to Pennsylvania, Chicago, Duluth, Celo (a collective, experimental community in the North Carolina mountains),

Dust jacket for Tyler's 1972 book, the first of her novels set in Baltimore, which she calls "wonderful territory for a writer"

and finally to Raleigh, North Carolina. She finished her undergraduate work (in three years) at Duke University, during which time she was the student of Reynolds Price, published short stories in the school's literary magazine, twice won the Anne Flexner Award for creative writing, and graduated with a degree in Russian. She completed her doctoral course work (but not the dissertation) in Russian at Columbia University and then worked as a Russian bibliographer at Duke.

In 1963 Tyler married Iranian-born child psychologist (and novelist) Taghi Mohammed Modaressi. She and her husband moved to Montreal, where he completed his residency. During this time she published her first novels, *If Morning Ever Comes* (1964) and *The Tin Can Tree* (1965) and gave birth to her daughters – Tezh in 1965 and Mitra in 1967. The family then moved to Baltimore, where Tyler has raised her daughters, managed her household, and written ten more novels, more than fifty short stories, and many book reviews. Her prolific output is in part the result of the strictness with which she

has maintained the divisions between her work and her family and ruthlessly protected her free time.

Tyler is protective of her intellectual life as well, remaining, as Joseph C. Voelker says, "subtly evasive in all her nonfictional self-representations." She is as guarded of her characters as she is of her own privacy: "I think that what I most fear," she commented to Wendy Lamb, "is intrusion, but it doesn't happen with those characters because on paper you control them, you guard against that intrusion." She watches over her characters, not because she fears them – or for them – but, she says, because she likes them.

Tyler's readers appear to like them as well. Since the publication of *If Morning Ever Comes* she has received predominantly favorable reviews. The enthusiastic attention of John Updike, beginning with her sixth novel, *Searching for Caleb* (1976), has increased her standing. Her recent novels have been commercially successful as well, with her ninth, *Dinner at the Homesick Restaurant* (1982), selling 60,000 copies in hardcover and 655,000 in paperback. *Breathing Lessons* (1988), her eleventh novel, was published in a hardcover edition of 100,000 copies and won the Pulitzer Prize for literature in 1988. Her most recent novel, *Saint Maybe* (1991), was on the *New York Times* best-seller list for nine weeks.

Tyler's popularity rests in part on the apparent ordinariness of her subjects: the power of family, the struggle for personal growth, the accumulation of possessions, and the influence of religion. Yet this ordinariness is not simplicity: she treats each common situation with wry humor and fills each plot with eccentric characters and unconventional developments. For example, her attitude about religion, as Voelker says, "possesses no force of law . . . has no concept of sin and no eschatology . . . but . . . acknowledges as valid the Christian feeling of being out of place in the world, the spirit's restlessness." In this as in many areas, Tyler manages to maintain the spirit of an idea while still questioning many of its premises.

Tyler's view of the family is similar. In nearly every novel characters are both burdened with and supported by their families; for Tyler, families are something one simultaneously wants to escape and to create. Recent critics often point out the way in which Tyler disrupts conventional expectations about family and redefines the subject in her own terms. Doris Betts puts it well: "Tyler's homes are not merely broken but often crazed like a glass vessel but the vessels still hold; blood is still thicker than water."

Tyler is also interested in the growth and maturity of her characters, yet drift and inaction frequently constitute a kind of progress in them. Her characters are often engaged in a struggle to cast off belongings and hold on to what is important: as with Charlotte Emory in *Earthly Possessions* (1977) Tyler's female characters in particular remain at home, with their cosmetic cases packed and their sensible walking shoes on. For Tyler, the most interesting moments in a person's life are not the grand gestures of repudiation or reconciliation but the day-to-day reality following: what happens to Cinderella after she marries her prince (or divorces him). As Betts says, Tyler is interested in how "people survive and persist *beyond* crisis during the long, steady, three-meal-a-day aftermaths."

This attention to steady aftermaths is one of the reasons that Tyler's worlds are so full of objects. Margaret Morganroth Gullette notes that for characters in Tyler's world decisions about accumulation are "momentous . . . because early on in life whether you can become an adult seems to hinge on it, and later, how you want your adulthood to be — whether you want it to be stationary (with a family, house and furniture), or whether you need it to be mobile and sparse." Some characters need it to be both; opposing forces in Tyler's novels operate between what Anne R. Zahlan identifies as "accumulating and gathering and clearing out and moving on." Tyler, too, finds herself drawn by these forces: "I build a house for them," she told Michaels about her characters, "and then I move on to the next house."

Tyler's first fictional house, occupied by Ben Joe Hawkes and his family in *If Morning Ever Comes,* is the prototypical Tyler home: cluttered with people and objects, it is the place characters often leave and always miss. Ben Joe's leave-taking, as is often the case in Tyler's works, is fraught with difficulties, which she establishes in the first lines of the novel: "When Ben Joe Hawkes left home he gave his sister Susannah one used guitar, six shelves of *National Geographic,* a battered microscope, and a foot-high hourglass. All of these things he began to miss as soon as he hit New York." Ben Joe, the only boy in a family of girls and the only man in the house after the desertion (and subsequent death) of their father, finds it hard to leave his things — and home — behind. His discomfort is echoed by later Tyler characters. Voelker cites Ben Joe as Tyler's first "gentle agoraphobic male," who later develops into such central characters as Jeremy Pauling in *Celestial Navigation* (1974) and Macon Leary in *The Accidental Tourist* (1985).

Ben Joe's family, however, does not find it hard to have him gone; in fact, when he returns, supposedly to help with what he alone regards as the crisis his sister Joanne has caused by leaving her husband, "he suddenly saw how closed-off his family looked. They went peacefully on with what they were doing; Ben Joe, having vanished, might as well not exist." They continue with their jobs, their quarrels, and their lives in apparent unconcern, but they are happier to have him back than is immediately apparent. Ben Joe comments, " 'You had to be a sort of detective with his mother; you had to search out the fresh-made bed, the flowers on the bureau, and the dinner table laid matter-of-factly with your favorite supper, and then you forgot her crisp manners.' " Like many mothers in Tyler's fiction, Ben Joe's is not expressively maternal; her care and concern have to be ferreted out.

Once he is home, the problem for Ben Joe becomes one that is typical in Tyler's later works — whether to remain trapped in old circumstances or to strike out for new territories. "Every place I go," he says, "I miss another place." In talking with Joanne, who thinks returning to her husband would be "going backwards," Ben Joe helps her work out her dilemma, telling her that " 'sometimes it's not the same place when a person goes back to it, or not the same,' " but then he runs out of explanation. He ends up marrying his high-school sweetheart, Shelley, and taking her back to New York, effectively combining his past and his future, which he sees as "a long, deep rug, as real as the past or the present ever was." The important thing here, Voelker says, is that "Tyler imagines sane people who know that life is a trap, but that grace is a distinct possibility." Even in this first Tyler novel Ben Joe Hawkes sees the trap — his home and family of women who appear to depend on him — and believes that in his marriage to Shelley he will find grace.

In *The Tin Can Tree,* Tyler's second novel, grace is harder to find, perhaps because the traps are deeper, the hold stronger, and the number of characters larger. As in *If Morning Ever Comes* a death precedes this novel, but the loss of six-year-old Janie Rose plunges her mother, Lou Pike, into a depression that causes her to neglect her remaining child, Simon. The accident reaches out to envelop a relative and their neighbors as well — the Pikes' boarder and niece, Joan Pike; brothers James and Ansel Green; and elderly sisters Faye and Lucy Potter, who share a three-family house with the Pikes and the Greens. Each of these groups is caught in its own trap as well: Joan can neither live with her parents, feel at home with the Pikes, nor progress in her relation-

Dust jacket for Tyler's 1974 novel, which examines the complex interrelationships of a reclusive artist and the tenants in his boardinghouse

ship with James; James is unable to extricate himself from a destructive relationship with his hypochondriac brother; and the maiden sisters are virtual prisoners of their fears and idiosyncrasies.

Photographs become emblematic of this stasis, as they do in many other Tyler novels. Ansel calls James's pictures "very *remaining* things," but their ability to remain also causes him distress when he finds that James has accidentally captured an image of Janie Rose on film shortly before her death. His distress is similar to Simon's; Ansel comments that "unliving things last much longer than living."

Yet, while photographs last longer than the human lives they capture, they also reveal a solidity in people. After Simon – in the hope that his mother will notice him again – runs away to Ansel and James's family and Joan comes back after an abortive attempt to return to her parents, the extended family has a party in the Potters' quarters, and James takes a picture. Joan thinks that "whole years could pass, they could be born and die, they could

leave and return, they would marry or live out their separate lives alone, and nothing in this [camera view] finder would change. They were going to stay this way, she and all the rest of them, not because of anyone else but because it was what they had chosen, what they would keep a strong tight hold of."

This keeping a "strong tight hold" becomes increasingly important in Tyler's fiction. Anne G. Jones poses the issue: "Tyler's novels present a meditation on mutability. How can identity persist if someone changes?" For the Pikes and the rest of their extended family, identity persists by keeping a "strong tight hold" of what matters – love, family, and neighbors.

For Evie Decker, the teenage heroine of Tyler's third novel, *A Slipping-Down Life* (1970), who carves the name of her rock-star idol into her forehead, the question of identity is a crucial one. Fat, unattractive, and trapped with her widowed father and an unsympathetic housekeeper, Evie thinks she finds what matters in Drum Casey, a local singer. Her self-mutilation gets Drum's attention as well as that of his "manager" (and drummer), and Evie becomes part of their publicity. To Evie's surprise, Drum proves to be as needy as she, and they marry. They are not well suited, in a typical Tyler way: Evie finds that the "importance of details seemed peaceful and lulling," but, for Drum, "life is getting too cluttered." As Zahlan observes, "Opposed to the tendencies of accumulating and gathering in are the centrifugal forces of clearing out and moving on."

When her father dies, Evie returns to his home, leaving Drum behind. But, just as for Ben Joe and the Pikes, there is the possibility that returning home is not giving up or moving backward. Drum asks her what she will say when people wonder why she has the name Casey on her forehead, and she says she will tell them it is her name, as it now is. Drum responds, " 'Now that you have done all that cutting . . . and endured through bleeding and police cars and stitches, are you going to say it was just for purposes of *identification?* ' " What Drum fails to realize is that it is for these very purposes that Evie, who is pregnant with his baby, has gone through all the trouble – she knows who she is; she has been identified. In this novel, to which Paul Binding accords "minor classic status," the growth from adolescence to adulthood involves enduring "bleeding and police cars and stitches" but ends with a clear sense of self.

Elizabeth Abbott, the main character in Tyler's fourth novel, *The Clock Winder* (1972), appears to lack this sense. When, after dropping out of college, she offers her help with odd jobs to widowed Mrs. Emerson, the older woman wonders "what kind of person would let herself get so sidetracked." On learning that Elizabeth has been looking for a job with another family, she asks, "Do you usually go at things in such a roundabout way?" Mrs. Emerson's son Timothy, who falls in love with Elizabeth and eventually kills himself (perhaps accidentally) out of jealousy, accuses her of "seeing life as some kind of gimmicky guided tour where everyone signs up for a surprise destination." Yet, when Elizabeth finally realizes that he is talking about her attitude toward life, she smiles "as fondly and happily as if he had mentioned her favorite acquaintance."

Mrs. Emerson's other son, Matthew, who also loves and eventually marries Elizabeth, thinks he will give her life direction and stability: "His life had solidified. He was a man in his thirties who lived by himself, encased in a comfortable set of habits and a plodding, easy-going job. He liked things the way they were. Change of any kind he carefully avoided." But Elizabeth sees the flux in their (and every) relationship: "Life seemed to be a constant collision and recollision of bodies on the move in the universe; everything recurred. She would keep running into Emersons until the day she died; and she and Matthew would keep falling in love and out again." The only reality for Elizabeth is constant motion.

This novel also contains Tyler's first extended discussion of the internal dynamics of the family. All of Mrs. Emerson's seven children, she says, "are always moving away from me; I feel like the center of an asterisk. They *work* at moving away." Another of Tyler's apparently ambivalent mothers, she has a "way of summing up each child in a single word, putting a finger squarely on his flaw." Also, everything she says to her children is "attached to other things by long gluey strands, calling up other days, none of them good, touching off chords, opening doors." Yet her children are "split between wanting to defeat [their] mother's expectations and wanting to live up to them." Elizabeth sees Matthew's life — and hers within it — "as a piece of strong twine, with his mother and his brothers and sister knotting their tangled threads into every twist of it, and his wife another thread, linked to him and to all his family by long, frayed ropes."

Since she is not yet one of Mrs. Emerson's children, Elizabeth can still work free of the ropes, and she runs home to marry her former sweetheart, Dommie Whitehill. She bolts during the ceremony,

however, and eventually ends up back at the Emersons' house, nursing Mrs. Emerson through a stroke, being shot by her son Andrew in retaliation for Timothy's death, marrying Matthew, having a series of children, and becoming thoroughly incorporated into the Emersons' troublesome domesticity.

Much of Elizabeth's transformation comes from a change in her attitude toward children. She realizes the amount of work it takes to raise children, in the process increasing her sympathy with Mrs. Emerson, her own family, and Matthew's desire to start a family with her. "Human beings are born so helpless, and stay helpless so long," she tells Mrs. Emerson. "For every grownup you see, you know there must have been at least one person who had the patience to lug them around, and feed them, and walk them nights and keep them out of danger for years and years without a break." Early in the novel Elizabeth seems so mismatched with her own parents that Timothy imagines a federal law that requires people to switch parents: "There would be a gigantic migration of children across the country, all cutting the old tangled threads and picking up new ones when they found the right niche, free forever of other people's notions of them." Yet Elizabeth has migrated to the Emersons and is completely transformed by them, with Mrs. Emerson even giving her a new name, "Gillespie," which turns her into "someone effective and managerial who was summoned by her last name, like a WAC."

The novel ends with a final vision of Elizabeth (now calling herself Gillespie) with a baby at her breast and dinner in the oven, smoothing over the usual Emerson hysteria. This happiness is not unmitigated. (Tyler told Clifford A. Ridley that she thinks this ending is sad and is surprised when others do not.) Mrs. Emerson's youngest son, Peter, has returned with his (as yet unannounced) wife, P. J., who comments that his family is "depending on someone that is like the old-maid failure poor relation you find some places, mending their screens and cooking their supper and fixing their chimneys and making peace – oh, she ended up worse off than *them*."

But P. J. may not have the last word. Peter is torn between wanting to go after his wife and having Gillespie take care of him. "Maybe they're right," he says to her, "you shouldn't hope for anything from someone that much different from your family." Gillespie responds, "You should if your family doesn't *have* it," and goes to check the oven; Peter goes after his wife. George (Matthew and Gillespie's son) watches him depart "absently, as if,

Dust jacket for Tyler's 1976 novel, which depicts the conflicts among rebels and traditionalists in several generations of an aristocratic Baltimore family

every day of his life, he saw people arriving and leaving and getting sidetracked from their travels." It seems that Gillespie is not the only one who has changed; the Emersons have become as "sidetracked" as she. Perhaps the last words come from Mrs. Emerson and Andrew. When she asks, " 'Why are my children always leaving?' " he answers, " 'Why are they always coming *back?* . . . Scratching their heads and saying, "*What* was it you wanted me to do?" ' " Mary F. Robertson has noticed this movement: "Because the boundary between insiders and outsiders is continually transgressed, the progress of Tyler's novels is felt more as an expansion of narrative disorder than as a movement toward resolution and clarification." For Tyler, adding new members, getting sidetracked, and coming back home are what families do.

Celestial Navigation – Tyler's fifth novel and, according to Voelker, her "most theoretical book" – addresses even more directly the issues of family disintegration and reformation. The novel opens, as do six of Tyler's first twelve, with a death, this time of artist Jeremy Pauling's mother. Jeremy has no immediate family members in his house, but he is surrounded by a surrogate family of boarders. Shortly

after his mother's death he takes in Mary Tell and her four-and-a-half-year-old daughter, Darcy, who have left home in the company of a man who promises to marry her but never does. In their way Jeremy and Mary fall in love and raise a large family in the boardinghouse, always with the help and observation of their boarders. Theirs is clearly a complex and unusual love story, as are all Tyler love stories.

Jeremy is also severely agoraphobic, unable to leave his block without having profound anxiety attacks, but he is not primarily an object of humor or pity. Voelker says that Tyler "recasts the novelist's inventive processes in the guise of a consciousness so fragmentary and fleeting that it approaches autism" and calls *Celestial Navigation* "a meditation on the connection between disorientation and insight." Jeremy thus becomes a figure for the writer, and his character type is repeated in several novels, most particularly in Ezra Tull in *Dinner at the Homesick Restaurant* and Macon Leary in *The Accidental Tourist,* as well as in many minor characters throughout her works. Voelker observes that Tyler often sees the "phobic moment as an initial imaginative conception."

Jeremy's attitude toward his collages and sculptures does seem analogous to Tyler's, in particular to the absolute necessity of cutting himself off from life in order to re-create it. "All his eye for detail goes into cutting and pasting. There is none left over for real life," his sister Amanda says. When people look at him, he thinks that all they see is the artist; they never guess at "the cracks inside, the stray thoughts, tangents of memory, hours of idleness, days spent leafing through old magazines or practicing square knots on a length of red twine or humming under his breath while he tapped his fingers on the windowsill and stared down at the people on the street." After the breakup of his marriage (Mary tries to protect him from the outside world, and he thinks she no longer needs him), he realizes that "humanity was far more complex and untidy and depressing than it ever was in his pieces."

Yet for a while Jeremy's struggle to fit into his household, into his family, is the source of much of the tension in this novel. Alice Hall Petry points out that "Tyler's characters try to integrate the seemingly antithetical fragments of the world, rendering incongruous images, ideas, and events into meaningful wholes over which they, as artists, exert control." At first integration seems impossible. Jeremy is " '*always* himself. That's what's wrong with him,' " as Amanda says, and to him it seemed that "life was a series of hurdles that he had been tripping over for decades, with the end nowhere in sight." A boarder, Miss Vinton, notices that he "*lives* at a distance. He makes pictures the way other people make maps – setting down the few fixed points that he knows, hoping they will guide him as he goes floating through his unfamiliar planet. He keeps his eyes on the horizon while his hands work blind."

Still, Jeremy and Mary manage to have children, and he comes to realize that she is more vulnerable, though also stronger, than he is because "the deepest pieces of herself were in those children and every day they scattered in sixty different directions and faced a thousand unknown perils; yet she sailed through the night without so much as a prayer. There was no way he could ever hope to match her." After their breakup he thinks "he had waited for love like a man awaiting salvation. The secret, the hidden key. Was it love that failed Jeremy, or was it Jeremy who failed love? Was there anything to hope for *after* love?" Mary, in self-imposed exile with her children in Jeremy's agent's waterfront cabin, decides that "all events, except childbirth, can be reduced to a heap of trivia in the end." Jeremy determines that "steadfast endurance" is what life is all about, and he continues to live with his elderly boarders, recognizing that although

"he had heard that suffering made great art . . . in his case all it made was parched, measly, stunted lumps far below his usual standard." Without his family around him, no matter how difficult or painful their presence may have been at times, Jeremy is unable to create.

Marriage and family are not just two of the subjects of Tyler's sixth novel, *Searching for Caleb;* they are its lifeblood. In this novel Justine Peck marries her first cousin Duncan, reluctantly follows him in his attempted escape from the rigidities of life in the Peck family, and simultaneously helps her grandfather Daniel try to find his long-lost brother, Caleb, who did manage to escape the family. The reason someone even mildly unconventional would want to escape is fairly clear: the Pecks are a family united in their "perfect manners" and their disapproval of "sports cars, golf, women in slacks, chewing gum, the color chartreuse, emotional displays, ranch houses, bridge, mascara, household pets, religious discussions, plastic, politics, nail polish, transparent gems of any color," and on and on. This escape pattern, however, is complicated by Justine and Duncan's daughter, Meg, who turns out to be afflicted with "total Peckness" and whose marriage to a man unlike her parents, but like the other Pecks, nevertheless makes her miserable.

Justine, too, has ambivalent feelings about the Pecks. She remembers childhood evenings at the Peck houses, where family members would piece together a memory, "each contributing his own little patch and then sitting back to see how it would turn out. Long after the children had grown calm and loose and dropped off to sleep, one by one, the grownups were still weaving family history in the darkness." Later, exiled to a goat farm with her new husband and trimming grass around their electric fence, "the smell of cut grass swung her back over years and years and she found herself sitting on a twilit lawn, nestled between her parents, listening to the murmur of her family all around her." She has to be pried from the fence by Duncan, even though "the throb of electricity caused a distant, dull ache."

In an attempt to gain some control over her life, Justine turns to fortune-telling. When asked whether people can choose their destiny, her mentor, Madame Olita, replies, "No, you can always choose to *some* extent. You can change your future a great deal. Also your past." Justine's grandfather, in his search for his brother, is also engaged in trying to change the past, yet, when he finally finds Caleb, he writes that "it appears that my ties to the present have weakened. I cannot feel that what happens today is of any real importance to me." Caleb tries a

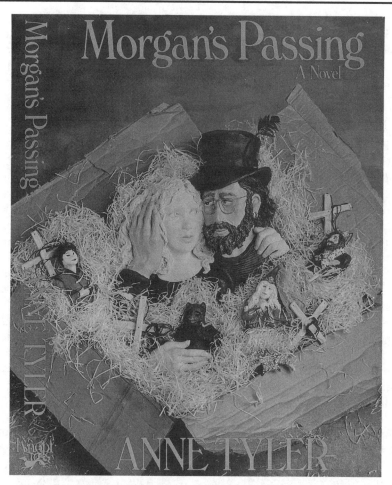

Dust jacket for Tyler's 1980 novel, the title character of which she calls "the inveterate impostor, who is unable to stop himself from stepping into other people's worlds"

brief return but again cannot remain part of the Peck family. He runs away but remembers to send a bread-and-butter note, in the best Peck tradition. Most un-Peckishly, Justine and Duncan escape, too, by going off to join a carnival. Along with others Frank W. Shelton has considered the rebellion of Tyler's characters "against restrictive institutions, especially the family." The most successful of Tyler's heroes – and Justine Peck is among them – "balance distance and sympathy" in a struggle toward clarity and fulfillment.

Midway through Tyler's oeuvre such thematic connections as the creation of family and identity, the passage of time, and the importance of details clearly emerge. Of even more interest is the connection between characters. The iron-willed orderliness of the Pecks (and the way the children flee from and return to it) recalls Mrs. Emerson in *The Clock Winder*. The "angular, slapdash lives" of Justine and Duncan anticipate Morgan Gower in *Morgan's Pass-*

ing (1980), and Justine's "lacking finality" foreshadows Muriel in *The Accidental Tourist*. The longing of Aunt Lucy for "her wing chair in which she could sit encircled, almost, with the wings working like a mule's blinders to confine her gaze to the latest historical romance" looks both forward and backward to Jeremy Pauling and Macon Leary. The cooking ability of the long-lost brother Caleb, who shows his friendship not in words but by choosing "to cook them their favorite foods instead – the comfort foods that every man turns to when he is feeling low," anticipates Ezra Tull in *Dinner at the Homesick Restaurant*. Tyler appears to try out characters in minor roles before she lets them onstage for command performances.

Tyler's seventh novel, *Earthly Possessions,* directly tackles one of her most important issues: the relationship between people and their possessions. Charlotte Emory has decided to leave her husband Saul, a minister, but during a final visit to the bank she is abducted by a robber, Jake Simms, who takes her on a long car ride, first to pick up his pregnant girlfriend and then to visit an old jail buddy Jake thinks can help him. While it is Jake who has the gun, it is Charlotte who ends up supporting this mission, trying to patch up the relationship between Jake and Mindy, consoling him when his friend rejects him, and finally deciding when it is time for her to leave, even though Jake says he needs her to stay.

The road trip is interspersed with reflections into Charlotte's life. Like James in *The Tin Can Tree,* she is a photographer, albeit a reluctant one, having taken over her father's photography shop after his death. As a photographer, she says, "I was only a transient. My photos were limpid and relaxed, touched with that grace things have when you know they're of no permanent importance." Charlotte thinks of herself as a transient in her entire life, although she also longs for the security of home. The twin worries of her life as a child, she says, were "that I was not their true daughter, and would be sent away" and "that I *was* their true daughter and would never, ever manage to escape to the outside world."

After her father's car accident, which cuts short her college career, "it had hit finally where I was: home, trapped, no escape. My mother couldn't even sit him up without me there to help. I saw my life rolling out in front of me like an endless, mildewed rug." Charlotte feels "locked in a calendar; time was turning out to be the most closed-in space of all." In order to cope with this feeling, especially after her marriage to Saul and all the physical possessions and human encumbrances he brings into her life, she "loosened her roots, floated a few feet off, and grew to look at things with a faint, pleasant humorousness that spiced my nose like the beginnings of a sneeze. After a while the humor became a habit; I couldn't have lost it even if I'd tried. My world began to seem . . . temporary. I saw that I must be planning to leave, eventually."

When her mother becomes ill with cancer, she spends time alone with her, asking questions. Unsatisfied with the answers she cannot "let loose of her yet. She was like some unsolvable math problem you keep staring at, worrying the edges of, chafing and cursing." Saul tells her that he believes that "we're given the same lessons to learn, over and over, exactly the same experiences, till we get them right. Things keep circling past us."

Like Emily Meredith in *Morgan's Passing,* who always keeps a cosmetic bag packed for that day when she knows she must leave, Charlotte says her whole life "has been a history of casting off encumbrances, paring down to the bare essentials, stripping for the journey." Charlotte has been ready her entire life for the trip she takes, but after she returns she redefines, or metaphorizes, her notion of travel. Her husband, perhaps suspecting that their marriage might not have been as perfect as he imagined, suggests they take a trip together. She declines, saying, "We have been traveling for years, traveled all our lives, we are traveling still. We couldn't stay in one place if we tried. Go to sleep, I say."

Morgan's Passing received a slightly more negative critical reaction than all Tyler's earlier novels, except *If Morning Ever Comes.* Shelton refers to it as "one of her most unruly and untidy novels," and *Morgan's Passing* is mentioned only in a dismissive remark in Voelker's book. The critics' objections center around the main character, Morgan Gower; yet Tyler stressed to Lamb as she wrote *Morgan's Passing* that she likes all her characters: "This is very important to me." She also told Patricia Rowe Willrich that Morgan's situation is "not unrelated to being a writer: the inveterate imposter, who is unable to stop himself from stepping into other people's worlds." Nominated for the 1980 National Book Critics Circle Award, *Morgan's Passing* thus appears to extend the characterization of the eccentric artist first seen in *Celestial Navigation;* this time she just takes him outside his house. Clearly Tyler has an affinity for the eccentric that some of her critics do not share.

The familiar Tyler issues are all here as well: the comfort and restrictions of family life, the urge to accumulate and to cast off, and the materials out of which one creates identity and direction. Morgan has a fairly stable external identity: he is married to Bonny, has six daughters, lives in a large old house, and works in a hardware store. Yet he also masquerades as a prospector, an explorer, and people of various nationalities — discontented, it seems, with the prospect of living just one kind of life.

Early in the book he performs a characteristic transformation: Emily Meredith, a young woman who puts on puppet shows for a living with her husband, Leon, goes into labor during one of their shows, and Morgan identifies himself as a doctor. Probably he assumes he can bluff his way through the charade by merely offering comfort on the ride to the hospital, but the baby arrives quickly, and Morgan must actually assume his role. Later the Merediths wonder "if they had imagined the man — just conjured him up in time of need" because there seems to be something magical about him, as if he could be a gnome or elf. Their sense of his unreality

Dust jacket for Tyler's 1982 novel, in which three grown children confront the emotional pain caused by a verbally abusive mother and a father who walked out on the family

increases when Morgan takes to following them, attracted by what he perceives to be the bohemian simplicity of their lives. He thinks Emily – who wears only leotards, wrap skirts, and ballet slippers – "looked stark, pared down. She had done away with all the extras." Morgan feels "awed by the Merediths – by their austerity, their certitude, their mapped and charted lives."

As he becomes part of the baggage of the Merediths' lives, he begins to cast away encumbrances from his own life, even his children, "The trouble with fathering children," he thinks, "was, they got to know you so well. You couldn't make the faintest little realignment of the facts around them. They kept staring levelly into your eyes, eternally watchful and critical, forever prepared to pass judgment. They could point to so many places where you had gone permanently, irretrievably wrong." After a disastrous vacation at the beach, Morgan thinks they could abandon him there: "He pictured how calm he would

grow, at last. The breakers would act for him, tumbling about while he lay still. He would finally have a chance to sort himself out. It was *people* who disarranged his life."

Emily, too, is becoming dissatisfied with her life, feeling "the world [is] split in two: makers and doers. She was a maker and Leon was a doer. She sat home and put together puppets and Leon sprang onstage with them, all flair and action." In spite of the fact that Morgan, too, is a "doer," Emily and Morgan have an affair, and she gets pregnant. By the end of the novel they have decided, like Justine and Duncan Peck, to join the circus and give puppet shows, with Morgan assuming the role of Leon, both for the shows and for the circus proprietor, who does not know about the divorce. The novel ends with Morgan – ensconced in a trailer with the baby and Emily – feeling "suddenly light-hearted. He started walking faster. He started smiling. By the time he reached Emily, he was humming. Everything he looked at seemed luminous and beautiful, and rich with possibilities." In order to enjoy what Jones has called the "blessed profusion" of Tyler's novels, the reader must learn to see life as Morgan (and Tyler) do – as rich with a nearly unlimited variety of possibilities.

The variety of possibilities for constructing and reconstructing a family is the major concern of Tyler's ninth novel, *Dinner at the Homesick Restaurant*. It tells the story of the Tull family and the ways they each find to mend cracks formed when the father, Beck Tull, a salesman, leaves his wife and children, whose difficult situation is exacerbated by abuse from the abandoned mother, Pearl. Throughout most of the novel Beck is the "absent presence," the "invisible man" whose purpose seems to be (for Pearl) to "show how little importance a father has." Pearl, on her deathbed as the novel opens, spends the rest of the time she is alive trying to come to terms with her job as a single parent, wondering when, if ever, she is going to be forgiven by her children.

Cody, the oldest son, seems obsessed by the past; he "catalogues grudges," as his sister Jenny says. Like many of Tyler's characters, he finds that photographs are a useful metaphor for his attitude about the past: "Isn't it just that time for once is stopped that makes you wistful? If only you could turn it back, you think. If only you could change this or that, undo what you have done, if only you could roll the minutes the other way, for once," he says to his son, Luke. One of the things he may want to undo is stealing his brother Ezra's fiancée, Ruth, and marrying her himself. The marriage is vaguely unsatisfying, Cody says, because he has

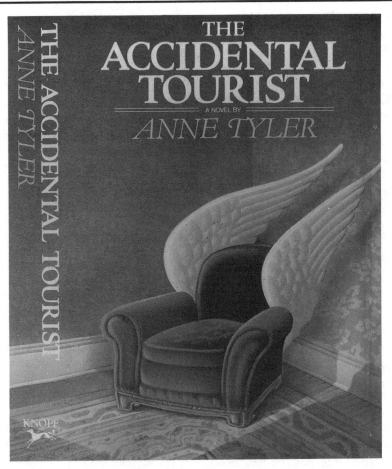

Dust jacket for Tyler's 1985 novel, in which a reclusive travel writer finds love and happiness with an extroverted dog trainer

"always had the feeling it wasn't my marriage, anyhow. It was someone else's. It was theirs. Sometimes I seemed to enjoy it better when I imagined I was seeing it through someone else's eyes."

How the characters choose to imagine the present — or the past — is vitally important to their happiness in this novel. When Cody tells his son about his life, he always prefaces his remarks with " 'This really happened,' " but, while the stories seem to him "unthinkable, beyond belief," his son finds that they "never seemed so terrible" to him. Beck returns for Pearl's funeral and remarks at the family dinner afterward that " 'it looks like this is one of those great big, jolly, noisy, rambling . . . why, *families!*' " It is, of course. Cody's response is to try to set the record straight: "You think we're some jolly, situation-comedy family when we're in particles, torn apart, torn all over the place, and our mother was a witch."

The stories of Pearl's other children, Jenny and Ezra, do not necessarily prove Cody wrong but show him to be no more right than Beck: at times

their mother was a witch, but they were also a family, or at least they have become a family. Middle child Jenny was afraid of her mother, dreaming that she "laughed a witch's shrieking laugh; dragged Jenny out of hiding as the Nazis tramped up the stairs; accused her of sins and crimes that had never crossed Jenny's mind. Her mother told her, in an informative and considerate tone of voice, that she was raising Jenny to eat her." Jenny also finds her family "too small" and too intense, so she marries in part for the "*angularity* of the situation — the mighty leap into space with someone she hardly knew." This marriage fails, but she ends up with that larger family she desires — her own daughter, the stepchildren of her new husband, Joe, and the children surrounding her daily in her job as a pediatrician. Her attitude becomes what she tells the worried teacher of her stepson Slevin: "I don't see the need to blame adjustments, broken homes, bad parents, that sort of thing. We make our own luck, right? You have to overcome your setbacks. You can't take them too much to heart."

The baby of the family, Ezra, makes his own luck too, first by working in a restaurant run by Mrs. Scarlatti and then in "a place where people come just like to a family dinner" – the Homesick Restaurant. There he cooks "what people felt homesick for," and there he tries to feed his family. Cody, always the pessimist, notices that his family has never finished one of Ezra's dinners. Cody wonders why Ezra does not see it, why he cannot see "the theme" of his family – that "it was almost as if what they couldn't get right, they had to keep returning to." Ezra keeps trying, calling the family back, tracking down missing members, and asking them, as at the funeral dinner, to " 'take up where we left off.' "

Pearl, the narrative and emotional focus of the book, also tries to make sense of her family. Her initial meditations lead her to the conclusion that "her family has failed. Neither of her sons is happy, and her daughter can't seem to stay married." At first she blames herself but then decides that "it's simply fate, and not a matter for blame at all." Her disappointment comes, Ezra realizes, because she "had imagined a perfectly wonderful plot – a significance to every chance meeting, the possibility of whirlwind courtships, grand white weddings, flawless bliss forever after." Yet she does find that she had at least one moment where she was "absolutely happy," and Ezra sees himself and his mother "traversing the curve of the earth, small and steadfast, surrounded by companions." Her last thoughts are of her version of a happy family, and she dies, being "borne away to the beach, where three small children ran toward her, laughing, across the sunlit sand."

Cody also comes to a kind of reconciliation with his past, including a pivotal memory of the day he accidentally shot his mother with an arrow:

> He remembered the archery trip, and it seemed to him now that he even remembered that arrow sailing in its graceful, fluttering path. He remembered his mother's upright form along the grasses, her hair lit gold, her small hands smoothing her bouquet while the arrow journeyed on. And high above, he seemed to recall, there had been a little brown airplane, almost motionless, droning through the sunshine like a bumblebee.

The elegiac quality of the last lines is intentional: each of the three children has created a satisfying surrogate family, Pearl has come to a final sense of her own identity, and even Beck has been reintegrated into the family circle. A novel that in other hands could have become a horrific chronicle of the violent legacy neglectful and cruel parents hand down to their children becomes instead a meditation on the ways people can produce sustaining families instead of reproducing destructive ones.

Both *Dinner at the Homesick Restaurant* and Tyler's next novel, *The Accidental Tourist,* create what Voelker calls a "utopian emotional state," in which characters achieve distance from the complex of emotions they have toward their families: "sickness for home (longing, nostalgia) but also sickness of it (the need to escape from the invasiveness of family) and sickness from it (the psychic wounds the human beings inevitably carry as a result of having had to grow up as children in families)." For Ezra, Voelker says, utopia is a "restaurant that is not a home but is as a home might be." For Macon Leary, it is his winged armchair, the logo of his books for reluctant business travelers – a chair that both travels and "dream[s] of staying put."

Macon, who "above all else" is an "orderly man," who believes "that there must be an answer for everything, if only you knew how to set forth the questions," writes books that make travelers feel that they are journeying "in a capsule, a cocoon." He therefore is stunned by the violent death of his son, Ethan, and the sudden departure of his wife, Sarah, and holes up in his house, devising elaborate timesaving measures that threaten to turn him into a recluse and result eventually in a broken leg. His injury sends him back to live with his unmarried sister and brothers in the family house, where the favorite meal is baked potatoes and all the kitchen products are ruthlessly alphabetized.

Macon's reaction to this disruption is to feel "content with everything exactly the way it was. He seemed to be suspended, his life on hold." He even wonders if "he had engineered this injury – every elaborate step leading up to it – just so he could settle down safe among the people he'd started out with." He is jolted out of this safe suspension by Muriel Pritchett, an extravagant dog trainer who has offered her services, ostensibly for his unruly dog, Edward. The training of Edward becomes a retraining in life for Macon, and soon he and Muriel – and her young son, Alexander – are living together.

Things do not turn out happily ever after, however, as they rarely do in Tyler's novels. Macon's brother Charles is worried about him: " 'You're not yourself these days and this Muriel person is a symptom. Everybody says so.' " Macon responds, " 'I'm more myself than I've been my whole life long,' " to which his brother replies, " 'What kind of remark is that? It doesn't even make sense!' "

Dust jacket for Tyler's eleventh novel, for which she received the Pulitzer Prize

Perhaps it does not – to someone who does not understand Tyler's notion of identity. Macon – like Jeremy Pauling (who is always himself) and the children in *Dinner at the Homesick Restaurant* – tries on roles and partners, until he finds ones that fit. These characters also chafe under their families' notions of who they have always been. Still, Macon is not sure he has made the right choice, fearing that he may have chosen a woman like his mother, Alicia – "silly, vain, annoying" – who "darted in and out of their lives leaving a trail of irresponsible remarks, apparently never considering they might be passed on." He also realizes that "the world was divided sharply down the middle: Some lived careful lives and some lived careless lives, and everything that happened could be explained by the difference between them."

There is also the question of Muriel's son, Alexander. Macon begins to care for him, easing the boy out of his mother's tight hold, comforting him when he is bullied by other children, and buying

him real boy clothes. At one point Macon feels a "pleasant kind of sorrow seeping through him. Oh, his life had regained all its old perils. He was forced to worry once again about nuclear war and the future of the planet. He often had the same secret, guilty thought that had come to him after Ethan was born: *From this time on I can never be completely happy.* Not that he was before, of course."

In spite of this connection he returns to his wife, Sarah, after a trip to Canada, during which he has a crisis in identity, "pictur[ing] himself separating, falling into pieces, his head floating away with terrifying swiftness in the eerie green air of Alberta." Muriel, however, follows him on a subsequent trip to Paris, and then Sarah shows up after he hurts his back. Sarah's solicitous practicality smothers rather than consoles him, and he crawls from his bed and limps away to catch up with Muriel and her careless enthusiasm for life. The final lines echo other Tyler endings: "A sudden flash of sunlight hit the windshield, and spangles flew across

SAINT
MAYBE

A NOVEL

ANNE TYLER

Dust jacket for Tyler's 1991 novel, which stayed on the New York Times best-seller list for nine weeks

the glass. The spangles were old water spots, or maybe the markings of leaves, but for a moment Macon thought they were something else. They were so bright and festive, for a moment he thought they were confetti." Like Justine and Duncan, like Morgan and Emily, this unlikely couple walk out — not into a sunset, but into a celebration, a carnival, a circus.

Breathing Lessons, Tyler's eleventh novel, begins with the death of Max, the husband of (the main character) Maggie's best friend. According to Karin Linton, such opening crises "eliminat[e] the safe and well-established routines of life and jol[t] the temporal perspective of the main character." Tyler sees this jolt in time and perspective as positive, both for the characters and for the novelist. For example, what she most admires about novelist Gabriel García Márquez, she stated in the *New York Times Book Review* (4 December 1977), is that "he has somehow figured out how to let time be in literature what it is in life: unpredictable, sometimes circular, looped, doubling back, rushing through 60

years and then doddering over an afternoon, with glimmers of the past and future just beneath the surface." *Breathing Lessons* moves effortlessly between the present trip to the funeral, the past of Maggie's courtship and marriage to Ira, the recent past of the breakup of her son's marriage, and the future of his former wife and Maggie's grandchild as Maggie tries to combine them all into some meaningful whole.

Although Ira loves Maggie, he cannot bear the disorganized way she goes about life, "how she refused to take her own life seriously. She seemed to believe it was a sort of practice life, something she could afford to play around with as if they offered second and third chances to get it right. She was always making clumsy, impetuous rushes toward nowhere in particular — side trips, random detours." She and her friend Serena also disagree about the progress of life, with Serena saying that what life comes down to is " 'pruning and disposing . . . shucking off your children from the moment you give birth.' " Maggie responds, " 'I don't feel like I'm letting go; I feel they're taking things away from me.' " Unlike Serena and Ira, Maggie wants to hold onto everything, no matter how cluttered and disorderly it makes her life.

The experience of traveling to the funeral creates a distanced perspective in Maggie that Serena describes: "Just to look around you one day and have it all amaze you — where you'd arrived at, who you'd married, what kind of person you'd grown into." This distance leads Maggie to discover that, although she might be easily classified by Ira as "teary and nostalgic," "if she was locked in a pattern, at least she had chosen what the pattern could be. She felt strong and free and definite."

One of the patterns, she realizes, involves her marriage. In order to keep from being like her mother, Maggie avoids any man like her "bumbling and well-meaning and sentimental" father, whom she loved. But, in comparison with her serious husband, Maggie drinks, talks, eats, laughs, and cries too much; she discovers she has turned into her father. At the funeral, however, she finds that she has fallen in love with her husband again, the "convenience" of which pleases her "like finding right in her pantry all the fixings she needed for a new recipe."

Maggie is not so lucky with her son, Jesse, whose marriage has failed and whose child is no longer a part of his life. No matter how hard she tries, she is unable to get Jesse, Fiona (his wife), and Leroy (their daughter) back together. Maggie thinks that she is perhaps not "compatible" with Jesse: "All they had to rely on was luck — the proper personality genes turning up like dice. And in Jesse's case, maybe the luck had been poor."

Maggie's new insight helps her to realize as well that "there was a single theme to every decision she had made as a parent: The mere fact that her children were children, condemned for years to feel powerless and bewildered and confined, filled her with such pity that to add any further hardship to their lives seemed unthinkable. She could excuse anything in them, forgive them everything. She would have made a better mother, perhaps, if she hadn't remembered so well how it felt to be a child."

Maggie's inability to effect any change in Jesse leads her to feel that her life has "forever repeated itself, and it was entirely lacking in hope." But this feeling does not last long. On the last page of the novel she and Ira are in bed, trying to sleep prior to an early-morning trip to take their daughter to college: "She felt a little stir of something that came over her like a flush, a sort of inner buoyancy, and she lifted her face to kiss the warm blade of his cheekbone. Then she slipped free and moved to her side of the bed, because tomorrow they had a long car trip to make and she knew she would need a good night's sleep before they started."

Tyler's twelfth novel, *Saint Maybe,* addresses most directly another important Tyler concern: religion. Tyler has a well-known skepticism about the premise of most religions: "It's not that I have anything against ministers," she told Lamb in a discussion about *Earthly Possessions,* "but that I'm particularly concerned with how much right anyone has to change someone, and ministers are people who feel they have that right." Still, she is interested in the subject, as she told Willrich about the genesis of *Saint Maybe:* "All I knew at the start was that I wondered what it must feel like to be a born-again Christian, since that is a kind of life very different from mine."

This emphasis on religion does not obscure the familiar Tyler issues – family, identity, marriage, and children. Ian Bedloe, who is not born again until later in the novel, lives in his street's version of "the ideal, apple-pie household." His family "believed that every part of their lives was absolutely wonderful." This belief wavers when Danny, the oldest son, brings home Lucy, a divorced woman with children, as his fiancée; falters when their baby is born "premature"; and finally is shattered when Danny runs his car into a wall after hearing from Ian that he suspects that Lucy has been having an affair and that their child, Daphne, is not Danny's. Lucy dies shortly afterward, overdosing on sleeping pills, and Ian's family is left with Agatha

and Thomas, the children from her first marriage, and Daphne.

Ian has an immediate connection to Daphne: "It seemed she had reached out and pulled a string from somewhere deep inside him. It seemed she *knew* him." Yet this connection contrasts with his sense of "the monotony and irritation and confinement" of children. After he takes over the child care, Ian feels that he is "travelling a treadmill, stuck with these querulous children night after night after night." Yet he also perceives the dual nature of his responsibility for them – his role in the loss of their father and mother and their helplessness: "Why being a child at all was scary. Powerlessness, outsiderness. Murmurs over your head about something everyone knows but you."

The Church of the Second Chance gives him another reason for taking care of the children: penance, a chance for forgiveness. While the church comforts him, Ian wonders: "Why didn't he, after all these years of penance, feel that God had forgiven him?" Yet he also understands that what he is doing is not exactly penance, as the children were "all that gave his life color, and energy, and . . . well, life." Daphne especially brings out in him "laughter and an ache." He realizes finally that he has to accept, for his children and others, "that the day would never arrive when [he] finally understood what they were all about," and this realization makes him "supremely happy."

There is also the question of how the children – and Ian's need to atone through them – are restricting the rest of his life. He wonders, "When is something philosophical acceptance and when is it dumb passivity? When is something a moral decision and when is it scar tissue?" After resuming a long-suspended romantic life with "clutter counselor" Rita diCarlo (a figure reminiscent of both Elizabeth Abbott and Muriel Pritchett), he concludes that dramatic events, personal or religious – happiness, tragedy, sin, atonement, salvation – are really part of the fabric of life. Ian knows that the children have completely changed his life, but "people changed other people's lives every day of the year. There was no call to make such a fuss about it."

Ian Bedloe's situation at the end of *Saint Maybe* is not so different from that of Ben Joe Hawkes at the end of Tyler's first novel or that of Maggie Moran, Ezra Tull, Charlotte Emory, or many other Tyler characters. They hope, early or later in life, to escape from the burdens and responsibilities of their families, but they find they are not trapped, and they learn that they do not really want to escape. In *Saint Maybe* Agatha confronts Daphne with the anal-

Tyler, circa 1988 (photograph by Diana Walker)

ogy that "living in a family is like taking a long, long, trip with people you're not very well acquainted with. At first they seem just fine, but after you've traveled awhile at close quarters they start grating on your nerves." Daphne responds, " 'Well, I guess I must not have traveled with them long enough, then.' "

While their families smother them, force them into restrictive roles, and place unwanted obligations on them, Tyler's characters still want to keep traveling with them, in close quarters. Those who escape the confines of their original families – Morgan Gower and Emily Meredith, Duncan and Justine Peck, Jenny Tull, and Elizabeth Abbott "Gillespie" Emerson – do not go off alone but take with them, or create, new families that do not re-create the problems of their first families but that are nevertheless families with responsibilities and problems of their own. Theirs is not a question of never being able to go home again – or worse, never being able to get out of home – but of remaking that home into what they want it to be, or finding out that they never really wanted to leave after all. After thirty years of writing novels Tyler continues to concentrate on the family – with insight, humor, and hope.

Interviews:

Clifford A. Ridley, "Anne Tyler: A Sense of Reticence Balanced by 'Oh, Well, Why Not?,' " *National Observer* (22 July 1972): 23;

Marguerite Michaels, "Anne Tyler, Writer 8:05 to 3:30," *New York Times Book Review,* 8 May 1977, pp. 42–43;

Wendy Lamb, "An Interview with Anne Tyler," *Iowa Journal of Literary Studies,* 3 (1981): 59–64;

Laurie L. Brown, "Interviews with Seven Contemporary Writers," *Southern Quarterly,* 21 (Summer 1983): 3–22.

Bibliographies:

Stella Ann Nesanovich, "An Anne Tyler Checklist, 1959–1980," *Bulletin of Bibliography,* 38 (April–June 1981): 53–64;

Elaine Gardiner and Catherine Rainwater, "A Bibliography of Writing by Anne Tyler," in *Contemporary American Women Writers: Narrative Strategies,* edited by Rainwater and William J. Sheick (Lexington: University Press of Kentucky, 1985), pp. 145–152.

References:

Doris Betts, "The Fiction of Anne Tyler," *Southern Quarterly,* 21 (Summer 1983): 23–27;

Paul Binding, "Anne Tyler," in *Separate Country: A Literary Journey through the American South* (New York: Paddington Press, 1979);

Elizabeth Evans, *Anne Tyler* (New York: Twayne, 1993);

Margaret Morganroth Gullette, *Safe at Last in the Middle Years: The Invention of the Midlife Progress Novel: Saul Bellow, Margaret Drabble, Anne Tyler, John Updike* (Berkeley: University of California Press, 1988);

Anne G. Jones, "Home at Last, and Homesick Again: The Ten Novels of Anne Tyler," *Hollins Critic*, 23 (April 1986): 1–14;

Karin Linton, *The Temporal Horizon: A Study of the Theme of Time in Anne Tyler's Major Novels* (Uppsala, Sweden: Acta Universitatis Upsalensis, 1989);

Stella Ann Nesanovich, "The Individual in the Family: Anne Tyler's *Searching for Caleb* and *Earthly Possessions*," *Southern Review*, 14 (Winter 1978): 170–176;

Alice Hall Petry, *Understanding Anne Tyler* (Columbia: University of South Carolina Press, 1990);

Mary F. Robertson, "Medusa Points and Contact Points," in *Contemporary American Women Writers: Narrative Strategies*, edited by Catherine Rainwater and William J. Sheick (Lexington: University Press of Kentucky, 1985), pp. 119–152;

Frank W. Shelton, "The Necessary Balance: Distance and Sympathy in the Novels of Anne Tyler," *Southern Review*, 20 (Autumn 1984): 851–860;

C. Ralph Stephens, ed., *The Fiction of Anne Tyler* (Jackson: University of Mississippi Press, 1990);

Joseph C. Voelker, *Art and the Accidental in Anne Tyler* (Columbia: University of Missouri Press, 1989);

Patricia Rowe Willrich, "Watching Through Windows: A Perspective on Anne Tyler," *Virginia Quarterly*, 68 (Summer 1992): 497–516;

Anne R. Zahlan, "Anne Tyler," in *Fifty Southern Writers After 1900: A Bio-Bibliographic Sourcebook*, edited by Joseph M. Flora and Robert Bain (New York: Greenwood Press, 1987), pp. 491–504.

Papers:

The Perkins Library at Duke University holds the manuscripts for three unpublished novels by Tyler as well as some of her correspondence.

John Updike

(18 March 1932 –   )

Donald J. Greiner
University of South Carolina

See also the Updike entries in *DLB 2: American Novelists Since World War II, First Series; DLB 5: American Poets Since World War II: Part Two; DLB Yearbook: 1980; DLB Yearbook: 1982;* and *Documentary Series 3: Saul Bellow, Jack Kerouac, Norman Mailer, Vladimir Nabokov, John Updike, Kurt Vonnegut.*

BOOKS: *The Carpentered Hen and Other Tame Creatures* (New York: Harper, 1958); republished as *Hoping for a Hoopoe* (London: Gollancz, 1959);

The Poorhouse Fair (New York: Knopf, 1959; London: Gollancz, 1959);

The Same Door (New York: Knopf, 1959; London: Deutsch, 1962);

Rabbit, Run (New York: Knopf, 1960; London: Deutsch, 1961);

The Magic Flute (New York: Knopf, 1962; London: Deutsch & Ward, 1964);

Pigeon Feathers (New York: Knopf, 1962; London: Deutsch, 1962);

The Centaur (New York: Knopf, 1963; London: Deutsch, 1963);

Telephone Poles and Other Poems (New York: Knopf, 1963; London: Deutsch, 1964);

Olinger Stories (New York: Vintage, 1964);

The Ring (New York: Knopf, 1964);

Assorted Prose (New York: Knopf, 1965; London: Deutsch, 1965);

A Child's Calendar (New York: Knopf, 1965);

Of the Farm (New York: Knopf, 1965; London: Deutsch, 1966);

Verse (Greenwich, Conn.: Fawcett, 1965);

The Music School (New York: Knopf, 1966; London: Deutsch, 1967);

Couples (New York: Knopf, 1968; London: Deutsch, 1968);

Midpoint and Other Poems (New York: Knopf, 1969; London: Deutsch, 1969);

Bottom's Dream (New York: Knopf, 1969);

Bech: A Book (New York: Knopf, 1970; London: Deutsch, 1970);

Rabbit Redux (New York: Knopf, 1971; London: Deutsch, 1972);

Seventy Poems (London: Penguin, 1972);

Museums and Women (New York: Knopf, 1972; London: Deutsch, 1973);

Buchanan Dying (New York: Knopf, 1974; London: Deutsch, 1974);

A Month of Sundays (New York: Knopf, 1975; London: Deutsch, 1975);

Picked-Up Pieces (New York: Knopf, 1975; London: Deutsch, 1976);

Marry Me: A Romance (New York: Knopf, 1976; London: Deutsch, 1977);

Tossing and Turning (New York: Knopf, 1977; London: Deutsch, 1977);

The Coup (New York: Knopf, 1978; London: Deutsch, 1979);

Too Far to Go (New York: Fawcett Crest, 1979); republished as *Your Lover Just Called* (Harmondsworth, U.K.: Penguin, 1980);

Problems and Other Stories (New York: Knopf, 1979; London: Deutsch, 1980);

Rabbit Is Rich (New York: Knopf, 1981; London: Deutsch, 1982);

Bech Is Back (New York: Knopf, 1982; London: Deutsch, 1983);

Hugging the Shore (New York: Knopf, 1983; London: Deutsch, 1984);

The Witches of Eastwick (New York: Knopf, 1984; London: Deutsch, 1984);

Facing Nature (New York: Knopf, 1985; London: Deutsch, 1986);

Roger's Version (New York: Knopf, 1986; London: Deutsch, 1986);

Trust Me (New York: Knopf, 1987; London: Deutsch, 1987);

S. (New York: Knopf, 1988; London: Deutsch, 1988);

Self-Consciousness: Memoirs (New York: Knopf, 1989; London: Deutsch, 1989);

Just Looking (New York: Knopf, 1989; London: Deutsch, 1989);

John Updike

Rabbit at Rest (New York: Knopf, 1990; London: Deutsch, 1990);

Odd Jobs (New York: Knopf, 1991; London: Deutsch, 1992);

Memories of the Ford Administration (New York: Knopf, 1992; London: Hamish Hamilton, 1992);

Collected Poems: 1953–1993 (New York: Knopf, 1993);

Brazil (New York: Knopf, 1994).

A reader would be hard pressed to name a contemporary author other than John Updike who is more in tune with the way most Americans live. Unconcerned with apocalypse in his fiction, undeterred by the universal absurdity that threatens to negate the bravest and the best, Updike writes about little people leading little lives. Man, wife, home, children, job – these mundane concerns have rested at the heart of his art since he published his first book, a volume of poetry titled *The Carpentered Hen and Other Tame Creatures,* in 1958, and they have continued to help him dissect, lovingly and clearly, the daily routine of middle America in small town and suburb.

War is generally not an issue for Updike, and neither are the problems of space weapons, world-wide hunger, or the fouling of the planet. The concerns in Updike's writing do not make front-page news. But the concerns do matter because Updike knows that "something fierce goes on in homes." He may not write about murder and mayhem and madness, but, in an exquisitely lyrical style that even his detractors admire, he probes the crises that sear the human spirit: how does a man cling to a mistress when he fears leaving his wife; how does he explain his guilt to his children when he knows that love is all that matters; how does he get his life going again when the applause heaped on him in high school has shattered into silence; how does he fill the void when religious faith seems faltering and false; and how does he grow along with his children who, overnight, seem to know more but care less?

Moralist, stylist, chronicler of the American middle class, Updike investigates the inner lives of families and the common details that define them. He knows that the insignificant particulars of a life are both signs of God's handiwork and hints of humanity's needs: finely crafted furniture, a carefully mown field, a perfect tee shot, a groping prayer, and, unfortunately, the halting march toward death.

Updike can tell of these lives because he has been there. Born on 18 March 1932 in Shillington, Pennsylvania, Updike grew up an only child in a relatively poor family. His father, Wesley R. Updike, taught mathematics in the local high school, but at age thirteen Updike, his father, and his mother, Linda G. Hoyer Updike, moved from the town to a farm from which he and his father had to commute daily. His memoir "The Dogwood Tree: A Boyhood" (*Assorted Prose*, 1965) captures the centrality of his Shillington years, and he has since implied that the loneliness uncovered by the move to the farm fired his imagination.

He now jokingly confesses that his adolescent imaginings were partly devoted to the problem of "how to get out of here," and his exquisitely paced short stories "A Sense of Shelter" and "Flight" (*Pigeon Feathers*, 1962) examine the contradictory urges that define most high-school students: longing to break free from home yet fearing the flight itself. Updike "flew" imaginatively through the cartoons and fiction in *The New Yorker* and physically when he won a scholarship to Harvard University. His lifelong commitment to prose style, to the sheer sound of words artfully selected and rhythmically grouped to suggest resonance and tone, was developed at Harvard. While an undergraduate English major, he drew cartoons and wrote for *The Harvard Lampoon*, which he later edited; and after he was graduated summa cum laude in 1954, he studied for one year on a Knox Fellowship at the Ruskin School of Drawing and Fine Arts in Oxford, England.

Updike has revealed that his true ambition was to be a cartoonist, if not for Walt Disney then at least for *The New Yorker:* "What I have become is a sorry shadow of those high hopes." Still, the beginnings of his career as a writer are associated with *The New Yorker,* for that magazine published his first professional story, "Friends from Philadelphia," on 30 October 1954. Following his return from Oxford in 1955, he joined the staff of *The New Yorker,* and for the next two years he contributed to the "Talk of the Town" columns. Although he ended his formal ties with the magazine's editorial staff in 1957 and moved to Ipswich, Massachusetts, to concentrate on writing, he continued his relationship with the periodical, which has been publishing his poems, stories, essays, and reviews regularly for more than four decades. The move from New York to Ipswich brought the anticipated results, for by 1959 Updike had had three books published: *The Carpentered Hen and Other Tame Creatures, The Poorhouse Fair* (1959), and *The Same Door* (1959).

Critical recognition soon followed. In 1959 he was awarded a Guggenheim Fellowship and then the Rosenthal Foundation Award of the National Institute of Arts and Letters for *The Poorhouse Fair* in 1960; his novel *The Centaur* (1963) won the National Book Award in Fiction in 1964; his short stories have been honored with O. Henry Awards; and he was elected to the National Institute of Arts and Letters in 1964 and to the American Academy of Arts and Letters in 1977. *Rabbit Is Rich* (1981) won the Pulitzer Prize, the National Book Critics Circle Award, and an American Book Award; and his collection of essays, *Hugging the Shore* (1983), won the National Book Critics Circle Award for criticism. *Rabbit at Rest* (1990) won the Pulitzer Prize and the National Book Critics Circle Award.

Although his popular reputation rests primarily on his novels, Updike is a master of four genres: novel, short story, poetry, and essay. In each case his care for the rhythms of language shapes his dismay at the secularization of life, but this is not to suggest that he writes in the 1990s the way he began in the 1950s. Committed in his novels, for example, to the realistic depiction of mundane affairs, he has nevertheless written about the comic intransigence of language in *A Month of Sundays* (1975), about the way that language controls both culture and global politics in *The Coup* (1978), and about the fine line between fantasy and reality in *The Witches of Eastwick* (1984), a humorous novel that is closer to the magical realism of contemporary Latin American authors than to Updike's earlier work.

Similar variations mark the development of his short fiction. The most accomplished American short-story writer since John O'Hara, Updike has moved from the nostalgia of *The Same Door* and some of the tales in *Pigeon Feathers* to the lyrical meditations of such stories as "Wife-wooing" (*Pigeon Feathers*) and "The Music School" (*The Music School*, 1966), toward the irony of *Museums and Women* (1972), *Problems and Other Stories* (1979), and *Trust Me* (1987). His decades-long love affair with this peculiarly American genre has helped change the shape of the short story, for the narrative element associated with the tales in *The Same Door* is often subordinated to a lyrical, meditative use of language in later pieces. The general topic is diminishment, and the reader of Updike's short-story collections will note how the loss of the high-school years in *The Same Door* and *Pigeon Feathers* gives way to the loss of family through betrayal and divorce in *The Music School* and *Museums and Women,* which looks toward, in *Problems* and *Trust Me,* the declining potency brought on by the specter of loss of life. Updike stirs the emotions while he challenges the intellect.

Varied interests also direct Updike's poetry. Blessed with a sense of humor and thus able to laugh at the flaws of life and the foibles of language, he has always been intrigued by the intricate verbal demands of light verse. Indeed, most of the poems in *The Carpentered Hen and Other Tame Creatures* and the first half of *Telephone Poles and Other Poems* (1963) sparkle with linguistic wit. But while Updike has maintained his joyous appreciation of the playfulness of words in his later volumes of verse, he has altered his emphasis. The decline of religious sureties is a prominent consideration in *Telephone Poles and Other Poems* and *Midpoint and Other Poems* (1969), and the diminishment of life itself results in the somber tone of many of the poems in *Tossing and Turning* (1977). The odes to natural processes in *Facing Nature* (1985) are challenging displays of intellect and humor, but they also indicate, however indirectly, the inadequacy of humanity before the inexorable increments of nonhuman otherness.

Updike formally discusses many of these concerns in the fourth genre at which he excels – the essay. *Assorted Prose, Picked-Up Pieces* (1975), *Hugging the Shore, Just Looking* (1989), and *Odd Jobs* (1991) illustrate not only a curious mind but also an astonishing range of interests. Small-town America, Central Park, baseball, mimesis, Nathaniel Hawthorne, the general state of the art of fiction, theology, and painting are just a few of the topics that engage his delighted enthusiasm for the things of his world. Yet, as with all his work, significant changes have marked his essays since *Assorted Prose*. Largely a collection of parodies, occasional pieces that Updike wrote for the "Talk of the Town" section of the *New Yorker*, autobiographical memoirs, and reviews, *Assorted Prose* is primarily notable for four distinguished essays: "The Dogwood Tree: A Boyhood"; "Hub Fans Bid Kid Adieu," a justly famous account of Ted Williams's last baseball game for the Boston Red Sox; "Faith in Search of Understanding," an analysis of Karl Barth's rigorously conservative theology; and "More Love in the Western World," an essay on the history of romantic love in literature.

Picked-Up Pieces, on the other hand, is necessary reading for the student of Updike primarily because it includes his speeches on the genre of fiction and his essay-reviews of the work of many non-American authors in which he develops his understanding of mimesis. European writers continue to hold Updike's focus in *Hugging the Shore,* but in this collection he discusses for the first time some of his American predecessors: Walt Whitman, Herman Melville, and Hawthorne. His interest in American literature also often prompts him to invoke the achievement of Henry James when evaluating the books of other writers.

In *Just Looking* Updike shifts his focus from writers to painters. Despite the self-effacing tone of his title, he offers nearly two dozen essays on artists as various as Richard Estes, Jan Vermeer, and Andrew Wyeth. Of special interest, when one considers Updike's long association with the *New Yorker,* are the essays on *New Yorker* cartoonist Ralph Barton and on writers who were also artists of sorts, including Edgar Allan Poe, Oscar Wilde, and Updike himself. *Odd Jobs* has a similarly self-deprecatory title, but Updike's seriousness is apparent in the sheer bulk of the collection – nearly nine hundred pages of essays and reviews. Commentaries on William Dean Howells, Franz Kafka, Isak Dinesen, and Graham Greene are especially illuminating, as are the multiple reviews of Updike's contemporaries John Cheever and Philip Roth. Typically, however, Updike features analyses of non-American writers, especially those from Africa and Europe.

The concerns that Updike elaborates in his essays shape the themes that he develops in his novels: the malaise of the spirit, the glory of common details, the shrinking of the family center, the enticing lure of adultery, and the ever-beckoning shadow of decay. His first novel, *The Poorhouse Fair,* is a case in point. Unlike most beginning authors who write about youthful initiation from the perspective of personal experience tentatively explored, Updike considers the plight of old folks in a charity home who have no place to turn except toward death. Published in 1959, *The Poorhouse Fair* is set in the imagined future of the 1970s as Updike predicts a welfare society where all needs but spiritual health are met. Writing in the lyrical style that would become the hallmark of his achievement, he exposes the potential sterility of a nation that supplies everything except the right to be eccentric, individual, and alone.

Detailing the one day in the county poorhouse when the inmates are permitted to hold a fair for the citizens of the town, the novel centers on the conflict between Conner, the efficient administrator, and Hook, the aging ward. The problem is not that Conner fails to care but that he fails to see. He can offer blankets for the beds and food for the table, but he cannot understand that marking the rocking chairs with nameplates denies the individuality of choice. The former schoolteacher Hook senses that "not busyness but belief" is the issue, that belief means not only that God dwells in both telephone

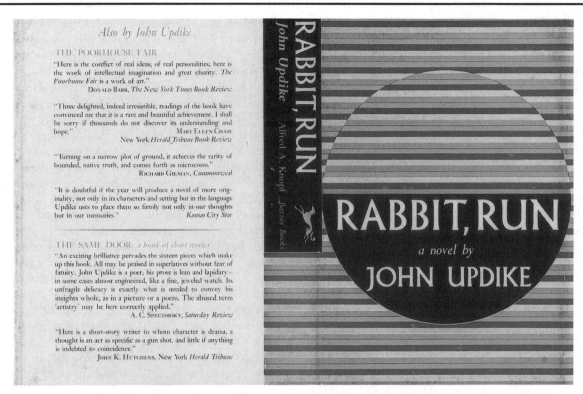

Dust jacket for the first novel of Updike's tetralogy concerning Harry "Rabbit" Angstrom

poles and trees but that faith inspires the craftsmanship that shapes everything from handcarved furniture to the nation itself. What happens to the soul of a country, asks Updike, when machine-sewn blankets count for more than hand-stitched quilts? On the day of the fair, the poorhouse inmates show off their carved peachstones and trinkets, and Updike celebrates their feeble yet stubborn rebellion against manufactured welfare and impersonal regard.

Announcing his presence in American fiction with an admirable first novel of verbal skill and significant concerns, Updike also previewed a theme that would become increasingly important in his canon: the necessity for belief – for faith – above all else. An informal student of modern theology, he has shaped his own religious thought from the strict tenets of Karl Barth and his predecessor Søren Kierkegaard. Drawn especially to Barth's insistence that God is "Wholly Other," that humanity cannot reach God and that only God can touch humanity, Updike stresses Barth's call for belief. Hook has this belief and thus a faith that permits him to maintain calm in the face of care. Harry "Rabbit" Angstrom has belief, too, but he lacks Hook's capacity for thought.

Rabbit, Run (1960), the first of the Rabbit chronicle that includes *Rabbit Redux* (1971), *Rabbit Is Rich,* and *Rabbit at Rest,* continues to be Updike's most shocking novel, but many of its themes are variations of those initiated in *The Poorhouse Fair.* Although Rabbit is only twenty-six while Hook is ninety, both sense the dead ends of their lives. Both also accept Barth's notion of religious commitment. But whereas Hook possesses the serenity that comes with age and the ability to articulate his faith, Rabbit reveals the uncertainty of youth and the inability to express his fear.

Named by Stanley Edgar Hyman as "the most gifted novelist of his generation," Updike began to fill the void left by the decline of William Faulkner and Ernest Hemingway. But, while initiated readers responded to Updike's lush style and sympathetic probing of the pain of American life, the general public was shocked by Rabbit's sexual exploits and by his wife's accidental drowning of their baby. *Rabbit, Run* continues to disturb readers because of Updike's skill at generating sympathy for a troubling young man who inadvertently causes pain. Updike takes a common American experience – the graduation from high school of a star athlete who has no life to lead once the applause diminishes and the headlines fade – and turns it into a subtle exposé of the frailty of the American dream.

Rabbit's dilemma has occupied Updike for his entire career (see, for example, "Ex-Basketball Player" in *The Carpentered Hen and Other Tame Creatures* and "Ace in the Hole" in *The Same Door*), and it is now clear that he has written a saga of middle-class America in the second half of the twentieth century. Not liking what he has but not defining what he wants, Rabbit is a decent, unintelligent man who finds that the momentum that sustained him during his basketball years has slowed to a crawl in a dingy apartment where the dinner is always late and the wife has stopped being pretty. Written entirely in the present tense – an unusual technique in American fiction – and thus stressing the immediacy of Rabbit's crisis, the novel details the sterility of a society that offers television sets and cars but ignores spiritual loss and belief.

Bewildered by her husband's restless agony, by his inarticulate need to run, Janice personifies all that clogs Rabbit's life. Updike's astonishing facility with language is used not only to suggest Rabbit's need for order and style but also to describe the junk that surrounds him via Janice: dirty ashtrays, droning television sets, disorganized closets. All she wants is for him to be like other husbands, to give in to the nine-to-five routine of selling Magi-peelers in the local dimestore, but Rabbit senses that loss of life's momentum means loss of life itself. So he runs.

And as he runs he becomes Updike's religious quester, momentarily stalled between the right way (Janice) and the good way (freedom), but determined to save himself despite the consequences. The Reverend Jack Eccles tries to help him, but Updike shows that Eccles lacks Rabbit's Barthian sense of belief, that in his passion for good works Eccles is a cousin of Conner in *The Poorhouse Fair*. When the frustrated Eccles badgers Rabbit to explain what he wants, all the inarticulate quester can do is hit a perfect tee shot on the golf course, point to the fluidity and grace of the soaring ball, and shout, "That's it!" The last word of the novel – "Runs." – suggests Rabbit's inability to find that grace.

A decade later, in 1971, Updike reintroduced Rabbit at age thirty-six. In *Rabbit Redux* ("Rabbit led back"), however, the junk of ashtrays and closets that Harry has run from earlier is replaced by national events that threaten to overwhelm him: Vietnam, the civil rights movement, and the drug culture. Framing these disasters – as Rabbit considers them to be – is the excitement of the first moon shot; but try as he might to turn the space flight into a metaphor for his own need to soar gracefully and far, he understands that the moon adventure is sterile, merely a triumph of impersonal technology

making contact with a dead rock. In *Rabbit Redux* Harry's dash for open territory has taught him that America no longer promises places to run to, so he returns to his dingy house in the plastic suburb.

What he finds is a metaphor for the upheaval of the 1960s: Janice has left him for a lover, although she would come home if Harry would ask; his son, Nelson, is suddenly a teenager who needs and deserves guidance; a hippie girl and a black Vietnam vet, both drug-crazed, invade his house; and Rabbit finds himself succumbing to physical sloppiness and spiritual despair. The fire that destroys the Angstrom house at the end is Updike's ironic apocalypse, his signal that nothing earth-shattering is going to happen to Rabbit, that Rabbit will have to rebuild his little life by himself. Rabbit attempts to rebound when, in the final scene – all but forgetting his earlier need for grace – he leads Janice to a motel. The last words of the novel – "Sleeps. O.K.?" – are a long way from "Runs."

Rabbit Redux is the least intriguing of the Rabbit tales, for Harry is a more interesting character when he quests instead of halts. But the third Rabbit novel, *Rabbit Is Rich,* is one of Updike's best, and it was published within a year of a resurrection of another of Updike's favorite characters, Henry Bech, in *Bech Is Back* (1982). Read together as installments in Updike's sagas, the two volumes illustrate the expanse of his range: Rabbit sells Toyotas; Bech writes books.

Each Rabbit novel records the tone of a decade. *Rabbit Is Rich* is about the 1970s, and the rainbow that Harry chases in the 1950s and 1960s has shrunk as the American dream goes sour with the bad taste of middle age and aimless youth. Farmland turns into shopping malls; overflowing garbage cans stand beside unsuccessful plywood restaurants; and people reel from a combination of less energy and higher prices. Now forty-six years old, Rabbit does not blame anyone for *Skylab*'s falling or Exxon's greed, but death leers on the horizon, and he is afraid of running out of gas. When Rabbit looks over his shoulder at the glory of early fame too easily won on the basketball court and thinks of himself as "king of the lot" and "the star and spear point" of the flourishing Toyota dealership his family owns, the reader knows that he has not changed much from the man whose value system was defined in terms of athletic prowess.

But he has changed some: golf has replaced basketball, and he rumbles rather than runs with a forty-two-inch waist and a tendency to avoid mirrors when he used to love reflections of himself. Still, Rabbit is rich in the ironic sense of being able to afford cashews instead of peanuts. Life is sweet. For the first time in twenty-five years he is happy to be alive, even happy with his marriage to Janice. Deserted by Harry in the first Rabbit novel and deserting him in the second, Janice fits snugly into a middle-age routine, plays tennis at the country club, and, says Rabbit, "never looked sharper." She still drinks too much, and she rarely serves meals on time, but she finally enjoys sex and even manages now and then to stand up to her husband.

Despite Janice, golf, and money, Rabbit needs to run, not as fast and not as far, but somewhere. He muses on "the entire squeezed and cutdown shape of his life," and he realizes that middle age is upon him, a time when dreams decline to awareness of limits and stomachs take on a noticeable sag. The strained jollity of the country-club set, "the kind of crowd that will do a marriage in if you let it," makes him uneasy, but his flight in this novel is not as urgent as it is in *Rabbit, Run* and thus not as poignant. He knows that he is a "soft and a broad target."

Aiming at the target is his son, Nelson, twenty-two years old, a surly college dropout, and, in Rabbit's eyes, "humpbacked and mean, a rat going out to be drowned." Hitchhiking home to a hurry-up marriage to a pregnant secretary, Nelson wants a job at Rabbit's Toyota dealership. Updike sketches the father/son tension with superb detail so that the reader understands Rabbit's lament: "How can you respect the world when you see it's being run by a bunch of kids turned old?" But that old bunch was once Rabbit's bunch, and Nelson will be right behind them. He is tired of being young, but he does not know how to grow up. Nelson lacks fluidity and grace. Sympathy for his fear of being trapped is not easy because, unlike his father, he has no intuitive sense of joy, no yearning. His wife is correct: he is a spoiled bully. Nelson runs but without Rabbit's faith; the son runs from while the father runs toward.

Later Rabbit "glimpses the truth that to be rich is to be robbed, to be rich is to be poor." In part he means spiritually poor, though he would not say it that way, so he and Janice break from his mother-in-law and buy their own home. Maybe his rainbow is in the suburbs. He still longs for a world without ruts, but God has become a "raisin lost under the car seat." In the earlier novels Rabbit runs toward transcendence, toward what he calls "it," but now he has only a vacation in the Caribbean to rejuvenate him. There, engaged in wife-swapping where he once pursued life's rhythm, he even misses his dream girl when he is paired with his second choice.

Sex is part of Rabbit's scampering, his questing, as Updike established years ago.

Rabbit returns home to find his son drifted back to college but his granddaughter born. The birth calms him for a moment, soothes his undefined sense of unsettledness, but he knows that it is also a giant step toward extinction: mortality looms beyond the middle years.

Late in *Rabbit at Rest,* apparently the final novel of the celebrated tetralogy about Harry Angstrom, Rabbit looks at his overweight, middle-aged body and sees "an innocuous passive spirit that doesn't want to do any harm, get trapped anywhere, or ever die." All three desires are denied him. At long last, Updike's Rabbit stops running.

Like James Fenimore Cooper's Leatherstocking, Hawthorne's Hester, and Mark Twain's Huck, Harry is one of the immortal characters who first absorb and then define a national culture. Now fifty-six and stuck in the United States of the 1980s with its cocaine addiction and condos – in what Rabbit calls "Reagan's reign" – Harry still worries about sex and death, religion and belief, but he is not as certain as he used to be, not as confident. Personal limitation mirrors national malaise. His America is depleted and his dreams are deferred. He now lives part of the year in a Florida condo, but, when he looks at the imported Toyotas that have brought him the easy life of golf and profits, he thinks not of success but of the eerie presence of lurking death: "Most of American life is driving somewhere and then driving back wondering why the hell you went." Similar witticisms throughout the novel create a comic frame for Rabbit's gloom.

No longer the hopeful Rabbit of his basketball-playing days in the 1950s, he is similarly distanced from the grace he once pursued with inarticulate fear. Like many Americans of his indulgent generation, Harry suffers from heart trouble, the physical sign of his spiritual dread. Never articulate, he continues to define abstractions with the metaphors of sports. Golf, he reasons, now has a greater relevance to his life than basketball: the golf ball starts wide before falling into a small hole in the ground. Perhaps the only immortality he will find is the "little genetic quirk" that he passes on to his granddaughter: "You fill in a slot for a time and then move out." Death means making room for someone else.

Yet, for all his fear, Harry continues his quest to break free of limitations. He is Updike's American dreamer, a mundane Jay Gatsby whose dissatisfaction cloaks a lifelong spiritual yearning. In *Rabbit at Rest* Updike describes the hairstyles, the inane

*Dust jacket for Updike's 1965 novel, in which a middle-aged son must come to terms with his mother, who has
dreamed of his becoming a poet before she dies*

pop songs, the dismal TV programs, such as *Rose-anne,* the physical-fitness nuts, and the racial prejudices to illustrate the uneasiness of the United States in 1988–1989 and to generate sympathy for a character who is similar to many readers who will buy the novel but is one they normally will not much like.

Despite material accumulation during the Reagan years, life in America is usually a matter of "mostly missed signals." Rabbit fails to acknowledge both his son's drug addiction and his own failing heart. His youthful running has been slowed to gliding over immaculate fairways in golf carts, aware, sadly, that the most depressing agony about aging is "the lessening of excitement about anything."

Clearly, Updike reread the earlier Rabbit novels in preparation for the finale. Harry's many memories include events dramatized in the first three books, and quotations of his thoughts from past years indicate the long continuity of his quest, the never-ending fever of his fear. In this way Updike suggests that a person's life establishes unalterable patterns, as when Rabbit nearly loses his granddaughter in a boating mishap and thus relives the horror of his wife's accidental drowning of their

daughter decades ago when he still believed in the promise of possibility. Harry's wife thinks that he is at peace now. Updike and the reader know better.

Watching a TV monitor to see inside his own heart during angioplasty, Rabbit witnesses a preview of his own death. Yet, with an irony that readers of the entire tetralogy will appreciate, Updike shows how Harry's wife accepts middle age as a springboard to move enthusiastically into the world even as her husband retreats inside his own shrinking space.

Despite the transgression of adultery, then, the reader cheers when, in the last movement of the novel, Rabbit runs one final time – away from complications, away from stasis, away from a catastrophe that he himself has helped cause. He no longer runs toward his ill-defined goal of "it," but at least he moves forward, "jostling for his space in the world as if he still deserves it." He even returns to the basketball court despite his weight, his age, his heart. In short, he tries. But his fear presages the final stillness. The last word of this splendid novel is "Enough." Death is, as it always was, the still center of Rabbit's frantic life of motion.

It is sad to think of death setting its snare for Rabbit Angstrom because, after four decades and four long novels, he has joined the pantheon of American literary heroes. Yet a glimpse of final defeat is the price to be paid for membership in that exclusive club. Like Natty Bumppo, Ahab, Huck Finn, Gatsby, Ike McCaslin, Holden Caulfield, and many others before him, Harry learns that, no matter how far he runs in space, he cannot outrace time.

Henry Bech has all but stopped running. In *Bech Is Back* Henry returns to the literary scene with a new wife and a new novel, but his old bewilderment is still intact. His former mistress knows that his book is lousy, but the ad-fed public adores it anyway. Henry suspects that her judgment is correct; yet, after suffering through a silence lasting more than a decade, he wonders how he can reject the royalties and the fanfare, since he has poured enough sex and violence into his latest novel to guarantee a best-seller all but created by media hype. Silence, he reasons, offers only limited rewards.

Bech is Updike's favorite writer, a character who promises to have the longevity of Rabbit in the Updike canon and who allows Updike the opportunity to work out the frustrations that inevitably trap the successful artist in America. When last seen in *Bech: A Book* (1970), Bech had published enough fiction to shape a reputation with the intelligentsia; had fallen into the hell of writer's block that, ironically, increased his reputation; and had emerged as a kind of artifact that Uncle Sam paraded around the globe to fulfill various cultural exchanges. Bech is Updike's joke on himself. More to the point, he is also Updike's joke on the discouraging hoopla with which Americans surround their authors in order to worship not the writing but the writer.

The laughs begin on the first page of *Bech: A Book*. There Updike reveals a letter to himself from Bech in which Bech says, with his ego showing, "Well, if you must commit the artistic indecency of writing about a writer, better I suppose about me than about you." The laughs continued through the 1970s when Updike kept up the charade of Henry Bech as real author by publishing bogus interviews between Bech and himself in the *New York Times*.

Yet there is a serious tone to the laughter. The jokes about Bech may illustrate the appalling way America treats its authors, but Updike is just as concerned with the fate that dooms many American writers to lesser and lesser achievement. While the royalty checks jump to six figures and the talk-show appearances multiply, the quality of the writing diminishes. In 1974 Updike said in a speech, "Why Write?": "*To remain interested* – of American novel-

ists, only Henry James continued in old age to advance his art."

How right he is – but only up to a point. Those who care about American fiction may now place Updike's name beside James's. The point is not that he rivals James but that, unlike Hawthorne and Melville, unlike Twain and Hemingway, unlike, arguably, even Faulkner, Updike has continued to advance his art.

Henry Bech is not so lucky. In *Bech Is Back* irony irritates his life. Even enduring reputation smarts: "Though Henry Bech, the author, in his middle years had all but ceased to write, his books continued, as if ironically, to live, to cast shuddering shadows toward the center of his life, where that thing called his reputation cowered." This sentence begins the book, and one thinks immediately of Bech's fellow author J. D. Salinger. But Salinger's silence seems noble. Rejecting the show biz of bigtime publishing, he may be writing his books only for himself. Bech's silence is more demeaning. Languishing in the success of his first novel, he is paralyzed by an old-fashioned writer's block. Silent before his public for almost fifteen years, Bech has become, to his dismay, a kind of myth.

But silence does not mean invisibility. If Americans cannot recognize true artists, they are proficient at worshiping stars. Rather than let Henry suffer privately from his inability to write, they send him around the world again to give speeches on "The Cultural Situation of the American Writer" and inadvertently to act the patsy to third-world audiences who use literature for political ends.

Henry's travels are the slowest part of *Bech Is Back,* but the entire book is a delight. Rebounding, for example, from the disillusion of meeting an avid collector who hoards Bech's novels for their potential value on the rare-book market, Henry agrees for a price to sign his name to 28,500 of his books. Transported to a balmy island for the chore and ministered to by his mistress, Bech confronts a stunning silence: he cannot even write his own name.

When he finally does dodge the spotlight for a moment and inches his way toward true literary recognition, he is selected for, of all things, the Melville Medal, "awarded every five years to that American author who has maintained the most meaningful silence." This kind of humor sparkles throughout *Bech Is Back*. Success, it seems, is unavoidable. Marrying his mistress's sister and moving to her family home in Ossining, New York, he gives in to his wife's nudges to free his blocked inspiration with pep talks, changes the working title of his novel in progress from *Think Big* to *Easy Money,* and accepts the degradation of advertising's stranglehold on literature when Madison Avenue turns the book into a best-seller. "Bech is back," scream the hucksters, but, Henry and Updike muse, at what cost? Lionized as the latest rage, surrounded by New York's prettiest at a gaudy white-on-white party, he closes with a word that typifies the entire experience: "unclean."

For all Bech's troubles, however, one hopes that he will rebound again in ten years or so. For Updike has more to say about the paradox that afflicts writers: their craving for applause and their need for privacy. The conflict between easy money and noble silence is deadly to American artists. Rather than pontificate about this cultural trap in ponderous essays, Updike uses sharp wit and evocative prose to create a memorable character who lives the dilemma.

Standing between the silent but articulate Bech and the questing but inarticulate Rabbit are Updike's family novels (*The Centaur;* and *Of the Farm,* 1965); his marriage novels (*Couples,* 1968; *A Month of Sundays; Marry Me: A Romance,* 1976; and *The Witches of Eastwick*); and his unexpected novel about language and Africa (*The Coup*). Updike has occasionally named the award-winning *The Centaur* his favorite. One can see why. Beautifully written and imaginatively conceived, *The Centaur* is an homage to his father, Wesley Updike, who sacrificed his own dreams to keep his family together during the disruptive trauma of the Great Depression.

Interestingly, Updike originally thought of *The Centaur* as a contrasting companion to *Rabbit, Run.* Both novels suggest that the threat of death can be defined as a loss of grace before an onslaught of the mundane yet overwhelming details that any head of a family faces in his daily routine; but, whereas Harry scampers from drudgery in pursuit of "it," George Caldwell plods painfully through the snow to escort his teenaged son Peter back home. Harry is a rabbit while Caldwell is a horse, and the story of his sacrifice is a modern tale of heroism.

Told from Peter's perspective while he is a middle-aged, second-rate painter in New York, *The Centaur* develops in a complicated manner along two parallel lines of narration. The first is the realistic level as Peter recalls his high-school days in Olinger, Pennsylvania, and the agony that his mocked and martyred father suffers while teaching science to uncaring clods. The second is the mythic level as Peter adapts the Greek tale of Chiron, the centaur injured in war but beloved by Zeus, to highlight Caldwell's heroism. Dreading the shrinking of his

future by the dispiriting grind of the high school and the destruction of his body by disease, Caldwell bravely yet comically bumbles his way through the day, unselfishly giving himself, unaware that the unruly students love him. Mocked, jeered, and metaphorically shot through the ankle with the "arrow" of laughter, Caldwell rarely challenges his duty and never dodges his fate.

The primary question in the novel, then, is not whether Caldwell will succumb to routine duties but whether Peter will step toward a creative life. Updike's style works its magical best in *The Centaur* as Peter's reminiscence transforms ancient Olympus into modern Olinger via lyrical descriptions of love, uncertainty, and fear. The epigraph from Karl Barth once again recalls Updike's insistence on the tenet of belief, and at the end of the novel George Caldwell trudges back through the snow toward his high school in order to guarantee the stability his son needs while growing up. Peter's narration is both an expression of gratitude and his greatest "painting," and the reader suspects that Peter is ready now to break out of his skepticism, ready now to live.

Of the Farm is the companion novel to *The Centaur.* Although the characters' names are changed, the situations are similar: both novels explore how a middle-aged son comes to terms with an aging parent who has personal myths of the family's past. The focus in *Of the Farm,* however, is on the mother, and Mrs. Robinson (whose husband is named George) is one of Updike's most intricately conceived characters. Strong, willful, jealous, brave, and afraid, Mrs. Robinson is an old woman who fears that death will beckon before her grown son, Joey, can fulfill the myth that she has dreamed for him and that he resists. She has set her life on his becoming a poet and a protector of her farm, but Joey has fled her distorting myth for a career in advertising and the concrete of New York. This short but highly charged novel is a psychological thriller that takes place during one weekend when Joey brings his second wife, Peggy, and his stepson to the farm for Mrs. Robinson's blessing.

He does not get it. In many ways *Of the Farm* is about the failure of forgiveness: Joey blames his mother for ruining his first marriage and threatening his second; Mrs. Robinson blames Peggy for enticing her son beyond poetry and the farm with the lure of uninhibited sexuality; and Peggy blames Mrs. Robinson for destroying Joey's father by forcing him to move to the lonely farm.

Framing these crosscurrents of guilt and fear is the counterpoint between the weakness of the son's

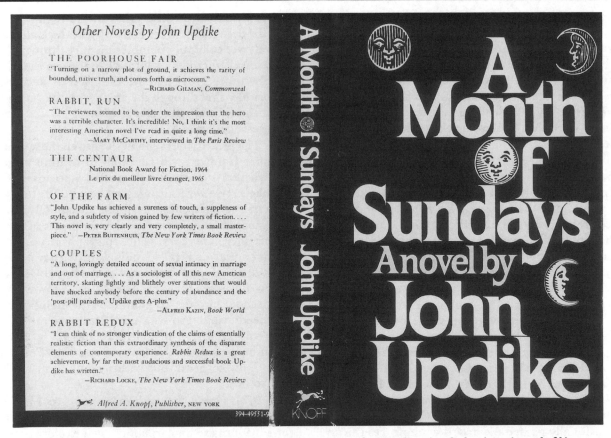

Dust jacket for Updike's 1975 novel, in which a minister must atone for his indiscretions by keeping a journal of his spiritual recovery

resolve and the strength of the mother's myth. Joey admits that he is weak, that he has turned to Peggy's earthy sexuality as a substitute for the farm: "My wife is a field." But he also understands the force of his mother's ability to reshape her past to accommodate her present. Trapped within her warping myth of the farm as a "people sanctuary," he falls victim once again and betrays Peggy to Mrs. Robinson's disparaging dismissal. Listening to a sermon in which the minister quotes Barth on the notion that women are "an appeal to the kindness of Man," Joey must realize that he has fallen short. Unlike Peter Caldwell in *The Centaur,* he cannot use the proven glory of his command of words (the novel itself) to illuminate the potential glory of his own life.

Updike's marriage novels continue his probing of the relationship between the physical and the spiritual, but in these particular books he wonders whether sexuality can fill the void left by the decline of faith in the "post-pill paradise." In the short story "The Music School" (*The Music School*), for example, the narrator muses, "We are all pilgrims, faltering toward divorce." Separation seems the ironic

goal of Updike's married couples. But the reader should understand that, although adultery is a consequence, unbridled sensuality is not the issue. Like Rabbit and Bech, the men in these novels fear for the loss of their souls, and, when they fail to find assurance in religion, they look to the carnal for the promise that they will never die.

The fate of Piet Hanema in *Couples* is an example. A builder who, like Hook, appreciates the strength of Calvinism and the permanence of fine carpentry, Piet becomes afraid when he suspects the inability of contemporary religious practices to hold back the darkness of his doubt. Thus when he abandons wife Angela (angel) for mistress Foxy (animal), he knows that his search for love triggers his fall to the world. Like the falls suffered by Hawthorne's characters (for example, in *The Marble Faun,* 1860), however, his plunge from grace may mean the fulfillment of his humanity. Piet's predicament is the most complex of the various adulteries in *Couples,* and the novel itself is Updike's most detailed evocation of the microcosm of the middle-class suburb. The reader must thus be careful to keep the lyrical descriptions of sex from obscuring the seriousness of Updike's concern for the ineffectuality of religion.

Updike's uncertainty about the value of Piet's effort is reflected in *Marry Me: A Romance,* a novel that exchanges the realism of *Couples* for the fable of Hawthorne, what the earlier author called "romance." Clearly not meant to be realistic, *Marry Me* proposes three illusory endings to Jerry Conant's adulterous affair with Sally, but in each case Jerry is still searching for assurance – be it spiritual or physical – that his life matters. Exclaiming that "I am married to my death," he cannot understand his wife Ruth's calm in the face of mortality. Neither can he understand how Ruth's own adulterous affair causes her blossoming as a woman. Although relatively slight as a novel, *Marry Me* contains Updike's finest portrait of a woman in Ruth. She, too, remains trapped by the Puritan insistence on the separation of the body and the soul, and her quest for love and selfhood parallels Jerry's quest for faith.

If *Marry Me* is the slightest of the marriage novels and *Couples* the most famous, *A Month of Sundays* is the most important. It is also the most difficult, the most comic, and the most ignored. Once again openly bowing to Hawthorne, Updike places his minister, Tom Marshfield (the echo of Dimmesdale is clear), in an omega-shaped motel in the desert to which he has been banished for seducing his organist, and in which he is to write a journal about his spiritual recovery. Marshfield has as much trouble with the intransigence of his language as with the flimsiness of his vows, and much of the comedy in this rich novel derives from the inadvertent puns and Freudian slips that he finds himself writing. Language, suggests Updike, is just as troubling to master as faith, and *A Month of Sundays* is on one level a novel about an author writing a novel in which the novelist is the main character.

But the comedy also has its serious side, for Marshfield is another of Updike's Barthian believers. Armed with his faith and aware of the weakness of his flesh, the wayward minister is convinced (as is Updike) that body and soul must be reunited if belief is to survive in a secular world. He pursues this conviction through a progression of often specious theological speculations and a longing for physical contact with women. His final affair with the mysteriously silent Ms. Prynne (a modern Hester) signals his success, and the novel ends with a serious prayer shaped by a comic embrace of the flesh.

A decade after *A Month of Sundays,* Updike published two novels that, when added to that work, comprise his trilogy on Hawthorne's *The Scarlet Letter* (1850). In *Roger's Version* (1986) and *S.* (1988) he reimagines Roger Chillingworth and Hester Prynne from a late-twentieth-century perspective. *Roger's Version* is especially challenging because of its focus on the antagonism between computer technology and theology.

Those readers who regard Updike as only the deft describer of suburban sexuality and prayerful flight should recall his careerlong fascination with science. From the astonishing first chapter of *The Centaur,* through the poem "Midpoint" (1969), to the collection *Facing Nature,* Updike has argued that, while science may be a metaphor for the mystery of creation, it is not a substitute for faith. In *Roger's Version* he offers a dazzling display of arcane knowledge that takes shape around the proposition that "wherever theology touches science, it gets burned." To, one suspects, the secret joy of most humanists, the person who gets burned in this novel is a computer freak.

Epigraphs from Karl Barth and Kierkegaard suggest not only that Updike is calling on past thinkers whose intellectual complexities have echoed throughout his work but also that he is setting a confrontation between faith and reason. To his usual interplay of sex, sin, and salvation, he adds the murky theories of science. One thinks immediately of Hawthorne's Aylmer ("The Birthmark") and Rappaccini ("Rappaccini's Daughter").

The Reverend Roger (that is, Chillingworth) Lambert, professor in a divinity school, prefers the sanctuary to the laboratory. As he says, " 'It is very important for my mental wellbeing that I keep my thoughts directed away from areas of contemplation that might entangle me.' " But entangled he becomes with the introduction of Dale (that is, Dimmesdale) Kohler, a research assistant in the computer lab. Roger tells his tale with a droll self-irony that enhances his wit and extols his modesty. No self-righteous fundamentalist, he is skeptical and irreverent, but he does believe. His faith in "the Lord's unsleeping witness and strict accountancy" has little patience with the crass *1*s and *0*s of a mainframe computer.

Yet Dale, himself one of the faithful, thinks that he can use computers to prove God's existence, and he needs Roger's help in securing a grant to support his research. Wondering whether the proof of reason will diminish the mystery of faith, Roger suspects that to reveal God's face is to eliminate God's majesty. (Updike's original title for the novel was "Majesty.") Thus Updike explores the ancient dilemma of humanity's need to know and its fear of knowledge, and he asks an equally ancient question: is religious faith stronger when long-held beliefs are protected from scrutiny or when they are subjected to challenge? Why, asks Roger, should he revere a God who allows himself to be "intellectually trapped?" Lambert knows his Barth: such a God would not be God. But he also argues that universities should fund something more "substantial than black or feminist studies," and thus he ostensibly backs Dale's project while indirectly teaching Dale a hard lesson: that the formulas of science are no match for the unreason of faith.

But this is an Updike novel; domestic crises also matter: Roger's wife Esther (that is, Hester) is bored. Like many of Updike's women, Esther is a nonbeliever. Domestic disaster masks religious uncertainty, because God, Updike insists, blesses the flesh as well as the spirit. Updike dovetails these various strands confidently, convincingly, and comically. When, for example, Roger calls on Tertullian's ancient opinion that carnal attraction does not threaten religious belief and that flesh does not oppose soul, he illustrates Updike's interest in America's disturbing need to separate body and spirit.

Comic, troubling, and erudite, *Roger's Version* is Updike's most intellectually challenging novel. In addition to Barth and Kierkegaard, Updike refers to, among others, Friedrich Nietzsche, Gian Bernini, Lucretius, Martin Luther, Marcion, Thomas Aquinas, Paul Dirac, Albert Einstein, Paul Tillich, Ludwig Wittgenstein, Ferdinand de Saussure, Dietrich Bonhoeffer, and Charles Darwin as well as the physics of the Big Bang Theory, Boolean algebra, and Christian heresies. Hawthorne would have been pleased.

Hawthorne's Hester finds her contemporary voice in *S.* Updike has explained that *S.* is an effort to placate feminist detractors of his canon by celebrating "a woman on the move." But as Sarah Worth, the forty-two-year-old discontented heroine, flees the rich life of her patriarchal, philandering husband, she moves from gaudy materialism to Asian spiritualism in such a rush that she unconsciously personifies feminism gone delightfully wacky. Sarah descends from the Prynnes and bears a daughter named Pearl, but she wants no part of Hester's stateliness and reserve in public. Where Hester is unusually quiet, *S.* (Sarah) is usually talking – or writing, one should say: *S.* is an epistolary novel built on Sarah's lively letters to husband, daughter, mother, hairdresser, and dentist.

S. begins her rebellion by moving out of her present and into her future, resentful of her husband of twenty-two years and of all the "dark unheeding illegible male authority." American women, she complains, are raised to enjoy "the smell of a man in the house." Updike's grin is delightfully wide as he details Sarah's swing from an American love of things to a religious pursuit of spirit. For Updike refers again to arcane theology, and thus he understands that chasing the spirit means enjoying the erotic: "Ego is the enemy," S. preaches; "love is the goal." Love, she decides, may be found by joining an arhat's religious commune in Arizona, and she fills her letters with the exotic words of Eastern worship while she dresses in "love colors" and helps build an eyesore called the Hall of Millionfold Joys.

The reader soon realizes that Updike's voluptuous S. is much more sexually active than Hawthorne's voluptuous Hester. Much of the fun of this witty novel comes from following Sarah's account of her pilgrimage to what she hopes is the perfect theological blending of active body and prayerful spirit. Her arhat asks, for example, whether she has "any venereal disease and how much money was I bringing to the Treasury of Enlightenment." Updike's bemused tone undercuts the illusion of blissful freedom for female or male, and, unlike S., the reader understands that the arhat lusts after both women and cash. Some of the wittiest moments are shaped in letters that S. types for the bogus spiritual leader and that expose his oily methods of soliciting funds. Alluding to the religious scandals of Jim Bakker and Jimmy Swaggert, *S.* is as timely as it is funny. Religion sells, and in America a sucker is born every minute. S. is one of those suckers. She even defends the arhat's nationwide chain of "regional meditation and massage centers." The reader waits, of course, for the moment when the arhat lures her to his lair.

Although a Christian believer, Updike is no puritan. He is amused by Sarah's diatribe against "the atrophied Puritan theology" that has, she insists, conspired for centuries against the liberation of women. Trying to free her willing body from the outdated Christian notion of Eve as defiler, she explains feminine power convincingly. Yet her naive belief in total freedom and in a huckster who builds a residence "Park" for the faithful suggests that her independence is an illusion.

As if she were aware of Updike's final joke in *The Witches of Eastwick* when the divorced women remarry, S. is horrified to learn that her daughter plans to drop out of college and marry a man. Men and women, it seems, need each other. Worse, she discovers that the arhat from India is really Art from Massachusetts. Her lesson takes hold: "Follow the fashion and trust biology to override culture." One assumes she means that gender politics is finally sterile. "We all have a number of skins," writes S., "especially women ... because society makes us wriggle more." At the end Sarah has wriggled herself into a tentative freedom with money and goodies to spare. *S.* is Updike's funniest novel, a meditation on the unexpected combination of American femininity and spiritual grace.

The comedy is even more audacious in *The Witches of Eastwick,* a novel that lacks the weight of *A Month of Sundays* and *Roger's Version* but that extends Updike's novelistic experiments beyond his earlier commitment to realism. The magical realism of such Latin American masters as Carlos Fuentes, Gabriel García Márquez, and Isabel Allende is in the background. Tennis balls turn into furry things, and suburban witches cast a spell of adultery, but the novel is finally a celebration of duty and art. The time is the late 1960s, the place is Rhode Island, and the witches are three thirtyish mothers who have divorced their husbands in the name of womanhood and freedom. Updike's sense of history sets the frame. Famous at its founding as a refuge for liberal believers looking to escape the rigors of Massachusetts Puritanism, Rhode Island was once described by Cotton Mather as the "fag end of creation." Anne Hutchinson, banished to Rhode Island in 1637, hoped to found a covenant of grace there, but today's witches of Eastwick have established instead a coven of transgression.

Jane, Sukie, and Alexandra shrink from the word *man* as an "assertive" noun that can negate the peaceful aura of a calm morning. *Man* carries such dreary connotations for the three divorced women that they deny witchhood to a friend merely because she still has a husband. "Magic," writes Updike, "occurs all around us as nature seeks and finds the inevitable forms, " and for much of the novel the inevitable form for the three liberated witches is freedom from "the armor of patriarchal protector" in the hope of indulging the fecundity women think they will find when single.

Alexandra, for example, becomes a witch when, in her middle thirties, she realizes she has a right to exist, not as "an afterthought and companion – a bent rib" – and thus less than man, but as "the mainstay of the continuing Creation, as the daughter of a daughter." Her initial tricks are often the result of "maternal wrath," and she argues that "a conspiracy of women upholds the world."

But, if all this sounds good to today's housewife, consider Updike's irony: becoming a witch

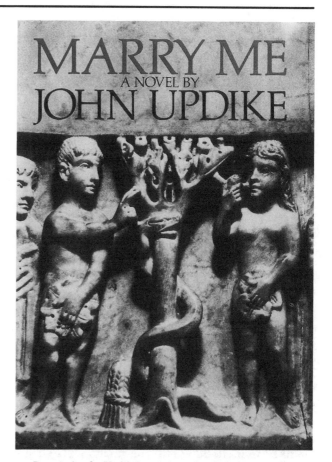

Dust jacket for Updike's 1976 novel, which proposes three possible endings to the central character's adulterous affair

frees Alexandra only from the obligations of wearing high-heeled shoes and controlling her weight. Blooming selfhood has its foolish extremes, too. As the narrator wryly says, "This was an era of many proclaimed rights." Updike's bemused tone directs the first half of the novel: "Being divorced in a small town is a little like playing Monopoly; eventually you land on all the properties."

In the post-Christian era, promiscuity is no more than a game. The only burnings these witches suffer are a hot bath with a ridiculous devil and "the tongues of indignant opinion." Although these women are a long way from Mather's scorched victims, they initially earn Updike's concern as well as laughter. When frustrated housewives receive Tofrinal from doctors; and suspect advice from ministers, domestic rebellion is just around the next corner, coming home with the children.

The complications begin when Darryl Van Horne, an unmarried, monied musician and dabbler in science, moves to Eastwick. In the waning 1960s, a time the narrator calls "this hazy late age of declining doctrine," the wealthy lord of the underworld easily makes his way. He may be ineffective and New York vulgar, but he fascinates the locals. Van Horne is, after all, their dark prince, the odd defiler who does not bother with God.

But Updike finally sympathizes not with the sexy witches and their mysterious mentor but with the anonymous citizens who plod "through their civic and Christian duties." While Van Horne sardonically collects the "permanized garbage" of the culture as mocking works of sculpture, the dutiful suburbanites have to live with the junk. The devil in the novel is not godless science but ministers who exchange belief for the latest college course, dropouts who do not wash and cannot think, and wives who save the world but ruin their homes.

The Witches of Eastwick laughs at these absurdities until a murder and suicide change the tone. Satire and sadness mix. Updike has written a novel of ebb and flow, spring and fall, life and death; a novel in which evil seems so potent that nothing can combat it except art. In an age of little faith, Johann Sebastian Bach counts for more than war protesters, Paul Cézanne for more than politics. Love, too, matters. The witches regain humanity when they find new husbands.

Updike's commitment to art and duty reaches a comic climax in *The Coup*. Africa has long been for Updike "an invitation to the imagination": "I've always been attracted to hidden corners." Drawing on that strange land as "the emptiest part of the world I could think of," he made *The Coup* a novel with noticeable though not dramatic differences from his other fiction. The most obvious difference is that the land of Kush is a long way from the lawns of suburbia. In addition, *The Coup* has a comic tone sustained largely by the sardonic observations of the narrator, Colonel Ellelloû. Ellelloû describes Kush, for example, as a constitutional monarchy "with the constitution suspended and the monarch deposed." Among Kush's natural resources, which seem largely to be comprised of drought and desert, is what Ellelloû calls "the ample treasury of diseases." Finally the narrator's conscious manipulation of narrative voice is distinctive in the Updike canon. Col. Hakim Felix Ellelloû, the recently ousted president of Kush, tells of his presidency primarily in the third person even while he is very much aware of the first person who experienced the events. A narrator watching his own presence in the tale, he interrupts his story, for example, to comment on how his manuscript is blurred in places by a wet ring from a glass of Fanta.

Part of the comedy, then, results from Ellelloû's distancing himself from himself with the device of third-person narration and yet relying on first person when convenient: "There are two selves: the one who acts, and the 'I' who experiences. This latter is passive even in a whirlwind of the former's making, passive and guiltless and astonished. The historical performer bearing the name Ellelloû was no less mysterious to me than to the American press." The point is that Ellelloû writes his story as much to find out who he is, to distinguish public mask from private man, as to explain the coup that has forced him to take up his pen. He understands now that the "he" carried the "I" here and there, and that the "I" never knew why but submitted. As a result, the "I" suffers the effects of the "he's" actions. A man of disguises and anonymous travels throughout Kush, he is a leader whose "domicilic policy is apparently to be in no place at any specific time." Even his languages are "clumsy masks" that "his thoughts must put on."

Ellelloû is a mystical leader without pragmatic talent because he believes primarily in "the idea of Kush." Yet one of his problems is that his obsession with his country is but the other side of his distrust of the world, an obsession that nurtures his determination to burn food offered by bungling America while his people go hungry. A true son of the Third World, he understands how gifts bring humans who in turn bring oppression, but his hatred of America is comically undercut by the clichés of revolution in his speeches. In light of the childish rhetoric of the Iranian revolution, Updike's portrait of the Islamic nationalist is especially interesting. America, for example, is "that fountainhead of obscenity and glut," but in Kush "the land itself is forgetful, an evaporating pan out of which all things human rise into blue invisibility."

The first meeting between Ellelloû and a goodwill bureaucrat from America is simultaneously ludicrous and pointed. Updike's two-pronged satire of the misguided American gift of a mountain of Trix cereal and potato chips to drought-stricken Kushites and of the indignant Ellelloû, who burns both the junk food and the bureaucrat, is a comic set piece that underscores how America's mindless need to be loved and the Third World's rigid ideology clash while people starve. One is reminded of Updike's earlier story "I Am, Dying, Egypt, Dying" (*Museums and Women*) with its portrait of the benign, rich American who cannot return the affection he seeks.

The comedy of this ideological sparring match depends upon the speech of the antagonists. Full of pop slang and bureaucratese, the American urges, " 'These cats are *starving*. The whole world knows

264

it, you can see 'em starve on the six o'clock news every night. The American people want to help. We know this country's socialist and xenophobic.' " Ellelloû's response is little better: " 'Offer your own blacks freedom before you pile boxes of carcinogenic trash on the holy soil of Kush!' " Updike's control of speech tones and language is so superb in *The Coup* that in one sense language itself is the hero of the novel.

Style is the triumph of *The Coup,* the primary means by which Updike makes fun not only of America's need to help despite its vexation by Vietnam and President Richard Nixon but also indirectly of President Jimmy Carter's fortune in peanuts. Typical of the comic tone is the following comment by one of Ellelloû's advisers when he learns that the national fad of dieting in America has caused a drop in consumption of peanut butter and a corresponding increase in the exporting of peanuts: " 'Nothing more clearly advertises the American decline and coming collapse than this imperative need, contrary to all imperialist principles, to export raw materials.' " The laughter cuts both ways, for American peanuts on the open market threaten Kush's own crop of peanuts, which it must sell to purchase Czech dynamos. Updike understands that the intricacies of shifting political alliances often depend upon the supply of hardly strategic items such as peanut oil, so he creates Ellelloû, an African revolutionary educated in America, a leader who despises that country as a meddling superparanoid, to personify these contradictions that may be ridiculous but are nevertheless lethal.

Longing to find a mystical cause for Kush's deprivation, Ellelloû travels the country only to collide with his Americanized side in a metropolis of McDonald's and Coke. On his final journey through Kush, he stumbles into a surprise, a bustling, illegal city named for him. Drugstores sell deodorant ("God sees the soul; men smell the flesh"), women wear miniskirts and halters, and the people go Western. Ready capital and comfort undermine Spartan tradition and myth. In this plastic town, with its commitment to upward mobility and declining quality, Ellelloû discovers that he is considered the curse on Kush. The coup achieved, he takes refuge as a short-order cook and parking attendant, searching the newspapers for news of himself, before accepting exile in France to write *The Coup.* The last lines reemphasize his dual narrative perspective: "He is writing his memoirs. No, I should put it more precisely: Colonel Ellelloû is rumored to be working on his memoirs."

Black Muslims, prejudiced whites, doublespeak bureaucrats, liberal college students, revolutionary Africans, dull Russians – all are targets for Updike's comic darts. His love for caricatures and parodies, for James Thurber and Max Beerbohm, once manifested in his boyhood desire to draw cartoons for the *New Yorker,* works itself out in *The Coup.*

A similar comedy of politics and language informs *Memories of the Ford Administration* (1992). In 1974, at the beginning of the Gerald Ford presidency, Updike published *Buchanan Dying,* the most curious but least read of his many books. A closet drama in three acts with an eighty-page afterword, *Buchanan Dying* chronicles the presidency of James Buchanan, Updike's fellow Pennsylvanian. Updike claims the play remains, "my favorite among my books." The statement appears to be accurate, for Buchanan reappears in *Memories of the Ford Administration* as the obsession of the narrator, Alfred Clayton.

A history professor at Wayward Junior College, Clayton receives a request from a historians' association for his memories of the Ford era. He obliges, but accounts of both his domestic chaos and his scholarly research on Buchanan's doomed administration become entangled in his explanations of the sexually liberated 1970s associated with Ford. The result is a comic novel of such erudition as to confirm once again Updike's preeminence among contemporary American novelists.

Clayton's rationalization to the historians who solicit his analysis of Ford is that he hopes not to rehabilitate but to reanimate Buchanan. One of Updike's jokes, however, is that the narrator becomes more sedentary as Buchanan becomes more lively. Stories tend to consume storytellers. Thus part of the fun of *Memories of the Ford Administration* is its occasional self-reflexivity, its use of footnotes and asides to the reader to document not only the difficulty of writing but also the proximity of history and fiction.

The breakup of the family unit during what Clayton calls the "paradise of the flesh" in the Ford administration parallels the shattering of the Union under Buchanan. Skillfully detailing his familiar subject matter of husband, wife, mistress, child, Updike suggests – albeit humorously – that Clayton's refusal to choose between wife and mistress reflects Buchanan's failure to embrace either South or North. "There is a civilized heroism to indecision," explains Clayton.

No wonder, then, that Clayton cannot finish his study of Buchanan. Satirizing scholarship even

Rabbit is Rich

Running out of gas, Rabbit Angstrom thinks, standing behind the summer-dusty

windows of the Springer Motors display room watching the traffic go by on

somehow thin and scared
Route 111, traffic ~~xxxxthxnxthxnxxxnxxxxxxxxx~~ compared to what it used to be.

The fucking world is running out of gas. But they ~~xxxxx~~ won't catch ~~him~~ me,

not yet, because there isn't a piece of junk on the road gets better mileage

than my Toyotas, while still standing up as a solid dependable machine. Read

Consumer Reports, April issue, page 221. ~~xxxxxxxxxxxxxxxxxxxxxxxxxxxxxx~~

That's all he has to tell the people when they come in. And come in they do,

the people out there are getting frantic, they know the great American ride is
at ninety-nine ~~xxxxx~~ point nine cents a gallon, ~~some stations~~
ending. ~~Axxxxxxx~~ Gas lines, The governor of the Commonwealth ~~xxxxxxxx~~ of
a   sales
Pennsylvania calling for five dollar minimum to ~~xxx~~ stop ~~this~~ the panicky
who can't get diesel
topping up.   And ~~xxxxxx~~ ~~the~~ striking truckers shooting at their own trucks,
~~last night,~~
there was an incident right in the county, along the ~~Rxx~~ Pottsville Pike,
People are going wild, their dollars are going rotten, theycome in
~~laxtxxnightxxxxx~~Today is the last Saturday in June, ~~the first Saturday of summer.~~
and shell out like there's no tomorrow. He tells them, when they buy a Toyota,
It hailed ~~last night on Brewer, stones the size of marbles, and then a~~
they're putting their ~~money in~~ yen. ~~Two~~ hundred cars new and used moved since
~~deluge that flooded~~ (dollars into) Nearly three   a
last Labor Day, at an average mark-up of ~~xxx~~ $1000 makes ~~thxxxxxxxxxxxxxxxxxxx~~

^{575} net profit of ~~quxxxxx~~ a ~~xxxxxxx~~ quarter of a million, less the six K for rent
twenty-seven
and ~~a~~ ~~twenty~~ plus for Stavros and about twelve for the two kids who come in
afternoons
~~xxxxxxxx~~ to work on comission and fifteen for old Mildred ~~Xxxxx~~ Kroust in billing
bless her, over seventy and
and bookkeeping, she's still hanging on, ~~xxxxxxxxxxxxxxxxxxxxxxxxxxxxxxxxxx~~
the peppy little ~~Polack Cissy~~ ~~bitch who~~
~~faxxxxxxxxxxxxxxxxxxxxxxxx~~ not to mention ~~xxxxxx~~ eight for ~~thxxxxxxxxxxxxx~~
comes in to do part-time
~~Roxxxxx~~ Doreen who does ~~xxxxxxxxxxxxxxxx~~ secretarial ~~three days a week~~ and

~~the~~ Fred ~~an~~ the old rummy who comes in to do clean-up and the heat and the) Blue Cross

(and heywprfs and the
advertising~~x~~ in the local rags and the uniforms for their softball team and
else ~~theyxxxxxxxxxxxxx~~ that are ~~necessary expenditures,~~
all ~~xxxxxxxxxxx~~ the other expenditures ~~they~~ they tell him~~xx~~ are necessary
better /
expenditures, still leaves one fifty mighty bills of which he pays himself a

salary of ~~xxxxxx~~ ~~xxxxxxxxxxxx~~ eighty grand

First page of the typescript for Rabbit Is Rich *(by permission of John Updike and the Houghton Library, Harvard University)* as he shows off his own research with an astonishing re-creation of America on the eve of the Civil War, Updike smiles at lesser mortals who cannot turn research into narrative, history into action. Intermingling direct quotations from Buchanan's papers, Clayton's unfinished book on Buchanan, and Clayton's memories of the Ford years, Updike implies that all history is fiction. Clayton writes from the perspective of 1992, and he has as much trouble remembering Ford as refashioning Buchanan. He mocks – with, one understands, Updike's blessing – the current academic fad known as deconstruction, and his struggle to complete both his book and his memoirs shows not only that history is narrative but also that reconstruction of the past is infinitely more important than deconstruction of texts.

Updike's subject, as always, is the mystery of America. Like Buchanan before the disaster of the Civil War, and like Ford after the near disaster of Watergate, he ponders the national quandary: "Our American problem is, we have land and climate enough for a number of nations, and seek to be only one." Updike succeeds admirably in the daunting task of counterpointing the formal vocabulary of Buchanan's nineteenth-century American oratory and the informal speech rhythms of Clayton's contemporary slang, and he does not hesitate to mock his own ornate style to illustrate humanity's tendency to embroider the historical record: "the careless desperate cascade of Mankind's enormous annals." The accounts of Buchanan's meetings with Andrew Jackson and Hawthorne are Updike's gems of historical reconstruction. Yet the value of *Memories of the Ford Administration* is finally its concern with language, humanity's primary means of communication. Late in the novel the narrator muses, "When . . . what we strive to achieve has been undone by history, the words we write remain, and will plead for us." Updike's artist figures – Marshfield, Roger, Sarah Worth, Ellellou, and Clayton among them – know this truth.

Despite the triumphs of his African novel and his reconstruction of James Buchanan, Updike remains fascinated primarily by the intricate workings of the American family. His short stories illustrate that interest. Beginning with *The Same Door,* he has traced the changing curve of the stability of family life. Read as a whole, his short-story volumes offer a social commentary on American domesticity since midcentury, and, while the prose is always lyrical and the observations always sharp, a tone of sadness – wistfulness – prevails. For Updike shows in his tales that the instability of the family reflects the shakiness of the nation, and the nostalgia associated

with *The Same Door* and *Pigeon Feathers* finally gives way to the incisiveness of irony and the shadow of mortality in *Problems and Other Stories* and *Trust Me.*

An important example of that family instability in *Problems* is the end of "Separating," where the father, Richard Maple, tells his oldest son about the impending divorce. When the son asks " 'Why,' " the query cuts Richard to the quick. Facing a darkness that is suddenly grim, he realizes that he has no answer: "*Why*. It was a whistle of wind in a crack, a knife thrust, a window thrown open on emptiness. The white face was gone, the darkness was featureless. Richard had forgotten why." Depicting that one lapse of memory, Updike dissects the breakdown of traditional values that seemed inviolable in the 1950s and became baffling in the 1970s. (The Maple stories are collected in *Too Far to Go,* 1979.) Paul Theroux (*New York Times Book Review,* 8 April 1979) writes, "Updike is one of the few people around who has given subtle expression to what others have dismissed and cheapened by assuming it is a nightmare." The point is well taken. No American author is currently writing about the mystery of family with such patience and grace as Updike.

Problems is largely a gathering of stories about such trauma. Teenaged sons criticize the rest of the family, daughters go away to live with red-bearded harpsichord makers, unhappy fathers forget why, and guilt creeps through suburbia. The stories were written from 1971 to 1978, a period of unsettling family conditions for Updike himself. Although the tales are not autobiography, the specter of domestic loss, of love moving forward from all sides toward a contact barely reached, hovers around most of them. It is not that love is denied but that it is difficult to sustain. Updike supplies a definition in "Love Song, for a Moog Synthesizer": "Love must attach to what we cannot help – the involuntary, the telltale, the fatal. Otherwise, the reasonableness and the mercy that would make our lives decent and orderly would overpower love, crush it, root it out." These stories detail the problems suffered when the threats to love do not stay hidden behind the bedroom wall. As Updike writes in the author's note, "Seven years since my last short-story collection? There must have been problems . . . the collection as a whole, with the curve of sad time it subtends, is dedicated lovingly" to his children.

The plunge to domestic problems takes place immediately, for in "Commercial," the first story, Updike contrasts the manufactured familial snugness of a television commercial for natural gas with the calm, unspoken, and finally hesitant familial tension of a suburban home. "Commercial" is vintage Updike in many ways. Nothing "happens": a husband, having watched the ad for natural gas late at night, shuffles and urinates, tosses and turns, tries to doze. Yet the reader knows that all is not well: the husband's fretfulness, the wife's sleepiness, the cold room. The little details are exact: the cat's need to go out, the noise of the hamster's wheel. The prose is exquisite: "The sharp bright wires of noise etched on darkness dull down into gray threads, an indistinct blanket." And the saving grace of comedy occurs here and there: "GRANDMOTHERLINESS massages her from all sides, like the brushes of a car wash." Tone is finally all. In eight pages Updike conveys the bewilderment of sadness, the bleakness of loss. The implied question is why cannot the long years of the man's domestic life equal the thirty seconds of the commercial's ideal family? The particulars behind this question are not important, but the final word of the story is "Nothing."

Other stories touch on the unspectacular but felt burden of religious belief in a secular community: the comic allegory "Minutes of the Last Meeting" and the thoughtful "Believers." "How to Love America and Leave It at the Same Time," a lyrical meditation reminiscent of the stories in *The Music School,* contrasts with Nabokov's satire of America's ubiquitous motels and fast-food restaurants in *Lolita* (1955): "American is a vast conspiracy to make you happy." The most unusual stories are "Augustine's Concubine," a meditation in defense of the saint's mistress that recalls the less successful "Four Sides of One Story" (*The Music School*), and "The Man Who Loved Extinct Mammals," a comic tale of the relationships between love and extinction that echoes "The Baluchitherium" (*Museums and Women*) and has in it the following metaphor, an example of Updike's sparkling language: "And the child's voice, so sensible and simple up to this point, generated a catch, tears, premonitions of eternal loss; the gaudy parade of eternal loss was about to turn the corner, cymbals clanging, trombones triumphant, and enter her mind."

But, except for the two stories about the Maple family, the finest tale in *Problems* is "The Gun Shop." With touches of *The Centaur,* "Home" (*Pigeon Feathers*), and "Leaving Church Early" (*Tossing and Turning*), "The Gun Shop" is a story of fathers and sons filled with the gestures of domestic particulars that Updike at his best details with delicacy and care. In this portrait of generations, in which the unnecessary tension caused by a grandson's disappointment with a malfunctioning .22 rifle is eased into harmony, Updike shows the ambiguities of love that bind grandfather,

son, grandson, and surrogate father into a moment of communication free of the embarrassment that close proximity always nurtures.

"The Gun Shop" is not a lyrical meditation as are "Leaves" and "The Music School"; that is, dialogue, characterization, and pacing carry the burden instead of meditative prose. Yet nuance takes the place of overt drama as Updike writes of the complications encountered when a country-bred but city-dwelling father brings his city-bred son back to the farmhouse of his parents. To the father the farm is a field of memories and echoes, but to the son it is a promise of experience: he is always permitted to shoot the old Remington .22 following Thanksgiving dinner. Updike focuses on the contrasts between the ways fathers handle sons. Aware that his own tendency to respond to his son's distress with gentle irony is a reaction against his own father's embarrassing habit of good-humored acceptance, the father watches as the grandfather turns the boy's disappointment into the expectation of adventure. The grandfather knows just the man to fix the rifle.

Dutch, the gunsmith, is the hero of the tale, a man to be admired and loved, for although gruff, grimy, and direct he is an artist with machine tools, a country-bred man who can both repair the firing pin and communicate with a stranger's boy familiar with the language of skiing and golf but not of gun shops. The father is out of place in the shop. Rejecting the grandfather's life of blundering forays and unexpected breakdowns, he has made his life in Boston a model of propriety and caution. He says all the wrong things in the gun shop, makes all the wrong gestures. The grandfather makes most of the right ones. With the insight of a man who is open to the world, the grandfather knows that the grandson is like Dutch and that even the father should have had Dutch for a parent. The rare combination of love and skill emanates from the gunsmith. The story ends with the father remembering his childhood and the son firing the rifle. Pride and relief are heard in the father's final laugh. The irreconcilable tensions between generations of a family will never completely dissolve, but for the moment communication offers its balm.

None of these touches is forced, for "The Gun Shop" is a story not of commentary but of reverberation. Nor does the father have an epiphany that promises to narrow the distance between his son and himself. His retort to his wife's comment that he is too hard on the boy shows that the lesson in the gun shop is observed but not absorbed: " 'My father was nice to me, and what did it get him?' " In-

Dust jacket for Updike's 1986 novel, in which he presents characters based on Nathaniel Hawthorne's Hester Prynne and Roger Chillingworth

deed the final paragraph suggests that the son is on the verge of his own rebellion. But, for the moment at least, the family holds on, as it does in another story, "Son," where the boy is the family's "visitor" and "prisoner." Fathers always fail their children, who are always beautiful.

It is not outrageous to say that *Problems* will eventually be judged as one of the major collections of American short stories published in the twentieth century. John Romano (*New York Times Book Review,* 28 October 1979) supports this opinion: "*Problems and Other Stories* won't be surpassed by any collection of short fiction in the next year, and perhaps not in the next 10. Its satisfactions are profound, and the proper emotion is one of gratitude that such a splendid artistic intelligence has been brought to bear on some of the important afflictions of our times." Updike remains America's foremost family chronicler because he understands that little incidents, grace notes as it were, make up the true drama of a home. The woman in "Nevada" who cries out "that it was nobody's *fault,* that there was nothing he could *do,* just let her *alone*" is a more convincing snapshot of a troubled wife than a dozen descriptions of women who survive on tranquilizers and thoughts of suicide. In this sense *Problems* is a volume of middle age. Wives' accusations are "mor-

alistic" reflexes and husbands' responses are full of "predictable mockery." As Updike writes in "The Egg Race," "The stratum of middle age has its insignia, its clues, its distinguishing emotional artifacts." Unlike *The Same Door* and *Pigeon Feathers,* which focus on the nostalgia felt for a time left far behind with the dogwood tree and youth, this collection is closer to *Museums and Women,* which details the love that lingers after the marriage goes bad. Not every story is about family, and not every story is about loss, but the fact remains that *Problems* reemphasizes Updike's move in his fiction from pastoral Olinger, Pennsylvania, to surburban Tarbox, Massachusetts. He took this step a long time ago, of course. The difference is that, whereas in *Museums and Women* he occasionally glances back over his shoulder at the tranquil, "voluptuous" 1950s, a time "when everyone was pregnant," in *Problems* his stories document the plunge into middle age when wives and husbands finally separate, when children unexpectedly grow up, when "the soul grows calluses," and when guilt, oddly, both lacerates and soothes.

A similar diminishment informs *Trust Me.* With a title that is largely ironic, the collection chronicles the crumbling of domestic order in what would seem at first glance to be an impregnable citadel of trust and ease: the civilized suburbs and rural retreats of the upper middle class. "The Ideal Village" concludes, "Man was not meant to abide in paradise," and this acknowledgment of dwindling expectations illustrates the enormous difference between the tales in *Trust Me* and the early, much-admired "Pigeon Feathers" (*Pigeon Feathers*) which ends with David Kern's certainty that God would let him live forever.

The title story sets the tone for the collection as a middle-aged man recalls the shock of recognition in his youth. Trusting his father's promise to catch him in the swimming pool if he will only jump from the safety of the side, he remembers that the father instead let him hit the water and slip chokingly to the bottom in a botched lesson of sink or swim. The parallel to "The Gun Shop" and the contrast with *The Centaur* are intriguing. Yet most of the variations on trust in *Trust Me* are less dramatic. Quiet, subtle, and lurking, the undermining of confidence more often takes its time, inching its way through a life or a marriage toward its final goal of disintegration and pain.

Adultery and divorce are not always the issues, as Updike shows in the stately "Made in Heaven." Once again ironic, the title refers to the long, apparently successful marriage of Brad and Jeanette Henderson. Interestingly for an Updike story, Brad is first attracted to Jeanette not by her promise of carnal mystery but by her confidence in what she calls "the salvation of my soul." Her surety negates his gloom, his sense that Karl Marx and H. L. Mencken were correct when they announced the death of religion. But, as Brad becomes more active in the church during the many years of their marriage, Jeanette becomes less so, even to the point of rejecting an offer of Communion as she confronts her final illness. Only then does he learn that his trust in her religious certainty violated her belief that spiritual matters are a private undertaking, an exploration that cannot tolerate crowding: " 'Since you took it from me. . . . It didn't seem necessary, for the *two* of us to keep it up.' " Recrimination is not the issue. Loss is, and, as Updike shows in *Trust Me,* little losses sear.

Similar variations direct Updike's poetry, except that the comic element is more pronounced in the verse than in the tales. Updike takes his poems seriously, as much more than diversions between completing one novel and planning the next, but the public wrongly defines his poetry merely as light verse in the spirit of Ogden Nash. This misconception is unfortunate, for his collections of poems show a change in tone and mood from the humor of *The Carpentered Hen and Other Tame Creatures,*

through the lyrics of *Telephone Poles* and the autobiographical poems of *Midpoint,* to the meditations on death in *Tossing and Turning* and the celebration of nature in *Facing Nature.* This is not to say that he abandons humor after *The Carpentered Hen* but only to suggest that the poems of comic rhyme and verbal pyrotechnics are but one side of Updike the poet. The place to begin a reading of his verse is not with *The Carpentered Hen* but with his essay "Rhyming Max," a review of Beerbohm's parodies first published in the *New Yorker* (7 March 1964) and collected in *Assorted Prose.*

Understanding Beerbohm's verse parodies to be a kind of verbal cartooning, Updike points to the art of rhyme as an agency of comedy. Replete with regularity and rigidity, rhyme reflects the mechanical action that Henri Bergson termed a primary cause of laughter. Updike writes, "By rhyming, language calls attention to its own mechanical nature and relieves the represented reality of seriousness." Assonance and alliteration perform a similar function and join rhyme as means by which humanity asserts control over things. Light verse for Updike "tends the thin flame of formal magic and tempers the inhuman darkness of reality with the comedy of human artifice . . . it lessens the gravity of its subject." *The Carpentered Hen* illustrates his argument. Beneath his celebration of the delightful artificiality of words is a respect for language itself.

Many of these early poems take to task the inane writing of journalists, advertisers, and editors. Combining verbal acrobatics such as puns, and traditional stanza forms organized with amusing twists, he often parodies the venerable art of the occasional poem when he appends to many of the verses prose statements usually lifted verbatim from an ad or editorial. Thus "Duet, with Muffled Brake Drums" pokes fun at an advertisement in the *New Yorker* claiming that the meeting of Rolls and Royce made engineering history, while "An Ode: Fired into Being by Life's 48-Star Editorial, 'Wanted: An American Novel' " comically exposes the muddled thinking of those who argue that the Great American Novel may be written to order to reflect the surface prosperity of the 1950s. Quoting parts of the editorial and designating sections of his poem as strophe, antistrophe, and epode (parts of the Pindaric ode), he writes a parody of inspiration.

Not all the poems are this amusing. As if foreshadowing the more somber poetry of his later collections, Updike also includes serious pieces of social observation such as "Ex-Basketball Player" and "Tao in the Yankee Stadium Bleachers." These poems illustrate his lifelong interest in sports, but, more important, they comment upon the ephemeral nature of physical prowess, reputation, and life itself. Readers of the story "Ace in the Hole" (*The Same Door*) and the novel *Rabbit, Run* will recognize the situation in "Ex-Basketball Player" as Updike describes the plight of the aging athlete whose current circumstances no longer equal the glory of past headlines. "Tao in the Yankee Stadium Bleachers" is a better poem, which muses on the proposition that "Distance brings proportion." Referring to passages of Eastern philosophy such as the dead rule longer than any king, Updike couches his thoughts on mutability in a metaphor of athletics. The inner journey is "unjudgeably long," and every man eventually flies out while small boys in the grandstands wait to take their places.

These two poems look forward to the short stories in which Updike effectively comments upon the sense of diminishment and loss that age inexorably brings. Yet the dominant tone of *The Carpentered Hen* is not melancholy but joy. The book appropriately ends with the twelve-page poem "A Cheerful Alphabet," which is an updated *McGuffey's Reader* designed to teach his son the wonder of a versatile vocabulary. *A* stands no longer for the apple of sin and Eden but for the still lifes of Cézanne. Designating *T* for trivet, for example, and *X* for xyster, Updike shows that alphabets can be cheerful and that language is alive.

Updike's witty efforts to guard language from the stultifying effects of jargon and cliché, a primary feature of *The Carpentered Hen,* are continued in the first half of *Telephone Poles.* The occasional poem is again parodied, as in "Recital," which quotes a headline in the *New York Times,* "Roger Bobo Gives Recital on Tuba," and which goes on to play with the outrageous rhymes associated with light verse. For all the pleasures of the light verse, however, *Telephone Poles* is a significant collection primarily because of the serious lyrics in the second half. These poems treat many of the themes that readers of Updike's fiction have come to expect: the attractions of memory, the threat of mutability, and the pleasure of the mundane. As Updike writes in the foreword to *Olinger Stories* (1964), he needs the "quiet but tireless goodness that things at rest, like a brick wall or a small stone, seem to affirm." These poems look more to Shillington than to Ipswich, as if he were trying to secure a still point before facing the changes of middle age. A testimony to his close observation of common things, the volume illustrates his statement that "a trolley car has as much right to be there, in terms of aesthetics, as a tree."

The title poem is the center of the collection. Praising the relative permanence of human-made objects and their place in the modern imagination, Updike writes, "The Nature of our construction is in every way / A better fit than the Nature it displaces." He does not mean that trees, for example, are less valuable that telephone poles, but that poles testify to humanity's ingenuity in meeting its needs in the natural world, which must endure the yearly cycle of death and rebirth. Telephone poles may not offer much shade, but unlike elms they are both stable and utilitarian. Since their "fearsome crowns" at the top may literally "stun us to stone," the poles also serve as updated versions of ancient myths, in this case the myth of Gorgons' heads.

Perhaps the most memorable poem in *Telephone Poles* is "Seven Stanzas at Easter." Noting how contemporary humanity is caught between the demands of reason and faith, Updike insists that the miracle of Resurrection must withstand the challenge by the mind if the Christian Church is to survive: "Make no mistake: if He rose at all / it was as His body." The dilemma is nicely suggested in the key word *if* and in the speaker's description of the miracle in the rational discourse of scientific language. *If* Christ rose, he did so not metaphorically but literally. Symbols may not replace fact as the cornerstone of faith. The poet's uncertain tone reflects the predicament of intelligent modern people who would believe even while they doubt.

Updike's most ambitious collection of poems is *Midpoint.* Published when the poet was thirty-seven years old, the title poem is a forty-one page analysis of his life to age thirty-five, midpoint in the biblical span of three score and ten years. "Midpoint" is an impressive combination of autobiography, homage to past poets (Dante, Edmund Spenser, Alexander Pope, Walt Whitman, and Ezra Pound), scientific knowledge, experimental typography, and comic tone. Defining the intellectual bearings of his first thirty-five years in order to prepare for the second half of his life, Updike explains that the poem is both "a joke on the antique genre of the long poem" and "an earnest meditation of the mysteries of the ego." "Midpoint" is not entirely successful because the parts are more impressive than the whole, but it must be read carefully by those interested in Updike's career.

The general movement of the poem illustrates the poet's growth from youthful solipsism to an acceptance of his connection with all humanity. *Point* is the key word both thematically and in terms of the poem's arrangement, for Updike not only shows

Autographed front sheet for Just Looking: Essays on Art *(1989), with a drawing by Updike (collection of Dennis Lynch)*

that he needs an acceptable point of view to understand his relationship with the highpoints of history, but he also fills the second canto with a maze of dots that take shape as photographs from his family album when held at arm's length.

From his mid-life perspective he understands that as a child he saw himself as the most prominent point in a radius of dots all secondary to him. Each person may view experience from a single point of view at a given moment in his or her life, but the solipsism of the child must be toned down if the child is to accept his or her place in the world. The pointillistic photographs illustrate Updike's most immediate connection – the family – and the opening line parodies Whitman's celebration of self: "Of nothing but me, me / – all wrong, all wrong – ." Whitman may be a significant dot in the myriad points of Updike's past, but nineteenth-century beliefs are not necessarily reliable for a twentieth-century person. The importance of appropriate points is again established in the third canto, about the composition of solids, which Updike now understands to be made up of compressed particles and dots. Finally he accepts the truth that identity

depends upon love and the willingness to see life as a progression toward a metaphorical point that clears the vision of the eye / I.

Three other sections join the title poem to make up *Midpoint:* "Poems," "Love Poems," and "Light Verse." Of the three, "Love Poems" is the most impressive because the mixed emotions of desire and guilt that are a hallmark of Updike's best short stories are poignantly expressed. These poems reflect what the shift from remembering his past to concentrating on his present has meant to his imagination.

Updike's recognition in *Midpoint* that he is on the downside of what he calls the "Hill of Life" forms the emotional center of *Tossing and Turning,* his most accomplished volume of poetry. He does not abandon the subject of his past, as the fine "Leaving Church Early" shows, but he focuses more than ever on the challenges of success and suburbia. The persistence of memory, a primary factor in his earlier poems and tales, gives way to the encroachment of age. The title of the collection suggests his restlessness, and a line from "Sleepless in Scarsdale" describes his dilemma: "Prosperity has stolen stupor from me."

Two of the three long poems in *Tossing and Turning* recall Updike's boyhood in Shillington and youth at Harvard: "Leaving Church Early" and "Apologies to Harvard," the Harvard Phi Beta Kappa Poem for 1973. The aloneness that later becomes insomnia is detailed in the former as Updike describes the absence of communication in his family "kept home by poverty, / with nowhere else to go." The need to forgive is a condition of their misery. The latter poem may be read along with "The Christian Roommates," a story from *The Music School,* as one of Updike's few accounts of university days.

Yet the richest poems in *Tossing and Turning* are the shorter lyrics in which Updike acknowledges his step across midpoint in the direction of what he calls "Nandi." Surrounded in suburbia by the trappings of material success and a happy family, he nevertheless finds himself restless and afraid. The stupor that prosperity steals has a double meaning. He cannot find the stupor he needs to sleep because his life is now "too clean," and his success has lulled him into a stupor that clouds his artistic vision, his spiritual sustenance. Too much success "pollutes the tunnel of silence."

It also makes him afraid. More than the other collections, *Tossing and Turning* shows the poet's uncertainty about death and annihilation. In "You Who Swim" and "Bath After Sailing," two of his finest poems, Updike uses water to illustrate the unbeatable immensity of nonhuman otherness. The former is a sixteen-line description of his lover, who is such an expert at the dead man's float that she seems at home on both land and water. She splashes and plays and excels at love, but death lurks just out of sight. The final line – "We swim our dead men's lives" – suggests that all people return to the water that made them. The fear is just as great in "Bath After Sailing." Safely back from another confrontation with the deep, the poet is aware of the ironic change from overwhelming ocean to soothing tub. The "timeless weight" of the sea may threaten, and the gentle swell of the bath may cleanse, but the tub so resembles a coffin that his fingertips shriveled by the water remind him of death. The last trip to the final destination is described in "Heading for Nandi" as the lonely poet takes a night flight across the endless ocean.

Not all the poems in *Tossing and Turning* are as bleak, for Updike also includes a section of light verse that recalls the verbal antics and dedication to a lively language that characterize *The Carpentered Hen*. Burlesques such as "The Cars of Caracas" and "Insomnia the Gem of the Ocean" are fun to read. But the public's misconception of Updike the poet as a mere versifier of witty rhymes and sparkling puns could be corrected by close reading of his more serious poems, especially those in the second half of *Telephone Poles* and most of *Tossing and Turning*.

The light verse placed at the end of *Facing Nature* similarly recalls the linguistic fun of *The Carpentered Hen,* but in his fifth collection of poetry Updike searches primarily for a balance between dread and desire. The sonnets in this volume meditate on mutability and death, but these inexorable laws of nature are then celebrated in "Seven Odes to Seven Natural Processes," in which Updike suggests that nature's "rot," "evaporation," and "fragmentation" are inextricable from nature's "growth," "crystallization," and "healing." Death and life are one. In these challenging odes Updike reveals intellectual curiosity and verbal precision to hint that the order of art reflects the wholeness of nature.

Supporting Updike's achievement in poetry, short stories, and novels is a body of essays large and varied enough to fill a half-dozen volumes. Including everything from parodies and autobiography, to celebrations of baseball and golf, to erudite ruminations on the practice of fiction, Updike's collections of nonfiction testify to a lively mind joyously receptive to worldly vagaries and little details.

What finally amazes the reader is the range of his curiosity, a range illustrated by the heart of each volume: the essay-reviews.

Beginning with *Assorted Prose* and *Picked-Up Pieces* and expanding in *Hugging the Shore,* Updike has assembled a substantial body of commentary on authors that not only directly investigates the literature of his day but also indirectly analyzes his own writing. The award-winning *Hugging the Shore* shows him at his most challenging, as one of the few men of letters who can write intelligently about Edmund Wilson and Nabokov, Henry Green and Iris Murdoch, Saul Bellow and Kurt Vonnegut, Louis-Ferdinand Céline and Robert Pinget, Italo Calvino and Günter Grass, Karl Barth and Paul Tillich, Roland Barthes and Claude Levi-Strauss. Few other contemporary writers can clarify so much or can help the reader see relations among so many branches of knowledge. Few except Updike have managed such enthusiasm for the life of the mind and continued to comment sanely and generously on artists who do not write or think the way he does.

As *Hugging the Shore* illustrates, Updike is primarily an appreciator. Not driven to possess his subject with an academic thoroughness, he nevertheless responds with such knowledge and wit that he cannot be dismissed as a dilettante. In *Hugging the Shore* he writes about theology, New England churches, and – incredibly – more than 130 authors with so much tact that the reader feels comfortable in the presence of his sparkling mind.

He does not rant and rave, he does not scold and scorn, and he does not stumble into the trap that ensnares many critics and makes them unable to treat other authors' books as anything except disappointing versions of what they themselves might have written. The hallmark of *Hugging the Shore* is sympathy for the writer's dilemma, concern for the writer's chore. About Nabokov, Updike writes, "He asked, then, of his own art and the art of others a something extra – a flourish of mimetic magic or deceptive doubleness – that was supernatural and surreal in the root sense of these degraded words." About Muriel Spark and Murdoch: "The two of them together reappropriate for their generation Shakespeare's legacy of dark comedy, of deceptions and enchantments, of shuddering contrivance, of deep personal forces held trembling in a skein of sociable truces." Such sympathy abounds.

Yet, for all the joy of reading this book, the initiated reader might squirm just a bit. Updike's insistence on realism echoes throughout. It is not that he regards realism as a literary convention like romanticism or modernism but that he somehow drags in his acknowledged Christian perspective and affirms the marriage of realism and morality. Of Calvino's fiction, for example, he writes, "There is little that sticks in the mind as involuntarily real, as having been other than intellectually achieved." Updike clearly prefers the touch of grace gained by hard contact with the real. His uneasiness with writers who stress the play of language over the reflection of the world is disquieting.

Especially rewarding are three longish lectures on three American giants – Hawthorne, Whitman, and Melville – which, he explains, were undertaken to "educate the speaker as much as the audience." That one comment perhaps best catches the spirit of *Hugging the Shore.* Updike learns as he reads and does not pontificate as he writes.

One is finally grateful for such gems as "A sensation of blasphemous overlapping, of some vast substance chemically betraying itself, is central to the Gothic tradition of which Hawthorne's tales are lovely late blooms." The question of religious belief not only unites the lectures on Hawthorne, Whitman, and Melville but also defines Updike's attitude toward his own life and art. A believer himself, he is drawn as if by paradox to the shudder of Melville's uncertainty: "Moby Dick represents the utter blank horror of the universe if Godless, a horror so awesome as to excite worship."

If, as Updike suggests in *The Witches of Eastwick,* art counters emptiness, then his essays on painters collected in *Just Looking* (1989) are more than an amateur's mere musings, as the self-effacing tone of the title might imply. Reading this wideranging volume one remembers Updike's boyhood appreciation of Disney, his own drawings for the *Harvard Lampoon,* and his year of study at the Ruskin School of Drawing and Fine Arts in Oxford following graduation from Harvard. His initiation into the complexities of cartoon art recalls his skill with light verse and is amply illustrated in the twenty-page essay on Ralph Barton, perhaps the most famous of the *New Yorker* cartoonists: "A cartoon traditionally aims to give all its information at a glance; it is a kind of calligraphy, which reduces marginal details to the most quickly readable scribble. But in Barton the background presses toward the foreground with an insistence found in Oriental art, and again in Cubism."

Although Updike discusses the seriousness of melancholy as the frame of Barton's drawings, he devotes most of *Just Looking* to remarks on what many readers would call "true" artists. Of Pierre-Auguste Renoir he writes, "Renoir does not quite rank with the heroic masters of early modern painting – specifically, with his friends Monet and Cézanne. Compared with either, he didn't look hard enough"; of John Singer Sargent: "Sargent had an underindulged instinct for the marginal"; of Edgar Degas: "This scrupulous realist found the perfect modern excuse for the female nude . . . bathing"; of Jan Vermeer (one of Updike's favorites): "He could paint anything." An appreciation of precision, of the objects of the world observed fondly and rendered accurately, marks these essays, and thus Updike's interest in painting reflects his commitment to writing. Both are means of investigating what he calls "details."

A similar discriminating curiosity sparkles throughout his most comprehensive collection of essays, *Odd Jobs.* Comically blaming the sheer bulk of the book on his acquiring a word processor, Updike describes himself as "aging into a shaky sort of celebrity" as he writes more and more "prefaces and puffs." Yet the bantering tone belies the seriousness illustrated, as in *Hugging the Shore,* by his sympathetic but astute opinions about writers from South America, Europe, Asia, and Africa. He muses, for example, on John Barth's use of Latin American authors to distinguish between modernism and postmodernism, on Zhang Xianliang's novel about love in the "drastically desexed culture" of China, on the fusing of oral narrative and written fiction in recent novels from Nigeria, and on such American giants as Ralph Waldo Emerson and William Dean Howells.

Part of *Odd Jobs* is composed of what Updike terms "Fairly Personal" and "Literarily Personal," and, in the absence of biographies, journals, and collections of letters, the reader who longs to know more about the writer might consult these sections. But such a reader would be better off with *Self-Consciousness: Memoirs* (1989), a sly, partly revealing portrait of the author written, Updike explains, as a repudiation "of someone wanting to write my biography – to take my life, my lode of ore and heap of memories, from me! The idea seemed so repulsive that I was stimulated to put down, always with some natural hesitation and distaste, these elements of an autobiography."

In a series of six chapters Updike tells only what he wants to tell – eloquently and, more important, shrewdly – for in these pieces he nudges the reader away from biography and back toward what should be the reader's primary interest: the novels, tales, poems, and essays. Thus the exquisitely paced "A Soft Spring Night in Shillington," a memoir of Updike's return to his hometown in middle age, should be read in context with the short sto-

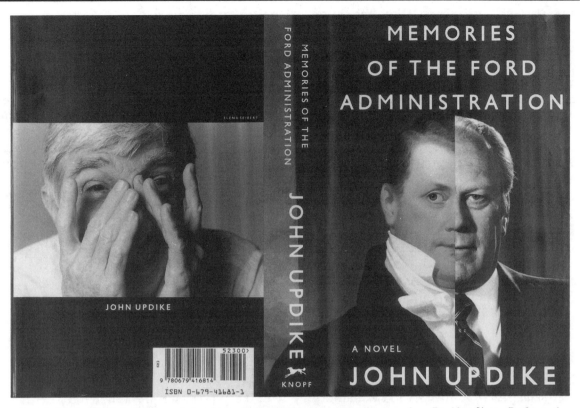

Dust jacket for Updike's 1992 novel, in which a history professor entangles his research on President James Buchanan in his memoir of President Gerald Ford

ries in *The Same Door* and *Pigeon Feathers*. "On Not Being a Dove," a revelation of his complex and perhaps unexpected position during the Vietnam War, should be read with *Rabbit Redux* and "Marching through Boston" (*Museums and Women*). The long "A Letter to My Grandsons" is especially notable when one understands that Updike's daughter is married to a West African, and thus the "letter" gives added resonance to *The Coup* and to Updike's many essays about African writers. Readers who have followed the subtleties of Updike's struggle with religion and who know his essay "Faith in Search of Understanding" (*Assorted Prose*) and his various analyses of Karl Barth and Kierkegaard will profit from "On Being a Self Forever." Yet perhaps the most revelatory chapters in *Self-Consciousness* are "At War with My Skin" and "Getting the Words Out," in which Updike describes his decades-long battle with psoriasis and stammering. The story "From the Journal of a Leper" (*Problems,* 1979) is relevant here, but more significant is that Updike refuses to use his afflictions as a catalyst for complaint. Rather, he shows how physical problems shape his response to the world and thereby his writing: "I groped for the exact terms I knew were there but could not find. . . . My stuttering feels like an acknowledgment, in con-

versation, of the framework of unacknowledged complexity that surrounds the simplest exchange of words." One need hardly reiterate that Updike "got the words out."

There are those who argue that Updike does not demand enough in his essays, that he refuses to ask hard questions. To insist, however, on more than the enormous amount that he already offers is to require academic specialization from one of America's finest creative writers. The happy union of lyrical prose and intellectual probing that is the highlight of his fiction shows itself everywhere in his nonfiction. John Updike may hug the shore in his criticism, but he remains one of the most perceptive men of letters in America since Edmund Wilson and Henry James.

References:

Harold Bloom, ed., *John Updike: Modern Critical Views* (New York: Chelsea House, 1987);

Rachael C. Burchard, *John Updike: Yea Sayings* (Carbondale: Southern Illinois University Press, 1971);

Robert C. Detweiler, *John Updike,* revised edition (New York: Twayne, 1984);

Donald J. Greiner, *Adultery in the American Novel: Updike, James, and Hawthorne* (Columbia: University of South Carolina Press, 1985);

Greiner, *John Updike's Novels* (Athens: Ohio University Press, 1984);

Greiner, *The Other John Updike: Poems/Short Stories/Prose/Play* (Athens: Ohio University Press, 1981);

Alice and Kenneth Hamilton, *The Elements of John Updike* (Grand Rapids, Mich.: Eerdmans, 1970);

George Hunt, *John Updike and the Three Great Secret Things: Sex, Religion, and Art* (Grand Rapids, Mich.: Eerdmans, 1980);

William R. Macnaughton, ed., *Critical Essays on John Updike* (Boston: G. K. Hall, 1982);

Joyce B. Markle, *Fighters and Lovers: Theme in the Novels of John Updike* (New York: New York University Press, 1973);

Modern Fiction Studies, issue on Updike, 20 (Spring 1974);

Modern Fiction Studies, issue on Updike, 37 (Spring 1991);

Judie Newman, *John Updike* (New York: St. Martin's Press, 1988);

Dilvo I. Ristoff, *Updike's America: The Presence of Contemporary American History in John Updike's Rabbit Trilogy* (New York: Peter Lang, 1988);

Charles Thomas Samuels, *John Updike* (Minneapolis: University of Minnesota Press, 1969);

James A. Schiff, *Updike's Version: Rewriting "The Scarlet Letter"* (Columbia: University of Missouri Press, 1992);

George J. Searles, *The Fiction of Philip Roth and John Updike* (Carbondale: Southern Illinois University Press, 1985);

Larry E. Taylor, *Pastoral and Anti-Pastoral Patterns in John Updike's Fiction* (Carbondale: Southern Illinois University Press, 1971);

David Thorburn and Howard Eiland, eds., *John Updike: A Collection of Critical Essays* (Englewood Cliffs, N. J.: Prentice-Hall, 1979);

Suzanne Henning Uphaus, *John Updike* (New York: Ungar, 1980);

Edward P. Vargo, *Rainstorms and Fire: Ritual in the Novels of John Updike* (Port Washington, N.Y.: Kennikat, 1973).

Papers:
Updike's manuscripts and letters are at the Houghton Library, Harvard University.

Alice Walker

(9 February 1944 –   )

Donna Haisty Winchell
Clemson University

See also the Walker entries in *DLB 6: American Novelists Since World War II, Second Series* and *DLB 33: Afro-American Fiction Writers After 1955.*

BOOKS: *Once: Poems* (New York: Harcourt, Brace & World, 1968);

The Third Life of Grange Copeland (New York: Harcourt Brace Jovanovich, 1970);

In Love and Trouble: Stories of Black Women (New York: Harcourt Brace Jovanovich, 1973);

Revolutionary Petunias and Other Poems (New York: Harcourt Brace Jovanovich, 1973);

Langston Hughes: American Poet (New York: Crowell, 1974);

Meridian (New York: Harcourt Brace Jovanovich, 1976);

Good Night, Willie Lee, I'll See You in the Morning (New York: Dial, 1979);

You Can't Keep a Good Woman Down (New York: Harcourt Brace Jovanovich, 1981; London: Women's Press, 1982);

The Color Purple (New York: Harcourt Brace Jovanovich, 1982; London: Women's Press, 1983);

In Search of Our Mothers' Gardens (New York: Harcourt Brace Jovanovich, 1983);

Horses Make a Landscape Look More Beautiful: Poems (New York: Harcourt Brace Jovanovich, 1984);

Living by the Word: Selected Writings, 1973–1987 (New York: Harcourt Brace Jovanovich, 1988);

To Hell with Dying (San Diego: Harcourt Brace Jovanovich, 1988);

The Temple of My Familiar (New York: Harcourt Brace Jovanovich, 1989);

Her Blue Body Everything We Know: Earthling Poems, 1965–1990 Complete (New York: Harcourt Brace Jovanovich, 1991);

Finding the Green Stone (San Diego: Harcourt Brace Jovanovich, 1991);

Possessing the Secret of Joy (New York: Harcourt Brace Jovanovich, 1992);

Alice Walker, circa 1989 (photograph by Jim Marshall)

Warrior Marks: Female Genital Mutilation and the Sexual Blinding of Women, by Walker and Pratibha Parmar (New York: Harcourt Brace, 1993).

OTHER: *I Love Myself When I Am Laughing . . .: A Zora Neale Hurston Reader,* edited by Walker (Old Westbury, N.Y.: Feminist Press, 1979).

Alice Walker knows firsthand the social and political consequences of being a black woman coming of age during the second half of the twentieth century. In her fiction, nonfiction, and poetry she confronts bluntly the history of the oppression of her people and, more recently, the oppression of her planet. Her wish for black men and women is that they not merely survive, but survive whole, as she has done. From the time she first appeared on the literary scene in 1968 with a collection of poems called *Once,* Walker has viewed her writing as a means of survival. Nearing fifty, she expressed surprise that she was not a suicide before the age of thirty, but she explains in the introduction to her fifth volume of poetry, *Her Blue Body Everything We Know* (1991), "I have climbed back into life over and over on a ladder made of words, but knitted, truly, by the Unknowable."

Walker's optimism is ultimately born of her belief that something of the divine exists in every human and nonhuman participant in the universe. The inhabitants of her fictional world search, with varying degrees of success, for that divine spark that makes them uniquely who they are, in spite of the forces of sexism and racism that often deny them their identities. Walker contends that definition of self must come from within and that the right to say who one is and who one should be must never be surrendered to another person.

Walker was born 9 February 1944 – the youngest of eight children, five boys and three girls – to Willie Lee and Minnie Tallulah Grant Walker, sharecroppers in Eatonton, Georgia. She remembers generally hating the southern sharecropper's life with its backbreaking field work and its string of shabby houses but loving to recite in church, in her starched dresses and patent leather shoes, and declaring smugly at age two and a half, "I'm the prettiest." In *In Search of Our Mothers' Gardens* (1983) she writes, "It was great fun being cute. But then, one day it ended." She was eight when a game of cowboys and Indians with her brothers took a tragic turn as one of them shot her in the eye with his BB gun. The injury left her blind in her right eye, with a scar that she felt made her ugly and disfigured.

As a result Walker cast her eyes down, and for six years she did not raise her head. When she was fourteen, her favorite brother, Bill, paid to have the scar tissue removed. During the intervening years, however, Walker perceived herself as an outcast; in her isolation she turned to reading and began to write poems. She became a keen observer of human nature, taking time to see people and things around her in depth, to notice human relationships and to care how they turned out. According to a 1973 interview with John O'Brien, she also "daydreamed – not of fairy tales – but of falling on swords, of putting guns to [her] heart or head, or of slashing [her] wrists with a razor."

Walker was blessed with a mother who, in spite of the fact that she had never read a book herself, appreciated her youngest daughter's need to do so, even if it meant stepping over and around her daughter to get the housework done. Minnie Lou Walker knew the value to her children of the education that she never received and resisted indignantly any white landowner's hints that sharecroppers' children did not need to go to school. One of Walker's sisters turned out to be what Walker calls in the O'Brien interview "one of those Negro wonders – who collected scholarships like trading stamps and wandered all over the world."

Walker started school at age four, when her mother could no longer take her into the fields with her, and went on to become valedictorian at her high school. Walker recalls her mother's buying her, out of the less than twenty dollars a week she made as a domestic, three gifts that gave her increasing degrees of freedom: a sewing machine to provide the independence of making her own clothes, a suitcase to allow her the freedom to travel, and a typewriter to enable her to pursue her art. When, because of her injured eye, the state of Georgia offered Walker a "rehabilitation scholarship" to Spelman, a black women's college in Atlanta, she was able to put all three gifts to use.

Willie Lee Walker greeted with less enthusiasm his daughter's foray into the world beyond rural Georgia. Education seemed only to make his daughters more critical of him. In "My Father's Country Is the Poor" (*In Search of Our Mothers' Gardens*) Walker writes, "This brilliant man – great at mathematics, unbeatable at storytelling, but unschooled beyond the primary grades – found the manners of his suddenly middle-class (by virtue of being in college) daughter a barrier to easy contact, if not actually frightening." Her "always tenuous" relationship with him virtually ended when she went to Spelman.

Walker felt that her father and brothers had largely failed her as the role models that they should have been. The Walker boys were encouraged to experiment with sex, but the girls were told not to come home if they ever got pregnant. Violence was a commonplace in her family as well as in the communities in which they lived in the course of their frequent moves. In her own family the violence was usually rooted in her father's need to dominate. Only later in her life did her readings in feminism make her understand that Willie Lee Walker was merely a product of his society and its sexism. Generally in her fiction Walker's male characters mellow with age and become more benevolent as they become less of a threat sexually. She saw both of her grandfathers mellow into kind and gentle old age in spite of the brutality that she knew had characterized their youths. Unfortunately, she never saw that change in her father, who died in 1973. Walker feels that she has been reconciled with him only since his death. She has remained devoted to her mother, who still has never read her daughter's books.

Walker spent two and a half years at Spelman, where she was an active participant in the civil rights movement, before transferring to Sarah Lawrence, a women's college in Bronxville, New York, where she was one of only six black students. At Sarah Lawrence, Walker's childhood dreams of suicide nearly became a reality. She returned from a trip to Africa the summer between her junior and senior years "healthy and brown . . . and pregnant." For three nights she slept with a razor blade under her pillow before a friend saved her by providing the phone number of an abortionist.

The poems in *Once* were written either in Kenya or in rapid succession at Sarah Lawrence in the week following her 1965 abortion. She reports in "From an Interview" (*In Search of Our Mothers' Gardens*) that during that week she wrote first about Africa "because the vitality and color and friendships in Africa rushed over [her] in dreams the first night [she] slept." She wrote about marches, picket lines, southern jails, and police brutality from her years in Atlanta. She wrote about love and the feelings she experienced those three days she waited to die. Walker slipped the poems daily under the cottage door of Sarah Lawrence's writer in residence, Muriel Rukeyser, her teacher and mentor. Rukeyser passed them on to her editor, who eventually became Walker's.

Publication of *Once* came with little effort on Walker's part and was met with a positive critical response; the volume went almost immediately into a second printing. In *In Search of Our Mothers' Gardens* Walker explains, however, that by the time the poems appeared in print "the book itself did not seem to me important; only the writing of the poems, which clarified for me how very much I loved being alive. . . . Since that time, it seems to me that all of my poems . . . are written when I have successfully pulled myself out of a completely numbing despair, and stand again in the sunlight. Writing poems is my way of celebrating with the world that I have not committed suicide the evening before."

Death and dying are at the heart of the first story that Walker wrote, "The Suicide of an American Girl" (unpublished), and the first one that she published, "To Hell with Dying" (*Best Short Stories by Negro Writers: An Anthology from 1899 to the Present*, 1967; collected in *In Love and Trouble: Stories of Black Women*, 1973). The difference in the titles is telling. Inspired by the death of an old guitar player beloved by Walker and her family, she wrote "To Hell with Dying" during that same critical senior year at Sarah Lawrence. Each time the fictional Mr. Sweet is on his deathbed, a character based on Walker's father herds all his children into the sickroom to kiss and tickle Mr. Sweet back to life. The narrator is at work on her doctorate in Massachusetts when, at age ninety, Mr. Sweet hovers on the brink of death one last time. She flies home, but the ritual does not save him this time. Walker was actually in New York at the time of her old friend's final illness, too poor to return home either to save him or to attend his funeral.

In "The Old Artist: Notes on Mr. Sweet" (*Living by the Word*, 1988) she tells how, on the day of his burial, she turned her back on the razor blade and wrote "To Hell with Dying" with tears pouring down her cheeks: "I was grief-stricken, I was crazed, I was fighting for my life. I was twenty-one."

Walker was unable to save Mr. Sweet, but she was able to save herself. As she contemplated suicide, she thought of all that he had had to endure as a black man in the South. In spite of it all, he had continued to sing: "He went deep into his own pain and brought out words and music that made us happy, made us feel empathy for anyone in trouble, made us think. We were taught to be thankful that anyone would assume this risk." Walker chose to take the same risk. In the story Mr. Sweet symbolically passes down his gift of song by leaving his guitar to the narrator. Walker accepts with great seriousness her responsibility as an artist to pass down the creative spark that those who have gone before her have kept alive.

The creative legacy is the subject of the title essay in *In Search of Our Mothers' Gardens*, a collection of essays, articles, reviews, and speeches Walker wrote between 1966 and 1982. The title essay celebrates those black women throughout the generations who kept the spark of creativity alive in spite of the racism and sexism that often denied them the means of expressing their art. Walker writes of mothers and grandmothers who were "driven to a numb and bleeding madness by the springs of creativity in them for which there was no release." Artists denied the proper materials of their art died unknown, but, in the absence of material goods, the possibility of art became a legacy passed down from mother to daughter.

Elsewhere in *In Search of Our Mothers' Gardens* Walker expresses outrage that the "education" she received, first at a prestigious black college and then a prestigious white one, left her largely ignorant of black literary models. Toni Morrison has said that she writes the sort of books she wanted to read. Walker's goal is rather to write the sort of books she should have been able to read. Walker had to discover on her own the works of early black women writers who, once found, spoke to her across the generations. One of those who spoke most clearly to her was Zora Neale Hurston, whose works Walker encountered while researching voodoo practices of southern blacks in the 1930s for her short story "The Revenge of Hannah Kemhuff" (*Ms.*, July 1973; collected in *In Love and Trouble*).

In Hurston, Walker found a kindred spirit. Hurston, who grew up in the all-black Florida town of Eatonville, studied anthropology at Barnard College in New York City in order to return to the South and record the folklore and language patterns, the courting rituals, and the humor of the rural black community. She wanted to preserve her heritage in all its complexity, all its wholeness. Hurston, like Walker, was concerned not only with the survival of a people but with their survival whole. The theme of surviving whole emerges as a major thrust of Walker's first novel, *The Third Life of Grange Copeland* (1970).

Walker has also been instrumental in helping Hurston's works survive after they were largely out of print and threatened with obscurity. "Looking for Zora" (*In Search of Our Mothers' Gardens*) is Walker's account of traveling to Florida to find and buy a marker for Hurston's unmarked grave. She has said that there is no book more important to her than Hurston's *Their Eyes Were Watching God* (1937); she made portions of that novel and Hurston's other works more accessible by editing a Hurston reader, *I Love Myself When I Am Laughing . . . And Then Again When I Am Looking Mean and Impressive* (1979).

Among the pieces in *In Search of Our Mothers' Gardens* is Walker's first published essay, "The Civil Rights Movement: What Good Was It?," which won first prize in the 1967 *American Scholar* essay contest. She wrote it during the winter of 1966–1967, when she was living in New York with law student Melvyn Leventhal, whom she met in 1966 after she left her job with the New York City Welfare Department to go to Mississippi to work in the voter registration campaign. Walker gave up a Mc-Dowell Colony Fellowship to marry Leventhal in March 1967. They moved to Mississippi, where he prosecuted the Jackson school-desegregation cases. For several years they were the only interracial, home-owning married couple in the state, even though it was against Mississippi law for them to live together.

During her seven years in Mississippi, Walker went through another suicidal period. She felt the pressure of trying to define her role as an artist in time of revolution, a theme she explores in the novel *Meridian* (1976), and she also felt the pressures of motherhood, which she explores most eloquently in the 1979 piece "*One* Child of One's Own: A Meaningful Digression Within the Work(s)" (*In Search of Our Mothers' Gardens*). During the late 1960s Walker tried to have a child so that her husband could avoid the draft. A week after she marched in Martin Luther King's funeral procession in April 1968, she suffered a miscarriage. In November 1969, when Walker was twenty-five, she had her only child, Rebecca, three days after she finished *The Third Life of Grange Copeland*.

When that novel was published in 1970, Walker suffered the same fate that Hurston had at the hands of reviewers. Critics seemed incapable of focusing on the work itself, choosing instead to seize the opportunity to comment on her lifestyle, a tactic that Walker sees as typical of the way critics respond to works by black women. Walker, however, has never flinched at accepting responsibility for her life choices. In the afterword to the 1988 Pocket edition of *The Third Life of Grange Copeland*, she writes:

> I believe wholeheartedly in the necessity of keeping inviolate the one interior space that is given to all. I believe in the soul. Furthermore, I believe it is prompt accountability for one's choices, a willing acceptance of responsibility for one's thoughts, behavior and actions, that makes it powerful.

This is the lesson that Grange Copeland has to learn.

The Third Life of Grange Copeland covers three generations of the Copeland family, beginning with the patriarch, Grange Copeland, who in the 1920s is caught up in the vicious cycle of the sharecropping system that Walker knew well from her childhood in Georgia. In the first of his three "lives" he makes the mistake of blaming the white man in whose fields he labors for the cycle of despair in which he finds himself. For as long as Grange lets him, the white man owns his soul along with his labor. Unable to take out his frustrations on the white boss, he unleashes them instead on his wife, Margaret, and their son, Brownfield. Here in

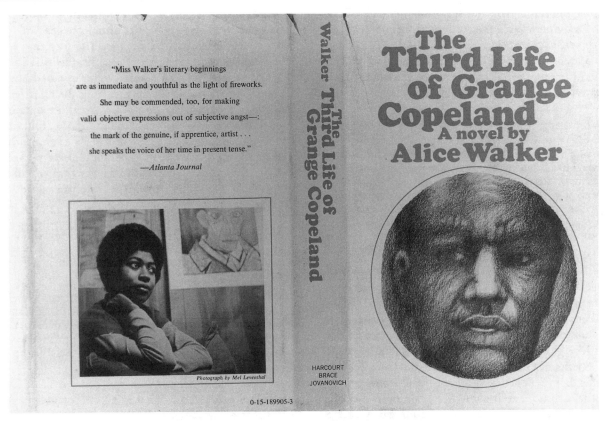

Dust jacket for Walker's first novel, which she completed at age twenty-five

Walker's fictional world is the brutality and need to dominate, born out of frustration and a sense of powerlessness, that she knew in her own community and family. Here, too, though, is her first fictional statement that men can change.

Grange's first life is one of resignation. His final act of resignation in that life comes when he deserts Margaret and fifteen-year-old Brownfield, driving Margaret to kill herself and the new baby born out of her recent infidelity. The benevolent old man who years later comes back from New York is difficult to identify with the brutal young one who left. Grange returns from his second life with the knowledge that other men have the power of gods only if one gives it to them. He finds his son caught up in the same cycle of despair from which he tried to escape, and Grange tries to save him by teaching him that only he can save himself.

Brownfield is even more of a monster than Grange was, beating his lovely young wife, Mem, into a hag old before her time, terrorizing his three daughters, and blaming all his problems on the white folks who refuse to let him be a man. He is unwilling to accept the salvation Grange offers him. Brownfield feels that he has no control over his own

life and therefore assumes no responsibility. When Mem proves stronger than he is by attempting to raise their family out of the depths to which they have sunk, he responds by shooting her in the face.

Mem is a precursor of Walker's later female characters in that she has a fighting spirit. Fighting back usually leads only to another beating, but at one point she aims a shotgun at Brownfield's testicles and threatens to blow away his manhood if he refuses to reform. Mem's tragic flaw is that she is too willing to forgive, too willing to believe in Brownfield's power to change. Once her finger is off the trigger, Brownfield irrationally refuses to enjoy the comfortable life in town that Mem's efforts win for them and their children. He forces additional pregnancies on her until she is too weak to hold a job, and they must go back to a sharecropper's shack even more dilapidated than those they have dwelled in before. Brownfield believes Mem when she threatens to get well and leave him. He shoots her before she can.

In her afterword to *The Third Life of Grange Copeland* Walker states, "The white man's oppression of me will never excuse my oppression of you, whether you are man, woman, child, animal or tree, because the self I prize refuses to be owned by him. Or by anyone." Walker's characters frequently seek which self to prize. Grange Copeland learns the fallacy of accepting the white man's definition of who he is. In trying to make Brownfield see the error of his ways, Grange says:

> When they [white people] got you thinking that they're to blame for *everything* they have you thinking they's some kind of gods! You can't do nothing wrong without them being behind it. You gits just as weak as water, no feeling of doing *nothing* yourself. Then you begins to think up evil and begins to destroy everybody around you, and you blames it on the crackers. *Shit!* Nobody's as powerful as we make them out to be. We got our own *souls,* don't we?

In his third "life" Grange tries to keep a part of himself inviolate, a place within himself where no white man can come. He tries to preserve what Walker would call his soul, yet Grange believes that his inability to forgive has spoiled his soul. His granddaughter Ruth knows better. She alone reaps the benefits of Grange's benevolent old age after her mother is murdered and her father goes to prison for the crime. Feeling only a numbness within where the ability to forgive should be, Grange would like to protect Ruth's soul from the numbing effects of the outside world by keeping her forever behind the barbed-wire barrier that he has built up around the farm. Ruth, however, is not one to be confined.

Besides, while Grange has been retreating within, the world outside has begun to change. The civil rights movement marches right up to his door one day in the persons of four workers, two black and two white. Their message, plus what she sees daily about the movement on television, convinces Ruth that she can forgive the crackers the evil they have done if they are willing to change. Yet she proves stronger in the one area where Mem proved weak: Ruth refuses to forgive Brownfield. Grange eventually kills Brownfield rather than surrender Ruth to him and is killed himself as a result. Ruth survives because, in leaving her unarmed to wait for his killers, Grange gives them no excuse for murdering her. Violence is not to be her way. Her toughness and her willingness to be unforgiving when necessary, combined with the compassion that makes forgiveness possible when it has been earned, are Ruth's defense against the future. The combination will enable her to survive whole rather than merely survive.

In the essay "Beauty: When the Other Dancer Is the Self" (*In Search of Our Mothers' Gardens*) Walk-

er reports that a period of personal healing began when she was twenty-seven and Rebecca was almost three. Walker had dreaded the day that her daughter would notice the blue "crater" that still marked where the scar tissue on her eye had been. Rebecca, however, grew up watching the children's television program *Big Blue Marble,* with its opening shot of the earth as viewed from the moon. She suddenly looked deep into her mother's eye one day and exclaimed, "Mommy, there's a *world* in your eye.... Mommy, where did you get that world in your eye?" At that point Walker realized that her affliction was all a matter of perspective. Where she had seen a flaw, her daughter, in her innocence, had seen the world. Walker writes of the dream she had that night:

> That night I dream I am dancing.... As I dance, whirling and joyous, happier than I've ever been in my life, another bright-faced dancer joins me. We dance and kiss each other and hold each other through the night. The other dancer has obviously come through all right, as I have done. She is beautiful, whole and free. And she is also me.

The women in Walker's first collection of short stories, *In Love and Trouble,* have not yet come through whole and free, but their struggle for wholeness is at the heart of Walker's fictional world. Walker told O'Brien, "In my new book *In Love and Trouble: Stories of Black Women,* thirteen women – mad, raging, loving, resentful, hateful, strong, ugly, weak, pitiful, and magnificent, try to live with the loyalty to black men that characterizes all of their lives." Some lose a life-or-death struggle for survival; more often, their struggle is for psychological wholeness.

Walker was certainly not alone in feeling a sense of disillusionment with the civil rights movement when, after fighting alongside black men for racial equality, black women still had to fight their own black men for sexual equality. A significant portion of *In Love and Trouble* consists of Walker's fictional musings on what happens to black women when their loyalty to black men proves misplaced. "My Sweet Jerome" most clearly illustrates the black revolutionary male who fails to realize that equal rights should exist in the home as well as in society at large.

Jerome makes a show of being a revolutionary, spending his evenings with stylish and politically correct black women who speak of violent overthrow, while his unattractive and politically naive wife spends her days straightening hair in her beauty parlor. Jerome beats her even before they are married. After their marriage he occasionally spends an evening at home quietly reading, but only if she promises not to touch him or talk to him. Convinced by his frequent evenings away from home and by the neighborhood gossips that she has reason to be jealous, his wife haunts the streets armed with axes, knives, and pistols, searching for "the other woman." When she finds out that her rival is not another woman but a cause, she burns herself to death along with stacks of her husband's books about revolution.

Two other stories in *In Love and Trouble* further illustrate the limiting definitions of black womanhood that men try to impose on their women. In "Roselily" a young mother of four from Panther Burn, Mississippi, is about to sacrifice her identity to marry a Muslim from Chicago who can offer her children financial security but can offer her only more children and the veil that represents women's inferior position in Muslim society. During the wedding that veil, the purdah, merges in her mind with the wedding veil, and the references to union merge in her thinking with images of chains.

Myrna in "Really, *Doesn't* Crime Pay?" is chained by marriage to a husband embarrassed by her aspirations to be a writer. He encourages her to take on more feminine pursuits, such as shopping or having babies. Enough of her own woman to take the Pill religiously, Myrna is still vulnerable enough to fall for the first man who takes her writing seriously. Unfortunately, Mordecai Rich takes it so seriously that he steals her work, publishing one of her stories as his own. Myrna responds by trying to cut off her husband's head with a chainsaw, but, when she fails, she surrenders to the image of herself for which her husband has longed. Myrna will never trade her Helena Rubenstein hands for the bitten nails and jagged cuticles of a serious writer. Like Roselily, she will sacrifice her own image of herself to conform to her husband's expectations.

The black women in *In Love and Trouble* more often than not operate from such positions of vulnerability that they allow others to dictate who or what they should be. The occasional rebel – such as the daughter in "The Child Who Favored Daughter," who takes a white lover – suffers (the "child's" enraged, aroused father cuts off her breasts) or, instead, finally succumbs to external pressures, like Myrna or the title character in "Diary of an African Nun." The young nun longs to respond to the African drums of her heritage and to the sensuality stirring within her at their call, yet she remains loyal to her vows and accepts a loveless, barren marriage to the church. This most hopeless and discontent of

characters – because she chooses to fit someone else's image of what she should be and disregards her own inner stirrings – contrasts sharply with the character in the collection who is most at peace with her image of herself, Mrs. Johnson of "Everyday Use," probably Walker's most anthologized piece of fiction.

Mrs. Johnson dreams of appearing slender of body and quick of wit on a late-night talk show but accepts with an easy satisfaction the reality of who she is, "a large, big-boned woman with rough, man-working hands." She takes pride in her ability to slaughter a hog, and her fat keeps her warm in zero-degree weather as she breaks ice to get water for washing. In addition, she provides an early example of the androgynous figure that appears more prominently in Walker's later works. Mrs. Johnson is content with life's little pleasures: a clean-swept yard, a pinch of snuff, the soothing movements of the milk cows. The absence of a man in her life seems irrelevant. She exists largely as a foil for her daughter, Dee, who exemplifies just how shallow a young black woman can be when she sees pride in her heritage as a fad rather than as a way of life.

From 1972 to 1973 Walker and Rebecca left Mississippi for eighteen months, during which Walker taught at Wellesley College and the University of Massachusetts – Boston. She believes that her course in black women writers was the first of its kind. In "*One* Child of One's Own" she explores the effect motherhood has on the artist and explains that during those months in New England she began to see "that [Rebecca's] birth, and the difficulties it provided us, joined me to a body of experience and a depth of commitment to my own life hard to comprehend otherwise. Her birth was the incomparable gift of seeing the world at quite a different angle than before, and judging it by standards that would apply far beyond my natural life."

Walker calls *Revolutionary Petunias* (1973) – her second collection of poems, which won the Lillian Smith Award and was nominated for the National Book Award – "a celebration of people who will not cram themselves into any ideological or racial mold." Petunias are, for Walker, an image of survival. She recalls how her mother once climbed down from the family wagon to salvage a single lavender petunia plant growing in the yard of a deserted house. She kept it alive throughout the dozen or so moves that the family made over the course of thirty-seven years. Each winter the plant would appear dead, but it came back to life each spring. Walker's characters in *Revolutionary Petunias* are "incorrect" by society's standards. In *In Search of Our*

Mothers' Gardens she explains, "They are told that they do not belong, that they are not wanted, that their art is not needed, that nobody who is 'correct' could love what they love." Yet, like the hardy petunia, they resist those forces that would deny them the chance to blossom; they, like Walker, have learned to judge the world by standards that apply far beyond their natural lives.

In Walker's works the nurturing of flowers is synonymous with art. Her search for "our mothers' gardens" is a quest for the forms that art took for those women denied more conventional art forms. A slave woman's only art form might be piecing a quilt, and her granddaughter's might be sweeping the dirt in her yard into original designs. Minnie Lou Walker's art took the form of the beautiful flower gardens that she planted wherever her family's itinerant life took them. Walker describes her mother's work in her garden as work that her soul had to have. In a larger sense art is the soul of the people.

In *Revolutionary Petunias* Walker specifically explores the role that art plays in time of revolution. In the poem "Lost My Voice? Of Course." a bully claims that the revolution cannot afford poems about love and flowers. Yet love and flowers blossom even under fire, a point that Walker makes in "While Love Is Unfashionable," which is dedicated to Leventhal. In the poem she suggests that they walk bareheaded and gather blossoms under fire, which she and Levanthal certainly did by living together as husband and wife in pre–civil rights Mississippi. She opens the title section of *Revolutionary Petunias* with a quotation from Albert Camus: "Beauty, no doubt, does not make revolutions. But a day will come when revolutions will have need of beauty."

That day comes in Walker's fictional world in her second novel, *Meridian,* which explores at length the role of the artist in time of revolution. The question had plagued Walker since her days in Mississippi, when she fantasized about dropping bombs in the laps of white oppressors and agonized over the feeling that her art was not enough. Meridian Hill, like her creator, is thrust into the heart of the civil rights movement after she receives a scholarship to a black women's college in Atlanta. Saxon College tries to produce ladies while looking the other way when those ladies land in jail or return to campus beaten by the police as a result of their activism. Amid this atmosphere Meridian proves a failure as the type of revolutionary her friends demand that she be. She can say that she would be willing to die for the cause, but not that she would be willing to

kill for it. A question haunts her: "If they committed murder – and to her even revolutionary murder was murder – *what would the music be like?*"

Where Walker had to learn that her role in the revolution was to record the lives of some extraordinary people, Meridian has to learn that her part is to walk behind the real revolutionaries – "those who know they must spill blood in order to help the poor and the black and therefore go right ahead – and when they stop to wash off the blood and find their throats too choked with the smell of murdered flesh to sing . . . [to] come forward and sing from memory songs they will need once more to hear." Meridian continues, "For it is the song of the people, transformed by the experiences of each generation, that holds them together, and if any part of it is lost the people suffer and are without soul. If I can only do that, my role will not have been a useless one after all."

Meridian comes to this realization after suffering debilitating guilt for having failed in the other roles imposed on her. She shares with other early Walker female characters vulnerability to the dictates of others. She "loses" her mother and thus fails as a daughter when she finds herself unable to love God with the same mindless intensity that her mother does. She fails as a mother, according to others' standards, when she gives away her infant son in order to free herself to attend Saxon, even though she feels that to do so is to save both his life and hers. As early as *Meridian* and as recently as her 1992 novel, *Possessing the Secret of Joy,* Walker has been about the business of debunking some of the myths of black motherhood.

At Saxon, Meridian lets her body wither away, believing that if she could become pure spirit, perhaps she would be deserving of her mother's love. Oblivious to her mother's utter failure as nurturer and further burdened by the guilt of being forced by Saxon's rules to deny that she ever had a child, Meridian aborts the second child that she conceives and removes any possibility of further children by having her tubes tied.

Ostracized by her fellow revolutionaries, Meridian – like Walker, who spent summers during her college years in Mississippi and Georgia – devotes herself to nonviolent means of furthering the cause of civil rights. As she travels about the South registering voters and aiding her people in any way she can, whether they register or not, she performs selfless acts of bravery that, more often than not, benefit the children. When the novel opens, for example, she is facing down a tank to win for the children the simple right to see a freak show on a day

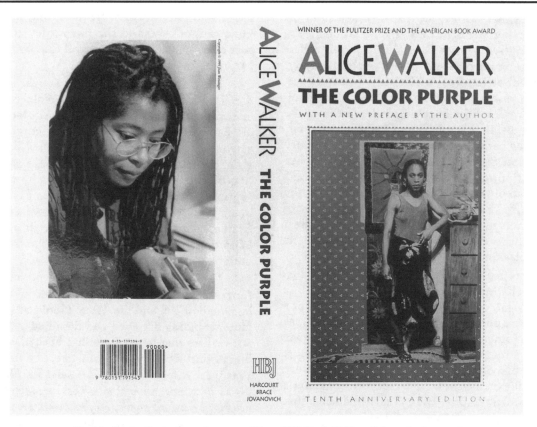

Dust jacket for the tenth-anniversary edition of Walker's Pulitzer Prize–winning novel

other than that set aside for blacks. She concludes each "performance" by slipping into a deathlike trance, her body paralyzed and useless. Each time, though, like the hardy petunia, she slowly comes back to life.

Meridian has received relatively little critical attention in spite of the fact that it offers a glimpse, rare in fiction, of the civil rights movement from the perspective of a young black woman. From a purely literary standpoint the novel is crucial to an understanding of the evolution of Walker's female characters. Meridian is described from the beginning as a woman in the process of changing her mind. Early on she perceives herself as a character in a novel whose existence presents a problem that will be solved only by her death. She dreams of releasing her mother, by dying, from the burden that motherhood has been.

She agonizes over her role in the revolution long after Truman Held, the father of her aborted child, tells her that it was only a fad. By the time Truman catches up with her one final time in Alabama, she has given away virtually all her material possessions. Even her near-death trances seem a rehearsal for death. The final performance is not to take place, however. Meridian is in the process of changing her mind about dying. She chooses eventually not to be a martyr, telling herself:

> The only new thing now ... would be the refusal of Christ to accept crucifixion. King ... should have refused. Malcolm, too, should have refused. All those characters in all those novels that require death to end the book should refuse. All saints should walk away. Do their bit, then — just walk away.

Meridian has recovered her spiritual health, and the fact that her thinning hair has begun to grow back suggests that she is on the road to recovering her physical health as well. She has fought back successfully against those forces that would deem her "incorrect," that would deny her her own definition of self. Truman compares her to Lazarus raised from the dead but feels the comparison not wholly accurate since Lazarus had to have help. Meridian is strong enough to do it alone. Her symbolic resurrection comes once she realizes that her duty to her own life is to live it, even if that means literally fighting for her life.

Meridian is linked thematically with a collection of fighters who populate Walker's second collection of short stories, the title of which sums up the increasing strength of Walker's women: *You Can't Keep a Good Woman Down* (1981). In this collection Walker confronts such issues as pornography, rape, and abortion from a blatantly womanist perspective, *womanist* being her term for a black feminist. Walker's politics have shaped her art from the beginning, yet here some critics felt she goes too far, blurring too completely the line between short story and political tract; feminist critics applauded her use of fiction, or pseudofiction, to advance their cause. Two of the most controversial pieces in the collection, "Porn" and "Coming Apart: By Way of Introduction to Lorde, Teish and Gardner," deal with the threat that pornography poses to relations between black men and black women.

The latter story was intended as the introduction to a chapter of a book on pornography, *Take Back the Night*, edited by Laura Lederer. Walker's piece first appeared in *Ms.* (February 1980) as "When Women Confront Porn at Home." One woman's attempt to cure her husband of his sexist attitudes provides an excuse for quoting Audre Lorde, Luisah Teish, and Tracey A. Gardner's views on pornography. Here is early evidence that Walker's work is least successful as fiction when it is most polemical. Walker admits that she would have treated the material differently had she intended it as a story in the first place. Elsewhere in the volume Walker further experiments with form, providing two endings to her treatment of interracial rape, "Advancing Luna — and Ida B. Wells," and presenting her views on God in the form of a letter in "A Letter of the Times, or Should This Sado-Masochism Be Saved?"

Two of the most conventional works in the volume, both in subject matter and in form, are among the most successful. In both Walker returns to her focus on art — in this case on the relationship between art and life. In "Nineteen Fifty-Five" the young white singer Traynor, who seems suspiciously like Elvis Presley, makes a fortune and a name for himself recording a song written by Gracie Mae Still. However, in spite of fame and fortune, Traynor remains spiritually bankrupt because he is never successful in forging the link between art and life. He sings Gracie Mae's song, yet his own experience is so divorced from the words that he fails to understand what he is singing. Gracie Mae has come to her understanding of both art and life through suffering. Like most of the characters in *You Can't Keep a Good Woman Down*, she has worked her way through her suffering to achieve a private peace that Traynor never finds. Through her music

she has found a form of freedom that money and fame cannot buy, and she has achieved the same sort of contentment with herself that characterizes Mrs. Johnson in "Everyday Use."

Autobiographical elements appear in "A Sudden Trip Home in the Spring" as Walker confronts once more the issue of the black artist's lack of models. Sarah Davis has left her native Georgia to study art on a scholarship at Cresselton, a prestigious girls' school in New York where she is one of only two black students. Sarah wonders how she is to capture her people on canvas if she has only one black face other than her own to serve as a model. Besides, she finds herself unable to draw or paint black men because she cannot bear "to trace defeat onto blank pages."

Called home suddenly to attend her father's funeral, Sarah learns at his graveside an important lesson about art and life. As she looks at her grandfather standing dry-eyed and dignified at the grave, she realizes that her mistake has been always to see him against a background of white. She thinks, "*It is strange . . . that I never thought to paint him like this, simply as he stands; without anonymous meaningless people hovering beyond his profile; his face turned brownly against the light*. The defeat that had frightened her in the faces of black men was the defeat of black forever defined by white."

There is no trace of that defeat on her grandfather's face now: "He stood like a rock, outwardly calm, the comfort and support of the Davis family. The family alone defined him, and he was not about to let them down." Sarah realizes that she can capture this strength on canvas, but her grandfather tells her to capture him, rather, in stone. As Grange Copeland learns to say no to the system that would deprive him of his manhood, Sarah learns that her art will be her way of saying "NO with capital letters" to the system that killed her mother and broke her father's spirit.

In "Source," the last story in *You Can't Keep a Good Woman Down,* one character tells another, " 'Your dilemma was obvious. You, even *objectively* speaking, did not know who you were. What you were going to do next; which "you" would be the one to survive.' " The self that survives in this second collection of Walker's stories, more often than in the earlier collection, is a self not dictated by others. These women represent a step toward spiritual health and self-definition. They fight sexist stereotypes and, in "Elethia" and "How Did I Get Away with Killing One of the Biggest Lawyers in the State? It Was Easy," racist ones as well.

Typical of their progress is Imani in "The Abortion." Like Walker, Imani has an abortion while in college. Seven years later, married and the mother of a two-year-old, she has another one. Where the first was a freeing experience, the second leaves her feeling that she is losing her own identity in her roles as wife and mother. She returns to her husband and daughter feeling "that the only way she could claim herself, feel herself distinct from them, was by doing something painful, self-defining but self-destructive." She demands that her husband have a vasectomy or stay in the guest room. He has the operation, but it comes too late to save the marriage. Imani's loyalty to her husband is not so strong that she will sacrifice herself to it. Two years later she completes the process of self-definition by ending the marriage.

Walker's marriage to Leventhal had ended by 1975. She left Mississippi for good in 1974 to become an editor at *Ms.*, and in 1977 she became an associate professor of English at Yale University. In 1978 she moved from Brooklyn to San Francisco with Robert Allen, a writer and former member of the board of directors of *Black Scholar* and one of her partners at Wild Trees Press since 1984. Her third volume of poetry, *Good Night, Willie Lee, I'll See You in the Morning,* came out in 1979. When the Guggenheim Fellowship she received in 1978 began to run out, she and Allen sought a place for her to write a novel that had been on her mind for some time but whose rural characters would not speak to her freely in New York or San Francisco. Royalties from *You Can't Keep a Good Woman Down* plus a retainer from *Ms.* to serve as a long-distance editor enabled her to take a year off from public appearances and move to Mendocino County, California, where the mountains reminded her of her native Georgia, and she pieced a quilt as the characters told her the story that became *The Color Purple* (1982).

In *The Color Purple* Walker succeeds in doing what she fails to do in the more polemical stories in *You Can't Keep a Good Woman Down:* she makes her case against sexual oppression by letting an abused woman from the rural South speak in her own voice rather than in words borrowed from her creator or other modern-day feminists. The voice, in reality, was borrowed, but from Walker's stepgrandmother, Rachel, who in her poverty had no legacy to leave, save the memory of the sound of her voice. The victim of the abuse, Celie, is based on Walker's great-great-grandmother, who was raped at the age of eleven by her white master.

An irate mother in California proposed that *The Color Purple* be banned from the Oakland public schools because of the crude language that fourteen-year-old Celie uses in the opening pages to describe her repeated rape by the man she believes to be her father but who is much later found to be her stepfather. In "Coming in from the Cold" (*Living by the Word*) Walker defends her decision to let Celie speak in her own voice. To have Celie speak in the voice of her oppressors would be to falsify her existence, to murder her and attack those ancestors who spoke as she does. Her words are the only words available to her – and a part of the self that she must eventually learn to respect. Because Celie dares not speak aloud, she writes letters to God.

After she has borne two children by her stepfather and he has taken them from her with no explanation, marriage for Celie means merely being passed like a piece of property from one domineering and abusive male to another. Albert would prefer the younger and prettier sister, Nettie, but settles for the unattractive, "spoiled," and now sterile Celie – once a cow is thrown into the deal – because he needs someone to care for the children he already has. The letters to God continue as Celie focuses on merely surviving Albert's cruelty and looks toward heaven as a final release from her suffering. When Nettie tells her to fight, Celie responds, "But I don't know how to fight. All I know how to do is stay alive." Her letters, however, provide a record of her growth out of this initial passivity into self-affirmation.

"A Letter of the Times" clarifies how the epistolary form that Walker also chose for *The Color Purple* aids Celie's process of self-definition. In that story Walker speaks through a character named Susan Marie, yet the definition of God that Susan Marie offers is Walker's own: "the inner spirit, the inner voice; the human compulsion when deeply distressed to seek healing counsel within ourselves, and the capacity within ourselves both to create this counsel and receive it." Susan Marie reads slave narratives and finds in them this inner spirit, "this inner capacity for self-comforting, this ability to locate God within." Each of these slave women "found within her own heart the only solace and love she was ever to know. It was as if these women found a twin self who saved them from their abused consciousness and chronic physical loneliness; and that twin self is in all of us, waiting only to be summoned."

This twin self was the same one Walker danced with the night Rebecca discovered a world in her mother's eye. Celie also finds the twin self within. The letters that constitute the first half of *The Color Purple* are a one-way correspondence

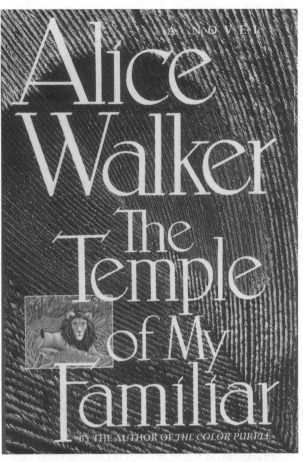

Dust jacket for Walker's 1989 novel, which stayed on the New York Times *best-seller list for more than four months*

between the abused and lonely Celie and her own inner self — that part of herself that eventually makes her fight back. In writing to God she is corresponding with the part of her personality that is growing progressively stronger until she is able to acknowledge the God within herself and demand the respect due her.

From childhood Celie has blindly accepted the image of God presented in the white man's Bible. She finally rejects that God in anger when, pushed too far, she can no longer reconcile his supposed benevolence with the evil that has been done her. Celie lost the only person who truly loved her after her sister Nettie fled her own home to avoid the sexual advances of her stepfather, and then Celie's home to avoid Albert's. Celie's anger flares up when she learns that for years Nettie has been writing to her from Africa, but Albert has been hiding the letters in revenge for Nettie's having rejected him. Because God let that happen, Celie writes him off as just like all the other men that she has ever known, "trifling, forgitful and lowdown," and stops writing him letters. She starts

writing to Nettie instead. She also takes up the needle and starts to sew to save herself from taking up the razor and murdering her husband.

When Celie loses faith in the only God that she has ever known, the flamboyant Shug Avery, Albert's longtime lover, steps in to offer her a genderless God that perhaps she can accept. Shug tells Celie, "God is inside you and inside everybody else. You come into the world with God. But only them that search for it inside find it. . . . God ain't a he or a she, but a It." She offers Celie the image of a God human enough to share Celie's need for love and compassionate enough to rejoice with its people when they find it, even in its most blatantly sexual forms. Shug arouses in Celie the sexuality that has lain dormant all her life. Walker knew early in her planning of *The Color Purple* that she was writing a book about two women who felt married to the same man. Celie and Shug's love for each other completes this love triangle.

A cry of outrage went up from some in the black community when in 1985 *The Color Purple* was made into a film, but not because of the hint of lesbianism. (In the novel it is more than a hint.) The complaint, rather, was that the story offers not a single positive black-male role model. Walker points out that what her critics too often miss, however, is that Albert also changes, a change that she feels is even more noticeable in the film adaptation than in the novel itself.

Walker remains concerned with the survival whole of a people. She argues that Celie and Albert both suffer from a sense of dis-ease that derives from their culturally defined sex roles. They grow toward wholeness by becoming more like each other, achieving wholeness and finding peace only when they achieve an androgynous blend of traditionally male and female characteristics. By the end of the novel Celie is wearing pants, running her own business that makes unisex pants, and smoking a pipe. Albert is keeping house for himself, even cooking, and late in the novel is shown sewing on the porch with Celie, designing shirts to go with her pants.

They have both lost Shug to a younger man, but they both now have enough inner strength to live without her as well as a newfound bond forged by their mutual love of her. Near the end of the novel Celie can say of Albert, " 'He ain't Shug, but he begin to be someone I can talk to.' " When Albert proposes that they remarry, she responds, " 'Naw, I still don't like frogs, but let's us be friends.' " Albert's son Harpo and his wife, Sofia, also find peace after years of battling one another once they decide to ignore what society tells them about sex roles. Sofia goes to work in the store that Celie has inherited from her father, while Harpo stops trying to prove his manhood by beating her and stays at home.

By placing Nettie in Africa with a family of missionaries, Walker is able to draw parallels between the oppression of black women in the American South and their oppression in Africa, a theme she develops more fully in *Possessing the Secret of Joy*. She is also able to wrap up all the loose ends of Celie's life when, by a strange twist of fate, Nettie becomes stepmother to Celie's two children, Adam and Olivia. When her family all come home in one wave of emotion, Celie thanks her new pantheistic God: "Dear God. Dear stars, dear trees, dear sky, dear peoples. Dear Everything. Dear God."

Walker allowed herself five years to write *The Color Purple*. It took her less than one. In 1983 the novel won both the Pulitzer Prize for fiction and the American Book Award for fiction; in that year also came the publication of *In Search of Our Mothers' Gar-*

dens. In January 1984 Walker wrote in her journal, "Next month I will be forty. In some ways, I feel my early life's work is done, and done completely. The books that I have produced already carry forward the thoughts that I feel the ancestors were trying to help me pass on." Her ancestors were not through with her yet, however.

One of Walker's disappointments with the response her works have received is that many black men have proved themselves incapable of empathizing with the black woman's suffering under sexism. Some used the controversy surrounding *The Color Purple* to draw attention to themselves, as though they were the ones being oppressed. Related to the denial that sexual brutality exists in the black community is the denial that racism does as well. What few noticed in *The Color Purple* is Albert's white blood. Albert never marries Shug, in spite of a love for her that lasts for decades, because his father, the son of a white master, objects to the color of her skin, which he describes as "black as tar." Old Mister feels a need to dominate anyone darker than he is, including his son. Walker takes it as a sign of psychic health that Albert is able to love himself in spite of his father's repudiation of him. For Albert as for Celie, learning to love himself is requisite to becoming whole.

Just as Albert has to come to terms with the entirety of who he is, Walker has had to come to terms personally and professionally with the entirety of who she is, including the fact that she is descended from slaveowners as well as from slaves. Her fourth volume of poetry, *Horses Make a Landscape Look More Beautiful* (1984), and her second collection of essays, *Living by the Word*, reflect Walker's coming to terms with both her Indian blood and her white blood. If Walker is the great-great-granddaughter of the eleven-year-old victim of rape who was her model for Celie, she is also the great-great-granddaughter of the white rapist. She believes that — just as Celie and Albert in *The Color Purple* exist in a state of dis-ease because of the limitations placed on them by culturally derived sex roles — individuals who try to deny the mixture of races within themselves often suffer from psychic illness. Dedicating *Horses Make a Landscape Look More Beautiful* to her white great-great-grandfather and to her part-Cherokee great-grandmother was Walker's acknowledgment of the "peaceful coming together racially, at last, of [her] psyche."

In *Living by the Word* Walker presents herself, like Meridian, as a woman in the process of changing her mind. For years she had withdrawn into her rural world in Mendocino County to escape the daily news of death and destruction, feeling that writing was no longer necessary. The essays in *Living by the Word* are her record of her journey out of isolation in search of the planet she had known and loved as a child. Here is Walker the environmentalist expressing her anguish over what human beings have done to each other and to the planet in the name of progress. Here also is Walker the optimist, who takes it as a positive sign that concern for the future of the planet has made differences based on gender or race seem insignificant by comparison. When Walker was arrested in 1987 for joining others in blocking one of the gates of the Concord Naval Weapons Station in California, most of her fellow protesters were white. Concern for the planet makes comrades of individuals who in another time and place might have been separated by a range of socially imposed barriers.

Walker's fourth novel, *The Temple of My Familiar,* came out in 1989, seven years after her third. In spite of the time lapse, encompassing those years when Walker felt writing was no longer necessary, *The Temple of My Familiar* is a logical extension of her earlier fiction and a further step in the evolution of her female characters. Once Walker had shown her women capable of breaking the bonds of oppression and defining themselves as whole persons and once she had, at the same time, discovered divinity in all human and nonhuman elements of the universe, it was a small step to making women into goddesses, which she does in *The Temple of My Familiar.* With one possible exception the novel's goddesses constitute part of womankind's distant past, yet the ancient matriarchal religions discovered by Walker's contemporary characters in the novel allow them to redefine relationships between the sexes. They are thus able to cure themselves of some of the same varieties of dis-ease based on societal expectations that plague characters in Walker's earlier works. The lessons they learn about the need for balance between the flesh and the spirit help them redefine themselves.

Early in her career Walker accused critics of focusing on her lifestyle rather than on her work. Her lifestyle today can be described as at times eccentric rather than inflammatory. In *Living by the Word* she provides verbal snapshots of herself lying across the path in a public park, in intense dialogue with the trees; munching seaweed off the rocks along the California coast during one of her vegetarian phases; and painting her "privy" snapdragon-yellow, with a blue seat and Oriental-red door. The eccentricities of her characters in *The Temple of My Familiar,* though, were enough to draw critics' atten-

tion from the author to the novel. The sheer magnitude of the undertaking was enough to arouse some initial skepticism.

Walker has called her fourth novel a romance of the past five hundred thousand years. One character, Miss Lissie, has lived through all of those half million years. Transmigration of the soul provides Walker with a handy, if somewhat artificial, means of encapsulating in one character centuries of the history of black womanhood. Miss Lissie boasts (inaccurately, it turns out) that in every one of her past lives she was fortunate to have been a black woman. Not so fortunate, however, were the black women that Miss Lissie was. One was burned at the stake, another died on a Virginia plantation after stepping in a bear trap while trying to escape slavery, and another was forced into prostitution when she was unable to prove on her wedding night that she was a virgin. Not all her lives have been tragic; the life that she is living in the novel's present has been rich with loving relationships.

The novel focuses on three couples. Miss Lissie and her husband, Hal, represent a bonding of the spirit. Now elderly, they stopped having sexual intercourse once Hal saw the pain childbirth caused his wife. Such is the oneness of their spirits that, when they paint self-portraits, each paints the other, and the portraits consist of an outline of a man and a woman, respectively, but with nothing but blue sky where the faces should be.

In spite of their spiritual bond, Miss Lissie is never able to be completely truthful with Hal regarding her past lives. Because he is terrified of cats, she never tells him that in one life she was a lion. She also fails to tell him that her soul once inhabited the body of a white man. She could be honest about the entirety of who she was only with Rafe, her lover. Miss Lissie contrasts the two men: "Hal loved me like a sister/mystic/warrior/woman/mother. Which was nice. But that was only part of who I was. Rafe, on the other hand, knowing me to contain everybody and everything, loved me wholeheartedly, as a goddess. Which I was." Such claims were in part what led critics to declare that the willing suspension of disbelief that Walker calls for in the novel is too much to demand of her readers.

When Miss Lissie meets Suwelo, a member of the history faculty at a California university, shortly after his Uncle Rafe's funeral, she realizes immediately that his refusal to confront the pain that his mother went through while married to his father and the tragedy of the car crash that killed both his parents prevents him from seeking anything more than a physical union with a woman. He is having an affair with Carlotta, a member of the women's studies department, whom he links in his mind with the women in the pornographic magazines into which he delves while his wife is on an extended trip to Africa. He concludes, wrongly, that she is a woman "without the kind of painful past that would threaten his sense of himself as a man or inhibit his enjoyment of her simply as a woman."

If he feels that he is using her, however, she feels the same about him. She describes him as "just a figment of my imagination. A distraction from my misery. He was just 'something' to hold on to; to be seen with; to wrestle with on the kitchen floor." Fanny, Celie's granddaughter and the wife from whom Suwelo is separated at the time of his uncle's funeral, sees the irony of the situation: "They were both wrong. There had not been a victim and an oppressor; there'd really been two victims, both of them carting around lonely, needy bodies that were essentially blind flesh."

Only when Suwelo, on Miss Lissie's advice, goes to Carlotta to seek her forgiveness for using her as a being with no substance can the two add a spiritual dimension to their relationship. Not surprisingly, given Walker's penchant for the symbolism of androgyny, Carlotta has by that time shed the voluptuousness of their early days together and now sports a slender, flat-chested body and closely cropped hair. Suwelo cannot help observing that she no longer looks like a woman. Carlotta retorts: " 'Obviously this is how a woman looks.' "

One source of discord in Suwelo's marriage to Fanny is her unusual habit of falling in love with spirits, another aspect of the novel that strains the reader's suspension of disbelief. When she and Suwelo make love, he never knows whether it is really he who is there for her or an Indian chief who has been dead for a century. Fanny finally succeeds in finding the perfect union of flesh and spirit, not with her husband but with Arveyda, Carlotta's husband.

The rather contrived plot of *Temple* exists primarily as a skeleton on which Walker can hang her theories on the historical bases of sexism. She traces both African and South American religions back to goddesses who were dethroned because of man's jealousy. Miss Lissie has lived long enough to recall the days of mother worship in Africa and to see a pattern emerge in relations between men and women – what she calls a pattern of freedom. Over the centuries, according to Miss Lissie, the sexes have alternated between periods when they could live together in harmony and periods when they could

achieve peace only by living apart. The novel shows a swing back toward a time when men and women can best preserve their freedom through segregated living.

Near the end of the novel Carlotta and Arveyda are still married, but they maintain separate dwellings. Fanny and Suwelo, their close friends, are divorced yet living together in a house modeled on the prehistoric ceremonial house of the Ababa tribe, a house with two wings, each with its own bedroom, bath, study, and kitchen, and a common space in the middle for those times when the man and woman choose to be together. *The Temple of My Familiar* has proved too much a novel of ideas for many readers, although it stayed on the *New York Times* best-seller list for more than four months. Spiritual history does not make light reading, nor does the subject of Walker's fifth novel, *Possessing the Secret of Joy*.

Walker comes across in her writing from the 1980s and 1990s as a woman at peace with herself and with the universe. Some of the anger of her youth remains, but it is more tempered and more focused. The sheer magnitude of her undertaking in *The Temple of My Familiar* is overwhelming; in *Possessing the Secret of Joy* she devotes her attention to one specific means of oppressing women and once more, as in *The Color Purple,* lets one woman represent the thousands who have shared her fate. *Possessing the Secret of Joy,* then, is much more concise, more controlled, and more successful as art than its predecessor.

Walker sees *Possessing the Secret of Joy* not as a sequel to *The Color Purple* or *The Temple of My Familiar,* although they all share some characters, but as a novel due the character of Tashi, who appears briefly in both of the earlier novels. Tashi is the best friend in Africa of Celie's daughter, Olivia, and at the end of *The Color Purple* marries Celie's son, Adam. When Tashi arrives in America with Adam, her face bears tribal scars, and Adam has had his face scarred as well in an act of support for her efforts to preserve the tradition of her tribe, now nearly wiped out by the white man in the name of progress. Mentioned only in passing is the fact that she has also undergone what is referred to vaguely as the female initiation ceremony. She has, in other words, been the willing victim of genital mutilation in the name of tradition. The novel records Tashi's attempts throughout the rest of her life to come to terms with what has been done to her body and to the bodies of generations of African women.

Under psychoanalysis Tashi retrieves the buried pieces of her past. From her childhood comes the memory of her tears on the day Adam and his family arrived. Her sister Dura had just died, having bled to death as a result of the female initiation. As a child, Tashi could not comprehend what had really happened, knowing only that she was terrified by the sight of her own blood and learned to play in such a way as to take no risks. Buried even deeper is the memory of having been outside the hut that day to hear her sister's screams. Walker's imaginative re-creation of Carl Jung helps Tashi finally to bring to the surface of her consciousness the repressed memory of what she calls her sister's murder.

As a middle-aged woman, Tashi is on trial for murdering M'Lissa, who killed Dura by performing female circumcision on her. As Tashi awaits the proper moment to kill M'Lissa, the old woman finally makes her understand that, in choosing to let herself be mutilated in what she believed was a noble gesture of tribal loyalty, Tashi was only making herself a false martyr to a dying culture. Convicted of M'Lissa's murder and sentenced to death, Tashi, however, becomes a true martyr. She breaks the silence that has too long surrounded female circumcision, a silence that made it taboo even to talk about any of the range of crude operations that deprived the African woman of any opportunity for sexual gratification and that made sexual intercourse painful and childbirth a nightmare. (Tashi's own son was born retarded as a result of the trauma of birth.)

Women come from all parts of the country to sing beneath Tashi's prison window. The men beat them into silence and on the day of the execution use machine guns to keep them quiet, but in silent protest the women who line the path that Tashi will travel drop the wrappings from the babies they carry to reveal the bare and natural bottoms of their little girls. Tashi's final thought – "*Resistance* is the secret of joy!" – could well become their new motto.

In a concluding note to the reader in *Possessing the Secret of Joy* Walker points out that an estimated 90 million to 100 million women and girls living in Africa, the Far East, and the Middle East have undergone some form of genital mutilation. She has pledged a portion of the royalties from the novel to help educate women and girls – and men and boys – about the hazardous effects of the tradition.

Her Blue Body Everything We Know collects all the poems from Walker's four previous volumes of poetry, adding a new introduction to each, along with a section of sixteen previously uncollected works. Walker introduces the collection by expressing her amazement that she has been writing poetry for twenty-five years, when her expectation was that she would be a suicide by thirty. She has been writing prose just as long.

Widely viewed – on the strength of her fiction, nonfiction, and poetry – as a major voice for contemporary black women, Walker will probably continue to add to her list of works in all three genres until her Great Spirit calls her home or until she decides for herself that her life's work is done. When she sacrifices art to social and political ideology, her critics and her public will let her know. When she blends art and activism effectively, as she does in *The Color Purple* and *Possessing the Secret of Joy*, there are few writers currently at work in America who outshine her.

Interviews:
John O'Brien, "Alice Walker," in his *Interviews with Black Writers* (New York: Liveright, 1973), pp. 185–211;
Mary Helen Washington, "Alice Walker: Her Mother's Gifts," *Ms.,* 10 (June 1982): 38;
Claudia Tate, "Alice Walker," in her *Black Women Writers at Work* (New York: Continuum, 1983), pp. 175–187;
Sharon Wilson, "A Conversation with Alice Walker," *Kalliope,* 6, no. 2 (1984): 37–45;
Donna Britt, "Alice Walker and the Inner Mysteries Unraveled," *Washington Post,* 8 May 1989, pp. B1, B4;
Gregory Jaynes, "Living by the Word," *Life,* 12 (May 1989): 61–64.

Bibliographies:
Louis Pratt and Darnell D. Pratt, *Alice Malsenior Walker: An Annotated Bibliography, 1968–1986* (Westport, Conn.: Meckler, 1988);
Erma Davis Banks and Keith Byerman, *Alice Walker: An Annotated Bibliography, 1968–86* (New York: Garland, 1989).

References:
Harold Bloom, ed., *Alice Walker* (New York: Chelsea House, 1989);
David Bradley, "Telling the Black Woman's Story," *New York Times Magazine,* 8 January 1984, pp. 24–37;
King-Kok Cheung, " 'Don't Tell': Imposed Silences in *The Color Purple* and *The Woman Warrior*," *PMLA,* 103 (March 1988): 162–174;
Barbara Christian, "Alice Walker: The Black Woman Artist as Wayward," in *Black Women Writers (1950–80): A Critical Evaluation,* edited by Mari

Evans (Garden City, N.Y.: Anchor/Double-day, 1984), pp. 457–477;

Christian, "The Contrary Women of Alice Walker: A Study of Female Protagonists in *In Love and Trouble*," in her *Black Feminist Criticism: Perspectives on Black Women Writers* (New York: Pergamon Press, 1985), pp. 31–46;

Christian, "Novels for Everyday Use: The Novels of Alice Walker," in her *Black Women Novelists: The Development of a Tradition, 1892–1976* (Westport, Conn.: Greenwood Press, 1980), pp. 180–238;

Thadious M. Davis, "Alice Walker's Celebration of Self in Southern Generations," *Southern Quarterly,* 21 (Summer 1983): 38–53;

Peter Erickson, " 'Cast Out Alone/To Heal/And Re-create/Ourselves': Family-based Identity in the Work of Alice Walker," *College Language Association Journal,* 23 (Spring 1979): 71–94;

Karen C. Gaston, "Women in the Lives of Grange Copeland," *College Language Association Journal,* 24 (March 1981): 276–286;

Trudier Harris, "From Victimization to Free Enterprise: Alice Walker's *The Color Purple*," *Studies in American Fiction,* 14 (Spring 1986): 1–17;

Harris, "On *The Color Purple,* Stereotypes, and Silence," *Black American Literature Forum,* 18 (Winter 1984): 155–161;

Deborah E. McDowell, "The Self in Bloom: Alice Walker's *Meridian*," *College Language Association Journal,* 24 (March 1981): 262–275;

Bettye J. Parker-Smith, "Alice Walker's Women: In Search of Some Peace of Mind," in *Black Women Writers (1950–80): A Critical Evaluation,* pp. 478–493;

Karen F. Stein, "*Meridian:* Alice Walker's Critique of Revolution," *Black American Literature Forum,* 20 (Spring–Summer 1986): 129–141;

Wendy Wall, "Lettered Bodies and Corporeal Texts in *The Color Purple*," *Studies in American Fiction,* 16 (Spring 1988): 83–97;

Mary Helen Washington, "An Essay on Alice Walker," in *Sturdy Black Bridges: Visions of Black Women in Literature,* edited by Roseann P. Bell and others (Garden City, N.Y.: Anchor/Doubleday, 1979), pp. 133–149;

Donna Haisty Winchell, *Alice Walker* (New York: Twayne, 1992).

Edward Lewis Wallant

(19 October 1926 – 5 December 1962)

Phillip A. Snyder
Brigham Young University

See also the Wallant entries in *DLB 2: American Novelists Since World War II, First Series* and *DLB 28: Twentieth-Century American-Jewish Fiction Writers.*

BOOKS: *The Human Season* (New York: Harcourt Brace, 1960; London: Gollancz, 1965);

The Pawnbroker (New York: Harcourt, Brace & World, 1961; London: Gollancz, 1962);

The Tenants of Moonbloom (New York: Harcourt, Brace & World, 1963; London: Gollancz, 1964);

The Children at the Gate (New York: Harcourt, Brace & World, 1964; London: Gollancz, 1964).

OTHER: "I Held Back My Hand," in *New Voices 2: American Writing Today,* edited by Don M. Wolfe (New York: Hendricks, 1955), pp. 192–201;

"The Man Who Made a Nice Appearance," in *New Voices 3: American Writing Today,* edited by Charles I. Glicksberg (New York: Hendricks, 1958), pp. 336–353;

"When Ben Awakened," in *American Scene: New Voices,* edited by Wolfe (New York: Stuart, 1963), pp. 94–100;

"The Artist's Eyesight," in *Teacher's Notebook in English* (New York: Harcourt Brace Jovanovich, 1963).

Edward Lewis Wallant (photograph by Bob Anthony)

Edward Lewis Wallant remains an important but minor Jewish-American writer of post–World War II America — one whose career was cut short by his death at age thirty-six, just as he had placed himself in a position to devote his full time and energy to his writing. His literary legacy includes four relatively short novels — *The Human Season* (1960), *The Pawnbroker* (1961), *The Tenants of Moonbloom* (1963), and *The Children at the Gate* (1964) — the last two published posthumously, and several stories, only three of which were published. These texts provide enough evidence of Wallant's fine developing artistic vision and talent to make one wonder

where his career might have led. His most enduring legacy among the general public may be the 1965 film adaptation of *The Pawnbroker,* for which Rod Steiger won critical acclaim for his subtle but powerful portrayal of its protagonist, Sol Nazerman. The film's excellence inspired more than one reviewer to comment that it surpasses the novel.

Nevertheless, Wallant's neorealistic, neonaturalistic novels of the early 1960s still stand up under critical gaze because they represent well the emergence of an American revisioning of the Holocaust outside the boundaries of traditional Judaism; of multicultural perspectives, particularly as located in a decaying urban environment; of the tension between the self-containment of individual isolation and the need for communal integration; and of the epiphanic search for faith and meaning in a cold war world of privileged affluence set daily against the physical and emotional deprivation of marginal lives. Wallant's work anticipates the further development of these issues and themes by such writers as Saul Bellow, E. L. Doctorow, Joseph Heller, Bernard Malamud, Philip Roth, and John Updike, marking him as a significant transitional writer between modern and contemporary periods in American literature.

Edward Lewis Wallant was born on 19 October 1926 in New Haven, Connecticut, the only child of Sol Ellis and Ann Mendel Wallant, a couple from the Jewish middle class. Wallant was only six years old when his father, a World War I veteran disabled by mustard gas, died of tuberculosis. Many critics point to this loss as the source of his fictional preoccupation with father-son themes. Wallant was raised by his mother, who never remarried, and two aunts in a modest, secure environment that provided him only minimal experience and education in the practice of Judaism. However, according to Wallant's widow, Joyce, he did go through the bar mitzvah ceremony as a young man.

Wallant's grandfather, a Russian immigrant, told him stories of Jewish life in the "old country," but most of Wallant's knowledge and interest in Judaism came to him as an adult. This circumstance may account for the errors he made in his novels regarding Jewish culture and religious rites as well as Hebrew and Yiddish. In fact, some reviewers and critics have taken him to task for what they deem inaccurate or inappropriate articulation of the Jewish experience, particularly in connection with the Holocaust.

Wallant attended New Haven High School, developing an obvious talent for art and writing before his graduation in 1944. During his high-school years he was employed as a plumber's assistant and a pharmacy delivery boy, occupations that figure respectively in *The Human Season* and *The Children at the Gate*. He also frequented a relative's Harlem pawnshop, which provided the technical details and urban background for which *The Pawnbroker* was praised by reviewers.

Wallant attended the University of Connecticut for two semesters, one in 1944 and the other in 1946, between which time he served in the U.S. Navy as a gunner's mate in the European theater of World War II. After the war he married Joyce Fromkin, a childhood friend, and they moved to Brooklyn in 1948 so he could study drafting at the Pratt Institute. After graduation in 1950 Wallant immediately took a position as a commercial artist with the advertising firm of L. W. Frohlich, the first of several similar positions he held with various New York advertising agencies. He built a solid career in commercial art that allowed his family to live comfortably in New Rochelle, New York, and then Norwalk, Connecticut, during the 1950s.

The Wallants had three children – Scott, born 1952; Leslie, born 1954; and Kim, born 1957 – and raised them in the tradition of Reform Judaism. By all accounts Wallant was a devoted husband and father who stayed close to his family despite his demanding dual career. He balanced his daily efforts at reaching the mainstream American consumer with his nightly efforts at articulating the lives of those who exist outside that mainstream.

In 1950 Wallant began taking creative-writing courses at the New School for Social Research. His instructors, Charles I. Glicksberg and Don M. Wolfe, encouraged his development as a fiction writer, and he produced his first serious writing for them, most notably "Tarzan's Cottage," a novel-length manuscript. In 1951 Wallant took a course in modern American literature at Hunter College. An enthusiastic reader all his life, he traces his evolving tastes in literature in "The Artist's Eyesight" (1963), his only published memoir, listing his early influences as Sherwood Anderson, Edgar Rice Burroughs, Charles Dickens, John Dos Passos, Ernest Hemingway, Howard Pease, Mark Twain, Edgar Wallace, and Thomas Wolfe. His later influences include Willa Cather, Fyodor Dostoyevsky and other nineteenth-century Russian novelists, F. Scott Fitzgerald, and Sinclair Lewis.

As he matured, Wallant's reading gradually turned away from popular fiction: "I was beginning to appreciate and to *require* art." For example, he portrays his response to Twain's *The Adventures of Huckleberry Finn* (1885) as reflective of "the queer power of someone I had actually known"; describes his fascination with the "dark poetry" of Anderson's *Winesburg, Ohio* (1919); and expresses his delight in the virile, suggestive style of Hemingway's *The Sun Also Rises* (1926) with the "rakishness of [its] great unsaid." In his own writing Wallant generally avoided obvious imitation of the writers he admired, but he made ample use of their examples in cultivating his own style and insights.

Writing mostly at night after his workday was completed, he tenaciously pursued his development as a fiction writer and eventually succeeded in having his first story, "I Held Back My Hand," published in a 1955 anthology edited by his mentor Don M. Wolfe. After "Tarzan's Cottage" and "Odyssey of a Middleman," another novel-length manuscript, were rejected by publishers in the late 1950s, *The Human Season* (originally titled "A Scattering in the Dark" after a line in the Archibald MacLeish poem "Einstein") was published in 1960. It received the Harry and Ethel Daroff Memorial Fiction Award (later renamed for Wallant) given by the Book Council of the National Jewish Welfare Board as the finest novel of that year on a Jewish theme.

The modest success of *The Human Season* helped Wallant secure an invitation to the 1960 Breadloaf Writers Conference. The publication of *The Pawnbroker,* which was nominated for the National Book Award, established Wallant as a notable emerging fiction writer and helped him receive a 1962 Guggenheim Fellowship. He resigned as art director at the McCann Erikson agency to pursue his writing career full-time and spent the summer in Europe, gathering information for a projected comic novel, "Tannenbaum's Journey." After his return to the United States he worked in a rented room to complete the revisions requested by Harcourt on *The Tenants of Moonbloom* and *The Children at the Gate.* After a four-month illness, during which his condition was misdiagnosed by his physicians, Wallant suffered a cerebral aneurysm, fell into a coma, and was admitted to a hospital where he died on 5 December 1962.

Since the beginning of Wallant's career, reviewers and critics have commented on his persistent combination of thematic binaries — such as individual/society, outsider/insider, despair/hope, ignorance/epiphany, victimization/survival, escape/engagement, stasis/progress, and Jewish/Christian mythos — which creates the axes of tension along which his narratives struggle as they develop toward some kind of resolution, however limited. Jonathan Baumbach and John G. Parks have characterized this resolution process as a "pilgrim's progress" toward self-realization, and others have described it as a search for father, faith, connection, community, regeneration, or God. In his insistence on writing about what Nancy A. Benson calls "quotidian worlds," Wallant reflects the realistic tradition; in his determination to write what Nicholas Ayo (1970) calls "accounts of human weakness and depravity," he reflects the naturalistic tradition.

But Wallant also represents the contemporary confessional tradition of the 1960s, with its focus on the individual psyche in all its psychological and social dimensions. This tradition also involves a frank, sometimes explicit, confrontation with the existential issues of the day as enacted in the conditions of the extreme. Wallant seems particularly interested in the dissolution and reconstitution of the family and its members. Richard Ruland and Malcolm Bradbury place him among those post-1945 Jewish-American authors who write less about the afflictions of immigration and more about "the nature of the American Dream, the rise of materialism, the experience of the modern city, the bonds that linked person to person in the moral chain." Clearly, as befits a writer of his generation, Wallant embodies multiple literary traditions.

It is difficult to describe Wallant's evolution as a novelist because he produced all four of his published novels while writing part-time during a four-year period. Each of his novels seems to be a different kind of fictional experiment, and he died before his career settled into a clearly discernible pattern. Wallant simply did not provide enough evidence over time to allow any definitive conclusions on his authorial development beyond some limited speculation. His extant manuscripts reveal his compositional practice to consist of careful outlining followed by systematic drafting according to such variables as imagery and point of view to produce several different versions of essentially the same story, or plot, from which he constructed the final draft. There are various manuscript versions for each of his published novels. Wallant's writing apprenticeship seemed geared toward his development following the prevailing notions of fictional craftsmanship based on the formalist aesthetic of the well-wrought novel. Indeed, most of his reviewers and critics base their critiques on this same formula, privileging restraint and realistic detail while criticizing Wallant's occasional melodramatic lapses, heavy-handed symbolism, and runaway lyricism.

According to David Galloway and others, Wallant's unpublished manuscripts and published stories also reveal his early investigation of the issues and settings that characterize his published novels. For instance, Wallant explores parental loss in the unpublished manuscripts for the stories "Robert" and "The Days to Come"; extreme individual isolation in "The Man Who Made a Nice Appearance" (1958); haunting memories of past failures in "I Held Back My Hand"; hospital settings in the unpublished manuscript for the story "Fathers"; multiracial relationships in the unpublished manuscripts for the stories "Fight Night" and "The Willy Novels"; Holocaust backgrounds in "Tarzan's Cottage"; and bildungsroman initiation patterns in the unpublished manuscript for the novel-length "Odyssey of a Middleman." Wallant used ideas and passages from his unpublished writing in his later publications after significant reordering and revision. He believed that experimentation with multiple approaches to a given story produced a better final product, particularly as he was learning his craft, because it allowed him the freedom to explore the many possibilities of fictional narrative before settling on one approach.

The Human Season received generally positive reviews that emphasized Wallant's promise as a writer. The *Times Literary Supplement* (15 April 1965) characterized it as a typical first novel, an apprenticeship exercise with too narrow a focus on the protagonist and no well-developed minor characters. *Time* magazine (5 September 1960), however, called it a tour de force. Later critics have compared *The Human Season,* as they have *The Pawnbroker,* to Saul Bellow's *Mr. Sammler's Planet* (1969), which focuses on the individual process of grief and the intensity of a personal quarrel with God. Critics have also pointed out parallels between *The Human Season* and the Book of Job as well as *J. B.* (1958), MacLeish's contemporary version of Job's story. William V. Davis (1972) argues that *The Human Season* is the least successful of Wallant's novels but that it represents his most central themes of redemption and reconciliation as set against the background of personal grief, ritual, and mysticism.

Certainly, *The Human Season* features a typical Wallant protagonist in Joe (Yussel) Berman, an aging Jewish widower who struggles to cope with the death of his wife, Mary, and the associated earlier loss of their only son, Marvin, in World War II. Berman's character is based on Wallant's father-in-law, whose grief over the loss of his wife apparently moved Wallant so deeply that he felt compelled to explore it in fiction. The novel is dedicated to his mother-in-law, Mae Fromkin, "who was a plumber's wife, too." Nevertheless, it would be inaccurate and naive to view *The Human Season* as a simple exercise in autobiography, for Wallant seems to use his experiences as a jumping-off point for his imagination and fictional experimentation, not as an opportunity for direct transcription.

The setting of *The Human Season* reinforces its narrow narrative focus on Berman and its individual-in-isolation theme by restricting virtually all the action to the interior of the Berman house, mostly during the month of June 1956, as a parallel to Berman's bruised psyche. The house, with its furnishings and souvenirs, represents for Berman, a

Dust jacket for Wallant's first novel, which Time *magazine called a tour de force*

Russian immigrant, the material acquisition of his hard work according to American-dream ideology, but the house seems empty of the most significant acquisition of all, his wife. Her social status as a blond, middle-class, born-and-bred American further reinforces Berman's sense of success, along with his grief. That Mary married him in the first place seems miraculous to Berman, even though his heroism and earnestness qualify him as worthy, so her loss seems doubly painful to him. He cannot take Job's words – "The Lord giveth and the Lord taketh away" – to heart.

Berman's flashbacks present his relationship with Mary as rich, with a multifaceted companionship and intimacy, sexual and otherwise. He is enclosed both literally and figuratively within a house and a head full of memories, each item or recollection emblematic of Mary's absence, which is so present that he sometimes calls out her name, forgetting she is gone. In this sense, like *The Pawnbroker, The Human Season* revolves around the persistence of memory, its chronological advance being counterpointed by the reverse chronology of flash-backs as Berman's life goes literally forward at the same time his memory of its past goes figuratively backward. Fourteen of the novel's eighteen chapters are divided into present and past narratives that represent Berman's benchmark experiences of life and death: Mary's illness and death; Berman's oper-ation and hospitalization, his own near-death expe-rience; his mother's death; the report of his son's death; a family vacation at the beach, full of life and laughter; his tender, grace-filled courtship and hon-eymoon; his brutal fight with an Irish foreman who, ironically, hates Berman's ethnicity; his New York City disembarkment; the ship crossing from Russia, with the emblematic birth of a baby; the death of his rabbi father, boyish games and his first sexual ex-perience with "crazy Rachel," a marginal play-mate "given to hysterical shrieking and hectic laughter"; his fainting in a synagogue during Yom Kippur and his father's pride at Berman's refusal to break his fast; his father's accidental killing of a Gentile peasant who was whipping a fellow Jew; and his sleeping in a wagon on a family journey, probably his earliest memory. All these pres-ent/past counterpoints emphasize Berman's intu-itive, ritualistic struggle to come to terms with his present life by seeking touchstones of meaning in memories of ritual and family. The novel ends with Berman's eventual acquiescence to his daughter Ruthie's insistence that he move in with her and her family, an agreement that symbolizes his final relinquishing of his pent-up isolation by his return to the family circle.

The Pawnbroker continues the theme of individ-ual isolation so pervasive in The Human Season but with far more deeply tragic and naturalistic setting, symbolism, characterization, and tone. Davis (1973–1974) regards it as the finest expression of Wal-lant's belief in the possibility of growth toward love. Ernest Becker sees it as a Kierkegaardian explora-tion of the human condition and the prospect of in-dividual hope and growth, going so far as to argue that Wallant's death may have resulted from the in-tensity of that exploration and its impact on his health. However, Dorothy Seidman Bilik censures Wallant for his unsympathetic treatment of Holo-caust survivors, and Alan L. Berger criticizes the novel for universalizing, and thus trivializing, the Jewish Holocaust experience by comparing it to the African-American experience in Harlem. S. Lillian Kremer, on the other hand, praises The Pawnbroker as a prototypical American revisioning of the Holo-caust foregrounded in fiction and represented, in its memory/dream sequences, by a "survivor-chorus"

that takes the Holocaust out of the realm of the symbolic.

Reviewers were divided on the novel's merits, with some, including those for the Times Literary Supplement (2 March 1962) and Newsweek (14 August 1961), complimenting its accuracy of detail and top-ical theme. Other reviewers, including the one for Time (18 August 1961), called it flawed, unconvinc-ing, and melodramatic. The reviewers' criticism tended to center more on formal issues and less on substantive ones, almost as if the sheer impact of the novel's subject matter were too profound for much argument, except among the Jewish scholars who are in such positions of critical authority that Wallant's editor at Harcourt Brace Jovanovich, Dan Wickenden, made it a point to emphasize that the novel's authenticity originated in Wallant's close friendship with an actual Holocaust survivor. The Pawnbroker may be, in fact, one of the most impor-tant popular literary expressions of how the Holo-caust affects contemporary American society and its collective psyche, reminding Americans that they have their own history of racist and genocidal acts. In a certain sense the novel helped make possible such sites of Holocaust documentation as the Holo-caust Museum in Washington, D.C., in addition to the continuing creation and collection of Holocaust narratives.

The New York City setting in The Pawnbroker establishes its location on the margins of main-stream American society, a place inhabited by dis-tressed, disadvantaged, and displaced people from virtually every immigrant and ethnic group. The lit-eral and figurative center of the novel is the pawn-shop run by Sol Nazerman, a well-educated Polish Jew who lost most of his family to the Holocaust. Like Berman, Nazerman lives in the world of the past as well as the present, and, as the fifteenth anni-versary of his family's death approaches, he finds himself more haunted by the past and less able to keep his daily ghetto business separated from his nocturnal, nightmarish memories.

The suburban Mount Vernon home Nazer-man shares with his sister's family gradually loses its protective power as the novel progresses. The pawnshop is filled with artifacts of lost lives – items ranging from wedding rings to men's suits – that present an authoritative associated image of Holo-caust booty – the tangible remainders of the Nazis' wholesale destruction of European Jews – the ex-change value of which cannot begin to approximate its actual cost.

Like a profane kind of confessor-priest, Nazer-man operates the pawnshop for the Murillio Mafia, whose pattern of cruelty and exploitation eventually causes him to associate the Mafia with the concentration-camp Nazis, especially in their mutual prostitution of women for profit and pleasure, and finally forces him to renounce his Mafia ties. His last view of his wife, Ruth, was as she was forced to fellate a camp guard while Nazerman was compelled to watch. When he realizes his profits are connected to the Murillio brothels, he breaks out of his acquiescent, isolated materialism and recovers his sense of ethics and power of personal action.

The literal and symbolic sacrifice of his assistant, Jesus Ortiz, in foiling a robbery of his own devising and saving Nazerman's life underlines and parallels Nazerman's redemption and subsequent change of heart, particularly in its messianic symbolism. In this transformation Nazerman represents a postmodern Shylock who forsakes his profit hunger and justice fixation for reconciliation and forgiveness. Like Berman, he abandons his alienation from life, but, unlike Berman, who is able to mourn from the moment of his loss, Nazerman must work on his willingness to open up his heart enough to mourn for his own dead, as well as for the dead of others, particularly Tessie Rubin's, his mistress, who also lost her family to the Holocaust. *The Pawnbroker* explores various modes of mourning – from the denial engaged in by Nazerman's sister's family in their Waspish Americanization to the exploitation engaged in by Goberman, a confidence man and possible Nazi collaborator, who plays on collective Jewish guilt for profit – but Nazerman, in his reaching out to Tessie and his alienated nephew, Morton, at the end of the novel exemplifies the mode with the greatest potential for possible healing and reconnection to the human race.

According to Wickenden, *The Children at the Gate* was the most troublesome of Wallant's novels to bring to final form, and, in fact, Wickenden himself readied it for publication following Wallant's death. Although it was published after *The Tenants of Moonbloom*, Wallant had drafted it much earlier. The manuscript developed under many titles – "A Many-Storied City," "View of a Marvelous City," "Sammy and Angelo," "Angelo and the Wandering Jew," and "In the Time of Sammy" – all of which reflect Wallant's changing sense of the novel's focus from the city to Angelo to Sammy before he settled on the final title, a reference to T. S. Eliot's "Ash-Wednesday" (1930). Wallant's difficulty with the text tempted him to set it aside permanently, but, with the encouragement of Wickenden and especially Joyce Wallant, who pronounced it her favorite of his novels, he persisted in its completion.

Davis (1968) describes *The Children at the Gate* as a type of Christian parable based on the mythic story of Cain and Abel as well as Christ's atonement. But Robert Sklar complained in *Congress Bi-Weekly* (12 October 1964) that Wallant's theology seems confused and inconsistent. Reviewers had difficulty dealing with Sammy's character, particularly the theatricality of his stereotyped, Yiddish personality, his contradictory sinner/saint status, his illustration of Wallant's tendency toward mixed Jewish/Christian metaphors, and his melodramatic death, with its obvious Crucifixion symbolism. Galloway notes that Wallant toyed with the idea of adapting the novel for the stage, which may account for its overly dramatic qualities.

The Children at the Gate features dual protagonists – Angelo DeMarco as the primary one and Sammy as the secondary one – a primary/secondary duality also present in *The Pawnbroker* with Nazerman and Ortiz, respectively. The narrative focus on Angelo does not diminish Sammy's role as the messianic figure (like Ortiz) of sacrifice and redemption so important in Wallant's fiction. That focus also preserves the mysterious nature of Sammy's origins and character. Like Nazerman, Angelo lives and works in an environment on the edges of American existence, one full of grotesques in the tradition of Southern fiction, especially the writing of William Faulkner and Flannery O'Connor, where grace and epiphanic understanding come in the most extreme and unusual circumstances.

Angelo's dysfunctional family provides a non-nurturing locus for his social isolation, and his pharmacy-delivery job with his uncle takes him to a hospital full of the ill and dying. Angelo's only real human connection is to his retarded sister, Theresa, for whom he likewise represents the only real human connection. Angelo's association with Sammy, an unusually eccentric hospital orderly, wrenches him out of his social rut and studied isolation by demanding Angelo's interaction with the grotesque, mostly in the form of the strange stories Sammy tells. One of these tales involves a pedophile who donates his corneas to restore a child's sight because "I never read or go to the movies anyhow, and I've seen everything at least a dozen times already." Another concerns a pimp who freezes to death holding the hand of one of his hookers, who is trapped in the wreckage of an accident, because "she shouldn't die without anyone who knows her to hold her hand."

The central event in the novel – the attempted rape of Maria Alvarez, a young patient, by Lebe-

Dust jacket for Wallant's last novel

dov, a hospital orderly – becomes the embodiment of one of Sammy's stories as he takes it upon himself to secure everyone's forgiveness of Lebedov. Sammy eventually attempts his own atoning sacrifice/suicide: a leap from the hospital steps that ends in his impalement on the wrought-iron fence surrounding Sacred Heart Hospital. He becomes the victim of his empathic theatricality and perhaps Angelo's betrayal. Angelo's subsequent breakdown and return to the family from which he has become estranged echo the conclusions of *The Human Season* and *The Pawnbroker*, offering a limited hope that, through the endurance of pain, one can become more alive to oneself as well as to others.

Wallant seems to have had a much easier time composing *The Tenants of Moonbloom*, which he started as an entry in the journal he began in October 1961. He had nearly completed the novel by his death at the end of 1962. Unlike *The Children at the Gate*, *The Tenants of Moonbloom* was com-

posed with what Galloway calls an almost effortless assurance, requiring much less substantive revision by Wallant. It was published posthumously under Wickenden's direction. *The Tenants of Moonbloom* differs from Wallant's other novels because of its humorous tone set alongside its serious theme. In his review of the novel John C. Pine (*199 Ways to Review a Book*, 1971) calls it "extravagantly funny" and "hauntingly sad." This combination of comedy and pathos also appears in *The Children at the Gate* in the character of Sammy, but not to the same extent.

Several reviews praised the humor in *The Tenants of Moonbloom* as a triumph over tragedy. *Saturday Review* (10 August 1963), for example, insisted that the comic spirit of the novel redeems its sentimentality, and the *Times Literary Supplement* (30 April 1964) noted its affinity to Bellow's comic masterpiece *Henderson the Rain King* (1959). However, the humor in *The Tenants of Moonbloom* does not detract from what Christopher Salvesen

(*New Statesman*, 8 May 1964) describes as its powerful social content. Davis (1982) argues that in combining Jewish characters and Christian symbols within an existential ideology Wallant originated a new genre.

The original title of *The Tenants of Moonbloom*, "The Man of Responsibility," reveals Wallant's most central issue in the novel and with its protagonist, Norman Moonbloom. The title change also reveals the thematic shift in Moonbloom's attitude from a self-centered egotism to an outer-directed altruism. The novel describes the transformation that tenement inhabitants bring about in Moonbloom, who changes his role from the collection of weekly rents for his brother (in a scheme to exact the most profit for the least amount of capital expense) to the renovation of living conditions simply for the sake of his own and his tenants' lives.

The Tenants of Moonbloom concerns yet another isolated escapist who finds a sense of community integration. Moonbloom goes from reluctant employee to subversive landlord, even using his own money to finance repairs. Wallant also creates a rich tableau of memorable minor characters, whose interaction with Moonbloom provides the most consistently funny scenes from any of Wallant's novels and demonstrates his ability to deal with serious issues in a comedic context.

Previously a professional student – accounting, art, dentistry, podiatry, and rabbinical studies – Moonbloom seems ill-equipped for his role but gradually grows into it as his relationships with his tenants become more intimate. The last act of his renovation project, plumbing repairs for the terminally ill Basellecci, literally demonstrates Moonbloom's willingness to immerse himself in sewer excrement so he can be, in his own words, reborn: "'I'M BORN!' he howled, with unimaginable ecstacy. 'See, Basellecci, I'm born to you. See, see, smell me, see me. . . . Everything will be all right!'"

Galloway concludes *Edward Lewis Wallant* (1979), the only book-length treatment of Wallant's life and literary career, by observing that he was a "minor writer with major talent." Wallant undoubtedly demonstrated a remarkable potential in the short time he wrote fiction seriously. He produced some intriguing, engaging novels that explore contemporary American culture in such a way that they seem prescient in their anticipation of the literature that developed in the decades following his death, most notably in that literature's emphasis on bringing the marginal and the multicultural more into the mainstream and on giving diverse voices a site from

which to speak. Other writers have certainly carried on the legacy that Wallant left incomplete.

Bibliographies:
Nicholas Ayo, "Edward Lewis Wallant, 1926–1962," *Bulletin of Bibliography*, 28, no. 4 (1971): 119;

"Edward Lewis Wallant," in *Jewish American Fiction Writers: An Annotated Bibliography*, by Gloria L. Cronin, Blaine H. Hall, and Connie Lamb (New York & London: Garland, 1991), pp. 1121–1140.

References:
Nicholas Ayo, "The Secular Heart: The Achievement of Edward Lewis Wallant," *Critique*, 12, no. 2 (1970): 86–94;

Jonathan Baumbach, "The Illusion of Indifference," in his *The Landscape of Nightmare: Studies in the Contemporary American Novel* (New York: New York University Press, 1965), pp. 138–151;

Ernest Becker, "*The Pawnbroker*: A Study in Basic Psychology," in his *Angel in Armor: A Post-Freudian Perspective on the Nature of Man* (New York: Braziller, 1969), pp. 73–99;

Nancy A. Benson, "When this World Is Enough: The Vision of Edward Lewis Wallant," *Cross Currents*, 34, no. 3 (1984): 337–342;

Alan L. Berger, "Symbolic Judaism: Edward Lewis Wallant," in *Crisis and Covenant: The Holocaust in American Jewish Fiction*, edited by Sarah Blacher Cohen (Albany: New York State University Press, 1985), pp. 164–172;

Dorothy Seidman Bilik, "Wallant's Reborn Immigrant and Redeemed Survivor," in her *Immigrant Survivors: Post-Holocaust Consciousness in Recent Jewish American Fiction* (Middletown, Conn.: Wesleyan University Press, 1985), pp. 81–100;

William V. Davis, "The Impossible Possibility: Edward Lewis Wallant's *The Tenants of Moonbloom*," *Studies in American Jewish Literature* [Albany], 2 (1982): 98–114;

Davis, "Learning to Walk on Water: Edward Lewis Wallant's *The Pawnbroker*," *Literary Review*, 17, no. 2 (1973–1974): 149–165;

Davis, "The Renewal of Dialogical Immediacy in Edward Lewis Wallant," *Renascence*, 24, no. 2 (1972): 56–69;

Davis, "The Sound of Silence: Edward Lewis Wallant's *The Children at the Gate*," *Cithara*, 8, no. 1 (1968): 3–25;

L. S. Dembo, "The Tenants of Moonbloooo-ooo," in his *The Monological Jew: A Literary Study*

(Madison: University of Wisconsin Press, 1988), pp. 44–53;

David Galloway, *Edward Lewis Wallant* (Boston: Twayne, 1979);

Leo Gurko, "Edward Lewis Wallant as Urban Novelist," *Twentieth Century Literature* 20, no. 4 (1974): 252–261;

Charles Alva Hoyt, "The Sudden Hunger: An Essay on the Novels of Edward Lewis Wallant," in his *Minor American Novelists* (Carbondale: Southern Illinois University Press, 1970), pp. 118–137;

S. Lillian Kremer, "From Buchenwald to Harlem: The Holocaust Universe of *The Pawnbroker*," in her *Witness Through the Imagination: Jewish American Holocaust Literature* (Detroit: Wayne State University Press, 1989), pp. 63–80;

Robert W. Lewis, "The Hung-up Heroes of Edward Lewis Wallant," *Renascence*, 24, no. 2 (1972): 70–84;

Thomas M. Lorch, "The Novels of Edward Lewis Wallant," *Chicago Review*, 19, no. 2 (1967): 78–91;

Sanford E. Marovitz, "A Prophet in the Labyrinth: The Urban Romanticism of Edward Lewis Wallant," *Modern Language Studies*, 15, no. 4 (1985): 172–183;

David R. Mesher, "Con Artist and Middleman: The Archetypes of Wallant's Published and Unpublished Fiction," *Yale University Library Gazette*, 56, nos. 1–2 (1981): 40–49;

Gabriel Miller, "Those Who Walk in Darkness," in his *Screening the Novel: Rediscovered American Fiction in Film* (New York: Ungar, 1980), pp. 167–191;

John G. Parks, "The Grace of Suffering: The Fiction of Edward Lewis Wallant," *Studies in American Jewish Literature* [Albany], 5 (1986): 11–18;

Richard Ruland and Malcolm Bradbury, *From Puritanism to Postmodernism* (New York: Viking, 1991).

Papers:

Wallant's papers and unpublished manuscripts are in the American Literature Collection at the Beinecke Rare Book and Manuscript Library, Yale University.

Eudora Welty

(13 April 1909 –)

Ruth D. Weston
Oral Roberts University

See also the Welty entries in *DLB 2: American Novelists Since World War II, First Series*; *DLB 102: American Short-Story Writers, 1910–1945, Second Series*; and *DLB Yearbook: 1987*.

BOOKS: *A Curtain of Green, and Other Stories* (Garden City, N.Y.: Doubleday, Doran, 1941; London: Lane, 1943);

The Robber Bridegroom (Garden City, N.Y.: Doubleday, Doran, 1942; London: Lane/Bodley Head, 1944);

The Wide Net, and Other Stories (New York: Harcourt, Brace, 1943; London: Lane/Bodley Head, 1945);

Delta Wedding (New York: Harcourt, Brace, 1946; London: Bodley Head, 1947);

Music from Spain (Greenville, Miss.: Levee, 1948);

The Golden Apples (New York: Harcourt, Brace, 1949; London: Bodley Head, 1950);

Short Stories (New York: Harcourt, Brace, 1950);

The Ponder Heart (New York: Harcourt, Brace 1954; London: Hamilton, 1954);

The Bride of the Innisfallen, and Other Stories (New York: Harcourt, Brace, 1955; London: Hamilton, 1955);

The Shoe Bird (New York: Harcourt, Brace & World, 1964);

A Sweet Devouring (New York: Albondocani Press, 1969);

Losing Battles (New York: Random House, 1970; London: Virago, 1982);

One Time, One Place: Mississippi in the Depression; A Snapshot Album (New York: Random House, 1971);

The Optimist's Daughter (New York: Random House, 1972);

A Pageant of Birds (New York: Albondocani Press, 1974);

Fairy Tale of the Natchez Trace (Jackson: Mississippi Historical Society, 1975);

The Eye of the Story: Selected Essays and Reviews (New York: Random House, 1978);

Eudora Welty

Women!! Make Turban in Own Home! (Winston-Salem: Palaemon, 1979);

Acrobats in a Park (Northridge, Cal.: Lord John, 1980);

Bye-bye Brevoort (Jackson, Miss.: New Stage Theatre/ Palaemon, 1980);

Moon Lake and Other Stories (Franklin Center, Pa.: Franklin Library, 1980);

White Fruitcake (New York: Albondocani Press, 1980);

Miracles of Perception (Charlottesville, Va.: The Library, 1980);

Twenty Photographs (Winston-Salem: Palaemon, 1980);

Retreat (Winston-Salem: Palaemon, 1981);

One Writer's Beginnings (Cambridge, Mass.: Harvard University Press, 1984);

Four Photographs by Eudora Welty (Northridge, Cal.: Lord John, 1984);

In Black and White: Photographs of the 30's and 40's (Northridge, Cal.: Lord John, 1985);

The Little Store (Newton, Iowa: Tamazunchale, 1985);

Photographs (Jackson: University Press of Mississippi, 1989).

Editions and Collections: *Thirteen Stories,* selected by Ruth M. Vande Kieft (New York: Harcourt, Brace & World, 1965);

Welty: An Exhibition at the Mississippi State Historical Museum, Jackson, Mississippi. Photographs and Text by Eudora Welty, selected and edited by Patti Carr Black (Jackson: Mississippi Department of Archives and History, 1977);

Ida M'Toy, edited, with a foreword, by Charles Shattuck, George Scouffas, and Daniel Curley (Urbana: University of Illinois, 1979);

The Collected Stories of Eudora Welty (New York: Harcourt Brace Jovanovich, 1980; London: Boyars, 1981);

Eudora, selected and edited by Black (Jackson: Mississippi Department of Archives and History, 1984);

The Complete Works of Eudora Welty, 9 volumes, edited by Isuzu Tanabe (Kyoto, Japan: Rinsen, 1988);

A Writer's Eye: Collected Book Reviews, edited by Pearl Amelia McHaney (Jackson: University Press of Mississippi, 1994).

OTHER: *The Norton Book of Friendship,* edited by Welty and Ronald A. Sharp (New York: Norton, 1991).

Although Eudora Welty has considered herself primarily a short-story writer, and although her earliest critical acclaim resulted from her brilliant experiments with form in that genre, it was not until the publication of her novel *Losing Battles* (1970) that reviewers began to speak of her as a novelist of major rank. *U.S. News & World Report* (15 February 1993) noted that when *The Optimist's Daughter* was published in 1972, Welty's "place in the pantheon [of American letters was] . . . formally ratified."

Among Welty's many awards are the Pulitzer Prize for fiction, for the novel *The Optimist's Daughter*; several O. Henry prizes for short stories; the William Dean Howells Medal, for the novella *The Ponder Heart* (1954); the Gold Medal for Fiction, given by the National Institute of Arts and Letters,

for her entire body of fiction; the Presidential Medal of Freedom; the P.E.N./Malamud Award for excellence in the short story; and the National Endowment for the Humanities Frankel Prize. In 1983 she was named Woman of the Year in Mississippi. In 1987 the French consul general traveled to her hometown, Jackson, Mississippi, to dub her a knight of France – Chevalier de L'Ordre d'Arts et Lettres – one of France's highest civilian awards. "It's not like anything I could have ever imagined," Welty commented on the honor, "to be a knight, or a knightess."

When Welty was awarded the Peggy V. Helmerich Distinguished Author Award (including twenty thousand dollars and an engraved crystal book) by the Tulsa, Oklahoma, Library Trust in 1991, the program for the black-tie dinner presented her as "our national treasure." The event was sold out two weeks in advance to 450 guests at eighty-five dollars a plate, and the following morning Welty spoke to an overflow crowd of more than 750 admirers in the library. In that same year the Eudora Welty Society was organized to promote the study of her work, and she also became the first recipient of the Cleanth Brooks Medal for distinguished achievement in southern letters. Also in 1991 she was honored by the National Book Foundation, whose tribute declared, "For the past five decades she has produced a body of fiction equal to any other writer of our time – and some say preeminent." Those present for her acceptance of the ten-thousand-dollar prize commented on her "modest acceptance speech [compared to] Saul Bellow's boorish one" the previous year, according to *Publishers Weekly* (6 December 1991).

Welty has received Guggenheim, Yaddo, and Bread Loaf fellowships and appointments to both the National Council of the Arts and the National Institute of Arts and Letters. She has been a guest lecturer at Harvard University, Smith College, Bryn Mawr College, Cambridge University, and Millsaps College, the last of which has named an endowed chair for her. Her fiction has been adapted for Broadway, Off-Broadway, and community-theater productions. These works include *The Robber Bridegroom* (1942), *The Ponder Heart,* and *The Shoe Bird* (1964), the last a children's story that became *The Shoe Bird Ballet* (performed by the Jackson Ballet Guild in 1968). *Bye-bye Brevoort* (1980), a sketch Welty wrote for the theater in 1949, was staged Off-Broadway in 1956. Other dramatic presentations include collages of her fiction that are sometimes staged as one-woman shows, as is *Sister and Miss Lexie,* taken chiefly from "Why I Live at the P.O."

(*A Curtain of Green, and Other Stories,* 1941) and *Losing Battles.* The monologue is usually accompanied by two pianos and a ukelele. Another collage is *A Season of Dreams,* which includes excerpts from "A Piece of News" (*A Curtain of Green*), "Lily Daw and the Three Ladies" (*A Curtain of Green*), "The Petrified Man" (*A Curtain of Green*), and "Why I Live at the P.O." Welty's strong interest in and support of the dramatic arts have led to the establishment of the Eudora Welty New Playwrights Series at the New Stage Theater in Jackson. Its March 1985 premiere production was *Private Contentment,* by Reynolds Price.

Welty is also a longtime literary critic, having been a reviewer for the *New York Times* and other publications, both under her own name and, during World War II, the pseudonym Michael Ravenna. A collection of these reviews, *A Writer's Eye: Collected Book Reviews,* was published in 1994. In fact, because of her many essays and lectures on her own and others' creative-writing techniques, she is also recognized as an astute literary theorist. Her most important critical essays are collected in *The Eye of the Story: Selected Essays and Reviews* (1978). Her international stature is often related to the world's extraordinary general interest in the literature of the American South. Her fiction has been translated into all the major languages of the world and a dozen or so others, including Greek, Burmese, Rumanian, Argentinean, and Pakistani. The Modern Language Association Bibliography (CD-ROM) for the years 1981–1992 lists a total of 334 separate items relating to Welty, including 8 in foreign languages; for the years 1988–1992 it lists 82 articles, 24 doctoral dissertations, and 7 books on Welty's works. The *Eudora Welty Newsletter* Checklist of Welty Scholarship for 1988–1989 reported the first Japanese book on Welty. Conferences devoted to Welty were held at the University of Mississippi (1977), Oberlin College (1978), the Gorky Institute, Moscow (1985), the University of Akron (1987) as well as in Jackson, Mississippi (1990) and Dijon, France (1992).

Eudora Alice Welty was born on 13 April 1909 in Jackson, Mississippi, the eldest of three children of Christian Webb Welty, from Hocking County, Ohio, and Chestina Andrews Welty, from the mountains near Clay, West Virginia. Welty was named for her maternal grandmother, Eudora Carden Andrews. Her maternal grandfather, Edward Raboteau (Ned) Andrews, was a cousin of Walter Hines Page – novelist, influential literary critic, advocate of public education and social reform in the New South, and founder of Doubleday, Page and

Welty with her father, Christian Welty

Company, which evolved into Doubleday, Doran, Welty's first publisher.

When Welty's parents married, they decided to settle in a place completely new to them. Christian Welty suggested either the Thousand Islands or Jackson, Mississippi; his bride chose Jackson. Thus her mother's decision determined that Eudora Welty would grow up as a Southerner, although the equally profound influence of her father, whom she distinguishes as "a Yankee and a Republican," may have enhanced her ability to achieve the artistic distance necessary to write about the South. Welty says that her love of reading and her having grown up in a home with books in a region with a vital oral-storytelling tradition, which she "helped [her]self to," were also important factors in her becoming a writer.

Welty attended public schools and read as fast as the Jackson Public Library would let her have books (no more than two a day). She enrolled in the Mississippi State College for Women and after two years transferred to the University of Wisconsin, where she earned a B.A. in English in 1929. At her father's suggestion she then spent a year at the Columbia University School of Business in New York City in order to prepare herself to earn a living while trying to become a writer. When her father died of leukemia in 1931, she returned to Jackson to live with her mother.

During the Depression years Welty held various jobs: with a radio station, as a newspaper correspondent, and as a "junior publicity agent" traveling around the state to gather information for the Mississippi Works Progress Administration (WPA). During this time she began to take the photographs that were, along with her WPA interviews with the people of her state, such a great influence on the stories she was beginning to write. Through taking pictures she said she became aware of "a story-writer's truth: the thing to wait on, to reach there in time for . . . the moment in which people reveal themselves." Some of the pictures have been published, primarily in *One Time, One Place: Mississippi in the Depression; A Snapshot Album* (1971) and *Photographs* (1989); but the great majority remain, as negatives and contact prints, in the Eudora Welty Collection, Mississippi Department of Archives and History, in Jackson.

Though news stories often call her "the first lady of American letters," her visitors and interviewers report that she remains modest, unassuming, and gracious. As her health permits, she is still, as she once remarked, "locally underfoot" in Jackson, living alone in the home where she lived with her parents, across the street from Belhaven College. She has never married. Her ability to write is now impaired by the crippling rheumatoid arthritis that afflicted her two younger brothers, Edward and Walter, both deceased. In spite of that limitation, as well as back problems and some hearing loss, she still enjoys informal talk and storytelling with friends. She travels occasionally, accepting a few invitations to read from her works. The public library in Jackson is now named the Eudora Welty Library, and she loves to tell the tale of someone who called the library, expecting to find her there.

Welty came to maturity as a writer during the prolific years of the great modernists – T. S. Eliot, Virginia Woolf, James Joyce, and William Faulkner – whose literary experiments were not lost on her. Her best works are marked by many of the tenets of modernism, especially myth structure, irony, symbolism, and the privileging of character over action. The entire Welty canon superbly exemplifies Eliot's concept of the artist as a blender of "tradition and the individual talent." Especially modernistic is Welty's virtuosity with language, as evinced by her ability to create – with great economy – subjective mood, realistic visual effects, and a near-musical poetics of prose. Further, because of her perfectly tuned ear and a fine sense of the power of grammar and punctuation to achieve natural speech rhythms, she is able to suggest nuances of character through dialogue without the distortions of dialect, notably in such dramatic monologues as *The Ponder Heart,* "Why I Live at the P.O.," and her magnum opus, *Losing Battles,* which Welty calls "pure talk . . . [without any] introspection."

Much has been written about the influence on Southern letters of the canonical, widely anthologized modernists, especially those known as "Fugitives" from the sentimental literature of nostalgia for the antebellum agricultural South. However, the works of Welty and many other women writers – such as Ellen Glasgow, Zora Neale Hurston, Carson McCullers, Caroline Gordon, Evelyn Scott, and even Katherine Anne Porter – were at first not recognized as important contributions to this twentieth-century literary flowering, as were those, for example, of Faulkner, Robert Penn Warren, John Crowe Ransom, and Allen Tate. Now Welty's position as a leading modernist and distinguished contributor not only to the Southern Renascence of the 1930s but also to the contemporary period is unquestioned.

Like Porter and Faulkner, Welty explores the theme of human vulnerability to the tyranny of time, especially to the influence of the past, often through the interior monologue, a technique appropriate to the depiction of a character's inner struggles with a living memory. Welty's early work has some common ground with McCullers's use of the grotesque, but comparisons between Welty and Flannery O'Connor are apt to be misleading. By the time O'Connor was publishing, in the 1950s and 1960s, Welty had long since abandoned the technique of creating physically deformed characters to suggest spiritual deformity, a technique basic to O'Connor. In spite of O'Connor's overt religious stance and Welty's more secular one, both writers do share a gift for capturing the idiomatic language of the South and an ability to select the exact phrase to define a character. More significant, they both possess a profound respect for the reality of mystery and a recognition that, in O'Connor's words, "art requires a delicate adjustment of the inner and outer worlds in such a way that, without changing their nature, they can be seen through each other."

The academic-canon revisionists of the 1980s and 1990s continue to demonstrate new significance in Welty's themes and narrative strategies. For example, commentators recognize connections between Welty's work and that of other American writers, especially the early "serious romancers," such as Nathaniel Hawthorne, and the Southern women writers who published from the 1920s to the 1940s. Feminist scholars note that, from early on, Welty's fiction has developed as an increasingly sophisticated critique of culture that questions many of the givens in the patriarchal value system that in many ways remains a force in the South. One mark of this cultural critique is her fiction's valorization of intellectual daring and lust for life in women and men alike. As Ruth M. Vande Kieft points out in *The Female Tradition in Southern Literature* (edited by Carol S. Manning, 1993), "Welty's fiction subverts conservative codes and attitudes toward love, including the idea of a woman's destiny to submit to traditional gender role expectations."

In many respects Welty's fiction creates a female aesthetic with a clear relation to that which contemporary feminist critic Elaine Showalter has described in the fiction of Dorothy Richardson, Katherine Mansfield, and Virginia Woolf – one based on a worldview that is "mystically and totally polarized by sex." Similarly, Welty contrasts male and female viewpoints and explores the ramifications of gender-role expectations. Her interest, however, is not so much in matriarchy versus patriarchy as in claims on behalf of individual (male or female) integrity versus those of culture.

The Fugitive group as such had disbanded by the time Welty began to publish her short stories in 1936; however, by her own account she was fortunate in having her work read and accepted by important Fugitive authors, such as Warren, then an editor at the *Southern Review*. She was also aided and encouraged by such major figures as Porter, Cleanth Brooks, Albert Erskine, and Ford Madox Ford. Even so, the then-unknown young writer encountered great difficulty in placing her first collection of short stories. In the publishing climate of the pre–World War II years, publishers were willing to invest in little more than the public's proven preference – mostly historical and romance novels. Welty's mysterious "interior life" short stories, with little plot or action, would have failed to satisfy such an audience and were thus an economic risk most publishers were unwilling to take.

Nevertheless, as Michael Kreyling (*Author and Agent: Eudora Welty and Diarmuid Russell*, 1991) makes clear, through the efforts of Diarmuid Russell, of Russell and Volkening, who offered to act as Welty's literary agent (her "benevolent parasite," as

Welty's mother, Chestina Andrews Welty

he called himself), and of John Woodburn, an editor at Doubleday, Doran who also recognized her merit, *A Curtain of Green* was published in 1941. Porter wrote the introduction, defending Welty's chosen genre, the short story, over the public's preference for novels. Some reviewers wrote reductively of the stories in *A Curtain of Green* as merely Southern Gothic grotesque, and even Porter's comments on the stories' exposés of "vulgarity" now seem superficial. These stories, however, immediately established some of Welty's most important literary theories, which she has explained in *The Eye of the Story*: that place is a vital determinant in a person's life, that human feelings "are bound up in the local," and that all the arts "celebrate . . . [the] mystery" of place, which "has a more lasting identity than we have."

One of Welty's favorite bits of advice, from E. M. Forster, is "Only connect." One of her basic attitudes is that a person must write, "not in self-defense, not in hate . . . not in any kind of militance, or in apology, but with love." It is a comment worthy of two of Welty's declared mentors: Woolf and Chekhov, whom Woolf cites in "Modern Fiction" (*The Common Reader*, 1925) as a model of the great Russian writers whose love and compassion give eternal value to their works. Testimony that Welty's fiction does "connect" in terms of those values comes from a former British officer, Tony Strachan, imprisoned by the Nazis; in 1993 he told Welty that rereading his copy of *A Curtain of Green* comforted him with "images that delighted him and fed his brain," helping him to survive a German prison camp from 1940 to 1945.

The fact that major literary figures helped to launch Welty's career facilitated acceptance of her stories by magazines with far greater circulation and power of remuneration than the small academic reviews that had published her stories in the 1930s. This success, along with the O. Henry Award for "A Worn Path" (*A Curtain of Green*) seemed to validate her choice of genre. In December 1942, however, Russell reminded her that publishers "have been – and will – plague you" for a novel. She had been working on a group of stories set in the Natchez Trace country near the Mississippi River; these culminated in *The Robber Bridegroom* and *The Wide Net, and Other Stories* (1943). Perhaps her decision to extend *The Robber Bridegroom* into a novella instead of including it in a collection of short stories prefigures her eventual development into a novelist. In this longer format Welty was able to explore more fully many of the themes she has written about throughout her career: the individual and the family, the need for both love and separateness, and the mystery and complexity of the human personality.

The Robber Bridegroom, which she has said is "not a *historical* historical novel" but rather an adult fairy tale, is set on the Mississippi River end of the old Natchez Trace, an area that was once the home of the now-extinct Natchez Indian tribe. This tale of pioneer cotton planter Clement Musgrove; his shrewish second wife, Salome; and his beautiful daughter Rosamond combines elements of "The Fisherman and His Wife" by the Brothers Grimm with American tall tales and legends. Welty achieves a middle distance from the romantic nature of this material by treating it with an irony that is humorous, even playful, but never bitter. The idea for the story grew directly out of Welty's work for the WPA and the Mississippi Advertising Commission, for which she had needed to read extensively about the Natchez Trace. She thus encountered the legendary bandits, itinerant preachers,

and other larger-than-life characters whose lives had colored the history of the Trace.

The novella met with virtually no public response at first. When an interviewer said she had missed reading it, Welty responded, "Everybody did; I swear, everybody did." But a wide public came to know it through its adaptation as a folk musical for the stage. Often billed as a "bluegrass musical," it focuses on the romantic drama and broad humor and eliminates much of the actual history and satire of the original. It was a hit on Broadway in 1976 and is still performed by college, little-theater, and touring repertory companies.

The Robber Bridegroom is also informed by the myth of Psyche, the quintessential story of female liberation and of the competing claims of male and female integrity. As in the myth of Psyche, in *The Robber Bridegroom* the heroine is abducted and kept in ignorance of the identity of her lover, who comes to her, as does Eros to Psyche, only at night. And, like Psyche, Welty's Rosamond, with the help of her "evil" stepmother, comes by night with a potion that removes the berry stains from Jamie Lockhart's face to reveal his true identity. After Jamie seduces Rosamond, her refusal to play the dishonored heroine, her insistence upon her right to an equal relationship that brings their love into the light of knowledge, and her chastisement of Jamie for "depriv[ing] a woman of giving her love freely" make the tale a virtual coda for the feminist content of Welty's mature canon. Rosamond is a fairy-tale feminist empowered by the help of a "good-enough mother," to use the term of modern psychoanalytic theorist Nancy Chodorow. Thus Welty introduces the theme of female individuation, self-authority, and daring that comes full circle in *The Optimist's Daughter*, where she creates a robber bride instead of a robber bridegroom.

The Wide Net, and Other Stories was another stepping-stone toward Welty the novelist, for here she explores a modernist technique of narration that she ultimately adapted for the novel. As Kreyling shows in *Author and Agent: Eudora Welty and Diarmuid Russell*, the method combines the modernists' distortion of time and their stream-of-consciousness technique with a feminine, nonlinear narrative logic, demonstrating a decidedly female literary imagination that at first seemed obscure to male readers, including her agent, as her correspondence with him makes clear. But it was understandable to Mary Louise Aswell, Welty's editor at *Harper's Bazaar*, first publisher of "The Winds," which was later included in *The Wide Net*. Aswell not only rec-

Welty in the backyard of her Jackson, Mississippi, home, 1941

ognized the merit of Welty's narrative method but, by encouraging Welty to articulate her technique, may have nurtured the development of Welty as a literary theorist.

Welty's experimental technique is revealed in "The Winds" through a complex narrative structure, one aspect of which is based on the contrasting attitudes of the males, father and son, who plot strategy against the storm, and the females, mother and daughter, who secretly seem to welcome and internalize any change as an interesting and somehow inevitable piece of news from the outside world. Once this thematic structure is recognized, the relevance of other details, such as the significance of names, becomes clear: the single syllable of Will's identifies the willful and emphatic male opposition to change, while the feminine ending on the trochee of Josie's, a more subtle and thus more appropriate technique than overt symbolism, suggests female ambivalence and flexibility.

A strong relation exists between this story and "A Piece of News" (*A Curtain of Green*), the novel

Delta Wedding (1946), and the title story of *The Wide Net*. In the last the mysterious inwardness of the pregnant Hazel is contrasted with the reactions of her husband, who organizes a community dragging of the river when he finds her suicide note. Far from committing suicide, however, Hazel has been watching with secret delight as he reads of her imaginary adventure. As for William Wallace and the men he recruits to search with the wide net for his wife's body, their odyssey into the watery underworld takes on the significance of a mythic quest, exciting their imaginations, too. The comic story concludes, as does "A Piece of News," with the young couple newly appreciative of each other's inherent and inviolable mystery.

The cyclic nature of life in the world is part of this mystery. William and Hazel's dual journeys into fantasy constitute a cyclic narrative superstructure that overlays and complements the contrasting male and female attitudes. In the stories of *The Wide Net* characters make circular journeys, essentially deep into themselves, toward knowledge and understanding, which they take back into a world that no longer seems mundane. In "The Wide Net" Hazel has been at home all along; she simply needed to awaken her husband to the wonder of the new life she was carrying, a mysterious "piece of news" that he had taken for granted.

Images of circles, spirals, and other dynamic designs suggesting psychic journeys inward toward, and outward away from, the still center of the self are nowhere more pervasive than in *Delta Wedding*. Welty's first full-length novel grew out of her close relationship with John Fraiser Robinson, whose family she visited while Robinson served overseas during World War II. After reading the journals of one of Robinson's female ancestors, an early settler in the Mississippi Delta, Welty wrote "The Delta Cousins" (unpublished). Her agent, Welty relates, recognized immediately that the story was the basis for a novel. *Delta Wedding* was first serialized in the *Atlantic* from January through April 1946 and was published in book form later that year.

Although reviewer Diana Trilling (*Nation*, 11 May 1946) charged *Delta Wedding* with sentimentalism over a South that was disappearing, the book is actually a harbinger of one of Welty's signature themes: the delicate balance between the past and the present moment, which at crisis points in her characters' lives becomes the still moment of vision. The novel also explores the equally delicate balance between culture – manifested as family or community, representing the tie that binds – and the individual who will not be bound by its codified expectations. Welty is interested in showing the joys and frustrations brought about by the human need to love and yet to protect the separateness that is necessary to one's psychic growth and intellectual integrity. This major Weltian theme of "love and separateness" was first identified in a 1944 essay by Warren. In much of Welty's fiction, including all her novels, this theme is worked out through relationships in families. In fact, Welty has said that in an early story, "Acrobats in a Park," unpublished until 1980, she found the subject of her fiction: the family.

Delta Wedding includes both a robber bride and a robber bridegroom as well as their counterparts, the captive and captivated loved ones. The lower-class Troy Flavin captures plantation aristocrat Dabney Fairchild just as the aptly named Robbie Reed has caught George Fairchild, the family's designated upholder of family honor and tradition. The novel continuously juxtaposes closely related opposites: death and life, past and present, insiders and outsiders. It begins and ends with the story of nine-year-old orphan Laura McRaven, who has come to visit her recently deceased mother's large family in Shellmound, Mississippi. Like Robbie Reed and Ellen Fairchild, Laura recognizes that the "shelly" veneer of the family at Shellmound is physically fluid yet emotionally impossible to penetrate.

Ellen, the present matriarch of the clan, is loosely modeled on Welty's own mother, a West Virginian who was just such an outsider in Jackson, Mississippi. In the novel such outsiders are lost in a wilderness of family, which closes smoothly around them without admitting their sometimes desperate individual needs. The novel depicts an intricate interlacing of family and of certain incorrigible free spirits who break into and out of its self-perpetuating but vulnerable shell. Welty's domesticated metaphor of the wilderness is central to the narrative shape of *Delta Wedding*, in which Laura completes a circular, initiatory journey through the dangerous forest of Fairchilds.

Delta Wedding is notable not only for its themes but also for its lyrical language, which creates a dreamlike counterpart to the realistic surface narrative with its specific Mississippi Delta setting. Welty's ability to infuse her novel with a richly allusive and mythic atmosphere has an older heritage than modernist symbolism. Her fluency in such techniques constitutes a major link between her work and that of Hawthorne, who explained his fiction as a moonlight-induced transformation of the familiar into what is a dramatic locus. He called it a "neutral territory, somewhere between the real world and fairy-land, where the Actual and the Imaginary may meet." In 1986, in celebration of its sixtieth anniversary, the Book-of-the-Month Club placed *Delta Wedding* on its list of sixty American novels in "the well-stocked bookcase."

The theme of the confining family wilderness in *Delta Wedding* is extended to that of the inhibiting, incarcerating society in *The Golden Apples* (1949), considered by many to be Welty's best collection. *The Golden Apples* is sometimes called a story cycle, sometimes a novel, since all its stories involve a basic cast of characters who either reside in or have ties with the fictional community of Morgana, Mississippi. The town, which in some stories is represented as an entity by a first-person-plural narrator, tries to hold its inhabitants to some unspoken standard of behavior.

Realizing that the thematically related "Music from Spain," "Golden Apples" (now called "June Recital"), and "Moon Lake" were longer than most short stories, Welty thought of these three as a book. More than any of her other works, these sto-

John Woodburn, Welty's editor; Welty; Ken McCormick, chief associate editor at Doubleday; Eugene Armfield of Publishers
Weekly; *Robert Simon, president of Carnegie Hall; Diarmuid Russell, Welty's agent; and agent Henry Volkening at
Doubleday's party to celebrate the publication of* A Curtain of Green, and Other Stories *(1941)*

ries grew out of Welty's love of Greek myths and
her admiration for William Butler Yeats, the Irish
poet who was himself a modern mythmaker. *The
Golden Apples* takes its title from Yeats's lines in
"The Song of Wandering Aengus" (*The Wind Among
the Reeds,* 1899), "The silver apples of the moon, /
The golden apples of the sun," which define the extent of the romantic search by a mythic hero for a
silver trout that, once caught, magically transforms
itself into an elusive, wandering, "glimmering girl."

Each of the seven stories in *The Golden Apples* focuses on at least one "wanderer." "Shower of
Gold" introduces the Zeus-like King MacLain, who
has spent his life wandering in and out of Morgana.
Both his sexual exploits and his absences are legendary in the town. His infrequent and mysterious
visits only add to his stature as a "demigod," and,
like a god, he appears in various guises. The title of
this opening story alludes to the myth in which
Zeus impregnates Danaë by coming to her as a
shower of gold in her lap. On one of King
MacLain's visits to his weak-eyed albino wife,
Snowdie, she has become pregnant with their twin
boys. When she tells Katie Rainey about it, she
looks, like Danaë, as if "a shower of something had

struck her, like she'd been caught out in something
bright."

MacLain is always represented as willful and
as physically dazzling and disorienting to those who
catch a glimpse of him. In another story, "Sir Rabbit," a title that suggests his many offspring, King
looks "like the preternatural month of June" as he
appears in the woods to Mattie Will. He is always
described in swanlike colors of white and golden
yellow, and here he wears a white linen suit and a
yellow hat. In "Sir Rabbit" King is the Zeus of
Yeats's "Leda and the Swan." He rapes Mattie, an
act that "put on her, with the affront of his body,
the affront of his sense too . . . [after which] he let
her fall and walked off . . . [while a] dove feather
came turning down through the light that was like
golden smoke."

King MacLain is perhaps Welty's archwanderer,
but there are many more throughout her fiction,
some characterized as demigods or other preternatural beings who refuse to be bound by the world's
terms. In "June Recital" the artist figure is combined
with that of the wanderer, both in Miss Eckhart, the
piano teacher, and in her pupil Virgie Rainey. Both
are outsiders in Morgana, and their tragic stories

are played out against the comedy of the town's willful astonishment at the audacity of these musicians, whose lives conform only to their personal rhythms.

"Music from Spain" is set in San Francisco, the site of Welty's five-month visit to be near her writer friend Robinson after World War II. It is the story of Eugene MacLain, one of King and Snowdie's twins, whose marriage has failed, perhaps because of the lack of a sustained relationship with his perennially absent father. His brother, Randall, whose similar despair is the subject of "The Whole World Knows," is now the mayor of Morgana but none the happier for it. He has married Jennie Love Stark, the child from "Moon Lake" who had admired the willful daring of the orphan Easter but was too conventional to emulate her. "The Wanderers" concludes the volume; a now middle-aged Virgie has had her fling in "wicked Memphis" but has come home to care for her mother. The story recounts Katie Rainey's wake, during which the town passes judgment on Virgie. After the funeral Virgie is at the edge of town, about to resume her wanderings.

Because the story lines of all the characters in *The Golden Apples* are brought together in the final story, set almost two generations later than the first, the cycle of episodes has a decidedly novelistic feel. A further connection of *The Golden Apples* with Welty's novels is that in both forms she shifts between what she calls "inside" and "outside" narrative techniques. "Sir Rabbit" is a third-person narrative told through the viewpoint of Mattie Will. The circular structure begins and ends with the objective description of Mattie's sexual frolic in Morgan's Woods with Eugene and Ran, the teenage twin sons of King MacLain. What seems to be a déjà vu experience for Mattie shifts her thoughts a generation back to her similar experience with their father. The "inside" (subjective) narrative here is richly suggestive; its ambiguity has even caused critics to disagree as to whether Mattie's ravishment actually happened or is imagined, perhaps her wishful thinking about being chosen for the "favors" of the legendary King. The lead story, "Shower of Gold," on the other hand, which is told by the garrulous Katie Rainey, the self-proclaimed spokeswoman of Morgana, maintains the "outside" (objective) technique. *The Golden Apples,* then, although composed of brilliant individual pieces, might also be seen as a cyclic experimental prelude to Welty's true novels, in which dramatic and interior monologues alternate.

The Ponder Heart is a short novel that was adapted for the stage in 1956 for what Welty calls a "modest Broadway run," starring David Wayne. Welty prefers another adaptation of the novella, one created for the New Stage Theater in Jackson in 1956, because it is truer to her original in its preservation of the viewpoint of the novella's narrator. The book is a brilliant example of "talk," a pastime that Welty and Southerners in general have always enjoyed. "Let's just talk," Edna Earle Ponder says to a captive audience at the Beulah Hotel, an establishment that she does not mind admitting has seen better days: "*You're* only here because your car broke down," she tells her silent guest, variously seen as a traveling salesman and a woman Edna Earle is setting up to be her Uncle Daniel's next wife. The narrative, through its perfectly cadenced Southern idiom, reveals personalities that are representative of a place and a time yet are distinctly individual.

The title of *The Ponder Heart* puns broadly on the trials and frailties of the human heart. Its most obvious reference is to the great heart of Uncle Daniel Ponder, whose weakness is his largess. He enjoys giving away anything and everything he owns: "a string of hams, a fine suit of clothes, a white-face heifer calf, two trips to Memphis, pair of fantail pigeons, fine Shetland pony (loves children), brooder and incubator, good nanny goat, bad billy." The title also suggests the weak heart of Bonnie Dee Peacock Ponder, the young second wife whom Uncle Daniel keeps a virtual prisoner of love, buying her whatever he thinks she might want.

Bonnie Dee runs away to Memphis whenever she can, but she comes back once too often. Trying to take her mind off a thunderstorm that frightens her, Daniel literally tickles her to death. The second half of the novella is the account of his trial for murder in a courtroom packed with cheerfully unruly partisans, before a judge who interrupts a witness to count the raised hands of those who mean to take their dinner at Edna Earle's hotel. Yet another allusion in the title is to Edna Earle, whose heart is not free to call her own or to bestow on a lover because of her status as the self-appointed caretaker of her uncle and as the mistress of the only boarding hotel in Clay, Mississippi.

Early reviewers of *The Ponder Heart* saw little but the tour de force of language and the slapstick comedy. V. S. Pritchett (*New York Times Book Review,* 10 January 1954) called it "a sardonic comic brio," describing Edna Earle as "a respectable young scold with a long tradition in English sentimental comedy . . . in the world of feminine tongue rattling" deriving from similar characters in the

Dust jacket for Welty's 1954 novella, which V. S. Pritchett called "a sardonic comic brio"

works of Sir Walter Scott, Robert Louis Stevenson, and Mansfield. Later critics have taken the story a bit more seriously, seeing the narrator as both victim and victor in family and city politics. Not until the emphasis on women's literature in the 1980s and 1990s, however, have readers thought to listen more carefully – in the text's strategic silences between her talk of others – for hints of Edna Earle's own story. Indeed, like Daniel Ponder, many readers "wouldn't dream [she] had one."

Contemporary research into Welty's American matrilineal literary heritage reveals that Edna Earle has the same unusual name as the heroine of Augusta Jane Evans Wilson's novel *St. Elmo* (1866), suggesting also that the Beulah Hotel's name may derive from Evans Wilson's novel *Beulah* (1859). Further, the two Edna Earles may share a similar sexual anxiety. Although Welty's novel is a thoroughly delightful farce, it has its shadow side, as does all good comedy. Thus *The Ponder Heart* is not a comic aberration in Welty's canon but rather a coherent part of her fictional exploration of nurturing/ confining families, of contrasting male and female views of life, of captive and captivating loves, and certainly of the Southern love of life and storytelling.

The Bride of the Innisfallen, and Other Stories (1955) provoked the strongest critical outcry of obscurantism. Orville Prescott (*New York Times,* 8 April 1955) saw it as a denial of Welty's best gifts (presumably that of the comic grotesque) for something "wanly Bowenesque" in "No Place for You, My Love" and "Ladies in Spring" and for something "gruesomely Faulknerian" in "The Burning." The tag "wanly Bowenesque" surely damns with faint praise an artistic relation to Elizabeth Bowen, with whom Welty maintained a treasured friendship until Bowen's death. In fact, "The Bride of the Innisfallen" was partly written while Welty was visiting the Anglo-Irish writer at Bowen's home in county Cork. Some of the description of "No Place for You, My Love" bears a close resemblance to an account Welty wrote to Bowen of a visit to Venice, Louisiana.

The many handbooks and literary dictionaries that persist in labeling Welty as a writer of the Southern Gothic grotesque short story may do so because of such critics as John Davenport (London *Observer,* 16 October 1955), who rejoiced at Welty's return to the short-story genre in *The Bride of the Innisfallen* but could not forgive her straying from "the

Southern Gothic." Welty is not a Gothic writer, though she employs some conventions of the Gothic tradition as narrative techniques in support of themes of women's enclosure in, and escape from, cultural stereotypes. Davenport, who was admittedly "churlish," conceded, "Even when she is at her least good . . . Miss Welty's eye and ear and her fastidiously disciplined prose put her . . . above most practitioners in her chosen field, whether in [England] or in her native America."

Ironically, in the same article, Davenport praised Walter de la Mare for qualities Davenport failed to *observe* (pun on the name of his newspaper intended) in Welty's work – namely, what he called de la Mare's ability to create "dreams on the borderline" of life and an authorial innocence that is not naive. Davenport gave low marks to Welty's "Circe," for example, which more perceptive reviewers recognize as concerned with the great mystery of human life and the equally great difficulty of communicating human feelings.

"Circe" is a retelling, from Circe's point of view, of Homer's episode of the same name in the *Odyssey*. The story powerfully validates Welty's concept of the unknowable core of the human personality, seen in Circe's regret that she cannot fathom the human Odysseus, even with all her powers. In fact, "Circe" is central to *The Bride of the Innisfallen,* which in turn provides a key to the entire Welty canon through its series of female wanderers, who have much in common with wanderers in her novels. Some, such as the bride in the title story and Gabriella in "Going to Naples," go on actual journeys, but all are on psychic searches similar to that of Circe, who in Homer's tale is merely an interlude for a male wanderer. Welty, along with other contemporary writers, reimagines narrative theory with stories in which women are not merely objects of questers such as Aengus, or waiting women, like Homer's Penelope, but rather heroic questers in their own right – many, like Shelly in *Delta Wedding* and Virgie in *The Golden Apples,* for the sheer joy they suspect is out there in the world. In the fiercely independent characters of *The Golden Apples,* Welty perfected the technique she was to use in her novel-length portraits of heroic loners: the besieged but optimistic female protagonists in *Losing Battles* and *The Optimist's Daughter.*

During the years after World War II, Welty herself was something of a wanderer, with extended visits not only on both coasts of the United States but also to England and Ireland, during which time she continued to write and take pictures. As her visit to San Francisco provides the setting for "Music from Spain," so her shipboard travels led to those of "Going to Naples" and "The Bride of the Innisfallen." After this period of travel, writing, and publishing, however, came a fifteen-year interlude when Welty was overwhelmed with family responsibilities, caring for her mother through a series of serious illnesses and often helping out with her brother Walter's children as his arthritic condition worsened. He died in 1959, and in 1966, four days apart, so did her mother and her brother Edward.

A further problem was the civil unrest of the 1960s. It affected the entire country, and the sensitive writer in Jackson, Mississippi, who both loved her region and hated its racial intolerance, felt it acutely. Welty did her writing in brief moments snatched from the trying circumstances; nothing was finalized, but finally, Welty says, she had "a suitcase full of earlier drafts" of what would become her longest novel. Indeed, the episodic nature of *Losing Battles* may in part result from the episodic nature of its composition. "I worked in scenes," she recalls, a comment also telling for its relevance to the dramatic, objective quality of that novel. Welty intended its title to suggest "all the battles which we always seem to be losing – battles against everything: poverty, disgrace, misunderstanding, and also funny battles, I hope; trying to make a go of it, trying to survive. And old age. And the teacher's battle against ignorance . . . all of our daily battles."

Losing Battles is important for these universal themes but also for its technical virtuosity, for the intertextuality that relies on traditions of all the genres Welty has always enjoyed: the classic romantic and Gothic tales of heroes and villains as well as fairy tales, Bible stories, myths, legends, and ghost stories. In developing her canonwide themes of human limitations versus possibilities and of safe enclosures versus perilous freedoms, Welty utilizes some significant narrative devices from sources as different as the heroic epic and the female Gothic. She creates (especially female) characters who suffer various physical and psychological constraints, and she depicts them through narrative codes and conventions of image, structure, and character that both she and her readers recognize from lifetimes of wide reading. For Welty knows that genres and literary conventions themselves constitute convenient "shorthand" codes for depiction of cultural behavior: one recognizes the actions of a Sleeping Beauty character, a questing hero, or an evil stepmother, even when an author revises expectations about them for a new purpose; and one expects certain actions to happen in certain kinds of settings.

Dust jacket for Welty's longest novel, the title of which, she says, suggests "all the battles which we always seem to be losing — battles against everything: poverty, disgrace, misunderstanding, and also funny battles, I hope"

In *Losing Battles* the professional woman, pariah of both patriarchy and matriarchy, opts for the authoritative but lonely existence of schoolteacher instead of the cultural confinement of marriage. Welty realistically portrays the situation of teachers in the first few decades of the twentieth century, when female educators were not allowed to marry. Julia Mortimer – the recently deceased, heroic teacher whose wake becomes the Renfro-Beecham family reunion in *Losing Battles* – is modeled closely after Welty's teacher Miss Duling, who was considered "almost supernatural . . . [and] all powerful." Julia, like Welty's later protagonist in *The Optimist's Daughter,* is the hero-victim of romantic self-imprisonment, a Byronic isolate who strives and suffers apart from community; and her isolation deprives her of fully balanced humanity in the eyes of the community and perhaps in fact. Further, her scientific insistence on having "everything brought out in the wide open, to see and be known" recalls the intellectual pride of a Faust or a Hawthornian amoral scientist, while it conflicts with the family's human reluctance to face some painful truths. Julia Mortimer, at great personal cost, eschews the intimacy of family in favor of some self-ordained model of integrity, which the community acknowledges in reluctant tributes to her intelligence, courage, generosity, and inspiration, though she "never did learn how to please."

Miss Julia is contrasted in the novel with its ostensible hero, Jack Renfro, the quixotic young adventurer who is Welty's stated reason for extending into her longest novel what began, like *Delta Wedding,* as a short story. Jack is obviously cut from the demigod pattern she uses in earlier works. Yet, though his family accords him heroic status, and though he enters the tale as a weary knight with a "torn sleeve that flowed free from his shoulder like some old flag carried home from far-off battle," his "mythic" ring quest has led only to the mundane test he endured in Parchman Prison, and his only "heroic" escape was an easy ride out of the penitentiary fields on a mule. Thus Jack is only a mock hero; as long-awaited savior for this Depression-poor, hill-country family's drought-ruined fields, he is "ever out of sight when most needed."

Torn between Miss Julia, who wanted her to be a teacher, and her young, family-bound husband is Gloria Short, who has given birth to their baby girl while Jack was in prison. One of Miss Julia's losing battles has apparently been with Gloria, who, "struck down by tender feelings," chose to give up a teacher's life for marriage and motherhood. But the teacher's battle has not been totally lost on Gloria, one of Welty's forward-thinking young women who refuse to be bound by family or custom. As the women of Jack's "mighty family" initiate her with watermelon, the red pulp is viciously "shoved down into her face . . . swarming with seeds, warm with rain-thin juice . . . as hands robbed of sex spread her jaws open." But Gloria is not in the least subdued because Miss Julia's words encouraging her independence are apparently inscribed "in letters of fire on her brain." In general, however, the family continues to smother her with attention in a manner that recalls Welty's description of her Grandmother Carden's "over-familiar" pigeons, who fed each other by placing their entire heads in one another's mouths. This act, which caused "agitation and apprehension" in the young Welty, appears consistently in the fiction as a trope for the repressive nature of love.

Through multiple points of view the discursive narrative of *Losing Battles* reveals Julia Mortimer's profound influence in the lives of many who have gathered to celebrate Granny's birthday. Throughout the two days of the novel's time frame, frenetic comic chases and rescues alternate with a veritable battle of storytellers. Another battle occurs between those, like Jack, who are content to rest in the traditional bosom of family and others who are, as Joyce Carol Oates says of Gloria, "desperate in this web of love."

Both *Losing Battles* and *The Optimist's Daughter* involve family rituals and incorporate ghostly settings. In both, the stories of several complex lives are spun out, weblike, from the still center of a corpse; and in both, female protagonists are measured against the community. *The Optimist's Daughter* is the story of Laurel McKelva Hand, a young widow who, having lived in Chicago since her husband's death, returns to the South for her father's last illness, death, and funeral. Obvious parallels with *Losing Battles* are the oral storytelling tradition, which characterizes the wake of Judge Clinton McKelva, and the female protagonist who struggles to free herself from the past and its traditions. Like Julia Mortimer, Laurel is self-imprisoned. She lives in the memory of her brief but idyllic marriage before her husband was killed in World War II. She is horrified at her widowed father's recent marriage to Wanda Fay Chisom, a vulgar, self-serving young woman – a robber bride who has stolen away the fair-haired son of Mount Salus, Mississippi, and whose very presence Laurel cannot forgive. Upset because the dignity of the wake in the McKelva parlor is profaned by the "common" extravagances of the

young widow's grief, Laurel spends a wakeful night after the funeral in the attic of her childhood home, where the desk and papers of her long-dead mother have been exiled. There she comes to realize the unfair comparison she has made between her short marriage and that of her parents, finally understanding that tragic betrayals can happen even in a good marriage when it is burdened with long years of trials, such as her mother's last years of blindness and near madness.

Welty's narrative virtuosity in *The Optimist's Daughter* provides continuing evidence of her modernist experimentation with the interior monologue and other narrative techniques, including character role reversals and split protagonists. As Kreyling shows in *Eudora Welty's Achievement of Order* (1980), Welty's technique in this novel owes much to Woolf. Welty is concerned primarily with the inner life; that is, with the mind itself, which, in Woolf's words, "receives a myriad impressions – trivial, fantastic, evanescent, or engraved with the sharpness of steel." Like Woolf, Welty is interested in the relation of the inner self to its store of memories as well as to the outer world, including the difficulty of relationships between people.

In *Losing Battles* Welty makes Jack a nurturing father and Gloria an aggressive, independent mother; and in *The Optimist's Daughter,* too, character role reversals are important to the novel's structure. Wanda Fay Chisom McKelva is a life-force character, a role Welty had earlier assigned only to male demigods, such as King MacLain in *The Golden Apples.* Fay is an "evil stepmother" like Salome in *The Robber Bridegroom,* but she is also an urban wanderer like Eugene MacLain in "Music from Spain," the brides of *The Bride of the Innisfallen,* and, indeed, Welty's other failed brides and bridegrooms. She is also a fay (a fairy) who wields various "wands" in the novel with varying degrees of success, including a cigarette, with which she gives the dying judge one of his last sensuous experiences, and a wooden breadboard, a family heirloom that Laurel contests her right to keep.

Ironically, it is the genteel Laurel who, provoked to an uncharacteristic anger, seizes the breadboard and comes close to striking Wanda Fay with it. Laurel's husband had made it and her mother had used it, but in Laurel's hand it is neither an artifact lovingly carved nor an instrument of nurture; it is a weapon. With the board raised above the other young widow's head, Laurel stops in horror when she perceives a mirror image of herself in Wanda Fay. Laurel realizes that she has been as self-centered as her "wicked" stepmother, even to "making a scene" like the actual tantrums Wanda Fay has staged in the hospital and in "black satin . . . running" through the mourners in the McKelva parlor to pounce on the judge's body in his coffin. This identification of opposites connects the novel with analogous Perseus-Medusa images throughout the Welty canon, especially in *The Golden Apples.*

As in *The Robber Bridegroom,* so in *The Optimist's Daughter* an "evil stepmother" acts as a catalyst for a heroine to gain the knowledge she needs for personal integrity and full humanity. Conflating several fairy-tale characters into one and inverting gender roles, Welty also makes Wanda Fay the unlikely hero who awakens the Sleeping Beauty character Laurel has been. Wanda Fay has failed to make Judge McKelva live, but she succeeds in rousing Laurel from her glass coffin of the past to a liberating knowledge of both her common humanity with the likes of Wanda Fay and her true superiority through the power of her artist's imagination, freed now that she has relinquished the symbolic breadboard, the final tie to false ideals and imprisoning memories.

In *The Optimist's Daughter* Welty demonstrates a distinctly feminine and feminist perspective that valorizes female wholeness, and she concludes the novel by giving both Wanda Fay and Laurel new options for life. As with Gloria in *Losing Battles,* she stops short of combining the professional and the sensual woman into a truly whole female hero; yet she shows in both novels that culture has prescribed roles for women that often grotesquely limit or distort their human nature. Like many other Welty protagonists, Laurel is able to walk away from stultifying security, reversing the spin that has held her in an orbit of cultural sameness and "desperate in this web of love."

Welty spent two years reading and selecting brief works for inclusion in *The Norton Book of Friendship* (1991), which she coedited with Ronald A. Sharp. To date the nearest thing to a biography of Welty is *Author and Agent,* Kreyling's account of her publishing history as seen through the long, close working relationship between her and Russell until his death. In her autobiography, *One Writer's Beginnings* (1984), Welty is at her finest both as storyteller and literary theorist. In a little more than one hundred pages it provides a remarkably rich picture of her life, while it reveals the autobiographical nature of her fiction, notably *The Optimist's Daughter. One Writer's Beginnings* is also a text so clearly focused on how the experiences of her life worked together to make her a writer that it is easily adaptable as a writing textbook.

Autographed title page for Welty's 1970 novel (collection of David Marshall James)

Based on the Massey Lectures in the History of American Civilization that Welty delivered at Harvard University in 1983, *One Writer's Beginnings* is divided into three sections: "Listening," "Learning to See," and "Finding a Voice." It features pictures of her home and family, including one of her mother and "a mission-style oak grandfather clock standing in the hall, which . . . [made Welty] time-minded" and thus mindful of narrative chronology and which "was one of a good many things I learned almost without knowing it; it would be there when I needed it." The importance of time in Welty's fiction and her experimentation with Bergsonian distortions of time constitute another significant link with the works of Woolf, Faulkner, and other major modernists. "The events in our lives happen in a sequence in time," she explains, "but in their significance to ourselves they find their own order, a timetable not necessarily — perhaps not possibly — chronological. The time as we know it subjectively is often the chronology that stories and novels follow: it is the continuous thread of revelation."

One Writer's Beginnings spent forty-six weeks on the New York Times best-seller list – the only best-seller in the history of Harvard University Press. This slim volume so charmed the general reading public that it not only increased the popular appeal of her novel The Optimist's Daughter, to which it bears a close relation, but also renewed public interest in her other works. All of Welty's major works remain in print; according to Publishers Weekly just under a million copies of her works were in print in 1991. First editions are now collector's items. One major collector is Welty bibliographer William U. McDonald, Jr., whose extensive private collection was exhibited in two separate showings at the University of Toledo: short-fiction texts in 1983 and longer fiction and nonfiction texts in 1987–1988. The Eudora Welty Newsletter, edited by McDonald and devoted to bibliographic scholarship and general news about Welty and her works, is published twice a year.

In 1987 Pennyroyal Press published a limited edition of 150 copies of The Robber Bridegroom, illustrated with twenty-three wood engravings by Barry Moser, each copy signed by Welty and Moser; it sold for five hundred dollars a copy. At the same time, Harcourt Brace Jovanovich brought out a trade issue with ten Moser illustrations. In 1988 the University Press of Mississippi reprinted an illustrated edition of the Morgana stories, for which the demand was so great that a second printing was ordered two months after publication. In 1989 Photographs, including pictures chosen from some sixteen hundred Welty took from the 1930s to the 1950s, was published in fifty-two leather-bound and more than four hundred other signed copies, all of which were sold out before publication. A fifty-dollar coffee-table trade edition went through a first printing of sixty-five hundred and a second of fifteen thousand three months later. In 1991 Harcourt Brace Jovanovich brought out a fiftieth-anniversary edition of A Curtain of Green as well as eight other Welty books repackaged as Harvest paperbacks, all with wood-engraving cover illustrations by Moser, each based on one of Welty's own photographs.

Welty's stories have been anthologized in college texts for many years now, and these anthologies are where young readers are often introduced to her fiction. By this means – and through her ability to communicate to both a popular and academic audience through several media, including television – Welty has gained a well-deserved worldwide audience for her fiction. Her works have clearly influenced many younger writers, such as Anne Tyler, Lee Smith, Reynolds Price, and Ellen Gilchrist. In 1994 many would say that Welty is the most important living author in the United States.

Interviews:

Bill Ferris, *Images of the South: Visits With Eudora Welty and Walker Evans* (Memphis, Tenn.: Center for Southern Folklore, 1977);

Conversations with Eudora Welty, edited by Peggy Whitman Prenshaw (Jackson: University Press of Mississippi, 1984).

Bibliographies:

Noel Polk, "A Eudora Welty Checklist," *Mississippi Quarterly,* 26 (Fall 1973): 663–693;

Victor H. Thompson, *Eudora Welty: A Reference Guide* (Boston: G. K. Hall, 1976);

Alain Blayac, "The Eudora Welty Collection at the Humanities Research Center, The University of Texas at Austin," *Delta,* 5 (November 1977): 83–88;

Peggy Whitman Prenshaw, "Eudora Welty," in *American Women Writers: Bibliographical Essays,* edited by Maurice Duke, Jackson R. Bryer, and M. Thomas Inge (Westport, Conn.: Greenwood Press, 1983), pp. 233–267;

Bethany C. Swearingen, *Eudora Welty: A Critical Bibliography, 1936–1958* (Jackson: University Press of Mississippi, 1984);

Suzanne Marrs, *The Welty Collection: A Guide to the Eudora Welty Manuscripts and Documents at the Mississippi Department of Archives and History* (Jackson: University Press of Mississippi, 1988);

Noel Polk, *Eudora Welty: A Bibliography of Her Work* (Jackson: University Press of Mississippi, 1993).

References:

Alfred Appel, Jr., *A Season of Dreams: The Fiction of Eudora Welty* (Baton Rouge: Louisiana State University Press, 1965);

Marilyn Arnold, " 'The Magical Percussion': Eudora Welty's Human Recital on Art and Time," *Southern Humanities Review,* 23 (Spring 1989): 101–118;

Harold Bloom, ed., *Modern Critical Views: Eudora Welty* (New York: Chelsea House, 1986);

Will Brantley, *Feminine Sense in Southern Memoir: Smith, Glasgow, Welty, Hellman, Porter, and Hurston* (Jackson: University Press of Mississippi, 1993);

Robert H. Brinkmeyer, Jr., "An Openness to Others: The Imaginative Vision of Eudora

Welty," *Southern Literary Journal*, 20 (Spring 1988): 69–80;

Mary Hughes Brookhart, "Do You Know This Author?: Eudora Welty According to the Handbooks and Histories," *Eudora Welty Newsletter*, 16 (Winter 1992): 6–11;

J. A. Bryant, Jr., *Eudora Welty* (Minneapolis: University of Minnesota Press, 1968);

Barbara Harrell Carson, *Eudora Welty: Two Pictures at Once in Her Frame* (Troy, N.Y.: Whitson, 1992);

John F. Desmond, ed., *A Still Moment: Essays on the Art of Eudora Welty* (Metuchen, N.J.: Scarecrow Press, 1979);

Albert Devlin, *Eudora Welty's Chronicle: A Story of Mississippi Life* (Jackson: University Press of Mississippi, 1983);

Devlin, ed., *Mississippi Quarterly*, special Welty issue, 39 (Fall 1986);

Louis Dollarhide and Ann J. Abadie, eds., *Eudora Welty: A Form of Thanks* (Jackson: University Press of Mississippi, 1979);

Elizabeth Evans, *Eudora Welty* (New York: Ungar, 1981);

Mary Ann Ferguson, "The Female Novel of Development and the Myth of Psyche," *Denver Quarterly*, 17 (Winter 1983): 58–74;

Franziska Gygax, *Serious Daring from Within: Narrative Strategies in Eudora Welty's Novels* (New York: Greenwood Press, 1990);

Nancy D. Hargrove, "Humor in Eudora Welty's *The Shoe Bird*," *Children's Literature in Education*, 23 (June 1992): 75–82;

Alun R. Jones, "The World of Love: The Fiction of Eudora Welty," in *The Creative Present: Notes on Contemporary American Fiction*, edited by Nona Balakian and Charles Simmons (Garden City, N.Y.: Doubleday, 1963), pp. 175–192;

Michael Kreyling, *Author and Agent: Eudora Welty and Diarmuid Russell* (New York: Farrar, Straus & Giroux, 1991);

Kreyling, *Eudora Welty's Achievement of Order* (Baton Rouge: Louisiana State University Press, 1980);

Lucinda H. MacKethan, "Prodigal Daughters: The Journeys of Ellen Glasgow, Zora Neale Hurston and Eudora Welty," in *Daughters of Time: Creating Woman's Voice in Southern Story* (Athens: University of Georgia Press, 1990), pp. 37–63;

Carol S. Manning, *With Ears Opening Like Morning Glories: Eudora Welty and the Love of Storytelling* (Westport, Conn.: Greenwood Press, 1985);

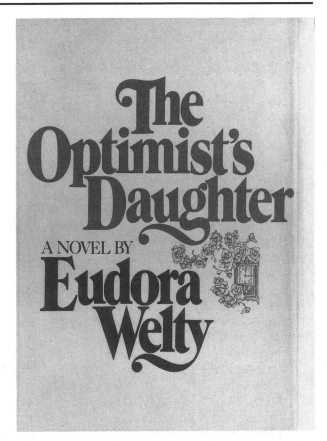

Dust jacket for Welty's Pulitzer Prize–winning 1972 novel

Manning, ed., *The Female Tradition in Southern Literature* (Urbana: University of Illinois Press, 1993);

Marie-Antoinette Manz-Kunz, *Eudora Welty: Aspects of Fantasy in Her Short Fiction* (Bern: Verlag, 1971);

Rebecca Mark, *The Dragon's Blood: Feminist Intertextuality in Eudora Welty's "The Golden Apples"* (Jackson: University Press of Mississippi, 1994);

Suzanne Marrs, "The Making of *Losing Battles*: Jack Renfro's Evolution," *Mississippi Quarterly*, 37 (Fall 1984): 469–474;

Sara McAlpin, "Family in Eudora Welty's Fiction," *Southern Review*, 18 (Summer 1982): 480–494;

Lisa K. Miller, "The Dark Side of Our Frontier Heritage: Eudora Welty's Use of the Turner Thesis in *The Robber Bridegroom*," *Notes on Mississippi Writers*, 14 (1981): 18–25;

Gail L. Mortimer, "Image and Myth in Eudora Welty's *The Optimist's Daughter*," *American Literature*, 62 (December 1990): 617–633;

Joyce Carol Oates, "Eudora's Web," in *Contemporary Women Novelists: A Collection of Critical Essays*, edited by Patricia Meyer Spacks (Englewood Cliffs, N. J.: Prentice-Hall, 1977), pp. 167–172;

Gina D. Peterman, "*A Curtain of Green:* Eudora Welty's Auspicious Beginning," *Mississippi Quarterly,* 46 (Winter 1992–1993): 91–114;

Peggy Whitman Prenshaw, "The Antiphonies of Eudora Welty's *One Writer's Beginnings* and Elizabeth Bowen's *Pictures and Conversations,*" *Mississippi Quarterly,* 34 (Fall 1986): 639–650;

Prenshaw, "The Harmonies of *Losing Battles,*" in *Modern American Fiction: Form and Function,* edited by Thomas Daniel Young (Baton Rouge & London: Louisiana State University Press, 1989), pp. 184–197;

Prenshaw, ed., *Eudora Welty: Critical Essays* (Jackson: University Press of Mississippi, 1979);

Jennifer Lynn Randisi, *A Tissue of Lies: Eudora Welty and the Southern Romance* (Washington, D.C.: University Press of America, 1982);

Ann Romines, *The Home Plot: Women, Writing & Domestic Ritual* (Amherst: University of Massachusetts Press, 1992);

Louis D. Rubin, Jr., "Art and Artistry in Morgana, Mississippi," in his *A Gallery of Southerners* (Baton Rouge: Louisiana State University Press, 1982), pp. 49–66;

Peter Schmidt, *The Heart of the Story: Eudora Welty's Short Fiction* (Jackson: University Press of Mississippi, 1991);

Thelma Shinn, *Radiant Daughters: Fictional American Women* (Westport, Conn.: Greenwood Press, 1986);

Lewis Simpson, ed., *Mississippi Quarterly,* special Welty issue, 26 (Fall 1973);

Dawn Trouard, ed., *The Eye of the Storyteller* (Kent, Ohio: Kent State University Press, 1989);

Craig W. Turner and Lee Emling Harding, eds., *Critical Essays on Eudora Welty* (Boston: G. K. Hall, 1989);

Ruth M. Vande Kieft, *Eudora Welty* (Boston: Twayne, 1987);

Robert Penn Warren, "The Love and the Separateness in Miss Welty," *Kenyon Review,* 6 (Spring 1944): 246–259; reprinted as "Love and Separateness in Eudora Welty," in *A Robert Penn Warren Reader,* edited by Albert Erskine (New York: Vintage, 1988), pp. 196–206;

Louise Westling, *Eudora Welty* (Totowa, N. J.: Barnes, 1988);

Westling, *Sacred Groves and Ravaged Gardens: The Fiction of Eudora Welty, Carson McCullers, and Flannery O'Connor* (Athens: University of Georgia Press, 1985);

Ruth D. Weston, *Gothic Traditions and Narrative Techniques in the Fiction of Eudora Welty* (Baton Rouge: Louisiana State University Press, 1994);

Sally Wolff, "Eudora Welty's Autobiographical Duet: *The Optimist's Daughter* and *One Writer's Beginnings,*" in *Located Lives: Place and Idea in Southern Autobiography,* edited by J. Bill Berry (Athens: University of Georgia Press, 1990), pp. 78–92;

Patricia S. Yaeger, "The Case of the Dangling Signifier: Phallic Imagery in Eudora Welty's 'Moon Lake,' " *Twentieth Century Literature,* 28 (Winter 1982): 431–452.

Papers:

The primary collection of Welty's letters and manuscripts is at the State of Mississippi Department of Archives and History, Jackson. Another important Welty collection is at the Harry Ransom Humanities Research Center, University of Texas at Austin. Also at the Harry Ransom Humanities Research Center is the Elizabeth Bowen Collection, which includes letters from Welty to Bowen.

John Edgar Wideman

(14 June 1941 –)

Keith E. Byerman
Indiana State University

See also the Wideman entry in *DLB 33: Afro-American Fiction Writers After 1955.*

BOOKS: *A Glance Away* (New York: Harcourt, Brace & World, 1967; London: Allison & Busby, 1986);

Hurry Home (New York: Harcourt, Brace & World, 1969);

The Lynchers (New York: Harcourt Brace Jovanovich, 1973);

Hiding Place (New York: Avon, 1981; London: Allison & Busby, 1984);

Damballah (New York: Avon, 1981; London: Allison & Busby, 1984);

Sent for You Yesterday (New York: Avon, 1983; London: Allison & Busby, 1984);

Brothers and Keepers (New York: Holt, Rinehart & Winston, 1984; London: Allison & Busby, 1985);

Reuben (New York: Holt, 1987; London: Viking, 1988);

Fever (New York: Holt, 1989; London: Penguin, 1991);

Philadelphia Fire (New York: Holt, 1990; London: Viking, 1991);

The Stories of John Edgar Wideman (New York: Pantheon, 1992);

Fatheralong (New York: Pantheon, 1994).

SELECTED PERIODICAL PUBLICATIONS –
UNCOLLECTED: "Frame and Dialect: The Evolution of the Black Voice in Fiction," *American Poetry Review,* 5, no. 5 (1976): 34–37;

"Defining the Black Voice in Fiction," *Black American Literature Forum,* 2 (Fall 1977): 79–82;

"*Of Love and Dust:* A Reconsideration," *Callaloo,* 1 (May 1978): 76–84;

"The Architectonics of Fiction," *Callaloo,* 13 (Winter 1990): 42–46.

John Edgar Wideman has firmly established himself as one of the most respected contemporary

John Edgar Wideman

writers, as evidenced by his receipt of the P.E.N./Faulkner Award in 1984 and 1991. The author of ten books of fiction and an autobiographical dialogue/meditation, he has won consistent praise for his polished style and his serious consideration of contemporary issues, including the deterioration of African-American urban life, the meaning of modern black manhood, and the role of violence and criminality in American life. His success as a writer has not led to predictability in his style, methods, or concerns. His career has been a persistent search for new modes of expression and deeper exploration of themes; he has challenged both conventional perceptions of black life and the methods of telling about it.

This discontent with fixed patterns seems to have been established early in his life. John Edgar Wideman, born on 14 June 1941 in Washington, D.C., to Edgar and Bette French Wideman, was raised in a poor African-American neighborhood, Homewood, in Pittsburgh. The community was made up primarily of those who came from the South at various points to seek freedom and economic opportunity; Wideman traces his ancestry to a woman who left slavery with the white man who wanted to marry her. In Pittsburgh, Wideman's love of sports, especially basketball, began, and he was able to listen to the storytellers in the family. When he was twelve the family moved to the predominantly white area known as Shadyside, where he attended Peabody High School, one of the best in Pittsburgh.

Because basketball and other sports in his new neighborhood tended to be played as organized school activities rather than in informal playground settings, he devoted his free time to becoming even more of an avid reader than he had been. This pastime, in addition to the encouragement that he received all through his school years as a writer, led him to develop a romantic notion of the literary artist as an adventurer and explorer. He had discovered that well-constructed stories could gain him attention and praise. He achieved success and popularity in every endeavor: he was a basketball star, senior-class president, and valedictorian.

At another level the shifts from black environments to mostly white ones and back again had profound effects on his identity. He has talked about the need, in essence, to set aside his racial identity in order to accomplish what he did at Peabody and later at the University of Pennsylvania. This need meant moving not only physically but psychologically away from Homewood and the values and expectations associated with that community. It meant – at the University of Pennsylvania, which he attended on a Benjamin Franklin scholarship and where he again played basketball – focusing on becoming racially invisible so as to achieve individual recognition. He operated successfully in a privileged white environment and came to apply its standards to his life. He was inducted into Phi Beta Kappa. His collegiate literary efforts, which were encouraged in writing courses, made use of such modern canonical authors as T. S. Eliot and William Faulkner. He became a Rhodes Scholar, only the second African-American to do so, and studied in England from 1963 to 1966, receiving a B.Ph. from Oxford University, with research interests in eighteenth-century British literature. In 1965 he married Judith Ann Goldman, whom he had met in Philadelphia.

After a year as Kent Fellow in the creative-writing program at the University of Iowa, Wideman joined the faculty of the University of Pennsylvania Department of English. He was also involved in creating the Afro-American Studies program, which he chaired from 1972 to 1973. During this same period he began publishing fiction, including his first novel, *A Glance Away* (1967).

This work reflects Wideman's early ambivalence about racial issues by focusing on two characters, one black and the other white. Moreover, as James W. Coleman has suggested, the theme is essentially one of modernist despair, in which black culture offers little hope for the characters. The story centers on a day in the life of Eddie Lawson, who has just come back from a drug-rehabilitation program to the troubled environment of the black community. The fact that his day of return is Easter is ironic: there is little evidence of possible resurrection for Eddie. He reenters a world in which his dying mother is bitter about her life, especially the death of her firstborn, a son named Eugene; she focuses her hostility on her daughter, Bette, who has sacrificed her own opportunities to care for her mother. Eddie must also deal with the anger of his girlfriend, Alice, who has never forgiven him for his sexual relationship with a white woman. There is little in his environment and relationships to keep Eddie from sliding back into his addiction and hopelessness. In the world Wideman creates here, there are no sources of strength to mitigate self-destruction.

In another ironic turn two characters who would be expected to aggravate the situation in fact offer what little hope there is for Eddie. The first is his best friend, Brother Small, who is Alice's brother and also an addict. Brother Small's contribution to Eddie's new life, in addition to his friendship, is his relationship to Robert Thurley, a white English professor who financially supports Brother Small's habit in exchange for sex. Thurley, though the other central character in the novel, is generally ineffectual. He grew up with a domineering mother, has endured a marriage in which he was incapable of sexually satisfying his wife, has little to offer students in the classroom, and finds his only sexual gratification with young black men he picks up in bars. He is the modern antihero, suffering through his life rather than living it.

Nonetheless, Brother Small and Thurley provide Eddie with some hope for his life, largely through Thurley's vision of possible renewal. In the last pages Wideman generates the image of a community of alienated, burned-out men that suggests the promise of Easter. It is a community created not by deeds or spoken words, but by a blending of thoughts and feelings in a multiple stream-of-consciousness. As Eddie experiences the pain of his own life and that of his family (his mother dies shortly before the final scene), Thurley strives to sustain him by recalling a church service he has just attended. Their thoughts alternate and then merge as death becomes a means to new life. The sense of renewal is brought together in the closing thoughts of Brother Small:

> I wonder how far it [the sky] is somebody should find out and tell people cause I'm sure they want to know look at them both closer to the fire now and both looking at the flames I wonder what it feels like to burn if it always hurts once your hand is in it deep if it pops and sparks like wood . . . kids do it stick their hands right in you gotta keep them away or they'll do it like bugs who get too close and burn up I see why they try once why they want to touch I can see it in Eddie's eyes in the white man's eyes that stare at the flame they want to touch to put them in and see if it keeps hurting I can understand why kids do it cause I want to touch myself just like one I want to put my hand in I want to go to smoke and see how high.

Wideman offers a traditional religious vision in which the self is found by being lost, in which suffering serves as purification, and in which all must become as children in order to discover the depths of faith. Whether the vision can bring about lasting change or is just a moment of insight is not made clear by the text, but the possibility exists in a world in which sexual relationships, family, high culture, and African-American traditions have all failed.

The book received somewhat mixed reviews. Roger Ebert (*American Scholar,* Autumn 1967) complained that the author "has the materials of a good novel, but his command of language is concealed by a bagful of stylistic tricks." In contrast Stephen Caldwell (*Saturday Review,* 21 October 1967) asserted that what "move[s] us is Wideman's artistry, his one- and two-paragraph evocations of joy and sorrow that first appear in his fine prologue and are echoed and revised time and again through the course of the book."

Wideman's second book, *Hurry Home* (1969), gives more attention to its central black character, but it still sees the frustrated individual as the central concern. The protagonist, Cecil Otis Braithewaite, is isolated from the black community from the beginning of the narrative. The author is less interested in how the character reached this position than in its effects on him. The novel is a blend of narrative and interior monologue; the point of view is primarily that of Cecil but also that of his wife, Esther, and a white man, Webb, whom Cecil meets during his travels. In addition, it is not always clear what are external events and what are Cecil's imaginings. This ambiguity is significant in understanding the role of the black community in the protagonist's life.

For example, in an early scene Cecil's isolation from his environment is emphasized when he is confronted on his way to getting a haircut. His arrogance and the community's hostility are clear here. Near the end of the book, however, he is seen working in a salon, giving a neighborhood man a "process" (an often painful chemical method of softening tight curls). In this scene, while Cecil ruminates beyond the immediate situation, he is still a part of the group. The text offers no indication of the means by which the change in relationship may have occurred, or even if it has occurred. Wideman remains unclear about the resolution of Cecil's conflict with the community. This fluctuation between fantasy and reality is central to Wideman's method in *Hurry Home.*

The story begins on the day Cecil is to receive his law degree after years of attending school. He has also been working as a janitor in an apartment building, where he lives in the basement with Esther, whom he has offered to marry this same day. They have been living together for several years and earlier had a stillborn child. Cecil regularly takes to his bed with a bottle of whiskey, and Esther must perform his maintenance tasks. At the end of this crucial day – which includes the confrontation on the way to the barbershop – and after Esther has fallen asleep, Cecil walks out the door, not to return for three years. He travels to various places and does various jobs, finally ending up in Spain with Webb, a wealthy man who seems to see Cecil as a surrogate for the son he had by a black woman.

Webb, who resembles Robert Thurley in his despair and ineffectiveness, takes the young black man on a tour of the great museums of western Europe. The narrative suggests that this generosity is given in exchange for sexual favors. This part of the text is permeated by a sense of corruption, frustra-

Dust jacket for Wideman's 1973 novel, which involves a conspiracy by a group of black men to lynch a white policeman in Philadelphia

tion, and self-pitying reflection. Cecil finally breaks away from Webb, and, after another period of wandering, including time in North Africa, he decides to go home – partly out of a realization that he would spiritually die if he gave himself over to those like Webb, that is, whites who would never acknowledge his identity.

The other crucial element in Cecil's decision to return is an imagined conversation with his uncle Otis, who tells him in a variety of ways that he should live his life with intensity; he uses a parable of a dwarf with progeria, a disease that causes rapid aging. He quotes the victim as saying that every moment of his life is like a day in a normal life. Otis ends by stating, "I kissed the dwarf when he slept hoping I would be infected." Cecil must not lose his life by constantly searching out its meaning; he must live it deeply and thereby create its meaning. At the end of the novel he returns to Esther in the middle of the night, reversing the process of his leaving. Whether this in fact is a resurrection or a Joycean epiphany is not made clear; as in *A Glance Away,* the conclusion is ambiguous. As in the earlier work, however, the potential for a truly new life is present.

Hurry Home received generally positive reviews. Joseph Goodman in the *New York Times Book Review* (19 April 1970) remarked on Wideman's "formidable command of the techniques of fiction," while John Leonard (*New York Times,* 2 April 1970) described the book as "a rich and complicated novel." Wideman's first two novels focus on the despair and search for personal meaning of individuals, some of whom are African-American. The quests of characters such as Eddie and Cecil are not distinct from those of white characters, nor is Wideman's style different from that of other modernist writers. Though African-American culture and community are significant parts of the characters' experiences, *The Lynchers* (1973) makes black life and history much more central, but it is also a transitional work in that the main characters are still concerned with meaninglessness and a sense of isolation. In fact, the black community itself is the source of alienation and despair. Wideman chooses to focus his attention on this flawed community rather than on a specific individual.

The plot involves a conspiracy by Philadelphia black men who decide to respond to ongoing racism and the continued victimization of the black community by carrying out the public lynching of a white policeman. Such a gesture will, they believe, inspire an insurrection on the part of African-Americans that will lead to a profound change in their condition. The choice of lynching as the initiating act is considered appropriate because it has great significance as a symbol of American racial oppression. Wideman reestablishes its historical importance in the "Matter Prefatory" to the narrative. This section includes a variety of texts by white writers revealing their racial attitudes; newspaper reports of racial violence; and petitions, tales, and commentaries by African-Americans addressing the reality of racial violence. A litany of lynchings serves as the centerpiece of this record that covers more than two hundred years of American history.

The lynching planned by the conspirators, then, has ritual significance for American society. Since such acts have been the extreme means by which oppression has been sustained, this one can serve as a symbolic reversal of the racial order of the society. The selection of a policeman whose behavior has not been especially brutal supports the point that he is an emblem of the larger society and that white society as a whole is the true enemy.

The very abstractness of this notion becomes an issue in the text. Because the conspirators are committed to an idea rather than a response to a concrete grievance, their plan is doomed to failure. In addition, Wideman makes it difficult to distinguish motivations for their scheme. Each of the major figures is limited in some way and has been a victim himself; moreover, the black community itself is shown to be in a state of self-destructive decline. Thus, it is not clear that Littleman, Wilkerson, Saunders, and Rice would be capable of carrying out their plan, nor is it clear that their scheme would have the desired effect. The conspiracy seems more a fantasy of frustrated men than a meaningful social action.

Littleman conceives the idea and is able to articulate it to his friends. While he offers a certain violent logic for the lynching, his anger at the world appears to be his real motivation. A paraplegic, he has suffered repeated humiliations as a result of his condition, which requires him to rely on others to carry out the plan. He deeply feels the troubled nature of the black community and out of his despair comes to believe that only a spectacular act of violence can save it. But he is also self-hating at some level and in fact acts in a manner that guarantees the failure of the conspiracy. He ends up beaten by the police and hospitalized on the day of the proposed lynching. Finally, his scheme involves the

murder of a black prostitute, a death that will be blamed on the policeman, thereby justifying the lynching. But the intention to kill her reveals an acceptance of the indifference to black life that is at the heart of racism. Littleman's conception of the black community's salvation therefore expresses a contempt for that which his plan aims to better.

The second conspirator, Thomas Wilkerson, understands this fundamental flaw in his friend's logic and tries to think his way through it. Like Cecil Braithewaite, he is more committed to words and thoughts than to action. He is able to see the complexities of any such action, and this ability makes him hesitant at the very time he needs to act forcefully. His condition is further complicated by his family, which seems to represent the community in the novel. He sees in his alcoholic father a man whom he both pities and loves. In addition, the father, known as Sweetman, has been imprisoned for the killing of his best friend, who died during an argument over a trivial amount of money. For Thomas, this incident suggests the fundamental randomness and meaninglessness of life in the ghetto. If African-American men have been brought to the point that they will kill each other for nothing, what hope can there be for the creation of a new kind of black life? All of this thoughtfulness on Thomas's part is itself ineffectual because it brings about no changes in his family's life and in fact may lead to his own death when one of the plotters, Rice, attempts to kill him out of anger at his indecisiveness.

Rice and Saunders are different from Littleman and Wilkerson in that they do not think about the implications of their behavior. Ironically, they are the ones most capable of carrying out the lynching, precisely because they act rather than think. While Rice is essentially a tool to be used by the others, Saunders is shown to have developed his cold-bloodedness in early life as part of a self-destructive family that was also manipulated by various social agencies. His humanity has been sapped, and all that remains is rage. His participation is motivated by this anger and not by any interest in the life of the community. He is prevented from acting only by the failures of the others, but it is clear that any action he would have taken would have been meaningless.

Thus, in his first work centered in the black community, Wideman demonstrates the same despairing perspective he had shown earlier. *The Lynchers,* in fact, can be said to be his most hopeless book in that, in contrast to *A Glance Away* and *Hurry Home,* meaninglessness and alienation are not individual but social and cultural. There is no way out, even when characters are both thoughtful and committed to social change.

Reviews of the novel tended to be negative, with critics agreeing that Wideman tended to explain more than he dramatized. F. L. Ryan (*Best Sellers,* 1 June 1973) complimented the author for his "keen ear for dialect, a hungry curiosity about the low life in a big city, a rich awareness of the necessity for symbolic structure, and a passion for a cause" but then argued that the book "breaks in two. The first half is determined by the desire to be a fictionizer, the second by an impulse to be an expositor." Richard P. Brickner (*New York Times Book Review,* 29 April 1973) identified the problem by noting that "the book lacks drive because it often uses words as a curtain on dramatic feeling."

This book came at a time of crisis in Wideman's career, and its hopelessness may reflect his situation. He was working to establish the Afro-American Studies program at the University of Pennsylvania, but he had to this point in his life done little reading in black literature. In 1973 he moved from teaching at the University of Pennsylvania to the University of Wyoming, an act of seeming self-exile from his racial and cultural roots. But, in fact, this period became the time of what he has called his "second education." He stopped publishing fiction for several years and immersed himself in black literature and history. His published writings during this time took the form of criticism addressing aspects of African-American cultural forms, including but not limited to literature.

Wideman's move west also became, ironically, a time of spiritual return to Homewood. He began to think about what that community had meant to his life and the ways it could be represented in fiction. A crucial event to Wideman was the arrest and life imprisonment in 1975 of his brother, Robby, for murder. This experience led him to deeper consideration of those forces at work in Homewood that led one brother to a life of crime and the other to academic and literary success. The issue of violence and its relationship to African-American families and communities became an important theme when Wideman began publishing fiction again eight years after *The Lynchers.*

In 1981 Wideman reemerged on the literary scene with the publication of the novel *Hiding Place* and the short-story collection *Damballah.* Both works, along with the later novel *Sent for You Yesterday* (1983), treat the history and culture of Homewood as clearly relevant to the present-day experiences of the characters, who take on aspects, and even the names, of some of Wideman's own family members. Thus, in this Homewood trilogy personal history becomes a vehicle for exploring social and cultural history. He even provides a family tree that traces the line from the slave woman Sybela Owens in the 1840s to the children of "John" – Danny and Jake, the names of his own sons – in the 1960s.

Hiding Place focuses on two members of the family: Tommy, a young man in trouble with the law, and Mother Bess, a recluse three full generations older. Tommy attempts to rob a local shop and is then accused of killing his accomplice. Though innocent, he runs to a place that might provide sanctuary, his great-aunt Bess's home. Since the deaths of her husband and son, Bess has kept herself in isolation from the community, having interaction only through a retarded boy, Clement. When she first discovers Tommy, she is not certain she knows him or wants to help him. She establishes contact – and thus relationship – through recitation of family history.

This litany is crucial throughout the narrative as the means by which both Tommy and Bess are brought back into a connection with the world. Tommy is like black men in Wideman's earlier works in that he has no sense of purpose or meaning in his life. He has drifted not only away from the community and anything in it that might sustain him but also from the responsibility for his wife and son. But his time with Bess recalls to him who his family is and the value of his life. At this point, at the end of the novel, he decides to return to the world and face the consequences of his behavior rather than continue to live afraid and ashamed. At the end Bess decides that she has the responsibility to do what she can to save him, even though it means going back into the world from which she has insulated herself.

It is not clear whether either of their choices will produce positive results; the black community of this book is not a more hopeful or peaceful place than the ones described in the earlier novels. The police are coming after Tommy at the end, and Bess, though determined to help, is both feeble and forgetful. What is clearly different in this work is that the traditions of the community and the black family can humanize those who have been alienated. Tommy and Bess have separate last chapters, but each speaks to the other in terms of the family, and each recalls the value of the blues as a solace in troubled times. Thus, Wideman has not sentimentalized African-American experience in making it central to the novel. The world remains as harsh and destructive as ever, but Wideman has discov-

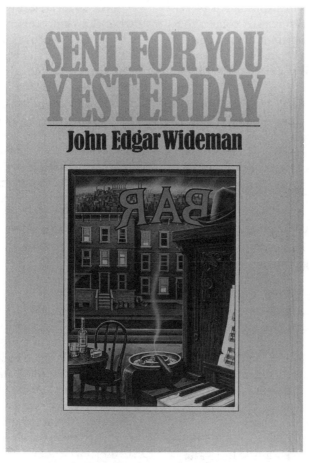

Dust jacket for Wideman's 1983 novel, which won the P.E.N./
Faulkner Award for fiction

ered resources that provide strength in dealing with it.

Damballah, a collection of twelve stories, retraces the beginnings of the family saga. The book begins in Africa, as the title story features Orion, a "crazy" slave who refuses to speak English and is killed for attacking an overseer. But even in death he suggests the power of his homeland: according to the little boy whose point of view is taken, all the blacks are afraid to enter the barn where the body lies, and the white men who commit the murder are terrified of him even as they behead him. The book circles back in the concluding "The Beginning of Homewood," which includes among the memories of Sybela, the founder of the family, an image of "old heathen Orion" as she is running away from the plantation. This running is also legendary: her lover, the son and heir of her owner, steals her and her children away from Maryland when he learns that his father is about to sell them. They settle in Homewood, where Sybela produces another eigh-

teen children. Out of this progeny come both the characters and storytellers of *Damballah.*

The title is explained in a prefatory note about the Haitian *loa* (spirit), of African origin, who is the father of humankind and who is appealed to as the one who "gathers up the family." The book, in fact, gathers the stories of the family, links generations, and seeks to find meaning for the present in the experiences of the past. There are stories of John French, the narrator's grandfather, a strong-willed man who finds the body of an abandoned infant ("Daddy Garbage"), saves his daughter by eating a caterpillar, and is saved in turn from a shooting by his wife (both in "Lizabeth: The Caterpillar Story"); of Tommy ("Tommy" and "Solitary"); and of Freeda, the grandmother, and the miraculous saving of Lizabeth as a baby ("The Chinaman"). But these stories are not so much about individuals as about the family within the community of Homewood. "Solitary," for example, does not concern Tommy as much as it does his mother's visits to him in prison, meetings that are as much spiritual as physical journeys. The title "The Chinaman" comes from an African-American oral tradition of representing death as a Chinaman, and the story involves the various ways in which family confronts death and remembers the dead.

Beyond the familial concerns in the collection Wideman focuses on the nature of storytelling itself. The character John gathers family tales as a way of recovering his relationship to his relatives past and present. The book opens with a message "To Robby," the author's imprisoned brother and the model for Tommy both here and in *Hiding Place*. Wideman describes the stories as letters meant to reestablish contact between these brothers whose lives have gone in such different directions. That contact is to be made through memory, through retelling what they both have come from and been a part of. Within stories, the telling is a central element. People have different versions of the same experience, and the telling becomes a means of keeping alive the reality of those who have gone before. Thus, "John" discovers for himself (and Wideman for his brother) the meaning of his identity through this oral tradition. The self is not separate and alienated, as suggested in earlier works. Its truth is in a communal memory that can be recovered.

Hiding Place and *Damballah,* which tended to be reviewed together, received relatively little attention when they were first published. In the *New York Times Book Review* (11 September 1982) Mel Watkins stated that Wideman's collection was "possibly his most impressive work." But Watkins was not taken with *Hiding Place:* "Despite some impressive passages in which Mr. Wideman displays his command of the language and of the voices of his characters, this is a static novel." In a later analysis James W. Coleman observes that the novelist's "portrayal of black language, rituals, myth, and folkways is skillful, accurate, and effective."

The third work of the Homewood trilogy, *Sent for You Yesterday,* won the P.E.N./Faulkner Award in 1984 as the best work of fiction published the previous year. It continues the saga of the community and the role of the descendants of Sybela Owens in it. Of the three books, however, it focuses least on the family and the relationships within it. John and Freeda French play important secondary roles, and their son Carl is one of the central characters, but the story really belongs to Albert Wilkes, a friend of John and Homewood's greatest blues artist, and Brother Tate, an albino African-American who does not speak for sixteen years after the death of his child.

As suggested by the role of Wilkes, music rather than storytelling is the key expressive form in the novel. According to John French, Wilkes's skill at the piano holds Homewood together. When he is forced to run away because he has killed a white policeman in a dispute about a woman, the spirit of the community is lost. Wideman implies that the blues gives shape to the social and psychological disorder that is experienced in black life. In this sense *Sent for You Yesterday* is consistent with Wideman's earlier works in viewing the urban black situation as constantly verging on, and often falling into, violence and meaninglessness. In this work, however, the community has available to it a creative form that offers solace and meaning, even if the reality itself cannot be changed.

When Wilkes returns after seven years, his presence is regenerating, although it threatens the safety of the black community, since the police will come after him. While Freeda is anxious that her husband not be found with his old friend, stories immediately begin about who was the first witness to Wilkes's return. He is killed by the police while playing piano at the Tate house. The shooting itself is ambiguously creative because Carl, Brother, and his sister Lucy, who witness the killing, devote themselves to carrying on the blues tradition. They keep the music alive, along with the legend of Brother, who has no musical training or special skill, sitting at a piano one night and perfectly recreating Wilkes's music.

More important for the novel, they must live and try to make sense of their blues-filled lives. Brother's son, also an albino, dies in a fire; the child's mother ends up in an asylum. Brother, Carl, and Lucy all become drug addicts as they try to cope with the disintegrating conditions of Homewood. Finally, according to the story told by Carl and Lucy, Brother dies as a means of escape. The survivors continue into the present to make lives for themselves.

Storytelling enters the narrative in the form of Doot, a child who left the community to lead a life parallel to that of Wideman himself. He comes back, like "John" in *Damballah,* to gather the tales of Homewood. He claims the tradition of Wilkes and Brother Tate by taking an improvisational approach to his material. He lets the various stories, fantasies, dreams, and lives find a shape in the telling rather than impose a rigid form on them. Thus, the book itself becomes the final blues.

Like the two earlier books of the trilogy, *Sent for You Yesterday* received little attention when it came out. Despite this neglect one reviewer believed it to be a powerful work. Alan Cheuse (*New York Times Book Review,* 15 May 1983) stated, "In this hypnotic and deeply lyrical novel, Mr. Wideman again returns to the ghetto where he was raised and transforms it into a magical location infused with poetry and pathos."

In his next book, *Brothers and Keepers* (1984), Wideman turns away from fiction to consider in autobiographical terms some of the issues he raises in his earlier works. Here he is concerned with his own life, but more centrally that of his brother, Robby. In *Brothers and Keepers* Wideman raises the question of how two brothers, reared in the same environment, can have led such different lives. But Wideman is not just interested in why his brother turned out so "bad" but also in how he ended up so much outside his brother's life and that of the black community. The book combines Robby's move into a life that leads to crime and violence, John's successful but alienating effort to escape such a world, and his thoughts on the American judicial and prison systems. Wideman incorporates narratives of the brothers' lives, conversations between them after Robby has gone to prison, and expository passages about prison conditions.

The theme running through the work is the loss of African-American men to their communities and to society as a whole; the cause is shown to be racism. In Wideman's view the desire to escape the constrictions of the inner city leads him into an essentially white world with little interaction with Homewood, and those same constrictions lead the younger brother to shape his life in terms of petty crime – primarily theft – rather than education. The book traces the journey of each of them to an understanding of the other.

In prison Robby discovers the power of learning for his self-esteem and his connection to a larger world. Wideman includes a speech made by Robby at a graduation ceremony held in the prison. Through reflection on his relationship with his brother, John finds a connection with what he had left behind. Each brother has been in a sense a fugitive; prison ironically brings them together. But for Wideman the reunion is essentially tragic, since it does not liberate Robby, whose rehabilitation is absurdist in the sense that it cannot be acted upon in the larger world. *Brothers and Keepers* is clearly related to Wideman's fiction in its pessimism, its exploration of the black intellectual's relationship to other forms of black experience, and its focus on family dynamics and voices. Giving Robby a voice out of the hell of the American prison system is the author's way of being his brother's keeper.

Wideman's next novel, *Reuben* (1987), continues his pattern of exploring the harsh reality of black inner-city life. The title character is an eccentric, somewhat misshapen black man who lives in a dilapidated trailer on an abandoned lot in Homewood. He provides legal aid to members of the community who need someone to speak for them downtown. The novel is made up of the stories told to Reuben and those that he tells to his clients. As in *Hurry Home,* it is often difficult to determine what is reality and what is fantasy as the tales unfold. One narrative concerns Kwansa Parker, a young mother whose child is kidnapped by the little boy's father. She seeks Reuben's help in getting him back; in the process she reveals aspects of her past and her current relationship with Toodles, a woman who is seen by the community as cold-blooded but who is willing to help Kwansa in any way she can.

The other narrative concerns Wally, formerly a successful basketball player and now a recruiter for a university. He initially comes to Reuben because he knows of corruption in the athletic department that is about to be exposed, and he wants to protect himself. But, in telling of this, he describes a murder he committed while on one of his trips. He has never been implicated in the crime and does not expect to be. Reuben must determine whether it in fact happened or whether it is an imagined act of violence designed to relieve Wally's obvious racial frustration and hostility.

Consistent with this textual concern for reality and responsibility is the question of Reuben's motivations and qualifications. A mystery to the community, he seems to earn little from his legal efforts; he also seems to be well educated and capable of succeeding elsewhere. Near the end of the book the reader learns that he is not a lawyer, and he is arrested for impersonating one. At the end, however, he goes to retrieve Kwansa's child, whom she can have back because Toodles has killed the father.

In *Reuben* Wideman tries to capture the nature of ghetto life in a blend of violence, casual sexuality, drugs, fantasy, memory, and a day-to-day reality of suffering and invisibility. The effect is an often surrealistic narrative in which ordering principles of love, law, and faith seem largely irrelevant. Reuben survives by being a version of the trickster figure whose true identity is never certain, but who in this case uses his abilities to aid those even more vulnerable and troubled than himself.

Given the experimental nature of the text, it is not surprising that it received mixed reviews. Walter Kendrick (*New York Times Book Review,* 8 November 1987) stated that "Homewood must really have

Dust jacket for Wideman's 1990 novel, about which the Newsweek *reviewer observed, "This book's brilliance bleaches out the reality it seeks"*

fallen, or perhaps 'Reuben' fails because Mr. Wideman has mined that vein to depletion and needs to move on." In contrast, Michael Gorra in the *Hudson Review* (Summer 1980) praised the author's control of African-American English. He also observed, "Page by page this is the most exciting new fiction I have read this quarter, marked by an energy and passion that makes its story of poverty, violence, and prostitution anything but depressing."

Wideman's second collection of stories, *Fever* (1989), deals with issues of death and failed communication, both personal and racial. "Valaida," for example, is in one sense an appreciation of the little-known jazz figure Valaida Snow. She is granted heroic status by an old Jewish man who tells of being saved by her when he was a child in a concentration camp. But the deeper message of the story lies in his difficulty in talking to the black woman who has cleaned for him for many years. He sees her as alien, and she has little identification with his history of suffering. "Doc's Story," the narrative of a blind man who plays basketball in the neighborhood, is told by a man seeking to understand the failure of his marriage. He believes that Doc's remarkable performance might carry a message for

his relationship, but he never has the opportunity to tell it to the one person who matters.

The title story links these issues to American history. "Fever" has as its central character the Revolutionary-era African-American church leader Richard Allen. In 1793 Philadelphia experiences a yellow fever epidemic. The reputation of blacks is doubly harmed by the outbreak, since they are accused of being responsible for it in the first place and then are said to be immune from it because of their race. Wideman uses a variety of voices to describe the situation, but he focuses on Allen as he devotes himself to aiding the sick and helping to remove the dead. He offers himself as a kind of sacrifice yet is constantly aware of the hatred whites have for him. The connection is also made across generations to the catastrophic 1985 police bombing of a house occupied by the black radical group Move in Philadelphia. Thus, the author indicates that the true "fever" of the city and America in general is racial hatred.

Reviews of *Fever* tended to be positive, especially about the title story. Susan Fromberg Schaeffer (*New York Times Book Review*, 10 December 1989) said that the collection "is almost majestic in its evocation of the goodness and evil of the human heart." Some commentators noted the experimental nature of Wideman's technique, which Francis Poole (*Library Journal,* 1 November 1989) described as "echoes of Faulkner in the post-Joycean narrative methods." Herbert Mitgang (*New York Times,* 5 December 1989) contended, however, that, except for "Fever," the stories "do not add to the author's reputation. They are fragmentary in their plots, strained in writing, and not always able to persuade the reader to suspend disbelief."

The late 1980s brought more change and trouble for Wideman and his family. In 1986 he took a position in the English department at the University of Massachusetts in Amherst. During this period his son Jacob, sixteen at the time, was convicted of murdering another teenager during a summer-camp trip to Arizona. Jacob was tried and imprisoned for life.

This family tragedy forms a part of Wideman's seventh novel, *Philadelphia Fire* (1990). Picking up on a section of "Fever," the book treats the 1985 bombing of the Move house in fictional form. The central plot concerns Cudjoe, an African-American writer who has been living as an expatriate in Greece. He returns after the bombing and subsequent neighborhood-wide fire, determined to find Simba, a young boy who was seen running from the house as it went up in flames. He is the only known survivor of the assault. For Cudjoe, the child represents a means of understanding what has happened. In his quest Cudjoe talks to a woman who once belonged to Move and who reluctantly agrees to help him find Simba. She resists his efforts, in part because she sees the man as an outsider whose questions and search can only aggravate the problems of the community and the boy. Cudjoe never entirely convinces her of his sincerity, even though he grew up in the neighborhood. He also talks to a friend who now works in city government and who tries to explain and rationalize the mayor's actions.

This doomed quest takes up part 1 of the novel. In part 2 Wideman shifts to a voice that resembles his own to provide a literary, historical, and sociological perspective on the events. He interweaves commentary on the role of Caliban in William Shakespeare's *The Tempest,* the history of Philadelphia, and his feelings about and the experiences of his imprisoned son. In this section he echoes what he does in *Brothers and Keepers.* At the same time he suggests a larger meaning of the Move fire: it represents not merely a flawed political/police

decision but a pattern of the interaction of political and racial oppression. Blacks, and especially black men, who are different are not accommodated within society but attacked by it. Thus, the leader of Move is seen by both black and white leaders as a threat to the existing social order, someone who becomes so prominent that he must be destroyed. Similarly, the imprisoned young man – whose difficulties, Wideman claims, would be diagnosed and treated if he were white – is dealt with as simply another young black sociopath who must be locked up.

The final two sections of the novel focus first on a homeless man who is ignored by society and then on Cudjoe's attendance at a service designed to address the meaning of the Move assault. He speculates on the significance of the meager attendance, feeling that all Philadelphians should participate in this event as a ritual of penance and cleansing. The fact that so few do reinforces the book's argument about the coldness and indifference of contemporary society. In this sense *Philadelphia Fire* continues the theme of despair and violence that runs through Wideman's work.

The book received the P.E.N./Faulkner Award and the American Book Award. Rosemary L. Bray (*New York Times Book Review,* 30 September 1990) found the passages dealing with Wideman's son "heartbreaking," while Mike Phillips (*New Statesman,* 1 February 1991) called it a "rehash of Ralph Ellison, Richard Wright and George Lamming, decorated with a magpie selection of classical and contemporary allusions." In *Newsweek* (1 October 1990) Jack Kroll contended that Wideman's skill with language weakened the story: "This book's brilliance bleaches out the reality it seeks."

Wideman's most recent work brings his short fiction together in a single collection. *The Stories of John Edgar Wideman* (1992) combines *Damballah* and *Fever* with a new group of tales, *All Stories Are True.* The new material continues his interest in family and Homewood history as well as in experimentation with narrative voice. As in parts of *Fever* and *Philadelphia Fire,* Wideman seems to be talking in his own voice. In "All Stories Are True" he describes a visit to his mother and then a conversation with his brother in prison. "Backseat" returns to friends in Homewood and memories of his first sexual experience, which is linked to the illness and death of his grandmother, at whose house the encounter occurred.

The narrative voices cover a wide range. "Signs" takes the perspective of a young black woman at college who seems to receive a series of racially insulting, and even threatening, messages. They may, however, be self-generated as a means of justifying her own insecurity. "Newborn Thrown in Trash and Dies" is spoken by a baby sliding down a garbage chute. "Everybody Knew Bubba Riff " is an unpunctuated, stream-of-consciousness narrative spoken at the funeral of a young black man.

All Stories Are True adds to Wideman's saga of the violence, suffering, and daily struggle in the contemporary inner city. He uses memory to suggest that, while earlier generations of African-American residents grappled with economic and racial oppression, they at least had a strong sense of family and community on which to fall back. His vision of the present is that the conditions have not improved, but the elements of support have been lost.

During his literary career Wideman has consistently faced the chaos and despair of black life, and this subject matter has ironically been fertile soil for his writing. It has led him from essentially modernist techniques in his early novels to highly sophisticated experimentation in his more recent works. He consistently finds new means of telling a tragic and sorrowful story, in part because he believes that all the different voices of suffering deserve to be heard.

Interviews:

John O'Brien, ed., *Interviews with Black Writers* (New York: Liveright, 1973), pp. 213–223;

Wilfred D. Samuels, "Going Home: A Conversation with John Edgar Wideman," *Callaloo,* 6 (February 1983): 40–59;

Charles H. Rowell, "An Interview with John Edgar Wideman," *Callaloo,* 13 (Winter 1990): 47–61;

Jessica Lustig, "Home: An Interview with John Edgar Wideman," *African American Review,* 26 (Fall 1992): 453–457.

References:

Jacqueline Berben, "Beyond Discourse: The Unspoken versus Words in the Fiction of John Edgar Wideman," *Callaloo,* 8 (Fall 1985): 525–534;

James W. Coleman, *Blackness and Modernism: The Literary Career of John Edgar Wideman* (Jackson: University Press of Mississippi, 1989);

Trudier Harris, *Exorcising Blackness: Historical and Literary Lynching and Burning Rituals* (Bloomington: Indiana University Press, 1984), pp. 129–147;

Ashraf H. A. Rushdy, "Fraternal Blues: John Edgar Wideman's Homewood Trilogy," *Contemporary Literature,* 32 (Fall 1991): 312–345.

Books for Further Reading

This is a selective list of general studies relating to the contemporary novel. Fuller bibliographies can be found in Lewis Leary, *Articles on American Literature, 1950–1967* (Durham, N.C.: Duke University Press, 1970); the annual MLA International Bibliography; and *American Literary Scholarship: An Annual* (Durham, N.C.: Duke University Press, 1965–   ).

Aldridge, John W. *Classics and Contemporaries.* Columbia: University of Missouri Press, 1992.

Aldridge. *The Devil in the Fire: Retrospective Essays on American Literature and Culture, 1951–1971.* New York: Harper's Magazine Press, 1972.

Aldridge. *In Search of Heresy: American Literature in an Age of Conformity.* New York: McGraw-Hill, 1956.

Aldridge. *Talents and Technicians: Literary Chic and the New Assembly-Line Fiction.* New York: Scribners, 1992.

Aldridge. *Time to Murder and Create: The Contemporary Novel in Crisis.* New York: McKay, 1966.

Allen, Mary. *The Necessary Blankness: Women in Major American Fiction of the Sixties.* Urbana: University of Illinois Press, 1976.

Alter, Robert. *After the Tradition: Essays on Modern Jewish Writing.* New York: Dutton, 1969.

Auchincloss, Louis. *Pioneers or Caretakers: A Study of Nine American Women Novelists.* Minneapolis: University of Minnesota Press, 1965.

Bachelard, Gaston. *The Poetics of Space.* New York: Orion, 1964.

Baker, Houston A. *Blues, Ideology, and Afro-American Literature: A Vernacular Theory.* Chicago: University of Chicago Press, 1984.

Baker, ed. *Three American Literatures: Essays in Chicano, Native American, and Asian-American Literature for Teachers of American Literature.* New York: Modern Language Association of America, 1982.

Balakian, Nona, and Charles Simmons, eds. *The Creative Present: Notes on Contemporary American Fiction.* Garden City, N.Y.: Doubleday, 1963.

Baumbach, Jonathan. *The Landscape of Nightmare: Studies in the Contemporary American Novel.* New York: New York University Press, 1965.

Bell, Bernard W. *The Afro-American Novel and Its Tradition.* Amherst: University of Massachusetts Press, 1987.

Bellamy, Joe D. *The New Fiction: Interviews with Innovative American Writers.* Urbana: University of Illinois Press, 1974.

Bercovitch, Sacvan, ed. *Reconstructing American Literary History.* Cambridge, Mass.: Harvard University Press, 1986.

Bergman, Ronald. *America in the Sixties: An Intellectual History.* New York: Free Press, 1968.

Bigsby, C. W. E., ed. *The Black American Writer*. Deland, Fla.: Everett/Edwards, 1969.

Blotner, Joseph. *The Modern American Political Novel, 1900–1960*. Austin: University of Texas Press, 1966.

Boelhower, William. *Through a Glass Darkly: Ethnic Semiosis in American Literature*. New York: Oxford University Press, 1987.

Bone, Robert A. *The Negro Novel in America,* revised edition. New Haven: Yale University Press, 1965.

Bradbury, John M. *Renaissance in the South: A Critical History of the Literature, 1920–1960*. Chapel Hill: University of North Carolina Press, 1963.

Bredahl, A. Carl, Jr. *New Ground: Western American Narrative and the Literary Canon*. Chapel Hill: University of North Carolina Press, 1989.

Bryant, Jerry H. *The Open Decision: The Contemporary American Novel and Its Intellectual Background*. New York: Free Press, 1970.

Byerman, Keith E. *Fingering the Jagged Grain: Tradition and Form in Recent Black Fiction*. Athens: University of Georgia Press, 1985.

Campbell, Jane. *Mythic Black Fiction: The Transformation of History*. Knoxville: University of Tennessee Press, 1986.

Carr, John, ed. *Kite-Flying and Other Irrational Acts: Conversations with Twelve Southern Writers*. Baton Rouge: Louisiana State University Press, 1972.

Chametzky, Jules. *Our Decentralized Literature: Cultural Mediations in Selected Jewish and Southern Writers*. Amherst: University of Massachusetts Press, 1986.

Christian, Barbara. *Black Women Novelists: The Development of a Tradition, 1892–1976*. Westport, Conn.: Greenwood Press, 1980.

Conversations with Writers, 2 volumes. Detroit: Bruccoli Clark/Gale, 1977–1978.

Cook, Bruce. *The Beat Generation*. New York: Scribners, 1971.

Cook, M. G., ed. *Modern Black Novelists: A Collection of Critical Essays*. Englewood Cliffs, N.J.: Prentice-Hall, 1971.

Core, George, ed. *Southern Fiction Today: Renascence and Beyond*. Athens: University of Georgia Press, 1969.

Cowan, Louise. *The Fugitive Group: A Literary History*. Baton Rouge: Louisiana State University Press, 1959.

Cowley, Malcolm. *The Literary Situation*. New York: Viking, 1954.

Cunliffe, Marcus, ed. *American Literature Since 1900*. New York: Peter Bedrick, 1987.

Darby, William. *Necessary American Fictions: Popular Literature of the 1950s*. Bowling Green, Ohio: Bowling Green State University Popular Press, 1987.

Dekker, George. *The American Historical Romance*. Cambridge: Cambridge University Press, 1987.

Drake, Robert, ed. *The Writer and His Tradition*. Knoxville: University of Tennessee Press, 1969.

Eco, Umberto. *Travels in Hyperreality*. San Diego: Harcourt Brace Jovanovich, 1983.

Eisinger, Chester E. *Fiction of the Forties*. Chicago: University of Chicago Press, 1963.

Elliott, Emory, ed. *The Columbia History of the American Novel*. New York: Columbia University Press, 1991.

Elliott, ed. *The Columbia Literary History of the United States*. New York: Columbia University Press, 1988.

Etulain, Richard W., and Michael T. Marsden, eds. *The Popular Western: Essays toward a Definition*. Bowling Green, Ohio: Bowling Green State University Popular Press, 1974.

Federman, Raymond, ed. *Surfiction: Fiction Now and Tomorrow*. Chicago: Swallow Press, 1975.

Feldman, Gene, and Max Gartenberg, eds. *The Beat Generation and the Angry Young Men*. New York: Citadel, 1958.

Folsom, James K. *The American Western Novel*. New Haven: Yale University Press, 1966.

Fox, Robert Elliott. *Conscientious Sorcerers: The Black Postmodernist Fiction of LeRoi Jones/Amiri Baraka, Ishmael Reed, and Samuel R. Delany*. New York: Greenwood Press, 1987.

French, Warren, ed. *The Fifties: Fiction, Poetry, Drama*. Deland, Fla.: Everett/Edwards, 1970.

Friedman, Melvin J., and John B. Vickery. *The Shaken Realist*. Baton Rouge: Louisiana State University Press, 1970.

Fuller, Edmund. *Man in Modern Fiction: Some Minority Opinions on Contemporary American Writing*. New York: Random House, 1958.

Gado, Frank, ed. *First Person: Conversations on Writers and Writing*. Schenectady, N.Y.: Union College Press, 1973.

Galloway, David D. *The Absurd Hero in American Fiction: Updike, Styron, Bellow, Salinger,* revised edition. Austin: University of Texas Press, 1970.

Gass, William H. *Fiction and the Figures of Life*. New York: Knopf, 1970.

Gass. *On Being Blue: A Philosophical Inquiry*. Boston: Godine, 1976.

Gates, Henry Louis, Jr. *The Signifying Monkey: A Theory of Afro-American Literary Criticism*. New York: Oxford University Press, 1988.

Gayle, Addison, Jr. *The Way of the New World: The Black Novel in America*. Garden City, N.Y.: Anchor/Doubleday, 1975.

Gayle, ed. *Black Expression: Essays by and about Black Americans in the Creative Arts*. New York: Weybright & Talley, 1969.

Geismar, Maxwell. *American Moderns: From Rebellion to Conformity*. New York: Hill & Wang, 1958.

Gerstenberger, Donna, and George Hendrick. *The American Novel, 1789–1959: A Checklist of Twentieth Century Criticism*. Chicago: Swallow Press, 1970.

Gilman, Richard. *The Confusion of Realms*. New York: Random House, 1969.

Glicksberg, Charles I. *The Sexual Revolution in Modern American Literature*. The Hague: Nijhoff, 1971.

Gold, Herbert, ed. *First Person Singular: Essays for the Sixties*. New York: Dial, 1963.

González Echevarría, Roberto. *The Voice of the Masters: Writing and Authority in Modern Latin American Literature*. Austin: University of Texas Press, 1985.

Gossett, Louise Y. *Violence in Recent Southern Fiction*. Durham, N.C.: Duke University Press, 1965.

Green, Martin. *Re-appraisals: Some Commonsense Readings in American Literature*. London: Hugh Evelyn, 1963.

Gruen, John. *The Party's Over Now: Reminiscences of the Fifties*. New York: Viking, 1972.

Guttmann, Allen. *The Jewish Writer in America: Assimilation and the Crisis of Identity*. New York: Oxford University Press, 1971.

Hamilton, Cynthia S. *Western and Hard-Boiled Detective Fiction in America: From High Noon to Midnight*. Iowa City: University of Iowa Press, 1987.

Handy, William J. *Modern Fiction: A Formalist Approach*. Carbondale: Southern Illinois University Press, 1971.

Harap, Louis. *In the Mainstream: The Jewish Presence in Twentieth-Century American Literature, 1950s–1980s*. New York: Greenwood Press, 1987.

Hardwick, Elizabeth. *A View of My Own: Essays in Literature and Society*. New York: Noonday Press, 1962.

Harper, Howard M., Jr. *Desperate Faith: A Study of Bellow, Salinger, Mailer, Baldwin, and Updike*. Chapel Hill: University of North Carolina Press, 1967.

Harris, Charles B. *Contemporary American Novelists of the Absurd*. New Haven: Yale University Press, 1971.

Haslam, Gerald W., ed. *Western Writing*. Albuquerque: University of New Mexico Press, 1974.

Hassan, Ihab. *Contemporary American Literature, 1945–1972: An Introduction*. New York: Ungar, 1973.

Hassan. *The Postmodern Turn*. Columbus: Ohio State University Press, 1987.

Hassan. *Radical Innocence: Studies in the Contemporary American Novel*. Princeton: Princeton University Press, 1961.

Hassan. *The Right Promethean Fire: Imagination, Science, and Cultural Change*. Urbana: University of Illinois Press, 1979.

Hauck, Richard Boyd. *A Cheerful Nihilism: Confidence and "The Absurd" in American Humorous Fiction*. Bloomington: Indiana University Press, 1971.

Hicks, Granville. *The Living Novel: A Symposium*. New York: Macmillan, 1957.

Hicks, Jack. *In the Singer's Temple: Prose Fictions of Barthelme, Gaines, Brautigan, Piercy, Kesey, and Kosinski*. Chapel Hill: University of North Carolina Press, 1981.

Hilfer, Tony. *American Fiction Since 1940*. London & New York: Longman, 1992.

Hill, Herbert, ed. *Anger and Beyond: The Negro Writer in the United States*. New York: Harper & Row, 1966.

Hobson, Fred. *Tell about the South: The Southern Rage to Explain.* Baton Rouge: Louisiana State University Press, 1983.

Hoffman, Daniel, ed. *Harvard Guide to Contemporary American Writing.* Cambridge, Mass.: Belknap Press of Harvard University Press, 1979.

Hoffman, Frederick J. *The Art of Southern Fiction: A Study of Some Modern Novelists.* Carbondale: Southern Illinois University Press, 1967.

Hurm, Gerd. *Fragmented Urban Images: The American City in Modern Fiction.* Frankfurt am Main & New York: Peter Lang, 1991.

Jackson, Blyden. *The History of Afro-American Literature,* 1 volume to date. Baton Rouge: Louisiana State University Press, 1989–

Johnson, Charles R. *Being & Race: Black Writing Since 1970.* Bloomington: Indiana University Press, 1988.

Jones, Peter G. *War and the Novelist: Appraising the American War Novel.* Columbia: University of Missouri Press, 1976.

Karl, Frederick Robert. *American Fictions, 1940–1980: A Comprehensive History and Critical Evaluation.* New York: Harper & Row, 1983.

Kazin, Alfred. *Bright Book of Life: American Novelists and Storytellers from Hemingway to Mailer.* Boston & Toronto: Atlantic/Little, Brown, 1973.

Kazin. *Contemporaries.* Boston: Little, Brown, 1962.

Kazin. *An Interpretation of Modern American Prose Literature.* Garden City, N.Y.: Doubleday, 1956.

Kennard, Jean E. *Number and Nightmare: Forms of Fantasy in Contemporary Fiction.* Hamden, Conn.: Archon, 1975.

Kim, Elaine H. *Asian American Literature: An Introduction to the Writings and Their Social Contexts.* Philadelphia: Temple University Press, 1982.

Klein, Marcus. *After Alienation: American Novels in Mid-century.* Cleveland & New York: World, 1964.

Klein, ed. *The American Novel Since World War II.* Greenwich, Conn.: Fawcett, 1969.

Klinkowitz, Jerome. *Literary Disruptions: The Making of a Post-contemporary American Fiction.* Urbana: University of Illinois Press, 1975.

Klinkowitz. *The Life of Fiction.* Urbana: University of Illinois Press, 1977.

Klotman, Phyllis Rauch. *Another Man Gone: The Black Runner in Contemporary Afro-American Literature.* Port Washington, N.Y.: Kennikat Press, 1977.

Kort, Wesley A. *Shriven Selves: Religious Problems in Recent American Fiction.* Philadelphia: Fortress, 1972.

Kostelanetz, Richard. *The End of Intelligent Writing: Literary Politics in America.* New York: Sheed & Ward, 1974.

Kostelanetz. *Master Minds: Portraits of Contemporary American Artists and Intellectuals.* New York: Macmillan, 1969.

Kostelanetz, ed. *The New American Arts.* New York: Horizon, 1965.

Kostelanetz, ed. *On Contemporary Literature: An Anthology of Critical Essays on the Major Movements and Writers of Contemporary Literature*. New York: Avon, 1964.

Kostelanetz, ed. *The Young American Writers: Fiction, Poetry, Drama, and Criticism*. New York: Funk & Wagnalls, 1967.

Krim, Seymour. *Shake It for the World, Smartass*. New York: Dial, 1970.

Lebowitz, Naomi. *Humanism and the Absurd in the Modern Novel*. Evanston, Ill.: Northwestern University Press, 1971.

Lehan, Richard. *A Dangerous Crossing: French Literary Existentialism and the Modern American Novel*. Carbondale: Southern Illinois University Press, 1973.

Ling, Amy. *Between Worlds: Women Writers of Chinese Ancestry*. New York: Pergamon Press, 1990.

Lipton, Lawrence. *The Holy Barbarians*. New York: Messner, 1959.

Litz, A. Walton, ed. *Modern American Fiction: Essays in Criticism*. New York: Oxford University Press, 1963.

Lord, William J., Jr. *How Authors Make a Living: An Analysis of Free Lance Writers' Incomes, 1953–1957*. New York: Scarecrow Press, 1962.

Ludwig, Jack. *Recent American Novelists*. Minneapolis: University of Minnesota Press, 1962.

Lutwack, Leonard. *Heroic Fiction: The Epic Tradition and American Novels of the Twentieth Century*. Carbondale: Southern Illinois University Press, 1971.

Madden, Charles F., ed. *Talks with Authors*. Carbondale: Southern Illinois University Press, 1968.

Madden, David. *American Dreams, American Nightmares*. Carbondale: Southern Illinois University Press, 1970.

Madden. *Rediscoveries: Informal Essays in Which Well-Known Novelists Rediscover Neglected Works of Fiction by One of Their Favorite Authors*. New York: Crown, 1971.

Malin, Irving. *New American Gothic*. Carbondale: Southern Illinois University Press, 1962.

Margolies, Edward. *Native Sons: A Critical Study of Twentieth-Century Negro American Authors*. Philadelphia & New York: Lippincott, 1968.

May, John R. *Toward a New Earth: Apocalypse in the American Novel*. Notre Dame, Ind.: University of Notre Dame Press, 1972.

McHale, Brian. *Postmodernist Fiction*. New York & London: Methuen, 1987.

Milton, John R. *The Novel of the American West*. Lincoln: University of Nebraska Press, 1980.

Moore, Harry T., ed. *Contemporary American Novelists*. Carbondale: Southern Illinois University Press, 1964.

Myers, Carol Fairbanks. *Women in Literature: Criticism of the Seventies*. Metuchen, N.J.: Scarecrow Press, 1976.

Newman, Charles. *The Post-modern Aura: The Act of Fiction in an Age of Inflation*. Evanston, Ill.: Northwestern University Press, 1985.

Newquist, Roy. *Counterpoint*. Chicago: Rand, McNally, 1964.

Nin, Anaïs. *The Novel of the Future*. New York: Macmillan, 1968.

O'Brien, John, ed. *Interviews with Black Writers*. New York: Liveright, 1973.

Olderman, Raymond M. *Beyond the Waste Land: A Study of the American Novel in the Nineteen-Sixties*. New Haven: Yale University Press, 1972.

Olster, Stacey Michele. *Reminiscence and Re-creation in Contemporary American Fiction*. Cambridge: Cambridge University Press, 1989.

Panichas, George A. *The Politics of Twentieth-Century Novelists*. New York: Hawthorn, 1971.

Parkinson, Thomas, ed. *A Casebook on The Beat*. New York: Crowell, 1961.

Pearce, Richard. *Stages of the Clown: Perspectives on Modern Fiction from Dostoyevsky to Beckett*. Carbondale: Southern Illinois University Press, 1970.

Peden, William. *The American Short Story: Front Line in the National Defense of Literature*. Boston: Houghton-Mifflin, 1964.

Pinsker, Sanford. *The Schlemiel as Metaphor: Studies in the Yiddish and American Jewish Novel*. Carbondale: Southern Illinois University Press, 1971.

Podhoretz, Norman. *Doings and Undoings: The Fifties and After in American Writing*. New York: Farrar, Straus, 1964.

Rocard, Marcienne. *The Children of the Sun: Mexican-Americans in the Literature of the United States,* translated by Edward G. Brown, Jr. Tucson: University of Arizona Press, 1989.

Rosenblatt, Roger. *Black Fiction*. Cambridge, Mass.: Harvard University Press, 1974.

Rubin, Louis D., Jr. *The American South: Portrait of a Culture*. Baton Rouge: Louisiana State University Press, 1980.

Rubin. *The Faraway Country: Writers in the Modern South*. Seattle: University of Washington Press, 1963.

Rubin, and Robert D. Jacobs, eds. *South: Modern Southern Literature in Its Cultural Setting*. Garden City, N.Y.: Doubleday, 1961.

Rubin, and others, eds. *The History of Southern Literature*. Baton Rouge: Louisiana State University Press, 1985.

Ruoff, A. Lavonne Brown, and Jerry W. Ward, Jr. *Redefining American Literary History*. New York: Modern Language Association of America, 1990.

Scholes, Robert. *The Fabulators*. New York: Oxford University Press, 1967.

Scholes, and Robert Kellogg. *The Nature of Narrative*. New York: Oxford University Press, 1966.

Schraufnagel, Noel. *From Apology to Protest: The Black American Novel*. Deland, Fla.: Everett/Edwards, 1973.

Schulz, Max F. *Black Humor Fiction of the Sixties: A Pluralistic Definition of Man and His World*. Athens: Ohio University Press, 1973.

Schulz. *Radical Sophistication: Studies in Contemporary Jewish-American Novelists*. Athens: Ohio University Press, 1969.

Scott, Nathan A., Jr. *Three American Moralists: Mailer, Bellow, Trilling*. Notre Dame, Ind.: University of Notre Dame Press, 1973.

Sherzer, Joel, and Anthony Woodbury. *Native American Discourse: Poetics and Rhetoric*. New York: Cambridge University Press, 1987.

Simonson, Harold P. *Beyond the Frontier: Writers, Western Regionalism and a Sense of Place*. Fort Worth: Texas Christian University Press, 1989.

Smith, Valerie. *Self-Discovery and Authority in Afro-American Narrative*. Cambridge, Mass.: Harvard University Press, 1987.

Sollors, Werner. *Beyond Ethnicity: Consent and Descent in American Culture*. New York: Oxford University Press, 1986.

Spiller, Robert, ed. *A Time of Harvest: American Literature, 1910–1960*. New York: Hill & Wang, 1962.

Stark, John. *The Literature of Exhaustion: Borges, Nabokov, and Barth*. Durham, N.C.: Duke University Press, 1974.

Stepto, Robert. *From Behind the Veil: A Study of Afro-American Narrative*. Urbana: University of Illinois Press, 1979.

Stuckey, William J. *The Pulitzer Prize Novels: A Critical Backward Look*. Norman: University of Oklahoma Press, 1966.

Sutherland, William O. S., ed. *Six Contemporary Novels: Six Introductory Essays in Modern Fiction*. Austin: University of Texas Department of English, 1962.

Tanner, Tony. *City of Words: American Fiction, 1950–1970*. New York: Harper & Row, 1971.

Tanner. *The Reign of Wonder: Naivety and Reality in American Literature*. Cambridge: Cambridge University Press, 1965.

Tate, Claudia. *Black Women Writers at Work*. New York: Continuum, 1983.

Taylor, J. Golden, and Thomas J. Lyon, eds. *A Literary History of the American West*. Fort Worth: Texas Christian University Press, 1987.

Tilton, John W. *Cosmic Satire in the Contemporary Novel*. Lewisburg, Pa.: Bucknell University Press, 1977.

Turner, Darwin T. *Afro-American Writers*. New York: Appleton-Century-Crofts, 1970.

Tuttleton, James W. *The Novel of Manners in America*. Chapel Hill: University of North Carolina Press, 1972.

Tytell, John. *Naked Angels: The Lives and Literature of the Beat Generation*. New York: McGraw-Hill, 1976.

Waldmeir, Joseph J., ed. *Recent American Fiction: Some Critical Views*. Boston: Houghton-Mifflin, 1963.

Watkins, Floyd C. *The Death of Art: Black and White in the Recent Southern Novel*. Athens: University of Georgia Press, 1970.

Watson, Carole McAlphine. *Prologue: The Novels of Black American Women, 1891–1965.* New York: Greenwood Press, 1985.

Weber, Ronald, ed. *America in Change: Reflections on the 60's and 70's.* Notre Dame, Ind.: University of Notre Dame Press, 1972.

West, James L. W. *American Authors and the Literary Marketplace Since 1900.* Philadelphia: University of Pennsylvania Press, 1988.

Westbrook, Max, ed. *The Modern American Novel: Essays in Criticism.* New York: Random House, 1966.

Whitlow, Roger. *Black American Literature: A Critical History.* Chicago: Nelson Hall, 1973.

Wiget, Andrew. *Native American Literature.* Boston: Twayne, 1985.

Wiget, ed. *Critical Essays on Native American Literature.* Boston: G. K. Hall, 1985.

Wilde, Alan. *Middle Grounds: Studies in Contemporary American Fiction.* Philadelphia: University of Pennsylvania Press, 1987.

Williams, John A., and Charles F. Harris, eds. *Amistad I: Writings of Black History and Culture.* New York: Knopf, 1970.

Williams and Harris, eds. *Amistad II.* New York: Knopf, 1971.

Writers at Work: The "Paris Review" Interviews, 4 volumes. New York: Viking, 1958–1976.

Contributors

Robert J. Butler...*Canisius College*
Keith E. Byerman...*Indiana State University*
William M. Clements ....*Arkansas State University*
Brenda Daly ....*Iowa State University*
Thomas Deegan...*Saint Xavier University*
Robert E. Fleming ....*University of New Mexico*
William A. Francis ....*University of Akron*
John Gerlach...*Cleveland State University*
Donald J. Greiner ....*University of South Carolina*
Denise Heinze ....*Western Carolina University*
John D. Kalb...*Salisbury State University*
Philip W. Leon ....*The Citadel*
Dianne C. Luce...*Midlands Technical College*
Edward C. Reilly...*Arkansas State University*
Carol A. Senf...*Georgia Institute of Technology*
Allen Shepherd...*University of Vermont*
Phillip A. Snyder ....*Brigham Young University*
Michael P. Spikes ....*Arkansas State University*
Caren J. Town ....*Georgia Southern University*
Alan R. Velie...*Oklahoma University*
Ruth D. Weston ....*Oral Roberts University*
Donna Haisty Winchell ....*Clemson University*
Susan L. Woods...*Iowa State University*

Cumulative Index

Dictionary of Literary Biography, Volumes 1-143
Dictionary of Literary Biography Yearbook, 1980-1993
Dictionary of Literary Biography Documentary Series, Volumes 1-11

Cumulative Index

DLB before number: *Dictionary of Literary Biography*, Volumes 1-143
Y before number: *Dictionary of Literary Biography Yearbook*, 1980-1993
DS before number: *Dictionary of Literary Biography Documentary Series*, Volumes 1-11

Cumulative Index

Cumulative Index

S

Whitgift, John circa 1533-1604 .....DLB-132

Smith, W. H., and Son DLB-106

Whiting, John 1917-1963 ....DLB-13

Whiting, Samuel 1597-1679 ....DLB-24

Whitlock, Brand 1869-1934 ....DLB-12

Whitman, Albert, and Company DLB-46

Whitman, Albery Allson
1851-1901 ....DLB-50

Whitman, Alden 1913-1990 ....Y-91

Whitman, Sarah Helen (Power)
1803-1878 ....DLB-1

Whitman, Walt 1819-1892 ....DLB-3, 64

Whitman Publishing Company DLB-46

Whitney, Geoffrey
1548 or 1552?-1601 ....DLB-136

Whitney, Isabella
flourished 1566-1573 ....DLB-136

Whitney, John Hay 1904-1982 .....DLB-127

Whittemore, Reed 1919- DLB-5

Whittier, John Greenleaf 1807-1892 ...DLB-1

Whittlesey House DLB-46

Wideman, John Edgar
1941- DLB-33, 143

Widener, Harry Elkins
1885-1912 ....DLB-140

Wiebe, Rudy 1934- DLB-60

Wiechert, Ernst 1887-1950 ....DLB-56

Wied, Martina 1882-1957 ....DLB-85

Wieland, Christoph Martin
1733-1813 ....DLB-97

Wienbarg, Ludolf 1802-1872 ....DLB-133

Wieners, John 1934- DLB-16

Wier, Ester 1910- DLB-52

Wiesel, Elie 1928- DLB-83; Y-87

Wiggin, Kate Douglas 1856-1923 ....DLB-42

Wigglesworth, Michael 1631-1705 ...DLB-24

Wilbrandt, Adolf 1837-1911 ....DLB-129

Wilbur, Richard 1921- DLB-5

Wild, Peter 1940- DLB-5

Wilde, Oscar
1854-1900 ......DLB-10, 19, 34, 57, 141

Wilde, Richard Henry
1789-1847 ....DLB-3, 59

Wilde, W. A., Company DLB-49

Wilder, Billy 1906- DLB-26

Wilder, Laura Ingalls 1867-1957 .....DLB-22

Wilder, Thornton 1897-1975 ....DLB-4, 7, 9

Wildgans, Anton 1881-1932 ....DLB-118

Wiley, Bell Irvin 1906-1980 ....DLB-17

Wiley, John, and Sons DLB-49

Wilhelm, Kate 1928- DLB-8

Wilkes, George 1817-1885 ....DLB-79

Wilkinson, Anne 1910-1961 ....DLB-88

Wilkinson, Sylvia 1940- Y-86

Wilkinson, William Cleaver
1833-1920 ....DLB-71

Willard, L. [publishing house] DLB-49

Willard, Nancy 1936- DLB-5, 52

Willard, Samuel 1640-1707 ....DLB-24

William of Auvergne 1190-1249 ...DLB-115

William of Conches
circa 1090-circa 1154 ....DLB-115

William of Ockham
circa 1285-1347 ....DLB-115

William of Ockham
1200/1205 - 1266/1271 ....DLB-115

The William Chavrat American Fiction
Collection at the Ohio State University
Libraries Y-92

Williams, A., and Company DLB-49

Williams, Ben Ames 1889-1953 ....DLB-102

Williams, C. K. 1936- DLB-5

Williams, Chancellor 1905- DLB-76

Williams, Charles 1886-1945 .....DLB-100

Williams, Denis 1923- DLB-117

Williams, Emlyn 1905- DLB-10, 77

Williams, Garth 1912- DLB-22

Williams, George Washington
1849-1891 ....DLB-47

Williams, Heathcote 1941- DLB-13

Williams, Hugo 1942- DLB-40

Williams, Isaac 1802-1865 ....DLB-32

Williams, Joan 1928- DLB-6

Williams, John A. 1925- DLB-2, 33

Williams, John E. 1922- DLB-6

Williams, Jonathan 1929- DLB-5

Williams, Miller 1930- DLB-105

Williams, Raymond 1921- DLB-14

Williams, Roger circa 1603-1683 ....DLB-24

Williams, Samm-Art 1946- DLB-38

Williams, Sherley Anne 1944- DLB-41

Williams, T. Harry 1909-1979 ......DLB-17

Williams, Tennessee
1911-1983 ....DLB-7; Y-83; DS-4

Williams, Valentine 1883-1946 ......DLB-77

Williams, William Appleman
1921- DLB-17

Williams, William Carlos
1883-1963 ....DLB-4, 16, 54, 86

Williams, Wirt 1921- DLB-6

Williams Brothers DLB-49

Williamson, Jack 1908- DLB-8

Willingham, Calder Baynard, Jr.
1922- DLB-2, 44

Willis, Nathaniel Parker
1806-1867 ....DLB-3, 59, 73, 74

Willkomm, Ernst 1810-1886 ....DLB-133

Wilmer, Clive 1945- DLB-40

Wilson, A. N. 1950- DLB-14

Wilson, Angus 1913-1991 ......DLB-15, 139

Wilson, Arthur 1595-1652 ....DLB-58

Wilson, Augusta Jane Evans
1835-1909 ....DLB-42

Wilson, Colin 1931- DLB-14

Wilson, Edmund 1895-1972 ....DLB-63

Wilson, Ethel 1888-1980 ....DLB-68

Wilson, Harriet E. Adams
1828?-1863? DLB-50

Wilson, Harry Leon 1867-1939 ....DLB-9

Wilson, John 1588-1667 ....DLB-24

Wilson, John 1785-1854 ....DLB-110

Wilson, Lanford 1937- DLB-7

Wilson, Margaret 1882-1973 ....DLB-9

Wilson, Michael 1914-1978 ....DLB-44

Wilson, Thomas
1523 or 1524-1581 ....DLB-132

Wilson, Woodrow 1856-1924 ....DLB-47

Wimsatt, William K., Jr.
1907-1975 ....DLB-63

Winchell, Walter 1897-1972 ....DLB-29

Winchester, J. [publishing house] DLB-49

Winckelmann, Johann Joachim
1717-1768 ....DLB-97

Windham, Donald 1920- DLB-6

Wingate, Allan
[publishing house] DLB-112

Winsloe, Christa 1888-1944 ....DLB-124

Winsor, Justin 1831-1897 ....DLB-47

John C. Winston Company DLB-49

Winters, Yvor 1900-1968 ....DLB-48

Winthrop, John 1588-1649 ......DLB-24, 30

Winthrop, John, Jr. 1606-1676 ......DLB-24

Cumulative Index

ISBN 0-8103-5557-4

90000

9 780810 355576